About the Authors

Desmond Norton, MA, PhD holds postgraduate qualifications in economics, mathematics, statistics and electrical engineering and is currently a Senior Lecturer in Economics at University College Dublin. He has been a visiting professor to the University of New Hampshire and Cornell University in the United States, and has extensive experience in Irish, European and multinational organisations. This work is much more than just a revised and updated edition of *Economic Analysis for an Open Economy* published by the Irish Management Institute in 1980.

Alan Matthews is Associate Professor, and Head of the Economics Department at Trinity College, Dublin.

Martin Kenneally is College Lecturer in Economics at University College Cork.

Patrick McNutt is Professor at the School of Public Policy, University of Ulster, Jordanstown.

Rory O'Donnell is Director of the National Economic and Social Council, Dublin Castle.

Irish Studies in Management

Editors:

W.K. Roche
Graduate School of Business
University College Dublin

David Givens
Oak Tree Press

Irish Studies in Management is a new series of texts and research-based monographs covering management and business studies. Published by Oak Tree Press in association with the Graduate School of Business at University College Dublin, the series aims to publish significant contributions to the study of management and business in Ireland, especially where they address issues of major relevance to Irish management in the context of international developments, particularly within the European Union. Mindful that most texts and studies in current use in Irish business education take little direct account of Irish or European conditions, the series seeks to make available to the specialist and general reader works of high quality which comprehend issues and concerns arising from the practice of management and business in Ireland. The series aims to cover subjects ranging from accountancy to marketing, industrial relations/human resource management, international business, business ethics and economics. Studies of public policy and public affairs of relevance to business and economic life will also be published in the series.

Economics for an Open Economy: Ireland

Desmond Norton

with contributions from
Alan Matthews,
Martin Kenneally,
Patrick McNutt and
Rory O'Donnell

Oak Tree Press
Dublin

in association with
Graduate School of Business
University College Dublin

Oak Tree Press
4 Arran Quay, Dublin 7

© 1994 Desmond Norton
Chapters 7 and 8 © 1994 Alan Matthews
Chapters 21 and 22 © 1994 Martin Kenneally
Chapter 28 © 1994 Patrick McNutt
Chapter 33 © 1994 Rory O'Donnell

A catalogue record of this book is
available from the British Library.

ISBN 1-872853-38-2 (pbk.)
ISBN 1-872853-76-5 (hbk.)

Cover Design: Robin Hegarty

Printed by Colour Books Ltd., Dublin

Contents

[v]

PART TWO
SUPPLY AND DEMAND

PART FOUR

HIGHER LEVEL MACROECONOMIC THEORY

PART SIX
MICROECONOMIC ANALYSIS

PREFACE

Economics for an Open Economy: Ireland is not designed to be in competition with any particular existing textbook. In fact, I hope that it can usefully be used as the core text in first year third-level courses on macroeconomics and microeconomics, and *also* that it can be used as a reference, or as the principal text, in some other courses up to the Master's Degree level. For example, I think that Chapters 9 to 20, plus Chapter 23 are suitable for adoption as the core references in introductory macroeconomics courses, while the contents of Parts Three to Five, plus Part Seven, cover more than enough material to form the basis of a respectable MBA course on macroeconomics. Some of that same material will hopefully be of value to second and third year undergraduates in courses on the national economics of Ireland. The contributions by Martin Kenneally will, I hope, mean that part of the text will be of relevance to those studying banking and finance. Turning to microeconomics, the contribution of Patrick McNutt should improve the usefulness of the book to courses in that branch of economics. Finally (but not least), it is hoped that the analysis of European economic integration by Rory O'Donnell, taken in conjunction with earlier chapters (especially those by Alan Matthews), will mean that the book is of value to those taking courses up to the Master's Degree level in European studies or in European economics.

The book is not a new edition of my old text of a similar name (published by the Irish Management Institute in 1980). Nor is it merely an exposition of ideas readily available elsewhere. It contains some analysis which is new and a moderate amount of material which is not readily available elsewhere — for example, the discussion of terms of trade effects and of national wage agreements, and large sections of the chapters written by the other four contributors.

The foregoing has indicated that the book is quite different from most other texts which can be used in first year at university. But there are other important differences: the emphasis is on an open economy, and the reasoning is quite tight. For the latter feature I make absolutely no apologies. A problem with some textbooks intended for adoption in first year at university is that they have the style of a magazine or a novel: they are deficient in that the student is not *forced* to think deeply. Anyone who believes that they can master the elementary fundamentals of economic theory by means of a quick or relaxed reading should prepare for a shock

— that is the intention in the compactness of the reasoning in the present text. As a successful student remarked to me a few years ago, with reference to the 1980 textbook, "If you wanted to summarise it, you would make it longer". I hope that the same can be said of several chapters in the present book.

It is not assumed that the reader has ever studied formal economics before. The objective is to take the reader a relatively long way, starting virtually from scratch. Thus, the reader should not attempt to glide through the book in the fashion of a novel. "Hasten slowly" should be the motto of the reader who strives for success. With pencil and paper, comprehension of each chapter on microeconomics or macroeconomics should be tested before advancing to the chapter which follows. It is worthwhile emphasising that a long analytical argument can be understood on a quick reading only when it is very simple indeed, relative to the reader's prior knowledge of the material. As L.J. Savage wrote in the *Foundations of Statistics*, "Serious reading [of analytical subjects] is best done sitting bolt upright on a hard chair at a desk. Pencil and paper are nearly indispensable; for there are always figures to be sketched and steps in the argument to be verified." Fuzzy thinking and vague impressions, generated by a desire to get through the text as quickly as possible, will get the reader nowhere. Thus, this book is for the desk, not the couch.

I have often encountered quite advanced (not first year) students who are confused between the notions of theory and tautology, or between an equilibrium condition and an identity, or between the notions of equilibrium and the stability of equilibrium. The frequency of such confusion is unacceptable. If you are a lecturer, and if you do not believe me, simply ask your most advanced class to explain, for example, the quantity theory of money; or to reconcile the statements that "the quantity bought is *always* the same as the quantity sold, but it is *only* in equilibrium that supply is equal to demand"; or ask those students to distinguish between equilibrium and a stable equilibrium, and ask them to explain why the method of comparative statics is misleading, and yields predictions which are certainly wrong, unless the relevant equilibria are stable. I suspect that the answers which you will obtain will surprise you. Nevertheless, I do not believe that one could possibly know much economics without being razor-sharp in the answers to such questions. In this book I have tried to dispel such confusion at the outset.

The present manuscript was prepared mainly in the summer and autumn of 1994. Despite its tightness, it has turned out to be longer than I had expected. For two reasons, I have decided not to prepare an index: First, the detail in the Table of Contents partly obviates the need for an index; second, because a given stage in the reasoning (in both macro-economics and microeconomics) can generally be understood only if the earlier stages are understood, an index would be of relatively little assistance to the reader's understanding. I have, however, added a glossary at the end; although it is not exhaustive, some readers might find it helpful.

ACKNOWLEDGEMENTS

I must now thank a large number of people (though not necessarily in the order listed below):

First, although not all of them were successful, I thank the thousands of students (at five universities — Berkeley, Cornell, New Hampshire, UCC and UCD) to whom I have lectured on elementary economics, and whose examinations I have graded, over a period of almost thirty years: I thank them for teaching me, or for revealing to me, the key concepts which they did not understand, the sources of their confusion, and the concepts which they found difficult. I have also lectured on much of the material contained herein to business people and to students outside universities (for example, those preparing for professional examinations in accountancy); I have learned much from them also.

Second, I thank the four contributors to this lengthy manuscript — Martin Kenneally, Alan Matthews, Patrick McNutt and Rory O'Donnell. Each is an expert in the subject area in which he has written. I believe that their contributions are far more substantive than they realise. I can only hope that the small amount of editing which I applied to their chapters has not caused any error to appear under their names.

Third, I thank Alex Miller of the Irish Management Institute for permitting me to reproduce, in revised form, several chapters from my earlier *Economic Analysis for an Open Economy: Ireland*, which, as already indicated, was published by the IMI in 1980.

Fourth, I owe a debt to the Faculty of Commerce and the Graduate School of Business at UCD. For over a decade, the immediate environment in which I work has been made progressively more difficult. After some years of requests to a more immediate source, it was the Faculty of Commerce which ultimately provided my office with a main-frame computer terminal in the mid-1980s. And again, in the autumn of 1994 when the present manuscript was being printed in draft, it was the Faculty of Commerce which provided my office with a printer. Around the same time (during the late summer of 1994) the Graduate School of Business in Blackrock — more specifically, Fionnuala McCarthy and William Roche — provided administrative and technical facilities not available to me at Belfield. All of such assistance greatly facilitated the speed of preparation of the final product.

Fifth, there are two individuals in the Economics Department at Belfield who assisted me to an extent unknown to themselves. I refer to James Heslin and Gerard Quinn, who carefully read the entirety of the drafts on macroeconomics, and made a great many corrections and fruitful suggestions. All I can do now is thank them for their care and their time. Thanks are also due to John Sheehan of the Economics Department for assistance during the summer of 1994.

Sixth, as much by way of apology as by way of thanks, I must mention Deirdre and Shevawn: Deirdre obtained no vacation in the summer of 1994, and Shevawn did not get taken to the countryside, all because of the time which I allocated to the preparation of this book. Well, wait for some sun, perhaps at Christmas.

Finally, the professionalism, the drive and the efficiency of the people at Oak Tree Press astonished me. I mention David Givens who had overall responsibility, and Emer Ryan who must have had many headaches interpreting well over one hundred hand-drawn diagrams. These two individuals have been responsible for the processing, editing, and correction of the manuscript over a time-span of not very many weeks. I do not believe that there is any other publishing company in Ireland which could match their work. Apart from thanking them, I congratulate Oak Tree.

Because I am in agreement with the chapters of my four contributors, it remains a fact that nobody other than myself is responsible for any errors or deficiencies.

Desmond A.G. Norton
Department of Economics
UCD Belfield
11 November 1994

PART ONE

THE SCOPE AND METHOD OF ECONOMICS

CHAPTER 1

THE SCOPE OF ECONOMICS

Economic problems affect the daily lives of everyone. Economics encompasses the investigation of an extremely broad range of questions, including the following:

(1) Why, in recent years, has the per capita real income of Irish citizens — the purchasing power relative to some base or given year of the average citizen's money income — been higher than ever before? What can be done to increase the rate of growth of output and employment in Ireland?

(2) What determines the rate of inflation in Ireland? Is it due to the degree of aggression in the bargaining of trade unions? Could inflation be reduced substantially by action on the part of the monetary authorities, or by appropriate fiscal policies — public policies in regard to government revenues and expenditures? Or has the Irish rate of inflation been linked to the foreign exchange rate relationships which Ireland has maintained with other countries?

(3) To what extent can government create employment in the economy by increasing the National Debt — by financing government expenditures through borrowing?

(4) Suppose that the government's current budget is initially balanced (i.e. its current expenditures are matched by an equal sum in tax and other current receipts from sources other than borrowing), and that it next increases its expenditures and also raises tax rates so as to maintain a balanced budget. Would output and employment in the economy tend to increase, or would the two policy changes tend to offset each other in their effects on output and employment?

(5) In what manner must a firm allocate resources — its inputs to the production process — if it is to maximise profits obtainable from the employment of those resources? And how must a household allocate its expenditures between different goods if it is to maximise the satisfaction obtainable from its money income?

(6) In what sense, if any, do monopolistic market structures involve waste

of the economy's resources? What are the effects of public policy towards monopoly?

(7) Suppose a per unit tax is imposed on transactions (purchases or sales) in a competitive market. What are the effects? In what sense is it irrelevant whether the tax is administratively levied on sellers or on buyers?

(8) What effect would an increase in the demand for housing have on house rentals and on the incomes of landowners, construction workers and others? Would it be possible for the authorities (central government, urban corporations or county councils) to tax the resulting increase in the incomes of landowners without affecting their incentives concerning how they wish to utilise their land?

(9) Suppose that all income earners in the economy attempted to save 50 per cent of their incomes. Would aggregate (i.e. total) savings increase? Or would aggregate income fall, possibly leading to no permanent change in the level of national savings?

These questions are quite typical of those analysed in economics. Very frequently the answers which on first sight appear to be "obviously" correct turn out to be fundamentally erroneous when subjected to economic analysis. Note that the words "should" or "ought" appear nowhere in the questions: as is emphasised below, *economics describes rather than prescribes*. It examines the implications of pursuing objectives but is not concerned with whether the objectives are good or bad, desirable or not.

ECONOMICS DEFINED: ENDS AND MEANS

Perhaps because of the wide range of questions encompassed by economics and because of the rapid evolution of the discipline, economists themselves have not always agreed on a concise definition of the subject. The great economist Alfred Marshall (1842–1924) defined economics as "a study of mankind in the ordinary business of life; it examines that part of individual and social actions which is most closely connected with the attainment and with the use of the material requisites of well-being. Thus it is on the one side a study of wealth; and on the other, and more important side, a part of the study of man" (*Principles of Economics*, 8th edn., Macmillan, London, 1920, p. 1).

This definition is very broad indeed — so much so that it fails to pinpoint the central characteristics of *the* economic problem. In at least one respect it is typical of definitions in the English language economics literature until the early decades of the twentieth century. These tended to regard economics as the study of the causes of wealth or of economic welfare, with the latter defined as "that part of social welfare that can be brought directly or indirectly into relation with the measuring rod of money" (A.C. Pigou, *The Economics of Welfare*, 4th edn., Macmillan, London, 1932, p. 11). Thus, what many regard as the first truly influential book on economics, written by the Scotsman Adam Smith and published in 1776, bore the title *An Inquiry into the Nature and Causes of the Wealth of Nations*. In the century following Smith's work, economists tended to define their discipline as the study of the nature, production and distribution of wealth. But as the nineteenth century approached its close the emphasis shifted from wealth to welfare. These traditions in the perceived scope of economics reached their culmination in Pigou's *Wealth and Welfare* and in the same author's subsequent book *The Economics of Welfare* (final edition, 1932).

In 1932 Lionel Robbins suggested a concise definition which is acceptable in spirit to the majority of economists. What Robbins sought was an *analytical* rather than a *classificatory* definition. By this is meant a definition which would not focus on certain facts or actions or causes, which would be termed "economic", as distinct from others which would be deemed "non-economic"; rather, what Robbins sought was a definition which would pinpoint what the truly economic aspect of human behaviour is. By the standards of this requirement classificatory definitions, such as those which regard economics as the study of the causes of wealth or economic welfare, are rejected. A central objection to such definitions is that even if there were a precise concept "economic welfare" there would still remain the *economic* problem of how time, effort and other resources must rationally be allocated to the pursuit of "economic" and "non-economic" activities. Furthermore, classificatory definitions which regard economics as the study of the causes of wealth or of economic welfare subsume the study of technology as part of economics — but few if any of us would agree with that.

The Robbins definition is that "Economics is the science which studies human behaviour as a relationship between ends and scarce means which have alternative uses" (*An Essay on the Nature and Significance of Economic Science*, 2nd edn., Macmillan, London, 1935, p. 16).

Some clarification is appropriate. The ends (objectives, desires or goals) of individuals, governments and other groups, are many, and are usually capable of being ranked in order of priority. However, few if any decision-makers can attain all their objectives. (If they could they would have no further wants; for example they would desire neither more income nor more leisure.) The key constraint on our ability to attain all our ends is the fact that the means at our disposal are scarce. These means may be, for example, inputs to the production process, generically termed *factors of production* — land, labour, capital equipment and enterprise — and/or what are generally termed policy instruments, such as (in the case of government) tax rates, the exchange rate for the currency, administrative orders of various kinds, etc. Apart from being limited, the means usually have alternative uses. Thus, the use of a means to pursue one objective generally implies that the means cannot at the same time be used to pursue all other objectives, or that it can be used to do so to a limited extent only. For example, a government's decision to change the tax system in order to foster economic growth may imply that it must forgo the use of the tax system to promote what it regards as an equitable distribution of *disposable income* — income after payment of taxes on income and wealth — among individuals. Or if a person decides to allocate more time to the pursuit of income (through labour), that person must usually forgo leisure. Similarly, if at a given level of technical knowledge the nation wishes to produce more defence goods, it must normally utilise its labour and other resources more fully (thereby forgoing leisure) or it must forgo the production of those non-defence goods which it could have produced had it not decided to divert resources (away from leisure and the production of non-defence goods) towards expansion of defence. Hence, every decision involving time and scarce means for the pursuit of one end involves the relinquishment of their potential use for the pursuit of another end: it has an economic aspect.

Thus, given that a person has decided on a set of objectives and ranked them in order of priority, *the economic problem of any decision-maker is how to allocate rationally the available means among competing uses*. Note that if the means were not scarce (in the sense that they were unlimited, or in the sense that the use of means to pursue one objective never involved sacrifice in the use of those same means to pursue some other objective), an economic problem might not arise and there might be no need for the study of economics. For, if all objectives could be attained simultaneously we would indeed be in Utopia. The *choice* of means in the pursuit of ends, necessitated by the *scarcity* of means, is that aspect of human behaviour which is the core subject-matter of economics. Because the means are scarce the rational decision-maker seeks to make a sensible choice in the utilisation of those means in the pursuit of objectives. If the person is rational, that is, the person *economises*.

What, then, are the boundaries of the subject-matter of economics? In the words of Robbins (pp. 16, 17) the analytical conception of economics which has just been outlined

does not attempt to pick out certain kinds of behaviour, but focuses attention on a particular aspect of behaviour, the form imposed by the influence of scarcity. It follows from this, therefore, that in so far as it presents this aspect, any kind of human behaviour falls within the scope of economic generalisations. We do not say that the production of potatoes is economic activity and the production of philosophy is not. We say rather that, in so far as either kind of activity involves the relinquishing of other desired alternatives, it has an economic aspect. There are no limitations on the subject-matter of Economic Science save this.

The Robbins definition clarifies the distinction between economics and technology. The confusion which once existed on this point — for example, by defining economics as the study of the causes of wealth or of economic welfare "derived from the fact that both economics and technology were concerned with the phenomenon of production, and it was not always possible to distinguish in what way one was concerned and in what way the other." (Claudio Napoleoni, *Economic Thought of the Twentieth Century*, ed. A. Cigno, Wiley, New York, 1973, p. 35.) The distinction lies in the fact that technology is concerned with the feasibility of means for attaining certain ends, leaving entirely out of consideration both the degree of scarcity of means and the order of priority of the ends. Economics, on the other hand, accepting what technology has to contribute, evaluates the means according to their scarcity and the order of priority of the ends.

Notions of benefit and cost are implicit in the Robbins definition. As economists we do not attach any moral content to those words. In economic analysis the *benefit* of any decision in regard to the use of means is the contribution it makes to the attainment of specified objectives. The *economic cost* (termed *opportunity cost*) of utilising means in any particular manner is the best alternative forgone by so doing. A decision to utilise means in the pursuit of a particular objective usually implies forgoing the use of those means towards the attainment of other objectives. The notion "opportunity cost" is perhaps best understood with the aid of an example. To keep analysis simple, consider a case in which choice is being made between the production of only two goods.

Every nation makes choices between production of goods for consumption by individuals and production of goods for defence. Given the factors of production available to the economy in any year, the more defence goods it is decided to produce, the smaller the potential output of consumer goods. If the state of technology and the amount of labour-time and of the other factors of production are fixed, the key characteristics of the choice between defence and consumption are as depicted in Figure 1. The quantities of defence goods and of consumer goods are measured along the vertical and horizontal axes, respectively.

Figure 1

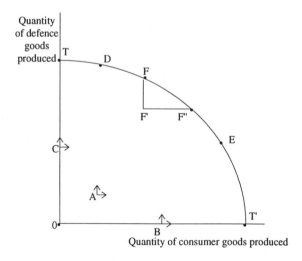

Any point in the diagram represents a certain output of both goods. If the economy's resources were unlimited, it could produce as much of each as might be desired. However, the fixity of available resources implies certain *trade-offs* between potential production of one good and that of the other; the more of one produced, the less the potential output of the other. Given its resource endowments, the downward-sloping curve TT' — called a *production possibility curve* — separates those combinations of goods which the economy can and cannot produce. If it allocated all its factors of production — all available land, labour, capital equipment and enterprise — to defence, it could produce OT of such goods; if, on the other hand, it allocated all its resources to production of consumers' goods, it could produce OT' of those goods. The production possibility curve represents the *maximum* amount of one good which the economy could produce if it has been decided to produce any particular amount of the other good. The key feature of the curve is that it slopes down from left to right. As we have depicted it, the curve is also strictly concave (bow shaped), but consideration of that property is deferred until Chapter 31. The downward slope reflects the fact that the more of one good the economy produces, the less of the other it can produce if it is fully utilising its resources.

Production levels above and to the right of TT' are unattainable. Combinations below TT' (such as points A, B or C) are attainable, but inefficient. They are inefficient because (as the arrows indicate) more of one good could be produced with the given resources without necessitating a reduction in the amount produced of the other good. But production levels along TT' are both attainable and efficient in the sense that along TT' it would be impossible to increase production of one good without (through reallocation of factors of production) reducing the quantity produced of the other. Given the government's preferences between defence and consumption, its central economic problem is to decide on how to allocate resources so that production will take place at the government's preferred point on TT'. (If the government behaves rationally, and if its choice is between consumption and defence only, it must seek to guide production to somewhere on TT'. Why?) If defence is paramount in its priorities, it may select a point such as D; if it attaches greater weight to consumption, it may seek to guide the economy to a point like E.

The production possibility curve is sometimes called a *transformation curve* because it indicates the extent to which one good can indirectly be transformed into another through reallocation of factors of production, away from production of one good toward production of the other. Its slope indicates the economic or opportunity cost of one good in terms of the other. Suppose, for example, that the economy is producing on TT' at point F. Then if the community wishes to have F'F" more consumer goods, it must forgo the production of FF' defence goods. This reflects the fact that because the means are scarce and have alternative uses, a decision to have more consumption goods implies a cost in terms of output of defence goods forgone. So, provided that resources are efficiently allocated to begin with, there is no free lunch: if the nation wants more of one good, given its leisure time and its factor endowments, it must forgo production of other goods.

The above can be summarised as follows: economics is the study of the relationship between human objectives and the scarce means, which normally have alternative uses, by which individuals and groups attempt to attain those objectives. It is the scarcity of means, which implies that not all objectives can be attained simultaneously, that gives rise to economic problems. The key aspects of the discipline are *scarcity of means* and the resulting necessity of *choice* in the *allocation* of those means among *competing ends*. The ends or objectives are many. But the scarcity of means which have alternative uses implies that the greater the extent to which one set of objectives is attained, the less is the potential attainment of others — there are *trade-offs* among the ends. That is because means must be diverted from the pursuit (or potential pursuit) of one set of objectives toward the pursuit of others. The ultimate economic costs, the opportunity costs, of pursuing any one set of objectives are the most beneficial alternatives forgone by utilising means in the pursuit of that set of objectives. Thus, economics investigates the implications for use of scarce means of pursuing actual or hypothetical ends; the effects, on the attainment of ends, of using particular sets of possible means; changes in the effectiveness of means (such changes may occur because of changes outside the economic system itself, but the latter changes are beyond the scope of the economic analysis of a particular economic system); and the trade-offs between actual or hypothetical ends.

Some comment on the meaning of *rationality* in economics is appropriate. In economics we accept the objectives of decision-makers as *given*; the economist *as economist* does not state what the objectives ought to be for behaviour to be rational. In economics the word rational pertains to the manner in which means are used in the pursuit of objectives. A particular utilisation of means is deemed rational in a specific context only if the means are utilised in such a manner as to make the greatest possible contribution to the decision-maker's objectives.

It is recognised that the Robbins definition of economics is rather abstract. However, the nine questions posed at the beginning of this chapter do fall within its scope. The reader is urged to refer back to confirm this claim. Each of the questions is concerned with actual or possible objectives of individuals or groups. And the answer to each inevitably involves consideration of, or implications for, means, as follows:

(1') The objective in question (1) can be construed as being high growth in national output and employment. The means by which these can be pursued pertain, *inter alia*, to the structure and size of the nation's physical capital stock (reflecting decisions in the past to incur costs by refraining from consumption); public policy concerning government revenues (tax rates, etc.) and expenditures (their levels and structures); restraint in wage demands, etc. Note that a higher level of national output in the future usually entails choice involving some sacrifice in earlier years. In the current year (apart from wage restraint) this might involve: refraining from consumption through saving, thereby increasing the national stock of productive assets; more time allocated to training; more resources allocated to marketing effort abroad, etc.

(2') A low rate of inflation may be the principal objective implicit in question (2). As will be indicated in later chapters, the means by which this could be attained involve considerations of exchange rate and monetary policies. However, at least in the short run, the orientation of such policies toward inflation control may imply some reduction in performance insofar as other policy objectives are concerned.

(3') The objective under (3) may be to increase employment in the year ahead, one of the possible means being government expenditure financed by borrowing. Note that the size of the National Debt (the total indebtedness of the government sector, reflecting all past borrowings) might itself be an objective, as well as a means for affecting employment. Contrary to what is sometimes assumed, this kind of situation (i.e. one in which a means is itself also an end) is *not* inconsistent with the Robbins definition of economics. If employment next year is positively related to (i.e. moves in the same direction as) government expenditure financed by borrowing, and if government wishes to maximise employment while simultaneously keeping borrowing as low as possible, then its central problem of choice is in deciding the extent to which it will increase borrowing in order to increase employment. Its task, that is, is to find the appropriate trade-off between borrowing and the creation of employment in the year ahead.

(4') The question posed under (4) concerns the effects of manipulating means (government expenditure and taxation) on possible ends, the two ends mentioned being national output and employment.

(5') The concern under (5) is allocation of means — factors of production or bundles of consumer goods — in order to pursue the two clearly stated objectives efficiently.

(6') The objectives under (6) are not explicitly stated. However, it can be shown that, depending on the objectives set for the operation of the economy as a whole, profit maximising monopolists *may* misallocate the nation's resources (its ultimate means, the factors of production) in the sense that these resources might not be allocated in the most rational way from the standpoint of society's objectives.

(7') An increase in government revenue may be the immediate objective here, the tax rate being a means. However, governments generally have objectives other than raising revenue. They will accordingly wish to know the several effects of the tax — its impact on resource allocation in the economy, how it affects standards of living of different social classes, etc. The extent to which imposition of the tax interferes with the attainment of other objectives is the ultimate economic cost of raising revenue through implementation of the proposed tax.

(8') If, for reasons unrelated to the prices of housing, consumers come to desire more housing than previously, then it is likely that either their incomes or their objectives (or both) have changed. Housing prices are likely to rise in consequence. It is also likely that increased housing demand would bid up the prices of scarce means — for example, land prices/rents and the wages of construction workers — reflecting their increased scarcity relative to demand. If factor prices have changed, then the pattern of income distribution in society has almost surely also changed. Governments may have certain objectives concerning income distribution, and may accordingly seek to devise means (such as lump-sum taxes) to affect the pattern of income distribution without significantly affecting the supply of factors of production such as land.

(9') Individuals saving, say, 10 per cent of their incomes may wish to save more. Their means may be longer hours of work, or simply decisions to refrain from consuming (say) 20 per cent of their incomes. It will be shown later that their objective of increased savings may be frustrated: one person's consumption expenditure is another's income, so if all individuals refrain from consuming, aggregate expenditure and income are likely to fall. It is therefore possible, following the attempt to save more, that aggregate savings will stay unchanged, or even fall, rather than rise.

THE NEUTRALITY OF ECONOMICS

Having established a working definition of economics, some of its implications can now be examined. The principal implication from the standpoint of scientific method is that economics is a positive rather than a normative science (if, indeed, there can be such a thing as a normative science); it is concerned with what is or could be rather than what ought to be. Normative disciplines (such as ethics or aesthetics) are concerned with what ought to be. Economics is entirely neutral between ends. There is nothing in economic analysis which indicates that certain ends are good or bad. For economics simply highlights implications (for use of means) of pursuing whatever ends may be chosen. Note that the use of the adjectives "economic" and "uneconomic" to describe particular policies can be misleading. For the criterion of economy following from the Robbins definition is the pursuit of specific objectives with least disposal of means. It does, therefore, make sense to say of a certain policy that it is uneconomical (economical) if, in order to achieve certain ends, it uses more (no more) scarce means than are necessary. But it may not be intelligible to use these adjectives to describe the ends themselves. For "there are no economic ends. There are only economical and uneconomical ways of achieving given ends" (Robbins, p. 145).

The Irish economist J.E. Cairnes (1824–75) of Trinity College Dublin, Queens College Galway (subsequently UCG) and University College London, was one of the first to emphasise forcefully the neutrality of economics. It is worthwhile quoting him in some detail:

> Political Economy [i.e. Economics] stands apart from all particular systems of
> social or industrial experience. It has nothing to do with laissez-faire [i.e.

unregulated private enterprise economies in which government plays little role] any more than with communism.... It pronounces no judgement on the worthiness or desirableness of the ends aimed at in such systems.... [Economics is to be regarded] as standing neutral between competing social schemes; neutral, as the science of Mechanics stands neutral between competing plans of railway construction, in which expense, for instance, as well as mechanical efficiency, is to be considered.... It is sometimes supposed that because Political Economy comprises in its expositions theories of wages, profits, and rent, the science is *therefore* committed to the approval of our present mode of industrial life, under which three distinct classes, labourers, capitalists and landlords, receive remuneration in those forms. Under this impression, some social reformers, whose ideal of industrial life involves a modification of our existing system, have thought themselves called upon to denounce and deride economic science.... But this is a complete mistake. Economic science has no more connection with our present industrial system than the science of mechanics has with our present system of railways. Our existing railway lines have been laid down according to the best extant mechanical knowledge; but we do not think it necessary on this account, as a preliminary to improving our railways, to denounce mechanical science. If wages, profits, and rent find a place in economic theories, this is simply because these *are* the forms [under which income distribution occurs] as society is now constituted. They are phenomena which need to be explained. But it comes equally within the province of the economist to exhibit the working of any proposed modification of the system. (*The Character and Logical Method of Political Economy*, 2nd edn., Macmillan, London, 1875, pp. 20–22.)

ECONOMICS AND PUBLIC POLICY

The fact that economics is a neutral science — that it is concerned with the relationship between ends and means rather than with the ends *per se* — may suggest that economics is irrelevant to policy. Such a conclusion (with which we certainly would not agree) might be inferred from Nassau Senior (1790–1864) who wrote that the conclusions of the economist, "whatever be their generality and their truth, do not authorise him in adding a single syllable of advice.... The business of a Political Economist is neither to recommend nor to dissuade, but to state general principles" (*An Outline of the Science of Political Economy*, reprinted by Augustus Kelley, New York, 1965, p. 3.) Note, however, that Senior himself was not an economist who hesitated from advising policy-makers.

When an economist suggests that a certain objective *ought* to be pursued that is a *value judgment* — an expression of an *opinion* concerning what ought to be, reflecting the economist's own personal values rather than making a conclusion within the confines of economics. In this context it is necessary to distinguish between economist *qua* economist and economist *qua* ordinary mortal. It is not the job of the economist *qua* economist to pronounce on the desirability of pursuing certain objectives; as an economist ends are of interest only insofar as they have implications for rational disposal of means. But an economist is as much a human as is a physicist, a labourer or an artist. As ordinary humans, economists often make pronouncements concerning the ends which they believe ought to be pursued. But strictly speaking, in doing so they are acting in their capacity as ordinary citizens rather than as economists. For there are no economic ends; there are only economic and uneconomic ways of pursuing given ends.

In the context of policy, economics consists of propositions of the form "if you want to attain those objectives efficiently, then you must do this"; "if that is your objective, then the manner in which you propose to go about it is not rational" or "is inconsistent with the pursuit of it"; "if you do that, the effects will be as follows". But granted that the role of economist *qua* economist is not to state what policy-makers ought to do — for views on such matters are left to the priest, the politician, the businessperson and the voter amongst others — the economist *is* concerned with the implications of what policy-makers want to do and with the effects of what they actually do. So we cannot conclude that economics has no vital role to play in the formation of policy. In practice economists make important contributions to the world around us, by advising decision-makers on how to pursue their chosen objectives (such as a high level of employment, more profits, economic growth, a target rate of inflation) in an efficient manner; by analysing the existing trade-offs between different objectives and indicating how, if possible, they might be improved; by estimating the effects of manipulating policy instruments in various ways (their analyses may then be guides in the formulation of new policies); by estimating the impact of changes in the environment such as new technology, an energy crisis, economic recovery abroad, etc., on the effectiveness of actual or potential means; by forecasting what would happen if there were no changes in policy (thereby possibly highlighting, but not prescribing, the need for changes in the instruments of policy); by educating the public so that they may assess public and private policies more intelligently.

The role of the economist in policy formation is very much similar to that of analysts in other sciences — nuclear physicists or missiles experts, for example. Thus, suppose that the Prime Minister of country Aggress wishes to exterminate the population of another nation, Unfortuna. Because he is unlikely to be an expert in missiles he will probably benefit from the advice of nuclear physicists and missiles experts in deciding on the design of a feasible offensive strategy. But this does not imply that the nuclear physicists or the missiles experts are in agreement with the policy-maker's objective of extermination. For apart from being professional scientists, they are also human beings who have their personal views concerning what ought to be done. But as scientists they can advise by making statements of the form: "if you want to do that, then the means which we suggest are consistent with the pursuit or attainment of your objective". A rational choice of offensive strategy would then be one which the missiles experts deem technically feasible and which is efficient (in the economist's sense).

The policy significance of economics should be reasonably clear. Its significance "consists in just this, that, when we are faced with a choice among ultimates, it enables us to choose with full awareness of the implications of what we are choosing.... It makes it possible for us to select a system of ends which are mutually consistent with each other" (Robbins, p. 152).

If economics appears to be such an objective science, "unadulterated" by ethics and politics, why, it may reasonably be asked, do economists so frequently disagree? One reason is that every economist, like everyone else, has personal views on what is good or bad, desirable or undesirable. If two economists disagree in regard to ends, the resolution to their conflict is not to be found in economics — for there are no economic ends. Under such circumstances they would be disagreeing, *not* as economists, but as ordinary mortals who have different views in regard to how the world ought to be. But if they disagree on how the economy actually works (ultimately a matter of fact), and hence on the possible means of pursuing a given end, then the resolution to their disagreement can it is hoped be found in economic (supplemented by statistical) analysis. However, the facts which we observe in the economy are often open to more than one interpretation. Therefore, even if two economists take the same ends as given, they might have differing views on the appropriate means for the pursuit of those ends, merely because they have differing explanations of how the economy actually works. Furthermore, in choosing between two competing explanations of how the economy works — both of which may appear to be equally consistent with observed facts — different economists might be influenced by how they would like it to work; they might therefore conflict in their advice to policy-makers (on the use of means). Nevertheless, most economists of high repute in the profession try clearly to distinguish those of their conclusions which follow from economic analysis from those which reflect mere value judgments, the latter reflecting their own personal views in regard to what ought to be. The reader should do likewise.

Objectives change over time. The environment in which we make decisions changes from instant to instant. Governments come and go. Individuals are being born at this moment while others are dying. Thus in what pertains to economics, the problems of decision-makers are not all resolved in some eternal cookbook of economic recipes. In this context, John Maynard Keynes (1883–1946) wisely wrote that economics

> does not furnish a body of settled conclusions immediately applicable to policy. It is a method rather than a doctrine, an apparatus of the mind, a technique of thinking, which helps its possessor to draw correct conclusions [in regard to efficient means, and effects, of pursing various objectives]. (J.M. Keynes in his *Introduction* to the Cambridge Economic Handbooks series of monographs.)

Although economics is neutral between ends, there can be no doubt that the impact of economists on the world around us has been enormous. Keynes may not have been exaggerating greatly when in his *General Theory of Employment, Interest and Money* (Macmillan, London, 1936, pp. 383–4) he wrote that

> the ideas of economists and political philosophers, both when they are right and when they are wrong, are more powerful than is commonly understood. Indeed the world is ruled by little else. Practical men, who believe themselves to be quite exempt from any intellectual influences, are usually the slaves of some defunct economist. Madmen in authority, who hear voices in the air, are distilling their frenzy from some academic scribbler of a few years back. I am sure that the power of vested interests is vastly exaggerated compared with the gradual encroachment of ideas. Not, indeed, immediately, but after a certain interval; for in the field of economic and political philosophy there are not many who are influenced by new theories after they are twenty-five or thirty years of age, so that the ideas which civil servants and politicians and even agitators apply to current events are not likely to be the newest. But, soon or late, it is ideas, not vested interests, which are dangerous for good or evil.

The thoughts expressed in this passage are surely good reasons for studying economics with a fresh, open mind. But to escape — and to remain escaped — from the incarceration of established modes of thought may not be easy, and is likely to require concentration and perseverance, as well as independence of mind and aloofness from herd-like thinking, on the part of the reader.

CHAPTER 2

THE METHOD OF ECONOMICS

It was stated in Chapter 1 that economics is a science. In this context it is noted that in recent decades there have been tendencies in popular usage to regard subjects described as scientific with acclaim; conversely, some people use the adjective "unscientific" to denote "sloppy". However, when in this book we refer to economics as a science, we purport merely to describe rather than to praise implicitly or to impute some judgment of value.

SCIENCE AND GENERALISATION

The central characteristic of science is the establishment of generalisations in regard to the relationships between categories of phenomena. Thus, if from some body of analysis (other than normative or prescriptive analysis, i.e. analysis of what ought to be) one can conclude "if this, then that", one has a scientific theory, hypothesis or law. The importance of scientific theories is that they may enable the analyst to make predictions about the world around us, and prediction is sought because it may permit control over phenomena. If scientific investigation predicts that "if you do A, then x will result, whereas if you do B, then y will follow", decision-makers may be able to control x or y or both. The relationship between scientific generalisations, prediction and control has been outlined by George Stigler as follows:

> That control requires prediction is self-evident, for unless one knows what "causes" a particular phenomenon, one cannot affect or prevent its occurrence. Prediction, however, requires a knowledge of *general* relationships. No matter how detailed our study of a particular phenomenon (say the price of wheat in March 1874) may be, we would never [on the basis of such raw facts alone] be able to predict the movement of the price of wheat in similar circumstances, because the "similar" circumstances would differ in literally an unlimited number of respects. It is for this reason that general laws are sought between classes of phenomena. (*The Theory of Price*, Macmillan, New York, 1946, pp. 3, 4.)

In similar vein the French mathematician Henri Poincaré (1854–1912), referring to the science of experimental physics, wrote that a good experiment

> is that which teaches us something more than an isolated fact. It is that which enables us to predict, and to generalise. Without generalisation, prediction is impossible. The circumstances under which one has operated will never again be reproduced simultaneously. The fact observed will never be repeated.... To predict ... we must generalise." (*Science and Hypothesis*, reprint of the first English translation, Dover, New York, 1952, pp. 141, 142.)

We have referred to scientific theories, hypotheses and laws as though the words were interchangeable. In this book we adopt the practice of Stigler (p. 4, footnote):

> It was once popular to call a *relationship* a *hypothesis* if it had not been tested, a *theory* if there were some evidence to support it, and a *law* if it were certain. This order contains a grain of truth, but it is essentially naive and mistaken (witness the fact that no sensible hypothesis can be made about a subject matter of which one is completely ignorant, and no scientific "law" is ever certain). Historical accident plays a large part in such matters (Boyle's "law" of gases is only an approximation), and everyday usage has corrupted any possible distinction (why is relativity a theory and "supply and demand" a law?).

Pure and Applied Science

When a researcher sets out on a scientific investigation, the objective of inquiry may be light-bearing or fruit-bearing — knowledge for its own sake or knowledge which increases understanding of the world around us and which may enable decision-makers to change that world. The two aspects may be present in varying degrees in different sciences. Some sciences purport to be primarily of the pure or light-bearing variety; others are mainly applied or fruit-bearing. At one side of the spectrum stand formal logic and pure mathematics; towards the other side, experimental physics, chemistry, and the biological and social sciences. In the case of light-bearing investigations the generalisations made purport to be logical implications of various assumptions, *whether or not such assumptions correspond to the world which was, which is, or which is likely to be*. The test for validity of such generalisations in pure science is to be found in logical consistency in determining whether the implications follow from the assumptions. Observed facts are irrelevant to pure science. The distinction between pure and applied science is apparent in the following lines from the philosopher-mathematician Bertrand Russell (*Principles of Mathematics*, 2nd edn., Norton, New York, 1937, p. 5.):

Pure mathematics has no concern with the question whether the axioms and propositions of Euclid hold of actual space or not: this is a question for applied mathematics, to be decided, so far as any decision is possible, by experiment and observation. What pure mathematics asserts is merely that the Euclidean propositions follow from the Euclidean axioms, i.e., it asserts an implication: any space which has such and such properties has also such and such other properties.... All propositions as to what actually exists, like the space we live in, belong to experimental or empirical [that is, applied] science.

The distinction drawn by Russell is applicable in principle to the field of economic investigation. As Pigou noted (*The Economics of Welfare*, 2nd edn., Macmillan, London, 1932, p. 6):

It is open to us to construct an economic science either of the pure type represented by pure mathematics or of the realistic type represented by experimental physics. Pure economics ... would study ... groups of persons actuated by any set of motives x. Under it ... would be included at once an Adam-Smithian political economy, in which x is given the value of the motives assigned to the economic man or to the normal man and a non-Adam-Smithian political economy ... under which x consists of love of work and hatred of earnings.... For pure economics both these political economies would be equally true. Contrasted with this pure science stands realistic economics, the interest of which is concentrated upon the world known in experience.

Economics is an applied science. Indeed the potential for empirical explanation (i.e. explanation of observed phenomena) and operational application characterises all the social sciences — those sciences which are concerned with human behaviour. Pigou, very much a pragmatic humanitarian in the tradition of Marshall, expressed his own motivation in studying economics by noting (p. 5) that "it is not wonder, but rather the social enthusiasm which revolts from the sordidness of mean streets and the joylessness of withered lives, that is the beginning of economic science."

Given that economics is an applied science it is not only concerned with the logical implications of assumptions — though such implications are certainly relevant. Logical consistency alone is not a sufficient test of an economic theory. Nor is economics confined to observation alone: infinite narration of facts does not enable us to derive scientific generalisations about the world around us. In order to explain what was, what is, or what plausibly might be, we need theory to relate *classes of facts* — to explain the relationship between some classes of facts and others. Thus, in applied science the facts are not simply brought together;

they are "compelled by thought to speak". Or, as Poincaré (pp. 141, 142–4, 150) wrote of the applied science of experimental physics:

> science is built up of facts as a house is built of stones; but an accumulation of facts is no more a science than a heap of stones is a house.... Detached facts cannot therefore satisfy us.... By generalisation, every observed fact enables us to predict a large number of others.... [Generalisation or theory] should always be as soon as possible submitted to verification.... If it cannot stand this test, it must be abandoned.

Similarly, quoting Pigou (p. 7) once more, every applied science

> through examination and cross-examination of the particular facts which it is able to ascertain, seeks to discover the general laws of whose operation these particular facts are instances. These laws ... are *generalisations*."

The above passages from Pigou and Poincaré can be summarised and linked together: All we observe are events or facts. Any proposed explanation of facts is a theory. Theories in applied science purport to explain why certain events occur; they purport to consist of the implications of one class of facts for another class of facts. They are therefore generalisations: rather than reporting that events A and B were observed simultaneously or sequentially, theory attempts to explain the manner in which events of category A are linked to events of category B. Some theories in applied science may be little more than assertions of causation (in contrast to normative, prescriptive assertions), but they may, on the other hand, be the logical implications of one set of apparent facts (the assumptions) for another class of apparent facts (the implications or conclusions). But logical consistency is no guarantee that theories in applied science are valid; because they purport to offer generalised explanations of facts, they must be substantively consistent with those facts. If in applied science the conclusions (predictions) of a theory are significantly inconsistent with observed facts, then that theory is deemed invalid. Note that this is in contrast to pure science, where logical rigour is all that matters. Thus, although theory is a vital aspect of applied science — for it attempts to explain why the facts are as they are, were the way they were, or how certain facts would be affected if other facts were to change or to be changed — it is not the only aspect; the second, complementary aspect is in appeal to the facts to ascertain whether those facts are consistent with the theory. (This is also in contrast to normative statements, which are themselves often described as theories or laws, but which cannot be refuted by appeal to facts alone.) If in applied science facts are significantly inconsistent with a theory (leading to rejection of that theory), it will be the endeavour of scientists to find a better theory

— one which is logically consistent and which is not refuted by facts.

It follows that statements of the form "that explanation is fine in theory but not in practice" are often misleading. For *any* proposed explanation of practice is a theory. If we do not agree with a theory because it is inconsistent with facts, it is up to us to construct a better theory. But to reject theory per se, while hoping to understand facts, is absurd. If we want to understand reality the choice is not between theory and observation, but between theories which are broadly consistent with observed facts and theories which are significantly inconsistent with them. In the discussion of theory in the remainder of this chapter, the context is confined to applied science.

Economic Theory, Abstraction and Generalisation

A well-specified economic theory has three aspects:

(1) A set of definitions indicating the meaning of technical terms.

(2) Assumptions concerning the general circumstances under which the theory purports to apply.

(3) Conclusions purporting to describe aspects of the world which was, is, or could plausibly be, and which purport to follow logically from the assumptions in (2).

The following is an example of an economic theory:

If:

(1) A firm seeks maximum attainable profits.

(2) Its average costs are constant.

(3) There is at least one level of output at which it can obtain some profit.

(4) It can vary output by small amounts.

Then:

The firm will produce an output at which marginal cost (the change in total cost due to small variation in output) equals marginal revenue (the change in total revenue due to small variation in output).

The definitions (often excluded because they are presumed known), the assumptions and the conclusion are clear in the statement of this theory. Note that the theory does not pertain to a single, isolated firm: provided assumptions (1) to (4) are satisfied, it purports to predict what any firm will produce; the conclusion is a generalisation. The assumptions may be true — in accordance with observation — or totally false or partially true. The conclusion is formally (though not necessarily empirically or factually) valid only if it follows logically from the assumptions.

In assessing the usefulness of a theory we note, first, that the assumptions may be true but the conclusions logically false. If the errors in logic are serious, the theory may be useless. Second, even though the assumptions may in some respects be unrealistic, the theory may nevertheless be a useful approximation to, or simplification (abstraction) of, reality. The theories outlined in this book and probably in any book on applied science fall into that category (i.e. they are abstractions of reality). Nevertheless, useful conclusions concerning reality may be drawn from the simplifying assumptions. The purpose of simplification or abstraction is merely to make analysis tractable in an otherwise unmanageably complex and/or partially unknown environment. Thus Stigler (p. 9) noted that

> reality is too complex ever to be described fully.... In order to reduce any problem to manageable proportions, we must ... concentrate our investigation on *important* and *relevant* factors — and this is nothing more or less than abstraction. As a corollary, no scientific law will ever fully describe reality; no theory of rent will ever predict the 196th word in the lease or the disposition of the farmer's second cousin on rainy days.

All applied scientific theories simplify or abstract from reality in specifying their assumptions. What is considered a good theory simplifies in a significantly useful way, in the sense that it yields explanations or predictions which approximate reality; a poor theory, even if it is logically consistent, does not. In attempts to explain how the economy, or particular sectors of the economy, operate, economists use theories (sometimes called *models* when the assumptions are complex and well specified, perhaps in mathematical form) like travellers use road maps. A map of Ireland does not indicate every traffic light, roundabout or minor road: it focuses on essentials. Though there are sure to be some exceptions, the map is, nevertheless, a fairly reliable indicator of how drivers will travel between, say, Belfast, Cork, Dublin, Galway, Limerick and Maynooth. Similarly (because they also focus on central features of reality only) economic theories purport to yield explanations and predictions which are only approximately correct (empirically), or are correct "on the average", with the dispersion of actual experiences away from the average being generally small.

Theory versus Tautology

We have seen that theories are typically propositions of the form, "if this, then that". But not all propositions of that form are theories. Propositions which are true *by definition* are not theories; they are *tautologies* or *identities*. Suppose for example that Y denotes the aggregate of all incomes in the economy (the national income) on an annual basis, that C is annual consumption expenditure in the economy and that investigation leads us to believe that the relationship between C and Y is represented by the equation

$$(1)\ C = 0.75Y$$

Equation (1) is a very simple theory. It states the hypothesis that if national income is at any particular level (in, say, £ million), then consumption expenditure must he three-quarters of that level, and that if national income changes by any amount, then consumption expenditure must change by three-quarters of that amount. Note that (1) may or may not be true, and if it is true, it is not true by definition. Two sets of remarks are appropriate in this context:

First, an alternative theory might be that the relationship between C and Y is represented by the equation

$$(2)\ C = 0.5Y$$

which states that if Y is at any particular level, then consumption expenditure must be one half of that level. This too is a theory which may or may not be true — it surely is not true if (1) is true, and if it is true, it is not true by definition.

Second, the propositions represented by (1) or (2) purport to hold, not for all conceivable values of C and Y, but only for those subsets of values of C and Y which satisfy the equations. For example, equation (1) is not satisfied by the values $Y = 1$, $C = 97$. But consider the following proposition:

If we denote $(u + w)^2$ by

$$(3)\ z = (u + w)^2,$$

then

$$(4)\ z = u^2 + 2uw + w^2$$

This (if, then) proposition is true but it is not a theory. It is a tautology or truism; (4) is merely another way of stating (3). The identity

$$(5)\ (u + w)^2 \equiv u^2 + 2uw + w^2$$

could not be refuted by any conceivable state of the universe; it could not be refuted by any choice of pair of values for u and w. (We use three bars in (5) to denote "identically equal to" rather than the customary two bars to denote "equal to" as in normal equations representing hypotheses.) Identities, such as (5), imply no testable hypotheses.

Tautologies can tell us nothing about the causes of phenomena. Defining a cow as x and stating that x is a cow tells us nothing about cows. Nor can the statement that if £x million of wheat was purchased then £x million of wheat was sold tell us anything substantive about reality; it is true by definition of the two-sided character of purchase and sale. Thus not all "if this, then that" propositions are theories; some are tautologies and as such are of little interest in scientific research.

Science is not concerned with defining terms so that propositions are true by definition. Thus commenting on meaningful theorems — what we call theories — in the applied science of economics, the Nobel prize-winning American economist, Paul Samuelson, has written as follows:

> By a meaningful theorem I mean simply a hypothesis about empirical data which could conceivably be refuted, if only under ideal conditions. A meaningful theorem may be false. It may be valid but of trivial importance. Its validity may be indeterminate, and practically difficult if not impossible to determine. Thus, with existing data it may be impossible to check on the hypothesis that the demand for salt is of elasticity -1.0. [As will be shown in Chapter 5 below, this is a hypothesis about the degree of sensitivity in the demand for salt to changes in its price.] But it is meaningful because under ideal circumstances an experiment could be devised whereby one could hope to refute the hypothesis. The statement that if demand were inelastic [to be interpreted as not particularly sensitive to changes in its price, as will be shown in Chapter 5], an increase in price will raise total revenue is not a meaningful theorem in this sense. It implies no hypothesis... and is true simply by definition." (*Foundations of Economic Analysis*, Harvard University Press, Cambridge, Mass., 1947, p. 4.)

The theories of economics are meaningful in Samuelson's sense: because they are not statements which are true by definition, they can in principle be tested by resort to data on empirical phenomena, and rejected if inconsistent with those phenomena.

Experiment, Ceteris Paribus and Statistics

In natural sciences such as chemistry, the scientist, having posed a theory, is often able to generate observations by means of *controlled experiments*, in order to provide evidence for or against the theory. Suppose, for example, that a theory states that some variable, z, depends in some specific manner on another variable, x. In a controlled experiment (perhaps a laboratory experiment) it is attempted to hold constant all variables apart from x which are believed to influence z, to vary x, and to observe the resulting variation in z, in order to test the hypothesis that z depends on x in the manner claimed in the theory. In controlled experiments researchers vary whatever independent variables they wish, controlling at constant levels yet other independent variables, and observe the consequences for the dependent variable (or dependent variables). However, such methods of testing theories are possible in social sciences to a much more limited extent than in the natural sciences.

Suppose we want to set up an experiment to test the theory that at times of economy-wide depression, increases in government expenditure financed by printing money will increase national output and employment. It is unlikely that it will be possible to conduct the experiment directly, because national output and employment depend on other variables apart from government expenditure financed by printing money, and it will surely be impossible to hold constant, during the experiment of varying government expenditure, all the other causal factors which influence output and employment. Even a dictator like George Orwell's Big Brother could not keep the age structure of the population constant during the experiment. Nor could he maintain constant weather and harvest conditions, or prevent fluctuations in income abroad which affect the demand for the home country's exports. Apart from government expenditure financed by printing money, these are all factors, uncontrollable or imperfectly controllable, which influence output and employment. It would therefore be virtually inconceivable to test the hypothesis posed by means of controlled experimentation, as in the natural sciences.

The main reason, then, why economists are not normally able to test their theories by means of controlled experiments is that most of the variables of interest to economists are influenced by a very large number of factors, many of which vary simultaneously and often in opposite directions, and which are beyond the full control of any individual.

We have seen that economic theories simplify reality. In order to make analysis tractable economic theories are generally conditional propositions of the form "other things being equal (or, using the Latin, *ceteris paribus*), if x becomes such-and-such, then z will be affected in such-and-such a manner", or "other things being equal, if you want z to be as you say, you must manipulate x in this manner". Even if the qualification "other things being equal" is not stated, it is usually implied in the specification of economic theories. By "other things being equal" the economist means (taking the example at hand) "if all variables apart from x which influence z remain constant". The economist does not necessarily believe that these "other things" can really be held constant as x varies; to do so would presumably mean advocating controlled experiments to test theories. But the effects on z of variation in these "other things" can also be theorised, with appropriate *ceteris paribus* qualifications applied to those theories also. If, as is likely, a given dependent variable depends on many independent variables, the approach of a large part of economic analysis is the construction of theories concerning the effects of variation in each of those independent variables in isolation (i.e. other things being equal, or holding constant in one's reasoning all other causal factors). Then combining and expanding on aspects of each of these theories makes it possible to predict the consequences of simultaneous changes in many independent variables.

If many explanatory factors underlying the phenomena of economic analysis are varying simultaneously, often in opposite directions, and if these explanatory variables cannot be held constant, so that controlled experiments are largely out of the question, how can we "appeal to facts" to test a theory? The answer is: (a) millions of *uncontrolled* experiments are taking place every year. Returning to our previous example, we do observe fluctuations in national output and employment simultaneously with variations in government expenditure, in agricultural output, in exports, demographic changes, and so on; (b) we can apply the methods of applied *econometrics* — that discipline which uses the tools of *statistical inference* from observed data in order to estimate the quantitative relationship between economic variables (but which is deferred for study in another course) to test whether observed facts are consistent with theory. If observed facts are significantly inconsistent with our simplified theories, we reject those theories and seek better theories.

Thus economics is both *logically deductive* and *empirical* in method. Economic theory starts with certain assumptions. These assumptions usually have an empirical element, because they purport to reflect broad features of reality (such as the general character of the cost structure of firms, the objectives of firms, the overall structure of the economy, etc.) Then, by a process of logical deduction, economic theory draws general conclusions to explain central features of the economy (such as the output levels which firms produce, or the effects on national income of variation in government expenditure). In highlighting the implications of the assumptions, logical deduction enables the economist to make predictions contingent on the postulated assumptions. Application of the methods of statistical inference in testing the correspondence between the conclusions/predictions of an economic theory on the one hand, and observed facts in regard to the variables which the theory purports to explain on the other hand, is an important empirical aspect of economic method. The role of statistical methods is at least twofold: (a) as just mentioned, they are used to test the conclusions of theories against empirical data. (b) We frequently assume in our theories that one thing is related to another in some very general way; if a sufficient number of observations on the variables is available, statistical methods can be used to improve our estimate of the quantitative manner in which one variable depends on another, or to suggest that one variable might depend on another in some manner of which we had not thought.

On the one hand, then, statistical analysis is used to test theories; but statistical analysis of the data may suggest new theories to the analyst. Theories which originate from analysis of, or even casual observation of, empirical data are sometimes called *inductive* hypotheses in contrast to *deductive* hypotheses. However, the distinction is nebulous.

Most theories in economics proceed by logical deduction from various assumptions. But they also have their inductive element: economists and others tend to theorise because they have some familiarity with the world around them, and wonder how that world can be explained or changed. That being the case, their theories have not only deductive, but also inductive, aspects. Thus, the Nobel prize-winning Swedish economist, Gunnar Myrdal, has written that

> there is an inescapable *a priori* element in all scientific work. Questions must be asked before answers can be given. The questions are an expression of our interest in the world, they are at bottom valuations. Valuations are thus necessarily involved already at the stage when we observe facts and carry on theoretical analysis, and not only at the stage when we draw political inferences from facts and valuations. (*The Political Element in the Development of Economic Theory*, translated from German by Paul Streeten, Routledge and Kegan Paul, London, 1953, p. vii.)

These considerations in no way detract from the neutrality of economics. A person may study economics in order to make the world what she regards a better place; this is an expression of values. But in analysing the implications for scarce means of pursuing that objective (given some criterion of "good" and "better"), the economist is acting as a positive scientist, not as a moralist.

A theory may be deemed significantly false, and hence rejected, if: (a) there are important logical discrepancies between its assumptions and conclusions; (b) there are important empirical discrepancies in its assumptions or in its conclusions. (Note that not all economists appear to agree on the latter issue: some have argued that the degree of realism in the assumptions is irrelevant, so long as the conclusions themselves are consistent with reality.) What matters from the standpoint of operational validity of a theory is whether it simplifies in a useful way, in the sense that it makes general assumptions which yield conclusions consistent with broad features of reality. But can we *prove* that a theory — an economic theory or a theory in any other applied science — about the world around us is true? The answer is no; we may say no more than that it is broadly consistent or inconsistent with facts in two billion controlled experiments or in two billion statistical studies. But we cannot prove that it will hold true in the next controlled experiment or in the next observation, although we can regard it as extremely probable. It is possible, indeed, that two alternative theories explain the facts equally well. Under such circumstances the criterion normally used by scientists in choosing between the theories is analytical simplicity; by this criterion that explanation which requires fewer assumptions, and is therefore the more general, is the preferred theory.

Economic Data

It has been indicated above that data on facts interact with economic theories in two main ways. First, they enable the economist to test the conclusions of theoretical models. For example, suppose that a theory leads to the conclusion that national income depends on the levels of government expenditure and on other specified variables. Then, if we have data on actual government expenditure and the other specified variables on, say, an annual basis for the past 25 years, we can use that data to test whether the theoretical model reasonably predicts (or explains) the level of national income which actually prevailed in each of those 25 years (assuming, of course, that we also have data on annual national income). Second, we can use data to improve our knowledge in regard to the quantitative relationships between variables in the assumptions of an economic theory or model (often referred to as the *structural relationships* between variables in the model).

The data used by economists are sometimes obtained by directly consulting firms or households. More often, however, the data used are those published by firms, trade associations, governments or international institutions. Data may be of two forms — time series or cross-section. A *time series* is a sequence of measurements of a particular variable at different points in time. For example, if we have data on national income on an annual basis for the past 25 years, then that is a national income time series. Data are in *cross-section* form if they indicate, at the same point in time, the value of a particular variable pertaining to different individuals or groups of individuals. For example, suppose that we have figures for per capita income in each of the counties of the Republic of Ireland in a given year — say 1995; those data on per capita income are in cross-section form.

In their analyses, or in reporting statistics on economic phenomena, economists sometimes use or refer to the absolute values of data. For example, an economist might note that according to statistics prepared by Irish government sources (by the Central Statistics Office), the national income of Ireland (in nominal terms — a concept explained below) increased from £3,575 million in 1976 to an estimated £11,866 million in 1985. Alternatively, the economist might use an index number to denote the relative change in national income over the period in question. An index number is a summary statistic indicating the value of data for given observations of a variable, relative to a base value (normally = 100) of that variable. Thus, for the example of national income growth just reported, we might choose 1976 as the base year (i.e. the year relative to which reference is made) and set national income in that year = 100. In index number form we could then state that (nominal) national income in 1985 was 322 [= (11,866/3,575)100]; thus national income increased by 232 per cent over the period in question. For both time series and cross-section data, the use of index numbers provides a convenient way of representing the magnitude of observations of a variable relative to a base observation value (usually set = 100) of the same variable.

If time series data on several different variables (such as the prices of various goods) are presented in index number form with the same time-period as base, then, at a glance, it is easy to read off the percentage change in one variable relative to that of the others. Suppose, for example, that we are interested in the prices of three goods, x, y and z, between 1970 and 1990. Suppose that, over the period in question, the price (of an arbitrarily defined unit — e.g. in tonnes, bushels, ounces, etc.) of x increased from £27 to £134, that of y increased from £64 to £280, while that of z went up from £8.1 to £40. The extent to which the percentage increase in one price differed from that of the others is not immediately obvious. Partly for clarity in exposition (but, as shown below, for other reasons also), economists often use index numbers to indicate how the prices of various goods have changed. Taking 1970 as the base year in the example at hand, and therefore setting the 1970 prices of the three goods = 100, we find (following the procedure outlined in the paragraph immediately above) that in 1990 the index for the price of x stood at 496, that of y was 437.5, while that of z came to 494. The rate of price increase was highest in the case of good x; its price increased by 396 per cent.

Some index numbers (e.g. one for a *composite*, or "bundle", of different goods) are special types of averages of other index numbers. For example, suppose that there are only three types of grain — barley (x), wheat (y) and oats (z), and that to base 1970 = 100, the indices for the prices of these three commodities are as indicated in the immediately preceding paragraph. With 1970 as base year, what is the value of the price index of the composite commodity, grain, in 1990? One possible approach — but generally an unsatisfactory approach — to constructing such an index number would be to take the *arithmetic average* of the three price indices in that year; for the example under consideration, this would involve computing (496 + 437.5 + 494)/3, yielding an index value of 475.8 in 1990 and thereby suggesting that the price of grain (the composite commodity) increased by 376 per cent over the period. But this approach could be extremely misleading: the construction of an index number for 1990 should assign appropriate *weights* to each of the individual components of the composite commodity in order to take account of the relative importance of the three types of grain in, say, overall grain production or consumption. The exact choice of weights depends on the purpose for which the (composite) grain price index is being constructed, but it is also in part a matter of judgment. Thus, suppose that we want to know the extent to which the price of grain faced by users of that composite commodity increased over the period in question; that in the base year (1970) barley (x) accounted for a proportion of only 0.003 of total expenditure on grain, wheat (y) accounted for a proportion 0.995 of such expenditure, while that on oats came to a proportion 0.002 of total grain expenditure; finally, suppose that the pattern (i.e. the shares) of such expenditure did not vary by much between 1970 and 1990. (Note that the sum of the shares must equal unity.) It would then make sense to construct a grain price index for 1990, to base 1970, by weighting the price indices of each of the component commodities in accordance with their shares in total expenditure on grain in the base year, (i.e. using a *weighted average*), as follows: Grain price index for 1990 (to base 1970) = 0.003(496) + 0.995(437.5) + 0.002(494) = 438, yielding a grain price increase of only 338 per cent (in contrast to 376 per cent as suggested by the earlier arithmetic average). Note that the weighted average price index for the composite commodity is a much more meaningful indicator of the general increase in the price of grain than was the arithmetic average of the individual components (where each commodity, regardless of its importance, was assigned the same weight, 1/3).

The logic behind the construction of a *consumer price index* — an index of the cost of living faced by consumers in general — is similar. The main points are that in constructing a price index for a composite variable, weights must be assigned to the individual component elements;

those weights should, in some meaningful sense, reflect the relative importance of the component elements; in order to make sense, the sum of the weights in the overall index should equal unity; finally, every index is always relative to some base observation(s).

The use of index numbers can clarify the distinction between the *nominal value* and the *real value* of an economic variable measured in terms of money. The distinction can be seen from the following example. To base year 1980 = 100, the index of average hourly earnings in Irish manufacturing industry is estimated to have attained a value of 199 in 1987; thus *nominal* earnings increased by 99 per cent. However, this provides no clue as to whether, per hour of work, workers became better or worse off. In order to make a judgment on that issue, it is necessary, at the very least, to know what happened to consumer prices. To base year 1980 = 100, the consumer price index stood at 191 in 1987. Given this evidence, we can estimate that to base 1980 = 100, the index for real hourly earnings — the purchasing power of nominal hourly earnings (before payment of taxes on income and wealth) — rose to only $(199/191)100 = 104.2$; thus, although nominal hourly earnings increased by 99 per cent over the period, their real value increased by only 4.2 per cent. The distinction is similar in the case of other economic variables measured in terms of money.

Having discussed index numbers, it is appropriate to comment briefly on time series for the absolute value of an economic variable which is measured in terms of money. Thus, suppose that the nominal value of consumers' expenditure on goods and services increased from £6,000 million in one year, say year 1, to £10,000 million in, say, year 5; alternatively we could report that the *money value* of consumption expenditure, or consumption expenditure measured at *current market prices*, increased from the first to the second figure over the period in question. But what was the absolute value of the increase in *real* consumption expenditure? To answer this question there are two (almost equivalent) procedures which we might adopt:

(1) Assuming that an appropriate index of consumer prices is available, and given a value for that index in year 5 (with that of year 1 = 100), we could *deflate* or *inflate* the absolute figure for nominal expenditure in year 5, using the index number of year 5. Thus, suppose that the price index for year 5 was 160. Our estimate of real consumption expenditure in year 5 would then be $(£10,000 \text{ m.})(100/160) = (£10,000 \text{ m.})(0.625)$; we therefore estimate that (relative to year 1) real consumption expenditure increased by £250 million over the period. This procedure involves

deflating the nominal value of consumption expenditure in year 5 by a factor of 0.625. (Note that we would have to inflate the nominal figure for year 5, by some factor greater than unity, if the price level had fallen over the period.)

(2) Alternatively, we could evaluate the goods and services upon which consumers incurred expenditures in year 5, using as our measuring-rod the prices which actually prevailed in year 1. This would yield an estimate of consumption expenditure in year 5 at *constant market prices* (i.e. those of year 1). This approach might yield an estimate of real consumption expenditure in year 5 of, say £6,260 million.

Methods (1) and (2) are two alternative ways of estimating real consumption expenditure in year 5 (real relative to that of year 1). Note that the two estimates can differ, though usually by relatively small amounts only. Method (2) is generally preferable because it implicitly allows the weights attached to the several components of overall consumption expenditure to change over time (as they in fact might), while method (1) assumes that they stay constant. The situation is similar in the case of other economic variables which are measured in terms of money. But whatever method is used, it should not be forgotten that a figure for the absolute value of an economic variable, interpreted in real terms and measured in terms of money (rather than in, say, tonnes or litres, and not to be confused with "the money or nominal value" of a variable) is always relative to some base period.

The Master Economist

Around the middle of the nineteenth century the economist-philosopher J.S. Mill wrote that a man is unlikely to be a good economist if he is nothing else. We are inclined to agree (though note that this implies a value-judgement on our part). To be a good economist one must be able to conceptualise in an empirically relevant way. Useful inductive hypotheses may be suggested by appreciation of the evolutionary forces underlying economic activity. Thus socio-historical intuition can be an asset to the economist. But it is also necessary to be able to conceptualise abstractly and think logically; indeed it may be nigh impossible to draw logically firm conclusions from the assumptions of many theories unless the theories are specified as formal (mathematical) propositions. And, finally, an economist must be down-to-earth when it comes to testing theories using the methods of statistical inference; but creativity and versatility in that direction also presume some mathematical abilities.

J.M. Keynes regarded his lecturer Alfred Marshall as perhaps the greatest of economists. There are millions of people who know a little economics and tens of thousands who describe themselves as economists, but few truly great economists. Why? We do not necessarily agree with all the views expressed, but perhaps the following passage from Keynes' essay on Alfred Marshall offers some insights:

> The study of economics does not seem to require any specialised gifts of an unusually high order.... Yet good, or even competent, economists are the rarest of birds. An easy subject, at which very few excel! The paradox finds its explanation, perhaps, in that the master-economist must possess a rare *combination* of gifts. He must reach a high standard in several different directions and must combine talents not often found together. He must be mathematician, historian, statesman, philosopher — in some degree. He must understand symbols and speak in words. He must contemplate the particular in terms of the general, and touch abstract and concrete in the same flight of thought. He must study the present in the light of the past for the purposes of the future. No part of man's nature or his institutions must lie entirely outside his regard. He must be purposeful and disinterested in a simultaneous mood; as aloof and incorruptible as an artist, yet sometimes as near the earth as a politician. Much, but not all, of this many-sidedness Marshall possessed."
> (*Essays in Biography*, Macmillan, London, 1933, pp. 170, 171.)

APPENDIX TO CHAPTER 2

FUNCTIONS, GRAPHS AND SLOPE

Here we review some simple technical concepts which should already be familiar. These are the *only* prior mathematical notions required for understanding the entire text. However, it is suggested that the reader will need much more mathematics if intending at a later stage to proceed to higher-level economic analysis.

Functions

We all recognise that consumption expenditure depends on income, and that the potential output of a good depends on the amounts of inputs to the production of that good. Instead of saying that consumption expenditure depends on income, we might alternatively say that consumption is a function of income. When we say that y is a function of x, what we mean is that y depends on x in some particular way, and we denote this as y =

f(x), which we read as "y is a function of x" or "y depends on x". (The mathematician would be more restrictive in defining function.) When we write $y = f(x)$ we are *not* saying that y equals f multiplied by x; the letter f (or any other letter unlikely to cause confusion) is used merely as shorthand to denote that the value of y depends on x.

Dependent and Independent Variables

In the above example, x (the variable on the right-hand side) is called the independent variable, while y (the variable on the left-hand side), is called the dependent variable. In that equation only one variable is postulated as independent: y depends on x and on x alone.

Functions of Many Independent Variables

We could likewise discuss functions of many independent variables. $Q = f(x_1, x_2, \ldots x_n)$ is an example. Q might be the number of motor cars (a particular model) produced per month. The variables $x_1, x_2, x_3 \ldots x_n$ might then be the amounts used of various inputs, n in number, per month. The variable x_1 might be the amount of engine assembly capacity used, x_2 might represent the amount of metal stamping capacity employed, and so on.

Equations

An equation tells us how variables are related. We read $y = f(x)$ as y depends on x. If we were told that $y = 7 + 2x$ we would know not just that y depends on x, but the precise manner in which y depends on x. If, for example (in the last equation), $x = 1$, then $y = 9$; if $x = 10$, then $y = 27$; if x increases by unity from 6 to 7, then y increases by two from 19 to 21, and so on. Equations normally enable us to calculate the values of dependent variables corresponding to any values of independent variables.

Variables and Parameters

Inspect the equation $y = 7 + 2x$. The x and the y are called variables, since they can take on different values in a single equation. The 7 and 2 are called parametric constants or, simply, parameters. A parameter is a symbol or number which remains constant in a given equation; if a parameter changes, the equation changes.

Standard Form of Linear Equations in Two Variables

A linear equation is one in which all variables are raised to the power of unity, and in which there are no products or quotients of variables. (Thus $y = ax^2 + bx$ or $z = 7uv$ are not linear.) The standard form of linear equations in two variables is $y = a + bx$, where x and y are variables, a and b being parameters. Note the standard mathematical convention of using letters at the end of the alphabet to represent variables, and those at the beginning to represent parameters, or constants. If an equation can be written in the standard linear form, the parameters provide us, on sight, some information about the graph of the equation.

The Rectangular Co-ordinate System

A graph is a pictorial representation of one or more equations. One method of constructing graphs of equations in two variables is to use the rectangular co-ordinate system, depicted in Figure 1. The two axes, X and Y, intersect at right angles at a point 0 (where x = 0 and y = 0). In mathematical convention the horizontal axis is assigned to the independent variable and the vertical axis to the dependent variable. (Note that this convention is not always abided by in economic applications.) The intersection of the X and the Y axes yields four quadrants. Any real number can be represented as a point on a line. The values of both x and y are positive inside quadrant I. Inside quadrant II, x is negative and y is positive. Both x and y are negative inside quadrant III, while inside quadrant IV, x is positive and y is negative. Along the axes themselves, at least one variable has a value of zero. For example, the point labelled A has the values x = 0 and y = 1; that labelled B has the values x = 2, y = 1; and that labelled C corresponds to x = -3, y = 1. Quadrant I is that most relevant to economic analysis, because economists seldom deal with negative quantities.

Figure 1

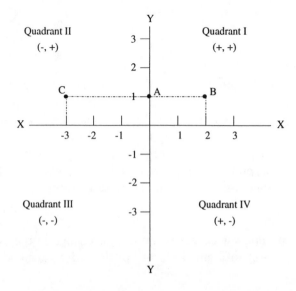

Return to the equation y = 7 + 2x. It is a simple matter to calculate that

If

$$x = 0, 1, 2, 3, 4, 5, 6, \ldots$$

then

$$y = 7, 9, 11, 13, 15, 17, 19, \ldots$$

Figure 2

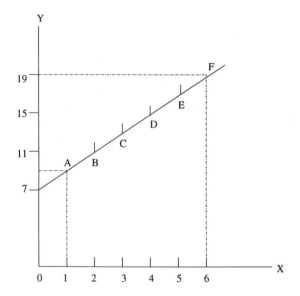

We can now plot the graph of y = 7 + 2x (concentrating on positive values of the variables). Taking various values of x and plotting the corresponding values of y in the (X, Y) plane, quadrant I, we get a set of points like A, B, C, D, E and F in Figure 2. If we join these points we get a smooth locus which is the graph of the equation as x varies from 0 to 6. The value of the dependent variable when the independent variable has a value of zero is called the intercept; in the present example, it is +7.

The Slope of a Line

The slope of any line (or curve) is the rate of change in the dependent variable with respect to a small change in the independent variable. It shows by how much the dependent variable will change if the independent variable changes by a small amount.

We saw, in the case of the equation $y = 7 + 2x$, that every time x increased by one unit, y increased by two units. Hence the slope, $\Delta y/\Delta x$ (read change in y with respect to change in x) is 2. (Note that we can speak interchangeably of the slope of an equation in two variables and the slope of the graph of that equation.) Note also that the slope of a straight line (a linear equation) is constant, and that this slope is given by the coefficient of (i.e. the parameter before) the independent variable. Thus the slope of the standard linear equation in two variables, $y = a + bx$, is b; the dependent variable y changes by b units for every unit change in the independent variable x.

Suppose that $x = 3$ in Figure 2 and ask the question: if x changes by a small amount — say by one unit from $x = 3$ to $x = 4$, by how much will y change? We can read from our graph that if $\Delta x = +1$, then $\Delta y = +2$. Hence the slope of the line between C and D — and, indeed, between any two points — is $\Delta y/\Delta x = 2$. This is exactly the value of the coefficient of x in the equation $y = 7 + 2x$.

But consider the equation $y = 7 - 2x$. The reader should recognise that, unlike the preceding example, the graph of this equation will slope down from left to right. It should also be recognised that the slope is -2, reflecting the fact that a unit change in x brings about a change of two units, in the opposite direction, in y.

It should now be obvious that we can tell the properties of the graph of any linear equation in two variables, $y = a + bx$, on sight, merely by inspecting the parameters of the equation. Thus the intercept is a and the slope is b.

Linear Equations: More Than Two Variables

A linear equation in more than two variables is of the form $y = a + b_1x_1 + b_2x_2 + \ldots + b_nx_n$ where y is the dependent variable, x_1 to x_n are independent variables, and a, b_1 to b_n are parameters. The main point to note is that the coefficient of any of the x's, say x_i, shows the amount by which y changes if x_i changes by one unit (assuming all the other x's are given).

Non-linear Equations: The Slope of a Curve

Not all equations are of the simple linear forms discussed above. If an equation in two variables cannot be reduced to the form $y = a + bx$, it is non-linear. Its graph is not a straight line. The slope of a curve — the graph of a non-linear equation — can change in both value and sign from one point to another. We defined slope as the rate of change in a dependent variable with respect to a small change in an independent variable. Alternatively, we can say that the slope of a curve at a point is the slope of the straight line tangent to the curve at that point. Thus we could measure the slope of the curve in Figure 3 below at, say, point A, by measuring $\Delta y/\Delta x$ along the tangent locus A'A'.

Convexity and Concavity

Consider a curve $y = f(x)$. This function is *strictly convex* if its slope continues to increase as x increases; if, on the other hand, the slope always decreases as x increases, the function is *strictly concave*. The curve in Figure 3 is strictly concave. However, if that curve were inverted it would be strictly convex. [On a more technical point note the following: non-mathematicians often confuse convexity (concavity) with strict convexity (strict concavity). A function $y = f(x)$ is simply convex if its slope does not decrease as x increases; it is simply concave if its slope does not increase as x increases. It follows that a straight line is both convex and concave, but it is neither strictly convex nor strictly concave. Similarly, a curve which is convex, but which is partly linear, is not strictly convex.]

Figure 3

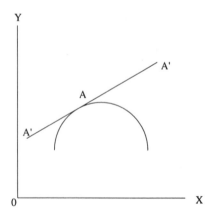

Inequalities: Notation

  A > B means A is greater than B.
  A ≥ B means A is greater than or equal to B.
  A < B means A is less than B.
  A ≤ B means A is less than or equal to B.

PART TWO

SUPPLY AND DEMAND

CHAPTER 3

INTRODUCTORY

There are two principal branches of economic analysis. *Macro-economics* is concerned with aggregates rather than the individual elements which make up those aggregates. In *microeconomics* we focus on individual markets and deal with questions of the form: What inputs, and how much of each input, will a firm operating in particular product and factor markets hire if its objective is to maximise profits? What would be the effects of a tax per unit on a good? What determines the price and quantity traded of a particular commodity? In macroeconomics we analyse questions such as: what determines the overall rate of infla-tion, the level of national output and the rate of economic growth? What can government do to avert large-scale unemployment? Suppose that the Irish monetary authorities attempted to generate a large increase in the money supply. Under what circumstances could that be done, independ-ently of what might be happening in the rest of the world? How would the national economy be affected?

An understanding of macroeconomics requires prior comprehension of some of its microeconomic foundations. This should come as no surprise, given that macro or aggregative variables are made up of micro components. Microeconomic theory tends to be quite abstract; macro-economics, while also necessarily abstract, is more public-policy oriented. Before attempting to understand macroeconomic theory, the reader should acquire some expertise in the elementary (microeconomic) analysis of individual markets.

THE ALLOCATION PROBLEM

What goods will be produced and in what quantities? *How*, or by what technique, will they be produced? *For whom* will goods be produced? (i.e. by what rules, of deservedness and the like, will production be distributed among individuals in society?) These questions constitute the allocation problem of every economy. The problem might, in principle, be solved by centralised planning without use of prices. A central plan-ning bureau could make orders concerning the amounts to be produced of each good, as well as directions in regard to choice of technique. It could then distribute the goods in accordance with the government's ethical

[41]

priorities. However, a private enterprise economy relies on a mechanism of markets and prices to solve its allocation problem. In that system prices (of both resources and final goods) serve as signals which allocate flows of factors of production into different productive activities and flows of products among consumers.

The questions what goods and how much of those goods will be produced, as well as how goods will be produced, are solved in an efficient manner in the *ideal* decentralised market economy. Part Six of this text will elaborate on the matter of efficiency of the market mechanism. The system is decentralised because, in its pure form, there is no controlling body co-ordinating activities in various markets. The market mechanism may also determine the pattern of income distribution — the question of who gets goods — but to say that it does so in a desirable or undesirable manner is a normative judgment (i.e. one which reflects personal values), and as such goes beyond the confines of economic analysis. The way in which the market mechanism solves the allocation problem is roughly as follows:

If consumers come to desire more of a particular good than previously, the price of that good will be bid upward. This acts as a *signal* for firms to expand production. In a competitive economy firms tend to produce only those goods which yield profit; furthermore, they expand output of any good up to a point at which they would be adding more to their total costs than to their total revenues if they were to expand output further. Only then can they be maximising profits. In this manner supply and demand determine the quantities of *what* will be produced. *How* goods will be produced — the choice of technology — is determined by supply and demand in the markets for the factors of production. Firms demand factors of production (or inputs) in order to gain profit from the production which the hire of those factors generates. The assumed increase in demand for a particular good, which increased its price, leads to an increase in demand by firms for certain inputs. The resulting increase in factor prices acts as a signal inducing resource-owners (labour, land-owners and the owners of capital equipment) to supply more inputs to the industry in question. Given these market-determined factor prices, firms, in maximising profits, choose those combinations of factors of production which minimise costs; this determines *how* goods will be produced. For example, if the price of labour is cheap relative to the price of capital equipment, firms tend to opt for labour-intensive techniques (i.e. methods of production involving high ratios of labour to capital equipment). Finally, the factor prices determined by supply and demand are the incomes of the factors of production. These accrue to households which indicate their "votes" for different goods by the pattern of their demands.

Thus the very process of factor pricing determines *for whom* goods are produced.

It follows that the configuration of prices emerging from the operation of markets is not independent of the pattern of income distribution. In a market economy some individuals earn very high incomes because they have skills very scarce in relation to the demand for them. Because of the high incomes thereby earned, they bid up the prices of Queen Anne furniture and choice residential sites in scenic locations. If all incomes were equal, the prices of such goods would not be bid up so high; but nor would other goods be low in price. The manner in which the pattern of income distribution emerging from the factor market of a decentralised market economy determines what goods are produced has been described as an "undemocratic" voting system in which some individuals (those on high incomes) have more votes than others. It is mentioned in passing that even some opponents of private enterprise (opponents mainly because of the manner in which the pattern of income distribution is determined in such a system) have been so impressed by the efficiency of the ways in which decentralised markets handle the questions *what* and *how* that they have advocated the adoption of those features in the economic systems which they have proposed as alternatives.

The mechanism of decentralised markets which solves the allocation problem is not one of chaos; it does operate in a systematic way despite the absence of conscious co-ordination. It has in fact been argued that resource allocation through free markets is efficient *because* of the absence of state intervention and control. That was the view of Adam Smith, who in 1776 wrote that

> it is not from the benevolence of the butcher, the brewer or the baker that we expect our dinner, but from their regard to their own interest. Every individual intends only his own gain, and he is in this led by an invisible hand to promote an end which was no part of his intention. By pursuing his own interest he frequently promotes that of society more effectually than when he really intends to promote it. (*The Wealth of Nations*, Bobbs-Merrill abridged edn., Indianapolis, pp. 14, 15, 166. The above quotation is a further abridgment).

The belief that each individual, in pursuing their own interests in a competitive economy, was also pursuing the interests of society as a whole by way of "an invisible hand", led Smith to oppose almost every kind of interference with the operation of free competitive markets, whether by government, by trade unions or in the form of conspiracies in constraint of free trade by employers.

Although the market mechanism does have several attractive features, these should not he exaggerated. First, an unregulated market mechanism would determine the pattern of income distribution in society, which may be very inegalitarian; depending on one's social philosophy, this might be deemed undesirable. Second, not all markets are freely competitive. There may be monopoly in both the product and factor markets, and this may interfere with the efficient functioning of the system. Thus, if only a single firm produces a final product, that firm might restrict output in order to obtain high prices and high profits. Or if wages are flexible in an upward direction but inflexible downward (due, for example, to monopoly power by trade unions), large-scale unemployment may result. More efficient operation of the economy may then require appropriate intervention by the public authorities. Third, unregulated firms, in maximising profits, may impose costs on third parties, as with environmental pollution, for example. Fourth, it may be felt that the public interest necessitates that the government should provide goods and services which profit-maximising firms would not have incentive to provide. In the century following the publication of Smith's *The Wealth of Nations*, British governments tended to apply Smith's *laissez-faire* philosophy (a political philosophy advocating non-intervention by government in the economy). One has only to read Cecil Woodham-Smith's classic, *The Great Hunger: Ireland 1845–9*, for details of how that government, by refusing to intervene in economic activity until it was largely too late, failed to prevent the starvation or emigration of millions of Irish people in the 1840s. Finally, although it may be granted that a free market economy would tend to be highly efficient if it were stable, it may be argued that such a system would be prone to oscillations in output and employment, or that it would take a long time to attain efficiency at what we will call equilibrium. Perhaps central planning or simply pragmatic intervention could bring the economy to equilibrium (a position of stability) more rapidly.

ECONOMIC GOODS, PRODUCTIVE ACTIVITIES AND THE MARKET

In this book when we refer to goods we mean physical goods as well as services (such as restaurant facilities, legal advice or banking services). However, lest the reader forget our meaning we will sometimes refer explicitly to "goods and services". Goods which command a price, or exchange value, are called *economic* or *scarce* goods in distinction to *free goods*, such as fresh air is or once was, which do not command a price. Alternatively it can be stated that for the economist, a scarce good is one for which the demand at a price of zero would exceed available supply. In order to possess exchange value a good must be subjectively *useful* (it must give satisfaction or utility to consumers) and *limited in supply*. It is only because economic goods are of subjective use that they are demanded. They cannot be produced in unlimited quantities because resources are limited. Provided that they can be reproduced at all (unlike the case of paintings such as "old masters"), the opportunity costs of scarce goods are positive; to provide more of them resources have to be induced away from other uses, including leisure. However, items which are low in supply, but which nobody wants, are not scarce in the sense of the economist. Utility and limitation of supply find their explicit expression in the demands of buyers and the supplies of sellers. By their interaction, supply and demand determine market price, or exchange value.

In modern economics any activity which creates economic goods is regarded as *productive* simply because it leads to satisfaction of human wants. That is the case whether the end product of the activity is a physical good or a service. In this respect modern economics is at variance with Adam Smith and other early economists who regarded activities the end product of which was a service, as unproductive.

The concept "market" is not amenable to a simple operational definition. In his *Principles of Economics* (8th edition, 1920) Alfred Marshall took eight pages to discuss the term, and since then a large number of refinements have been added. Any place in which buyers and sellers communicate to trade is a market. But the word "place" should not be interpreted too narrowly. We think of a market as a medium of communication between buyers and sellers rather than as a well-defined geographic location. The foreign exchange market is not well-defined geographically, but in that market there is constant communication, through electronic and other means, between buyers and sellers. The only essential requirement for market is that buyers and sellers can communicate — regardless of how — to carry out trading.

CHAPTER 4

SUPPLY AND DEMAND IN PERFECTLY COMPETITIVE MARKETS

As a starting point in the analysis of the allocation process, this chapter outlines the determination of price and output in a perfectly competitive market. Discussion of the allocation process will be completed only after a return to microeconomics in Part Six.

The market for a particular good is perfectly competitive if the following conditions are satisfied:

(1) There must be a very large number of both buyers and sellers such that no single trader can influence price. No single buyer could bargain down the established market price in their own favour. Buyers accept price as given, a datum beyond their control. If any seller tried to raise price above the established level no willing purchasers would be found. These conditions assume that traders have perfect knowledge about conditions in the market. In a perfectly competitive market each trader is accordingly a price-taker.

(2) The product traded must be homogeneous or identical, in the minds of buyers. Competitive advertising, trademarks and brand names are therefore ruled out — for their purpose is to differentiate, in buyers' minds, one firm's product from that of a competitor. The homogeneity requirement, along with that of perfect knowledge, ensures that buyers will not purchase from firms charging higher prices than others. (Pressed to its extreme, this assumption implies zero transport costs; strictly speaking, two physically identical goods are not homogeneous if costs must be incurred in bringing them to the same place.)

(3) There must be no collusion or conspiracy anywhere in the market; nor must there be institutional restrictions (for example, government rationing or maximum price orders) on supplies, demands or prices. The first condition implies that no group of traders organise together to influence price. The second condition (no institutional restrictions) ensures that all potential traders are free to enter the market and that prices are free to move if conditions underlying supply or demand change.

It should be obvious from these conditions that few if any markets are fully perfectly competitive. Other market structures will be analysed later on. But as indicated in Chapter 2, all theory abstracts, and a good theory abstracts in a useful way. Actual markets often approximate the requirements of perfect competition. Government intervention aside, Irish agriculture is in large measure perfectly competitive. The individual potato grower does not perceptibly affect price by deciding to sow a few acres under potatoes. One grower's supply is negligible compared with total market supplies of potatoes; it is like a grain in the bucket. Nor do individual growers collude with other farmers to restrict supplies, or attempt to promote their product over that of other growers by competitive advertising. Furthermore, because it is subject to brisk competition from firms in other EU countries, it is useful for some purposes to analyse the market conditions of much of Irish manufacturing industry as closely approximating perfect competition. That may be true even if each of the Irish firms in an industry is one of only a few producers (as distinct from sellers) in the domestic economy. If domestic firms in an industry are producing products which are very close substitutes for each other as well as for those of competitors located in other EU countries, and if the products in question are quickly and easily transported, then the individual Irish producer can have little impact on price. Even if the Irish producers colluded to restrict their outputs, and to raise their prices significantly above those of other EU producers, they would face the constraints imposed by external competition; thus they could not effectively collude to raise prices significantly above those of close substitutes in the form of competing imports. Nor would UK or Continental consumers be willing to buy Irish manufactures at prices significantly higher than those charged by UK or Continental firms for very similar goods.

Some markets diverge from perfect competition largely because of government intervention. To analyse the effects of such public policies it is then appropriate to start assuming perfect competition, and to superimpose the public policies on that analytic framework. That is what will be done in Chapter 6, where some applications of supply and demand analysis will be considered. Useful theories abstract in a useful way; they explain and predict central features of reality. It is our belief that the applications in Chapter 6 and subsequently will satisfy those criteria.

In the analysis of price determination which follows, it is assumed that the good under discussion is sold under conditions approximating perfect competition. It is emphasised that the analysis is offered as an explanation of price determination *only* in markets approximating perfect competition; for other types of market structure, such as monopoly, the analysis of the supply side can be significantly misleading.

MARKET DEMAND

Throughout this book it is assumed that consumers seek to maximise the utility (subjective satisfaction) obtainable by allocating their expenditures among goods. Unless indicated to the contrary, it is assumed that their tastes among goods are constant.

A market demand curve shows the various alternative quantities of a good which consumers would attempt to buy per period of time (e.g. per day, per week, etc.) at various alternative prices of that good, other things being equal. In order to clarify "other things being equal" it is necessary to consider the concept of a general demand function, implicit in the definition of demand curve. Suppose that many kinds of goods, say n different types of goods, are available and consider any one of them, say the nth. Upon what things does the quantity demanded of good n depend? (Note that the goods can always be listed in such a manner that any good is the nth.) To answer, consider a general demand function:

$$(1) \quad q_d^n = f(p^1, p^2, ..., p^{n-1}, p^n; m, pop, dist, g)$$

This demand function states that the quantity demanded of good n (q_d^n) depends on: the price of good n itself (p^n); the prices of all other goods ($p^1, ..., p^{n-1}$); total money income (m); the number of consumers (pop); the distribution of income (dist) and possibly on a variable (g) representing government interference in the market.

We assume here that there is no government interference; so $g = 0$. Quantity demanded of good n also depends on the tastes of consumers, but tastes are not included as an explicit independent variable in the demand function; rather, tastes determine the *functional form* of (1) — they determine the manner in which quantity demanded depends on the variables on the right-hand side. It is true that the quantity demanded of a good might depend on further independent variables (such as the stock of assets held by consumers) not listed on the right hand side of (1), but because such variables will be assumed constant in what follows, they need not be listed: like tastes, they will influence the functional form of (1).

We agree that quantity demanded of good n — say apples — depends on the price of apples (p^n). We expect that if all variables on which the demand for apples depends other than the price of apples remain constant, then the lower the price of apples, the more apples consumers will wish to buy. Apart from the good's own price, p^n, the demand for good n, apples, depends on the prices of all other goods, $p^1, ..., p^{n-1}$. That is the case for two reasons:

(1) Suppose p^1 is the price of pears. Then, given p^2, ..., p^n, the lower p^1 happens to be, the smaller will desired purchases of apples be. That is because apples and pears are *substitutes*.

(2) Consideration of substitute goods (and their opposites, complements, which will be discussed in the next chapter) aside, the demand for any good depends on the prices of all other goods which consumers buy. To see this we simplify and suppose that there are only three goods entering consumers' expenditure plans, their prices being p^1, p^2 and p^3. Then the demand function for good 3 would be of the form: $q_d^3 = f(p^1, p^2, p^3, m, ...)$. Substitutability (and complementarity) aside, q_d^3 depends on (for example) the price of good 2, p^2, because if the price of good 2 increased, while the prices of all other goods and consumers' money incomes stayed fixed, then consumers would experience a decline in general purchasing power — they could buy fewer goods with their fixed money incomes. Although they would experience no changes in their money incomes, their *real* incomes — the general purchasing power of their money incomes — would have fallen, and this could affect their demands for all goods.

Hence, returning to the general demand function (1) above, it can be stated that q_d^n depends on p^1, p^2, ..., p^{n-1} because (a) good n is likely to have substitutes (and complements) and (b) given their money incomes, the size of consumers' real incomes — their purchasing power in general — depends on the prices of all goods, i.e. on the price level in general.

To explain why q_d^n depends on the remaining variables is a more simple task. If total money income (m) or the number of consumers (pop) change, one would expect changes in the amount of any good demanded. Furthermore, as was mentioned in Chapter 3, one would expect the pattern of demand among goods to be sensitive to the pattern of income distribution among households (dist). Finally, the demand for a good may depend on government interference (g). For example, it is likely that if consumption of some good were banned, then the demand for that good would be reduced.

A demand function represents the amount of a good consumers would desire to buy *per period of time* if prices, money income, etc. were at various alternative levels. Thus the dependent variable is a *flow* over time rather than a *stock* at a point in time; it is so much per day, per month, or over some other specific time period. We are now ready to move from the general demand function (1) to a simple demand curve and to explain some implications of "other things being equal".

Reflect on the general demand function for good n, (1) above. If tastes and all variables inside parentheses on the right of (1) stay constant, except for p^n, there would be a definite relationship between q_d^n and p^n and we could write

(1') $q_d^n = f(p^n)$

This function states that quantity demanded of good n depends in some particular manner on the price of good n, so long as all other things upon which q_d^n depends remain constant. Alternatively, (1') states that other things being equal, quantity demanded of good n depends in some particular manner on the price of good n. Assume as before that q_d^n is the demand for apples and that p^n is the price of apples. Now suppose that using techniques of statistical inference an economist correctly estimates that the relationship between the quantity demanded of apples and their price (given tastes and specific levels of all other variables in the general demand function) is as in Table 1.

Table 1: A Schedule of the Demand for Apples (Bushels per Week)

Price (£)	18	15	9	6	3
Quantity Demanded (Bushels)	250	500	1,000	1,250	1,500

The dependence of q_d^n on p^n is represented in graphical form in Figure 1 below. Along the vertical axis we measure p^n. Quantity demanded is measured along the horizontal axis. We plot the demand schedule from Table 1 as a set of points. Joining these points yields the continuous demand curve DD.

Demand curves generally slope downward implying that more of a good will usually be bought at low than at high prices. In Figure 1 the demand curve DD traces the dependence of the demand for apples (q_d^n) on the price of apples (p^n). For any particular price of apples (good n) a specific quantity of apples would be demanded — but only on the assumption that tastes, p^1, ..., p^{n-1}, m, pop, dist and g remain constant as p^n varies. Hence we can say that other things being equal, if the price of apples falls from £12 to £6 per bushel, quantity demanded will increase from 750 to 1,250 bushels per week.

Consider what would happen if some of the things which were regarded as constant in constructing DD were to change. Suppose that tastes changed in favour of apples. Instead of demanding 750 bushels a week at a price of £12, consumers might now want to buy 1,250 bushels. Similarly, they might now seek to buy 1,750 instead of 1,250 bushels at a price of £6 per bushel. The change in tastes would have led to an outward shift in the demand curve from DD to D'D' in Figure 1. Other reasons why, at any particular price of apples, consumers might wish to buy more apples include an increase in the price of a substitute good (pears, for example), growth of money incomes, change in the distribution of income in favour of vegetarians, etc.

The demand curve for good n (apples) could shift to the left as, for example, from DD to D"D" in Figure 1. This might happen if tastes moved against the good, if money incomes fell, if the price level in general increased, thereby reducing the general purchasing power of consumers, or if the price of a close substitute for good n decreased. The shift to the left of the demand curve from DD to D"D" would reflect the fact that at any particular price of good n, consumers are now willing to buy a smaller quantity of good n than before.

Figure 1

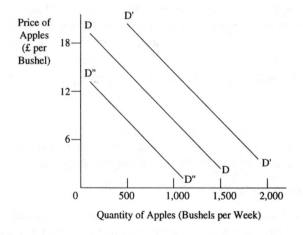

Quantity of Apples (Bushels per Week)

MARKET SUPPLY

It is only for markets which approximate perfect competition that the supply and demand analysis of this chapter is valid. As will be demonstrated much later, that is mainly because a well-defined supply curve does not generally exist in other market structures.

A market supply curve shows the alternative quantities of a good producers will supply per period of time at various alternative prices of that good, other things being equal. It will be assumed in what immediately follows that the objective of firms is to maximise profits, and that they act accordingly. Also, unless stated to the contrary, it will be assumed that the state of technical knowledge is given, and that the situation in regard to the availability of various factors of production to firms stays constant in whatever time period is under analysis. These considerations influence the functional form of the general supply function

(2) $q_s^n = F(p^1, p^2, ..., p^n; w^1, ..., w^m; g)$

which states that the quantity of good n supplied per period depends on the prices of all goods, n in number, on the prices of all resources (w^1, ..., w^m), m in number and possibly on government interference (for example, by taxes on suppliers) in the market. We continue to assume no such interference; so $g = 0$.

Quantity supplied of a good depends on the good's price; we expect producers to increase supply of a good if its price increases. It also depends on the prices of other goods. Suppose, for example that a farmer's land is equally suitable for oats and barley. Given the price of oats, the farmer would not grow oats rather than barley unless the price of barley were below a certain level. Quantity supplied also depends on the prices of resources which could be used as inputs, because these help determine production costs. And as already stated, our assumptions concerning the goals of producers, the state of technology and the availability of factors, influence the functional form of (2); they influence the precise manner in which q_s^n depends on the variables on the right-hand side of (2).

If all variables affecting quantity supplied of good n, except for p^n, remain constant, there will be a definite relationship between q_s^n and p^n, and this can be represented by the simple supply function

(2') $q_s^n = F(p^n)$

which states that other things being equal quantity supplied of good n (apples) per period depends in a particular way on that good's price. Suppose that an economist, on the basis of statistical analysis of market data, correctly estimates that the relationship between quantity supplied of apples and their price (given technology and constancy of all other independent variables) is as in Table 2.

Table 2: A Schedule for the Supply of Apples (Bushels per Week)

Price (£)	3	6	9	12	15	18
Quantity Demanded (Bushels)	550	850	1,150	1,450	1,750	2,050

The dependence of q_s^n on p^n in Table 2 is more clearly seen graphically, by the supply curve SS in Figure 2. Supply curves generally slope upward implying that other things being equal, in order to give producers an incentive to expand production, price must rise. But apart from the good's own price, if any of the conditions underlying the supply of good n change, then the supply curve will shift. For example, if technical change brings improved methods of production and lower unit costs, or if input prices fall, then the supply curve will shift to the right, from SS to, say, S'S', reflecting the fact that at any particular price of apples, producers are now willing to supply more than before. If changes in the reverse directions take place, the supply curve will shift to the left, perhaps to S"S" in the diagram.

Figure 2

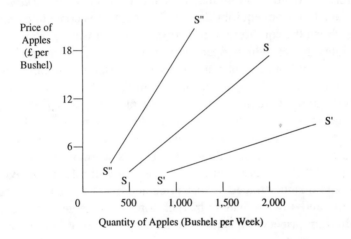

Quantity of Apples (Bushels per Week)

Thus the only independent variable which changes in moving along any particular supply curve is the good's own price; if technology or any other independent variable changes, then the supply curve shifts. Some general comments are in order at this stage.

First, the demand and supply curves DD and SS in Figures 1 and 2 have been drawn as straight lines. That is only because the numbers in Tables 1 and 2, to which these curves correspond, *happen* to imply linear demand and supply curves.

Second, in the above exposition it was assumed that good n was apples; it could in fact have been *any* good which is traded in markets approximating perfect competition.

Third, in the analysis which follows the focus will be on what are called the equilibrium price and quantity traded in a single market, on the assumption, except where otherwise indicated, that all "other things" remain "equal" (i.e. that all factors underlying the demand and supply of

the good under consideration, except the good's own price, remain
constant). Because we will be dealing with a specific good there can be
no confusion concerning the price and quantity to which we refer; so we
can dispense with superscripts above variables and denote the price of
the good under analysis by p and its quantity by q (with subscripts below
those variables representing different levels of p and q).

PRICE DETERMINATION BY SUPPLY AND DEMAND

Quantity traded and price are in *equilibrium* if, given all things discussed
earlier governing supply and demand, there is no tendency for price or
quantity to change. By equilibrium we mean a position of rest, a situation
in which there is no tendency toward change, a balance between oppos-
ing forces. An equilibrium may be stable or unstable. It is *stable* if, when
any deviation from equilibrium takes place, forces come into operation to
re-establish the equilibrium. It is *unstable* if a deviation from equilibrium
generates forces which operate in a cumulative manner to drive the
system away from equilibrium. Thus an egg standing unobstructed at the
side of a smooth table is in unstable equilibrium. But as we will see, most
of the equilibria studied in this text are plausibly stable: if the phenomena under study are not in a position of rest, then they tend to converge
toward such a position unless they are continuously prevented from
doing so because of outside shocks. Unless we indicate to the contrary,
given that they are assumed to be stable, we will refer to the equilibrium
price and quantity traded as that price and quantity traded which tend to
prevail, and toward which market forces converge. To see how the
equilibrium price and quantity traded are determined in a perfectly competitive market we simply enter the supply and demand curves on the
same diagram, as in Figure 3.

Figure 3

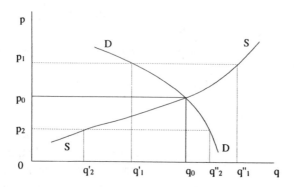

The curve DD in Figure 3 relates quantity demanded of a good per period of time to its price, when tastes, the prices of all other goods, per capita money incomes, etc., are given. The curve SS relates quantity supplied of the good (over the same time period) to its price, given all other conditions underlying supply. Equilibrium price and quantity traded are determined by the intersection of the supply and demand curves; this occurs at p_0 and q_0. They are equilibrium values because once p and q have attained those levels, they will remain unchanged unless some disturbance (a change in the things we are assuming constant underlying either curve) causes one or both of the curves to shift. The equilibrium at p_0 and q_0 is assumed to be stable; other things remaining constant, if these variables are at any other levels, it is assumed that they tend to converge toward their equilibrium values.

To see why the equilibrium price and quantity traded are those corresponding to the intersection of the supply and demand curves, and why that equilibrium is plausibly stable, consider the kinds of pressures which would prevail if price were at any level other than p_0. If price were above p_0, say p_1, suppliers would attempt to sell q''_1 units but buyers would be willing to take only q'_1 units. Quantity supplied would exceed quantity demanded — there would be an excess supply to the extent of $(q''_1 - q'_1)$ units. To avoid such undesired inventory accumulation, suppliers are likely to reduce prices. As competition among sellers forces prices down, quantity supplied decreases and quantity demanded increases. The excess supply disappears only when price has fallen to p_0. Symmetrical reasoning would apply if price were below p_0. If price were p_2, quantity demanded would be q''_2 and quantity supplied would be q'_2; there would be an excess demand of $(q''_2 - q'_2)$ units per period, and the ensuing competition among buyers would drive price up toward p_0. As price rises, quantity demanded decreases while quantity supplied increases. The excess demand disappears only when price has been bid up to p_0 per unit.

Only at p_0 is there neither excess demand nor excess supply. Thus price and quantity traded remain constant only when they have attained the levels corresponding to the intersection of the supply and demand curves. No other price or quantity traded could be maintained for long. Hence p_0 and q_0 represent market equilibrium. So long as the conditions underlying supply and demand remain constant, that price and quantity combination will continue to prevail.

Consider next what would happen if either of the curves were to shift (because of changes in the conditions underlying the supply or demand curves). The supply curve might shift to the right because of some technical development leading to lower unit costs. At any particular price

producers are now willing to supply more than previously. The supply
curve therefore shifts to the right from SS to S'S' in Figure 4, leading to
reduction from p_0 to p_3 in equilibrium price and increase from q_0 to q_3 in
equilibrium quantity. Note that the equilibrium price could also fall as a
result of a shift of the demand curve. Suppose that the conditions underlying the supply curve remain constant but that there is a movement in
tastes away from the good. The demand curve then shifts to the left from
DD to D'D' in Figure 5. Equilibrium price falls from p_0 to p_4, and equilibrium quantity declines from q_0 to q_4. The reader should now be crystal
clear on the question of how supply and demand determine equilibrium
price and quantity traded in a perfectly competitive market, and on how
changes in either (or both) of those curves cause a rise, a fall or no
change in equilibrium price and quantity.

Figure 4

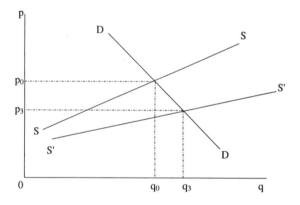

Figure 5

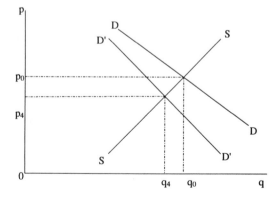

"Change in Demand" and "Change in Quantity Demanded"

It is important to distinguish between a change (increase or decrease) in demand and a change in quantity demanded. A *change in demand* reflects a change in the conditions underlying a demand curve. It is represented by a shift of the demand curve, due to the fact that at least one of the determinants of demand, other than the good's own price, has changed. A *change in quantity demanded* is represented by a movement along a demand curve, reflecting a situation in which the only independent variable in the general demand function which has changed is the good's own price. In Figure 4 there is a change (an increase) in quantity demanded (a movement along a demand curve); in Figure 5 there is a change (a decrease) in demand (a shift of a demand curve).

The distinction between change in supply and change in quantity supplied is similar. A *change in supply* reflects change in the conditions underlying the supply of a good (other than variation in the good's own price). It is represented by a shift of the supply curve. A *change in quantity supplied* is represented by a movement along a supply curve. In Figure 4 there is a change (an increase) in supply. In Figure 5 there is a change (a decrease) in quantity supplied.

CHAPTER 5

ELASTICITIES OF SUPPLY AND DEMAND

Firms are interested in the effects of changes in price on their receipts from sales. In order to know how much they can raise in tax revenue, governments must estimate the response in quantity demanded of various goods to changes in their prices entailed by taxation. In long-term economic planning, change in the demand for various goods, as income increases over time, has to be considered. In the formation of a price support policy for agricultural products, government wants to know the response in quantity supplied of such goods to changes in their prices. If estimates of the relevant elasticities are available, positive answers can be given to such questions.

An elasticity of demand (or supply) is a measure of the degree of responsiveness in the demand for (or in the supply of) a good to changes in the value of some independent variable. *Price elasticity of demand* is a measure of the responsiveness in quantity demanded of a good to changes in the good's own price. *Income elasticity of demand* is a measure of responsiveness in the demand for a good to changes in money income. *Cross elasticity of demand* is a measure of the responsiveness in the demand for a good to changes in the price of some other good. *Elasticity of supply* is a measure of the responsiveness in quantity of a good supplied to changes in its price.

PRICE ELASTICITY OF DEMAND

Subject to a qualification stated in the next paragraph, we use the symbols E_d to denote price elasticity of demand. If, in absolute value, the proportionate change in quantity demanded of a good exceeds a proportionate change in its price, the demand for that good is *elastic*. If the absolute value of the proportionate change in quantity demanded of a good is less than the proportionate change in price, the demand for the good is *inelastic*. If the absolute value of the proportionate change in quantity demanded equals the proportionate change in price, demand is of *unit elasticity*.

We can measure E_d by the formula E_d = (proportionate change in quantity demanded)/(proportionate change in price). Thus

(1) $E_d = (\Delta q/q)/(\Delta p/p) = (\Delta q/\Delta p)(p/q)$

An important convention should be noted. Because price and quantity are almost always inversely related (if price rises, quantity demanded falls) $\Delta q/\Delta p$ is normally negative. Both p and q are positive. Therefore E_d is usually negative. However, Alfred Marshall laid down the convention of treating price elasticity of demand as a non-negative number. We will accordingly measure price elasticity of demand by the absolute (i.e. non-negative) value of E_d, written $|E_d|$.

Another issue liable to cause confusion in using measure (1) to calculate elasticity is best seen by taking an example. If price falls from £8 to £6 in Figure 1 below, leading to an increase in quantity demanded from 200 to 400 units per period of time, what is the numerical value of elasticity within the relevant range of price variation? Use the formula $E_d = (\Delta q/\Delta p)(p/q)$. The interpretation of Δq and Δp is straightforward: $\Delta q = 200$ and $\Delta p = -2$. So $\Delta q/\Delta p = -100$. But what about the measure of p and q in the formula? Does p refer to the first price ($p_1 = 8$) or the second price ($p_2 = 6$), or does it refer to some price between p_1 and p_2? Similarly, does q refer to q_1 (200 units) or q_2 (400 units) or to some quantity between q_1 and q_2? To resolve the ambiguity in the quotient p/q, the convention is to let $p = p_3$, the price *half-way* between the first and second prices. In like manner, let $q = q_3$, the quantity half-way between the first and second quantities. Hence we have, for the numerical example at hand, $p/q = p_3/q_3 = 7/300$. Thus $E_d = (-100)(7)/(300) = -2.3$, and adopting the convention of expressing price elasticity as a non-negative number, $|E_d| = |-2.3| = 2.3$. Interpreted in this way, formula (1) is identical to

$$(2)\ E_d = \frac{\Delta q}{\Delta p} \cdot \frac{\frac{1}{2}(p_1 + p_2)}{\frac{1}{2}(q_1 + q_2)} = \frac{\Delta q}{\Delta p} \cdot \frac{(p_1 + p_2)}{(q_1 + q_2)}$$

where p_1 and q_1 represent the initial price and quantity demanded, p_2 and q_2 are the new price and quantity demanded, and Δp and Δq are the changes in price and quantity demanded.

Note that if the demand curve were the dotted non-linear locus D'D' in Figure 1, the estimate of elasticity given by formula (2), when price falls from £8 to £6, would be exactly as we have calculated above. Thus the measure makes a linear estimate of elasticity between two points. If the demand curve is non-linear, formula (2) in effect assumes that the curve is linear over the range of price variation under consideration.

Figure 1

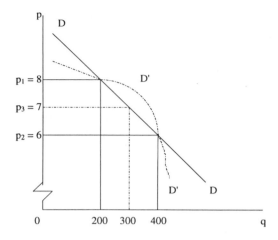

Figure 2

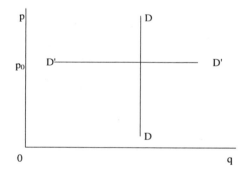

$|E_d|$ can have any value between zero and infinity, but there are five general possibilities:

(1) If $|E_d| < 1$, demand is *inelastic*. Quantity demanded is not particularly responsive to changes in price. If price changes by a given proportion, quantity demanded will change by a smaller proportion. If, for example, a 10 per cent change in price led to a 5 per cent change in quantity demanded, demand would be inelastic in the range of price variation in question.

(2) If $|E_d| > 1$, demand is *elastic*. Quantity demanded is quite responsive to changes in price.

(3) If $|E_d| = 1$, demand is of *unit elasticity*. A proportionate change in price would lead to an equiproportionate change in quantity demanded.

There are two limiting cases for the value of $|E_d|$:

(4) If $|E_d| = 0$, demand is *perfectly inelastic*. A change in price would lead to no change in quantity demanded. If a demand curve were perfectly inelastic for all ranges of price variation, it would look like DD in Figure 2.

(5) If $|E_d|$ is infinite, demand is *infinitely elastic*. If a demand curve were infinitely elastic throughout its domain it would look like D'D' in Figure 2. If price were increased to the slightest extent conceivable above p_0 in the diagram, then quantity demanded would go to zero.

Figure 3

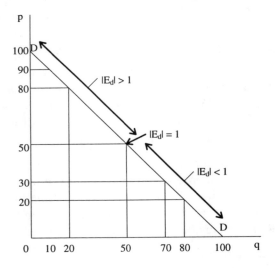

It is emphasised that the term price elasticity of demand refers to the response in quantity demanded in a neighbourhood of a specific point on a demand curve. Price elasticity varies along most demand curves; only in special cases is it constant. At high prices demand is normally elastic. At low prices it is likely to be inelastic. Except in the two limiting cases (4) and (5) above, the reader should never look simply at the steepness of a demand curve and on that basis alone declare the curve to be elastic or inelastic. Consider, for example, the straight line demand curve in Figure 3. Because slope in this diagram is constant, $\Delta q / \Delta p$ is constant. At very low quantities p/q is very high. Thus, $|E_d|$ is high; demand is elastic. At very low prices p/q is very low; demand is inelastic. Elasticity decreases as we move down a linear demand curve. It can be shown that elasticity equals unity half-way down a linear demand curve, and that it is elastic to the left, inelastic to the right, of the half-way point.

Price Elasticity of Demand and Changes in Total Revenue

Consider now the relationship between price elasticity of demand and changes in total revenue (TR). Total revenue from sales of a good is simply price multiplied by the amount sold, pq. There are three general cases:

(1) If $|E_d| < 1$ (inelastic demand) a rise in price increases TR and a fall in price reduces TR. The relationship between inelastic demand and changes in TR can be seen in Figure 3. We know that demand is inelastic in the price range (0, 50), i.e. to the right of the half-way point of this straight line demand curve. When p = 20, TR = (20)(80) = 1,600. If price is raised to p = 30, TR = (30)(70) = 2,100, an increase in TR. The converse would hold if price were reduced from p = 20 to p = 10.

(2) If $|E_d| > 1$ (elastic demand) a rise in price implies a fall in TR and a fall in price implies a rise in TR. The relationship between elastic demand and changes in TR can be seen in Figure 3. We know that demand is elastic in the price range (50, 100). When p = 80, TR = (80)(20) = 1,600. If price is raised to p = 90, TR = (90)(10) = 900, a fall in TR. The converse holds if price is reduced from p = 80 to p = 70.

(3) If $|E_d| = 1$ over some range of price variation, TR will be constant over that range of price variation. (Elasticity is unity only at a single point in Figure 3, but approximately unity throughout a small neighbourhood around that point.) If a demand curve were of unit elasticity throughout, pq = TR would stay constant for any paired p and q.

The three cases can be summarised as follows:

If $|E_d| < 1$: ΔTR has the same sign as Δp.
      $|E_d| > 1$: ΔTR has the opposite sign to Δp.
      $|E_d| = 1$: ΔTR = 0 regardless of sign of Δp.

Determinants of Price Elasticity of Demand

The most important factor governing price elasticity of demand is the extent to which a good has *close substitutes*. The more substitutes there are, the more elastic will demand for the good tend to be, given the prices of those substitute goods. As successive Ministers for Finance have long recognised, the demand for cigarettes, which for many people have no close substitutes, is quite inelastic — that is why they have been such reliable targets of annual taxation. The demand for a particular brand of cigarettes, by contrast, is very elastic; if only one brand were raised in price by a significant amount, smokers would consume considerably less of it, and more of other brands. If consumers regard some good as essential, then that good does not have close substitutes. As a group, food products are biological essentials. Essentials tend to be price inelastic; if the price of food fell by 50 per cent, people in developed countries would not consume as much as 50 per cent more food. The low price elasticity of demand of many agricultural products is important, and merits further consideration in Chapter 7.

Another factor governing price elasticity of demand involves consideration of goods which are the opposite of substitutes — *complementary goods*. When a good is purchased to be used jointly with a more expensive product, the demand for that good tends to be price inelastic. Two or more goods are in *joint demand* if they are all necessary for the satisfaction of a given want. Examples are automobiles and driving licences; golf clubs and golf balls; pipes and pipe tobacco. Goods which are jointly demanded are called complementary goods, as distinct from substitute goods. If the price of driving licences were doubled, it is unlikely that the percentage decrease in purchases of licences would be significant. For law-abiding people, licences are necessary to drive a car. However, a 100 per cent increase in the price of driving licences represents, on average, only a small rise in the annual cost of running a car. Therefore, driving licences, the cheaper of two complementary or jointly demanded goods, are price inelastic in demand.

INCOME ELASTICITY OF DEMAND

Income elasticity of demand, a measure of the responsiveness in the demand for a good to changes in money income, other things being equal, is measured as

$$(3)\ E_m = \frac{\text{Proportionate change in demand}}{\text{Proportionate change in income}}$$

$$= (\Delta q/q)/(\Delta m/m) = (\Delta q/\Delta m)(m/q)$$

where m denotes the average of the initial and new income levels, q denotes the average of the initial and new quantities of a particular good demanded and Δq and Δm are the change in the demand for the good and change in money income.

For any particular good, E_m can be greater than, equal to or less than zero. If $E_m < 0$ for some good, then the demand for that good *falls in absolute terms* as money income increases, and increases as money income falls. Such goods are called *inferior goods*. If $E_m = 0$ for some good, then a change in money income leads to no change in the demand for that good. If for some good $E_m > 0$, then a change in money income leads to a change in the same direction in the demand for the good. Goods for which $E_m > 0$ are called *normal goods*.

Among the positive values of income elasticity, $E_m = 1$ is a benchmark value. If for some good $E_m = 1$, then a given proportionate change in money income leads to an equiproportionate change (in the same direction) in purchases of the good. If $E_m < 1$ for a good, then the proportion of income spent on the good falls as income rises. (Under such circumstances the absolute amount spent on the good increases so long as E_m is positive.) If $E_m > 1$ for some good, the proportion of income spent on that good increases as income increases. (In this case sales of the good increase both absolutely and relatively as income increases.) Goods for which $0 < E_m < 1$ are called *necessities*; those for which $E_m > 1$ are termed *luxuries*. Goods for which income elasticity is close to zero are said to be *income inelastic*. Others, which have a higher (positive) income elasticity, such that purchases are significantly responsive to changes in income, are *income elastic*. Thus the demand for basic foods like cereals is income inelastic in developed economies; in very poor countries, however, it may be income elastic.

Whether a good or a group of goods is high or low in income elasticity of demand is a matter of great importance. In developed economies, on average, aggregate income has tended to double every twenty to thirty years. The demand for various goods has therefore increased. But the demand for some goods has increased proportionally more than others. For example, in Western Europe over the last fifty years the demand for food products as a group has increased proportionally much more slowly than the demand for manufactured goods such as automobiles and household durables. Partly because of the differing income elasticities of demand for different groups of goods, there are substantial changes in the structure of national output as an economy develops toward high levels of per capita income: agricultural output tends to decline relative to the output of the industrial and services sectors. Because of differing income elasticities of demand for output, the distribution of employment between sectors of the economy tends to change as the process of economic development unfolds.

CROSS ELASTICITY OF DEMAND

The cross elasticity of demand between two goods, A and B, measures the degree of responsiveness in the demand for A to changes in the price of good B, other things being equal. It is measured as

$$(4)\ E_{ab} = \frac{\text{Proportionate change in purchases of A}}{\text{Proportionate change in price of B}}$$

$$= (\Delta q^a/q^a)/(\Delta p^b/p^b) = (\Delta q^a/\Delta p^b)(p^b/q^a)$$

where, on the assumption that the change in the price of good B is small, p^b represents the price half-way between the first and second prices of B, and q^a denotes the quantity half-way between the first and second quantities of A.

The measure E_{ab} can take on any value between minus infinity and plus infinity. A widely used definition of substitute and complementary goods is that two goods A and B are substitutes if $E_{ab} > 0$; they are complements if $E_{ab} < 0$. For example, margarine (good A) and butter (good B) are substitutes. Their cross elasticity of demand is positive; if p^b increases ($\Delta p^b > 0$), q^a will also increase as some consumers substitute margarine for butter. Pipes (good A) and pipe tobacco (good B) are complements. Their cross elasticity of demand is negative because if p^b increases ($\Delta p^b > 0$), q^a will decrease ($\Delta q^a < 0$), as some consumers curtail their purchases of both pipes and tobacco.

ELASTICITY OF SUPPLY

Elasticity of supply is calculated as

$$(5)\ E_s = \frac{\text{Proportionate change in quantity supplied}}{\text{Proportionate change in price}}$$

$$= \frac{\Delta q}{\Delta p} \cdot \frac{(p_1 + p_2)}{(q_1 + q_2)}$$

where the variables are measured as in equation (2) for price elasticity of demand, except that q now represents quantity supplied rather than quantity demanded.

Because supply curves usually slope upwards like SS in Figure 4 below, E_s is normally positive. If $E_s < 1$ over a specific range of price variation, supply is *inelastic*. Note, however, that E_s normally varies from a neighbourhood of one point to that of another along a supply curve.

If E_s is infinite, then supply is infinitely elastic. If supply were infinitely elastic throughout the domain of a supply curve, its graph would look like S'S' in Figure 4. If $E_s = 0$ for a specific range of price variation, supply is of zero elasticity. If a supply curve were of zero elasticity throughout, its graph would look like S"S" in Figure 4. The possibility that E_s may be negative is often misunderstood. If $E_s < 0$, a reduction in price would be associated with an increase in quantity supplied. This possibility will be investigated in Part Six in the context of industry equilibrium in perfectly competitive product markets.

It was pointed out in Chapter 4 that supply curves pertain to flows of a good over time. Time periods may be long or short. Thus two crucial determinants of the elasticity of supply of a good are:

(1) The length of the time period under consideration. If an unanticipated increase in demand causes price suddenly to increase, producers will not be able to adjust outputs instantaneously. As time elapses they can respond to the higher price and increase their outputs by hiring more labour and buying more raw materials to use as inputs. Quantity supplied will then be more responsive to changes in price. As time elapses further, firms already in the industry can add to their plant and equipment and new firms can establish themselves in the industry. Thus, the longer the time period under consideration, the more elastic supply is likely to be.

(2) Other determinants of elasticity of supply of a particular good are the elasticities of supply of the various inputs used in its production. If the inputs are elastic in supply, the final product will tend to be elastic in supply. The converse will tend to prevail if the inputs are inelastic in supply.

Figure 4

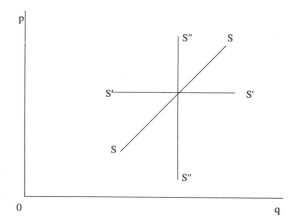

Figure 5

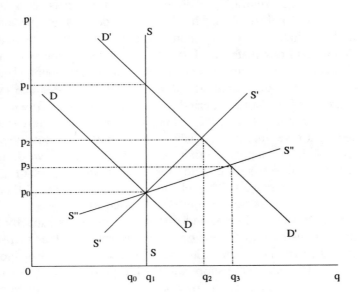

MOMENTARY, SHORT-RUN AND LONG-RUN EQUILIBRIUM

Because time is a crucial factor in determining elasticity of supply, an increase in the demand for a good will generally lead to different increases in price, depending on whether the time period under consideration is long or short. There is, of course, an infinity of time periods. But to make analysis tractable, we follow Marshall's analytic framework by distinguishing equilibria in the context of three conceptual time periods, *momentary equilibrium* (associated with what is perhaps best called the *very short run*), short-run equilibrium (associated with Marshall's *short run*) and long-run equilibrium (associated with Marshall's *long run*).

Suppose that starting at a full equilibrium which has long prevailed there is a permanent increase in demand for some good which cannot be stored — fresh fish, for example. The very short run is so short a period that firms can vary none of the variables which influence supply; supplies have already gone to market or are on their way to market, and will fetch any price, whether it be high or low, which equates the momentarily fixed supply of fish with the increased demand.

The initial situation is at (p_0, q_0) in Figure 5. The increase in demand is represented by an upward shift in the demand curve from DD to D'D'. Because supplies are momentarily fixed along SS, the new *momentary equilibrium* price is p_1. This high price is likely to be one at which suppliers earn large windfall profits. The high price acts as a signal for suppliers to expand supplies. The short run is defined as a period of time in which producers may vary their employment of certain factors, perhaps labour and raw materials, but are constrained by the fixed availability of certain other factors, such as plant and equipment. The former group of factors are called *variable factors*; the latter (i.e. whatever inputs are fixed in the time period in question) are *fixed factors*. Returning to the example of fish, the fishing industry in the short run is constrained by a given number of fishing boats, nets, etc.; however, if price has increased, the supply of fish can be increased by working longer hours, hiring more fishermen, etc., thereby utilising the existing number of boats more intensively. The relevant supply curve would then be S'S' in Figure 5, and the *short run equilibrium* price would be p_2.

In the long run the fishing industry could add to its capacity by waiting for the construction of new boats and by varying other factors which were fixed in the short run. Thus supply would be more responsive to change in price than in the short run; the long-run supply curve would be like, say, S"S" in Figure 5; and p_3 would be the new long-run equilibrium price.

The long-run supply curve is likely to slope upward, reflecting the fact that the fishing industry (in the present example) must bid up prices of some inputs to attract them away from other industries. Note that after the shift in demand from DD to D'D', the long-run equilibrium price is lower, and quantity supplied is higher, than in the short run, and the short-run equilibrium price is lower, and quantity supplied is higher, than in the very short run. This reflects the fact that elasticity of supply is generally higher, the longer the time period under consideration.

CHAPTER 6

GENERAL APPLICATIONS OF SUPPLY AND DEMAND ANALYSIS

Government intervention and legal restrictions are among the reasons why markets diverge from perfect competition. That is not to say that all government intervention in markets, or all legal restrictions on their operation, are inconsistent with perfect competition. But when they do involve significant departures from such assumptions in markets which would otherwise approximate perfect competition, the effects of public policies are best analysed by starting with the assumption of perfect competition and imposing the public policies on that analytical framework. That is what will be done in this chapter. It is assumed that apart from the effects of government intervention, the markets under analysis approximate the relevant assumptions of perfect competition. It is also assumed that if unregulated, the markets have unique and stable equilibria, and that if they are not in equilibrium they rapidly converge toward equilibrium.

The examples which follow in this and in the next two chapters indicate how supply and demand analysis is applied to situations in the world around us.

TAXES ON TRANSACTIONS

Governments raise revenue by taxes on sale of goods. What are the effects of such taxes? Does the burden fall on the seller, or is the tax mainly passed on in the form of higher prices? How much may government expect to raise in revenue from a tax on a good? Would it make any difference if the buyer rather than the seller were administratively liable for its payment? Suppose we are dealing with a per unit tax on a good, and that it is the suppliers who must pay the government so many pounds or pence per unit sold. If, as we assume, the good in question is traded in markets approximating in relevant ways the assumptions of perfect competition, it is easy to give definite answers to these questions.

Suppose that initially there is no government interference in the market and that next a tax of £t per unit sold is imposed on suppliers of a good. In Figure 1, SS is the pre-tax supply curve; equilibrium price and quantity are p_0 and q_0 respectively. The introduction of a per unit tax on sellers causes no change in the demand curve, for none of the factors underlying the demand curve have changed. But because the sellers are liable for payment of the tax (the variable g in the general supply function (2) of Chapter 4 has changed) the supply curve shifts upward by the full amount of the tax per unit to, say S'S'. The vertical distance between SS and S'S' is exactly £t, the amount of the tax per unit. For example, before the tax producers were willing to supply, say q_1 units, at a price p_1. After the tax they would be willing to supply that same quantity only if they receive the same net receipts per unit as before; they would therefore be willing to supply q_1 units at the price $(p_1 + t) = p_2$ pounds. Similarly after the tax they would be willing to supply q_2 units at the old supply price for that quantity plus the tax, i.e. at $(p_3 + t) = p_4$ pounds.

Figure 1

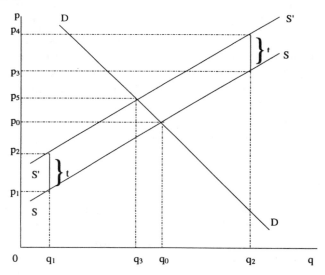

Figure 1 has become a little clogged, so we reproduce those supply and demand curves in Figure 2 below, where it is clear that the tax per unit sold causes the equilibrium price to increase from p_0 to p_5, and the equilibrium quantity to decrease from q_0 to q_3. (For the moment, the reader should ignore D'D' in the diagram.) Thus the theory predicts that a per unit tax on a good traded in a market approximating in relevant respects the assumptions of perfect competition, will increase the equilibrium price paid by consumers and decrease the equilibrium quantity traded. In the context of the discussion on methodology in Chapter 2, this is a meaningful theory. As such, it is not true by definition; its empirical validity could in principle be tested, and rejected if substantively inconsistent with facts.

Figure 2

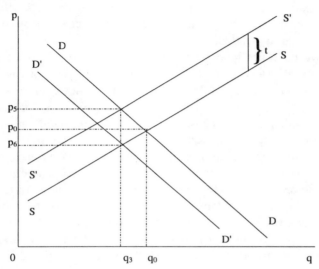

It may be worthwhile to point out that in the absence of foreign trade (which adds some complications) the conclusion concerning the effects of a per unit tax would be valid even if sellers were exempt from payment of tax, but if a tax of £t per unit were imposed, administratively payable by *buyers*. The reader should be able to show that in this case it is the demand curve which would shift to the left — to D'D' in Figure 2. The locus SS would remain the supply curve, but the new demand curve would be a vertical distance of £t below the pre-tax demand curve DD. The equilibrium after-tax quantity is again q_3, and the equilibrium effective price paid by buyers (though not that posted by sellers) is again $p_5 = p_6 + t$. In both cases the after-tax effective price paid by buyers has increased to p_5, and the after-tax net price received by sellers has decreased to p_6. Conclusions like these hold whether or not the supply and demand curves are linear. However, in reality it is sellers who are usually liable for payment of a per unit tax because there are usually fewer sellers of a good than there are buyers — and it is easier, from an administrative standpoint, to collect tax revenue from the fewer sellers. It will therefore be assumed that per unit taxes are administratively payable by suppliers. Before proceeding to the relevance of elasticities, it is noted in passing that a per unit subsidy is the exact opposite, and has the opposite effects, of a per unit tax. It is left it to the reader to analyse the effects of a per unit subsidy.

The Relevance of Elasticities

A central conclusion is that so long as supply curves slope upward and demand curves slope downward, a per unit tax will increase the effective price paid by consumers (though not the net price received by sellers) and will reduce quantity traded.

However, we have not investigated the determinants of the extent to which such a tax may lead to higher prices paid by buyers, or lower net (after-tax) prices received by sellers. Thus we have not examined what determines the extent to which a per unit tax on suppliers is "passed on" in the form of higher prices. These questions are intimately related to (price) elasticities of supply and demand.

Assume, starting from an equilibrium price-quantity combination, that a per unit tax of £t is imposed on the suppliers of a good. The curves SS in Figures 3a, 3b and 3c indicate some possible supply curves at the pre-tax equilibrium, (p_0, q_0). The demand curve DD is unaffected by the tax. In regard to supply, we warned earlier of the dangers of merely looking at the slope of a supply (or demand) curve and on that basis alone drawing conclusions in regard to price elasticity. However, in a neighbourhood of a given price-quantity combination (such as p_0 and q_0 in Figures 3a, 3b and 3c) we can legitimately conclude that the less steep the slope of a supply curve, the greater its price elasticity. Thus in a neighbourhood of the point (p_0, q_0) in the three diagrams, SS is infinitely elastic in Figure 3a; in 3b it is moderately elastic; in 3c it is inelastic. The loci S'S' (which lie a vertical distance of £t above the pre-tax supply curves SS) represent the after-tax supply curves in the three cases depicted.

It can be seen that the price paid by consumers increases by the full amount of the tax when supply is infinitely elastic (Figure 3a); in 3b, where supply is moderately elastic, price increases by about 50 per cent of the tax, and in 3c, where supply is inelastic, price increases by a smaller percentage of the tax. Hence although, as assumed, suppliers are administratively responsible for payment of the tax, the incidence or burden of the tax (by which is meant the question of who *ultimately* pays the tax, by having to offer a higher price for goods bought, or by having to accept a lower after-tax price for goods sold) may fall mainly on buyers or mainly on sellers, or on both more or less equally, depending on elasticity of supply (and, as will soon be seen, on elasticity of demand also). In the case of infinitely elastic supply, producers fully "pass on" the tax by charging consumers a higher price. In the opposite case, where supply is of zero elasticity, the tax leads to no change in price to consumers; in that case the entire burden of the tax falls on suppliers, who must accept an after-tax net price equal to the original price minus the per unit tax.

Figure 3a

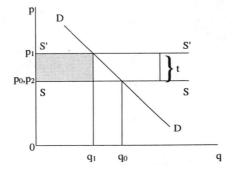

Figure 3b

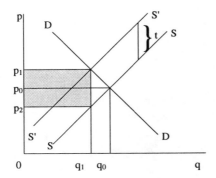

Figure 3c

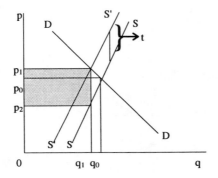

Price elasticity of demand is also of relevance. Figures 4a, 4b and 4c
illustrate three possible demand curves leading to the same pre-tax price-
quantity combination, (p_0, q_0). The initial pre-tax supply curve SS is the
same in each case. The demand curve in Figure 4a is perfectly inelastic,
and the per unit tax of £t, which causes the supply curve to shift upward
by a vertical distance of £t, to S'S', is fully passed on in the form of
higher prices paid by consumers; in 4b demand is more elastic, and price
rises by less than the tax; in 4c, where demand is infinitely elastic, the tax
leads to no change in price paid by consumers.

Figure 4a

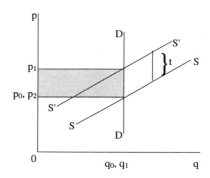

Figure 4b

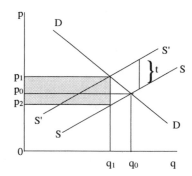

Figure 4c

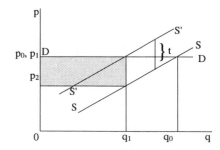

The results obtained for three different ranges of price elasticity of demand can be generalised by stating the proposition that the less elastic the demand curve in a neighbourhood of the pre-tax equilibrium price, the larger the increase in price charged to consumers entailed by a per unit tax (and the smaller the reduction in net after-tax price received by suppliers); on the other hand, the higher the price elasticity of demand, the lower the increase in price charged consumers after the tax (and the more the burden of the tax falls on suppliers).

We have not yet indicated what the net after-tax equilibrium prices received by suppliers actually are in the various cases considered. The net after-tax equilibrium price received by suppliers is the equilibrium price charged to consumers after the imposition of the tax minus the tax per unit. For example, in Figures 4a, 4b and 4c it is p_2.

This discussion can be concluded as follows: given a particular initial *supply curve*, a per unit tax levied on suppliers will raise price paid by consumers most, and reduce purchases least, the lower is price elasticity of demand; given a particular initial *demand curve*, the price paid by consumers, as well as purchases, will change least, and net after-tax price received by suppliers will fall most, the less elastic the supply curve. The tax tends to be passed on to consumers when the demand curve is very inelastic, but its burden tends to fall on suppliers when the supply curve is very inelastic. The reader should now use pencil and paper to ensure a full understanding of these assertions.

Per Unit Taxes and Government Tax Revenue

If government imposes a per unit tax of £t on sales of a good, the increase in tax revenue will be the tax rate multiplied by the number of units sold after the imposition of the tax. Thus, revenue raised by taxing a good may be high or low depending on the good's price elasticities of demand and supply. In Figure 3a to 4c, the pre-tax equilibrium prices and quantities are p_0 and q_0 respectively. The after-tax equilibrium prices and quantities are p_1 and q_1. In each case the net after-tax equilibrium price received by sellers is p_1 minus the tax per unit. The tax per unit is the height of the shaded rectangles; thus, in each case the net after-tax price received by sellers is p_2. In each case total revenue raised from taxation of the good is given by the area of the shaded rectangle. It can be seen from the diagrams that tax revenue is high or low depending on the elasticities of supply and demand.

There are two extreme cases, depicted in Figures 5 and 6, in which the introduction of a per unit tax on suppliers would cause no change in the equilibrium quantity bought.

The pre-tax equilibrium price-quantity combination is the same in Figures 5 and 6. In Figure 5, where demand may be of any elasticity other than zero (it may be infinitely elastic like DD, or less elastic like D'D'), supply is of zero elasticity. Under such circumstances a per unit tax would not affect the supply curve; all it can affect is the after-tax net price received by suppliers, which, in this example, falls to p_2, the shaded rectangle being the government's total receipts from the tax. In Figure 6, where the pre-tax supply curve, such as SS or S"S", may be of any elasticity other than zero in a neighbourhood of the initial price, the demand curve is of zero elasticity, and the tax (represented by the shift to S'S' or S'"S'" in the supply curve) again causes no change in quantity purchased. If the per unit tax has been the same in each diagram, the government's total receipts from the tax are the same in either case. The closer actual markets approximate the circumstances of Figure 5 or Figure 6 in a neighbourhood of the initial price–quantity combination, the larger a government's receipts from a per unit tax of a given size.

Finally, without making specific reference to elasticity of supply, we can state the generalisation that the more inelastic the demand curve in the neighbourhood of the pre-tax equilibrium price, the larger the increase in government revenue from a per unit tax.

Figure 5

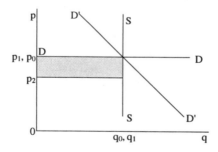

Figure 6

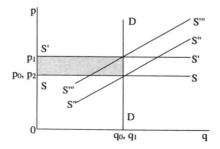

Price Elasticities of Tradable Goods and Tax Revenue in Small Open Economies

An open economy is one which, among other things, depends heavily on foreign trade, and which has relatively free mobility of goods (exports and imports) across its national frontiers. If an economy were fully open, there would be no tariffs or quantity quotas restricting the movement of goods across its frontiers. We regard an open economy as small if its output and consumption of tradable goods is only a small proportion of the total output and consumption of similar tradable goods in the countries with which there is relatively free mobility of goods. At given levels of tariffs and non-binding quantity quotas, tradable goods are those for which transportation costs are not prohibitive, and which are not impeded, on that count, from entering international trade. Other goods are called non-tradable. The Republic of Ireland is a small, open economy within the European Union (EU). Because EU countries do not maintain tariffs and import quotas against each other, and because Ireland's output and consumption of tradables is only a small proportion of EU output and consumption of tradables, Ireland, insofar as tradable goods are concerned, is in many respects close to being a perfectly competitive supplier and demander within the whole EU market. These considerations have important implications for elasticities of supply and demand for tradable goods in Ireland.

Consider first supply. The supply of a good to an individual in a market approximating perfect competition is infinitely elastic. That is because the individual can purchase in effect any quantity of the good at the going market price; individuals do not bid up price against themselves by increasing their purchases, simply because those purchases are a negligibly small fraction of total purchases of the good in the market. For tradable goods — comprising mainly manufactures and agricultural goods — Ireland is in a situation similar to such an individual buyer in a perfectly competitive market, except that now the market of relevance is the EU. Because there is freedom of movement of goods within the EU, and because Irish buyers are only a small fraction of all buyers in the EU, Irish buyers are, as a group, closely akin to price-takers: abstracting from some aspects of taxation, so long as they pay roughly the going market prices for tradable goods in the EU as a whole, they can buy in effect any quantities of those goods without bidding up prices against themselves. Thus, ignoring very short periods of purely localised shortages, the supply curve of a tradable good to the Irish market is, as an approximation, infinitely elastic (like SS in Figure 7). If, then, government imposes a per unit tax on supplies to Irish buyers the supply curve will shift upward by the amount of the tax, to S"S" in Figure 7.

Figure 7

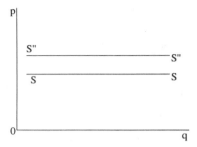

The demand curve of relevance to the pricing of tradable goods in the Irish economy reflects both domestic demand and export demand. If there were perfect information among buyers in the EU market; if transport costs were zero; and if the product under analysis and available to Irish consumers were identical to other goods available to all EU consumers, then the demand curve would, in effect, be infinitely elastic at the prevailing common EU market price. If, for example, Irish producers as a group conspired to raise their price for the tradable good under analysis above the level prevailing in other EU countries, they would lose all their sales. For then Irish consumers would import the good from abroad, and if originally there were any exports of the good from Ireland, those would fall to zero. Conversely, if Irish producers were to charge a lower price than the equilibrium price in the rest of the EU, Europeans would switch their purchases toward Irish sellers, thereby bidding the Irish price upward toward that prevailing in the rest of the EU.

However, the existence of inertia and imperfect information among buyers, and the fact that transportation costs are positive, implies that the demand curve of relevance to the pricing of a tradable good in Ireland is not generally infinitely elastic. In the case of manufactures, another reason why the demand for Irish goods is not generally infinitely elastic is the fact that many manufactured goods are not (in buyers' minds) identical substitutes for those produced in other EU countries; they may differ in design, packaging or brand names and in the effectiveness of advertising outlays. All of these considerations imply that the demand curves of relevance to the pricing of tradable goods in Ireland are not generally infinitely elastic. The central conclusions at this stage are:

(1) Very short periods of localised shortages aside, supply curves of manufactured goods to the Irish economy are likely to be very elastic in a neighbourhood of equilibrium prices.

(2) Demand curves for tradable goods are also likely to be quite elastic in a neighbourhood of equilibrium prices. They are more elastic than they would be if Ireland were a closed economy with little market dependence on the rest of the EU.

(3) Consideration (1) implies that if a per unit tax is imposed on tradable goods to the Irish economy, price is likely to increase by close to the full amount of the tax.

What has just been stated applies to tradable goods only. But not all goods and services are tradable; one does not go to Liverpool to get a haircut, or import a house (and the site upon which it is built) from Germany. Considerations of international trade are of less immediate relevance to the pricing of such goods and services. The supply curves for such non-tradables are therefore likely to be less elastic than in the case of tradable goods. Hence, for any given value of price elasticity of demand in a neighbourhood of a pre-tax equilibrium, the imposition of a per unit tax on sales of non-tradables would tend to raise equilibrium price by a smaller percentage of the tax than in the case of tradables. Correspondingly, the burden of a per unit tax on sales generally falls mainly on buyers in the case of tradables: for non-tradable it falls more heavily on suppliers.

DIRECT PRICE CONTROLS

Governments often invoke legislation enabling them to control the prices which may legally be charged for various commodities, both final goods as well as factors of production. During, and for a short period after, the Second World War, industrial wages in Ireland were regulated by Emergency Powers Orders, the general effect of which was to prohibit increases above "standard rates" in operation in April 1942. In more recent years maximum prices which could legally be charged for various consumer goods have been subject to control. Such maxima on permissible prices are called *price ceilings*.

　As examples of government interference in the market, price controls differ very substantively from per unit taxes. A per unit tax on the sale of a good usually shifts the supply curve; the equilibrium price and quantity traded are still determined by supply and demand. However, a price ceiling, if it has any effect at all (i.e. if the maximum permissible price is less than the market equilibrium price), is likely to prevent a market from attaining a determinate equilibrium.

　Suppose that the supply and demand curves for a good are as in Figure 8 below. The equilibrium price and quantity are p_0 and q_0, respectively. Suppose that government imposes an order to the effect that p_1 is the maximum price which may legally be charged; note that this is less than the market equilibrium price. At this ceiling price, buyers wish to purchase q'_1 but suppliers are willing to provide only q_1; there is an excess in quantity demanded over quantity supplied. Under these circumstances there no way of knowing which potential buyers will obtain what quantities of the good. All we can say for sure is that if the law is rigidly enforced there will be unsatisfied potential buyers who are willing to pay the price asked for by sellers, who in turn are not willing to supply the quantity demanded at the ceiling price. Early morning queues may develop, with sales on a "first come, first served" basis, leaving many at the end of the line, unable to buy because supplies have been exhausted by the time they register their desire to buy. Or suppliers may simply confine sales to "regular" customers. However, it may be impossible to enforce the law rigidly. If that is the case it is likely that at least some transactions will take place at prices in excess of the ceiling, in "black markets". If enforcement of the law is lax, suppliers may sell at prices between the ceiling and the equilibrium levels, but so long as actual prices are less than the equilibrium level there will be some unsatisfied demanders. There is of course the possibility that the ceiling price is rigidly enforced on the original suppliers, but not on secondary transactions in the good. Thus secondary markets may emerge, with middlemen buying the total supply, q_1, from the original suppliers at the ceiling price, but selling at prices, or at a single price, as high as p_2, in Figure 8. In this case the intent of the price ceiling is totally frustrated: compared with the initial unregulated market situation, quantity traded is reduced from q_0 to q_1, while price charged is increased from p_0 up toward p_2.

Figure 8

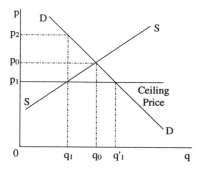

Figure 9

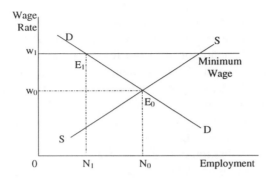

It has already been observed that if an effective price ceiling is imposed, there is no way of knowing which consumers will obtain what quantities of the good. Government may therefore seek to allocate the good in accordance with its own preferences (rather than the preferences of suppliers and demanders). It may try to do so by issuing ration coupons sufficient for the purchase of the quantity q_1 (the amount which suppliers offer at the ceiling price) in Figure 8. It may issue ration coupons on the basis of household size, for example. But we can be almost certain that a market for ration coupons would emerge, largely reflecting the fact that the preferences of individuals are not identical. The emergence of prices for ration coupons would mean that some individuals would be paying effective prices for the rationed good above the ceiling price. The effective price paid by a buyer for any particular unit of the good would then be the ceiling price, p_1, plus the price, if any, paid for a ration coupon enabling the consumer to buy that unit of the good. Thus, if a price ceiling is imposed, it is likely that "black markets" and effective prices above the ceiling level will emerge whether or not the good is rationed.

Minimum Prices

A law controlling the minimum or *floor price* at which a good or factor may be bought or hired can have no substantive effect if that floor is below the equilibrium price. Common kinds of floor prices which come to mind are those on factors of production such as labour (through minimum wage laws). Because these are normally designed to raise prices above their equilibrium market levels, thereby reducing the amount of such factors hired, these controls may harm many of those they are designed to help.

Suppose that the market for unskilled agricultural labour, for example, is initially free from government intervention, and that it approximates the assumptions of perfect competition in relevant ways. Figure 9 shows the initial market situation. The price of labour services, in hours, is the wage rate. It is assumed in the diagram that the lower the wage rate, the higher the demand for, and the lower the supply of, labour hours. The equilibrium wage and employment levels are given by the co-ordinates of point E_0. If the minimum wage is as in the diagram, the resulting wage and employment levels will be represented by the co-ordinates of point E_1. Those workers who remain employed will have obtained a higher wage, but others will be made unemployed.

It was assumed above that the wage floor was imposed by law. However, it could have been introduced by trade union organisation in a labour market which was previously unorganised. Under such circumstances the effect of trade union bargaining for a wage w_1 would be to increase the wage (from w_0), but at a cost of reducing employment from N_0 to N_1 in the diagram (where N denotes the number of hours worked).

Price Control, Allocation and Equity

It was observed in Chapter 3 that although one might not like the resulting pattern of income distribution, reliance on market forces in the ideal market economy would tend to solve the economy's allocation problem in an efficient manner. It has been seen in the present chapter that government interference with supply and demand may introduce inefficiencies. Thus, price ceilings may cause production of goods to be contracted and may make their allocation among consumers *a priori* indeterminate. Price floors may cause unemployment, which is obviously inefficient. Why, then, do governments introduce price control? In wartime, government seeks to control the allocation of an economy's resources toward the war effort; it seeks to encourage the release of resources away from production of consumer goods not considered essential, toward production of defence goods. Price control combined with rationing may be appropriate under such circumstances. In peacetime, governments may implement price control under the declared objective of curbing inflation, and on grounds of what they consider equity. But attempts to curb inflation by price control in an open economy like Ireland are likely to meet little success; the reader who is doubtful of this assertion is asked to wait until the chapters on macroeconomics. It might appear then that, wartime aside, the main arguments for price ceilings and floors involve considerations of equity. Consider these briefly.

Government may place a legal floor on the price of labour services in order to raise the wages of those who remain employed. But it may then find (given its objectives of "fairness" in income distribution) that it must use the tax system to finance income maintenance ("dole") payments to those made unemployed by the imposition of the price floor. Given its objectives, it may be more rational for government to place more reliance on the market mechanism by abstaining from such direct interference with the forces of supply and demand, by using the tax system to assist mobility of labour to more high-paying jobs and to finance retraining of workers in low-paying jobs for employment elsewhere in the economy — where rates of pay are higher. This would represent improvement in efficiency of resource allocation, for total production in the economy would then increase, while at the same time the pattern of income distribution could be improved by mildly influencing the market mechanism in the manner suggested, rather than blocking it by means of wage controls.

Government may try to control the price of a final product because it believes that excess profits are being reaped. But such controls may lead to "black markets", with large profits being pocketed by middlemen, a class not normally held in special esteem by government or the public. It was shown above that allocation of goods among consumers may be *a priori* indeterminate if a price ceiling is enforced; of all the consumers who are prepared to buy a reduced supply of a good at a ceiling price, the good may be sold to those who desire it least rather than most. If the objective of price control is the prevention of excess profits, that objective can usually be pursued more efficiently by means of the tax system.

It is perhaps worthwhile repeating that price controls, by affecting supply of goods and employment of factors, frequently harm those they are intended to benefit. For example, France had virtually no residential construction between 1914 and 1948, partly because of rent control, and the same kind of interference with the market mechanism led to decay (failure to repair and maintain) and ultimate abandonment by owners of dwellings in New York City in the 1960s, in Rome in the 1970s, and in Ireland for several decades after the Irish Free State was established. Unless politicians and civil servants have competent economic expertise to assess proposed measures of price control, their actions may involve serious misallocation of resources. We therefore do not advocate price controls as general policy measures unless their implications are competently analysed, and unless the principal alternative means of promoting the objectives motivating proposed price controls are competently assessed. If change in the pattern of income distribution is an important objective, this is normally more efficiently attained by manipulating the tax system and by further means other than blocking the operation of markets. Finally, to think that one can substantively, or for long, control the rate of inflation by means of ceilings on prices legally charged in a highly open economy like Ireland would be to indulge in fantasy.

CHAPTER 7

SUPPLY AND DEMAND
APPLIED TO AGRICULTURE

Alan Matthews

Agriculture is a very important sector in the Irish economy. In 1992 it accounted for 8 per cent of Gross National Product and 14 per cent of employment. These shares of economic activity are higher than in most other European Union Member States, apart from the Southern European countries (Table 1). Yet even in countries where agriculture now accounts for a relatively minor part of economic activity, there is extensive government intervention in agricultural markets. This intervention is designed to address a number of problems perceived to arise if agricultural markets are left unregulated, such as the relatively low incomes of farmers compared with non-farmers, unstable prices for agricultural products, rural depopulation, damage to the natural environment and, for some countries, a sense of vulnerability arising from undue dependence on food imports.

Table 1: Percentage of Working Population Engaged in Agriculture

Country	Per cent	Country	Per cent
Germany	3.4	United Kingdom	2.2
France	5.4	Ireland	13.8
Italy	8.5	Spain	10.7
Netherlands	4.5	Greece	21.6
Belgium	2.7	Portugal	17.5
Denmark	2.7	Luxembourg	3.1

Source: EU Commission, *The Agricultural Situation in the Community, 1993 Report*, Brussels.

Since Irish membership of the European Community (now the European Union) in 1973, government regulation of agricultural markets takes

[84]

place within the framework of the EU's Common Agricultural Policy (CAP). The way in which the CAP operates and its consequences are described in detail in the following chapter. The purpose of this chapter is to use the supply and demand analysis introduced in earlier chapters to illustrate why these farm problems exist and the consequences of different types of government intervention.

THE FARM PROBLEM

In most industrialised countries there is evidence that average farm incomes tend to lag behind the growth in non-farm incomes. Such comparisons are not easy to make and are subject to many measurement errors. For example, information on the number of people who work in agriculture can be difficult to obtain because of the family structure and seasonal nature of farming activity. Thus, figures for average farm income, obtained by dividing total farm income by the farm workforce, must be treated with caution. Another major criticism is that looking only at the income from farming of farm households ignores the substantial amount of income which farm families obtain from non-farming sources, including off-farm employment, social welfare payments and deposit interest. Despite these caveats, however, the tendency for average farm incomes to fall below average non-farm incomes is a widely-accepted characteristic of industrial economies.

To understand the causes of this income disparity it is useful first to examine the behaviour of agricultural product markets. The agricultural product market is where the price of agricultural products is determined by the supply of and demand for these products. Agricultural prices show a strong tendency to fall in real terms (i.e. adjusted for inflation) over time, and in particular, to fall relative to the prices of non-agricultural products. To see why this is so, consider Figures 1 and 2.

Figure 1 shows the agricultural product market in a closed economy with no international trade, and in the absence of government intervention in agriculture. The position of the supply curve SS is determined by the state of agricultural technology and the cost of the inputs used in agricultural production. If productivity improves because of technological progress or costs are reduced, then the supply curve will shift to the right. The demand curve for food in this economy, DD, is determined by population size, average income per capita, and tastes. In a growing economy, with an increasing population and rising income per capita, the demand curve will also shift over time to the right.

Figure 1

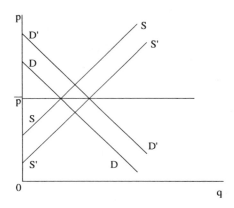

Figure 2

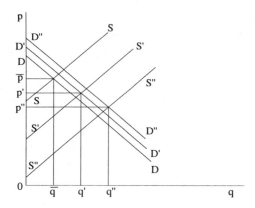

If both the supply curve and the demand curve shifted to the right at the same rate, then the initial equilibrium price level $\bar{p}$ would be maintained. Such a situation is shown in Figure 1 where the new supply curve in the subsequent period S'S' and the new demand curve D'D' intersect at the original price level $\bar{p}$. Throughout the post-war period, however, the rate of change in the position of the supply curve has been much faster than that of the demand curve. The factors shifting demand have been losing much of their force, at least in the industrialised countries. Population growth has virtually ceased and, while per capita incomes continue to increase, the proportion of additional income which is spent on food has fallen to a very low level. Thus, aggregate demand for food has stagnated. On the supply side, in contrast, there has been no let-up in the pace of technological innovation, and productivity growth has continued at a rapid rate. This situation is shown in Figure 2. The more rapid shift in the supply curve causes the equilibrium price level for agricultural products to fall from p̄ to p' to p" in subsequent time periods. The extent of the fall in price is exacerbated by another characteristic of agricultural demand, namely, its inelasticity with respect to price. This implies that the supply shifts bring about a larger fall in the market price than would occur with more elastic demand. This imbalance between the growth in supply and demand for agricultural produce over time is at the root of the farm problem in industrialised countries.

Are the same forces at work in an economy which is open to international trade? At first sight, for a small open economy the demand constraint may not appear to be binding. By definition, a small open economy can sell all it can produce at the prevailing world price. This is represented by the perfectly (infinitely) elastic demand curve at the world price p_w in Figure 3. Outward shifts in the supply curve (from SS to S'S') have no influence on the price which is received. However, the world price for agricultural products does not necessarily stay fixed but is itself determined by supply and demand forces on a global level. Despite the potential for greater growth in demand at the world level, particularly in developing countries, the shift in the global supply curve for agricultural products has exceeded the shift in global demand and the world price level for agricultural products has been gradually falling over time. Thus, even a small open economy cannot escape from the downward trend in agricultural prices.

Figure 3

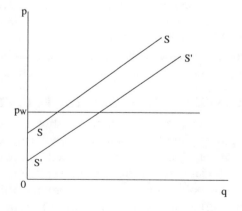

Lower agricultural prices because of the more rapid shift in the supply curve compared with the demand curve do not mean that the value of total farm income or even average income per farmer is reduced. Farmers' costs have fallen (this is the cause of the shift in the supply curve) generally by more than the fall in prices, and overall production has increased (for example, from $\bar{q}$ to q' to q" in Figure 2). Technological progress in agriculture does not make farmers as a group *worse* off, although individual farmers who are unable to adopt the new techniques will find their incomes disimprove. The fall in real agricultural prices does mean, however, that the growth in farm income tends to lag behind the growth in non-farm income which has also been boosted by productivity growth. Farmers whose incomes are determined by the prices they receive thus experience falling relative incomes over time.

We would not expect this fall in relative income to continue indefinitely. Individual farmers could expect to improve their incomes by moving out of the agricultural sector to take up higher-paying jobs in the non-farm sector. If there is easy movement between the two sectors we would expect the disparity in incomes to be kept fairly small. The fact that large disparities are observed, despite falling numbers at work in agriculture, implies that the movement of labour from the agricultural to the non-agricultural sector has not been sufficient to close the gap. This suggests that a second cause of the farm/non-farm income gap may lie in the operation of the labour market. Farmers or those about to enter farming may lack information about alternative employment opportunities. High unemployment in the non-farm sector may discourage those in agriculture from seeking non-farm employment. However, probably the most important explanation of lower average farm incomes is the fact that farmers, on average, have poorer educational qualifications and fewer marketable skills than those working in the non-farm sector. In a sector with declining employment, the average age of those still at work will tend to be high and older farmers have fewer opportunities to take up employment elsewhere. The higher average age of farmers and their lower educational qualifications mean that they would be relatively low earners whether working in the farm or in the non-farm sectors.

GOVERNMENT INTERVENTION TO RESTRICT SUPPLY

The previous section showed how the characteristics of agricultural supply and demand help to explain the problem of low farm incomes and declining farm employment. Farmers have lobbied successfully for government support to alleviate these problems. Governments have been very inventive in devising policy instruments to provide this support. Most operate by raising agricultural prices above the free market level, but the particular way in which support is provided determines whether taxpayers or consumers must bear the cost and how third countries are affected. The supply and demand framework can be very useful in illuminating these issues.

Consider first the case of a closed economy in which food markets are insulated from international trade and the price of food is determined solely by domestic supply and demand. Suppose the government wishes to raise agricultural prices as a way of improving farm incomes and discouraging migration from rural areas. One policy option would be to restrict supply. The supply of agricultural products can be reduced either by issuing marketing quotas to farmers which determine how much each farmer is allowed to produce, or by limiting the use of a particular input used in agricultural production. The requirement to set aside arable land is an example of an input limitation programme.

Figure 4 illustrates the market for milk in a closed economy. Suppose the government restricts the production of milk to some quantity less than the amount currently produced, q_c. Assuming that each dairy farmer is asked to reduce production by the same percentage amount, then the supply curve pivots around the point S. The new supply curve is shown as SS' where this curve is drawn to intersect the demand curve at the quota level q_0. As a consequence of the quota restricting the production of milk to q_0, the equilibrium milk price increases from p_c to p'. The tighter the quota, the greater the increase in the milk price which farmers receive. The effect on the milk price will also be affected by the slope of the demand curve for milk products. The more inelastic (steeper) the demand curve around the initial equilibrium, the greater the milk price increase resulting from a given quota restriction.

Figure 4

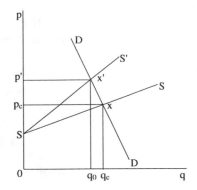

Whether farmers are better off as a result of a quota policy depends on whether the proportionate gain in price exceeds the proportionate reduction in the amount they are allowed to produce. This in turn is determined by the absolute size of the price elasticity of demand for agricultural products in a neighbourhood of the original price p_c. If this elasticity in absolute terms is greater than unity, then the percentage increase in price will be less than the percentage reduction in the quantity produced, and farmers' total revenue will fall. In the extreme case where demand is perfectly (infinitely) elastic, revenue will fall in the same proportion as the reduction in supply.

If, however, the demand for milk is inelastic with respect to its own price, then the price increase will be significantly greater than the reduction in the quantity supplied and farmers' total revenue will increase. This is the case in Figure 4 where it is clear that the area of the rectangle $0p'x'q_0$ which measures farmers' gross revenue with the milk quota is greater than the area of the rectangle $0p_cxq_c$ which measures their gross revenue before the introduction of the quota. As the price elasticity of demand for food products is generally quite low, farmers will usually benefit from the introduction of a quota policy at the expense of consumers who must pay a higher price for their food. In this example, consumers' expenditure on food equals producers' receipts, and increases by a corresponding amount.

This analysis assumes that supply restrictions are enforced by government legislation and apply to all producers or, at least, to those producers who account for the substantial bulk of production. Even if overall market demand were price-inelastic, individual producers could not increase their total individual sales revenues by reducing supply unless most other producers followed suit. This is because the demand curve facing an individual producer in a competitive market is, in effect, infinitely elastic. Individual producers can sell as much as they like without affecting the market price; they are described as *price-takers* in that the market price is given and beyond their individual control. Thus, co-ordinated or group action is necessary to influence the market price.

In principle, supply restriction could be co-ordinated by an agricultural co-operative or producer group (such action by non-agricultural producers would fall foul of anti-trust legislation designed to prevent such anti-competitive behaviour, but agricultural producers are often exempt from this legislation). However, the effectiveness of a producer group in raising prices may be limited if it cannot compel all producers to follow its instructions. Where a producer group implements a supply control programme to raise prices, there is a strong incentive for an individual producer to ignore these controls to take advantage of the higher prices made possible by the lower production of other producers. This is referred to as the *free-rider problem*; the non-complying producer gains a free ride from the discipline of the others. Obviously, if too many producers seek to gain a short-term advantage in this way, then the supply control programme will break down. For this reason, a government which wishes to encourage higher farm prices may make membership of a producer group mandatory if a farmer wishes to continue growing that crop.

The foregoing analysis examined the effect of introducing quotas in a market without previous government intervention. Sometimes quotas are introduced in a situation where market price support already exists. The purpose of quotas in this situation is not to raise the market price further but to limit the amount of production farmers are able to sell at the supported price. Farmers are clearly worse off when quotas are introduced for this purpose. The use of milk and sugar quotas in the EU agricultural policy is a good example of this second use of quotas.

This last point illustrates another aspect of supply and demand analysis as applied to agricultural policy. With the help of this framework the consequences of government intervention for agricultural output and revenue, consumer food expenditure (and, as we shall learn later, for other variables of interest such as government revenue and expenditure as well as for the level of imports and exports) can be determined. We can state, for example, that the introduction of a quota policy will, under specified conditions with respect to the elasticity of the demand curve, raise farmers' revenue at the expense of consumers. This is an example of what is referred to as *positive* economic analysis rather than *normative* analysis: the analyst merely makes the best possible estimate of what will happen to prices and quantities produced and consumed as the result of a specific government intervention, without comment on the desirability of the outcomes.

It is a further step to ask whether society as a whole will be better off as the result of this policy. To answer this question requires evaluating the benefits of higher food prices (in terms of higher domestic food production, higher farm incomes and a larger rural population) and comparing these benefits with the cost of the policy (in terms of the cost to consumers of higher food prices and the cost to the economy of using national resources to produce food which might have been used more productively elsewhere). Making these comparisons of social benefits and costs is part of what is called *welfare economics*. It is one of the most difficult areas of economics because it involves normative comparisons of welfare levels across different groups and individuals. Such comparisons invariably involve value judgments as to whether a given increase in income is worth more to one person (say, a poor person) than to another (say, a rich person). Economics is not equipped to make these value judgments although positive analysis can go a long way to illuminate the choices and the costs of alternative courses of action.

Supply Control in an Open Economy

The discussion so far has assumed that government intervention to restrict supply takes place in a closed economy with respect to international trade. Whether supply limitation programmes are effective in raising the price of an agricultural product in an open economy depends on whether or not the country is a price-taker on international markets for that commodity and, if so, on whether the *world* demand for that commodity is price inelastic. A country is a price-taker if it can sell as much as it wishes on the world market without any effect on the world price. In these circumstances it makes no sense for the country to restrict its production as there would be no offsetting benefits to its farmers in terms of a higher price.

Countries whose production is large enough to influence the world price are said to have *market power*. While Ireland on its own is a price-taker in most agricultural markets (beef is a possible exception) the EU is certainly large enough to be able to influence world prices. The impact on the world price of changes in EU supply and demand in response to changes in EU agricultural policy is discussed in the following chapter.

A particular case where countries tried to exploit their market power in commodity markets to raise world prices was the OPEC oil cartel in the 1970s. Saudi Arabia, as the world's largest oil exporter, has the market power to influence world oil prices on its own; this market power was considerably strengthened through the formation, by developing country oil producers, of the oil exporters' cartel, OPEC. The OPEC countries met together to decide on the total quantity of oil they were prepared to supply to the world market in the next period and to allocate this quantity between them. Because at least in the short run, the demand for oil was very inelastic in response to price, small reductions in OPEC export quantities caused very substantial increases in the price of oil. In 1973 and again in 1979 the world market price of oil was increased very substantially.

Since its heyday in the 1970s, the power of the OPEC cartel to influence world oil prices has considerably diminished. The reasons for this illustrate the limitations of cartel (i.e. group) action to influence market prices. In the first place, high energy prices gradually encouraged consumers to consume less energy; energy conservation measures were introduced, more efficient engines were developed for cars, and so on. In technical terms, the demand curve for oil, which was very price inelastic in the short term, became more elastic in the medium to longer term. On the supply side, the high price of energy encouraged the development of substitute sources of energy; for example, North Sea oil, which would not have been produced at previous oil prices, now became economic to exploit. As the UK, and other developed-country oil producers, were not members of OPEC, the cartel's power to influence the oil price diminished. Also on the supply side, the discipline of cartel members began to break down. Many oil exporters launched ambitious development programmes which required large amounts of foreign exchange, and were tempted to sell more than their quota of oil in order to acquire this. This is another example of the free rider problem mentioned earlier. As this extra oil found its way to the world market, the cartel's ability to influence the oil price was further undermined. Today, in terms of its influence on the oil market, OPEC is little more than a shadow of its former self.

The OPEC experience is a salutary lesson for other primary product (i.e. agricultural and natural resource) exporters hoping to exploit market power by restricting supply to the world market. In the first place, most other primary products face close substitutes in consumption (coffee and tea, copper and aluminium) and thus have quite a high price elasticity of demand. In the face of elastic demand, even successful group action to restrict supply will have little impact on the market price. Second, even where demand is (in the short run) inelastic, group co-ordination to restrict supply can be very difficult because of the free rider problem. As a result, agricultural schemes of supply restriction are invariably mandatory and backed by government sanctions.

GOVERNMENT INTERVENTION TO RAISE DEMAND

As an alternative to influencing supply in order to raise agricultural prices, governments can attempt to stimulate demand. A typical mechanism is the establishing of minimum guaranteed prices, with the government standing by to act as a buyer of last resort. The manner in which such a programme is often implemented is as follows.

Assume, for simplicity, that the country is closed to international trade for the commodity for which the government wishes to guarantee a minimum price, p_m. Figure 5 illustrates the market for this commodity. Suppose the demand curve for this commodity is represented by DD and the supply curve by SS. In this case the equilibrium market price, p', is higher than the minimum guaranteed price, p_m, and the government does not intervene. Suppose, however, that the supply curve moves out to S'S', in which case the equilibrium free market price would fall to p" which lies below the guaranteed price. In this case, government may add to market demand by buying the excess of the quantity supplied over the quantity demanded at the guaranteed price. In Figure 5 it would have to buy q_2q_4 per period in order to support the price at p_m. The quantity demanded would then be q_2 (demanded by consumers) plus q_2q_4 (bought by government). This would equal the quantity supplied, q_4, at the guaranteed floor price, p_m. If the government commits to buying all produce offered at an intervention price, then the effective demand curve for the commodity becomes perfectly elastic at this price. Producers will receive at least this price regardless of how much they produce.

Figure 5

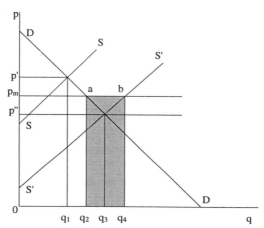

What will the government do with its purchases? As long as p_m is the guaranteed price and as long as the supply and market demand curves remain at S'S' and DD, it cannot release its purchases to be sold on the free market; if it did so, the equilibrium price would fall further below p''. Its purchases will, therefore, go into storage (this was the origin of the beef and butter mountains and wine lakes which plagued the EU during the 1980s). Intervention stores can be reduced if the government either gives the food away or sells it at a very cheap price to people who otherwise would not have consumed it, such as the poor (thus adding to, and not displacing, domestic demand); or (for this moment moving to the case of an open economy) if the government either gives it away to poor countries as food aid or sells it on the export market. In some cases, the food may be simply destroyed.

Just like supply controls, intervention purchases raise domestic prices to benefit farmers at the expense of consumers. In the absence of government intervention the price would be p''; after intervention it is higher, p_m. The farming community is better off; its receipts in the absence of intervention would be $p''q_3$; after intervention, farmers receive p_mq_4. Consumers are made worse off in that they consume less of the product than they would have done before intervention (q_2 instead of q_3) and they must pay a higher price (p_m instead of p") for this quantity. In this case, however, taxpayers must also foot some of the bill as it is they who finance the purchase of the excess supply at the guaranteed price. The cost to taxpayers is represented in Figure 5 by the shaded rectangle q_2abq_4.

OPEN ECONOMY INTERVENTIONS

A much wider range of options to support agricultural prices is available when the economy engages in international trade. If the country is a net importer, one approach to raising domestic prices is to place a *tariff* on imported products. Tariffs can be fixed rate or *ad valorem*. A fixed rate tariff applies the same import tax per unit regardless of the world price of the product. An *ad valorem* tariff is established as some percentage of the world price rather than a fixed per unit amount. The consequences of imposing a tariff on imports in a small open economy which cannot influence the level of world prices are shown in Figure 6.

Figure 6

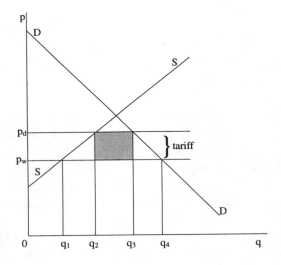

The domestic market price is initially equal to the world price, p_w. Suppose the government now imposes a tariff which raises the domestic market price from p_w to p_d. The protection afforded the domestic agricultural sector will encourage an expansion of domestic supply from q_1 to q_2. The higher price on the domestic market will reduce domestic demand from q_4 to q_3. The demand for imported products will decrease from q_1q_4 to q_2q_3. Farmers gain because they receive a higher price (p_d) on a larger quantity (q_2) than was the case before the tariff. Taxpayers also benefit because the import duties contribute to government revenue equal to the height of the tariff times the volume of imports (represented by the shaded area in Figure 6). The losers in this scenario are the consumers who must pay a higher price not only for domestic production but also for imported food.

Figure 7

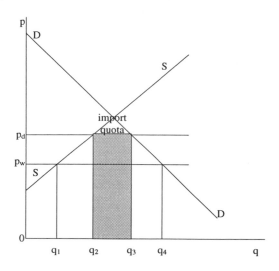

An alternative to imposing a tariff is to introduce quota restrictions on the volume of imports permitted. Such *import quotas* should be distinguished from the production quotas discussed earlier; import quotas seek to control the amount supplied from external sources, whereas production quotas control the amount of domestic production. In both cases, however, the intention is to raise the level of domestic prices by restricting supply to the market.

The impact of restricting imports through quotas is shown in Figure 7, where it is assumed that the quota is set at the quantity q_2q_3. This diagram looks similar to that showing the impact of a tariff and it may appear that it is a matter of indifference whether a country restricts imports by means of a tariff or a quota. However, there are some differences between the two instruments. First, if world prices are unstable, this instability will be transmitted to the domestic market under a tariff régime. A tariff raises the level of domestic prices in comparison to world prices but there generally remains a fixed relationship between the two. In contrast, under an import quota régime the domestic market is largely insulated from world market price fluctuations (except in the case where world market prices increase above the level of the protected domestic price). Second, the government of a net importing country benefits from a tariff régime as it obtains the revenue from the import duties. There is no such revenue in the case of an import quota. In this case, the higher protected price is also paid to exporters located abroad, who thereby obtain some compensation for the loss of some of their export market. The cost of import purchases under the quota régime is shown by the shaded area in Figure 7.

What happens if the country is an exporter instead of an importer? Some of the country's production must now be sold on the world market. In this case import protection at the border, whether by tariffs or import quotas, will not increase domestic prices above world market levels. If the price received for the last unit of output is the (constant) world price, in a competitive market the domestic price will be forced down to world market levels. To prevent this happening, a government can pay an *export subsidy* equal to the difference between the desired domestic price and the world price. The consequences are illustrated in Figure 8, where DD and SS denote the internal demand and supply curves, respectively, in the absence of foreign trade.

Figure 8

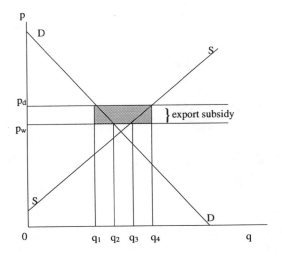

When producers must sell at the world price, p_w, domestic production is q_3. If the government now agrees to pay an export subsidy on all produce exported, in a competitive market, this will be reflected in the domestic producer price which will increase to p_d. Production will increase to q_4, while domestic consumption will fall from q_2 to q_1. The volume of exports will increase from q_2q_3 to q_1q_4. Farmers clearly gain from the export subsidy, while consumers lose. In the case of an export subsidy, moreover, taxpayers are now worse off as they must finance the cost of the subsidy, shown as the shaded area in Figure 8. Export subsidies are widely used to support farm prices under the EU's Common Agricultural Policy which is examined in greater detail in the next chapter.

PRICE INSTABILITY

Agricultural prices are not only falling over time, they can also be very unstable. The reason for this can again be understood with the aid of a supply and demand diagram (Figure 9). We now focus on the relative slopes of the demand and supply curves, rather than on their positions. Both curves for agricultural products are rather steep. In the short run, agricultural supply may be almost completely inelastic. The decision to undertake production has been made in the past and farmers have little choice but to market this production, regardless of the level of current prices. The inelasticity of the demand curve with respect to own price reflects the fact that consumers do not significantly alter the quantity of their purchases of food when food prices change.

Figure 9

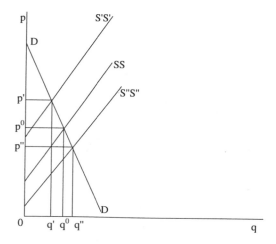

The position of the supply curve can vary considerably from year to year in response to weather conditions during the growing season, disease outbreaks, etc. Given the steepness of the slope of the demand curve, these shifts in supply can lead to substantial variations in prices within a short period. Looking at Figure 9 (where SS denotes the supply curve in an "average" year) the supply curve S'S' represents a position of tight supplies when price (p') is high; on the other hand, the supply curve S"S" represents a glut situation when price (p") is depressed. If the agricultural supply curve shifts frequently between these two positions, agricultural prices will be very unstable. This price volatility can bring hardship to farmers while the increased uncertainty which results can be a major source of inefficiency. Furthermore, agricultural supply has the characteristic that there is a lag between taking the decision to produce and this production becoming available. When this *supply lag* is considered, the potential arises for the generation of cycles of agricultural prices and production. This problem can be illustrated by extending the static supply and demand framework into a dynamic setting.

STATICS AND DYNAMICS

The difference between static and dynamic analyses can be briefly explained. The method of analysis used up to now is called *comparative static equilibrium analysis* or *comparative statics*. This method adopts the following procedure. Starting from an equilibrium, some disturbance causes a departure from equilibrium. This might be some shift in one of the underlying parameters or the introduction of a government policy such as a tax as described in Chapter 6. On the assumption that a new equilibrium will be reached, the method calculates the characteristics of the new equilibrium; what will be the new equilibrium price level? What will be the new equilibrium quantities traded? The new equilibrium which is assumed to be attainable (i.e. stable) can then be compared with the initial equilibrium. This method of comparative statics is very useful, but it has two deficiencies. First, it cannot tell us what happens out of equilibrium. Second, although an equilibrium may exist, the behaviour of the system out of equilibrium may be such that equilibrium is never reached. If an initial equilibrium is disturbed and if the behaviour of the system out of equilibrium is such that the new equilibrium is never reached (i.e. if that equilibrium is unstable), then the *predictions* yielded by the comparative static method will almost certainly be wrong. To avoid the deficiencies of the comparative static method we need dynamic analysis, which is the study of the behaviour of systems (e.g. whole economies or individual markets) in disequilibrium situations.

An Example of Dynamics: The Cobweb Model

As an example of dynamic analysis, this section discusses the cobweb model (so-called because of the pattern of graphs which it generates). This model helps to illustrate how supply lags in agricultural markets can generate cycles in agricultural production. Consider the market for an agricultural crop where the decision on planting is taken in the previous year. Three assumptions underlie the cobweb model explanation of agricultural cycles. First, there is a time lag between the planting decision and harvest. This means farmers must make their planting decisions on the basis of the price expected to prevail in the following period. There are many ways in which farmers might form expectations about the future price level. The second assumption made in the cobweb model is that farmers expect next year's price to be the same as this year's. The implication of this behaviour is that actual supply in any year is a function, not of the price in the current year (as has been implicitly assumed until now) but of the price in the previous year. Demand in the current year continues to be a function of the current year's price. The demand and supply functions thus take the following forms:

(1) $q^d_t = f(p_t)$

(2) $q^s_t = g(p_{t-1})$

where the subscript t indicates time (in, say, years). Equation (1) states that the demand in any year, t, is a function of the price in that year, t. Equation (2) says that the supply in any year, t, is a function of the price in the previous year, t-1. This year's supply is based on last year's price, next year's supply is based on this year's price, and so on.

The third assumption is that, once production has taken place, the price must adjust to ensure that the market clears. No storage is possible within the model. The operation of the model is shown in Figure 10.

Assume initially that the market is in equilibrium at price p_0 and quantity q_0. Next, suppose that in some year t the supply curve shifts outwards to S'S'. This may have occurred because of an improvement in technology, for example. In order to highlight the central issues, it will be assumed that S'S' remains the new supply curve. Consider now how the market reacts over time. On the basis of the original price p_0, producers plan to produce q_1 which becomes available for sale in time t+1 because of the time lag in the production process. Once produced, in order to sell q_1, given the demand relation DD, the market price must fall to p_1. On the basis of this price in year t+1, farmers prepare to produce q_2 in year t+2. This is turn leads to the price increasing to p_2 in year t+2 which in turn encourages production to increase to q_3 in year t+3. By following the direction of the arrows in Figure 10, we see that the market eventually reaches a new equilibrium at price p_e and quantity q_e. Thus the diagram indicates that the dynamics of the system are such that, starting from one equilibrium point (p_0, q_0), the time path is (p_1, q_1), (p_2, q_2) and so on as indicated by the arrows. The system oscillates but eventually converges to the new equilibrium (p_e, q_e). The cobweb pattern traced out on the graph is what gives the model its name. Note that for a clear cobweb the supply and demand curves must remain fixed in position after the initial shock.

Figure 10

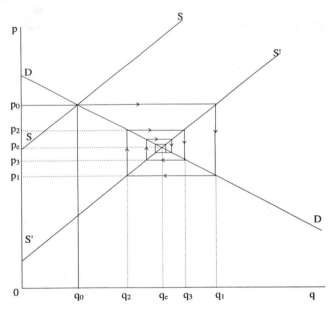

In Figure 10, the cobweb model converges and leads eventually to the new equilibrium (p_e, q_e). But this need not necessarily be the case. Figure 11, which is constructed in exactly the same way as Figure 10, illustrates a case where the cobweb model leads to diverging oscillations and where the market moves further and further away from equilibrium. Starting from the initial equilibrium (p_0, q_0), the reader should confirm that the time path of the system after the shift in the supply curve from SS to S'S' is (p_1, q_1), (p_2, q_2) and so on. The oscillations now become larger over time and the system explodes. Thus, although an equilibrium exists at (p_e, q_e), the dynamics are such that it will not be reached.

Whether a system converges (as in Figure 10) or diverges (as in Figure 11) in response to a shock depends, in practice, on the relative slopes of the demand and supply curves. Where the absolute value of the slope of the demand curve is smaller than the slope of the supply curve, then there is a tendency for the oscillations to converge. Conversely, where the slope of the demand curve is steeper than the slope of the supply curve, the oscillations tend to diverge. In the coincidental case where the slopes of the two curves are equal in absolute value, symmetric oscillations will be produced but the system will fail to settle at a new equilibrium. In the latter two cases, dynamic analysis results in a prediction different from comparative statics. The comparative static method would predict (in Figure 11) that the market price will eventually settle down at (p_e, q_e); the dynamic analysis shows that this will not be the case. While this disagreement is worrying, throughout this chapter and (except where otherwise stated) in the rest of the book we assume that markets are dynamically stable, and focus on equilibrium solutions.

Figure 11

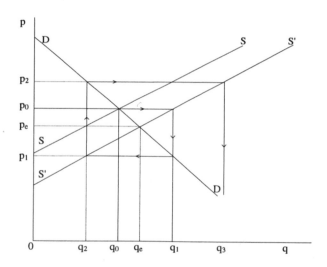

PRICE STABILISATION SCHEMES

Fluctuating prices increase the risk of investment for farmers and the possibility of making wrong decisions. Production cycles reduce capacity utilisation in the processing sector and drive up unit costs. For these reasons, governments, quite apart from trying to raise farm prices, have also attempted to stabilise them. Fluctuations in prices received by producers can be reduced through the creation of a stabilisation fund or, alternatively, through the use of buffer stocks. Under a fund scheme, money is accumulated by paying producers less than the current market price in years of scarcity, when market prices are high. The money thereby accumulated by the fund is then used to top-up prices to producers in years of good harvests, when market prices are low. A buffer stock scheme operates by storing a portion of the crop in years of high production and low prices and then releasing stocks in years of high prices. The operation of a buffer stock scheme in an economy closed to international trade is illustrated in Figure 12.

Figure 12

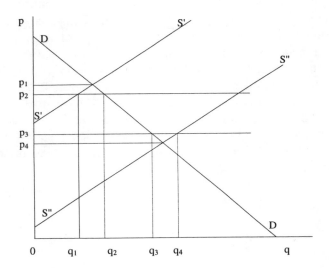

For simplicity, assume that good and bad years alternate with equal frequency and offsetting consequences. In Figure 12, the supply curve representing bountiful harvests is S"S" and the free market price in years of plenty would fall to p_4. In years of poor harvests (represented by the supply curve S'S'), the free market price would increase to p_1. Suppose, however, that the government wishes to stabilise market prices in the range between p_2 and p_3. In a good year, the government must step in and buy the amount q_3q_4 to support the price at p_3. Such purchases are then added to the government's buffer stock. In the following year, in order to prevent the market price from rising above p_2, the government can draw down its buffer stock to release to the market an additional supply, equal to q_1q_2. This action will ensure that total supplies are sufficient to meet the quantity demanded at price p_2. Note, in passing, that these buffer stock operations can be very profitable as the government is buying in years of low prices and selling in years when prices are high. It is, therefore, not surprising that private firms engaged in processing a commodity with a volatile price also engage in this arbitrage over time, building up stocks when prices are low and running them down when prices are high; they consequently contribute to evening out the amplitude of price fluctuations.

In discussing Figure 12, it was assumed that the agency operating the buffer stock knows precisely the extent of supply shifts and thus the average price around which the market should be stabilised. In practice, buffer stock managers must operate in a world of uncertainty and of conflicting interests. Producers will usually call for early intervention by the buffer stock manager whenever prices begin to fall; consumers will wish to delay buffer stock intervention to take advantage of the lower prices. If there is a tendency for commodity prices to fall over time (as we argued earlier in this chapter), then the buffer stock could find itself buying more and more in order to support the market price, but with fewer and fewer high-price periods in which to off-load these stocks. If this continues, eventually the buffer stock will run out of finance and must cease operations. In practice, many buffer stock schemes set up with the objective of stabilising prices turn out to be used as price support mechanisms as well.

CHAPTER 8

AGRICULTURAL POLICY IN THE EUROPEAN UNION

Alan Matthews

Within the European Union agricultural production, marketing and trade are regulated by the provisions of the EU's Common Agricultural Policy. The main purpose of this intervention is to provide support for EU farmers and to protect agricultural production in the EU from lower-cost competition outside. The extent of this support has risen over time and now accounts for a substantial proportion of the income of farmers within the Union.

There are various ways to measure the extent of government intervention in agriculture. One indicator is the size and proportion of the EU budget spent on agricultural policy. This has grown between 1983 and 1993 from ECU17 billion to ECU40 billion. The share of agricultural expenditure in the EU budget peaked at 70 per cent in 1984 but still remains at around 55 per cent. Providing support to EU dairy farmers alone cost around one-fifth of the entire EU budget over the decade 1983–92. Yet budgetary expenditure on agriculture underestimates the total extent of EU support. Regulation which requires EU consumers to pay more for their food than they otherwise would is an even more important means of supporting EU farmers. These consumer transfers do not show up in budgetary accounts but are nonetheless real.

A more comprehensive measure of agricultural support which has become widely used in recent years is called the Producer Subsidy Equivalent (or PSE for short). This measures the total amount of the transfer, from taxpayers and consumers to farmers arising from the set of government policies in place, to support agricultural production and income. It includes the cost of market price support (as discussed in Chapter 7), direct payments to farmers and the cost of grants and other development and structural assistance. The PSE can be expressed in aggregate terms (so that it measures the absolute amount of the total transfer to farmers), on a per farm basis (so that it measures the average transfer received by individual farms) or *on a percentage basis* (so that it measures *the percentage of the final value of agricultural production at domestic prices which is accounted for by these transfers*). PSEs for all the major industrialised countries, including the EU, are now published annually by the OECD and this permits comparisons of the trend in agricultural support over time as well as between countries.

For inter-country comparisons it is usual to use percentage PSEs (or, sometimes, average PSE per farm) in order to control for differences in the size of the agricultural sector between countries. Percentage PSEs for a selection of industrialised countries during the 1980s are shown in Table 1. A number of conclusions can be drawn from this table: (a) a high proportion of the value of farm output in the EU is now directly attributable to government policies which result in transfers to farmers from taxpayers and consumers; (b) while the size of the percentage PSE varies from year to year (largely in response to variations in world market prices) the relative amount of support appears to be growing over time; and (c) the amount of support provided to EU farmers is high relative to the support provided to farmers in other countries.

Table 1: Agricultural Support in Industrialised Countries (measured as net Producer Subsidy Equivalent, per cent)

Country	1979–86	1987	1988	1989	1990	1991	1992	1993
Australia	10	10	8	7	12	12	10	9
Canada	28	51	38	35	46	45	38	32
EU	37	49	46	40	46	48	47	48
Japan	64	74	72	68	65	62	71	70
New Zealand	24	13	7	5	5	4	3	3
United States	21	32	24	20	23	21	21	23
All OECD	34	47	42	37	42	42	41	42

Source: OECD, *Agricultural Policies, Markets and Trade, 1994 Report*, Paris.

The supply and demand framework applied to agriculture in Chapter 7 is also used in the present chapter to help analyse and understand the consequences of government support for agriculture in the EU. One important extension introduced in this chapter is that the EU is a large player in world agricultural markets. A consequence is that EU agricultural policy has implications beyond the EU's own borders. We shall see below that supporting agricultural prices in the Union above free market levels has the effect of lowering prices for agricultural commodities on the world market. These world market effects of the EU's agricultural policy help to explain the antagonism which other agricultural exporting countries, notably the US, display towards the Common Agricultural Policy. The disarray in world agriculture caused by massive subsidisation of agricultural production in nearly all indus- trialised countries led to the efforts to reduce agricultural support in the Uruguay Round of GATT talks which concluded at the end of 1993. The successful introduction of disciplines on the permitted extent of agri- cultural subsidisation in this GATT Round may mark the beginning of the end of the special protected status which agriculture has enjoyed in Europe in the post-war period.

The present chapter first sets out the historical context for the Common Agricultural Policy and its main institutional features. This is followed by a description of the main types of market intervention practised under the CAP and how such intervention has been altered by the reforms introduced by EU Commissioner for Agriculture, Ray MacSharry, in 1993. The chapter then extends the supply and demand framework used in the previous chapter to analyse how agricultural policy in a large country, or in a large economic union, affects the world market. Informed by this analysis, the chapter concludes by examining the consequences of the move towards agricultural trade liberalisation and the restrictions on agricultural support introduced by the GATT.

THE COMMON AGRICULTURAL POLICY

The objectives of the CAP were defined in the Treaty of Rome (1957) which established the European Economic Community, as it was then called. The policy was to increase agricultural productivity, to ensure a fair standard of living for the agricultural community, to stabilise markets, to assure the availability of supplies and reasonable prices for consumers.

This common agricultural policy was not created on a *tabula rasa*. Each of the original six Member States already intervened extensively in its own agricultural sector. The harmonisation of six systems of agri- cultural support with different price levels into a common agricultural policy with a common set of prices was a major political achievement. At an early stage three principles were laid down which have remained the cornerstone of the policy to this day. They were:

(1) Unity of the market. This means the elimination of all obstacles to intra-EU trade in agricultural products and the establishment of a common set of prices throughout the Union.

(2) Union preference. This means that the Union market is reserved in

the first instance for Union producers and that imports should only be permitted when internal production is insufficient to meet internal demand.

(3) Financial solidarity. This means that the costs of running the Union agricultural policy are a charge on the EU budget financed in common by the Member States and not specifically by the Member States which benefit from the policy.

The Common Agricultural Policy was formally launched on 1 January 1968. Its two arms are respectively: (a) price and markets policy; and (b) structures policy. The price and markets policy focuses on maintaining the level and stability of agricultural product prices deemed appropriate in the light of the CAP's objectives set out in the Treaty of Rome. The objective of the structures policy is to encourage the modernisation of farming and the food processing sector through the provision of grant aid and incentives, although more recently its brief has been widened to include agri-environment measures and rural development.

FEOGA, the agricultural budget of the Union, is in turn divided into two sections, the Guarantee Section which funds the price and markets policy, and the Guidance Section which funds the structures policy. FEOGA is the French acronym for the European Agricultural Guarantee and Guidance Fund (EAGGF). It is not hard to understand why the French acronym is preferred! Although the original intention had been to adopt a ratio of Guarantee to Guidance spending of two to one, in practice Guarantee expenditure has had the lion's share of the funds and has accounted for 95 per cent of total FEOGA expenditure over the decade. More recently, greater emphasis on using the EU's Structural Funds, which include the Guidance Section of FEOGA, to bring about economic and social cohesion within the EU, has led to increased funding and a more prominent role for agricultural structures policy.

Price and Markets Policy

The totality of market intervention arrangements used to regulate the market price for a farm commodity within the EU is referred to as the *market régime* for that commodity. The details of market intervention arrangements differ from commodity to commodity and have also been changed over time in response to budgetary and other pressures.

The cereals market régime was the first to be agreed and introduced the main policy instruments, many of which are carried over into other market régimes (see Figure 1). A *target price* is set each year for each of the main cereals as the price the EU wishes to maintain in the wholesale market in the EU region of greatest deficit (the Ruhr area of Germany).

To prevent this target price being undermined by cheaper imported grain the EU establishes a *threshold price* as a minimum import price for grain entering the Union through the port of Rotterdam. It is calculated so that the threshold price plus transport costs from the port to the Ruhr area of Germany is at least equal to the target price.

Figure 1

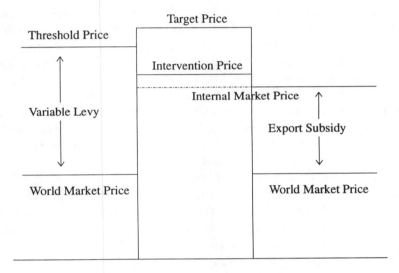

Each day *variable import levies* are calculated, making up the difference between the lowest offer price on the world market and the threshold price. These levies must be paid by any importer wishing to import cheaper world market grain into the Union and they ensure that Union producers are protected from lower-cost competition. Imports occur only if the Union market price rises above the target price level. In this case it would be profitable to import grain until the market price was driven down to the target price level. Thus the target price also represents a ceiling above which the market price is unlikely to rise for any extended period of time.

The one exception to this is where world prices are *above* the Union target price, in which case there would be an incentive to export grain out of the Community. This would have the effect of dragging the Union market price above the target price. To prevent this from happening there is provision in the CAP to turn the border import levies into export taxes. This prevents farmers and wholesalers from taking advantage of higher world market prices and keeps prices at the target price level to the benefit of EU consumers. In practice, world market prices have exceeded EU target prices for only one or two commodities on only one or two occasions in the past two decades.

If the Union remained a deficit market this border protection against imports would be sufficient to maintain the internal Union price at the desired target level. However, if internal production exceeds internal consumption, the excess supply would cause the market price to fall. To limit the extent of any such fall in the market price, provision is made for government purchases of excess supplies at an *intervention price*. If farmers, merchants and processors had unlimited access to this intervention arrangement, then the intervention price would set an effective floor price to the market. In practice, the EU restricts access to intervention in various ways (by limiting purchases to certain grades or qualities, for example) or makes it less attractive by delaying payment, so that the market price does frequently fall below the intervention floor. Increasingly, the intervention agencies issue invitations to tender and the buying-in price reflects the market situation. For some commodities, such as pork, wine and certain fruits and vegetables, the intervention arrangements are even more flexible. When supplies are plentiful, the Union may pay *aid for private storage* to take a proportion of output temporarily off the market. Once market prospects improve, the produce is released from storage and offered for sale. This is similar to the operation of a buffer stock scheme as discussed in Chapter 7.

The intervention system was designed to deal with short-term oversupply on EU markets. If a situation of structural oversupply emerges, then the surplus must be sold outside the Union. Given that the EU market price is usually well above the world price, export sales must be made attractive by providing *export subsidies* or *refunds* to compensate exporters for the difference. This system of external protection, intervention and export subsidies applies to the major Irish farm enterprises, including beef, pigmeat, cereals and dairy products, although the specific details of each market régime vary from commodity to commodity.

Two other forms of intervention can be used. In the sheep and oilseeds régimes, part of the market return to farmers comes through *direct payments* paid either directly to the farmer (in the form of ewe premia in the case of sheepmeat) or to processors (in the form of a subsidy to make up the gap between the EU price and the price of imports in the case of oilseeds). In the case of the dairy and sugarbeet régimes, the amount of production eligible for support is limited by *quota*. In the case of milk, production above the quota amount is prohibited and large levies are placed on above-quota milk production offered for sale. In the case of sugar, above-quota production is allowed but must be offered for sale outside the Union without the benefit of export subsidies. The use of direct payments and supply controls has been greatly increased under the so-called MacSharry reform of the CAP introduced in 1993. The next section examines the rationale for this reform and its likely impact.

The MacSharry CAP Reforms

From one perspective, the CAP has been an enormous success. The combination of high and guaranteed prices, by raising farm profitability and reducing the risk and uncertainty associated with farm production, has encouraged the rapid uptake of technical advances in farming and ensured an abundant supply of foodstuffs in Western Europe. It has been less successful in meeting some of the other objectives outlined in the Treaty of Rome. Consumer food prices are high (in comparison, for example, to the prices consumers pay in the United States or Australia) even though there is little evidence that European consumers are overly concerned about this. Considerable rural poverty persists despite the high transfers from taxpayers and consumers documented above. The budgetary costs of agricultural policy continue to rise and there is grow-ing antagonism from other major agricultural exporters to the EU's policy of dumping its export surpluses on world markets at their expense.

In February 1991 Ray MacSharry, then EU Commissioner for Agri-culture, launched his plan to reform the CAP (Commission, *The Develop-ment and Future of the CAP,* COM(91)100, Brussels, 1991). While rec-ognising the contribution of the policy in providing European consumers with a wide range of quality food products, he argued that the CAP had been created at a time when Europe was in deficit for most food prod-ucts. The EU's move into surplus for most of its agricultural production had revealed a number of deficiencies:

- The price guarantees stimulated output growth at a rate far in excess of the market's absorptive capacity. Between 1973 and 1988 the volume of EU agricultural production increased by 2 per cent per annum whereas internal consumption grew by only 0.5 per cent per annum.

- The encouragement given to the intensification of farming has had increasingly negative environmental effects.

- Income support is largely proportionate to the volume of production and therefore concentrates the greater part of support on the largest and more intensive farms. The effect of this is that 80 per cent of the support provided by FEOGA accrues to only 20 per cent of the EU's farms.

- The per capita purchasing power of those engaged in agriculture improved very little over the 15 years 1973–88, despite a fall of 35 per cent in agricultural employment and a massive growth in FEOGA budgetary expenditure.

The essence of the MacSharry plan was to substitute direct income payments for market price support. Support prices for major commodities were reduced (by up to 35 per cent in the case of cereals) but farmers were compensated for this reduction by direct payments per hectare (in the case of cereals and oilseed crops) or per animal (in the case of live-stock). To qualify for these compensation payments, larger cereal farmers have to set aside a proportion of their cultivated land for non-agricultural use, while payments to livestock farmers are limited by stocking rate pro-visions. In the case of both cereals and livestock, these changes introduce a significant degree of *decoupling* of income support from production decisions. Unlike price support, where higher prices give farmers greater incentives to produce more, the MacSharry compensation payments are limited to fixed volumes of production. Farmers will produce more only if additional production is profitable at the lower level of market prices now prevailing, irrespective of the level of direct payments.

Calculations suggest that, in a static framework, Irish agriculture has benefited from this CAP reform. The increased compensation and premia payments more than offset the expected reduction in market prices. (See the National Economic and Social Council report *Reform of the Common Agricultural Policy*, Dublin, Stationery Office, 1992 for details of how Irish farming is affected, although note that the proposals finally adopted in June 1992 were more favourable to Ireland than those considered in this report.) The Irish economy also gains because some of the transfer to farmers previously paid by Irish consumers (in the form of higher food prices) will now be paid by the EU taxpayer (because of the switch from market price support to direct payments). The reforms are to be phased in gradually over a three-year period 1993–5. In 1993 and 1994 market prices were stronger than expected, especially for beef and dairy products, and when the compensation and premia payments were added, Irish farm income reached record high levels. Whether this good fortune continues will depend, in part, on whether the EU will continue to fund direct payments on the present scale and on how market prices evolve in the future. More recently, farmers have attacked the GATT Uruguay Round agreement reached in December 1993, on the grounds that its disciplines on agricultural support go well beyond those agreed in the MacSharry CAP reform. The next section explains the background to the GATT negotiations on limiting agricultural support by examining how such support can distort world markets and world trade.

WORLD MARKET EFFECTS OF CAP SUPPORT

The impact of using policy instruments such as import restrictions, export subsidies and supply controls in the agricultural sector of a small economy was explored in Chapter 7. A small economy was defined as one where changes in its domestic policy had no impact on the world market or on other countries. But the European Union is a major participant in world agricultural markets. It accounts for 15 per cent of world cereal exports, 33 per cent of world dairy exports, 20 per cent of world meat exports, 18 per cent of world sugar exports and 75 per cent of world wine exports. In addition, it accounts for 45 per cent of world oilseed imports. Even small changes in EU supply and demand as a result of changes in agricultural support policy have important repercussions in world markets for these products. These consequences are explored in this section.

Figure 2

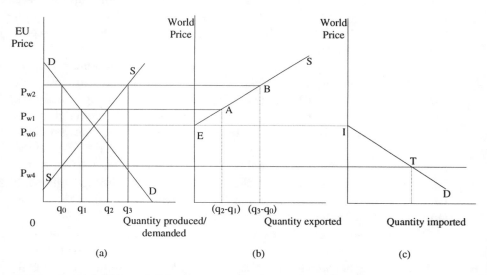

In Figure 2(a) DD and SS represent the demand and supply curves for a particular agricultural commodity, say, beef, in the EU. These curves show how the quantities of beef demanded and supplied within the EU vary with the EU market price (note that the vertial axis shows the price level in the EU). *Assume that, initially, the EU has no policy of agricultural protection.* Then the EU beef price will be determined by the world market price for beef and, in the absence of transport costs, will be equal to the world price. If the world price is p_{w1}, then the quantity demanded in the EU (q_1) will be less than the quantity supplied

(q_2) and the surplus (q_2-q_1) will be exported at the world price. If the world price (and thus the EU price) increases to p_{w2}, then the EU's export surplus will increase to (q_3-q_0). At the world price (and EU price) p_{w0} the EU will be exactly self-sufficient and its export surplus falls to zero; this is referred to as the *autarchic price*. At world prices (and EU prices) below p_{w0}, the quantity demanded in the EU will exceed the quantity supplied from within the EU, and the EU would move into deficit and become a beef importer.

These changes in the net trade position of the EU as the world price changes can be depicted using the *export supply* curve (sometimes called an *excess supply* curve), as shown in Figure 2(b). The export supply curve shows the quantity of exports which the EU is prepared to supply to the world market as the world market price changes. It is constructed as follows. Note that the vertical axis shows the price level on the world market. At the autarchic price p_{w0} the EU's export supply is exactly zero. This is point E on the export supply curve ES. At the price p_{w1} the EU's export supply equals (q_2-q_1). This is point A on the export supply curve ES. At price p_{w2} the EU's export supply equal (q_3-q_0). This is point B on the export supply curve ES. By joining these points together the export supply curve is derived.

Alternatively, if the world price is below the EU's autarchic price, we can construct an *import demand* curve ID showing the quantity of imports demanded at different levels of the world price using exactly the same procedure. Figure 2(c) shows the EU's import demand curve derived from the EU market diagram in Figure 2(a). At the autarchic world price p_{w0} imports are zero (shown as point I in Figure 2(c)). At the world price p_{w4} imports are equal to the horizontal distance between the DD and SS curves at that price, shown as point T on the import demand curve ID. The import demand curve is derived by joining these and similar points together.

These constructions of export supply curves and import demand curves provide a simple way of determining the equilibrium world price level. Suppose that we simplify the world market by assuming that it consists of only two regions, the EU and the Rest of the World. If the EU is an exporter at a particular world price, then the Rest of the World must be an importer of an equivalent amount. In Figure 3, the world market price is found at the point of intersection of the EU's export supply curve and the import demand curve ID of the Rest of the World. At this equilibrium price the quantity of world exports supplied and the quantity of world imports demanded are equal. In this two-region model, the quantity exported from the EU (q_e) equals the quantity imported by the Rest of the World at the equilibrium price p_{w1}.

Figure 3

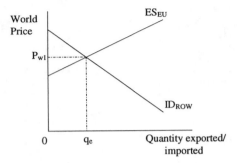

Up to this stage in the present section, it has been assumed that the EU has no policy of agricultural protection. Under such circumstances, suppose that the world (and EU) market is in equilibrium at p_{w1} (= p_{eu1}) to begin with. Starting from the situation just indicated, assume now that the EU introduces a fixed export subsidy of 20 per cent on exports of beef with the intention of raising EU beef prices by 20 per cent (see Chapter 7 for an explanation of an export subsidy). Some of the effects are analysed using Figure 4. At the new internal price (p_{eu2}) the EU will want to offer a much larger supply of beef to the world market (q_3-q_0) compared to its previous exports of (q_2-q_1), even if there were no change in the world price (Figure 4a). Recall that the export supply curve shows the quantity of exports the EU wishes to supply to the world market at different levels of the world price. Because we are examining what happens at a *given* level of the world price, the EU's greater export capacity cannot be the result of a movement *along* its export supply curve. Instead, we show this change in the EU's willingness to export as an outward *shift* in its export supply curve to ES' (Figure 4b).

There is now a disequilibrium in the world market. At the original world price p_{w1} the amount of exports available (e_1) exceeds the quantity of imports demanded (e_0). The world price will fall to restore equilibrium. This important result shows that raising prices to EU farmers lowers world market prices. It explains why exporting countries in the Rest of the World region become so annoyed with the EU's use of export subsidies, although importing countries in the Rest of the World will gain from the improvement in their terms of trade. (A country's "terms of trade" is the ratio of its export prices to its import prices. If a country is a net importer of food, and the price of food on the world market falls, then the cost of its imports is reduced relative to the price of its exports, and the country experiences an improvement in its terms of trade.)

Figure 4

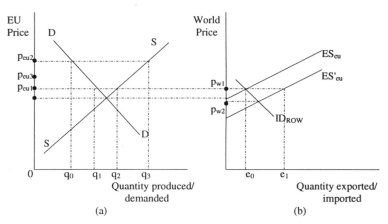

(a)

(b)

Note also a further consequence of the fall in the world price in Figure 4a. Because we assume that the EU introduced a fixed rate of export subsidy, the final level of the EU internal price is not p_{eu2} but p_{eu3} (where p_{eu3} is 20 per cent higher than the final world price equilibrium level p_{w2}). This illustrates that some of the transfer from EU consumers and taxpayers has not benefited EU farmers, which was the intention, but has instead benefited foreign purchasers of EU exports who can now buy these exports more cheaply.

In actual practice, the EU fixes its internal support price and operates a variable export subsidy scheme in order to ensure that this price level is maintained *regardless of the level of world prices*. This has a further consequence for world market prices which is illustrated in Figure 5. This diagram represents the world market under two alternative EU policies. The export supply curve ES represents an EU policy of a fixed rate of export subsidy (e.g. a subsidy of 20 per cent of the world price) and the export supply curve ES' represents an EU policy of a fixed internal price (and thus variable export subsidy — the export subsidy is variable because it must equal the difference between the fixed internal price and an uncertain world price). The second curve ES' is drawn vertically to reflect the fact that, under a variable export subsidy régime, the level of available EU exports is determined solely by internal EU circumstances and is not influenced at all by the level of world market prices. For purposes of illustration, it is assumed that, given the position of the Rest of the World import demand curve ID, both policies result initially in the same world equilibrium price.

Now examine what happens if the Rest of the World import demand curve is unstable, perhaps because of volatile weather conditions in the main producing regions elsewhere in the world. Under good weather conditions, import demand in the Rest of the World is reduced (for any given level of world prices) and the import demand curve shifts inwards to ID_1. Because of the lower demand for imports, world prices will fall. However, the fall is much greater when the EU has a variable export subsidy régime (when the world price falls to p_{w5}) than when the EU has a fixed export subsidy régime (when the world price falls to p_{w4}).

Similarly, if poor weather conditions lead to harvest failures in the Rest of the World, import demand increases and the import demand curve shifts outwards to ID_2. This will put upward pressure on the world price. Once again, the rise in the world price will be much greater when the EU adopts a variable export subsidy régime (when the world price would rise to p_{w3}) compared to what would happen under an EU fixed export subsidy régime (when the world price would rise to p_{w2}). As import demand in the Rest of the World fluctuates, the degree of volatility of world prices is much greater when the EU insulates itself from these fluctuations by maintaining a fixed target price for its own producers.

Figure 5

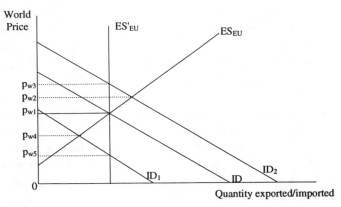

This illustrates a further paradox. Not only does the EU's policy of raising its own farm prices lower world prices for everyone else, but the EU's policy of stabilising its domestic farm prices destabilises world prices for all other countries. The advantages of stabilising agricultural prices were discussed in Chapter 7. The way the EU stabilises its prices, however, is at the expense of other countries. It is no wonder that the EU's Common Agricultural Policy is heavily criticised by its outside trading partners.

THE GATT URUGUAY ROUND

The way in which domestic agricultural policies distort world trade was at the centre of the agricultural negotiations in the GATT Uruguay Round which began in September 1986 and concluded in December 1993. Arising from these negotiations three main disciplines on agricultural support have been agreed:

(1) Variable import levies of the kind used by the EU to protect and stabilise its domestic market must be converted to fixed import tariffs and the level of these tariffs must be reduced by, on average, 36 per cent over six years. Access to up to 5 per cent of the domestic market must be opened up to imports.

(2) Budgetary expenditure on export subsidies must be reduced by 36 per cent over six years and the volume of subsidised exports must be reduced by 21 per cent over six years.

(3) The total amount of agricultural support must be reduced by 20 per cent over a six-year period. However, payments to farmers which are decoupled from production are excluded from this limitation. Examples of decoupled payments include the EU compensation payments introduced under the MacSharry CAP reform, as well as payments to farmers for environmental purposes. This important exemption means that the GATT agreement does not prohibit governments giving support to farmers. In future, however, this support must increasingly be given in ways which do not distort agricultural markets.

In the light of the graphical analysis outlined above, it is possible to indicate qualitatively the effects of these GATT disciplines. The tariffication of border levies required under (1) will mean that, in future, EU prices will be more responsive to changes in world market prices, even though, initially, this effect will be very limited. We know that this will lead to a somewhat more elastic EU export supply curve and thus greater stability in world market prices in the future (see Figure 5).

The restrictions on export subsidy expenditure under (2), insofar as they go beyond the reforms already being introduced under the MacSharry Plan, will force further reductions in either support prices or quota volumes within the EU. The extent to which this GATT discipline will require further reductions in agricultural support beyond those required in the MacSharry Plan is a matter of some dispute.

The exemption from GATT disciplines for decoupled payments to farmers under (3) will mean that, in future, we are likely to see a higher proportion of transfers to farmers taking the form of direct payments or payments for environmental services and a lower proportion in the form of traditional market price support.

Thus, in conclusion, the analysis in this chapter has shown how domestic agricultural price support can have important ramifications for other countries. Policies designed to increase prices to EU farmers lower world market prices. Policies designed to stabilise prices for EU farmers destabilise world market prices. Simple supply and demand analysis has been shown to be a powerful tool in understanding the consequences of wide-ranging government intervention such as has characterised the agricultural sector in the past.

PART THREE

MACROECONOMIC ANALYSIS

CHAPTER 9

THE NATIONAL ACCOUNTS

Macroeconomics is concerned with the determination of aggregate variables such as total output, unemployment and inflation. It gives insights into major policy issues, among them the following:

- *Rising prices*: Why does the price level increase? Why be concerned with rising prices if wages adjust at least proportionately?

- *Unemployment*: Why do we have unemployment? Why does the unemployment rate vary over time? Why is it lower in other EU countries?

- *Stability or instability of private enterprise*: Could a private enterprise economy manage its affairs without recurrent bouts of inflation and unemployment? Is government intervention necessary to stabilise the economy?

IDENTITY OF NATIONAL INCOME, PRODUCT AND EXPENDITURE

The primary task of macroeconomics is to explain what determines the size of national income and its growth and fluctuation over time. What is loosely termed the national income is a measure of the money value of total *production* of final goods and services by residents of the economy in a particular year. (Actually, national income statistics may pertain to any time period, but in Ireland complete national income data are published on an annual basis only.) Alternatively, it can be described as a measure of the sum of all *incomes* (wages and salaries, rents, interest and profits) accruing to resident factors of production as payments for their services in production during the year. As yet another alternative, we can say that it is a measure of total *expenditure* on the output of final goods and services produced by residents of the economy during the year.

Governments are interested in the size of the national income for several reasons. Given the price level, the volume of goods and services available to society as a whole obviously affects living standards. Thus, subject to some qualifications, economic welfare (that part of individual welfare which can be brought into relation with the measuring-rod of

[123]

money) is directly related to the size of the national income. Furthermore
— again subject to important qualifications — employment (unemployment) tends to move in the same direction as (opposite direction to)
changes in national income.

For advanced countries, official (government) national income
statistics date from the late 1930s and early 1940s. This timing of public
interest in national income data coincided with the commitment of
governments to policies of full employment in the aftermath of the Great
Depression of the 1930s; until then most governments played minor roles
in attempting to manage their economies. Private estimates preceded
official estimates of national income in Ireland. Our official estimates
date from 1938 and are available annually in the publication entitled
National Income and Expenditure.

Appropriately defined, national product, national income and national
expenditure are identical, since they represent three different ways of
calculating the same aggregate, which we denote by the symbol Y.
Although the three terms may be used interchangeably, the term "national
income" is most often used in a generic or general sense to denote Y in
all its aspects.

National Product and National Income

That national product and national income, appropriately defined, are
identical, can be seen by denoting the value of the economy's output of
final goods and services by Y (pounds), and by assuming that there are
no net taxes (taxes less subsidies) on goods (i.e. net taxes on expenditure). The output valued Y (pounds) must be fully accounted for by costs
of production incurred in payment of wages and salaries, rents and
interest, plus the residual between those payments and Y, i.e. profits or
losses. Thus, with profits/losses as a balancing item, total income
generated by production must exactly account for Y: national product and
national income are identical.

In reality there are taxes on expenditure. Therefore, the market prices
of goods diverge from their costs in terms of payments to the factors of
production — their *factor costs*. Thus national product measured at
market prices usually exceeds national income measured at factor cost.
If, then, national product is measured at market prices (and thereby
includes net taxes on expenditure), those expenditure taxes must be
added to national income at factor cost in order to preserve the identity of
product and income. Thus, (a) national product *exclusive* of net expenditure taxes is identical to national income at factor cost, and (b) national
product at market prices is identical to national income at factor cost *plus*
net expenditure taxes.

National Product and National Expenditure

Consider the identity of national product and national expenditure. The reader may try to refute this as follows: "Consider a producer of, say, widgets. Suppose that production during the year is 100 widgets priced at £x each. Total product is then valued at £100x. Suppose that only 90 widgets are sold. Then expenditure is only £90x; so product and expenditure are not identical."

The only objection to this argument is that it ignores an important convention: the firm must have ended the year with 10 extra widgets in stock or inventory; its inventory must have increased by £10x, and in national income accounting an increase in inventory is regarded as part of expenditure — the firm is regarded as spending on investment by increasing its inventory. The opposite treatment is applied if inventories are reduced. Hence, because of the way in which the components are defined, national product is the same as national expenditure. It has now been established that

(1) national income ≡ national product ≡ national expenditure ≡ Y

Note that lower case letters have been used throughout in identity (1). That is because reference is being made to national income in a generic sense (rather than in a very specific sense, as explained later).

Final Goods and Intermediate Goods: Double-counting

National income is a measure of the money value of all *final* goods and services produced by residents of the economy in a year. In this context domestic investment (increase in the economy's inventories or productive assets such as machinery and buildings) is regarded as final. Goods produced during the year but used up as inputs in the same year are not final; they are *intermediate*. Suppose, for example, that the economy produces bread using domestically grown wheat and that all the wheat is used in bread production. The bread is a final good and is therefore included in national product. The wheat is not final since it is all used as an input. If we included both the wheat and the bread in national product we would be double-counting.

Suppose that only part of the wheat is used during the year, and that some of it is allocated to warehouses, increasing the economy's wheat inventory. The wheat used in bread is not included in national product; however, because investment is regarded as final and because an increase in inventory is investment, the increase in wheat inventory is included in national product. The central point is that, in measuring national income from the product side, we count only production of final goods and services (including investment). Similarly, in estimating national income from the expenditure side we count only expenditures on final goods and services (including investment).

Value Added and Transfer Payments

It follows from the loose definition of national income, Y, that if we measure Y from the income side by summing payments to the factors of production, we should count only those payments made for productive activities. We should count only wages and salaries, rents, interest on capital, and profits (or losses, which are profits with a negative sign). Alternatively, it can be said that only those incomes representing *value added* by residents are counted. Consider bread production again. The creation of income at each stage of production is indicated in simplified form in Table 1.

Table 1: Generation of Value Added, £ million

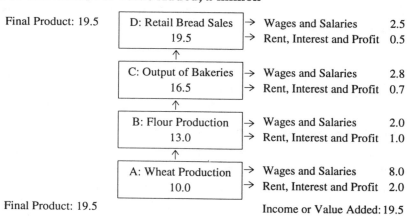

Final Product: 19.5		
D: Retail Bread Sales 19.5	Wages and Salaries	2.5
	Rent, Interest and Profit	0.5
C: Output of Bakeries 16.5	Wages and Salaries	2.8
	Rent, Interest and Profit	0.7
B: Flour Production 13.0	Wages and Salaries	2.0
	Rent, Interest and Profit	1.0
A: Wheat Production 10.0	Wages and Salaries	8.0
	Rent, Interest and Profit	2.0
Final Product: 19.5	Income or Value Added: 19.5	

Bread production at retail prices is £19.5 million, as indicated by box D of Table 1; this is part of national product, but boxes C, B and A are not. Income earned at any stage of production is the value added at that stage. The sum of such incomes, indicated by arrows outside the boxes, is also £19.5 million. For illustration it is assumed that there are only four stages in production, as follows:

Suppose farmers buy no raw materials from outside agriculture. (If this assumption were relaxed we would have to go further backward in the structure of production.) With land, labour and capital they produce wheat with a wholesale value of £10 million. This is accounted for by payments to the factors of production, including profit or loss as the residual, or balancing, item. Thus, value added in agriculture is £10 million. Farmers sell their wheat for £10 million to flour mills, where £3 million is added to the value of the wheat used as an input. (Assume that wheat is the only raw material used in milling, and make similar assumptions in regard to the bakery and retail stages.) Thus, income earned in milling is £3 million. Bakeries buy the flour for £13 million but sell their product to retailers for £16.5 million; value added is £3.5 million. Finally, the bread is sold to consumers for £19.5 million; value added by the retailers is £3 million.

The values added at each stage are the incomes of the factors of production; the sum of these comes to £19.5 million — the value of the final product at retail level. In calculating national product from the income side we simply sum the values added, or incomes, generated at each stage of production throughout the economy. Thus, national income is national value added.

In calculating national product from the income side, only those incomes earned from production are counted. A mere *transfer payment* (a transfer of income from A to B for reasons other than the provision of services in production by B) is not included. In the example in Table 1, wages and salaries in bakeries are £2.8 million; this is part of national income because it is in payment for productive activity. But suppose that of this sum bakery workers give £10,000 as gifts to their children. That £10,000 is transfer income to the children: it is not in payment for productive activity on their part. If we included it in national product we would be double-counting. Thus, in calculating national product via the income method, we do not include payments such as gifts, unemployment assistance or similar transfers.

FURTHER CONCEPTS IN NATIONAL INCOME ACCOUNTING

The provision of a service is productive (of utility) if it satisfies human wants. In this respect the services provided by performers at concerts (entertainment) are productive in the same sense as the output of manufacturing industry. However, in national income accounting exactly which services are regarded as productive and are therefore included in estimating national product is partly a matter of convention. For example, the services of a hired housekeeper are included in national income and are valued at the amount paid in cash and in kind. But the services provided by a spouse in taking care of the home are not included, presumably because of difficulty in assessing their market values. (It follows that measured national income falls when a person marries someone who had previously been that person's hired housekeeper!)

Investment

By *investment* in any time period (such as a year) the economist usually means that part of the flow of output which is not consumed in the same time period. This definition diverges from that of the plain person who speaks of investing when they buy a piece of land or an old security; the economist generally regards these as transfer payments — they are payments for the transfer of assets from one person to another. If there were no foreign trade, investment could be of only two forms: fixed investment, and investment in stocks of materials and finished goods. By *fixed investment* we mean additions to the nation's roads, buildings, machinery and equipment, etc. To avoid confusion we will describe the second form of investment — the change in the level of stocks of materials and finished goods — as *inventory investment*.

Capital is a stock of physical assets at a point in time; investment is the change in that stock over time. Thus, considerations of foreign trade aside, if the stock of fixed capital, and of inventories, were constant over time, net investment would be zero. If, however, the level of inventories or of fixed capital increased, then the relevant category of investment, in the period under consideration, would be positive. The two kinds of investment to which we have referred — fixed investment and inventory investment — comprise what is called *domestic investment*.

Foreign Trade and National Expenditure

Foreign trade complicates the calculation of national income from the expenditure side. Suppose the economy is closed, so that there is no foreign trade. Then the identity of national product and national expenditure can be written as

(2) $Y \equiv C + I + G$, where

Y: National product.

C: Personal consumption expenditure on goods and services.

I: Private fixed investment expenditure plus private inventory investment (change in level of inventories in private sector), private investment.

G: Government expenditure on goods and services (including fixed and inventory investment in the public sector).

Recognising that the economy is open — that there is foreign trade — changes identity (2) in two respects. First, part of the expenditures on national product are by non-residents; these are exports of goods and services, X. Because exports are a disposal of Irish production and generate income in Ireland, they are part of Irish national product. Second, part of the expenditures by Irish residents create income abroad rather than in Ireland. For example, expenditure by Aer Lingus on a fleet of new aircraft does not in itself generate income in Ireland; it creates income abroad. Therefore, expenditures on goods which are imported are not included in (Ireland's) national product. Thus, by *national expenditure* in an open economy, we mean expenditure by residents on home-produced output plus expenditure by foreigners on the output of the home country. Let M_c, M_i, M_g, and M_x denote the import content of C, I, G and X. For the open economy, identity (2) is then replaced by

$$(3)\ Y \equiv (C - M_c) + (I - M_i) + (G - M_g) + (X - M_x)$$

which says that national product is identically the same as total final expenditure on the output produced by residents of the home country.

Identity (3) can be simplified. Let M denote imports of goods and services; $M \equiv M_c + M_i + M_g + M_x$. The national product-income identity is then re-written as

$$(4)\ Y \equiv C + I + G + (X - M)$$

where Y, C, I and G are as defined at (2) and

X: Exports of goods and services.

M: Imports of goods and services, including those imports which form the category called net factor services from abroad.

Some initial comment on what is meant by imports of services is desirable at this stage. Ireland imports services when its imports or exports of (physical) goods are carried by shipping firms located abroad (an import of freight); when its residents use the services of foreign airlines (an import of "other transportation"); when Irish residents take holidays abroad (a tourism import); when Irish individuals or firms buy insurance cover or consultancy services from firms located abroad, etc. Such services — services in the ordinary sense of the word — are called *non-factor services*. For the moment it is merely noted that there exists another kind of services import and export, and that the net value of such services traded is called *factor services from abroad*, which may be positive or negative. In the hope of avoiding confusion at the present stage, explanation of the form and significance of net factor services from abroad is deferred to a subsection which will shortly follow.

Two technical terms are often applied to (X - M) in (4). If net current transfer payments from the rest of the world — denoted where necessary by the symbol R — were zero, then X - M would be the same as the balance of international payments on current account. (In practice, Ireland's current account balance of payments statistics do include certain transfer payments received from abroad. These take the form mainly of grants and subsidies from the EU. They also include remittances to Ireland from her emigrants. If net current transfer payments from abroad are not zero, then X - M + R denotes the balance of payments on current account.) Except where indicated to the contrary in this text, the existence of transfer payments to/from abroad will be ignored; this approach will be adopted in order to economise on notation and to highlight the key issues. The quantity (X - M) is also often termed *net external investment*, which may be positive or negative. Given the definition of investment (output not consumed), it is indeed part of national investment. However, we will describe (X - M) as the balance of payments on current account, and will reserve the word "investment" to denote domestic investment only, i.e. fixed investment plus change in inventory.

Government Services

National income purports to measure total production of final goods and services using money value (and hence prices) as the measuring rod in aggregation. In national income accounting, all government services (e.g. the civil service, the provision of defence, law and order) are regarded as final. However, they generally do not have explicit prices. For this reason the output of public administration and defence is measured in terms of its wage and salary cost. Note that it is only that part of government expenditure which is on goods and services that is included in the national product; transfer payments by government are not included.

Depreciation, GNP and NNP at Market Prices

National income can be measured on a gross or net basis. This leads to two concepts of national product: Gross National Product (GNP) and Net National Product (NNP). In producing the output of the economy, part of the nation's capital stock becomes worn out; there is some depreciation of the capital stock. Keeping capital intact then requires some investment to replace that part of it used up in the process of production. Thus, net investment equals gross investment minus depreciation. Hence, GNP equals NNP at market prices plus depreciation. In summary: *Gross National Product* (GNP) is a measure of total production of final goods and services valued at market prices, before deduction of depreciation. *Net National Product* (NNP) at market prices is GNP minus depreciation.

NNP at Factor Cost ("National Income")

Net taxes on expenditure (i.e. taxes less subsidies on goods and services) raise the market value of NNP, and of national expenditure, above the sum of incomes paid to resident owners of factors of production, called the *National Income*. (Note that those two words are now being used in a specific rather than in a generic sense; that is why capital letters have been used.) However, if we deduct expenditure taxes from, and add subsidies to, NNP at market prices, we get what is called *NNP at factor cost*, which is identically equal to National Income.

We could make a similar adjustment to national expenditure at market prices (or we could add net expenditure taxes to NNP at factor cost, and to expenditure exclusive of net expenditure taxes), thereby maintaining the identity of national income, national expenditure, and national product — whether on a factor cost basis or at market prices, and whether on a gross (before deduction of depreciation) basis or on a net basis.

NATIONAL PRODUCT VERSUS DOMESTIC PRODUCT

The careful reader should not be at all confused at this stage; we have stressed that certain concepts are equal merely by definition (i.e. they are identical), or that they are related, not because of any theory, but by definition. A similar remark applies to the oft-made distinction between *national* income (product) and *domestic* income (product), whether measured gross or net.

The distinction between *national product* and *domestic product* hinges on the particular way in which imports, M, are defined. In identity (4) above (which concerned national product), M was defined as imports of goods and services, including those imports which form the category called net factor services. The main components of (imported) net factor services are the net positions in regard to profits, dividends, royalties, etc. repatriated to abroad, as well as payments of interest on monies borrowed by the government from non-residents — interest payments on the externally-held national debt. Conceptually, these are reckoned as payments made in remuneration for production which takes place in the home country (i.e. *domestically*, say in Ireland); however, the payments are made to factors of production which are themselves located abroad (*outside* Ireland), rather than to factors of production which are located within the home country's *national* boundaries. Conceptually, the home country is reckoned to be importing the services (e.g. risk-taking and lending functions) of factors of production (e.g. enterprise) located abroad. For example, if a foreign multinational company earns profits from its production activity in Ireland, and if it repatriates such profits abroad, then although the profits have been earned from production located domestically in Ireland, they are paid to factors of production which are located abroad rather than in Ireland (e.g. to shareholders living in New York, Tokyo or Rome). Similarly, if a person resident abroad lends to the Irish government and thereby finances part of public sector output in Ireland, factor payments in the form of interest are paid to that foreign resident. Such payments are incomes accruing to non-national factors of production for production located domestically in Ireland. They are included in domestic product, but not in national product.

In short, domestic product measures production in the home country; national product measures payments to factors of production in the home country. The two measures differ only to the extent that there are net payments (in remuneration for productive activity in the home country) to factors of production resident abroad. Imports of goods and services are reckoned as in identity (4) when calculating national product; however, in estimating domestic product, the measure of imports includes goods and non-factor services only.

Because Ireland in recent decades has been a net importer of factor services — we pay more in interest and repatriated profits, etc. to the rest of the world than the value of factor incomes which we earn from there (e.g. profits of Irish companies in the USA repatriated to Ireland, etc.) — it follows that in Ireland, domestic product has exceeded national product in recent decades. In fact, in 1991 the absolute value of net factor income from the rest of the world (itself a negative figure) amounted to more than 10 per cent of domestic product, implying that measures of domestic product were more than 10 per cent higher than measures of national product (gross or net). This consideration implies that there can exist a wedge between the trend in economic activity and the trend in living standards. Domestic product is generally a better measure of the state of economic activity in Ireland; however, the trend in national product is the better measure of movement in living standards here (as indicated by the incomes of factors of production located in Ireland). Indeed (although domestic and national product do tend to move in the same direction) in a country which depends heavily on foreigners to finance investment, it is conceivable that domestic product could be increasing over time consistent with national product decreasing over time; in that case, the gains from growth in output would be accruing to foreigners rather than residents. (A formal model illustrating such a possibility can be found in this author's contribution to Renée Prendergast and H.W. Singer (eds), *Development Perspectives for the 1990s*, Macmillan, London, 1991, Chapter 4.)

Other Income Aggregates

National Income or NNP at factor cost is the sum of incomes of the factors of production earned in production; it omits transfer incomes.

Measures of GNP or of domestic product similarly exclude transfer payments. However, the categories Gross National Disposable Income, Private Income, Personal Income and Disposable Personal Income (what we call Disposable Income) do include transfer incomes.

Gross National Disposable Income (GNDI): As has been indicated earlier, receipts of transfer payments from abroad have been of some significance for Ireland, mainly because of grants and subsidies which we receive from the EU, and also because of much smaller amounts of emigrants' remittances. Payments such as these are called current transfers from the rest of the world. What is called Gross National Disposable Income (GNDI) is simply GNP at market prices plus net current transfers from the rest of the world, R:

(5) $GNDI \equiv GNP + R$

Private income is the sum of incomes of residents of the community, with the exception of incomes accruing to public authorities in their entrepreneurial or business capacity, whether or not the incomes are in payment for productive activity. Private Income equals, as an approximation, NNP at factor cost, less government trading and investment income, plus transfer income from government, plus transfer income directly from abroad. Not all of it accrues to persons; some accrues to corporate bodies in the private sector.

Personal Income equals Private Income less undistributed profits of companies before tax. Not all of this is available for personal consumption expenditure and savings; some of it goes to government as taxes on incomes and wealth.

Disposable Income equals Personal Income less taxes on personal incomes and wealth; it is accounted for by personal expenditure on consumer goods and services, plus the residual, personal savings.

THE IRISH NATIONAL ACCOUNTS

What is loosely termed the national income can be calculated by the income method (summing incomes from productive activity); by the expenditure method (summing expenditures on home-produced final goods and services); or by the output method (summing final outputs). Official estimates for Ireland are available annually, and are presented in detail in the Central Statistics Office publication entitled *National Income and Expenditure*, from which Tables 2, 3 and 4 below are drawn.

In principle, the three methods could be used simultaneously to arrive at independent provisional estimates, and then, in the face of incomplete information, they could be used to supplement and cross-check the ensuing provisional estimates. But in practice, using data obtained from the Revenue Commissioners and other sources, Ireland relies mainly on the income method; the estimates in Tables 3 and 4 below are therefore very much subsidiary to those in Table 2.

Table 2: The Income Method, 1986 and 1992, £ million

Year	1986	1992
Income from Agriculture, Forestry and Fishing:		
1. Income from self-employment and other trading income	1,190	1,939
2. Employee remuneration	142	201
Non-Agricultural Income:		
3. Profits, professional earnings, interest, dividends, and income from land and buildings	4,191	6,546
4. Employee remuneration	10,123	14,769
Equals Net Domestic Product at Factor Cost	15,646	23,455
5. Net factor income from abroad	-2,017	-3,158
Equals NNP at factor cost = National Income	13,629	20,297
Plus taxes on expenditure less subsidies	1,988	2,859
Equals NNP at current market prices	15,617	23,431
Plus provision for depreciation	1,885	2,859
Equals GNP at current market prices	17,502	26,290

Table 3: The Net Output Method, 1986 and 1992, £ million

Year	1986	1992
1. Agriculture, Forestry and Fishing:	1,338	2,141
2. Industry	6,104	9,043
3. Distribution, transport, communication	2,845	4,164
4. Public administration and defence	1,125	1,593
5. Other domestic	4,968	7,849
6. Adjustments to [1 to 5]	-734	-1,335
Sum: Net Domestic Product at Factor Cost	15,646	23,455

Table 4: The Expenditure Method, 1986 and 1992, £ million

Year	1986	1992
1. Personal expenditure on consumer goods and services	11,954	17,106
2. Net expenditure by public authorities on current goods & services	3,542	4,773
3. Gross domestic fixed capital formation	3,456	4,676
4. Value of physical changes in stocks (inventory investment)	+118	-60
5. Exports of goods and services, excl. factor services exports	10,377	18,673
6. Less imports of goods and services, excl. factor services imports	-9,929	-15,721
Sum: GDP at market prices	19,518	29,448
Net factor income from abroad	-2,017	-3,158
Sum: GNP at current prices	17,502	26,290

Source for Tables 2, 3 and 4: Central Statistics Office, *National Income and Expenditure 1992*, PL. 9878, Stationery Office, Dublin, July 1993, to which the reader should refer for further details. In the above tables, totals do not in all cases exactly match column sums, due to rounding of decimals.

For example, given the consistency requirement that the totals in Table 4 must be the same as those in Table 2, the important category "personal expenditure on consumer goods and services" in Table 4 is estimated by the Central Statistics Office as a residual. Therefore, according to *National Income and Expenditure*, this item "must bear the brunt of errors in the other constituents" of Table 4. Because the totals in that table are the same as those carried forward from Table 2, it is possible that other items in Table 4 also bear the brunt of errors in the estimation of the totals in Table 2.

It is appropriate to make two further observations in regard to Tables 2 to 4. First, GNP is measured at *current* market prices. The word "current" here refers to the market prices prevailing in the years tabulated. This is in contrast to GNP at *constant* market prices, discussed below. Second, the entry pertaining to public authorities in Table 4 is for public *current* expenditure on goods and services. The word "current" is here used in contrast to "capital" expenditure by public authorities; it refers to expenditure by public authorities on goods and services other than capital goods. In Table 4, fixed investment by the public sector is included along with private sector fixed investment, in the entry "gross domestic fixed capital formation".

Nominal GNP and Real GNP

It is necessary to distinguish between nominal GNP and real GNP. *Nominal* or *money* GNP, otherwise termed GNP *at current market prices*, measures the value of goods and services at the prices prevailing in the year in which they are produced. *Real* GNP, or GNP *at constant market prices*, measures the value of goods and services using the prices of a common base year. Table 5 indicates that nominal GNP in Ireland increased by just over 50 per cent — from £17,502 million to £26,290 million — between 1986 and 1992. However, much of this increase represents illusory money gains due to inflation; the table also shows that over the same period real GNP — GNP at constant 1985 market prices — increased from £16,310 to £20,923, or by about 28 per cent.

Table 5: Current Price versus Constant Price GNP (£ million)

Year	1986	1992	1990	1992
GNP at current market prices	17,052	19,782	23,675	26,290
GNP price index or deflator (1985 = 1)	1.07	1.13	1.20	1.26
GNP at constant (1985) prices	16,310	17,514	19,742	20,923

Source: *National Income and Expenditure 1992*, Tables 3 and 4.

The Consumer Price Index and the GNP Deflator

The most frequently used measure of the rate of inflation is the percentage change in the consumer price index (CPI). The CPI is an estimate of the cost of a "representative" basket of consumer goods and services in a particular year relative to some base year. In distinguishing real from nominal gains in GNP over time it is necessary to deflate nominal GNP by a price index which expresses the change in the prices of all goods which make up GNP, relative to some base year. The index used is called the GNP deflator. It is similar to the CPI except that it includes the prices of all goods and services which enter GNP. For example, the prices of new machines are included in the GNP deflator but not in the CPI. Real GNP = (Nominal GNP)/(GNP price deflator). The GNP price index or deflator in Table 5 is with reference to 1985 prices; 1985 has been chosen as the base year. It indicates that prices increased by about 26 per cent between 1985 and 1992. Deflating nominal GNP in each year by this price index gives the series for GNP at constant (1985) market prices.

In practice — and as explained in Chapter 2 above — price indices are usually assigned a value of 100 in the base year. Adopting this convention, Table 5 shows that with 1985 as base year, the GNP price index increased to 126 in 1992. (Under this convention, the GNP price deflator would be distinct from the GNP price index: the deflator would be the price index divided by 100.) Because of the dominance of consumer expenditure in GNP, the consumer price index and the GNP price index tend to move in phase. For example, with 1985 = 100, Ireland's official consumer price index was at 125.1 for 1992, a figure very close to that of the GNP price index.

FURTHER IMPORTANT NATIONAL ACCOUNTING IDENTITIES

A set of national accounting identities based on earlier discussion will now be derived. They have no *behavioural* content: they tell us nothing about what people are trying to do. However, they will be essential to an understanding in the chapters which follow. To understand how the levels of real national income and related variables are determined is the central objective of Part Three of this text. We will be constructing a series of models of the economy showing how it behaves in, say, a given year. Starting in the next chapter with a very simple model of a closed economy without government, we will relax restrictive assumptions and move in the direction of realism. In the identities below and in the analysis of national income determination which follows in the subsequent chapters, it will be assumed — unless indicated to the contrary — that all variables are expressed in real terms (i.e. at constant prices). This implies that either the price level remains constant or, if not, variables in nominal terms have been deflated (or inflated if prices are falling), thereby expressing them in real terms. Our interest in real rather than in nominal income is motivated by the fact that it is real income that affects living standards and, given the state of technology, the level of employment.

A. A Simple Closed Economy without Government

Assumptions:

(a) No depreciation.

(b) No taxes or subsidies on expenditure.

(c) No foreign sector.

(d) No government economic activity.

Assumptions (a) and (b) imply that real GNP equals real national income at factor cost and also equals real national expenditure at market prices.

The symbol Y denotes all three. The following identities hold in the closed economy without government:

(6) Output identity: $Y \equiv C + I$

(7) Income identity: $Y \equiv C + S$

Identity (6) states that output is divided between consumption, C, and investment, I. *Investment is defined as output not consumed.* Identity (7) states that income is divided between consumption and savings, S. *Savings are defined as income not consumed.* Together (6) and (7) imply:

(8) $S \equiv I$

In the simple economy without government activity, private savings are necessarily equal to private investment. That is true whether or not income is at what we will in the next chapter call its equilibrium level. Identity (8) says nothing about what determines savings or investment. It is important to observe that (8) does not state that the amount which people decide and try to save (what will later be called planned savings) must be the same as the amount which people decide and try to invest (what will later be called planned investment): it only says that the amount actually saved must be the same as the amount actually invested. As an identity, (8) tells us nothing about human behaviour. Whether or not planned savings in the simple economy are equal to planned investment will turn out to be crucial, and will be subject to detailed investigation in the next chapter.

Before moving on to consider more complex (and more realistic) economies than that assumed above, it is noted that some textbooks refer to (8) as the identity of *withdrawals* from the expenditure stream and *injections* to the expenditure stream. As will be seen below, measured withdrawals must be the same as measured injections *in any economy* — not only in the simple economy just considered.

B. Introduction of a Government Sector

Recognising the existence of economic activity by government, the output-expenditure identity becomes

(9) $Y \equiv C + I + G$

where C is consumer expenditure, I is private investment expenditure and G is government expenditure on goods and services (including public sector investment).

Further assumptions:

(e) Income earned by public authorities in their business capacity is zero. Thus all government revenue must come from taxation or borrowing.

(f) Undistributed profits of companies are zero. Thus if companies receive profits they are all distributed to shareholders. Then, private income equals personal income.

It is now necessary to distinguish between national income and disposable income, Y_d, which is that part of national income which households are free to dispose of as they wish, after they have paid income and property taxes:

$$(10) \ Y_d \equiv Y - T$$

where T denotes net tax receipts of government (i.e., tax receipts less government transfer payments to the private sector — which can be regarded as negative tax receipts). Disposable income is divided between consumption and personal savings:

$$(11) \ Y_d \equiv C + S$$

Together, (9), (10) and (11) imply:

$$C + S \equiv Y - T, \text{ or}$$

$$C + S \equiv C + I + G - T, \text{ or, letting C cancel out,}$$

$$(12) \ (S - I) \equiv (G - T)$$

which relates the excess of private sector savings over private investment to the government sector overall budget deficit. The government's overall budget deficit is the excess of government spending on goods and services, G, over net tax revenues, T. (If T exceeds G, the government's overall budget is in surplus; if T falls short of G, it is in deficit; while if T equals G it is balanced.) According to (12), measured private sector savings are no longer necessarily equal to measured private investment. If the government sector is running an overall deficit, then (12) states that the private sector must be saving more than it invests. Under such circumstances the government sector deficit is being financed, in some ultimate sense, by household savings. Under the assumptions stated — in particular, as a result of assumption (e) above — the amount (G - T) would denote what is called the public sector borrowing requirement (PSBR).

The identity (12) can be written and interpreted in various other ways. Suppose that G is explicitly decomposed into government current expenditure (such as payment of public servants) and capital expenditure by the government sector (such as public road-building programmes); let these be denoted by G_c and G_i respectively, while the interpretations of T, S and I are as already agreed. Identity (12) is then rewritten as:

$$(S - I) \equiv (G_c + G_i - T), \text{ or}$$

$$(12') \ (S + T - G_c) \equiv I + G_i$$

In identity (12'), $T - G_c$ denotes what is called the *current budget* surplus, which may be positive or negative. (A deficit is simply a negative surplus.) It can also be described as government sector (or public sector) savings, which may be positive or negative. (The word dissavings is often used to describe negative savings.) With these interpretations, identity (12') states that, in an economy of the kind under consideration, total measured savings (by private and public sectors combined) must numerically be the same as total measured investment (by private and public sectors combined). Thus, letting S_g denote government sector savings, (12') is equivalent to the identity $S + S_g \equiv I + G_i$. Finally, it is noted here that for the kind of economy under consideration, (12') can also be interpreted as a restatement of the identity of measured withdrawals from the expenditure stream and measured injections to the expenditure stream.

C. An Open Economy with Government

Further assumption:

(g) There are no transfer payments to abroad (e.g. foreign aid) and none are received from abroad.

The output-expenditure identity and the income identity now are, respectively,

$$(13) \ Y \equiv C + I + G + (X - M) \text{ and}$$

$$(14) \ Y \equiv C + S + T. \text{ Hence}$$

$$C + I + G + (X - M) \equiv C + S + T$$

which implies, for an open economy with government,

$$(15) \ (S - I) \equiv (G - T) + (X - M)$$

Referring back to the notation introduced in (12'), identity (15) is equivalent to

$$(15') \ (S + T - G_c + M - X) \equiv (I + G_i)$$

which highlights the fact that in the open economy under consideration, there are three ways in which domestic investment $I + G_i$ (often referred to as domestic capital formation) can be financed, namely, through private sector savings S, through public sector savings $T - G_c$, or through operating a deficit in the balance of payments on current account — i.e., through savings of foreign countries (which is equivalent to the home country borrowing abroad).

The identity (15) can in fact be interpreted in various ways. Once again rearranging terms, it is equivalent to

$$M - X \equiv I + G - (S + T),$$

From (11) this is equivalent to

$$M - X \equiv I + G - (Y_d - C + T)$$

and invoking identity (10) this is by definition the same as

$$M - X \equiv I + G - (Y - T - C + T), \text{ or}$$

$$(15'') \quad X - M \equiv Y - (C + I + G)$$

The sum inside the parentheses in (15'') is often called *absorption*. As before, Y denotes output. Thus, identity (15'') links the current account balance of payments to the difference between national output and absorption: if the current account balance of payments is in deficit (X - M negative), it must be the case that absorption exceeds output; if it is in surplus (X exceeding M), it must be the case that the absorption falls short of output. Hence, any policy or any other event which reduces absorption relative to output must be associated with a reduced deficit, or an increased surplus, in the balance of payments on current account; and any reduction in a current account balance of payments deficit (any increase in a current account balance of payments surplus) must be associated with a reduction in absorption relative to output. Note that this statement is true by definition; it is not a theory.

Finally, at this stage it is noted that X can be interpreted as an injection to the expenditure stream while M can be considered a withdrawal (because it is income which is earned but not spent on home-produced output). If the reader does wish to refer to withdrawals and injections, (15) can be rewritten as

$$S + T - G_c + M \equiv I + G_i + X$$

which, for the kind of economy under consideration, once again repeats the identity of measured withdrawals and measured injections. As before, however, this tells us nothing about human behaviour: it is merely true by definition.

It is extremely important that the reader avoid confusion in regard to the several identities mentioned above. With the subsequent chapters on macroeconomics in mind, the reader is now warned that the key identities to which particular attention should be assigned are those which have been numbered (1), (8), (12) and (15) above. What follows in the present chapter will not be crucial for an understanding of the chapters which follow on macroeconomics.

RECONCILIATION WITH THE IRISH NATIONAL ACCOUNTS: A DIGRESSION

In the exposition of the identities for an economy of types A, B and C above, certain assumptions have been made, purely in order to minimise the number of symbols employed. The simplifying assumptions have pertained to the kinds of economy being discussed: they have not been assumptions about human behaviour per se.

Ireland is an open economy with a government and with a system of taxation. In order to reconcile the identities with the many details in the Irish national accounts as published, two further modifications are necessary.

First, the assumption (e), initially specified in discussing an economy of type B (a closed economy with a public sector) is not necessarily empirically valid: Partly because state enterprises (in Ireland called semi-state bodies or state-sponsored bodies) can earn profits (positive or negative in sign), it is not true that all government sector revenue must come from taxation or borrowing — for example, some of it can come from the profits of state-owned enterprises.

Second, turning to assumption (g) introduced for an economy of type C — an open economy with government — in the case of Ireland it is not true that there are no transfer payments to/from abroad.

Taken together, these considerations mean that the identities outlined above for a C-type economy are not exactly valid for the economy of Ireland, and are not fully consistent with the data in Ireland's national accounts, as published: Reconciliation with Ireland's national accounts requires some slight further modifications, and some further notation.

In taking account of possible transfer payments to/from abroad (R), note that identity (5) is equivalent to

$$(5') \; GNDI \equiv C + I + G + X - M + R$$

Let all variables be measured (in real terms as before) at market prices. Now GNDI can also be viewed from another angle: it is either consumed (by the private sector or by the government sector) or it is not consumed. Recall that savings are defined as income not consumed. Thus,

(5") $\text{GNDI} \equiv C + G_c + S + S_g$

where S denotes private sector savings, as before, while S_g represents government sector savings.

Equating the right hand sides of (5') and (5"), and letting BOP denote the balance of international payments on current account $(X - M + R)$, which may be positive or negative in sign:

$I + G_c + G_i + \text{BOP} \equiv G_c + S + S_g$, or

$\text{BOP} \equiv S_g - G_i + S - I$, or

(16) $\text{BOP} \equiv \text{PSBR} + S - I$

where PSBR denotes what is called the public sector borrowing requirement.

Let O_g indicate all government sector receipts other than those raised through taxation (e.g. income of state-owned enterprises, capital grants to government from the EU, etc). Then (16) can be rewritten as

$\text{BOP} \equiv T + O_g - G_c - G_i + S - I$, or

(17) $I + G_i \equiv S_g + S - \text{BOP}$

which indicates that there are two ways in which domestic investment — the left hand side of (17) — can be financed: through domestic savings by the private and public sectors, or through a deficit in the balance of payments on current account (i.e. through borrowing from abroad). Lest the reader be confused, it is to be observed that if the current account balance of payments is in deficit, then the variable BOP in the above identity is negative in value. Note that it also has a minus before it. Equation (17) states that domestic investment is identically the same as domestic savings plus the absolute value of the deficit in the balance of payments on current account, or that domestic investment is identically the same as domestic savings minus the surplus in the balance of payments on current account.

In closing, the reader is again reminded that this chapter has been concerned with national accounting identities only. In itself, it gives no insights into human behaviour. Because it has been concerned with definitional relationships only, the chapter has not sought to explain what determines the values of the variables which were introduced, such as Y, C, S or I. It is extremely important to be aware that in the foregoing, all symbols represented the realised (i.e. *ex post*) values of the variables mentioned; they did not necessarily indicate the planned or desired (i.e. *ex ante*) values of the variables. For example, the symbol I denoted actual private investment, which is not necessarily the same as the amount which the private sector is desiring, planning or trying to invest. Similarly in the case of S, C, etc. The determinants of the planned magnitudes of macroeconomic variables will be discussed in the several chapters which immediately follow. However, the reader must be careful to distinguish the *ex ante* and the *ex post* values of macroeconomic variables; otherwise there is little prospect that the macroeconomic analysis which follows will be understood.

CHAPTER 10

A SIMPLE MODEL OF INCOME DETERMINATION: THE GOODS MARKET

The reader should be familiar with the key identities in Chapter 9 before proceeding to the present chapter or to those which immediately follow. The central task in Part Three is to explain what determines some of the variables in those identities, and in particular, to explain what determines the equilibrium level of national income. Recall from Chapter 4 the meaning of equilibrium and its stability: national income is at an equilibrium if it shows no *inherent* tendency to change (unless the equilibrium is disturbed by shocks from outside the model which explains how the equilibrium is determined). If the equilibrium were not stable, there would be little point in studying it, because it would then be unlikely that any actual economy would be close to an equilibrium — actual economies are in fact subject to frequent and unpredictable shocks. Given an assumption of stability, we can interpret equilibrium income as that level of national income toward which the economy tends to converge.

In this chapter (which is labelled "the goods market" because it deals with ordinary goods and services as distinct from money) we construct a simplified model of equilibrium national income determination which isolates aggregate demand, omitting any detailed consideration of aggregate supply. Except where indicated to the contrary, a change in a macroeconomic aggregate (e.g. national income or consumption expenditure) is a change in its real value at constant prices. It will also be assumed that firms are both willing and able to supply any level of output at those prices. These assumptions will be relaxed later. Thus the core question in the present investigation is: if firms are both willing and able to supply any amount of output at the prevailing price level, what determines the equilibrium national output — equilibrium national income?

Demand must enter the picture. Under the stated assumptions we would expect firms to produce just sufficient to meet aggregate demand, or planned expenditure. If output exceeded aggregate demand, firms would find their inventories piling up; conversely, if production fell short of aggregate demand, inventories would be falling (and/or households would be unable to buy what they want for consumption: queues would develop and firms might post "sold out" signs). Firms would respond to such unplanned inventory changes by altering their outputs. These considerations suggest a notion of equilibrium national income as that level of national output where aggregate demand, or planned expenditure, equals aggregate supply, implying that unintended changes in inventories would be zero and households' actual consumption expenditure would be equal to their planned or desired consumption expenditure.

Aggregate supply is determined by firms. When deciding how much to produce in a given period (say one year), firms calculate how much investment, including inventory investment, they wish to undertake. Then, if firms miscalculate households' planned consumption expenditures, aggregate supply will almost surely differ from aggregate demand (planned expenditures, including planned changes in inventories). If firms overestimate demand, it is likely that there will be unplanned inventory accumulation. If firms underestimate demand, they are likely to experience unplanned inventory decumulation, as attempts are made to meet the higher than anticipated level of demand by drawing on inventories carried forward from the close of the previous year.

Thus our claim (to be demonstrated) is that the equilibrium level of national income is that level of aggregate production at which actual ouput equals aggregate demand (planned expenditure): there would then be no unintended accumulation or decumulation of inventories. Call this Assertion No. 1. Alternatively, we can say that in a very simple economy (one with neither government nor foreign trade) the equilibrium level of income would be given by the equality of planned (or desired or intended) private savings and planned (or desired or intended) private investment. Call this Assertion No. 2. Because it has just been claimed that the two assertions are alternatives, it will be shown below that they are *equivalent*: either one implies the other. Distinct diagrams will be used to illustrate the validity of each assertion individually, but it will be shown that the two diagrams yield exactly the same information. Note that we have referred to the equality of *planned* private savings and *planned* private investment rather than to the identity of actual savings and actual investment. The reasons why we have added the adjectives "planned" or "intended" should become clear later in this chapter.

THE CONSUMPTION AND SAVINGS FUNCTIONS

As preliminaries to a demonstration that Assertions No. 1 and No. 2 are correct and are equivalent, it is necessary to introduce two concepts — the economy's personal consumption function (the consumption function) and its personal savings function (the savings function) — and to show that these two concepts yield the same information.

The Consumption Function

Personal consumption expenditure is a major component of aggregate demand. What determines personal consumption expenditure? Both introspection and empirical investigation indicate that disposable income is a major determinant. In what follows we will be discussing the determinants of aggregate personal consumption (and personal savings) in the short run — in a particular year and from year to year, rather than from, say, decade to decade. It is in this context that we will be referring to "the" consumption function (and to "the" savings function).

Definition: The consumption function is the relationship between the community's planned personal consumption expenditure and its disposable income. It expresses the amount the community would attempt to spend on personal consumption if aggregate disposable income were at various hypothetical levels, other things being equal. Thus

$$(1)\ C = f(Y_d, e)$$

where C denotes the amount households in aggregate attempt to spend on consumption, in real terms, Y_d is real disposable income and e represents the other things (objective and subjective factors such as the stock of real personal wealth, the age-distribution of the population, expectations in regard to the future, etc.) upon which aggregate consumption demand depends. (The operator f denotes a function: the reader who is unaccustomed to functional notation should refer to the Appendix to Chapter 2.) The exact manner in which real consumption demand depends on its determinants — the explicit form of the consumption function — can be expressed as an equation. Given e, we will assume, as a linear approximation

$$(2)\ C = a + bY_d$$

where $a > 0$ and $0 < b < 1$ (i.e. "a" is greater than zero and b is strictly between zero and one). This is demonstrated graphically in Figure 1 below.

What can sensibly be said about the form of the consumption function in Figure 1? First, note that the intercept "a" is positive: if Y_d were zero, some consumption would still take place. In the virtually inconceivable case in which Y_d approached zero, consumption would, in the short run, be positive, as the community sought to maintain some consumption by running down its inventories (i.e. by dissaving) — cattle would be slaughtered and finished food products carried forward from previous years would be consumed. Note also that b, the slope of the consumption function, $\Delta C/\Delta Y_d$, is positive but less than unity: if disposable income changes by £1 million, then consumption demand changes in the same direction but by a smaller amount. This reflects an assumption for which there is a great deal of empirical support: as aggregate disposable income increases, so too does aggregate consumption, but because of increased savings, the increment in consumption falls short of the increase in income. Later on it will be seen that if the slope of the consumption function were as high as unity (rather than being an ordinary positive fraction), then "the impossible would happen"; thus its slope must be less than unity. The slope of the consumption function is of vital importance in macroeconomic analysis.

Figure 1

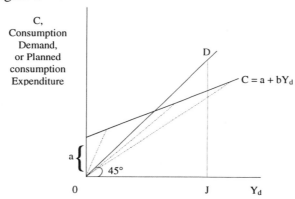

At this stage it is appropriate to note in passing that the reader may wonder why Irish data have not been tabulated here to show that the consumption function for Ireland can be approximated by an equation of form (2) above. The reason for not doing so is that in recent years at least, Ireland's official estimates of personal consumption expenditure and personal savings are extremely unreliable — to such an extent that they are virtually useless for analytical investigation. In this context, recall the discussion in Chapter 9, where it was observed that in Ireland, personal consumption expenditure is estimated as a residual. In some cases the official estimates for a given year have been subject to extremely substantial revisions in the following year. For example, consider the categories personal consumption expenditure and personal savings in Ireland for the year 1989. In the official publication *National Income and Expenditure 1991* the estimates (for 1989 and at the prices prevailing in 1989) are personal consumption £13,886 million and personal savings £1,654 million. But in *National Income and Expenditure 1992* the estimates (also for 1989 and at 1989 prices) are £15,032 million and £1,213 million, respectively.

Definition: C/Y_d is the average propensity to consume (APC).

Definition: $\Delta C/\Delta Y_d$ is the marginal propensity to consume (MPC). It shows the amount by which planned consumption increases per unit increase in disposable income.

The reader should be on guard not to confuse the APC and the MPC. The APC at any point on the consumption function is *the slope of a ray from the origin* to the point in question. In Figure 1 it can be seen that the slope of such rays decreases as Y_d increases; thus the APC falls as Y_d increases. The MPC at any point on the consumption function is *the slope of that function*. Even though the APC is falling as Y_d increases, the MPC is constant in Figure 1.

Before proceeding to consider the economy's savings function, it is worthwhile to note some properties of the 45 degree line in a diagram such as Figure 1. First, it is a *guide line only* — it is merely meant to guide us in our reasoning. In itself, it has no economic significance. Second, it has the property that the co-ordinates of any point on the guide line with respect to either axis are equidistant. Hence, a statement of the form "suppose income were 0J" is equivalent to the statement "suppose income were JD". Simple as this observation is, the fact that the co-ordinates of any point on the guide line to either axis are equidistant will be very helpful in understanding some of the reasoning which will follow. Third, the guide line emanates from the origin and has a slope of unity. Because the intercept "a" of the consumption function is positive, and because its slope b is positive but strictly less than unity, it follows that the vertical gap between the consumption function and the guide line must at first get smaller as Y_d increases, the consumption function must intersect the guide line from above, and thereafter the vertical gap between the two loci must increase as Y_d increases further. This third geometric property will also assist in reasoning to be conducted shortly.

The Savings Function

The savings function is the relationship between the community's planned personal savings and its disposable income. Because personal savings are the residual after personal consumption has been deducted from disposable income, if we know the consumption function, we know the savings function, and vice versa. Both give the same information. Thus:

Because $S \equiv Y_d - C$, and because planned consumption $C = a + bY_d$, it follows that planned savings

$$S = Y_d - a - bY_d = -a + (1 - b)Y_d \text{ or,}$$

$$(3) \ S = -a + sY_d,$$

where $s = (1 - MPC) = \Delta S/\Delta Y_d$ is the marginal propensity to save, MPS. The marginal propensity to save is the amount by which planned personal savings would increase if disposable income increased by one unit. Because an increase in disposable income is allocated to either consumption or savings, $\Delta C/\Delta Y_d + \Delta S/\Delta Y_d \equiv 1$. The higher the MPC, the lower the MPS, and vice versa. The savings function can be derived graphically from the consumption function, as in Figures 2a and 2b.

Figure 2a

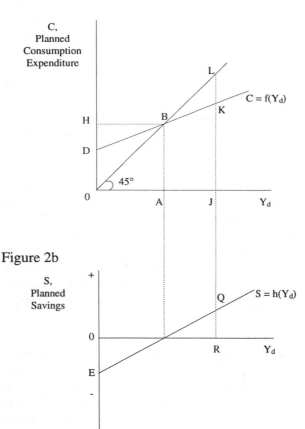

Figure 2b

From the consumption function diagram, Figure 2a, we see that if $Y_d = 0$, planned consumption = 0D. Since $S \equiv Y - C$, this means that planned savings = $0 - 0D = 0E$ in Figure 2b, a negative quantity. The economy would then be dissaving, i.e. consuming from the stock of assets (wealth) carried forward from the close of the previous year.

Turning to the 45 degree guide line in Figure 2a, 0A = AB = BH. So for $Y_d <$ OA, $C > Y_d$ and hence $S < 0$, as in Figure 2b. Note that the vertical gap between C and Y_d falls as Y_d increases in the direction of point A in Figure 2a; correspondingly, the absolute value of dissaving declines as income rises in the direction of point A. However, at $Y_d = 0A$, $C = Y_d$, so $S = 0$ in Figure 2b; the community is then neither saving nor dissaving. But for $Y_d >$ OA, $C < Y_d$, so $S > 0$. For example, suppose $Y_d =$ 0J = JL. At that disposable income, planned consumption equals JK. Thus, planned savings equal JL - JK = KL in Figure 2a = RQ in Figure 2b. In general it can be seen that for $Y_d >$ OA, the vertical gap between the guide line and the consumption function in Figure 2a increases as income increases; this vertical gap in Figure 2a is mirrored in Figure 2b where it can be seen that planned savings become progressively more positive as Y_d increases.

Figure 2b has just been derived from Figure 2a. Similarly, if we had been given Figure 2b to begin with, we could have derived Figure 2a. It should be clear to the reader that the two diagrams are equivalent: they yield exactly the same information.

Before proceeding the reader should observe that because

$$Y_d \equiv C + S \text{ and } \Delta Y_d \equiv \Delta C + \Delta Y_{d,,}$$

$$1 \equiv C/Y_d + S/Y_d$$

$$1 \equiv \Delta C/\Delta Y_d + \Delta S/\Delta Y_d$$

Thus, the higher the average propensity to consume, the lower the average propensity to save; and the higher the marginal propensity to consume, the lower the marginal propensity to save. But do not confuse the average and the marginal concepts. For example, the *average* propensity to consume could be high and the *marginal* propensity to save could also be high. The reader should not proceed until clear on these points.

THE SIMPLEST MODEL

We are now ready to construct a series of models of national income determination. Each successive development will move in the direction of realism. Start with the simplest model, by assuming:

(1) There is no depreciation.

(2) There is no government. Hence there can be no net taxes (i.e. taxes less subsidies) on expenditure.

(3) Companies retain no earnings. Any profits are distributed to shareholders.

(4) The economy is closed. Thus $X = M = 0$.

(5) Planned investment is determined *exogenously*, or *autonomously*, i.e. it is determined entirely outside the model, implying that it does not depend on the level of national income (which is *endogenous*, i.e., as will soon be seen, it is determined within the model).

Assumptions (1), (2) and (3) imply that real GNP, or Y, is here the same as real disposable income, Y_d; under the present assumptions, there is therefore no need for separate notation.

We now wish to demonstrate that given the earlier assumption that firms are willing and able to produce any quantity at prevailing prices, the equilibrium level of national income is determined by the level of aggregate demand (in this model, by private consumption and investment demand); alternatively, we will show that it is given by the equality of planned savings and planned investment. Turning to Figures 3a and 3b, the claim is that $Y = Y_e$ is the equilibrium level of national income.

Assertion 1: Using the Guide Line Diagram
Consider Figure 3a. Suppose first that income exceeds what we claim to be its equilibrium level, and observe what is likely to happen. Suppose that $Y = Y_1$. From the 45 degree line, $0Y_1 = Y_1A$. Thus, output is Y_1A. But planned expenditure, or aggregate demand, is Y_1B. Because actual expenditure is identical to output, it follows that actual expenditure exceeds planned expenditure. Hence, either the consumption plan or the investment plan or both will not be achieved exactly; at least one of them will be overachieved. Suppose that the consumption plan is achieved. Then consumption is Y_1D. Since output is Y_1A, actual investment is DA, which exceeds planned investment, DB. There is, then, unplanned investment equal in volume to AB. What is this unplanned investment, and why has it occurred? It must take the form of an unanticipated accumulation of inventories (which, as indicated in Chapter 9, is counted as part of actual national expenditure). The reason for this unplanned inventory accumulation is clear: aggregate supply, Y_1A, exceeds aggregate demand (planned expenditure), Y_1B. The economy is producing too much relative to the desires of firms to invest and of consumers to buy.

Figure 3a

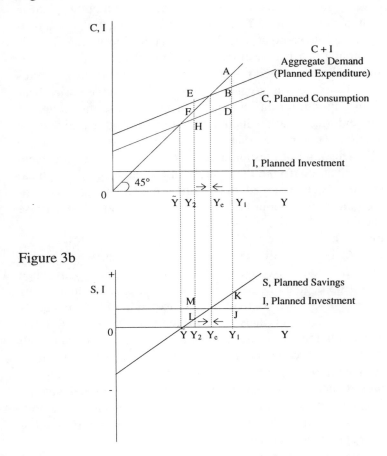

Figure 3b

The behavioural reaction of firms is also clear: in view of the build-up of inventories beyond their desired levels, retailers will reduce orders and manufacturers will cut back production. As production falls, so too will income — recall that firms' spending on inputs to produce output is income to the factors of production. So, by definition of equilibrium, the economy is not in equilibrium if $Y > Y_e$. Income will fall toward Y_e as long as $Y > Y_e$. This kind of reasoning applies for any Y to the right hand side of Y_e in the diagram.

Still focusing on Figure 3a, suppose next that income is initially below what we claim to be its equilibrium level. Suppose that $Y = Y_2$. From the 45 degree line it can be seen that output is Y_2F. But aggregate demand, or planned expenditure, is then Y_2E. Because actual expenditure is identical to output, planned expenditure then exceeds actual expenditure. So either the consumption plan or the investment plan or both will not be achieved. Suppose, as before, that the consumption plan is achieved. Then consumption is Y_2H. Actual investment, HF, must then fall short of planned investment, HE. What is happening is that there is unplanned decumulation (disinvestment) in inventories.

The reason for the unplanned run-down in inventories is clear: aggregate demand, Y_2E, exceeds aggregate supply, Y_2F, and inventories bear the brunt of this disequilibrium situation. In face of the unanticipated run-down in inventories, retailers increase their orders and manufacturers expand production. This implies that income will increase toward Y_e so long as $Y < Y_e$. This kind of reasoning applies for any Y to the left hand side of Y_e in the diagram. (Note that, purely in the interests of graphical clarity, it has just been assumed that with a moderately-sloped consumption function, Y_2 was about half way between $\tilde{Y}$ and Y_e: otherwise there would be danger that visual clarity would be obscured.)

It has now been seen that if $Y > Y_e$, income will fall toward Y_e, whereas if $Y < Y_e$, income will rise toward Y_e. Hence, starting from any level of income the economy converges toward Y_e. What happens when $Y = Y_e$? From the 45 degree line we see that national product then equals aggregate demand — actual output (actual expenditure) then equals planned expenditure. Thus all plans are achieved exactly; there is no unanticipated accumulation or decumulation of inventories. Because all plans are achieved, producers have no reason to change their behaviour. The market is voluntarily absorbing exactly what producers are supplying. There would then be no change in output. Thus national income would stay at Y_e indefinitely, unless some shock causes either the consumption function or the investment function (the locus representing planned investment expenditure) to shift.

Using Figure 3a it has been shown that: (a) The equilibrium level of national income is given by the intersection of the aggregate demand function (in the present simple model, the sum of the consumption and investment functions) and the 45 degree guide line. At that point aggregate demand, or planned expenditure, equals actual output. (b) The equilibrium income is plausibly stable, so if the economy is not in equilibrium, it is likely to move towards equilibrium.

Assertion 2: Using the (Planned) Savings and Investment Diagram
The determination of equilibrium national income in a simple macroeconomic model has now been explained with the aid of Figure 3a. It has also been shown, earlier, that if we know the consumption function, then we know the savings function, and vice versa. Figure 3a shows the consumption and the investment functions. Figure 3b shows the same

investment function and the savings function corresponding to the consumption function in Figure 3a. Because the two figures are equivalent it should be possible to explain the determination of equilibrium income using Figure 3b, and the explanation should be equivalent to that already outlined. It is easy, as an equivalent explanation, to show that the equilibrium level of national income is given by the equality of planned savings and planned investment. In Figure 3b the claim is that Y_e is the equilibrium income. This claim can be verified as follows.

First, suppose that $Y > Y_e$, say $Y = Y_1$. Then planned savings exceed planned investment by an amount KJ. But actual savings are identical to actual investment. Thus, either the savings plan or the investment plan or both will not be realised exactly. In line with the earlier assumption in discussing Figure 3a, that the consumption plan is realised, assume now that the savings plan is realised; thus actual savings equal KY_1 in Figure 3b. Then, because of the identity of actual savings and actual investment, actual investment must also be KY_1 in Figure 3b. Thus actual investment exceeds planned investment by an amount KJ, which represents unplanned investment. This takes the form of unplanned inventory accumulation. The reason for this is that too much is being produced relative to the level of aggregate demand. As before, output will be reduced and the system will approach Y_e.

Suppose next that $Y < Y_e$, say $Y = Y_2$ in Figure 3b. Then, planned investment, MY_2, exceeds planned savings, LY_2, by an amount ML. But actual investment is identical to actual savings. Thus, either the savings plan or the investment plan or both will not be realised exactly. Assume that the savings plan is realised. Then actual and planned saving is LY_2, and by the identity of actual savings and actual investment, actual investment is also LY_2. Thus, actual investment falls short of planned investment by the amount ML, which is unplanned decumulation of inventories of raw materials and finished goods. The reason for this is that too little is being produced relative to the level of aggregate demand. Because inventories are being run down below their desired levels, retailers increase their orders and manufacturers expand production. Thus, output and income increase toward Y_e.

When $Y = Y_e$, planned savings equal planned investment (and, as always in this simple model, actual savings are the same as actual investment). All plans are being realised: there is no unplanned accumulation or decumulation of inventories. Nobody has reason to change behaviour. Thus income and output stay at Y_e for as long as the savings function or the investment function do not shift. Hence Y_e is the equilibrium income. It has now been demonstrated, for a simple closed economy without government, that the equilibrium level of national income is given by:

(1) The equality of aggregate demand, or planned expenditures, with actual output, or, equivalently, by:

(2) The equality of planned (private) savings and planned (private) investment.

Equilibrium Conditions versus Identities

For the simple model which has just been analysed, the *equilibrium condition* (i.e. the condition under which national income is in equilibrium) may be written in two equivalent forms, one of them corresponding to the analysis using Figure 3a, the other corresponding to that using Figure 3b). The first way of writing the equilibrium condition is

$$(4)\ Y = C + I$$

where Y is aggregate output, C is consumption demand or *planned* consumption expenditure, and I is *planned* investment expenditure, including planned change in inventories. Writing equation (4) as $Y - C = I$, where Y is now interpreted as national income and C and I are as just defined, yields the *equivalent* equilibrium condition

$$(5)\ S = I$$

where I is *planned* investment expenditure and S is income which it is planned not to spend on consumption, i.e. it denotes *planned* savings.

It is essential to recognise that for the model which has just been developed, equations (4) and (5), in which C, I and S are interpreted as planned magnitudes, are *not true by definition* — they are *not identities*.

Close to the end of Chapter 9 it was seen that at *any* level of national income it would be true, for a closed economy without government, that

$$(4')\ Y \equiv C + I,\ \text{and}$$

$$(5')\ S \equiv I$$

where C, I and S denote the actual values of the variables.

Equations (4) and (5) hold *only* in equilibrium; (4') and (5') are true *whether or not* national income is at its equilibrium level; they are identities, not theories (i.e. they do not purport to be an explanation of anything).

Generalisation and Qualification

It has now been demonstrated, for a macroeconomic model in which producers are willing and able to supply any quantity at the prevailing price level, that the equilibrium level of national income is determined by

(a) the level of aggregate demand, or equivalently in the simple model, by (b) the equality of planned private savings and planned private investment. Condition (a) still holds when, by introducing government expenditure and foreign trade, we complicate aggregate demand in the direction of realism. But if we do add further complications, condition (b) must be modified. Further qualifications will be needed when we come to consider aggregate supply more explicitly.

Equilibrium Income versus Full Employment Income

Although the matter is more complex than is suggested at this stage, the economy's full employment output can be defined as that level of output which, given the state of technology, and given the economy's factor endowments and the distribution of fixed capital across different sectors of the economy, corresponds to the maximum the economy is capable of producing. Thus either the capital stock or the labour force or both would be fully employed. Full employment output is more or less fixed in the short run.

The full employment level of output tends to increase if the economy's factor endowments increase. Thus if there is positive net investment in the economy, implying that its capital stock is increasing, full employment output will also tend to be increasing. However, in the short run, net investment can add only marginally to the existing capital stock inherited from the past. That is why full employment output is usually taken as more or less given in a short-run analysis. (Note that we are here on the fringe of consideration of the determinants of aggregate supply, but discussion of such matters is being deferred until later.)

There is nothing necessarily "good" about being in equilibrium. Equilibrium national income is not necessarily the full employment level of national income — it is not necessarily a level of output at which all the economy's labour force and/or its capital stock are fully utilised. An economy could be in equilibrium with a great deal of capital and labour unemployed. In fact, we will see, when we bring government into the model, that one of the rationales for government intervention is to affect aggregate demand so as to drive the economy into a specific equilibrium — an equilibrium in the neighbourhood of full employment.

Some Effects of Shifts in the Functions

Suppose we start with the economy in equilibrium at Y_0 in Figures 4a and 4b, and, because of a campaign urging frugality, the average propensity to save, S/Y, increases. This means that on aggregate people are trying to save more at any level of income. The immediate effect of the attempt to save more is an upward shift in the savings function, from S to

S', in Figure 4a. If, as has been assumed, planned investment is autonomous, implying that it does not depend on the level of income, and if the investment function does not shift, an effect is a reduction in the equilibrium level of income from Y_0 to Y_1. Note that in this case, although the community has tried to save more, it ends up in the new equilibrium at Y_1 saving the same amount as at Y_0. With private investment demand autonomous, the situation in which an attempt to save more causes no change in equilibrium savings is called *the weak version of the paradox of thrift*.

Figure 4a

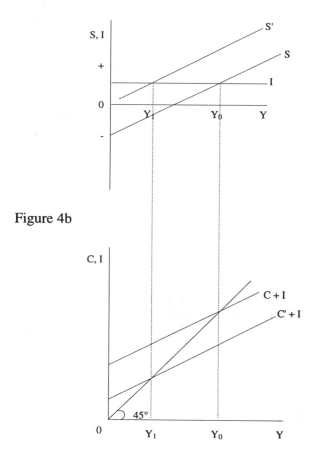

Figure 4b

The upward shift in the savings function in Figure 4a is equivalent to a downward shift in the consumption function from C to C' (neither plotted individually) in Figure 4b. Thus Figures 4a and 4b give the same information.

At this stage it is worthwhile noting that Figures 4a and 4b illustrate more than just the weak version of the paradox of thrift: inspection of the diagrams shows that in each case the absolute value of the change in equilibrium income exceeds the absolute extent of the vertical shift in the savings or consumption functions. Why this has occurred will be the subject of the next principal section.

The present paragraph, which will illustrate what is called the strong version of the paradox of thrift, is a digression because it involves a *temporary* change in one of the key maintained hypotheses carried forward until now, namely, the assumption that investment demand is autonomous. On the assumption that planned investment is autonomous, it has just been seen that an attempt by the community to save more will lead to no change in equilibrium savings. Suppose, however, that planned investment is not entirely autonomous, but that it increases with income. In that case the investment function — the relationship between planned investment and national income — will have a positive slope, as in Figure 5. There are several reasons why planned investment might be high at high levels of income and low at low levels of income. For example, if in the short run national income increases, then greater pressures will be imposed on the existing stock of machinery and equipment, so firms might want to add to their capital stocks.

Figure 5

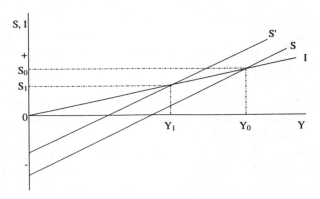

Also, given the aggregate capital stock, it is likely that the profitability of investment will increase as national income increases. Figure 5 indicates that if planned investment is an increasing function of income, if the slope of the investment function is less than the marginal propensity to save, and if the community's average propensity to save increases (i.e. if the savings function shifts upward, so that S/Y at any level of Y is now greater than before) then the community will end up in a new equilibrium at Y_1, saving less than initially at Y_0. It can be seen from the diagram that aggregate savings fall from S_0 at the initial equilibrium to S_1 after the upward shift in the savings function. Thus the attempt to save more not only causes income to fall; it also causes a reduction in equilibrium savings. This is known as the *strong version of the paradox of thrift*. The paradox holds when planned investment (with the slope of the investment function less than the slope of the savings function) is an increasing function of national income. In order to avoid confusion, the reader is reminded that the foregoing consideration of the strong version of the paradox of thrift has been a digression. Therefore, until further notice, it will be assumed (as before) that private investment demand is entirely autonomous, or exogenous.

THE MULTIPLIER IN THE SIMPLE MODEL

Suppose that planned investment is entirely autonomous, and that the economy is initially in equilibrium at Y_0 in Figure 6a. Then, because aggregate demand equals C + I, and because investment demand is assumed autonomous (the investment function has a slope of zero), the slope of C + I *is* the slope of the consumption function, the MPC, b in equation (2) above.

Consider the effect of an upward shift in the investment function. (This might have occurred because firms have become more optimistic in regard to the future.) Suppose that $\Delta I = £1$ million. Then C + I shifts up by £1 million to C + I' (where $I' = I + \Delta I$), and the new equilibrium is at Y_1 in Figure 6a. The central point to observe is that $\Delta Y > \Delta I$, or $\Delta Y/\Delta I > 1$; although planned investment has increased by £1 million, equilibrium income has increased by more than £1 million.

Suppose that the economy depicted by Figure 6a is economy A, and consider next another economy, economy B, identical to economy A in every respect except for the fact that the marginal propensity to consume in B is higher than the marginal propensity to consume in A. Economy B is depicted by Figure 6b. As was also the case in economy A, because investment demand in economy B is assumed autonomous, the slope of the aggregate demand function (the sum of the consumption function and the investment function) in Figure 6b is the slope of the consumption function.

The main respect in which Figure 6b differs from Figure 6a is that the implied consumption function in Figure 6b has a steeper slope — the

MPC, b, is higher. Starting at Y_0 in Figure 6b, suppose that the investment function shifts upward by the same amount as the shift in economy
A: $\Delta I = £1$ million. Figure 6b also indicates that $\Delta Y > \Delta I$. But in this case
the increment in income generated by a £1 million increase in planned
investment is more than the increment in income which occurred in
Figure 6a. By assumption, there was only one respect in which the two
economies initially differed — the second economy had a higher marginal propensity to consume — and the larger response of equilibrium
income to a unit change in investment demand in the second economy
must therefore be due to the higher marginal propensity to consume
applicable in that second economy.

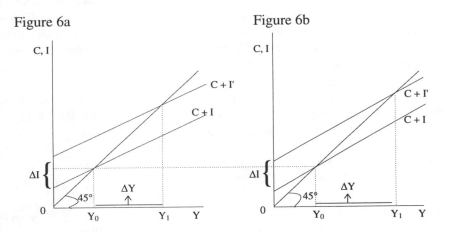

Figure 6a   Figure 6b

The geometry of Figures 6a and 6b has shown (a) that if planned
investment increases by £1 million, equilibrium national income will
increase by more than £1 million, and (b) the increment in equilibrium
income generated by a unit increase in planned investment will be higher,
the greater the slope of the consumption function, the MPC, b.

Note that the same kinds of results as above would have been
obtained if, instead of $\Delta I = £1$ million, there was an increase in the intercept of the consumption function, equation (2) above, such that $\Delta a = £1$
million, i.e. if the consumption function were to shift up by £1 million.

To clarify the economic process implicit in the two diagrams we turn
to a concept called a national income multiplier.

Successive Rounds of Expenditure

Suppose that an economy is at an initial equilibrium with an annual rate
of net investment equal to £100 million, and that next the rate of

investment permanently increases to £101 million; so ΔI = £1 million. Assume that the overall MPC is 3/4 and examine what will happen.

Because investment has increased by £1 million, the factors of production are paid an additional £1 million in wages, profits, etc. On this count, ΔY = £1 million. But there are further effects. Because income has increased by £1 million, and because the MPC is 3/4, the recipients of this £1 million spend an additional £(3/4) million. This is an increment in national expenditure, so it must be matched by an equal increment in output. The producers of this output experience an increment in incomes of £(3/4) million on this count.

In the second round effects just described, incomes have increased by £(3/4) million. The recipients of this additional income will not save all of it; they will, on the assumption that their MPC is 3/4, spend three quarters of it. Hence their expenditures will increase by $(3/4)£(3/4)$ million, or by $£(3/4)^2$ million. But this increase in expenditure is a further increment in incomes somewhere in the economy, because the expenditure of one group is income to another group.

Because incomes have increased by a further $£(3/4)^2$ million (in the third round) and because the recipients of this income are also assumed to have an MPC of 3/4, those income recipients will spend $(3/4)£(3/4)^2$ million - $£(3/4)^3$ million. But as before, one group's expenditure is another group's income. Those in the latter group therefore experience an increase in their incomes of $£(3/4)^3$ million. If, as we assume, their MPC is also 3/4, they will spend an additional $£(3/4)^4$ million, thereby generating an increment of $£(3/4)^4$ million in the incomes of some other group in the economy. And so the process continues, each increment in incomes generating further increments in expenditure, which in turn generate further increments in income.

For ΔI = £1 million, we thus have (in £ million):

$$\Delta Y = 1 + (3/4) + (3/4)^2 + (3/4)^3 + (3/4)^4 + \ldots +$$

or, in general,

$$(6)\ \Delta Y = 1 + b + b^2 + b^3 + b^4 + \ldots +$$

where b is the marginal propensity to consume.

According to a theorem which the reader should recall from the elementary mathematics of infinite series, for any real number b such that $0 < b < 1$, the infinite series (6) converges to, or equals, $1/(1 - b)$. Because of the plausible assumption that in the case at hand the number b (the MPC) is indeed strictly between zero and unity, we have, for ΔI = 1:

(7) $\Delta Y = 1/(1 - b)$ or, for any arbitrary value of ΔI,

(8) $\Delta Y = \{1/(1 - b)\}\Delta I$

It should be clear to the reader that the higher b happens to be, the greater the change in national income due to a change in investment. Thus if $\Delta I = £1$ million, and if $b = 3/4$, then equation (8) shows that $\Delta Y = £4$ million; if, on the other hand, $\Delta I = £1$ million while $b = 1/2$, then $\Delta Y = £2$ million. The reason for the different results in Figures 6a and 6b should now be very obvious: the slope of the consumption function, the MPC, b, is closer to unity in the second diagram than in the first; hence, from (6), the successive rounds of expenditure generated by a unit change in investment demand converge to a larger number for economy B (represented by the second diagram) than in the case of economy A (represented by the first diagram). The coefficient $1/(1 - b)$ above is called a national income multiplier.

Definitions: A national income multiplier is a coefficient relating change in equilibrium national income to changes in autonomous (or exogenous) demand, or to policy-induced shifts in aggregate planned expenditure. In any particular model of national income determination, *autonomous demand* is that part of aggregate demand which is determined outside, rather than within or by, the model under consideration. In any given model of income determination, if investment demand is determined by forces outside the model, then it is autonomous. Similarly, that part of planned consumption expenditure which does not depend on national income — the intercept "a" in the consumption function (2) — is autonomous. However, that part of planned consumption expenditure in any given year which is dependent on income in the same year is not autonomous (exogenous); rather, it is *endogenous*, meaning that its value is determined by, or within, the model under consideration. (The equilibrium level of national income is the most obvious example of an endogenous variable in the macroeconomic models considered in this text.)

Writing the multiplier expression in the form $1/(1 - b)$ may suggest that when autonomous demand changes, the economy will instantly move to the new equilibrium level of national income. That in fact will not be the case, as is suggested by the multiplier expression in form (6), where the multiplier is seen to operate in a convergent lagged fashion, as income increases by successively smaller increments over time, ultimately reaching its new equilibrium level. However, comparative statics — comparative static equilibrium analysis — forms the main methodology of this expository text. Thus, in allocating relatively little attention to disequilibrium, the principal focus is on equilibrium solutions, and although questions involving disequilibrium adjustment over time are sometimes addressed in the text, the limitations of the method of comparative statics — the comparison of one equilibrium solution with another — should always be kept in mind.

The Savings Leakage

The reason why the multiplier which we have just derived is a finite number (rather than infinite) is that savings are a leakage from the expenditure stream as the multiplier process works itself out: only part of the income earned in each round of expenditures is subsequently spent. The greater the savings leakage — the higher the marginal propensity to save — the lower the multiplier. Because the marginal propensity to save, MPS, equals 1 - MPC, we can write the multiplier derived above as

$$(9) \ 1/(1 - MPC) = 1/MPS$$

which indicates that the higher the savings leakage (as represented by MPS), the lower MPC must be and, in consequence, the lower the multiplier. For models of an economy more realistic than that just outlined above, it will be seen later that apart from personal savings, there are other leakages from the expenditure stream which lower the value of the multiplier. It will be shown in the next chapter that if governments were to believe that the multiplier for Ireland is $1/(1 - MPC)$ they would almost surely be led to pursue nonsensical policies.

The Simple Model in Algebra

The simple model of national income determination, as developed up to now, is easily represented algebraically. Thus we have

$Y = C + I$, equilibrium condition

$C = a + bY$, the consumption function

I autonomous

Simple substitution yields $Y = a + bY + I$, which implies:

$Y - bY = a + I$, or

$Y(1 - b) = a + I$, or

$$(10) \ Y = \{1/(1 - b)\}a + \{1/(1 - b)\}I$$

Equation (10) indicates that if "a" (the autonomous element of planned consumption) or I were to increase by £1 million, then the equilibrium level income would increase by $£1/(1 - b)$ million. Simple inspection shows that the higher the marginal propensity to consume, the larger the increase in equilibrium income generated by an increase in "a" or in I.

A glance at equation (10) indicates that there is a very simple way of interpreting a national income multiplier: it is simply the derivative (or rate of change) of equilibrium income with respect to any exogenous variable in the model under consideration. Thus, in equation (10) $\{1/(1 - b)\}$ is the derivative of Y with respect to "a", and it is also the derivative of Y with respect to I.

A Warning: It has been emphasised earlier in this chapter that the marginal propensity to consume, b, is a number strictly between zero and unity; therefore the marginal propensity to save is also strictly between zero and unity. This excludes any possibility that the MPC could be unity — that the MPS could be zero. Note that (in a simple linear model like that just investigated) any assumption that the MPC could equal unity (that the MPS could equal zero) would imply that the impossible was possible. Inspection of any of the equations (6) to (10) above shows that if MPC = 1 (MPS = 0), then the simple multiplier — and income — would become infinite!

CHAPTER 11

EXTENSIONS OF THE SIMPLE MODEL

The main conclusion in the previous chapter was that — assuming suppliers willing and able to provide any quantity at prevailing prices — equilibrium national income is determined by the level of aggregate demand. That still holds when the simple model is extended to include government and foreign trade. Given the assumptions in regard to supply, and alternatively phrased, it was shown that equilibrium income in the simple model is given by the equality of planned private savings and planned private investment; however, this statement of the equilibrium condition must be modified when the model is extended to include government and foreign trade. Before proceeding, the reader should ensure familiarity with the key identities in Chapter 9.

THE MODEL INCLUDING GOVERNMENT AND TAXES

Continue to assume:

(1) No depreciation.

(2) No taxes or subsidies on expenditure (no net taxes on expenditure).

(3) Undistributed profits of companies are zero; all company profits are distributed to shareholders. Thus private income equals personal income.

(4) No economic relationships with the rest of the world, so $X = M = 0$.

(5) Planned private investment is determined exogenously.

Assumptions (1) and (2), which are made only to avoid complexity, imply that we need not distinguish between GNP and national income at factor cost; we continue to denote both by Y. Similarly, assumption (3) is made only to avoid complexity: so long as it is satisfied, we need not distinguish between company savings and personal savings; all the private sector's savings are then personal savings, S.

In introducing government to the model, it is assumed:

(6) Income of public authorities in their business capacity is zero. Thus all the government sector's revenue must come from taxation or borrowing. In practice, taxation and borrowing are the main sources of public

finance, and because we will soon be investigating some impacts of each of those methods of financing, we will not want minor considerations to complicate our reasoning.

Because of assumption (2), taxation must be raised by means other than taxes on expenditure — by income taxes, for example. That assumption is not restrictive: in practice, what we call expenditure taxes — taxes on production or sale of goods and services — do exist, but their impact on the real purchasing power of consumers is similar to that of, say, income taxes. Both kinds of taxation mean that consumers can buy fewer goods with their disposable income; the impact on aggregate demand is similar. Therefore, the assumption that there are no expenditure taxes is not particularly restrictive.

The variable G in what follows denotes government (current plus capital) expenditure on goods and services; it does not include transfer payments. We can regard transfer payments by government as a form of negative taxation: they involve government giving to households rather than taking from them. Transfer payments may be incorporated in the analysis by treating them as part of net tax receipts (tax receipts as commonly understood, less transfer payments by government). The symbol T will be used to denote (net) tax receipts.

The existence of taxes on income implies that national income and disposable income are no longer the same. In what follows, disposable income equals national income less government (net) tax receipts.

Recall that in Chapter 10 private sector consumption demand was expressed as a function of disposable income. However because disposable income and national income were then the same (as a result of zero taxation), expressing consumption as a function of national income caused no particular problem in that chapter. In the present chapter it is convenient to continue using the 45 degree guide line diagram introduced in Chapter 10, and it is also convenient to represent Y rather than Y_d on the horizontal axis; thus we will continue to depict C as a function of Y in the guide line diagram. In this context (with taxation in the model) the reader should be aware that from now on, any time a consumption function is drawn in the (C, Y) plane, it is assumed that the tax régime (the levels and structure of tax rates, etc.) is given. Although a change in the tax régime need cause no change in consumption as a function of disposable income, a change in the tax régime usually *does* cause a change — a shift — in consumption as a function of national income.

For example, suppose initially that tax rates are given, that national income is given at some level Y_0 and that the ensuing level of consumption demand is C_0. Next, suppose that tax rates are increased. At the same level of national income as before, disposable income is now lower than before. Because consumption demand is an increasing function of disposable income, consumption demand C_1 will be lower than before, even if Y stays unchanged. Thus $C_1 < C_0$ even if $\Delta Y = 0$.

In summary, although a change in the tax régime need not cause any change in C as a function of Y_d, in general it will cause a change in C as a function of Y: for example, a rise in income tax rates means that at any Y, Y_d is lower than before; therefore a rise in tax rates causes the consumption function to shift downward when that function is expressed in the (C, Y) plane (with C on the vertical axis) — rather than in the (C, Y_d) plane.

As in the preceding chapter, all magnitudes in what follows are measured in real terms.

The Equilibrium Conditions

With government expenditure on goods and services included in the model, income is at an equilibrium when aggregate demand (including government demand) equals actual output, i.e. when

(1) $Y = C + I + G$, where

Y: National product, or aggregate supply.

C: Consumer demand. It will be assumed that consumers' expenditure plans are always realised; then C represents both actual and planned consumer expenditure.

I: Planned private investment expenditure, including planned inventory changes.

G: Planned government expenditure on goods and services. It will be assumed that those expenditure plans are always realised.

Equation (1) is *not* an identity. It holds only in equilibrium, because I denotes planned private investment rather than only actual private investment. (As in the model in Chapter 10, planned investment will equal actual investment only if income is in equilibrium; otherwise there would be unplanned accumulation or decumulation of inventories.)

Parallel to the analysis of the previous chapter, the equilibrium condition (1) can be rewritten in an *equivalent* form, by interpreting Y as national income rather than as product; then, disposable income, Y_d, is Y minus tax receipts, T:

(2) $Y_d \equiv Y - T$

Disposable income is either consumed or saved:

(3) $Y_d \equiv C + S$

From (2) and (3):

(4) $Y \equiv C + S + T$

Then, from (1) and (4), and interpreting all variables to represent their planned magnitudes:

$C + I + G = C + S + T$, or

(5) $S - I = G - T$

Because it has been assumed that the consumption plan is always realised, so too is the savings plan. Thus S denotes both planned and actual planned personal savings.

Just as equation (1) is an equilibrium condition rather than an identity, so too is (5), which has been derived using (1); for the simple closed economy with government, income is in equilibrium only when planned personal savings less planned private investment equals the government budget deficit (or the budget surplus, if $S - I$ is negative). Otherwise actual investment would differ from planned investment, in which case income would not be in equilibrium. (Recall from Chapter 9 that (5) would be an identity if all variables were defined as their actual magnitudes.) Both forms of the equilibrium condition — (1) and (5) — will be used to derive some important results in this chapter; however, the main reliance will be on representation (1) of the equilibrium condition.

The reader should now have the conceptual base to show why some modern economies have relied heavily on government intervention to regulate the level of national income and employment. However, because of the number of variables now involved in the model, graphical analysis is generally inefficient. But there are a few cases which can easily be shown graphically.

A Graphical Treatment

Consider Figure 1a. The $C + I$ function shows aggregate demand in the absence of government: $Y = Y_0$ is equilibrium income. We now recognise that there is some maximum output which the economy is capable of producing under normal working conditions. That is Y_F, the full employment level of output. If Y is less than Y_F, capital and labour will be unemployed. Government may then seek to steer the economy closer to full employment by adding to aggregate demand. Suppose government finances its expenditure by borrowing (in such a manner as to leave the private sector's consumption and investment functions unaffected). It can be seen from Figure 1a that if $G = \overline{G}$, and if the consumption and investment functions are unaffected, equilibrium income will increase to Y_F — the full employment level of national income. Thus, government may intervene to fill the gap which might otherwise prevail between aggregate demand and the full employment level of output.

Figure 1a

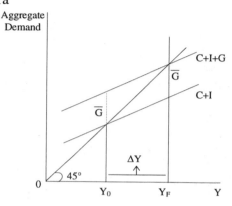

Figure 1b

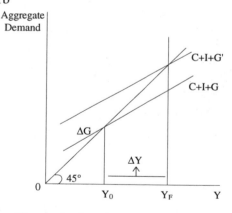

Note from Figure 1a that ΔY exceeds ΔG, which, because G was initially zero, is simply G. This reflects the operation of the multiplier introduced in Chapter 10. Because it is assumed that planned private investment is autonomous, the slope of the aggregate demand function is the MPC. It can be inferred that the higher the slope of the $C + I$ function in Figure 1a, the larger the increase in equilibrium income induced per unit of government expenditure; equivalently, the multiplier applicable to government expenditure is higher, the higher the MPC. In the model in Figure

1a, the multiplier is $1/(1 - MPC)$, as in the previous chapter: the upward shift in the aggregate demand function by the distance $\overline{G}$ changes equilibrium income by an amount $1/(1 - MPC)$ times $\overline{G}$. The MPC is a positive fraction which is strictly less than unity; therefore $\Delta Y > \Delta G$.

In the preceding paragraph it was assumed that G was initially zero. The initial aggregate demand function might in fact be $C + I + G$ in Figure 1b. In this case if G is raised to G' (so $\Delta G = G' - G$), equilibrium income is likewise raised to Y_F. The aggregate demand function has deliberately been drawn with a steeper slope in Figure 1b, implying (on the assumption that planned private investment is autonomous) that the MPC is higher than assumed in constructing the immediately preceding diagram. Figure 1b shows that although the economy starts in equilibrium well below full employment, a relatively small increase in government expenditure is needed in order to obtain the large increase in output necessary for full employment. Suppose, for example, that the MPC is 0.9. Then, if $\Delta G = £1$ million, ΔY is $1/(1 - MPC)$ times ΔG, £10 million.

The Balanced Budget Multiplier

One reason why government might wish to intervene in economic activity is that the private sector, if left to itself, might not generate a full employment level of output. In the preceding exposition it was assumed that the increase in government expenditure was financed by borrowing, in such a manner as not to affect the consumption or investment functions. But government often finances expenditure by increasing tax rates. Suppose, then, starting from equilibrium at Y_0 in Figures 1a or 1b, that the government increases its expenditure by £x million and also increases tax rates (in this case, from their initially assumed level of zero) so as to finance the increased expenditures fully. That is really a *composite* of two policies simultaneously: (a) an increase in G by £x million; (b) an increase in tax rates by a sufficient amount such that (taking account of any change in income which may ensue) the government will end up raising an extra £x million in tax receipts. It is important to understand that the two policies will not exactly offset each other; the composite policy will be expansionary, given that private investment demand is autonomous. That can be seen by considering the two polices in isolation:

Suppose that the MPC is 3/4. It has already been seen that if government increases its expenditure by £x million, the aggregate demand function will shift upward by an amount £x million, and $\Delta Y = \{1/(1 - MPC)\}$ times x: in this example, $\Delta Y = 4x$ (in £million).

Consider next the effect of raising the extra £x million in taxation. This implies that at any level of national income Y, disposable income

Y_d, and hence consumer expenditure C, will be less than before; the consumption function would shift *downward* in Figures 1a or 1b. The crucial question is whether the consumption function, and hence the aggregate demand function, could shift down by as much as £x million; if they did, there would be no net change in the aggregate demand function (the downward shift would offset the upward shift brought about by the increase in G).

Purely for simplicity in exposition and understanding, suppose that the new taxes are *lump sum*, the receipts from which do not depend on the level of national income. Thus we imagine the government raising the £x million by taxes on property or by simply assessing individuals regardless of their income or property position (a case of pure poll taxes). At any level of national income, disposable income then falls by £x million; however, consumption expenditure at any level of national income will not fall by as much as £x million because not all the disposable income taken from consumers would have been spent: of that sum they would have spent only the MPC times the disposable income taken from them. Thus the consumption function in the 45 degree diagrams shifts downwards by an amount £(MPC)x. Therefore the aggregate demand function shifts downward by an amount smaller than £x — by £(MPC)x. The multiplier is also applicable to this downward shift in aggregate demand. Thus $\Delta Y = -1(1 - MPC)$ times $(MPC)x$, or $-MPC/(1 - MPC)$ times x. With the MPC equal to 3/4, the £x million in increased taxes causes equilibrium income to fall by the amount $\Delta Y = -3x$.

Bringing the two sets of effects together:

(i) $\Delta Y = £4x$ million due to $\Delta G = £x$ million.

(ii) $\Delta Y = -£3x$ million due to $\Delta T = £x$ million.

Hence, the net effect is $\Delta Y = £x$ million $= \Delta G = \Delta T$.

The result just obtained is an illustration of what is called the balanced budget multiplier theorem. Note that despite the nomenclature the theorem does *not* require the budget to be balanced.

Balanced Budget Multiplier Theorem: Consider the demand side of a closed economy in which planned private investment is autonomous. Then, if government changes its expenditure on goods and services, and also changes (net) tax receipts by the same amount, so that there is no change in the initial budget surplus or deficit (or the budget stays balanced if it was initially balanced), $\Delta Y = \Delta G$, or $\Delta Y/\Delta G = 1$.

It will soon be shown that taxes need not be lump sum (as assumed in the illustration above) for the theorem to hold.

Changes in Autonomous Demand and Policy-Induced Expenditure Shifts

Close to the end of Chapter 10 a national income multiplier was defined as a coefficient relating a change in equilibrium national income to changes in autonomous demand or to policy-induced shifts in aggregate demand. We have not yet fully indicated what is meant by policy-induced shifts in demand. A policy-induced shift in demand occurs any time government policy causes a shift in the aggregate demand function. A change in government expenditure is perhaps the most obvious example of a policy-induced shift in aggregate demand. Similarly, if government changes tax rates, consumption as a function of national income will shift, leading to a shift in the aggregate demand function; this would also be policy-induced.

Algebraic Analysis

Because of the number of variables involved, the above analysis and its extensions are easier using simple algebra. We first assume that tax receipts T are fixed at some level by government policy; in that case tax receipts would be entirely exogenous. The model of income determination then is:

$Y = C + I + G$, equilibrium condition.

$C = a + bY_d$, consumption function.

$Y_d \equiv Y - T$, definition of disposable income.

T, G and I all exogenously determined.

By substitution, $Y = a + bY - bT + I + G$, which implies

(6) $Y = \{1/(1 - b)\}(a + I + G) - \{b/(1 - b)\}T$

The parameter b in (6) is the marginal propensity to consume. From (6) it can be seen that if "a", I or G increase by £1 million (so that the aggregate demand function shifts up by £1 million), then equilibrium income will increase by $£1/(1 - b)$ million. But because the coefficient of T has a negative sign, if the level of lump-sum taxes T is increased by £1 million, equilibrium income will *fall* by $£b/(1 - b)$ million; alternatively, if T is reduced by £1 million, income will increase by $£b/(1 - b)$ million. Thus a £1 million increase in government expenditure is more expansionary than a £1 million reduction in tax receipts. Equation (6) also illustrates the balanced budget multiplier theorem:

Let $\Delta G = £1$ million and also $\Delta T = £1$ million. Then, from (6),

$$\Delta Y = \{1/(1 - b)\}\Delta G - \{b/(1 - b)\}\Delta T, \text{ or}$$

$$(7) \; \Delta Y = 1/(1 - b) - b/(1 - b) = (1 - b)/(1 - b) = 1$$

Expression (7) is the balanced budget multiplier. It shows the amount by which equilibrium national income changes per unit change in government expenditure financed by taxation. The balanced budget multiplier for the simple closed economy model is unity.

The reader's understanding can be improved by noting that when government increases its expenditure on goods and services by £1 million, income initially increases by £1 million on that count; thus the *first-round effect* (see equation (6) of Chapter 10) is an increase in income by £1 million, some of which will be spent, thereby generating a further increase in income, leading to a further increase in expenditure, and so on. But when government raises taxes by £1 million, the immediate effect is *not* a £1 million reduction in consumer expenditure; rather, households would have spent (had they not been taxed) only the MPC times the £1 million taken from them. In this case the first-round effect is a reduction in expenditure by an amount £b million. So the change in income generated by a £1 million increase in government expenditure is (in £million)

$$(8) \; \Delta Y = 1 + b + b^2 + b^3 + b^4 + \ldots$$

whereas the change in income generated by a £1 million increase in tax receipts is

$$(9) \; \Delta Y = -b - b^2 - b^3 - b^4 - \ldots$$

Considering the two effects simultaneously ($\Delta G = 1$ and $\Delta T = 1$), it is readily observed that the sum of the two series (8) and (9) is unity, again illustrating that the balanced budget multiplier is unity. Generalising these principles, the reader should be able to show that if $\Delta G = \Delta T = x$, where x represents an arbitrary sum, then $\Delta Y = x$.

Endogenous Tax Receipts

Up to now it has been assumed that tax receipts are under the *direct* administrative control of the government — it has been assumed that tax receipts are entirely exogenous (determined outside rather than within the model under investigation). However, in reality the government does not determine total tax receipts directly; in practice a considerable portion of tax receipts depends on both tax rates (administratively determined by government) *and* on the level of national income (an endogenous variable which in turn depends on tax rates). It follows that in practice aggregate tax *receipts* are an *endogenous* variable, even though tax *rates* can be taken as *exogenous*.

In a modern economy some part of tax receipts in any year — such as lagged payments of tax liabilities incurred in earlier years but paid in the current year, some receipts from taxation on assets, etc. — are independent of income in the same year. Denote such tax receipts (those which are independent of current period income) by the symbol t_0. However, the bulk of tax receipts in any year depend on income in the same year and on the structure of the tax code applicable in that year. Furthermore, most modern economies adopt a *progressive* income tax structure — a structure in which higher bands of income are subject to progressively higher marginal rates of taxation. It follows that given the tax code, if one were to plot the relationship between tax receipts and aggregate income, with T on the vertical axis in the (T, Y) plane, the resulting locus would have a positive intercept term, t_0, and would be convex thereafter, the degree of convexity reflecting the progressivity of the tax code. However, in order to avoid non-linearities in the model which we are about to construct, it will be assumed, as an approximation, that $T = t_0 + t_1 Y$, where t_0 is that part of the current year's tax receipts which do not depend on income in the current year, and t_1 is the rate of income tax (assumed for simplicity to be constant and applicable at all levels of income). Still maintaining the closed economy assumption, the model then becomes

$$Y = C + I + G$$

$$C = a + bY_d$$

$$Y_d \equiv Y - T$$

$$T = t_0 + t_1 Y$$

I and G exogenous

Solving for equilibrium Y yields:

$$Y = a + b(Y - T) + I + G = a + bY - bt_0 - bt_1 Y + I + G$$

Hence, $Y(1 - b + bt_1) = a - bt_0 + I + G$, giving

$$(10) \ Y = \{1/(1 - b + bt_1)\}(a + I + G)$$

$$- \{b/(1 - b + bt_1)\}t_0$$

With tax receipts dependent on income, the multiplier for "a", I and G, is now less than that in (6); an increase in government expenditure *at unchanged tax rates* will now be less expansionary than previously, since, with an extra positive term in the denominator,

$$(11) \ \{1/(1 - b + bt_1)\} < \{1/(1 - b)\}$$

The reason why the multipliers are now lower than previously is because, apart from the savings leakage — represented by $1 - b \equiv 1 - MPC \equiv MPS$ — as the multiplier process works itself out in successive rounds of expenditure, the model now includes a second leakage represented by the (marginal) income tax rate t_1. Now, not all of the income earned at each round will be spent because, as before some of it will be saved, and because some of it will accrue to government in extra tax revenue. For example, suppose that the marginal propensity to consume is 0.75 and that the rate of income tax is 0.20; the multiplier on the left-hand side of (11) is then 2.5, while that on the right side is 4.0. Under these circumstances a £1 million increase in government expenditure financed by borrowing would generate a £4 million increase in equilibrium income if there were no taxes which depended on income, but only a £2.5 million increase in the contrary case.

The multiplier on the left-hand side of (11) has just been derived algebraically by solving the model for equilibrium Y. In order to focus more clearly on the economics involved, this multiplier will now be derived as an infinite series:

Suppose, at given tax rates and with tax receipts at least partly dependent on the level of national income, that the economy is initially in equilibrium. Next, suppose that the rate of private sector investment rises by £x due to the emergence of a boom in residential construction, for example. Because $\Delta I = x$, and because investment is part of output, *the impact effect — the first round effect —* is $\Delta Y = \Delta I = x$. The increased output must be accounted for by increased payments of £x to the factors of production — say to the construction workers. Construction workers, then, have increased their incomes by x. But their disposable incomes will have increased by less than this amount: With an income tax rate of t_1, they must pay $t_1 x$ of their increased incomes to the government; therefore their disposable income increases by only $x - t_1 x = (1 - t_1)x = \Delta Y_d$. Assuming a constant $MPC = b$ (implying a constant $MPS = 1 - b$), of that sum they will save a proportion $(1 - b)$ and spend $b\Delta Y_d = b(1 - t_1)x$. This is an increase in expenditure and it must be accounted for by an increase in output. Hence *the second round effect* is $\Delta Y = b(1 - t_1)x$. Suppose that all of this is increased output of spring water bought by the thirsty construction workers. In that case, incomes of factors of production in the spring water sector will have increased by $b(1 - t_1)x$, but because those factors of production must also pay a proportion t_1 to the government, their disposable incomes increase by only $\Delta Y_d = b(1 - t_1)x - t_1 b(1 - t_1)x = (1 - t_1)[b(1 - t_1)]x$. The factors of production in the spring water sector spend only a proportion b of that increase in their disposable income;

thus their expenditure increases by $b(1 - t_1)[b(1 - t_1)]x = [b(1 - t_1)]^2x$. This increase in expenditure corresponds to an increase in output elsewhere in the economy. Hence, *the third round effect* is $\Delta Y = [b(1 - t_1)]^2x$. As before, the factors of production which have increased their output and incomes in the third round pay a proportion t_1 of such increased income to the government, and spend a fraction b of the increment which remains. Along the lines of reasoning already sketched, their expenditure therefore induces a *fourth round* increase in output of $b(1 - t_1)[b(1 - t_1)]^2x = [b(1 - t_1)]^3x$. And so on, the pattern continues indefinitely. Summing the successive rounds of expenditure induced by $\Delta I = x$, the ultimate increase in income/output is represented by the infinite series:

$$\Delta Y = x + b(1 - t_1)x + [b(1 - t_1)]^2x + [b(1 - t_1)]^3x + \ldots$$

$$= \{1 + b(1 - t_1) + [b(1 - t_1)]^2 + [b(1 - t_1)]^3 + \ldots\}x, \text{ or,}$$

defining $b(1 - t_1) \equiv z$,

$$(12)\ \Delta Y = \{1 + z + z^2 + z^3 + \ldots\}x$$

A crucial question at this stage is whether each successive term in the infinite series is progressively smaller, and whether the infinite series itself converges to, or equals, a finite number. Now b and t_1 are both positive fractions strictly less than unity; therefore b and $(1 - t_1)$ are both positive fractions strictly less than unity. It follows that $z \equiv b(1 - t_1)$ must be a positive fraction which is strictly less than unity, and, from elementary algebra, the infinite series (12) converges to, or equals

$$(13)\ \Delta Y = \{1/(1 - z)\}x$$

Finally, substituting the definition of z into (13) yields

$$(14)\ \Delta Y = \{1/(1 - b(1 - t_1))\}x = [1/(1 - b + bt_1)]x$$

$$= [1/(1 - b + bt_1)]\Delta I$$

Note that the investment multiplier just obtained in (14) is exactly the same as that on the left-hand side of (11) above. But deriving this multiplier as an infinite series highlights the fact that there are now *two* leakages from the expenditure stream — a savings leakage as in the simplest model but also a tax leakage — which cause the multiplier to converge to a finite number.

The Balanced Budget Multiplier Theorem Once Again

With the model now developed in such a manner as to make tax receipts dependent on the level of national income, the reader may wonder whether the balanced budget multiplier theorem still applies. (It will be recalled that in the earlier illustration of the theorem it was assumed that tax receipts were lump-sum.) The answer, for the simple closed economy, is yes. Suppose that the government increases its expenditure by £x million and simultaneously changes tax rates in such a manner that tax receipts increase by exactly £x million at the new equilibrium. This £x million in increased tax receipts will be the net outcome of two forces simultaneously in operation: (a) increased revenue at any given level of national income due to higher tax rates. (b) increased revenue induced by changes in income at given tax rates.

To demonstrate that the theorem is still valid we use equilibrium condition (5) of a few pages back:

(5) $S - I = G - T$

which implies, in comparing the new equilibrium (following $\Delta G = \Delta T$) with the initial equilibrium, that

(15) $\Delta S - \Delta I = \Delta G - \Delta T$

By assumption, $\Delta G = bT = £x$ million; so the right-hand side of (15) is zero. Also by assumption of the theorem, $\Delta I = 0$. Equilibrium condition (15) then implies $\Delta S = 0$. But since planned savings depend on disposable income — they are a strictly increasing function of disposable income — and because there has been no change in planned savings, it must be the case that $\Delta Y_d = 0$. By definition, Y_d equals $Y - T$; thus $\Delta Y_d \equiv \Delta Y - \Delta T$. Hence, with $\Delta Y_d = 0$, $\Delta Y = \Delta T$, and recalling that $\Delta G = \Delta T$ it is concluded that $\Delta Y = \Delta G = £x$ million, or $\Delta Y/\Delta G = 1$, given that $\Delta G = \Delta T$. Therefore, the balanced budget multiplier theorem holds exactly for the simple closed economy, regardless of whether taxes are lump-sum. It follows that if the closed economy is at an initial equilibrium below full employment output, implying that capital and labour are idle, then increased government expenditure may drive the economy to an equilibrium in a neighbourhood of full employment, even if income taxes are used to finance that expenditure.

THE MODEL WITH FOREIGN TRADE

It is now appropriate to bring exports (X) and imports (M) of goods and services into the picture. As before, national income is in equilibrium when aggregate demand (including now export demand) for the output of the economy equals its actual output, i.e. when

(16) $Y = C + I + G + (X - M)$

The symbols Y, C, I and G are as defined earlier in this chapter. Imports are deducted from the right-hand side of (11) because they represent demand for output produced abroad rather than for that of the home economy. As before, it is assumed that the expenditure plans of consumers and government are realised, and we now add the further assumption that export and import plans are also realised.

Equation (16) is an equilibrium condition rather than an identity because it holds only in equilibrium; I denotes planned rather than only actual private investment. (Planned investment will equal actual investment only if income is in equilibrium: otherwise there would be unplanned accumulation or decumulation of inventories.)

Parallel to the analyses in Chapter 10 and earlier in the present chapter, equilibrium condition (16) can be written in equivalent form by interpreting Y as national income rather than as national product. Then

(17) $Y = C + S + T$

Taken together, equations (16) and (17) imply that in equilibrium

(18) $S - I = (G - T) + (X - M)$

where all variables are at their planned magnitudes. The equilibrium condition for the present model of an open economy with government can be expressed in the form of either equation (16) or equation (18).

What determines the levels of X and M? This is a question of great importance for an open economy like Ireland. Until further notice, it will be assumed that exchange rates between the home country and its main trading partners remain approximately constant. Then, in the short run, it can be assumed, as a first approximation, that export demand is determined by factors beyond the control of the home country — by the level of foreign demand. Thus, in the present short-run model, exports are determined exogenously. However, imports are endogenous — they are a function of the level of national income in the home country. That is because, in the case of a small open economy like Ireland, imports are both a precondition for growth in national income as well as an effect of such growth. The dependence of imports on national income can be expressed as

(19) $M = f(Y)$

where f is merely functional notation and where it is assumed that imports increase with national income: $\Delta M/\Delta Y > 0$.

In order to make progress in extending the model framework as developed up to now, it is desirable to know more about the functional form of (19). It is likely that some parts of imports in a given year are quite independent of national income in the same year; for example, they may reflect deliveries in connection with contracts arranged in the past. Let the parameter m_0 denote that part of aggregate imports. However, in an open economy like Ireland, imports of energy and other materials are necessary in order to facilitate current-period production; furthermore, part of the value added earned by households from expanded production will be spent on imports of final goods and services. As an approximation, and for tractability in the analysis which follows, it will be assumed that (19) has the simple linear form:

(20) $M = m_0 + m_1 Y$

where m_0 — that part of imports which does not depend on national income in the current year — is positive and m_1, called the *marginal propensity to import* $\Delta M / \Delta Y$, is strictly between zero and unity.

In order to focus on the role of imports in isolation, the impact of government and taxation will at first be ignored. The model then becomes

$Y = C + I + X - M$

$C = a + bY$

$M = m_0 + m_1 Y$

I and X exogenous

Simple substitution then yields

$Y - bY + m_1 Y = a + I - m_0$, which implies

(21) $Y = \{1/(1 - b + m_1)\}(a + I + G - m_0)$

Equation (21) indicates that the multiplier is now lower than it was in the simplest closed economy model:

(22) $1/(1 - b + m_1) < 1/(1 - b)$,

i.e. $1/(MPS + MPM) < 1/MPS$

Furthermore, the multiplier will be lower, the higher the marginal propensity to import, m_1. The reason is that changes in import volume, induced by changes in income, are a further leakage from the successive rounds of expenditure as the multiplier process works itself out.

An understanding of the multiplier on the left-hand side of (22) can be enhanced by deriving that expression from an infinite series. Thus, suppose that the economy is initially in equilibrium and that next, a disturbance to equilibrium causes the rate of investment to rise by £x. Because investment is part of output, and because output must be associated with payments to the factors of production, income increases by x (pounds); this is *the impact effect,* or *the first round effect* in the multiplier process. The factors of production (households) save a proportion (1 - b) of x; thus savings increase by (1 - b)x. A proportion m_1 of the increase in income will be spent on imports; thus imports increase by $m_1 x$. The residual part of the increase in income, namely x - (1 - b)x - $m_1 x$ = (b - m_1)x, will be spent on home produced output. Thus, $\Delta Y = (b - m_1)x$ in the *second round* of the multiplier process. This kind of reasoning is readily extended to the third and subsequent rounds. It follows that the ultimate change in income will be

$$\Delta Y = \{x + (b - m_1)x + (b - m_1)^2 x + (b - m_1)^3 x + \ldots\}$$

$$= \{1 + (b - m_1) + (b - m_1)^2 x + \ldots\}\Delta I$$

Assuming that $0 < (b - m_1) < 1$, the infinite series converges to

$$\Delta Y = \{1/(1 - b + m_1)\}\Delta I,$$

thereby yielding the same multiplier as on the left hand side of (22) above.

The tax leakage aside, Ireland's high marginal propensity to import explains why national income multipliers for the small open economy of Ireland are quite low. As a rough order of magnitude, b = 0.75 in the case of Ireland. If ours were a closed economy, and if there were no tax leakage, the ensuing multiplier applicable to autonomous demand would be 1/(1 - 0.75) = 4. But if one now recognises that Ireland's overall marginal propensity to import is about 0.6 (still ignoring the tax leakage), that multiplier is reduced substantially to 1/(1 - 0.75 + 0.6), which is approximately 1.2.

Three leakages from the expenditure stream — savings, tax and import — have now been identified. The effect of each of these is to lower the numerical value of national income multipliers below what they would otherwise be. All three leakages will now be included together in an economic model.

THE MODEL WITH SAVINGS, TAX AND IMPORT LEAKAGES COMBINED

Gathering the principal equations of relevance, the extended model of the goods market is now as follows:

$$Y = C + I + G + X - M,$$

$$C = a + bY_d$$

$Y_d \equiv Y - T$

$T = t_0 + t_1 Y$

$M = m_0 + m_1 Y$

I, G and X exogenous

Solving this set of simultaneous equations for Y, by substitution as before:

$$Y = a + b(Y - t_0 - t_1 Y) + I + G + X - m_0 - m_1 Y$$

which implies

$$Y - bY + bt_1 Y + m_1 Y = a - bt_1 + I + G + X - m_0$$

Hence,

$$(23) \quad Y = \{1/(1 - b + bt_1 + m_1)\}[a + I + G + X - m_0] + \{b/(1 - b + bt_1 + m_1)\}t_0$$

It can now be seen why multipliers for Ireland must be very small. Although no claim to spurious precision is pretended — recall some earlier observations in regard to the lack of precision of certain key national accounts statistics in Ireland — economists are in general agreement that for the economy of the Republic of Ireland, and as an approximation, the marginal propensity to consume $b = 0.75$, the marginal propensity to import $m_1 = 0.6$, and the marginal net tax rate $t_1 = 0.3$. Suppose government increases its expenditure by £1 million and that it finances this without affecting other components of autonomous demand (e.g. by issuing securities to the non-bank public). From equation (23) it can be calculated that the multiplier for government expenditure is $1/[1 - .75 + (.75)(.3) + 0.6] = 1/1.075$, a number just below unity, or approximately unity. Recall that with $b = 0.75$ in a closed economy with no tax receipts dependent on income, the government expenditure multiplier would be 4. Thus, recognising that we live in an open economy and that net tax receipts (including the level of dole payments) vary with national income makes an overwhelming difference in the formation of macroeconomic policy.

Does the balanced budget multiplier theorem still hold? Suppose that planned private investment is unaffected, that government increases its expenditure by £1 million and that net tax receipts are increased by exactly £1 million so as to match the increase in expenditure: will equilibrium national income increase by £1 million as it would in a closed economy? Assuming that imports depend on the level of national income, the answer is no; although income will increase, it will increase by less than £1 million. This is easily seen by assuming that the government collects its revenue by means of taxes which are independent of current year income; then $t_1 = 0$ in equation (23), where t_0 then represents the level of tax receipts, all determined independently of current year national income. The multiplier for an increase in G is given by the coefficient of G in equation (23); with $t_1 = 0$, $b = 0.75$ and $m = 0.6$, if $\Delta G = 1$, then $\Delta Y = 1/(1 - 0.75 + 0.6) = 1.2$ approximately. The change (it is a reduction) in income generated by a £1 million increase in non-income taxes is given by the coefficient of t_0 in equation (23). Thus if $\Delta T = 1$, then $\Delta Y = $ minus $0.75/(1 - 0.75 + 0.6) = $ minus $.85$ approximately. Therefore, if $\Delta G = \Delta T = £1$ million, then $\Delta Y = £(1.2 - 0.85)$ million $= £0.35$ million approximately. Note that although the balanced budget multiplier is now very low — it is very much less than unity — it is still non-zero, and in fact positive; hence an increase in government expenditure fully financed through extra taxation will have *some* effect in increasing output.

The considerations just outlined suggest that in the open economy of Ireland, a *broadly distributed* increase in government expenditure on goods and services financed by increased taxation would have only a marginal impact on the level of aggregate demand. It should not be forgotten, however, that the *structure* of increases in government expenditure is important in assessing the first-round import leakage, and hence, in estimating the overall value of the relevant multiplier. (In the present chapter it has not been possible to deal with the structure of government expenditures because the scope for formal disaggregation is minimal in an introductory exposition.) For example, a £1 million increase in government expenditure in recruiting extra police would have practically zero import leakage in the first round. But an extra £1 million spent on aircraft parts for the airforce would have virtually no impact on the domestic economy in the short run, because almost all the parts would be imported. The structure of investment expenditure by the private sector is also important in estimating the value of the multiplier applicable to such expenditure. Thus, because the direct import intensity is smaller, an increase in private investment in building and construction will have a higher multiplier effect than an equivalent increase in investment in machinery and equipment (which, because of high import intensity, will typically have a very small multiplier effect on the state of economic activity in the short run).

EXCESS CAPACITY AND PUBLIC POLICY

The multiplier analysis in this and in the preceding chapter is applicable in situations in which the economy under analysis is operating below full capacity utilisation. If the economy is operating at full employment — which at this stage can be taken to mean that it is actually producing the maximum it is capable of producing — any one form of real expenditure can be increased only if other real expenditures are reduced: In a sense, any real increase in one form of expenditure would "crowd out" other expenditures. If full employment prevailed, (in the short run) the economy could produce more investment goods, for example, only by diverting labour and capital away from production of consumption goods. The theory of the multiplier, therefore, is applicable in an expansionary direction only to situations in which less than full employment prevails. (Of course, the theory is applicable in a downward direction from Y_F throughout the domain of non-negative income levels.)

Subject to the full employment constraint on aggregate output which has just been mentioned, it has been assumed throughout the last two chapters that producers are willing to supply any quantity at the prevailing price level. This assumption remains to be investigated at later stages of the macroeconomic analysis, especially when the role of real wages is considered.

Demand Deficiency and Public Policy

Suppose, because of deficiency in the level of aggregate demand, that the economy is producing with excess capacity, and that public policy seeks to drive the system closer to full employment equilibrium. Because $Y = C + I + G + (X - M)$, government might do so, in the short-run, by generating an upward shift in the consumption function, or in the investment function, or by increasing its own expenditure: alternatively, it could possibly generate a downward shift in the import function (e.g. it could seek to reduce the parameter m_0 by raising taxes on imports, though in a longer-term context this might well turn out to be a short-sighted policy). The immediate effect of such shifts would be compounded by the multiplier process, even though national income multipliers are themselves small in an economy as open as Ireland. The principal instruments at the disposal of government in this context are fiscal policy (government policy in regard to the levels of its revenues and expenditures), *perhaps* monetary policy, and commercial policy (concerning tariffs, subsidies and quotas on international trade). Exchange rate policy might also be of some importance in influencing aggregate demand in the short run. The consumption function could be shifted upward by reduction in tax rates (an example of fiscal policy) or *possibly* by reducing the cost, and increasing the availability, of credit to households (issues involving monetary policy). The investment function could be shifted upward by offering various kinds of tax incentives for business investment, or *perhaps* by reducing interest rates. Conceivably, the import function could be shifted downward (thereby causing the aggregate demand function to shift upward, because imports appear with a negative sign in that function) by imposing tariffs or maximum quantity quotas on imports, though in the case of Ireland such actions, if applied unilaterally, would be contrary to international agreement in an EU context. Note that formal modelling of all of the aforementioned possibilities would require use of an economic model much larger than that finally constructed in the present chapter. Note also that reservations have just been expressed in regard to the ability of the authorities to increase aggregate demand by means of monetary policy. Detailed elaboration on this question will be provided later.

Figure 2

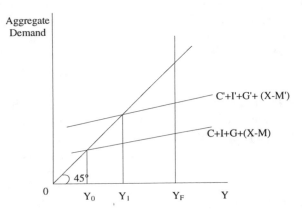

Suppose that the economy is initially in equilibrium at Y_0 in Figure 2 and that Y_F, which exceeds Y_0, is the full employment output. Corresponding to the final model of the goods market as developed in this chapter, the initial aggregate demand function, $C + I + G + (X - M)$, is drawn rather flat (but still with a positive slope) due to the simultaneous operation of savings, tax and import leakages. Nevertheless, the effect of the kind of policies which have just been discussed is an upward shift in the aggregate demand function to $C' + I' + G' + (X - M')$ and movement toward a higher equilibrium level of national income, closer to the full employment level of income. Note that if the aggregate demand function were steeper (as it would be in a closed economy), a much smaller upward shift of the aggregate demand function would be required in order to get the economy to full employment output.

THE GOODS MARKET MODELS:
OBSERVATIONS ON METHODOLOGY

A few remarks on some of the difficulties surrounding what has been done in this and in the immediately preceding chapter are appropriate.

First, the methodology has been mainly that of comparative static equilibrium analysis, usually termed comparative statics for brevity. Thus, the essence of the approach has been to start with a model of an economy at an equilibrium solution, to assume the application of some shock (e.g. a change in government expenditure) from outside the model, to calculate the new equilibrium solution for Y and to compare that solution value with the initial solution value of Y. It has also been assumed that all equilibria are stable; otherwise, even though an equilibrium solution would presumably exist, it would be extremely unlikely that it would ever be realised (attained). Relatively little attention has been addressed to the disequilibrium behaviour of the economy — in particular, nothing has been said on the question of how long in time it takes the economy to move from an initial equilibrium to a new equilibrium solution. Disequilibrium responses have been discussed in only two contexts — first, in arguing that the equilibrium level of national income is plausibly stable and second, in discussing national income multipliers expressed as infinite series.

Related to the foregoing is the fact that the key variables in each of the models were *behavioural* — they purported to represent what groups of individuals were trying to do — and the equations in the models therefore represented *equilibrium relationships*. For example, the consumption function purported to express *planned* consumption as a function of its underlying determinants, the symbol I in each of the models denoted *planned* private sector investment, etc. It follows that in solving any of the models for Y, we were finding that (unique) Y at which all of the relevant plans were simultaneously attained.

Actual economies are exposed to persistent disturbances to equilibrium; thus (even assuming accurate and instantaneous statistical information), the observed (actual) value of an endogenous macroeconomic variable (such as national income) is unlikely to coincide exactly with that predicted by macroeconomic equations which purport to apply to an equilibrium context alone (and which are used for predicting comparative static effects of changes in exogenous variables).

In fact, if equilibrium were unstable, the actual values of endogenous macroeconomic variables would tend to explode or cycle away from the values of those variables predicted by a model which expressed equilibrium behaviour alone: even if all of the statistical data utilised were accurate, the method of comparative statics would then yield predictions (e.g. of the effects of a change in government expenditure) which were fundamentally wrong. When an analyst is using the method of comparative statics, these observations underline the importance of being satisfied that the analyst is dealing with equilibria which are stable. The observations also reveal some of the limitations of the comparative statics method.

Some idea of the *orders of magnitude* to be assigned to key parameters in a macroeconomic model — for example, to b, t_1 and m_1 in the final extended model toward the end of the present chapter, is important for policy: otherwise — and by way of example — the government might have no idea of the (equilibrium) effects of its fiscal policies. In large-scale models the parameters are usually estimated using econometric methods. (Applied econometrics is a blend of mathematics, mathematical statistics, economic theory and empirical statistical data.) In the case of (comparative static) equilibrium models, precision in the parameter estimates usually assumes, among other things:

(1) Abundant accurate and up-to-date empirical statistical data. As already observed in Chapter 9, in this context the official Irish national accounts data leave much to be desired.

(2) Confidence that the model under investigation has a stable (and unique) solution for the endogenous variables, given the values of the exogenous variables. Otherwise there is a danger that as time elapses the observed values of endogenous macroeconomic variables will progressively diverge from their equilibrium values and if that is the case, it is likely that the ensuing values of parameters (estimated using, say, conventional econometric methods) in an equilibrium model will be hopelessly wrong.

The foregoing remarks notwithstanding, although few Irish economists would make claim to precision (to an order of, say, three decimal places in estimating the marginal propensity to consume, for example) in their estimates of key macroeconomic parameters, there *is* broad agreement on the order of magnitude assumed for the key parameters in the extended model of the goods market outlined above.

The reader is reminded that the focus of the macroeconomic analysis developed in this and in the immediately preceding chapter has been on the goods market (sector) alone — on the demand side of the economy exclusive of much (or any) discussion of the monetary sector or of the external sector (which includes the market for foreign exchange). The supply side — in particular the labour market (sector) — has been ignored almost entirely. It is an ultimate objective in this text to investigate all four sectors in detail, and to bring them together in a more complete (in principle, simultaneous equations) macroeconomic model. With this objective in mind, it is appropriate at this stage to move on to investigate some aspects of the money market.

CHAPTER 12

THE MONEY MARKET

It was assumed in the foregoing discussions of the goods market (Chapters 10 and 11) that private sector investment demand was exogenously determined at some level, and little effort was made to explain what determines that level (or changes in that level). It is now time to recognise that private investment demand depends on expected profits — the difference between the expected flow of returns from investment, and the initial costs of financing plus the expected flow of operating costs, associated with changes in the capital stock (investment projects). Because interest is a cost of financing investment, the decision to invest depends on the interest rate. The present chapter does not provide any detailed analysis of the relationship between the desire to invest and the rate of interest; that is reserved for investigation when we return to microeconomics — in Chapter 29 below. Here it is necessary only to point out that if the interest rate falls, the cost of financing investment falls and therefore investment demand rises.

In discussing the investment function in the preceding two chapters it was implicitly assumed that the interest rate, and hence the expected profitability of investment, were given. However, if the interest rate falls, the expected profitability of investment increases, causing the investment function to shift upward in the 45 degree guide line diagram (and in the savings–investment diagram). The immediate effect on income would be compounded by the relevant multiplier. Similarly, if the interest rate increased, the cost of financing investment would rise, so the investment function would shift downward causing equilibrium income to decline. These considerations suggest that it is now time to examine the determinants of the interest rate. In the analysis which immediately follows, a closed economy will be assumed. When this assumption is relaxed at a later stage, it will be found that the implications for interest rate determination and for monetary policy may be altered drastically in an open economy. The assumption that the price level is constant will be maintained until further notice.

FUNCTIONS OF MONEY AND DETERMINATION OF THE RATE OF INTEREST

Interest on money is the price for the services of money; alternatively, it is the cost of holding money. We sometimes think of interest as the cost of borrowed money. However — and more generally — we can also think of it as the cost of holding wealth in the form of money, which yields no financial return, rather than in the form of assets such as real estate, machinery or bonds (which usually do yield financial returns). A decision to hold wealth in the form of money is a decision to forgo earning interest. Thus, interest is the economic cost — the opportunity cost — of holding wealth in the form of money. This cost may be explicit or implicit. It is an explicit cost of holding borrowed funds. It is an implicit cost if the funds held (e.g. in your pocket or in safe-keeping "under the mattress") are not borrowed.

Functions of Money

The principal role of money is to separate the acts of buying and selling. In a pure barter economy, in which there is no money, every transaction would have to involve the exchange of goods or services on both sides of the transaction. The economist wanting a new suit might have to find a tailor who wants economic advice, while the tailor who wants butter might have to find a farmer who wants new clothes. The existence of money avoids such awkwardness, for money is a *medium of exchange*. It makes it unnecessary that there be direct coincidence of wants between parties entering trade. Money normally has three other functions. These are as a store of value, a unit of account and a standard of deferred payment.

A *store of value* is something which maintains value over time. An essential feature of a store of value is that it does not easily perish as fresh fruit or meat would if used as means of exchange. Note that there are many other stores of value apart from money — land for example. Money is not necessarily a perfect store of value, for (if the price level is not constant) inflation may erode its purchasing power.

Money is a *unit of account* because it is the common denominator (the *numéraire*) in which prices are normally expressed and in which accounting records are maintained.

Finally, as a *standard of deferred payment* money is the measure in which payment of loans is normally expressed. Someone who buys a car on credit does not usually contract to give the seller ordinary goods and services, or non-monetary assets, in exchange at future dates; rather, they agree to pay certain sums of money, including interest, which in this case would be a fee associated with a deferral of immediate payment in the form of money.

While money performs all the above functions, its most important role is that of medium of exchange. In fact, money is *anything* which is generally accepted as a medium of exchange. If people in general refused to accept payment in coin, banknotes or bank deposits (via cheques), such instruments would cease to be money. In practice, people do accept payment in coin, banknotes or transfer of bank deposits; these are the principal forms of money in modern economies. Note that money does not have to be "backed" by anything of intrinsic worth such as gold. All that is necessary for something to be money is that people generally *believe* that if they accept it in payment, it will also be accepted in payment by others.

Liquidity

Money is a perfectly liquid asset in the sense that it can be immediately converted into goods without significant risk of incurring a windfall loss. This is in contrast to less liquid assets such as real estate, consumer durables or bonds: if you suddenly decide to go on holidays, you cannot normally expect to finance that vacation by deciding instantly to sell your home while at the same time obtaining its full market value. Assets differ on a spectrum of liquidity, or ready convertibility into purchasing power without significant risk of windfall loss. At one end of the spectrum stands money; toward the other end stand assets such as real estate.

A *bond* is a piece of paper with a face value of £x, issued by a borrower and promising to pay the bearer (who might or might not be the original lender) a certain *fixed* sum (called the coupon) in money over a certain period of time (say each year) until the bond is redeemed. (Note that this definition has focused on the central characteristics of a bond; individual details may differ.) Suppose that the government seeks to borrow £100 for 20 years. It may issue a bond with a face value of £100 to Morton, the (original) lender. The government agrees to pay the bearer of the bond in 20 years' time the sum of £100; 20 years' time is then the redemption date of the bond. The government will have to pay interest, or a coupon which is equivalent to a fixed rate of interest on the face value of the bond. Suppose that the government agrees to pay Morton, or whoever might subsequently own the bond (the bearer) if Morton sells it, a fixed sum of £15 annually for the next 20 years. This coupon of £15 is then the interest on the face value of the bond. Perhaps Morton will wish to sell the bond in 10 years' time — before the redemption date. However, he may not be able to find buyers who are willing to pay the original price of the bond (£100) even though such potential buyers know that they would obtain £100 at redemption date, plus the fixed coupon annually in the interim. Therefore, Morton might have to accept incurring a windfall loss if his desire for liquidity leads him to sell the bond before it matures (i.e. before its redemption date). Thus, bonds are not perfectly liquid assets. In varying degrees the same can be said of all assets other than money — the only asset which is perfectly liquid.

The Demand for Money

The notion of the community's "demand for money" does not directly reflect any wish that people might have to be endowed with "lots of money" in the conventional sense. Rather, the words pertain to people's desire to hold some of their assets in perfectly liquid form (as money) rather than in alternative forms which are not perfectly liquid (e.g. land).

How is the rate of interest determined? Note that this reference is to "the" rate of interest. In reality there are many rates of interest — those applying to short-term loans and those applying to long-term loans as well as those applying to loans with different levels of risk of default. To facilitate exposition, when we refer to the rate of interest in what immediately follows, we will be referring to the rate of interest on a *new* gilt-edged government bond (so that there is no perceived risk of default) with no fixed redemption date. Thus, the rate of interest is "pure" or riskless. All other rates of interest tend to move in phase with this central rate.

Because interest is a price (either explicit or implicit), it is determined in much the same manner as any other price — by supply and demand; in the present case, by the supply of and the demand for money. As is the case with most ordinary commodities, the demand curve for money (quantity of money demanded as a function of the price of money) slopes down from left to right as in Figure 1 below. The lower the rate of interest, the more money will borrowers seek. Also, the lower the rate of interest, the more will asset holders be willing to hold their wealth in the form of money rather than in the form of assets which yield direct financial returns. The reader may wonder why anyone might prefer money, a liquid asset, to other forms of wealth yielding direct financial returns. Broadly speaking, there are three motives which underlie such liquidity preference (i.e. people's demand for money as distinct from their desire to hold less liquid forms of wealth). These are the transactions, precautionary and speculative motives.

(1) *The Transactions Motive*: One reason why people wish to hold wealth in the form of money is to facilitate current transactions. Most households receive their incomes weekly, fortnightly or monthly. Therefore, they need to hold money to meet day-to-day expenses. The transactions demand of households for money depends on the payment habits of the community (in particular, whether households receive their incomes at long or short intervals) and on the level of money income. Businesses

also hold money balances — normally in their bank accounts — to finance day-to-day transactions. They must hold money to meet the costs of raw materials, the wage bill, etc. The larger the turnover of the firm, the larger, other things being equal, the firm's transactions demand for money. It follows that the community's transactions demand for money is determined, broadly and primarily, by the level of national income, and that it is an increasing function of the level of national income.

(2) *The Precautionary Motive*: People hold money under the precautionary motive in order to guard against unforeseen contingencies, such as "acts of God" or "a rainy day". Those currently earning high incomes tend to have notions of their conventional needs which involve higher financial outlays than those earning lower incomes. For example, in contrast to lower income groups, those earning high incomes tend to hold higher money balances to meet contingencies such as breakdown of their mode of transportation, repair to their residential property following storm or flood damage, having a meal in a restaurant with someone who one met unexpectedly, etc. It is reasonable to assume that the overall demand for money under the precautionary motive depends mainly on the level of national income, and that it is an increasing function of the level of national income.

(3) *The Speculative Motive*: Money may be held under the speculative motive when the prices of other assets, such as bonds, are expected to decline. If prices of assets other than money do decline in the near future, the speculator who decides to hold assets in liquid (i.e. monetary) form now will have avoided incurring a windfall loss (which would have been incurred had illiquid assets been held now); also, if the prices of non-monetary assets do fall in the near future, the same speculator can then use the money to buy such assets more cheaply, in the prospect of holding them for a while and selling them at a profit later on, if and when their prices rise.

Consider an irredeemable gilt-edged bond issued in year zero, a time when the rate of interest is 10 per cent. If, as will be assumed, the face value of the bond is £100, competition in the market will ensure that the coupon on the bond will be £10 per annum. (By irredeemable we mean that the bond has no redemption date — the coupon will be paid forever. By gilt-edged we mean that there is no perceived risk of repudiation of the fixed annual coupon payments.) The bearer of such a bond is entitled to receive a *fixed* sum of £10 every year the bond is held. If the market rate of interest remains 10 per cent — if new lenders continue to receive £10 per annum for every £100 they lend — then the market price of the bond, indefinitely, will be £100. But if the market rate of interest rises to

20 per cent in year one (after the year zero bond has been issued), the market price of a year zero bond will fall. Borrowers in year one are now offering to pay a fixed sum of £20 per annum for every £100 they borrow. The price of the year zero bond will therefore fall to £50. This is because that bond gives an income of only £10 per annum, whereas a year one bond gives an income of £20 per annum. People will be willing to pay only £50 for the year zero bond (although it has a face value of £100) because it requires two of those bonds to provide the same income (£20) as a year one bond. Only then will they be obtaining a return of 20 per cent on new bonds and on any old year zero bonds which they may buy from, say, the original lenders. The converse would prevail if the interest rate fell to 5 per cent in year one. Borrowers would then have to pay only £5 per annum on every £100 they borrow. Someone with £200 to lend in year one could then earn a fixed return of £10 per annum by allocating the entire £200 to new (year one) bonds. But a year zero bond would also provide £10 per annum. Therefore the market price of the year zero bond would be bid up to £200 in year one.

In the above examples it was assumed that the bonds were irredeemable. That was to avoid complications which would arise in connection with the number of years remaining before redemption date. If the bonds in fact had fixed redemption dates, *qualitatively* the same kind of conclusions would have emerged. For example, consider a 20-year bond with face value £100 issued 19 years ago and providing an annual coupon of £10; thus, the bond has only one year remaining until maturity (redemption), at which date the principal of £100 will be paid to the bearer. With only one year remaining until maturity (and recall that the fixed coupon will be paid for that year), if the current rate of interest were to double, from say 10 per cent to 20 per cent, then the price of such a bond would indeed tend to fall from its existing level, but certainly not by as much as 50 per cent. (For this example, the price of the old bond with one year to redemption, P_b, is found as follows: The old £100 bond pays the bearer £10 in its final year. A new £100 bond would pay the bearer £20 in that year. Hence market forces would bid down the price of the old bond until its yield to a buyer is 20 per cent. P_b is calculated as £100 multiplied by the factor 110/120; hence P_b = £91.67.)

Thus, *the prices of bonds move inversely to the rate of interest*. In like manner, the price of any asset which yields income over time tends to move inversely to the rate of interest. For example, suppose initially that the current rate of interest is x per cent, and that the market valuation of, say, a firm (its plant and equipment, goodwill, etc.) is £y. This valuation of £y is revealed by the stock market quotation for the sum of all the shares in the firm: people in aggregate are willing to pay £y for the firm in anticipation of the future flow of profits of the firm. If the rate of interest rises to 2x per cent, the market will no longer be willing to pay £y for the firm because, *at that price*, the anticipated flow of future profits (and hence dividends) will seem unattractive *relative* to what could be earned at the new rate of interest of 2x per cent: indeed, other things being equal, the total stock market valuation of the firm will fall in the direction of £.5y. This reflects the fact that market forces tend to equate the expected percentage yields on the current cost of all assets traded. If one asset has a higher expected percentage yield on its current cost than other assets, the market would bid up the price of that asset (at least relative to the prices of other assets), thereby causing its percentage yield on current cost to fall; at the same time the prices of the lower-yielding assets would be bid downward. In this manner, the forces of supply and demand would tend to equate the expected percentage yields on the current costs of the two types of asset.

It is the immediately foregoing considerations which give rise to the speculative demand for money. People will desire to hold more of their wealth in perfectly liquid form rather than in other assets (bonds, equities, real estate, etc.) if they expect the rate of interest to rise. Conversely, if people feel that the future interest rate will be lower than now, they will attempt to hold more of their wealth in the form of bonds and other imperfectly liquid assets, rather than in the form of money. If they are correct in their anticipation, they will then be able to sell their bonds, etc., at a higher price.

At any point in time people have notions of "normal" levels or zones of the rate of interest. If the interest rate is low — say 2 per cent — more people than would otherwise be the case will feel that it is unlikely to fall any lower and will probably soon rise. This implies that they expect bond prices to fall. They will sell bonds and hold money. Therefore, at low interest rates the speculative demand for money is high. If the present interest rate is high, say 30 per cent, more people than otherwise will feel that a higher interest rate is unlikely, and that a fall in the interest rate (a rise in bond prices) is probable. At high interest rates more people therefore attempt to hold bonds rather than money. The speculative demand for money is low at high interest rates and high at low interest rates: it is a decreasing function of the rate of interest. The higher the current interest rate, the greater the perceived probability of a rise in bond prices and windfall gains. The lower the current interest rate, the greater the perceived probability of a fall in bond prices and windfall losses.

Note that it is not the present interest rate per se which determines the speculative demand for money; it is the relationship between the present and expected future rates that matters.

The Equilibrium Rate of Interest

The equilibrium rate of interest is determined by supply and demand. In regard to the supply of money, it will be assumed that it is fixed by the monetary authority. (We will later see how this is done, as well as some limitations on the effective powers of the monetary authority in an open economy.) The money supply curve is SS in Figure 1. It has already been shown that the overall demand for money consists of: (a) a transactions demand, which depends mainly on the level of national income; (b) a precautionary demand, which is also a function of the level of national income; (3) a speculative demand, which is a decreasing function of the rate of interest.

Figure 1

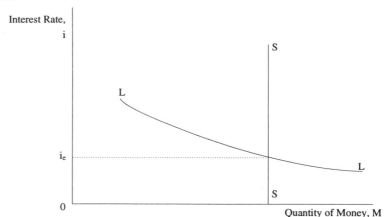

Let the community's demand for money at a given level of national income and at different interest rates be LL in Figure 1. This is often called the community's *liquidity preference curve*, reflecting its preference for money over other assets at different interest rates.

With the supply and demand curves for money like SS and LL in Figure 1, i_e is the equilibrium interest rate. If the authorities increased the money supply, SS would shift to the right, leading to a lower interest rate. Planned private investment would increase. If we start with the system in equilibrium below full employment, the initial impact on income of the increased investment demand would be compounded by a multiplier effect. In this manner, expansionary monetary policies can be implemented in order to boost the economy toward full employment output. (Note, however, that if the demand for money were infinitely elastic — if the liquidity preference curve were perfectly flat — as it probably would be at a very low interest rate, then an increase in the money supply would cause no change in the equilibrium rate of interest. This situation is known as "the liquidity trap". In such a case the rate of interest is so low that it cannot be forced any lower, in which case further expansionary monetary measures will be of little avail in getting the economy closer to full employment).

If (given the supply of money) the demand for money increases, the liquidity preference curve will shift to the right, implying that at any interest rate, the public wishes to hold more money than previously. The interest rate will be bid upward in consequence. Thus, at a given price level (recall that a more or less constant price level has been assumed up to now), if government expenditure is expanded, equilibrium national income will tend to increase, leading to an increase in the demand for money to facilitate a higher level of transactions and, on that count, the interest rate would rise. The rise in the interest rate would choke off some investment demand; though if the economy had initially been in equilibrium below full employment, one would expect the increase in government expenditure to exceed the reduction in investment demand induced by the rise in the interest rate, so there would be a net increase in income. Detailed treatment of the issues raised in the present paragraph will be deferred, mainly to Part Four.

In this paragraph the assumption that the price level is constant will momentarily be relaxed. People demand money under the transactions motive to facilitate the *money value* of their transactions; the demand for money is a function of the level of *money* income rather than *real* income. So, if the price level is increasing over time, the community's demand for money curve would tend to be shifting to the right over time. If the money supply is held constant, the equilibrium rate of interest would then be increasing. By choking off some investment demand (and perhaps some consumption demand also), such increases in the rate of interest would automatically reduce aggregate demand. Further consideration of the complications which have just been raised in this paragraph will be deferred until Chapter 13, when the process of inflation will be the subject for investigation.

Interest Rates

The reader is reminded that so far we have referred to "the" rate of interest as though there were only one rate of interest. There are in reality many interest rates. The rate of interest on a security the redemption date of which is far into the future will normally be higher than that on short-term loans. The longer the life of a security, the greater the sacrifice of liquidity, and the higher the price that usually must be paid in the form of interest. A further determinant of the levels of actual interest rates is the risk associated with the securities in question. A lender will demand a higher interest rate from a borrower whose character or financial standing is doubtful than from one of repute and sound financial standing. Although some reference will also be made to what will be called Bank Rate (described below), the central rate of interest to which we generally refer in the present and immediate subsequent chapters is the long-term rate on gilt-edged government securities with no redemption date. Because all interest rates tend to move in phase, this central rate serves as a proxy for the structure of interest rates. For simplicity we ignore considerations of risk (that the borrower might repudiate either the original debt or the interest payments) and we also for the most part ignore distinctions between short-term and long-term securities. Actual rates of interest will diverge from the long-term gilt-edged rate, depending on the degree of risk associated with the securities in question, and on the time which must elapse to maturity (i.e. to redemption date).

THE SUPPLY OF MONEY: DETAILS

Money has already been defined as anything that is generally accepted as a medium of exchange. In a modern economy it is of two general forms:

(1) Cash or currency or legal tender. (Cash or currency is not absolutely identical to legal tender but the distinction is of minor importance and may be ignored). In most economies cash is a liability of an institution — normally owned by the state — called the central bank.

(2) Deposits at commercial banks (those banks with whom the public normally deals). These deposits are money because transfers of bank deposits (by means of cheques) are generally accepted as means of exchange.

Central Banking

In many respects a central bank has a relationship with the commercial banks similar to that which the commercial banks have with the non-bank public. Although the precise role of central banks differs from country to country, the "classical" (or archetypal) central bank has the following functions:

(1) It is the bankers' bank. Thus it accepts deposits — and for reasons which will be considered later, it may even insist on (special) deposits — from the commercial banks.

(2) It is banker to the government, i.e. it holds the government account.

(3) It is lender of last resort. This technical function means that, upon presentation of appropriate securities by the commercial banks, the central bank is normally willing to lend to those banks, but only at a price (interest rate) determined by the central bank itself. If the central bank wishes to reduce the money supply, it will discourage the commercial banks from borrowing from it; it may therefore raise the interest rate at which it is willing to lend to them. In different countries and at different times, that rate of interest has been called Bank Rate, the central bank's Minimum Lending Rate, Discount Rate, Rediscount Rate, the Lombard Rate (in Germany) or the Short-Term Credit Facility (as in Ireland at present). In what follows the term *Bank Rate* will be used to describe all of the above — the interest rate at which the central bank is willing to lend to the commercial banks. This rate of interest may be punitive in the sense that, if the commercial banks are forced to borrow from the central bank at the rate of interest charged by the central bank, they may then incur losses. Any commercial bank must hold an appropriate level of liquid reserves in order to be able to meet the day-to-day demands of its depositors. If an individual commercial bank finds itself running short of liquid reserves, it may first try to borrow such reserves from other commercial banks. But if those banks (and other financial institutions apart from the central bank) are also short of reserves, the initial bank in question would seek to borrow from the central bank, but only "as a last resort"; hence the nomenclature "lender of last resort".

(4) The central bank is the issuer of currency. The way in which it does so is simple: it buys securities and gives its own liability — cash (or equivalently, a cheque drawn against itself, which can be converted into cash) — in exchange. In some countries the central bank may buy bonds directly from government, thereby financing government expenditure directly through the printing press. Alternatively, the central bank may buy bonds from commercial banks, insurance companies or other institutions.

(5) A central bank is usually charged by law to pursue monetary policies consistent with the perceived overall interests of the economy, in particular, the maintenance of currency stability.

Commercial Banking and Deposit Money

As already indicated, there are two kinds of money in modern economies: cash or currency, and deposit money (commercial bank deposits). It has been seen that currency, a liability of the central bank, can be created by central bank purchases of securities. Most of the central bank's liabilities are in fact reserves to the commercial banks. It is on the basis of such reserves that the commercial banks, along with the non-bank public, create deposit money.

Deposit money (in commercial banks) is a liability of the commercial banks. How is deposit money created? In what follows we can refer interchangeably to currency or cash held in commercial banks, and deposits made by the commercial banks held at the central bank. (Recall that the central bank is banker to the commercial banks.) That is because both are liabilities of the central bank, and either one can normally be converted into the other upon request by a commercial bank. Both cash on-hand and their deposits at the central bank are reserves to the commercial banks.

Suppose that the money supply is initially given, that the commercial banks are initially holding no more reserves than they need to hold, and that next, an additional £100 is injected into the system. Perhaps someone has sold a bond to the central bank for £100, and the central bank may have paid the seller £100 in cash (or equivalently the central bank may have paid the seller by means of a cheque drawn on itself; this cheque could be "cashed in" at the central bank, or, if it is deposited in a commercial bank, the commercial bank may deposit it in its account at the central bank — recall that such commercial bank deposits at the central bank are equivalent to cash held by the commercial banks).

Assume that the original recipient of the £100 has an account with commercial bank A, and that all of it is placed on deposit. The initial impact on the balance sheet of bank A is as follows:

Bank A

Assets		Liabilities	
Cash	+ £100	Deposits	+ £100

It is reasonable to assume that bank A is in business to maximise profits. It does so by lending, thereby earning interest. But it will not lend *all* of the increments in its assets: it will hold some of the additional cash as reserves — in the form of cash or as deposits at the central bank — to secure against the day-to-day contingency of withdrawals by depositors. But more importantly (for reasons to be understood shortly) the central bank is likely to require commercial banks to hold a specific minimum ratio between their reserves (their holdings of cash plus their deposits at the central bank) and their deposit liabilities. Suppose that this ratio is 20 per cent. Assuming that bank A can find a credit-worthy borrower, it will lend £80 of the increase in its assets, holding only £20 of the increment in assets as reserves. The change in its balance sheet then becomes:

Bank A

Assets		Liabilities	
Reserves	+ £20	Deposits	+ £100
Loans	+ £80		

The person who borrowed £80 from bank A presumably did not do so to hold it in idle cash balances — for there is interest being paid on it. Suppose £80 was borrowed to buy clothing. The retailer of clothing has an account with bank B. Assume that the retailer deposits the whole £80. So the liabilities of bank B increase by £80. However, given the assumed required ratio of 20 per cent between reserves and deposits, bank B will hold £16 of the increase in its assets as reserves, and the remaining £64 as loans and advances. The change in bank B's balance sheet is then as follows:

Bank B

Assets		Liabilities	
Reserves	+ £16	Deposits	+ £80
Loans	+ £64		

Presumably the £64 borrowed was used to buy some commodity, say tyres. The tyre dealer banks with bank C and deposits the whole £64. In accordance with the 20 per cent reserve ratio requirement, bank C puts £12.80 in reserve and increases its lending by £51.20. The change in the balance sheet of bank C is:

Bank C

Assets		Liabilities	
Reserves	+ £12.80	Deposits	+ £64
Loans	+ £51.20		

Following the preceding reasoning, the £51.20 in loans from bank C will become deposits in some other bank, say bank D. which, in turn, will generate further loans and hence further deposits in other banks. The process of credit creation will continue by way of successive rounds, each increment in deposits being progressively smaller.

Given the implicit (stated below) and explicit assumptions, it is easy to show that the *ultimate* effect of the original injection of £100 in cash will be an increase in the money supply of £500. Thus, letting ΔM denote the change in the money supply,

$$\Delta M = 100 + 80 + 64 + 51.2 + \ldots, \text{ or}$$

$$(1)\ \Delta M = [1 + (4/5) + (4/5)^2 + (4/5)^3 + \ldots](100)$$

From earlier discussion in the context of national income multiplier theory (see equations (6) and (7) of Chapter 10) it should be recognised that (1) is the same as

$$(2)\ \Delta M = \{1/(1 - 4/5)\}(100) = \{1/(1/5)\}100 = 500$$

The infinite series (1) converges to 500. Hence an injection of £100 in cash into the economy will lead to an ultimate increase of £500 in the money supply. Similarly if the required reserve ratio were 50 per cent, or 1/2, an injection of £100 in cash into the system would lead to an increase in the money supply of only £200. In general, if there is an injection of £x in cash into the system, the ultimate increase in the money supply will be £(the reciprocal of the reserve ratio)(x). More formally, if 1/r denotes the reserve ratio, and if x denotes an injection of cash into the system, then

$$(3)\ \Delta M = \{1/(1/r)\}x = rx$$

The multiple expansion of deposit money has just been outlined for a closed economy in which there are several commercial banks. In this context the number of commercial banks is irrelevant. Thus, consider a closed economy in which there is a single commercial bank — a monopoly commercial bank with many branches, and which therefore represents the consolidated commercial banking system. Suppose there is an increase in cash deposits of £100 and that the reserve ratio is 20 per cent. The money supply would then be increased by a further £400 as follows: in a relatively short period the bank could buy securities (i.e. lend) to the extent of £400 by writing cheques drawn on itself, knowing that the ultimate recipients of such cheques would deposit them with itself, the only commercial bank.

Two Qualifications

Some qualifications need to be added to the foregoing exposition of the multiple expansion of deposit money:

(1) It was assumed, when there was an injection into the system of £x in cash, that there was no permanent leakage of cash into hand-to-hand circulation. To the extent to which such leakages do in practice occur, commercial bank reserves would increase by an amount less than £x, and

therefore the ultimate increase in the money supply would be less than that indicated by equation (3).

(2) It was assumed that commercial banks kept no excess reserves. Thus, it was assumed that if commercial banks were required by law to hold a ratio of at least 20 per cent between their reserves and their deposit liabilities, they would hold that ratio exactly. But commercial banks might in fact find it in their interest to hold excess reserves, mainly because they might not be able to find enough credit-worthy borrowers. To the extent to which they do hold excess reserves, an injection to the system of £x would lead to a smaller increase in the money supply than is suggested by equation (3).

The discussion in the immediately preceding subsection pertained to changes in the money supply. However, it gives enough insight to see, *as an upper bound approximation*, that the total money supply is determined as:

$$(4) \quad M \cong r \text{ (Level of Central Bank Liabilities Outstanding)}$$

where $\cong$ denotes an upper bound approximation.

It is emphasised that (4) gives an upper bound estimate of the money supply: its actual level will be less than that predicted by (4). The actual money supply will fall short of that predicted by (4) to the extent to which some of the central bank liabilities outstanding stay in the hands of the non-bank public (implying that such balances are *not* part of commercial bank reserves) and to the extent to which the commercial banks hold excess reserves. However, (4) highlights the fact that the central bank influences the total money supply by varying the level of its own liabilities outstanding, and to the extent to which it can influence the actual (and not only the minimum) reserve ratio maintained by the commercial banks.

Further Qualification: Open Economy, Fixed Exchange Rates

Two key assumptions at the beginning of the present chapter were that the price level was constant and that the economy was closed. At this stage, and in the context of an *open* economy, it is appropriate to observe in passing that the exposition of the creation of money, as above, can be very misleading when applied to a small open economy which maintains fixed, or approximately fixed, exchange rates with its main trading partners. Because the question of exchange rate determination has not yet been addressed, the observations which immediately follow, and which pertain to a small open economy under approximately *fixed* exchange rates, will necessarily be brief.

Suppose that the central bank buys securities from the market, thereby increasing its liabilities by payment in cash (or equivalently, by issuing a cheque drawn against itself, which can be converted into cash). The reserves of the commercial banks would increase in consequence. Suppose that those banks, in their quest for increased profits, then begin to expand loans and deposits in the manner already indicated. Following the earlier analysis of the supply of and the demand for money, an effect of this, in a closed economy, would be a reduction in the rate of interest. However, let the country in question, called Home, be economically small relative to its main trading partners, called Abroad. Also, let the economy of Home be relatively open in the sense that there are few restrictions on the mobility of ordinary goods and services, or on movement of financial assets, across its frontiers to or from Abroad. Finally, suppose that the exchange rate between Home and Abroad is fixed, and that it is expected to stay fixed. (For most purposes this would be equivalent to assuming that Home and Abroad have a common currency.) Recalling that the Irish economy is relatively small, these assumptions characterise key features of the Irish economy *vis-à-vis* the UK in the 1960s and 1970s; they also capture some features of the Irish economy *vis-à-vis* the Federal Republic of Germany in the period 1979–93.

Under the circumstances specified, Home would be a price-taker rather than a price-maker in the market for financial assets. Its equilibrium rate of interest — the price of money — would tend to be the same as that Abroad, with the causation running from Abroad to Home rather than vice versa.

Suppose (under a fixed exchange rate with Abroad) that the rate of interest in Home is initially in line with that of Abroad. For ease of exposition, and because policy in Home does not significantly affect financial markets in Abroad, the rate of interest in Abroad will be taken as constant. Next, consider what would happen if Home's central bank tried to increase the money supply by, say, buying £x of domestic securities from a commercial bank. Considered in isolation, an immediate effect would be an increase of £x in the reserves of the commercial banks, which in turn would tend to expand credit along the lines already outlined. However, another immediate effect would be downward pressure on the rate of interest in Home. But given the fixed exchange rate with Abroad, the ensuing interest rate differential between Home and Abroad would simultaneously lead to capital outflows from Home to Abroad in order to avail of the higher interest rate obtainable there. (The reader should note that in contrast to our earlier usage of the word capital, when referring to capital outflows and inflows, and unless indicated to the contrary, the reference will always be to movement of financial assets.) The existence of capital outflows means that residents of Home are (in an ultimate sense) going to the central bank and buying foreign currency, in order to lend abroad, in exchange for domestic money; hence, for as long as the capital outflows continue, the domestic money supply *automatically* contracts. This automatic contraction of the money supply does not in itself reflect any new discretionary policy of the central bank; rather, it merely reflects the obligation of the central bank to exchange domestic money for foreign money, at a fixed rate, assuming that the Home currency is indeed convertible. The contraction in the Home money supply means that the rate of interest in Home will rise. The capital outflows will continue — and hence the Home money supply will continue to contract — so long as the Home interest rate is less than that in Abroad which, by assumption, has stayed constant. Hence, assuming that the fixed exchange rate is maintained, the expansionary monetary policy in Home has no *permanent* effect on the Home rate of interest, which falls in disequilibrium only, ultimately returning to its initial level, i.e. equal to the level of the rate of interest in Abroad. Nor is there any *permanent* increase in the Home money supply: because the price of money will not have changed (comparing the initial equilibrium with the new equilibrium), the quantity of money would not have changed. Thus, starting from an initial equilibrium, the prediction that if the central bank injects an additional £x of its own liabilities into the system, then $\Delta M \cong rx$, will be false; indeed, it has just been shown that $\Delta M = 0$ at the new equilibrium. What will really have happened is that the central bank will have bought £x of domestic securities in exchange for £x of its own liabilities (Home cash), but this £x in cash will have been sold to the central bank by Home residents in exchange for the currency of Abroad. Ultimately (i.e. comparing the initial equilibrium with the new equilibrium) there would be no change in the level of liabilities of the central bank; therefore, there would have been no change in the level of its assets. However, the *composition* of its assets would have changed: the central bank ends up holding £x more domestic assets and £x fewer foreign assets (foreign currency). Ultimately, the apparently expansionary monetary policy is not in fact expansionary; rather, it is merely tantamount to the central bank swapping foreign assets for domestic assets.

THE INSTRUMENTS OF MONETARY POLICY

In relatively closed economies (and, as will be seen at a later stage, in open economies in which the exchange rate is not approximately fixed) central banks affect the money supply mainly (a) by directly influencing the level of commercial bank reserves (i.e. commercial bank holdings of currency, plus commercial bank deposits with the central bank), and (b) by changing the required minimum ratio of commercial bank reserves to their deposit liabilities. The principal policy instruments available to central banks in this context are:

(1) *Open Market Operations*: By this we mean purchases or sales of securities by the central bank on the open market. For example, suppose that the central bank wishes to increase the money supply. It may do so by buying securities on the open market (e.g. from insurance companies or from commercial banks or from the general public). It pays for these securities in cash (or equivalently, by cheques drawn on itself). Through direct or indirect processes, the reserves of the commercial banks will increase: they will end up holding more currency or (equivalently in the present context) their deposits at the central bank will increase. This increase in commercial bank reserves will lead to multiple expansion of deposits in the manner already indicated. If the central bank sought to reduce the money supply, it could do so by selling securities. It would be paid in cash, or by cheques drawn on the commercial banks, or by direct commercial bank drawings on their deposits at the central bank. In either case the reserves of the commercial banks (their holdings of currency or their deposits at the central bank) would fall, and a multiple contraction of deposits would occur.

(2) *Changes in Bank Rate*: If the central bank wishes to reduce the money supply, it may raise the rate of interest at which it is willing to lend reserves to the commercial banks. This will discourage those banks from borrowing from the central bank, and will therefore tend to curtail growth in the money supply. If it wishes to expand the money supply, it will lower the rate of interest at which it is willing to lend to the commercial banks, thereby encouraging those banks to borrow reserves and hence to create more deposit money.

Note that if a central bank wishes to change the money supply it will normally manipulate instruments (1) and (2) *simultaneously*. Suppose that the central bank engages in open market sales of securities with a view to contracting the money supply. On that count the commercial banks will experience reduction in reserves, and will have to cut back their loans (and hence their deposits). However, if the interest rate at which the central bank is willing to lend to the commercial banks is relatively low, those banks might have incentive to borrow reserves from the central bank at the low interest rate, thereby generating the resources by which they could lend to their customers at a higher interest rate. In that case, the loss of reserves generated by the open market sales could be offset by an increase in the reserves due to commercial bank borrowing from the central bank. To prevent this happening — to make the open market sales effective — the central bank would also raise the interest rate at which it is willing to lend to the commercial banks.

(3) *Changes in the Minimum Reserve Ratio*: Suppose that the commercial banks have £x in reserves, and that the minimum reserve ratio, as stipulated by the central bank, is 20 per cent. Assuming that the commercial banks can find a sufficient number of credit-worthy borrowers, the amount of deposit money, from equations (3) or (4), will approximate £5x (as an upper bound quantity). If the central bank seeks reduction in the money supply, it can raise the required minimum reserve ratio to, say, 25 per cent. The total amount of deposit money would then approximate £4x.

In order to comply with the new higher reserve ratio, the commercial banks would have to call in loans or sell securities. They could also turn down applications for new loans. If, starting from a position in which the minimum reserve ratio was 20 per cent, the reserve ratio were increased to 25 per cent, the commercial banks might have to unload large quantities of securities on the market (in exchange for cash), thereby depressing security prices. This could force the commercial banks into substantial losses. For this reason, if the reserve ratio is raised, the commercial banks may be given ample prior notice. They could then gradually adjust toward a higher reserve ratio by not issuing new loans after loans are paid off, by not buying new bonds after other bonds in their portfolios have been redeemed at redemption date, etc. The case of an increase in the minimum reserve ratio has just been considered. If the central bank seeks to expand the money supply, it might reduce the required minimum reserve ratio.

(4) *Special Deposits*: It has earlier been noted that one of the usual functions of a central bank is that it acts as banker to the commercial banks, and in that capacity it accepts deposits from the commercial banks. It was also observed that such deposits are part of the reserves of the commercial banks. However, the central bank might insist that the commercial banks place special deposits at the central bank. (Central banks usually have the legal power to insist that such deposits be placed with them.) These deposits would be "special" in the sense that the commercial banks would not be permitted to reckon them as part of their reserves. A call for special deposits would therefore be tantamount to a reduction in the effective level of commercial bank reserves, and as such it would tend to induce multiple contraction of commercial bank loans to the public and hence contraction of commercial bank deposits from the

public. Similarly, if the central bank wants to expand the money supply, it may terminate any requirement for special deposits which had earlier been in force: this would tend to induce multiple expansion of the money supply along the lines already outlined.

(5) *Moral Suasion*: The central bank might make formal requests to the commercial banks, urging them to adhere to the central bank's guidelines in regard to monetary policy. Thus, the central bank might request — rather than demand — that the commercial banks maintain a specific minimum reserve ratio. Or it might seek to influence the structure of credit by urging the commercial banks to favour investors rather than consumers in their lending policies. Note that experience in Ireland and elsewhere suggests that moral suasion tends to be relatively ineffective unless the central bank is provided with statutory powers to implement punitive measures (such as an increase in the minimum reserve ratio) to which it could resort if suasion were ignored.

The reader should now understand how central banks in closed economies (or, as will become apparent at a later stage, in open economies under floating exchange rates) could change the money supply, thereby leading to changes in the cost and availability of credit. In turn, changes in the cost and availability of credit lead to shifts in the aggregate demand function. If we start with the economy in equilibrium below full employment, the effect on real income of such a shift will be compounded along the lines indicated by national income multiplier analysis. Thus, monetary instruments, fiscal instruments, or both, may be manipulated to drive the economy towards full employment.

It is emphasised in closing that the present chapter has merely outlined "the bare essentials" of monetary economics, necessary for an understanding of the chapters which immediately follow. The chapter has provided none of the complex details of money and banking in Ireland. These will be provided later by Martin Kenneally in Chapters 21 and 22.

CHAPTER 13

INFLATION: AN INCOMPLETE ANALYSIS

The assumption that the price level remains more or less constant will now be relaxed. By inflation, economists mean sustained — as opposed to once-and-for-all — increases in the price level. Price deflation is simply inflation with a negative sign — sustained decreases in the price level. Because inflation (as the word will be used below) is fundamentally a *dynamic* process, it tends to generate its own momentum: an experience of inflation over several years tends to generate expectations of further inflation. As will later be seen, the potentially adverse consequences of such expectations may then induce policies which in the outturn confirm those expectations. If those who expect inflation are correct in their anticipation of the policy responses to their actions based on those expectations, then inflationary expectations tend to be self-fulfilling prophesies. But if anticipations of the policy responses turn out to be wrong, then the consequences for output and employment may be adverse in the short-run. That is because once inflationary expectations have gained momentum through the experience of inflation, the breaking of inflationary expectations may require quite drastic action by government and the monetary authorities. By way of contrast, we will *not* regard a once-and-for-all increase (decrease) in the price level as inflation (deflation). This procedure is both convenient for exposition and is reasonable, especially in view of the likelihood that a once-and-for-all change in the price level will not have been generally anticipated.

The rate of inflation over any period is measured as the rate of increase in the price level, $\Delta P/P$, where P is an index of the price level at the beginning of the period and ΔP denotes the change in the price level during the period in question. *The inflation rate is therefore a proportional rate of change*; the percentage rate of inflation is merely that proportional rate of change, $\Delta P/P$, multiplied by 100. The following are among the principal effects of inflation:

(1) Erosion in the purchasing power of individuals on relatively fixed money incomes.

(2) Redistribution of real disposable income away from individuals to government. This can occur, for example, when personal allowances in

the tax code are not adjusted in line with inflation.

(3) Redistribution of real wealth away from lenders in favour of borrowers. This was occurring during Ireland's high inflation years in the 1970s (when we maintained a fixed exchange rate with the UK and the UK itself had high inflation). Redistribution of real wealth was occurring largely because *real* interest rates were in some years negative (i.e. nominal rates of interest were less than the rate of inflation). Thus, lenders obtained negative real returns. Because (nominal) interest rates were often lower than the rate of inflation, borrowers, when they repaid loans, were repaying less in real terms than the sum originally borrowed. The treatment of interest payments in the tax code (i.e. tax concessions on mortgage interest payments) further improved the position of borrowers.

(4) Inflation poses problems in accountancy. Indeed it is not always clear what the accountancy term "profit" means in an inflationary environment.

Note that it was *not* stated in the foregoing that inflation inevitably causes an immediate increase in aggregate unemployment. As will be seen later, if wages increase less rapidly than the rate of inflation, employment will almost certainly increase in the short-run. However, if wages later increase faster than the rate of inflation ("catching up" on past inflation and in anticipation of future inflation), then (at a given level of labour productivity) employment will tend to contract in the longer run.

THE DEMAND FOR MONEY AND INFLATION

Throughout most of the macroeconomic analysis as developed up to the present chapter, there was no need to use separate notation for *nominal* (or *money*) income and real income: the assumption that the price level stayed constant meant that the two magnitudes were the same. However, in the immediately preceding chapter it was briefly noted — but only in passing — that the transactions demand for money depends on nominal income rather than on real income. Allowing now for the possibility that the price level is variable, nominal income will be denoted by PY, where P (no longer held constant, in effect at a level of unity) denotes the price level and Y is real national income. The earlier analysis then suggests that if nominal income increases, so too will the transactions demand for money, while if the rate of interest increases, the opportunity cost of holding money will have increased and for that reason less money will be demanded. These considerations suggest, as a first approximation, that the demand for money function should be written as:

(1) $M = L(PY, i)$

The function (1) states that the demand for money, M, depends on PY and i. It was established earlier that $\Delta M/\Delta PY > 0$ and $\Delta M/\Delta i < 0$ — that the demand for money increases with nominal income but decreases as the rate of interest increases. Suppose now that the price level is steadily increasing over time, and think of i as some kind of average, or representative, *real* rate of return on all assets except money (on bonds, real estate, machinery, etc.). Note that we have just hinted toward a distinction between the real rate of interest and the nominal rate of interest. If there is no actual or expected inflation, then the real rate of interest is the same as the nominal rate of interest. However, if the rate of inflation is positive, then the real rate of interest (not observed directly) is simply the nominal rate of interest minus the rate of inflation. It must now be recognised that the function (1) is misspecified; it omits an important variable — the expected rate of inflation. In an inflationary environment there are two kinds of costs of holding wealth in the form of money:

(1) The loss of direct financial returns which could be earned by holding wealth in the form of bonds, machinery and equipment, etc.

(2) Loss in purchasing power of money over time: if people held their wealth in antiques, real estate or machinery they would not expect to experience such losses, for those assets would generally increase in nominal value in line with inflation. The erosion in the purchasing power of money is represented by the rate of inflation, which will be denoted by $\dot{P}$. Then, given PY and the *real* rate of interest, i, the higher the rate of inflation, the higher the actual and expected cost of holding money, and hence the lower the demand for money. The demand for money function will therefore be written as

(2) $M = L(PY, i, \dot{P})$

where $\Delta M/\Delta PY > 0$, $\Delta M/\Delta i < 0$ and $\Delta M/\Delta \dot{P} < 0$: the demand for money increases with nominal income but decreases if either type of cost of holding wealth in the form of money — the real rate of interest or the rate of inflation — increases.

A little more will be assumed in regard to the functional form of equation (2): it will be assumed, so long as i and $\dot{P}$ stay unchanged, that the demand for money is *proportional* to the level of money national income, but that the factor of proportionality between M and PY changes if either i or $\dot{P}$ changes. Hence:

(3) $M = k(i, \dot{P})PY$

where k is some positive number indicating the factor of proportionality between M and PY, and where $\Delta k/\Delta i < 0$ and $\Delta k/\Delta \dot{P} < 0$: the number k, (and hence the demand for money M) falls if i or $\dot{P}$ increase. The variables in parentheses after k are entered purely to remind us that k itself depends on i and on $\dot{P}$.

The hypotheses embodied in equation (3) are very plausible *a priori*. The equation states that *given* the costs (i and $\dot{P}$) of holding wealth in the form of money, the demand for money is proportional to the level of nominal income (which is a proxy for the nominal level of transactions). However, the equation also states that the factor of proportionality k itself depends on the *costs* of holding wealth in monetary form: given the level of nominal income, if those costs increase, then k will fall, and hence the demand for money will fall. Empirical studies have been undertaken to test whether an equation like (3) closely explains the observed demand for money; it turns out that for developed economies it is a satisfactory working hypothesis for year-to-year data.

One final assumption before proceeding: it will be assumed that the money market is always in equilibrium or always adjusts toward equilibrium so quickly that it can plausibly be assumed to be in equilibrium, i.e. that the interest rate always quickly adjusts equating the supply of and demand for money. For developed countries at least, this seems to be quite a reasonable assumption. The symbol M will therefore be used to denote both the demand for money and the supply of money. Equation (3) can then be transformed into the condition under which the money market is in equilibrium, as in equation (3'):

(3') Money Supply, $M = k(i, \dot{P})PY$, Money Demand

Observe that like *any* theory, equation (3') is not *necessarily* true (as a close approximation to reality), and if it is true, it is not merely true by definition. As a theory, it is a proposed explanation of some aspect of the universe, and *any* proposed explanation of any aspect of reality is a theory. Of course, not all theories are correct or acceptable. But to hope to understand reality without resort to theory is to deceive oneself. A "good" or "acceptable" theory is one which adequately explains the key phenomena under investigation, and which also satisfies other criteria discussed in Chapter 2 above. (It follows that those who describe some explanation as "all right in theory but not in practice" are usually showing their ignorance of the role of theory in applied science.) For the purposes of the investigations which will shortly be addressed, (3') is regarded as an acceptable theory. (Anyone who disagrees is asked to provide a better theory.) By way of contrast, an *identity*, which is always true by definition, could not conceivably be refuted, but in itself it could explain nothing.

CORRELATION BETWEEN INFLATION AND MONETARY EXPANSION

It seems probable that most people suspect that money supply and inflation are related. Thus, in popular parlance, inflation is often described as "too much money chasing too few goods". However, there has been a great deal of confusion in regard to whatever relationships might exist between monetary expansion and inflation.

Before beginning the analysis, note the often cited and often misinterpreted *identity*:

$$(4) \; MV \equiv PY$$

where M denotes the money supply while V is the *income velocity of money* — the ratio of nominal national product to the money supply (i.e. income velocity V is the number of times that the stock of money is turned over during the year in financing the purchase of the annual flow of final output). So the left-hand side of (4) is the purchase of national product. Moving to the right-hand side of (4), P is an index of the price level during the year and Y denotes the level of real national output. So the right-hand side of (4) represents total sales of the economy's final output. As it stands, (4) is an identity because it is true by definition. Like any identity, it does not in itself explain anything; nor does it enable us to make any interesting predictions. It states that the value of total final purchases must be the same as the value of total final sales. But this is always true because of the two-sided character of any transaction. Alternatively, remembering that V is by definition PY/M, (4) states that $M(PY/M) \equiv PY$, or $PY \equiv PY$, a finding which is not very informative. Hence (4) does not enable us to make predictions in regard to the consequences of an increase in M. For example, it is consistent with an increase in M being offset by a decrease in V, leading to no change in P or in Y. In practice, popular commentators and others often do invoke the identity (4) in arguing that there must be some relationship between variation in M and variation in P. However, such reasoning — based on the identity alone — is entirely spurious and provides no explanation of anything.

A theory in applied science is a proposed explanation of some aspect of the world or universe around us, the validity of which could in principle be tested, and rejected if demonstrated as false; if it is true, it is not true by definition. Good or useful theories enable the analyst to make interesting contingent predictions. Recall equation (3) for the demand for money. This is *not* an identity; it is not true by definition. Rather, it is a testable hypothesis or theory. When subjected to empirical tests it is found to be broadly consistent with the world of observed experience: it is therefore accepted as a satisfactory hypothesis. Recall also that it was assumed above that the interest rate would always adjust quickly to keep the money market in equilibrium — to equate the supply of and the demand for money. If we accept these assumptions as reasonable working hypotheses, and substitute the right-hand side of equation (3) into the left-hand side of the identity (4), we get

(5) $\{k(i, \dot{P})PY\}V = PY$, which implies

(6) $V = 1/k(i, \dot{P})$

Equations (5) and (6) are *not* true by definition: they are theories because equation (3), upon which they depend, is a theory. Equations (5) and (6) imply

(7) $MV(i, \dot{P}) = PY$

where V is assumed to depend in a predictable manner on i and $\dot{P}$: it is to remind us of this dependence that we have entered the elements in parentheses after V in (7). The assumptions made in connection with (3) were that k moves in the *opposite* direction to changes in i and $\dot{P}$; then from (6), V — the reciprocal of k — moves in the *same* direction as changes in i and $\dot{P}$. Equation (7), along with the assumptions that $\Delta V/\Delta i > 0$ and $\Delta V/\Delta \dot{P} > 0$, constitute *the quantity theory of money*. Although it looks like the identity (4), equation (7) is not an identity, for the hypothesis that V depends in a stable manner on i and $\dot{P}$ is not something which is true by definition. Note that equation (6) implies that V in (7) will be constant so long as i and $\dot{P}$ remain constant. After decades of often confused debate, the quantity theory of money, as outlined above, is now broadly accepted by economists.

Note that as is suggested by the nomenclature, the quantity theory of money is not a theory of inflation: it is partly a theory about the demand for money but more particularly it is a theory about the determinants of the income velocity of money, V. However, it does convincingly suggest that inflation is inevitably a monetary phenomenon in the sense that monetary expansion is either a causal force or a permissive force underlying any steady rate of inflation. Thus, either (a) a particular inflationary process may be *caused* by monetary expansion, or (b) if the initiating force behind any particular inflation is not monetary expansion, then that inflation will not proceed indefinitely unless monetary expansion permits it to proceed. The importance of these observations is that regardless of what may have initially caused any particular inflationary process, that inflation can be halted if the authorities can and do prevent the money supply from increasing.

Consider any variable, say z, and suppose that z = uw, where u and w are themselves variables. In analytical work, by a rate of growth (decline) we mean a *proportional* rate of change. Using elementary algebra, it can be shown that the rate of growth of z, denoted $\dot{z}$, equals the rate of growth of u ($\dot{u}$) plus the rate of growth of w ($\dot{w}$): $\dot{z} = \dot{u} + \dot{w}$. Hence:

$$(8) \quad \dot{M} + \dot{V} = \dot{P} + \dot{Y}$$

where the dots denote rates of growth. Suppose that the rate of inflation $\dot{P}$ and the real rate of interest i are constant. The quantity theory of money then says that V will be constant (and hence $\dot{V} = 0$), and that then

$$(8') \quad \dot{M} = \dot{P} + \dot{Y}$$

Equation (8') suggests that growth in M will be *associated with* growth in PY. But it does not tell us anything about *causal forces*. For purposes of illustration, suppose that the economy stays at full employment and that the supply potential of the economy stays fixed; then $\dot{Y} = 0$. Under such circumstances, and given the maintained assumptions, equation (8') states that

$$(8'') \quad \dot{M} = \dot{P}.$$

Perhaps the causal mechanism in this correlation runs from the left-hand side to the right-hand of (8''). For example, in a closed economy $\dot{M} > 0$ might reflect central bank financing of the government sector which persistently leads to excess demand relative to the supply potential of the economy, and therefore causes inflation. But the causal mechanism could also run from the right-hand side to the left-hand side of (8''). For example, consider a small open economy which maintains a fixed exchange rate with the rest of the world, and suppose that the rest of the world has positive inflation at a constant rate. Then, as will be argued later in the present chapter, $\dot{P} > 0$ in the small home economy. Suppose that this inflation is also at a constant rate, that the real rate of interest is constant and that the small country has full employment throughout. Then $\dot{M} = \dot{P}$ in the small economy. However, in this case the monetary expansion in the home country would have been induced by the externally determined rate of inflation. The mechanisms through which this would have occurred will be clarified in a later chapter.

Among the most important conclusions implied by the quantity theory of money is that regardless of the ultimate causes of a particular inflationary process, inflation could not persist for very long unless the money supply were increased. From equation (8) it can be seen that if P is increasing at a constant rate (and — in order to keep our reasoning sharp — if the real rate of interest is constant) it must also be the case that M is increasing unless Y is steadily decreasing. (Recall, under the assumptions specified that $\dot{V} = 0$.) In sum, increases in the domestic money supply *may* be the ultimate causes of inflation (though it will later be shown that they *could not* be the ultimate causes of significant inflation in small open economies operating under fixed exchange rates with the rest of the world). On the other hand, if increases in the money supply are not the ultimate causes of a particular inflationary process, expansion in the home money supply must be a *permissive factor* in that inflation. Thus, regardless of the initiating causes, domestic inflation could not prevail for very long if the domestic money supply were held constant. That is *not* to say that all economies are actually *able* to control their money supplies: as will later be seen, small open economies operating under *fixed exchange rates* with larger trading partners may not be able to control their money supplies, and on that count, they may not be able to control their rates of inflation (for as long as they are unwilling to change their exchange rate relationships): their rates of inflation are overwhelmingly determined abroad.

INFLATION IN CLOSED ECONOMIES

Inflations are often labelled "demand-pull" and "cost push". These are the two theories of inflation most frequently found in elementary economics textbooks, at least until fairly recent years. Although they have *not* been the dominant causes of Irish inflation, those concepts will now be reviewed, briefly.

Demand-Pull

In its simplest form demand-pull inflation prevails when aggregate demand exceeds the supply potential of the economy. In Figure 1, Y_F denotes the supply potential of the economy (the full employment level of output). It can be seen that the maximum real output which the economy is capable of producing is Y_FA. However, aggregate demand exceeds this by the amount AB, called an *inflationary gap* (the excess of aggregate demand over full employment aggregate supply). The price level will therefore be pulled up.

The inflationary gap AB could be eliminated by *discretionary policies*. For example, contractionary monetary and fiscal policies could be implemented, causing a downward shift in the aggregate demand function to D'D'. However, it would *automatically* shift to D'D' if the money supply were held constant. This could be described as a *passive policy* — in a sense, a policy of "doing nothing". Perhaps surprisingly to some, such a policy of "doing nothing" would resolve the demand-pull inflation problem.

Figure 1

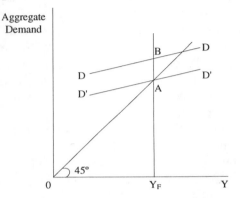

In order to show that the passive policy would cause the demand-pull inflation to "burn itself out", it will at first be supposed that both the inflation rate and the real rate of interest are constant; then, from the quantity theory of money, V will be constant. It will be argued that an assumption that M is constant is inconsistent with the assumption about the inflation rate. Thus, it will now be shown that if the money supply is constant, then the inflation rate will go to zero, and the reasoning will be along the lines of what mathematicians call "proof by contradiction".

With M and V both constant as assumed (implying that $\dot{M} = 0$ and $\dot{V} = 0$), equation (8) implies that $\dot{P} + \dot{Y} = 0$. With $\dot{P} > 0$, it must be the case that $\dot{Y} < 0$ — output must be falling, and output must continue to fall indefinitely. But (in the model as developed) falling output means falling demand. The inflationary gap must therefore be disappearing and it will ultimately become negative. The economy would then be subject to a problem of deficiency of aggregate demand rather than "excess" demand, relative to its supply potential. But this all means that the assumed cause of the inflation would no longer be applicable. Hence the maintained assumption that the inflation rate could stay at a positive constant level (because of excess demand) while the money supply stays constant leads to a contradiction.

An alternative approach to the central proposition at hand — that if $\dot{M} = 0$, then the demand-pull inflation will burn itself out — is along the following lines: if $\dot{P} > 0$ and if the economy is at full employment (as indeed it is in Figure 1) then the demand curve for money (the liquidity preference curve of the immediately preceding chapter) will be shifting upward because it is necessary to hold progressively more money to buy any volume of output, and if the money supply is held constant, then the nominal rate of interest must rise. At a given inflation rate this means that the *real* rate of interest will rise. A progressively rising real price of money, combined with a consistently falling real quantity of money to facilitate transactions, will mean that the investment function, and probably the consumption function also, will be shifting downward over time. Hence, the aggregate demand function will automatically be shifting downward over time — the demand-pull inflation would "burn itself out", provided, of course, that the money supply is not increased.

In the case just considered, the only way in which the aggregate demand function could remain at DD in Figure 1 would be if the money supply were increasing in line with inflation, thereby preventing the real money supply from falling; this could be described as a situation in which an increased money supply would be *accommodating* (or "validating" or simply "permitting") the excess demand. Thus, if increases in the money supply are not the ultimate or initiating causes of a demand-pull inflation (by, say, causing an upward shift in the investment function and thereby creating an inflationary gap), they must be regarded as permissive factors in the sense that if for any reason (such as an upward shift in the consumption function due to reductions in rates of income tax) an inflationary gap emerges, it could not prevail for very long unless increases in the money supply permitted it to do so.

In the simplified exposition just outlined it was assumed that "full employment" represented a well-defined level of output and that demand-pull inflation would not occur until after the economy had attained full employment. In reality that will not be the case, mainly because the economy generally will not attain full employment in all sectors simultaneously. Consider an economy expanding from a recession, aided, say, by successively larger doses of government expenditure over time. Ultimately, full capacity utilisation will be attained in certain sectors and/or regions. But this will generally be associated with a situation in which other sectors experience excess capacity. If demand is further expanded, inflationary gaps will emerge in those sectors which have already attained full capacity utilisation. Thus, demand-pull inflation will prevail before each sector has attained full capacity utilisation.

Furthermore, the demand-pull inflationary pressures will become more severe the closer the economy approaches full capacity utilisation in all sectors. These considerations suggest that some slack in the economy (some excess capacity in certain sectors, as well as some unemployment) will be necessary if demand-pull inflation is to be avoided entirely.

Cost-Push

Cost-push inflation is a process in which the factors of production *continuously* push up the prices of their services over time. For example, suppose that the economy is initially at full employment equilibrium, and that trade unions demand and obtain a higher money wage. If this cost-push pressure is to lead to an increase in the price level, it must be the case that firms react by raising output prices. But that would not in itself lead to (sustained) inflation; it would only yield a once-and-for-all increase in the price level. However, if trade unions demand and obtain a yet higher money wage (for example, to compensate for the increase in the price level) profit margins will fall unless employers raise their prices further. For cost-push inflation to proceed, it must be the case that trade unions again demand and obtain a yet higher money wage, leading to yet higher prices charged by employers, followed by further wage demands (and attainment of at least part of those demands), and so on in an upward spiral of wages and prices.

Continuous cost-push pressure by trade unions may be the initiating cause of an inflation, but if it is, it could not prevail for long unless increases in the money supply permit, or "validate", such inflationary forces. This is seen fairly readily by once again invoking the quantity theory of money. In order to stay clear in our reasoning, suppose that a wage-price spiral, initiated by (say) trade unions and the reactions of firms, leads to a constant rate of cost-push inflation at a constant real rate of interest. It is true that (starting from a zero inflation rate) V in equation (7) would initially increase; however, the quantity theory of money predicts that it would adjust to a new *constant* level. It will now be shown that the assumption that $\dot{P} > 0$ will ultimately be inconsistent with a constant level of the money supply: the manner in which it will be shown that the cost-push pressure would then burn itself out will be similar to that already applied for the case of demand-pull inflation. Under the maintained assumptions (M and V constant) equation (7) indicates that for P to increase steadily because of cost-push pressure on a sustained basis over time, it must be the case that the level of real national income Y is decreasing. Therefore the bargaining power of trade unions will be weakening, thereby mitigating the cost-push pressures. The longer the inflation prevails, the larger the contraction in output and the weaker the bargaining power of the unions. It can be concluded that cost-push pressures could not prevail for long unless increases in the money supply permitted them to prevail (that is, "validated" the cost-push pressures). If M is held constant, cost-push pressure by trade unions will lead to higher unemployment, progressively weakening that bargaining power. At some level of unemployment trade union bargaining power would be sufficiently weakened so as to eliminate the cost-push pressure.

Breaking Inflationary Expectations

The foregoing discussion gives some insights into understanding why, once inflationary expectations have gained momentum, it may be possible for the authorities to break those expectations only at a cost of an increase in the level of unemployment. For example, suppose that the money supply and the price level have been increasing for several years, at a constant or accelerating rate. Perhaps at first the trade unions, in their wage bargaining for any given year, sought compensation for the (unexpectedly) increased price level of the year in the immediate past. However, as the experience of monetary expansion and inflation endures, and following various rounds of wage bargaining, workers will start to feel themselves "cheated" by the inflation which actually occurs during periods of wage contracts. It is likely, in their wage bargaining, that they will start to seek compensation not only for past inflation, but for the *expected* rate of inflation in the immediate future. They may therefore push wages upward now in anticipation of the rise in prices which they expect to occur over, say, the next twelve months. This kind of possibility poses a dilemma for the authorities. If they do not increase the money supply (and thereby validate the cost-push pressure) then the price level will not increase by as much as anticipated when employers and unions were engaged in wage negotiation; however, *real* wages — nominal wages relative to prices — would have increased. Collapse in real profit margins is a likely counterpart. Firms would therefore respond by contracting output, and the unemployment rate would rise in consequence. Hence, if people in general come to expect inflation, it is likely that those expectations can be broken only at a cost in the form of reduced employment in the short-run at least (i.e. until the inflationary expectations have in fact been broken).

The considerations outlined in the above paragraph highlight the importance of *credibility* of statements by government in regard to commitments to control inflation. Despite repeated official statements of intent to control inflation, if there has been a steady or rising rate of inflation in the past, and if people have therefore come to discredit official statements that inflation will be controlled, then trade unions and others will tend to push wages upward to compensate for expected price inflation. Then, if the money supply is in fact held constant (i.e. if the authorities unexpectedly do act on their discredited promises that inflation will be controlled), real wages and unemployment will rise. However, if trade unions and others *do* believe a statement that the money supply will be held approximately constant, then it is likely that they will realise that if they do push wages upward, unemployment will ensue. In that case — a case where credibility is attached to official statements of intent — cost-push inflation could be reduced or eliminated at little or no cost in the form of increased unemployment.

Mixed Cost-Push and Demand-Pull

For the moment the assumption of a closed economy is maintained. Neither cost-push nor demand-pull inflation is likely to prevail in isolation; in a relatively closed economy most inflations are likely to be a combination of both. If there is a large margin of excess capacity, both demand-pull inflationary pressures and the bargaining power of trade unions will tend to be weak. But if an economy is near full capacity utilisation, demand-pull pressures will be stronger and trade unions will tend to act more aggressively in wage bargaining. But in either case, if the money supply is held constant, inflation could not prevail.

INFLATION IN SMALL OPEN ECONOMIES WITH FIXED EXCHANGE RATES

An open economy is one which depends heavily on foreign trade and which has a high degree of capital mobility (in the present context, meaning mobility of financial assets) across its frontiers. It will be assumed that there are relatively few institutional restrictions on the mobility of goods and financial assets between the small country and its main trading partners. If the economy is small, then the home country has little influence over the foreign-currency prices of the goods or assets in which it trades: in key respects the economy is akin to the perfectly competitive firm of microeconomics, which is a price-taker in a market in which there are very many buyers and suppliers. Ireland is a small open economy trading in a competitive international environment. From 1826 until March 1979, Ireland maintained a fixed change rate with the UK. Subject to certain qualifications, mainly in regard to taxes on expenditures and in regard to the composition of output, a consequence of this was that Ireland's rate of inflation was largely determined by the UK's inflation rate. Ireland's inflation was therefore largely beyond the control of the authorities in Ireland (for as long as those authorities had a commitment to a fixed exchange rate with the UK). Given the structure of taxation, domestic causes of high inflation can operate to a significant degree in a small open economy under a fixed exchange rate (to the extent to which they may in the long run operate significantly at all) only in those sectors of the economy which do not engage in international trade or which do not compete with imports.

It is an inescapable conclusion that if Ireland maintains a fixed exchange rate with *any* large diversified economy with which there is free trade, Ireland will tend in the long-run to approximate that country's rate of inflation; to deny this is to deny the existence of markets. This follows almost as readily as the conclusion that Kildare, which operates in a competitive environment with a fixed exchange rate *vis-à-vis* the rest of Ireland), must experience roughly the same underlying rate of inflation as the rest of Ireland. (The reader should be able to see what would happen if Kildare's inflation rate tended to differ from that of the rest of Ireland.)

The output of an open economy, such as Ireland, falls into two broad categories, *tradables* and *non-tradables*. As will be illustrated shortly, the distinction between these two categories is not necessarily watertight.

Tradables are goods produced domestically and which enter international trade or compete against imports on the domestic market. They consist of *exportables* and *importables*.

An *exportable* is a domestically produced good, some of which is exported. Because we in Ireland cannot have much effect on international prices — because of smallness we are close to being price-takers rather than price-makers on international markets — the rate of inflation for exportables, given a fixed exchange rate with a large diversified economy, is determined mainly abroad. Even exportables retained for home consumption would have their rates of inflation determined mainly abroad. That is because producers of such goods tend to withdraw supplies from the domestic market and sell abroad until the price obtainable at home is bid up toward that obtainable on the export market.

An *importable* is a domestically produced good which competes with imports on the home market. Given a fixed exchange rate with a large diversified trading partner country, and given rates of taxation on expenditure, the rate of inflation for importables in a small open economy would also tend in effect to be determined abroad. For example, consider the case of domestic production of basic clothing and footwear. Suppose that these are currently in the category called importables, because they compete at home with imports of similar manufactures. In terms of foreign currency, if the prices of foreign-produced clothing and footwear are steadily rising at x per cent per annum, then (under fixed exchange rates) the prices of home-produced basic clothing and footwear cannot persistently rise by significantly more than x per cent per annum: if there were any tendency for this to occur in the short-run, consumers at home would substitute foreign manufactures for their home-produced counterparts. On the other hand, if the rate of price increase of home-produced basic clothing and footwear were for long lower than that of competing imports, then (under fixed exchange rates) the small country's manufactures would become increasingly more attractive to consumers abroad; the underlying inflation rate for such goods would therefore tend to be bid up toward the inflation rate of the foreign-produced counterparts.

Non-tradables are domestically-produced goods which are neither exported nor compete with imports. To the extent that they use tradables as material inputs, their prices under a fixed exchange rate with a large trading partner country are directly subject to external influences. The extent to which the non-tradables sector can insulate itself from inflation (externally-determined under fixed exchange rates) in the tradables sector is further limited by the fact that the two sectors compete for factors of production such as labour and land. To some extent the prices of non-tradables may be subject to domestic demand-pull and cost-push pressures; an excess demand for non-tradables may pull up their prices, while domestic cost-push pressure may push them up. However, given the assumption about the exchange rate, such domestic causes of inflation are unlikely to be of significance for very long. The extent to which domestic causes of inflation can operate is very much limited, partly because a rise in the prices of non-tradables relative to tradables will reduce the demand for non-tradables, tending to increase unemployment in that sector. This in turn would mitigate the internal forces generating inflation. A further limitation on the extent to which inflation in the non-tradables sector can be insulated from that abroad (under fixed exchange rates) is clear when it is noted that the distinction between the tradables and non-tradables sectors is not watertight: whether a good is or is not in the non-tradable category itself depends on relative prices. Suppose, for example, because of transport costs, and at prevailing prices at home and abroad (under fixed exchange rates), that cement is currently in the non-tradables category. Suppose that the inflation rate for home-produced cement exceeds that abroad, and that a fixed exchange rate is maintained. Then, sooner or later, it will become profitable to import cement, at which stage the inflation rate for cement prices would in effect be determined abroad. (Home-produced cement would then be classified as an importable). Similar observations apply to the building and construction sector (usually classified among non-tradables): if building costs at home become sufficiently high, it will become profitable to import prefabricated structures.

The immediately foregoing paragraphs can be summarised, and

perhaps further clarified, by the following sequence of points:

(1) By demographic and economic criteria, Ireland is about the same size as Greater Manchester, England.

(2) Like Manchester, Ireland is fundamentally exposed to forces external to an economically small region's boundary: The sum of exports and imports of goods and services comes to almost 140 per cent of Ireland's net domestic product (measured at factor cost, i.e. exclusive of indirect taxes). Expressed in terms of foreign currency, the prices of that 140 per cent are overwhelmingly determined abroad.

(3) Define "the" exchange rate, e, as the price of a unit of foreign currency: it is the number of Irish pounds which must be paid for a unit of foreign currency, where the weights applicable in the definition of that unit reflect the structure of Ireland's trade. Then, subject to qualifications which are of fairly minor importance for present purposes, and as an approximation,

$$(9) \; P^{SOE} \cong eP^{F}$$

where $\cong$ denotes "approximately equal to", P^{SOE} is an index of the Irish price level (measured at factor cost), e is the exchange rate as already defined, and P^{F} is an appropriate index of the foreign price level. That a relationship like (9) must hold for goods and services actually traded follows from recognition that competition in markets does exist. That it must hold for goods which are not exported but which compete with imports on the home market, and that it must hold for goods only some of which are exported, is fairly obvious for the same reason. Also, as already indicated, even the non-tradables sector of the small economy cannot be insulated from outside forces — partly because it competes with the tradables sector for materials and for labour (to some extent) and because many of the non-tradables subsectors are potentially tradable. Brushing aside some qualifications (most of which are relevant in a short-run context only), the main points to note, because of openness and smallness of the Irish economy, are that:

(1) For any given P^{F} and e, Ireland's price level is largely determined by forces beyond the control of the domestic authorities.

(2) Unless they offset each other, changes in P^{F} or in e will tend to cause the Irish price level to change.

(3) If e is held constant, and if P^{F} is rising at, say x per cent per annum, then Ireland's underlying inflation rate will tend to be x per cent per annum; furthermore, because the small economy is close to being a price-

taker rather than a price-maker on international markets, the chain of causation runs from inflation abroad to inflation in Ireland, rather than vice versa.

Demand-Pull and Cost-Push Pressures under Fixed Exchange Rates

In the case of a small economy with a *fixed exchange rate* under free trade with any large diversified economy, domestic demand-pull and cost-push pressures are likely to have different effects on the tradables and the non-tradables sectors. It may be the case that such pressures, if sustained over time, will cause some inflation in the non-tradables sector. But any such domestic causes of inflation would be constrained by openness. However, domestic demand-pull and cost-push cannot cause much inflation in the tradables sector — for the prices of tradables are determined mainly outside the small open economy: even in the short-run, the demand for tradables produced in Ireland is rather price elastic.

If there is *cost-push wage pressure* in the tradables sector, and if, given output per employee, trade unions obtain higher money wage rates, an effect will be an increase in the share of value added (national income) accruing to labour, and a decrease in the share of value added accruing to profits, etc. Real wages will increase while real profits will decline. Because they are more akin to price-takers rather than dominant price-makers, employers in tradables will not normally be able to mark up their prices to an appreciable extent in order to compensate for wage increases. Because unit costs will have increased whilst output prices will not have increased proportionately, the principal effect of cost-push pressure will be on the level of employment (which will contract) rather than on the price level. (Note: This exposition of the effects of cost-push pressures has assumed that tax rates on the employment of labour stay constant, and that what is called the *terms* of international trade stays constant. Elaboration on these issues is deferred.)

Consider next domestic *excess demand (demand-pull) pressure*. This may, in the short run, bid up the prices of tradables, leading producers to post higher domestic prices for such goods. But the principal effect will be an increase in imports, combined, perhaps, with some fall in exports. Imports will rise because any rise in the price of importables relative to their foreign-produced counterparts will make the home-produced goods less attractive to domestic consumers, and also because it will tend to be the case that not all of the increased demand can be satisfied from domestic sources. There is also some possibility that exports will fall, as exporters temporarily divert supplies away from the export market in favour of domestic consumers. Thus the principal effect of an excess demand for tradables is on the balance of international payments on current account rather than on the rate of inflation. It is concluded that under a fixed exchange rate with a large country with which there is relatively free trade, excess domestic demand for tradables in a small open economy cannot be a major cause of inflation — by which we mean sustained increases in prices over time.

It follows that if Ireland maintains a fixed exchange rate with a large country with which there is free trade, Ireland cannot independently generate much inflation. Ireland cannot do so because (consideration of expenditure taxes aside) we can have little impact on the rate of change of prices of tradable goods on Irish or foreign markets. A very close matching of UK and Irish inflation rates — as measured by the consumer price index (CPI) in Ireland and by the retail price index (RPI) in the UK — in the decades immediately preceding 1979 (the year in which the Irish authorities abandoned their commitment to a rigidly fixed exchange rate with the UK) illustrates these propositions. Thus, like the UK, Ireland experienced mildly creeping inflation in the 1950s, significantly rising inflation in the 1960s, and a tendency toward accelerating inflation in the 1970s.

Very few (if any) economists would argue, under fixed exchange rates with a large diversified trading partner, that inflation rates in Ireland must be *exactly* the same as those in the larger partner country. In fact, although the inflation rates were indeed *approximately* the same, Ireland's measured inflation in the later part of the period just mentioned was slightly in excess of that in the UK. Analysis of the relevant data suggests that part of the increase in the Irish price level relative to that of the UK in the later part of the period was accounted for by an increase in expenditure (or indirect) taxes in Ireland. An important point in this context is that we export free of expenditure taxes, while imports to Ireland from the UK or other countries are subject to Irish expenditure taxes. Thus, an increase in the Irish consumer price index due to higher taxes on expenditure does not in itself affect the competitiveness of the Irish economy. Quite consistent with the maintenance of a fixed exchange rate, the fairly small divergence of the Irish inflation rate from that of the UK in the 1970s could have been accounted for by:

(1) Differences in the rates of taxation of expenditures.

(2) Possibly, differences in the method of calculating the CPI and the RPI.

(3) Differences in the *structure* of output or internal demand in the two countries. Consider two countries, A and B, which maintain fixed exchange rates with each other, and ignore expenditure taxes. Suppose

for illustration that they produce only two tradable goods, x and y, that there are no non-tradables, and that x accounts for 50 per cent of the output of A but for 90 per cent of the output of B. Finally, suppose that the price of x is increasing by 20 per cent annually in both countries and that the price of y is constant in both. Using the trend of output prices as a measure of inflation, country B has the higher overall rate of inflation (because its output is more heavily biased toward the good with the high annual rate of price increase) even though the price of any given good may be the same in both countries. This example explains why the earlier exposition of inflation in a small open economy under fixed exchange rates argued that the small economy would tend to have *approximately* the same inflation rate as a larger *diversified* economy with which there was relatively free trade. However, the earlier arguments also implicitly assumed that the small economy itself had a diversified structure of demand or output.

(4) Differences in the agricultural pricing policies of the two economies, in spite of the fact that both Ireland and the UK joined the EEC in 1973. Reflecting the fact that Ireland has long been a net exporter of food, whereas the UK has been a net importer of such produce, Ireland in the 1970s consistently adopted a "high price food policy" (by adjusting what is called its green exchange rate in line with its market exchange rates *vis-à-vis* the main EEC currencies other than sterling). By contrast the UK tended to adopt a "low price food policy". (In order to avoid being side-tracked, we have deliberately avoided technical details on these issues). The main point is that different agricultural (including green exchange rate) policies caused the rate of increase in Irish farm prices to rise above the rate of increase in UK farm prices in the 1970s. However, such price differentials were not sustainable in the context of the EC (EU) in the 1980s.

(5) Possibly, different rates of inflation in the non-tradables rather than the tradables sectors of the two economies.

(6) Possibly, increasing monopoly power of Irish manufacturers relative to those in the UK. However, because we are an open economy greatly exposed to world competition (especially from that of other EU countries), the extent to which Irish manufacturers as a group could have steadily increased their monopoly power on either home or foreign markets was greatly constrained.

(7) Increase in costs of Irish producers relative to their competitors in the UK. But if Irish costs did increase relative to those of the UK, the

increase in costs of tradable goods could independently be passed on in the form of higher prices only to a very limited degree.

Ireland's exports plus imports of goods and services have summed to almost 140 per cent of domestic product measured at factor cost. Inflation in the prices of such goods and, indeed, in the prices of exportables and importables generally was, under a fixed exchange rate with the UK, approximately that of the UK. Any tendency toward exact equality in the two inflation rates was of course subject to qualifications of the kinds just outlined above. Given the openness of the economy and given that Ireland had a fixed exchange rate with the UK which was inflating rapidly, Ireland inevitably had high rates of inflation in the 1970s without necessarily becoming *price* non-competitive.

INFLATION, MONEY WAGES, PRODUCTIVITY AND UNEMPLOYMENT

It has been indicated earlier that by inflation is meant sustained rate of increase — rather than a discrete once and for all increase — in the price level. In Ireland, the most frequently cited indicator of the trend of inflation is the rate of change in the consumer price index. The rate of change in wages is *not* a reliable indicator of inflation, for wages can increase, on a sustained basis over time, consistent with no increase in the price level (and consistent with no change in the share of profits in national income), simply because output per unit of labour (what will be called productivity) is also increasing. (Productivity tends to increase over time largely because of technical change and because net investment is positive; more and improved capital equipment enables output per unit of labour to increase.) There has been some confusion in regard to the relationship between inflation and employment in the small open economy of Ireland. High inflation does not *necessarily* have an adverse affect on the competitiveness of the Irish economy and thereby cause unemployment, at least in the short run.

Insofar as job creation is concerned, the crucial issue in the context of Irish inflation is not the rate of inflation itself but rather the relationship between the rate of inflation, productivity growth, and the rate of increase in wage rates. As was revealed by Table 2 in Chapter 9 above, wages and salaries (termed wages for brevity) are by far the dominant component of total domestic production costs. As a very close approximation, if the rate of increase in wage rates, minus productivity growth, exceeds the rate of inflation (which may be high or low and is basically determined abroad under approximately fixed exchange rates), then the share of profits in the value of output will decline. Under such circumstances Irish goods would become cost uncompetitive. Given the declining profits share under such circumstances, some potential exporters could not compete on export markets, and some home producers could not compete against foreign suppliers on the domestic market. A short-term effect would be decreased output and employment. But there would also be a longer-term effect: because of the declining profits share, the funds available to finance investment would be reduced, as also would the incentive of the private sector to invest. In consequence, job-creating productive capacity in the future would be less than it would otherwise tend to be. Thus, rather than there being any necessary trade-off between unemployment and inflation in Ireland, there is a trade-off between the rate of increase in real wages (i.e. in money wages relative to the price level) less productivity growth on the one hand, and employment on the other. For, if wage rates, minus productivity growth, rise more rapidly than factor-cost prices (i.e. prices excluding their expenditure-tax component), the share of profits in value added will fall, ultimately resulting in decreased employment.

(In the interests of simplicity and brevity, the above paragraph ignores the distinction between the cost of hiring labour as perceived by the employer, and the remuneration of labour as perceived by employees. Potentially important issues pertaining to changes in what are called the terms of international trade — not to be confused with the balance of international payments — were also ignored. Some attention will be assigned to these matters in later chapters.)

Aggregate Demand and Aggregate Supply

The preceding sub-section makes it clear that there is more to the determination of equilibrium national income than consideration of aggregate demand alone, given the supply *potential* of the economy. The reader should now realise that an expansion in aggregate demand will not increase equilibrium national income unless firms in aggregate are *willing* (as well as able) to increase supply. They will not be willing to increase supply unless their costs (including wage costs) make it profitable to increase supply. Investigation of the determinants of aggregate supply is one of the principal themes of the chapter which follows.

Irish Inflation and Fixed Exchange Rates

It has been argued in this chapter that as long as Ireland maintained a fixed exchange rate with the UK, Ireland tended to have the UK's inflation rate. The argument (which would be strengthened if it were further complicated by bringing international factor mobility into the analysis) was roughly as follows:

(1) Ireland is a small open economy. Subject to certain qualifications in regard to agricultural products, goods have moved freely between the UK and Ireland.

(2) Until 1979, the exchange rate between the Irish and the UK currencies was rigidly fixed.

(3) Consideration (1) implied that in the long run and subject to qualifications indicated, the prices of internationally tradable goods in Ireland had to be roughly the same as those prevailing in the UK; for if not, international competition would have tended to equate the prices of the goods in the two countries, and because the UK is the larger country *vis-à-vis* Ireland, the prices that tended to be given to Ireland were those of the UK.

(4) Therefore, under a fixed exchange rate with the UK, Ireland's rate of inflation had to approximate the UK's rate of inflation.

(5) Given a fixed exchange rate, and due mainly to the UK's high and rising rates of inflation in the 1960s and 1970s, Ireland had high and generally rising rates of inflation until 1979.

(6) Therefore, if Ireland were to experience a significantly different rate of inflation from the UK in the long run, Ireland had to abandon the fixed exchange rate relationship with the UK.

For the reasons just outlined, and because of high and rising inflation in the 1970s, it was argued that Ireland should end its commitment to a fixed exchange rate with the UK. Many economists proposed that Ireland should attempt to maintain a fixed exchange rate with a currency such as the West German mark (because West Germany tended to inflate far more slowly than the UK). That is what we in effect *nominally* committed ourselves to doing by joining the Exchange Rate Mechanism (ERM) of the European Monetary System (EMS) in March 1979. ERM membership involved breaking the 150-year parity link with the pound sterling within a matter of weeks after Ireland joined the system. A sketch of the operation of the EMS, which has been dominated by the West German currency unit, is deferred to a later chapter. For the moment it is merely noted that Ireland did not succeed in maintaining fixed exchange rates within the EMS in the 1980s. However, it is left to the reader to reason, along the lines already surveyed, and subject to relevant qualifications, that if Ireland had succeeded in maintaining a fixed exchange rate against the mark in the 1980s and early 1990s, then Ireland would have approached (West) Germany's underlying inflation rate much more speedily than actually proved to be the case. The core of the reasoning would amount to little more than recognising that markets do exist; thus, by analogy, Sligo goods must have roughly the same rate of inflation as Dublin goods, as long as there is a fixed exchange rate between goods in Sligo and goods in Dublin. However, the simplicity implicit in the latter statement disguises the fact that the smooth operation of a fixed exchange rate system may require disciplined macroeconomic policies, including labour market policies, which were not acceptable to, or recognised by, the Irish authorities. These issues will be addressed in later chapters.

Money Supply and Inflation in Small Open Economies under Fixed Exchange Rates

The present chapter has outlined *some* of the mechanisms by which inflation is transmitted to a small open economy under a fixed exchange rate with a larger country with which it has free trade. But there are further transmission mechanisms at work, one of them being monetary in form. We will analyse that transmission mechanism at a later stage. Suffice it for the moment to state that, for reasons already explained, if a small open economy with fixed exchange rates has (sustained) inflation, it must be the case that its money supply is increasing over time. That is not to say that a small open economy under fixed exchange rates can control its money supply. However, we will not be prepared to analyse in further detail the relationship between increases in the money supply and inflation in small open economies until exchange rate determination has been considered in detail, in later chapters.

Inflation and Floating Exchange Rates

The discussion of inflation in a small open economy has been entirely confined to the context of a *fixed* exchange rate relationship with some major country. The possibility that the exchange rate will be allowed to float — that it may vary from day to day in accordance with the free forces of market supply and demand — has not been investigated. Nor have the effects of discrete changes in the exchange rate been investigated. The conclusions of the last several pages in regard to inflation in small open economies must be substantively altered if the exchange rate is not approximately fixed *vis-à-vis* one or more major trading partners.

CHAPTER 14

INTERACTION OF AGGREGATE SUPPLY AND AGGREGATE DEMAND: THE MAIN ISSUES

With the exception of the material in the preceding chapter, it has been assumed until now in Part Three that:

(a) The price level stays more or less constant.

(b) Provided that they are not fully utilising their capacities, firms are willing to supply whatever outputs may be demanded at prevailing prices.

Assumption (a) was relaxed in Chapter 13, where it was shown that if a small country — say Ireland — maintains a fixed exchange rate with a large country (large in the sense that its level of economic activity is much greater than that of Ireland) with which there is free trade, Ireland's rate of inflation will tend to approximate that country's rate of inflation. It was also pointed out towards the end of Chapter 13 that expansion of aggregate demand will not increase equilibrium real income unless firms are willing to increase supply. In fact, the equilibrium level of real national income is determined by both aggregate demand and aggregate supply — just as, in an individual competitive market, equilibrium quantity traded is determined by demand and supply. Before proceeding, note that:

(1) When reference is made to *aggregate demand* we shall as before be referring to demand for (planned expenditure on) *home-produced output*, or C + I + G + X - M, where all variables are in real terms and are as defined earlier. Note that this is not necessarily the same as the demand for final goods and services by residents of the economy under investigation: it includes foreign demand for the home country's goods and services but does not include goods and services which are imported to the home country.

(2) When reference is made to *aggregate supply* we shall be referring to the planned supply of home-produced output in real terms (i.e. it

indicates how much firms in the home economy would be willing to supply under specified conditions). This is not necessarily the same as the supply of goods and services on the home market (some of which is produced abroad).

(3) From the exposition in Chapter 9 and subsequently, we know that actual expenditure on national output is identical to actual national output; however, it is only in equilibrium that aggregate demand equals aggregate supply.

(4) Throughout this chapter it will be assumed that the country under analysis is small and operates under a *fixed exchange rate* with a large country with which there is relatively free trade. However, the conclusions will not need to be modified greatly if the exchange rate is not exactly fixed, but is only approximately fixed. Because the small open economy does not determine the foreign price level, it will be assumed (except where otherwise indicated) that the price level abroad stays constant.

(5) Finally, it may be worthwhile to point out that it can be shown that provided people do not persistently suffer from *money illusion* — provided, that is, that they do not indefinitely confuse changes in nominal prices of goods and of factors (e.g. nominal wage rates) with changes in real prices of goods and factors (e.g. real wage rates) — *most of the key features of what follows will be valid, at least in the long run, even if the exchange rate is freely floating rather than fixed.*

AGGREGATE SUPPLY

Consideration of aggregate supply is crucial for an understanding of elementary macroeconomics. Until indicated to the contrary, it will be supposed that the state of technology is given and that the stock of machinery and equipment is more or less constant. (Thus, for the moment we ignore the impact of fixed investment on the capital stock, and hence, on the supply potential of the economy.) It will also be supposed that the *quality* of the labour force is constant; thus workers do not suddenly begin to work harder. These assumptions imply that the technical conditions underlying supply are more or less constant. Under these conditions potential aggregate output will depend on the level of employment (of the labour force).

Suppose also that the prices of final goods and services, as distinct from the prices of inputs, are more or less given. As is usual, it is assumed that firms seek to maximise profits.

Under the stated assumptions the output which firms plan to produce depends on the prices of the factors of production at home, on the prices of imported inputs, and on the technical opportunities available to firms. These technical opportunities determine how inputs may potentially be transformed into outputs. Input prices and the technical relationships between inputs and potential outputs together determine how costs of production vary with output. As Table 2 of Chapter 9 indicated, wages and salaries (we will say just wages) account for the bulk of domestic production costs. Thus, (a) given the price of output and (b) given the technical relationships between inputs and output, the output which firms plan to produce depends on (c) the prices of imported inputs and on (d) the costs of the factors of production at home, and especially since labour is the dominant domestic cost item, on wage rates.

If the technical conditions underlying potential supply are given, and if the prices of both products and inputs are also given, then firms will produce some specific level of output (i.e. that output which maximises profits), and hence they employ some specific amount of labour. These, then, are the considerations underlying aggregate supply, or the ability and willingness of firms in the home economy to supply output (and hence to vary their employment). There is little reason for believing that the aggregate supply and employment levels resulting from the profit-maximising calculations of firms will always lead to full employment.

From the reasoning just outlined, it can be seen that aggregate supply does not depend on the price level (for output) alone; nor does it depend on costs alone. Ignoring for the moment complications arising from the tax code, and as already indicated, there are two principal kinds of costs: (a) those of imported inputs and (b) those associated with the prices of the factors of production (at home). The foreign-currency prices of the first category are determined abroad, beyond the control of the small country; they are also beyond the control of the small country in terms of domestic currency if (as is assumed) that country operates under fixed exchange rates. Therefore, unless indicated to the contrary, the prices of imported inputs will be taken as given. Within the second category of costs, wage rates — we will say "the" (average) wage rate — are by far the most important. A central proposition is that, other things being equal, aggregate supply depends crucially on the ratio of wage costs (the dominant component of domestic costs) to output prices, i.e. the key consideration is the level of wage costs relative to the price level. Let W be the average money wage and let P be the price level; then, other things being equal, aggregate supply depends on (W/P), i.e. on *the real wage*. (In reality different real wage rates are associated with different categories of labour, but incorporating this consideration into the analysis would needlessly complicate rather than illuminate.)

Suppose that we start with national income in equilibrium; then aggregate supply is equal to aggregate demand and the real wage is at some particular level. (It is at that level which induces firms to produce the level of output they are actually producing.) Suppose that the price level and the technical possibilities underlying production (in particular, the state of technology and the stock of fixed capital assets) are in effect constant, and that the cost to employers of hiring any given amount of labour is increased. This may have occurred because trade unions have bargained upward the money wage (or for other reasons). The effective real wage, as seen by employers, has therefore increased. Because unit wage costs have increased relative to price, firms, in order to avert losses, will cut back production: aggregate supply will be reduced. Thus, national income will approach a new equilibrium at which aggregate supply again equals aggregate demand, but at a lower level of output and employment than previously.

It is important to note that under the circumstances indicated, we would not expect the full process of contraction in employment to be instantaneous with the rise in the real wage. Rather, we would expect employers to react with significant lags. That is because there are costs associated with the firing and hiring of labour. For these reasons if at given levels of labour productivity the real wage (as perceived by employers) is increased, employers will be cautious about shedding labour, for the increase in real wages may be only transitory. (The price level may soon increase, thereby moving real wages down again.) Given the state of labour productivity, firms tend to shed unskilled labour first if an increase in real wages is sustained over time. But they tend to be more hesitant in shedding skilled labour — they are likely to fear that without having to incur recruitment and other costs they may be unable to obtain skilled labour at a future date if they seek to re-employ workers. Thus, firms (which are interested in profits *over time*) tend to hoard skilled labour even at a short-run loss. Aggregate supply has at last been brought into the picture of macroeconomic income determination. The reader may wonder how the aggregate demand approach stands in the light of the issues just raised.

Aggregate Supply and Aggregate Demand

Suppose that the economy is initially in equilibrium: aggregate demand equals aggregate supply at some level of output and employment, and corresponding to this there is some level of the (average) real wage. Suppose also that the system is operating well below full capacity utilisation at the initial equilibrium. Given the money wage rate, an increase in aggregate demand will tend to induce firms to expand supply because (a) it enables them to sell more at the prevailing price level and/or (b) it increases the price level. Consider two possible sources of an expansion in aggregate demand:

(1) Export demand may increase because incomes are expanding abroad. The increase in aggregate demand abroad may cause some demand-pull inflation abroad, and because exchange rates are assumed constant it would then cause the prices of tradable goods in the small open economy to rise. If the money wage did not increase in proportion to the price level, then the real wage would have fallen, and (given the technical conditions underlying potential supply) the profitability to domestic firms of expanding output and employment would have increased. Ultimately the system would reach a new equilibrium at which aggregate demand again equals aggregate supply, at a higher level of output and employment, but at a lower real wage than previously. Note that if an expansion in aggregate demand causes prices to rise in the manner indicated, and if the money wage were simultaneously pushed up in the same proportion as the price increase, then the real wage would not have changed and firms might have little incentive to expand either output or employment.

(2) Aggregate demand may increase because of increased real government expenditure on goods and services. In this context it is a matter of great importance whether the increase in government expenditure is on tradables or non-tradables. Because its immediate impact on imports and the balance of international payments is low, government expenditure on non-tradables tends to have a more expansionary impact on national output and employment than in the case of tradables. Suppose that all of the increased government expenditure is on tradables (though this is unlikely in practice). To the extent to which this raises the prices of tradables it is likely to cause some expansion in output and employment. But if it does raise the prices of tradables, it is likely to lead (with a lag) to a rise in competing imports which will mitigate the upward pressure on the prices of tradables and will curtail expansion of output. If, on the other hand, the increased government expenditure does not raise prices, it may lead to diversion of output away from the export market in favour of home sales to the government sector; in that case it might lead to no change at all in output. Finally, if the technical conditions underlying supply remain more or less constant, and if increased government expenditure does raise the prices of tradables, the effect on output and employment may be zero if the money wage is increased in the same proportion as the increase in the price level. In fact, given the technical conditions underlying supply, if prices increase and if money wages are increased more rapidly than prices (so that the real wage increases), then firms will tend

to reduce their production and employment, for their costs per unit would have increased relative to the price of output.

A MORE FORMAL TREATMENT

The preceding analysis can be clarified using aggregate supply and demand diagrams: see Figures 1 and 2 below.

The general aggregate supply function for the output of the home economy can be represented as

$$(1) \ AS = AS(P, W, P^{MRM}, T)$$

where the dependent variable AS denotes aggregate supply and the symbols inside parentheses on the right-hand side denote the independent variables upon which AS depends. These independent variables are as follows: P represents the domestic price level (largely determined abroad due to the assumption of a fixed exchange rate); W, an index of the wage rate, is meant to proxy domestic production costs, a procedure which is well justified in view of the fact that employee remuneration accounts for the bulk of domestic value added in the Irish economy; P^{MRM} denotes the externally-determined prices of imported inputs (RM for "raw materials"); T represents the level of primary factor endowments in the economy (land, labour, capital and enterprise) as well as the state of technology. Phrased otherwise, it denotes all those of things which determine the *potential* output of the economy. We will refer to T in a very loose sense: thus, we will say that T increases if the productivity of inputs rises. This may be due to either an improvement in "the state of the industrial arts" (technology in a narrow sense) or to greater efficiency in the use of existing inputs (less "featherbedding" by the workforce, reduction in restrictive practices, etc.).

In general, it is sensible to draw an AS curve in the (price, output) plane, as in Figure 1, only on the assumptions that all of the variables which determine supply, apart from the price of output, stay constant. Then, given W, P^{MRM} and T:

$$(2) \ AS = AS(P), \text{ with } \Delta AS/\Delta P \geq 0$$

The function (2), representing the willingness and ability of firms in aggregate to supply, is depicted by a curve like AS in Figure 1. Note that this curve will *shift* if any of the independent variables other than P (namely W, P^{MRM} or T) change from the levels at which they are assumed constant along a given aggregate supply curve. Drawn in the (price, output) plane with price measured on the vertical axis, the aggregate supply curve is approximately zero-sloped at very low levels of output, it then becomes positively sloped and ultimately becomes vertical. The reasons are as follows:

At historically low levels of output, firms have excess capacity of machinery and equipment, etc.; hence, given the money wage rate, costs per unit may be roughly constant. (It is in fact conceivable that they could be falling as fixed overheads are spread over higher levels of output.) The aggregate supply curve AS in Figure 1 is therefore drawn fairly flat at low levels of aggregate output (national income), implying (given the things we are assuming constant) that little or no increase in prices is necessary in order to induce firms to expand output. But if output is increased toward historically high levels, machinery and equipment must be operated more intensively and less experienced workers may need to be hired, so costs per unit are likely to rise. At the higher levels of output, unit fixed costs become relatively insignificant and unit variable costs rise because of the law of diminishing returns. It then requires higher prices to induce firms to continue expanding production; the AS curve will slope upwards. If prices were to continue to rise (given money wage rates, etc.), suppliers would eventually provide the maximum they were technically capable of producing; no more could then be supplied from domestic sources, so the aggregate supply curve would be vertical at full capacity utilisation. (Recall that only supply from home sources is included in AS.) Consider now the effects of changes in W, in P^{MRM} or in T, given P.

First, note that increases in W or in P^{MRM} have the same kinds of effects: Given T, they both mean that costs have risen relative to the price of output. Production therefore becomes less profitable: at any P, firms will be less willing to supply, and the aggregate supply curve will swivel (or, to use equivalent expressions, it will pivot or swing) to the left, as with AS' in Figure 1. The opposite would occur if either W or P^{MRM} were to fall: the aggregate supply curve would swivel to the right — to, say, AS" in the same diagram. Observe that changes in W or in P^{MRM} cause swivelling rather than unambiguous shifts of the aggregate supply curve: they do not affect the asymptotic level of output — the level of output at which the aggregate supply curve becomes approximately vertical. Because the asymptotic level of output represents the maximum the economy is capable of producing, it is determined by technology T rather than by financial (cost) variables.

Consider next the effect of a change in T, given W and P^{MRM}. Suppose for example that improved work practices, or an improvement in technical knowledge, raise output per worker (at any level of employment). Because output per unit of measured input will have increased whilst the cost per unit of measured input would not have increased, firms will be willing to supply more at any given level of P. The supply potential of the economy will also have increased. Therefore, the aggregate supply curve would not merely have swivelled to the right; its asymptote would also have moved to the right. Thus, an improvement in T causes the entire aggregate supply curve to shift to the right, as illustrated by AS''' in Figure 1, reflecting the fact that firms would then always be both willing and able to supply more than before.

Figure 1

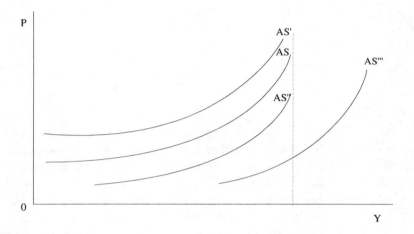

Figure 2a

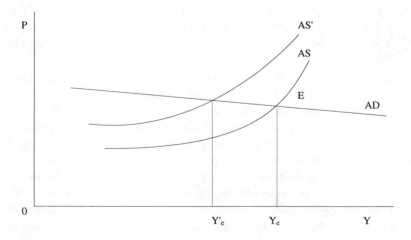

Figure 2b

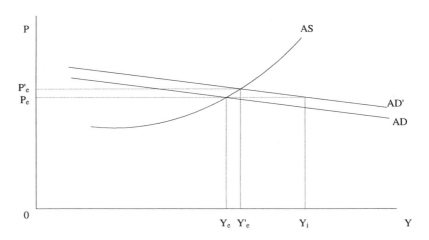

It should now be clear that the slope of the aggregate supply curve is determined mainly by whether the prevailing level of output is high or low relative to potential output (full employment output); its level in the plane — whether it is located largely toward the right or toward the left — reflects the levels of the variables which are constant along a given supply curve (i.e. on the levels of W, P^{MRM} and T).

Discussion of the level and slope of the aggregate demand curve (*for home-produced output*) will be brief at this stage. The *level* of the aggregate demand curve — whether it lies more toward the right or toward the left in the non-negative (P, Y) plane — reflects those components of demand which in the short-run are independent of the level of national income (e.g. part of government expenditure on goods and services). Because it is assumed that foreign prices and the exchange rate with a large country are both given, intuition (correctly) suggests that the *slope* of the aggregate demand curve reflects the degree of sensitivity of real net exports (real exports less real imports) to changes in the domestic price level. Reflecting the fact that a small diversified open economy is close to being a price-taker rather than a dominant price-maker on world markets, aggregate demand is quite sensitive to changes in the domestic price level (given the exchange rate and given foreign prices); the reader should be able to infer that at the equilibrium point E in Figure 2a, aggregate demand is price elastic, reflecting relative price-taking behaviour. (The foregoing discussion of the level and slope of the aggregate demand curve has been as brief as possible; more rigorous investigation is deferred, mainly until Chapter 19).

Suppose that starting at point E in Figure 2a trade unions bargain the money wage upward. Because costs have risen relative to prices, firms will be willing to supply less than before; the aggregate supply curve swivels upward to, say, AS' in Figure 2a. Inspection indicates that the price level rises by a small proportionate amount, but the main impact is on national income (and hence, though probably with lags, on employment); equilibrium real income falls from Y_e to Y'_e.

What is the effect of an expansion in aggregate demand? Suppose we start with real income in equilibrium at Y_e in Figure 2b, and that the government increases its real expenditure on goods and services. This increase in expenditure, along with the multiplier process, causes the aggregate demand curve to shift to the right, to AD'; at the initial price level P_e, demand increases to Y_1. But in order to induce an increase in supply, given the money wage, the price level will have to be bid upward: the domestic price level rises slightly, to P'_e, and equilibrium real income rises to Y'_e. Thus, the application of ordinary multiplier analysis, which assumes that aggregate supply is infinitely elastic (as in Chapters 10 and 11 above), would overstate the increase in equilibrium income. It is appropriate to add two important sets of observations:

(1) If, throughout a large interval around the initial equilibrium, there is a great deal of unemployed labour and capital equipment, and if the money wage remains constant, then the aggregate supply curve may be horizontal throughout that interval. In this case an increase in aggregate demand would enable more to be sold at the existing price level and, because of excess capacity, producers would be willing to supply more at that price level. Hence, an increase in demand could increase equilibrium income without causing any increase in domestic prices. However, if we start in equilibrium near full capacity utilisation, aggregate supply can be increased only with progressively greater difficulty (by employing less experienced workers, by bringing less efficient machines into operation, etc.), with the result that the AS curve must then slope upward. Under those circumstances an increase in aggregate demand, to the extent to which it leads to any increase in output in the home economy, must be accompanied by some increase in the price level. However, given the exchange rate and the foreign price level, the increase in domestic prices will induce an increase in imports. Thus, the level of imports at the new equilibrium will generally differ from that predicted using ordinary multiplier theory; firstly, because the increase in income will be less, and secondly, because of the increase in domestic prices.

(2) If the AD curve shifts to the right, and (given the technical conditions underlying production) if the AS curve also shifts, to the left (possibly

due to the implementation of new minimum wage legislation or to trade unions pushing money wage rates upward), the effect will be to reduce the expansion in output which the stimulus in aggregate demand would otherwise create. Indeed it is possible that equilibrium output and employment would actually fall under the circumstances specified. (It is left to the reader to demonstrate this proposition graphically. Note that it would hold even if the original aggregate supply curve were horizontal.)

MONEY WAGES, PRODUCTIVITY AND UNEMPLOYMENT

We have been assuming that the technical conditions underlying supply were given. This led to the conclusion that increases in money wage rates, at given levels of employment and with a more or less given price level, would reduce national income and, in lagged response, the level of employment. These conclusions, which are correct given our assumptions, suggest that if workers through collective bargaining obtain increases in real wages, then employment must fall. However, the assumption that the technical conditions underlying production remain given is not generally valid, except for fairly short periods of time.

In fact, the level of net fixed investment in any economy is usually positive, and this has effects on both aggregate demand and aggregate supply. However, the time dimension of these effects differs. The main effects of net fixed investment on aggregate demand are almost immediate, and should be well understood by the reader at this stage. The effects on aggregate supply are more permanent, or long-term. Net fixed investment affects aggregate supply in various ways, among them the following:

(1) At any given level of employment (of labour) it means that the amount of capital equipment per worker is increasing over time. This increases the productivity of labour.

(2) Investment in fixed assets — we will simply say investment — is a crucial mechanism through which technical change is transmitted to the economy. New machines tend to be superior to machines of earlier vintages because they embody more recent technical designs. Thus, even if new machines, etc., merely replaced old machines (i.e. even if gross fixed investment were at that level which is generally called replacement investment, implying a net fixed investment rate of zero), output per unit of employed labour would tend to be increasing over time.

Considerations (1) and (2) imply that output per unit of labour — what is generally called labour productivity — tends to be increasing over time because of increased and improved capital. Given money wage rates, as determined by collective bargaining or otherwise, the aggregate supply curve will therefore tend to be shifting to the right over time. This simply reflects the fact that corresponding to any wage-price combination, firms will be willing to supply more real output at higher levels of labour productivity. The effect of an increase in labour productivity is depicted in Figure 3, where AS is assumed to be the initial aggregate supply curve.

Figure 3

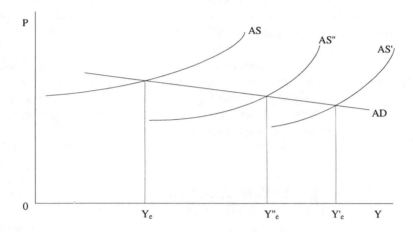

Given money wage rates, an increase in output per worker (which may be brought about by increased or improved capital per worker) means that firms are willing to increase supply at any particular price level; the aggregate supply curve shifts to the right to AS' in Figure 3 and equilibrium income increases to Y'_e. (There is also some slight downward pressure on the price level, which implies that real wages would have increased.) But if money wage rates increase as a result of, say, trade unions arguing that the increased output per employee is due to increased effort by those in employment, then the aggregate supply curve will not shift as far to the right as AS' in Figure 3; it may shift to, say, AS", in which case equilibrium income would expand to Y''_e only.

Money Wages, Inflation and Unemployment

For the most part, the foregoing expositions assumed that the price level in the larger country with which there is a fixed exchange rate stayed constant. However, the analysis is easily adapted to an inflationary environment. If inflation abroad is 20 per cent per annum, then (certain mainly minor qualifications set aside) the annual rate of inflation in the small economy will tend to be about 20 per cent. If the technical conditions underlying production are constant and if P^{MRM} is rising at the same rate as the overall rate of inflation, then domestic money wage rates may increase by about 20 per cent annually without causing increased unemployment; for the real wage (and the real profit margin) would then be constant. However, if technical conditions are constant, if inflation abroad is 20 per cent and if P^{MPM} is also rising by 20 per cent annually, then an annual increase in domestic money wage rates of more than (less than) 20 per cent represents an increase (a decrease) in the real wage (and movement in the opposite direction in the real profit margin), and output and employment would tend to fall (rise) on that count.

Assume next that the price level and P^{MRM} are increasing by 20 per cent and that labour productivity is increasing by 5 per cent. Money wage rates may then increase by more than 20 per cent annually — the real wage may increase — without causing any fall in the share of profits in national income and without inducing firms to reduce employment. However, if the real wage increases persistently faster than 5 per cent a year, then real profit margins and both national income and employment will fall.

FURTHER SUPPLY-SIDE ISSUES:
TERMS OF TRADE AND TAXES

Up to now the analysis of aggregate supply has almost completely ignored what are called changes in the terms of international trade — for brevity, the *terms of trade* — and has completely ignored some important issues pertaining to taxation.

What are loosely called the terms of trade (not to be confused with the balance of international payments) refer to the terms under which real exports are exchanged for real imports: directly or indirectly, they indicate how many "units" of exports must be traded in order to obtain one "unit" of imports. However, the terms of trade are most usually measured, not with reference to quantity units directly, but with reference to prices, in index number form. Let p_x be an index of the prices of a country's exports, constructed in such a manner that it equals unity in some given year, called the base year. Let p_m be an index of the country's import prices, constructed in such a manner that it also equals unity in the same base year. Then the terms of trade index, p_x/p_m, would equal unity in the base year. A 5 per cent rise in export prices relative to import prices — what is called a favourable movement in the terms of trade — would be indicated by a rise in the index from unity to 1.05; a 5 per cent fall in export prices relative to import prices — called an adverse movement in the terms of trade — would bring the index down from unity to 0.95. In practice, the terms of trade index in most common usage is one which is as defined above, multiplied by 100. Thus, the index has a value of 100 in the base year and would move to values of 105 or 95, respectively, in the two hypothetical examples used for illustration above.

Note that because a small open economy is a price-taker rather than a price-maker on world markets, such an economy cannot have any substantive influence on its terms of trade. Note also that the terms of trade index is independent of whether prices are expressed in domestic currency or in foreign currency units.

Given that export and import prices are both determined abroad, the reader may wonder how a small open economy maintaining fixed exchange rates could possibly experience a change in its terms of trade, p_x/p_m. The answer is quickly seen when it is observed that a small country might export goods and services (e.g. beef, tourism and finished goods) which are fundamentally different in composition from those which it imports (e.g. coal and oil for its energy requirements). Thus, a change in a small country's terms of trade reflects a change in *relative* prices abroad.

Changes in the terms of trade are of relevance to the aggregate supply function of a small open economy; it is therefore important to know how to incorporate terms of trade variables in that function, either directly or indirectly. One approach would be to include p_x and p_m explicitly as independent variables on the right-hand side of equation (1) above. An alternative and simpler approach — that adopted here — is as follows: In equation (1), it is reasonable to regard p_x as embodied in P, and to assume that other things being equal, it moves in phase with P; similarly, it is reasonable to assume that p_m and P^{MRM} move in phase. An adverse (a favourable) movement in the terms of trade will therefore be represented by a fall (a rise) of P relative to P^{MRM} in equation (1) above.

A deterioration in the terms of trade — an event itself beyond the control of policy-makers in a small open economy — has some effects identical to those of a wage increase, given productivity: Because it involves a rise in the prices of inputs relative to output (export) prices, it causes the aggregate supply curve to shift to the left, leading to contraction in output and employment, as well as to some rise in the domestic price level (unless the home country is a *perfect price-taker* — i.e. unless the aggregate demand curve is perfectly flat). Because it represents a supply-side shock, it may be possible for policy to assist in offsetting or neutralising its contractionary effects by appropriate supply-side policies. For example, policies of wage reduction/restraint might be implemented, shifting the aggregate supply curve to the right. In this manner the original levels of output and employment might be maintained. Furthermore, the government might respond to the terms of trade deterioration by adopting policies which maximise the pace of technical improvement, broadly interpreted. For example, a stiffer stance might be adopted against interest groups pursuing restrictive trade practices (e.g. antiquated "work to rule"), or against interest groups adopting "defensive" strategies preventing the implementation of technical improvement, more narrowly interpreted. It is true that it is likely that policies in regard to technical change will reveal their effects on aggregate supply more slowly than would wage restraint. However, those effects will tend to be more durable in the case of technical change than in the case of wage restraint. We will return to these and related issues in a later chapter.

Turning briefly to questions involving taxation, "the" wage rate W in the aggregate supply function, equation (1) above, has denoted the cost of hiring a unit of labour, *as perceived by employers*. In practice in Ireland there has existed a gap or wedge — the so-called tax wedge — between W as interpreted in this chapter, and the after-tax wage *as received by employees*. This wedge has consisted of two principal components: (a) employers' contribution to social insurance, which is reckoned as part of employee remuneration and is in effect a tax on employers on the amount of labour which they hire; (b) taxation of income levied directly on employees.

A rise in the rate of employers' contribution to social insurance has an effect similar to that of anything else which increases unit costs, given output prices: it causes the aggregate supply curve to swivel to the left, thereby contracting output and employment. Similarly, if increased rates of taxation levied on labour income lead workers to demand and obtain higher (pre-tax) wage rates (at given levels of productivity), then the aggregate supply curve will swivel to the left. Thus (considering the demand-side effect in isolation), the government may boost output and employment through its expenditure policies; however (taking supply-side effects in isolation), the manner in which the government finances its expenditures may cause output and employment to contract.

DIFFERENT KINDS OF UNEMPLOYMENT

Demand-Deficient or Cost-Constrained Unemployment

The analysis up to now suggests that, given the size of the labour force, unemployment is due to (a) deficiency in the level of aggregate demand and/or (b) downward rigidity, but flexibility in an upward direction, in money wage rates. Depending on how one looks at the matter, the ensuing unemployment can be regarded as *demand-deficient* or *cost-constrained*: it exists because demand is too low given the incentives of suppliers as determined by their costs relative to output prices; alternatively, it is due to a situation in which the costs of suppliers are too high given the level of aggregate demand. It follows, at least in a relatively closed economy, that effective policy responses could seek to operate on the demand-side, on the supply-side, or on both.

To the extent to which the analytic framework as developed up to now is *empirically* relevant, it implies (given the technical conditions underlying potential supply) that expansions in demand (due, say, to increased export demand or to increases in government expenditure on non-tradables), which generate some upward pressure on prices and downward pressure on real wages, might quite rapidly create full employment of the labour force, provided that increases in money wage rates (or increased costs of any other kind) do not cause the aggregate supply curve to shift to the left. However, it would appear that in the case of an open economy like that of Ireland, only rather limited reduction in rates of unemployment could be attained by domestic policies of demand expansion alone. That has been the case for several reasons, some of them listed below:

(1) Consideration of issues pertaining to aggregate supply for the moment aside, it has earlier been seen that national income multipliers for the Irish economy are very low. That is largely because of the high import leakages accompanying growth in output in Ireland. Therefore, if exports remain constant, an increase in income, by causing imports to rise, may cause balance of payments difficulties. The next chapter will indicate what those difficulties might be. Here it is merely noted that the high import leakages of the Irish economy place major restrictions on the ability of policy-makers to increase income and employment through short-run policies of aggregate demand expansion.

(2) An expansion in aggregate demand will not lead to any increase in equilibrium income unless supply from domestic sources is increased. If technical conditions and real wage rates are both constant, producers may have little incentive to increase aggregate supply if aggregate demand is increased. Given the technical conditions underlying supply, an expansion in aggregate demand in a closed economy would tend to cause real wages to fall and employment to increase by raising the price level. However, as already seen, the extent to which a country like Ireland can increase its price level (relative to that of countries with which it maintains approximately fixed exchange rates) through domestic policies of demand expansion (thereby inducing increases in aggregate supply) is greatly limited.

(3) In a free and efficient labour market, labour flows out of those activities and out of those regions where productivity (and hence real wages) are low, into those areas and those activities in which productivity is high. For many decades of the twentieth century, labour automatically flowed out of Kerry, Leitrim and Mayo, for example, and into the Dublin area (or abroad), where productivity and real wages were higher. These movements merely reflected the fact that Dublin and Kerry, etc., formed parts of the same labour market. It is probable that very few people blamed the County Council of (say) Kerry for not creating a situation of full employment in Kerry consistent with zero migration out of Kerry, toward Dublin or beyond. Today, near the end of the twentieth century, policy-makers in Ireland often claim (when circumstances, often financial, suit them) that Ireland is part of a Common Market — the European Union. If that were the case in all respects, labour would automatically tend to flow out of regions (perhaps entire countries) where productivity is low, toward regions where productivity is high, and it would not always be sensible to blame the Local Authority in Dublin for such migration, at least in the short-run. Considerations of language, cultural differences and family ties may also, of course, serve to deter outward migration. In practice, and in an Ireland–EU context, although claiming to pursue full European Union, policy-makers in Ireland prevent the labour market from operating effectively. Thus, migration out of Ireland is regarded as a national defect, and a system of relatively high unemployment relief (the "dole") discourages such migration out of Ireland and at times in fact encourages inward migration. Thus, the system of dole can be an immediate cause of measured unemployment in Ireland.

Quite apart from its affects on migration, the existence and the form of the dole may indirectly increase unemployment in Ireland through two mechanisms: (a) the levels of dole payment set floors on the levels of wage bargaining, and therefore raise wage costs, in at least some areas of productive activity; (b) the dole system has to be financed, and one of those ways has been by taxing employers on the jobs they do provide, through employers' contribution to social insurance. (Note that the author is not expressing any view that the dole system is morally or otherwise undesirable; as an economist, he is merely expressing observations on its implications. Similarly, no value-judgment has been expressed on the desirability of being part of a common EU labour market; however, note the *inconsistency*, in Irish circumstances in regard to productivity, in sometimes pretending a commitment to be part of a common European labour market, and in blaming the prevailing Irish government for both unemployment and emigration.)

The longer the period over which Irish governments prevent the relatively tiny Irish sector of the EU labour market from working, the more severe Ireland's unemployment problem must become — unless productivity can be advanced towards levels which apply in the more prosperous areas of the EU. Note that raising productivity implies measures affecting the supply-side rather than the demand-side, and involves the long-run rather than the short-run as time horizon. The sensitive issues which have just been raised will be discussed in a later chapter; for the moment it is noted that they are related to those in the paragraphs which immediately follow.

(4) Even if the balance of payments constraint mentioned in (1) were relaxed, if the dole system were modified and if money wage rates suddenly became flexible downwards, we in Ireland would still encounter difficulties in attaining anything like full employment for the *existing* workforce. That is largely because Ireland has historically had an abundant supply of labour relative to the capital stock. Thus, given the kinds of production techniques which have been carried forward from the past, a situation in which the economy was producing its maximum potential output, so that the capital stock was fully utilised, would probably be characterised by an excess supply of labour. These considerations lead us to the phenomenon of structural unemployment.

Structural Unemployment

Structural unemployment in any region (or country) is the outcome of particular structural features of the region. In developed economies it is often the result of permanent shifts in demand away from the products in which specific regions have specialised. Even in developed countries it can normally be effectively eliminated only over several years rather in the short-run, by manpower policies (retraining and possibly resettlement of labour) and by policies concerning industrial location (for example, by fiscal incentives designed to attract new industries to the structurally depressed regions). In less developed economies it typically takes the form of a long-run overall excess in the supply of labour relative to the capital stock, given the market prices of labour and capital. Even if the capital stock were fully employed under such circumstances, there would still be unemployment or under-employment of labour. Two kinds of policy are often advocated ultimately to eliminate this kind of structural unemployment:

(1) Policies encouraging rapid accumulation of capital throughout the economy. In Ireland the Industrial Development Authority has been one of the principal agencies in this context. Because net investment in the

short-run can amount to only a small proportion of the existing capital stock, such policies can have significant impact in eliminating widespread structural unemployment only in the medium or long term.

(2) Subsidies for the employment of labour, even if the capital stock is fully employed. Although the matter is complex, a case for wage subsidies can be argued as follows: The imbalance between the economy's labour force and capital stock is largely due to the wage rate, in the past, being high relative to the price of capital. This has encouraged firms to choose methods of production requiring large amounts of capital relative to labour (capital-intensive techniques). If the state subsidised employment of labour, the effective price of labour, as perceived by firms, would be lower than the market wage. They would therefore select more labour-intensive techniques than previously in new projects. However, because new investment projects, in the short-run, can amount to only a small proportion of existing projects, policies of subsidising the employment of labour, if they have a significant effect in reducing widespread structural unemployment, will do so only over relatively long periods of time.

It should be clear from the above that the effective elimination of the kind of structural unemployment that is typical of underdeveloped economies can be attained only over quite long periods of time. It should also be clear, in the absence of net emigration, that its effective elimination generally implies large-scale accumulation of capital (i.e., high rates of net investment). Furthermore, it is the supply-side rather than the demand-side effects which would be of paramount importance.

Frictional Unemployment

If among that part of the labour force which is looking for jobs, unemployment is neither demand-deficient nor cost-constrained nor structural, it is generally termed frictional. In a modern economy some firms will generally be in a period of decline while others are expanding: this inevitably gives rise to temporary unemployment as workers adjust to changes in the composition of labour demand. The existence of frictional unemployment reflects the fact that information in regard to job opportunities is not perfect. For example, in times of brisk demand for labour, new entrants to the labour market will not usually accept the first job opening that is available to them. Rather, they would generally be wise to spend some time investigating the opportunities open to them, ultimately opting for that job which is most attractive to them. Consider the case of a graduate seeking employment. Perhaps there would instantly be an offer of a post as gardener. But it would, in general, be foolish to accept such immediate employment, for it would be more beneficial to spend time investigating the alternatives, and opting for the best offer. Because it is voluntary and transitory, frictional unemployment is not considered as constituting a very serious social problem. The state can reduce its extent and duration by improving information on available job openings. However, it can also raise and prolong it by offering levels of unemployment compensation which are high relative to prevailing after-tax money wages; i.e. high levels of dole payment, especially when available over long periods, reduce the urgency of individuals in seeking employment.

THE EXTENT OF UNEMPLOYMENT IN IRELAND

The most commonly cited measure of unemployment in Ireland is the number of persons on what is called the Live Register. This comprises those persons registering for certain unemployment payments under social welfare legislation. Using this criterion, a measure of the rate of unemployment is the percentage of the labour force which is insured against unemployment and which is on the Live Register. Calculated in this manner the rate of unemployment in Ireland averaged over 18 per cent in the early 1990s. The Live Register is only one of two principal sources of information on unemployment in Ireland. Because it is compiled weekly and published monthly, it is the main indicator of short-run variations in unemployment. A second source of unemployment estimates is derived from the annual Labour Force Survey. This Survey is conducted in line with guidelines established by the International Labour Organisation and approved by the Statistical Office of the EU; the resulting measures of unemployment and unemployment rates are therefore those now normally used in making international comparisons. Because of differing coverage and differing definitions, estimates of Ireland's unemployment rate based on the Labour Force Survey have been slightly below those derived using Live Register data: the Labour Force Survey yielded estimates of Ireland's unemployment rate of around 16 per cent in the early 1990s. However, regardless of which particular measure one uses, rates of unemployment in Ireland in the early 1990s have been very high in comparison with other EU countries.

The analytical framework developed in the present chapter (and in subsequent chapters) suggests that Ireland's high unemployment rates can be reduced toward zero only by either:

(1) Recognising that Ireland is now part of a common labour market — that of the EU — and removing obstacles hindering the efficient operation of that market. Thus, if productivity levels in Ireland cannot be brought up towards levels elsewhere in the EU, either labour will flow out of Ireland and/or unemployment rates in Ireland will stay high. Under

the circumstances just specified, living standards for those who stay in Ireland will remain low relative to those of residents of some other parts of the EU. Or,

(2) Implementing policies which cause productivity levels in Ireland to converge toward those elsewhere in the EU. However, the potential gains from increased productivity will not be realised unless the economy is *cost* competitive, which implies that real wages cannot steadily increase at a rate in excess of the rate of productivity growth. Thus, in an economy like that of Ireland, demand-management may help in the short-run in smoothing or stabilising unemployment rates around a trend; but (in the absence of large-scale outward migration) the trend in unemployment rates will move steadily downward only if the supply-side environment is appropriate. Finally at this stage, note that (unlike demand-side policies) supply-side measures — especially those directly or indirectly affecting technical change — tend to operate relatively slowly. Thus, in the absence of large-scale outward migration, Ireland's unemployment problem cannot be resolved in the short-term.

AGGREGATE SUPPLY AND AGGREGATE DEMAND: DIGRESSION ON AN ALTERNATIVE APPROACH

Recall the definitions of aggregate supply and aggregate demand employed in this chapter: they *both* pertained to *domestically* produced output. Consider a small open economy under fixed exchange rates with the rest of the world, and let the world price level, say P^W, be given. Suppose that the distinction between tradables and non-tradables is ignored, and assume that the small country is a perfect price-taker. Thus, it is assumed that all goods are tradable, at a given price level. Let the choice of units be such that the exchange rate, e, equals unity. Under such circumstances, the price level in the small economy would be P^W: the domestic price level would be determined *entirely* beyond the control of the small economy.

The locus S in Figure 4 denotes the supply of domestic output, as defined earlier. That labelled S^W is the supply curve of goods from the world market. It is drawn perfectly flat reflecting the assumption that (in effect) unlimited supplies are available from the world market at the world price level. But *the aggregate demand curve* D in Figure 4 is *not* defined in the same way as earlier in this chapter. It is defined as *the demand by residents of the small economy* as a function of the price level. Thus, it includes that part of their demand which represents expenditure on imports, but it does not include demand for the small country's exports.

The way the curves have been drawn in Figure 4, there is an *excess demand* at the prevailing price level, P^W. Assuming that there are no net transfer payments from abroad, this excess demand represents the deficit in the current account balance of payments, $(X - M) < 0$, which is now brought very clearly into the picture. Equilibrium income in this model is given by Y_e in the diagram.

Figure 4

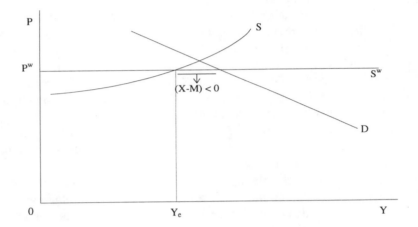

Figure 5

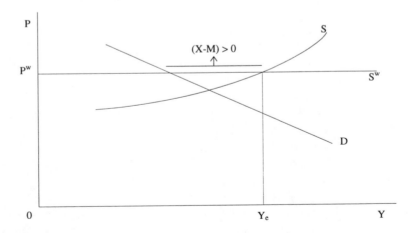

Once again defining the aggregate demand curve to represent the demand by residents of the small country, the curves S and D in Figure 5 intersect below P^W. The *excess supply* at the prevailing price level takes the form of a surplus in the balance of payments on current account, $(X - M) > 0$. Thus, the model outlined is easily adapted in order to analyse, *in an explicit manner*, the response of $(X - M)$ to changes in demand by residents of the small country. It also highlights, very clearly, some of the implications of complete price exogeneity (i.e. the implications of the assumption that price is determined entirely outside the model of the economy under investigation). We will refer to the model just outlined as "the alternative model".

The approach adopted in the earlier sections of the present chapter had the merit of relative simplicity. But this was simplicity at a cost. For example, by embedding changes in $(X - M)$ in the *slope* of the aggregate demand curve for domestic output, that approach could not *explicitly* indicate what would happen to $(X - M)$ when the aggregate demand curve was shifted (by, say, an increase in government expenditure). On the other hand — and unlike the alternative model — the approach adopted throughout most of the present chapter did not assume perfect price-taking behaviour, and it did not preclude a distinction between tradables and non-tradables.

Which approach to adopt depends on the context of one's investigations. Despite its simplicity (in some respects an advantage and in other respects a disadvantage) the approach adopted in the earlier sections of this chapter does yield many useful predictions. Thus, until further notice — from Martin Kenneally in Chapter 21 — we will continue to define aggregate demand as at the beginning of the present chapter; hence, for the moment, the present subsection has been a digression.

Chapter 15

THE BALANCE OF INTERNATIONAL PAYMENTS AND EXCHANGE RATES

THE BALANCE OF INTERNATIONAL PAYMENTS

The balance of international payments for any year is a systematic statement of all transactions between residents of the home country and the rest of the world in that year. When appropriate consideration is taken of balancing items, this set of records or accounts must balance exactly. This does not mean that transactions of a given category must balance. For example, the value of exports of goods may differ from the value of imports of goods. Likewise, inflows of financial capital from abroad (for example, to finance the purchase of land in Ireland or the purchase of Irish government securities) need not equal in value the outflows of financial capital from Ireland. The character and size of the balancing items in the balance of payments accounts is often of crucial importance.

The *balance of trade* is the difference between the value of merchandise exports and merchandise imports. If the value of merchandise exports exceeds (falls short of) the value of merchandise imports, the balance of trade is in surplus (deficit). The *balance of payments on current account* is found by adding *net* exports (i.e. exports less imports) of *non-factor services* (such as net receipts from tourism, external earnings of transportation companies, etc.) and net exports of *factor services* (as represented by interest and profits on assets held abroad by Irish residents, for example), as well as net receipts of transfer payments from abroad, to the balance of merchandise trade. If the value of exports of goods and services, plus net transfer payments from abroad, exceeds (falls short of) the value of imports of goods and services, then the current account is in surplus (deficit).

If transfer payments to and from abroad were zero, the balance of payments on current account would be the difference between the value of exports of goods and services and the value of imports of goods and services, X - M. Thus, as a first approximation (i.e. not taking net transfer payments from abroad into consideration), the balance of payments on current account indicates the extent to which transactions with the rest of the world contribute to aggregate demand in the economy.

The balance of payments on capital account indicates how the current account has been financed. Because the balance of payments on capital account must equal, in absolute value, the balance of payments on current account, as an accounting identity the balance of payments accounts balance exactly. However, this statement masks what is meant by an overall surplus or deficit in the balance of payments.

Suppose, for example, that transfer payments from abroad are zero and that in a given year we import goods and services valued £1,000 million and export goods and services valued £600 million. The net debt to foreigners thereby incurred is £400 million. Some of this debt may be paid off by running down our holdings of foreign exchange reserves (and paying foreigners those foreign monies); the residual must take the form of net borrowing from abroad. (It is noted in passing that the latter observation is subject to a possible qualification pertaining to the operations of the International Monetary Fund, which will be ignored for the present.) Thus, the current account deficit must equal (a) the reduction in Ireland's foreign exchange reserves plus (b) borrowing by Ireland from abroad, or, in the event that we borrow more from abroad than the current account deficit, it must equal (b') borrowing by Ireland from abroad minus (a') the increase in Ireland's foreign exchange reserves. If a country has a current account balance of payments deficit, its net claims on foreign countries are decreased, or equivalently, its net liabilities to foreigners are increased. The opposite holds if a country has a surplus in its balance of payments on current account. Thus, a balancing entry on capital account must offset the balance on current account, as in Table 1.

Table 1: Ireland's Balance of Payments, 1992, £ Million

Current Account		Capital Account	
Surplus on Merchandise Trade	(+) 3,361	Net Capital Outflow	(+) 2,736
Deficit on Services	(-) 3,566	Less Reduction in Reserves of Foreign Exchange	(-) 1,201
Net Transfer Payments from Abroad	(+) 1,740		
Surplus on Current Account	1,535	Matching Balance on Capital Account	1,535

Source: Central Bank of Ireland, *Annual Report 1993*, Table B7.

In the capital account in Table 1, the entry net capital outflow (inflow) has two broad components:

(1) The value of *direct investment* abroad by Irish residents minus direct investment in Ireland by foreigners. An example of direct foreign investment in Ireland (an inflow) would be a case of foreigners transferring foreign currency into Ireland in order to finance the purchase of land or the building of factories in this country. In this case Ireland would be reckoned as borrowing from (i.e. reducing its claims on, or increasing its liabilities to) the rest of the world. The opposite would apply if an Irish company bought foreign exchange in order to build factories or develop mines abroad. Note that capital flows (inflows or outflows) reflecting direct investment — which involves physical assets other than paper IOUs — tend to be long-term rather than short-term in character.

(2) *Portfolio investment*. This consists of purchase of foreign financial assets by Irish residents, less the purchase of Irish financial assets by foreigners. Examples of inflows (of foreign exchange) would be borrowing abroad by the Irish government, or by Irish companies; however, repayment of such borrowings, or the purchase of foreign securities by Irish residents, would give rise to outflows. The financial assets could include currency itself. Thus, if Irish residents speculate against the Irish pound by buying foreign currency (a foreign asset) and thereby adding to their deposits in a bank abroad, then a capital outflow will have occurred. A large part of portfolio investment tends to be speculative or short-term in character. In fact, the large net capital outflow recorded for 1992 in Table 1 — some £2,736 million — reflected speculative short-term movements out of the Irish pound in that year.

Although any individual entry in the balance of payments accounts can be interpreted as a balancing item, the change in the stock of foreign exchange reserves is the key balancing item in Table 1. These consist of changes in holdings of foreign exchange (or foreign government securities) at the Central Bank of Ireland. The table indicates that current account transactions generated a net gain in foreign exchange to the extent of £1,535 million. But the net outflow of foreign exchange on capital account, at £2,736 million, was £1,201 million in excess of that sum. This residual £1,201 million was obtained only by running down the nation's stock of foreign exchange reserves. This balancing item is what is usually meant by the balance of payments surplus or deficit: by this criterion — which is that adopted in this text — if foreign exchange reserves increase (decrease), then the balance of payments is said to be in surplus (deficit).

The reader may wonder in regard to the mechanisms through which the Central Bank lost some £1,201 million in foreign exchange reserves. The answer is that the immediate demanders of this foreign exchange either (a) bought it from the Central Bank in exchange for domestic money, or (b) bought it from the commercial banks; the commercial banks, in turn, obtained it from the Central Bank, giving Central Bank liabilities (i.e. Irish currency or commercial bank deposits at the Central Bank) in settlement.

Finally, in order to ensure understanding at this stage, consider a year in which the reserves of the Central Bank increased by £x million. By the criterion of overall surplus or deficit most commonly adopted, the balance of payments was therefore in surplus to the extent of £x million. The initial holders or recipients of this foreign exchange either (a) sold it to the Central Bank, receiving Irish money in return, or (b) sold it to the commercial banks; the commercial banks, in turn, sold it to the Central Bank, receiving Central Bank liabilities in settlement. It should now be clear that a surplus in the balance of payments causes an automatic expansion in the Irish money supply, while a deficit causes it to contract.

The magnitude of the change in the stock of foreign exchange reserves may be of crucial importance: if the home country's stock of foreign exchange reserves is decreasing, the nation may find it impossible to maintain approximately fixed exchange rates with trading partners.

DETERMINATION OF EXCHANGE RATES

An exchange rate is the price of a foreign currency. In this book "the" exchange rate is defined as the number of units of domestic currency required to purchase one unit of foreign currency.

(Note that "the" exchange rate is often defined as the amount of *foreign* currency required to purchase one unit of *domestic* money. But this is in confusing violation of convention: we usually define the price of a commodity such as wheat as the number of units of domestic money required to purchase, say, a bushel of wheat — *not* as the number of bushels of wheat required to purchase a unit of domestic money. Hence the definition in the paragraph above: the commodity under investigation is foreign exchange; the price is the amount of domestic money required to buy a unit of that commodity, foreign exchange. Observe that each of the two possible definitions is the reciprocal of the other; hence, if the exchange rate rises under one definition, it falls under the other. Thus, the reader should never refer to a rise or fall in the exchange rate unless it is clear that one particular definition of the exchange rate is being used.)

Like any other price, the exchange rate is determined by supply and demand. In the exposition which follows it will be assumed for simplicity that there are only two countries, Home and Abroad. Call the currency of Home the pound, and call the currency of Abroad the dollar. The two countries would be operating under *fixed exchange rates* if the central banks of the two countries intervene in the foreign exchange market in order to ensure that the total supply and demand for dollars (or pounds) in that market are equated at a fixed price. Thus, under a fixed exchange rate régime, a central bank acts as a residual supplier or demander for foreign exchange: it acts like an intervention agency in a market for agricultural produce by conducting intervention operations in order to peg price (in the present context, the price of foreign currency) at some target level. The two countries would be operating under *freely floating exchange rates* if the central banks refrained from intervention in the market for foreign exchange.

Consider the two-country example. From Home's standpoint, the exchange rate is the number of pounds required to obtain a dollar. The price of a dollar is determined by the total supply and demand for dollars in the foreign exchange market. The market *supply* of dollars is determined by Home's exports to Abroad, and by investment in Home by residents of Abroad. The market *demand* for dollars is determined by the desire of residents of Home to buy goods and services from Abroad, and the desire of residents of Home to invest in Abroad. Figure 1 illustrates the market supply and demand curves for dollars. These curves are to be interpreted as the supply and demand of all participants in the foreign exchange market, other than central banks.

Figure 1

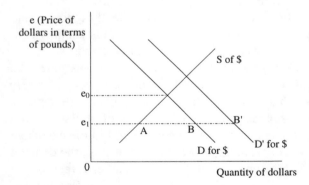

In discussing the slopes of the supply and demand curves, for simplicity in exposition we will lay focus on current account variables alone. The market *demand curve* slopes down from left to right, reflecting the fact that the lower the price of dollars in terms of pounds, the more anxious will residents of Home be to buy Abroad's goods. Thus, if the exchange rate were low, say 1/10, a Cadillac made in Abroad and priced at $50,000 in Abroad could be bought by residents of Home for £5,000. (We have ignored the impact of tariffs, transport costs, etc.) Home's residents' demand for Cadillacs would then be high; therefore, assuming that Home's demand for Abroad's goods is quite sensitive to their price denominated in Home money, the demand for dollars to pay the exporters of Abroad would be high. The opposite would hold if the exchange rate were high, say 10. (One would then have to pay £10 to get $1.) Home's residents' demand for goods made in Abroad, and hence for dollars, would be low.

The desire of Abroad's residents to import from Home is a factor determining the supply of dollars. If the exchange rate were low, say 1/10, residents of Abroad would have to pay $10 to obtain £1. Their demand for Home's goods — and hence the supply of dollars in payment for them, would be low. But if the exchange rate were high, say 10, a good priced at £10 in Home could be bought by Abroad's residents for only $I. (We have again ignored the impact of tariffs, transportation charges, etc.) The demand for Home's exports would be high. But since the price of Home's exports in terms of dollars would then be lower than in our previous example, Home might or might not earn more dollars than before, depending on the price elasticity of Abroad's demand for Home's goods. If Home did not earn more dollars as the price of dollars increased (the price elasticity of demand for Home's exports would then be less than unity), then the supply curve of dollars would have a negative slope. Although this would be a possibility if Home were a large country relative to the rest of the world, we can confidently ignore it and can assume that the supply curve has a positive slope. (This is equivalent to assuming that the demand for Home's exports is price elastic.)

The intersection of the market supply and demand curves gives the equilibrium rate of exchange, e_0 in Figure 1. Under a system of *freely floating exchange rates* this is the exchange rate which will tend to prevail; if the rate were higher than e_0, the supply of dollars would exceed the demand for dollars and market forces would bid the exchange rate down toward e_0; if the exchange rate were lower than e_0, the demand for dollars would exceed the supply of dollars and market forces would bid the rate up toward e_0. Thus, under a system of freely floating exchange rates, market forces will automatically tend to equate the supply and demand for foreign exchange.

Both the supply curve and the demand curve for dollars will tend to shift from time to time. For example, if national income in Abroad rapidly rises, Abroad's demand for imports from Home will tend to increase. This will cause the supply curve for dollars to shift to the right, leading to downward pressure on the exchange rate. If there were a rash of strikes in Home (causing domestically produced goods to become more scarce in Home), the demand by residents of Home for Abroad's goods — and hence for dollars — would tend to increase. Thus, the demand curve for dollars would shift to the right, leading to upward pressure on the exchange rate. If the exchange rate is allowed to float freely, periodic shifts in the supply and demand curves will cause the equilibrium exchange rate to fluctuate over time.

The main advantage of a system of freely floating exchange rates is that under such arrangements the exchange rate will tend to an equilibrium at which the supply and demand for foreign exchange are automatically equated. There would be no need for central banks to accumulate massive holdings of foreign exchange reserves (as buffer stocks for intervention in the foreign exchange market). In contrast to the case under fixed exchange rates, no country could have a balance of payments problem if rates were freely floating. However, a drawback is that a free float would tend to increase uncertainty. Consider, for example, a company in Home exporting to Abroad. Suppose that the company quotes its prices in terms of dollars, and that payment is made only when the goods arrive at the docks in Abroad. Unless the company makes special forward provisions (which involve extra costs), the company, when it accepts an export order, will have no way of knowing how much it will be paid in terms of pounds when the goods have arrived at Abroad's docks.

Consider next the case of *fixed exchange rates*. Suppose that the free market demand and supply curves (i.e. the demand and supply curves in the absence of any central bank intervention) remain as in Figure 1. If the Central Bank of Home attempts to maintain a fixed exchange rate, there is a danger that the fixed rate chosen may differ from the sustainable long-run equilibrium rate. If that is the case, it is possible that the pound will ultimately be forced into devaluation or revaluation. In this context we define a *devaluation* or *depreciation* of the pound as a *rise* in the price of foreign currency (implying that the Home currency would be "worth less": in the two-country example, more pounds would have to be paid for one dollar. We define an *appreciation* or *revaluation* of the pound as a *fall* in the price of foreign currency (implying that the Home currency would be "worth more"). Note that these present definitions are crucially contingent on the definition of an exchange rate which we have chosen to adopt: if we had chosen the alternative definition indicated in the second paragraph of the present subsection, then a devaluation would imply a fall rather than a rise in the exchange rate.

Suppose that the Central Bank of Home seeks to maintain the exchange rate at e_1 in Figure 1. (In what follows it will be assumed that the

Central Bank of Abroad acts passively.) At this low rate, and in the absence of central bank intervention in the foreign exchange market, the demand for dollars exceeds the supply of dollars by an amount AB per period. There would be upward pressure on the price of dollars. In order to maintain the rate e_1 — to prevent a depreciation of the pound — the Central Bank of Home must intervene in the foreign exchange market: it must resort to its foreign exchange reserves, selling AB dollars per period, in exchange for pounds. In this manner the total supply of dollars would be equated to the demand for dollars at the rate e_1 — the Central Bank of Home being the residual supplier of AB dollars per period. But, if there is no shift of either the market supply curve or the market demand curve, the Central Bank of Home will not be able to maintain the exchange rate e_1 indefinitely: in order to maintain e_1, the Bank has to sell AB dollars in each time period, but no central bank has infinite reserves of foreign exchange. Sooner or later the Bank would exhaust its holdings of foreign exchange; then it will no longer be able to supply the foreign exchange market with the requisite AB dollars per period. In the long run Home would have to devalue the pound from e_1 to e_0.

Suppose next that Home does devalue the pound to e_0, and that it wishes to keep the exchange rate fixed at e_0. The Central Bank of Home will still need foreign exchange reserves. That is because both the supply and demand curves will in fact tend to shift reflecting seasonal factors, fluctuations in income in the two countries, etc. In the summer there may be a temporary increase in the supply of dollars, reflecting expenditures by tourists from Abroad in Home; the supply curve of dollars would shift to the right. There would then be downward pressure on the exchange rate and (in the absence of central bank intervention) the pound would tend to appreciate. In order to maintain the rate e_0, the Central Bank of Home would act as a residual demander of dollars, buying dollars in exchange for pounds. In the autumn there may be an increase in the demand for dollars due to seasonality in imports of goods (e.g. coal and oil in the case of Ireland) from Abroad. The demand curve for dollars would then shift to the right putting upward pressure on the exchange rate. The Central Bank of Home, to maintain the rate e_0, would resort to its foreign exchange reserves and act as residual supplier of dollars. Thus, foreign exchange reserves will be needed in order to peg the rate at e_0.

In the above example in which Home devalued from e_1 to e_0, it was assumed that speculators remained inactive. However, given the kinds of macroeconomic policies being pursued, and ignoring any seasonal or other factors which themselves might cause the supply or demand curves to shift about, suppose that the curves D and S in Figure 1 represent the *underlying* (or "representative") demand and supply curves for foreign exchange, in the absence of action by potential speculators. Under the circumstances specified, e_0 is the underlying equilibrium rate. Suppose, furthermore, that the Central Bank of Home insists on pegging the rate at e_1. We have already seen that under the circumstances specified the central bank will have to devalue, sooner or later. However, we must now recognise that if it does not do so voluntarily, speculators will almost surely force it to do so, sooner rather than later. With the exchange rate e_1 fundamentally out of sustainable equilibrium, speculators will see that there is only one direction in which it is likely to move — upward toward e_0. Acting on these expectations they will buy dollars now at the low price, e_1, with the intention of converting these dollars back into pounds at a higher price — e_0 — after the anticipated devaluation of the pound. In this manner the expectations of speculators are likely to be self-fulfilling, in the sense that speculative activity based on expectation of a devaluation will tend to precipitate the expected devaluation. That is because the increased demand for dollars by speculators will cause the demand curve for dollars to shift to the right, so the Central Bank of Home will now have to sell more than AB dollars per period in its attempt to peg the rate at e_1. In Figure 1, speculation causes the market demand for dollars to shift to the right, from D to D'. At its target exchange rate e_1, the central bank now loses AB' instead of AB dollars per period of time. The Bank will therefore tend to run out of foreign exchange reserves more rapidly than would have been the case had speculators not entered the market. It is therefore very likely that the Central Bank of Home will be forced to devalue sooner than it would have done had there been no speculation against the pound.

Given our definition of an exchange rate, a currency is said to be *overvalued* if the present level of the exchange rate is too low relative to levels suggested by underlying market forces. These underlying market forces are often referred to as the *economic fundamentals* behind the exchange rate. If a currency is overvalued, speculators are likely to anticipate devaluation (depreciation), and may in fact precipitate devaluation. The devaluation of the Irish pound in January 1993 is an example in which calls for devaluation by the media and some politicians, which accentuated expectations of devaluation, precipitated devaluation. In the paragraph immediately above, the currency of Home was overvalued at the exchange rate e_1. A reverse kind of scenario would apply if a currency were *undervalued*.

We have seen that if a country is operating under a system of fixed (or approximately fixed) exchange rates, and if it is losing foreign exchange reserves, it may decide to devalue. However, there are other policy options.

Deflationary Fiscal Policies

If Home is losing foreign exchange reserves, it may adopt deflationary fiscal policies. If these lead to reduction in national income, the demand for imports will be reduced. This would imply that the demand curve for foreign exchange will shift to the left, thereby curtailing the loss of foreign exchange reserves. Deflationary fiscal policies also imply some downward pressure on the prices of factors of production such as labour. This may make Home's goods more competitive on export markets, thereby leading to a shift to the right in the supply curve of foreign exchange. This will also curtail reserve losses.

Restrictive Monetary Policies

Home might implement restrictive monetary policies, such as open market sales and/or increases in the permissible minimum reserve ratios to be maintained by the commercial banks. The ensuing higher domestic interest rates relative to those in Abroad would tend to attract capital inflows from Abroad. These would cause shifts to the right in the supply curve of foreign exchange and would therefore curtail reserve losses. Policy-induced monetary contraction and the associated rise in interest rates would also have a deflationary effect on aggregate demand: the demand for imports would therefore fall and hence the demand curve for foreign exchange would then shift to the left.

Restrictive Commercial Policies

Home might unilaterally increase tariffs and other controls on imports, thereby reducing the demand for imports and shifting to the left the demand curve for foreign exchange. Home might also make its exports more competitive by subsidising them. That would shift to the right the supply curve of foreign exchange. (But note that it might not be possible for a Member State of the EU, or for a member of the General Agreement on Tariffs and Trade, GATT, to implement policies of the forms just mentioned.)

Supply-side Policies

Although (as already indicated) discretionary monetary and fiscal policies may indirectly have some supply-side effects, in the short-run they operate largely through their effects on aggregate demand. Measures aimed directly toward the supply side of the economy are further alternatives. In fact, if the currency of a small country remains overvalued for long periods of time, it is usually the case that restrictive commercial policies and institutional restrictions on the international mobility of capital (implying that the Home currency is not freely convertible) are necessary in order to prevent speculators from forcing a devaluation. A very frequent counterpart to such overvaluation is that, given the exchange rate, domestic production costs are higher than those abroad. This consideration underlines the importance of supply-side measures — e.g. wage restraint, policies aimed at increasing productivity, etc. — in removing the underlying cause of overvaluation and the ensuing pressure for devaluation. However, such supply-side measures tend to operate rather slowly, relative to the effects of the actions of speculators in the foreign exchange market, which can become the dominating force in a matter of weeks, or even days.

Automatic Effects of Balance of Payments Deficits

It has already been seen in the present chapter that:

(1) If Home is experiencing balance of payments deficits, then, on a net basis, people in the market are selling domestic money to Home's central bank, receiving foreign exchange in settlement, and, on this count, contraction of the domestic money supply is an *automatic* effect of the foreign exchange reserve losses at the central bank (an automatic effect of the balance of payments deficits). If the central bank allows this automatic mechanism to operate — i.e. if it adopts a neutral policy stance by refraining from implementing added discretionary policy measures which would increase the money supply — then the balance of payments deficit may gradually, and automatically, disappear;

(2) If people in general feel, because of foreign exchange reserve losses induced by balance of payments deficits, that Home really cannot indefinitely maintain the present exchange rate, then a speedy build-up of speculation may force Home's central bank to devalue.

Thus, two key forces may be in operation simultaneously — the first tending to protect the existing exchange rate, the second tending to undermine it. In part, whether or not the force in (1) will dominate that in (2) depends on whether the central bank can convince speculators that it really will allow the mechanism in (1) to operate quickly. In practice it may not be willing to do so, because of the adverse short-run effects of the automatic mechanism on output and employment. This is an issue which will be investigated in detail in Chapter 18, which follows in Part Four of the present text.

FIXED VERSUS FREELY FLOATING EXCHANGE RATES

Compared to floating exchange rates, an advantage of a system of fixed exchange rates, if the rates really remain fixed, is that it avoids the uncertainty in regard to future exchange rates that prevails under floating rates. A disadvantage is that it may lead to a situation in which other short-run objectives of policy — such as full employment — are unattainable. Suppose, for example, that a country under fixed exchange rates is running out of foreign exchange reserves. In order to improve the current account balance of payments by reducing imports, government may have to depress demand through deflationary fiscal policies, thereby increasing unemployment. Such policies, for balance of payments reasons, were adopted to a severe degree by Ireland in the mid-1950s. The need to pursue deflationary fiscal policies for balance of payments reasons could not arise if the economy were under freely floating exchange rates: under such a system, the exchange rate would automatically tend to adjust to equate the free market forces of supply and demand for foreign exchange, and there would be no need for central banks to hold buffer stocks of foreign exchange reserves.

BUFFER STOCKS AND MANAGED FLOATING

In Chapters 7 and 8 it was seen that agricultural prices would fluctuate with weather and other conditions if the determination of those prices were left to the free play of market forces alone. It was also seen, in order to peg farm prices at target levels, that an intervention agency could engage in intervention purchases and sales, selling from buffer stocks when prices tended to rise above target levels and buying into intervention (thereby adding to buffer stocks) at times when they tended to fall below target levels. The operation of the foreign exchange market under fixed exchange rates is similar: if under free market pressures the exchange rate tends to rise above some target (the "fixed") level, then the central bank may prevent this by selling foreign exchange, thereby pegging the rate at the target level. Similarly, if under free market pressures the exchange rate shows a tendency to fall below a target level, the central bank may intervene by buying foreign exchange, again pegging the rate at a target level.

In reality the exchange rate may be neither fixed nor freely floating; rather, the home country may engage in a *managed float* of the exchange rate. Under a managed float there is a target band or range of fluctuation of the exchange rate. To some limited extent, the determination of the equilibrium exchange rate under managed floating is left to the forces of market supply and demand; however, the amplitude (i.e. upper and lower bounds) of fluctuation is constrained by central bank intervention in the event that the actual exchange rate would otherwise fall outside the target band.

Under a managed float it may be decided to maintain the exchange rate within a zone of, say, 10 per cent of some "central" or "ideal" rate x. Then the central bank would sell foreign currency if, in consequence of free market forces, the exchange rate tended to rise above x + 0.1x; it would buy foreign currency if the exchange rate would otherwise fall below x - 0.1x. Thus, a managed float is akin to a régime of rigidly fixed exchange rates if the central bank seeks to maintain a small range of fluctuation in the rate (i.e. if the acceptable upper and lower bounds for fluctuation in the rate are close to some ideal central rate): it is more akin to a freely floating exchange rate system if the central bank is content to permit the rate to fluctuate within a fairly broad interval around some central rate.

EXCHANGE RATE ARRANGEMENTS: A SPECTRUM

If the exchange rate has long been fixed, is fixed and really stays fixed, it is reasonable to assume that it will generally be expected to stay fixed. An example would be the case of the Irish pound *vis-à-vis* sterling over several decades up to 1979. However, a very different situation applies when the exchange rate is only *quasi-fixed*, meaning that it tends to stay fixed for a few months or a few years, is then discretely devalued or revalued, again stays fixed for a year or two, is again discretely devalued or revalued, etc. Such a system — that of quasi-fixed exchange rates — creates a speculator's paradise in which the expectations of speculators tend to be self-fulfilling prophesies. Under such a system, if non-speculative forces lead on average to an equilibrium (no foreign reserve change) in Home's balance of payments, then speculators may remain inactive in matters pertaining to Home's currency. However, if non-speculative forces would lead to deficits in Home's balance of payments, then it is likely that speculators will feel that there is only one direction in which the exchange rate can change — upwards (the case of devaluation). It is likely that as a group speculators will act now, and they may therefore force a speedy devaluation. (However, in the absence of any change in the "economic fundamentals" note that the devaluation would ultimately occur in any case, even with no speculation. The central bank would run out of reserves. It is the fact that the economic fundamentals are inconsistent with the overvalued exchange rate which causes the devaluation; speculation advances the time.)

Similarly, if, on average, non-speculative forces would yield surpluses in Home's balance of payments (implying a deficit in the balance of payments of some other country, because one country's surplus is another's deficit), speculators will tend to operate against a foreign currency, thereby possibly precipitating a devaluation of that foreign currency (which effectively means a revaluation of the Home currency). Thus, under an exchange rate régime which is merely quasi-fixed, speculators as a group, if they are wrong in their expectations, will lose little; however, if they are correct in their expectations (which tend to be self-fulfilling) they will gain, perhaps very substantially. These characteristics of a quasi-fixed exchange rate system would not apply under a freely floating exchange rate régime: Predictions about the *direction* of change in the exchange rate will tend to be far more accurate in the former case than in the latter.

We can briefly consider a spectrum of possible exchange rate arrangements: (a) perpetually fixed; (b) quasi-fixed; (c) managed floating; (d) a free float. In almost every important respect, the first option would be tantamount to abolishing the national currency unit and sharing the same currency with other countries in a *monetary union*. This would reduce speculation and uncertainty in regard to the exchange rate, but it would involve some perceived loss of national sovereignty, because domestic macroeconomic policies would be constrained by virtue of the *definite* fixity of the exchange rate. A free float would restore perceived national sovereignty, because domestic macroeconomic policies could be implemented without having to worry about what might happen to the exchange rate, in consequence of such policies. In practice it is likely that a system of quasi-fixed exchange rates would be characterised by periods of instability — when the authorities are attempting to maintain the current exchange rate contrary to the expectations and hopes of the speculators — followed by interludes of relative tranquillity. A managed float would share some of the characteristics of the quasi-fixed and freely floating systems. However, the question of which system *ought* to be implemented, or which system is "best", is resolved ultimately with resort to criteria which are *political* rather than economic. Nevertheless, if political decisions (in regard to the exchange rate) are to be sensible, they will be taken only after due regard to the economic implications of alternative exchange rate régimes.

CHAPTER 16

POLICY ISSUES IN SMALL OPEN ECONOMIES

Consider a small open economy. Monetary and fiscal policies will have different effects depending on whether the exchange rate is fixed or freely floating. (It was seen toward the end of the preceding chapter that managed floating of exchange rates is akin to fixed or freely floating rates, depending on the range of fluctuation in the exchange rate which the monetary authorities are both willing and able to permit.) Along the lines of many other textbooks, the discussion in the present chapter applies mainly to the short run. However, in order to avoid seriously misleading the reader in some cases where short-run and long-run effects of policy substantively differ, brief observations will be provided in regard to long-run effects. Unless otherwise indicated, when it is assumed that the exchange rate is fixed, it will also be assumed that it is *expected* to stay fixed.

(The reader may wonder why the latter assumption in regard to expectations is being made. The answer is that in the analysis which will follow shortly, we want to keep the central points as clear as possible. If there is free mobility of financial assets across national frontiers, then the owners of such assets will tend to allocate their portfolio holdings in such a manner as to equate the marginal expected yield of assets denominated in any currency. If exchange rates are expected to stay fixed, then the expected marginal yield in equilibrium is the rate of interest in any country. However, if for example the home currency is expected to depreciate over the next twelve months by x per cent against foreign currencies, then the equilibrium expected yield to residents of the home country from holding deposits abroad would be the foreign rate of interest *plus* their expected windfall gain of x per cent. If that is the case, then the equilibrium rate of interest in the small home economy would be higher than that abroad. However, for purposes of clarity as already indicated, such complications will be avoided in the present introductory exposition.)

Now, consider first the case of fixed exchange rates.

POLICIES UNDER FIXED EXCHANGE RATES

Fiscal Policy

Assume that we start with the economy in equilibrium well below full capacity utilisation and that the government pursues an expansionary fiscal policy by increasing its expenditure on, say, non-tradables. It is assumed that this is a pure fiscal policy (not a combination of monetary and fiscal measures); thus, the increased government expenditure on goods and services is financed either by borrowing from the non-bank public or through increased taxation (rather than by borrowing from the central bank). We know from elementary multiplier theory that as long as producers are willing to supply whatever quantity may be demanded, national income will increase by some (possibly small) multiple of the increase in government expenditure. However, as income increases, so too does the transactions demand for money. Thus, the demand curve for money will shift to the right. (Recall Figure 1, Chapter 12.) If the supply of money stayed constant, this would raise the interest rate, thereby choking off some of private sector investment demand and possibly some of consumption demand. (If this were to occur, the extended public sector, by inducing upward pressure on the rate of interest which chokes off some of private sector demand, would be said to be *crowding out* part of private sector demand.) The rise in equilibrium income would then be less than multiplier analysis alone would predict. However, a considerable rise in the domestic rate of interest relative to that abroad could only be temporary: the higher domestic interest rate relative to that abroad would attract capital inflows from abroad, increasing the reserves of the commercial banks and thereby automatically increasing the domestic money supply. Thus, the interest rate would be bid down toward its initial level. Under the circumstances outlined (with no change in the rate of interest in comparing the initial equilibrium with the new equilibrium), income would therefore increase more or less as predicted by ordinary multiplier analysis (of an open economy with a positive marginal propensity to import).

In practice (contrary to what was assumed just above) producers might not be willing to supply whatever quantity is demanded: the price level may have to be bid up slightly to induce them to expand output, though that is least likely to be the case if, as was assumed, we start with plenty of excess capacity. As was indicated in Chapter 14, the aggregate supply curve may be infinitely elastic (i.e. perfectly flat) around an equilibrium if there is abundant excess capacity. Under such circumstances (taking account of both aggregate supply and demand) increased government expenditure would raise income by an amount approximated by ordinary multiplier analysis of an open economy. However, if we start in equilibrium below but close to full capacity utilisation, then the aggregate supply curve will be positively sloped and an increase in aggregate demand will induce some small increase in the domestic price level. The reader should know, from Figure 2b of Chapter 14, that equilibrium income would then increase by less than the amount predicted by elementary multiplier analysis of an open economy under fixed exchange rates.

The conclusions at this stage are:

(1) If we start with the economy in equilibrium well below full capacity utilisation, increased government expenditure on non-tradables in a small open economy under fixed exchange rates will cause national income to increase (a) by an amount approximated by the relevant multiplier if the aggregate supply curve is infinitely elastic or (b) by a smaller amount than in (a) if the aggregate supply curve is positively sloped. The main point is that equilibrium income increases under the specified conditions. (It will be shown below that a crucial assumption yielding this conclusion is that the exchange rate *vis-à-vis* some large country is indeed fixed.) Cases (a) and (b) above are illustrated in Figure 1 where the aggregate demand curve shifts from AD to AD' corresponding to case (a), but the shift corresponding to case (b) would be from (AD) to (AD)' in the diagram. (The economy would be at full capacity utilisation — sometimes called full employment — only when AS is absolutely vertical.) Given that the horizontal distance of the shift of the aggregate demand curve has been drawn the same in both cases, the diagram clearly indicates that the increase in income is smaller in case (b) than in case (a).

Figure 1

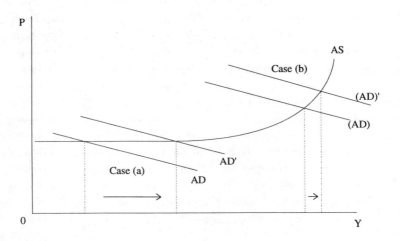

(2) In the first paragraph of the present subsection it was seen that the money supply in a small open economy under fixed exchange rates would *automatically* increase if there were an increase in income and hence an increase in the transactions demand for money, leading to no change in the equilibrium rate of interest. From this the reader may conclude, in a small open economy under fixed exchange rates, that the policies of the small country's central bank can have a significant effect on *neither* the domestic money supply nor the equilibrium rate of interest. As will be shown in the subsection which immediately follows, this conclusion is correct — though the assumption of a fixed exchange rate is crucial. However, before turning to monetary policy, some qualifications in regard to the long run are appropriate.

The foregoing was concerned with the effectiveness (in the sense of generating some variation in output) of fiscal policy in a small open economy under fixed exchange rates. Because we were concerned with a pure fiscal policy — rather than a combination of fiscal policy and discretionary monetary policy — it was assumed that the fiscal expansion was financed either through taxation or by borrowing from the non-bank public. Suppose that the fiscal expansion was financed by borrowing from the non-bank public, and consider some long-run effects of the fiscal expansion. In order to keep the analysis as clear as possible, suppose that the economy is initially in an equilibrium with government revenue equal to government expenditure, and that government expenditure on goods and services is *permanently* increased to some constant level, this increase being recurrently financed by borrowing from the non-bank public. If aggregate supply were infinitely elastic, short-run considerations would suggest that income would *permanently* increase by an amount predicted by (or approximated by) ordinary multiplier analysis. However, longer-run considerations indicate that even this will be an overestimate. That is because interest will have to be paid on the government borrowings. The necessary annual interest payments will be larger, the longer the deficit financing is maintained. The key point in the long run is that sooner or later, the government will have to increase tax rates in order to pay the interest on the national debt created by the cumulative borrowing, and this extra taxation, in turn, will exert a depressing impact on private sector demand. Thus, even if aggregate supply is infinitely elastic, the long-run effects of a fiscal expansion financed by borrowing from the non-bank public will be less potent than those suggested by short-run considerations alone.

Monetary Policy

Consider next the effects of an expansionary monetary policy in a small open economy under fixed exchange rates. Throughout this section we will be referring to monetary policy in the form of open market operations by the small economy's central bank. Suppose that the central bank buys securities on the open market. The money supply therefore increases and in the first instance there is downward pressure on the rate of interest. But this means that the domestic rate of interest falls relative to the rate of interest in the large economy, or large economies, with which the small economy has a fixed exchange rate. Domestic residents therefore prefer foreign interest-bearing assets, and a *capital outflow* occurs in consequence. The capital outflow means that the demand for foreign currency increases. We know from the preceding chapter that in the absence of central bank intervention to maintain the exchange rate, the domestic currency would depreciate on the foreign exchange market. Therefore, in order to keep the exchange rate at its fixed level the central bank must buy domestic money with foreign exchange. Thus, the central bank's holdings of foreign exchange reserves fall. In this manner the central bank will be forced to offset the initial expansion in the money supply by a more or less equivalent contraction in the money supply. The interest rate will then move back toward its initial level. Hence, under a fixed exchange rate with one or more relatively large countries, monetary policy (in the form of open market operations) can have little or no effect on equilibrium national income.

It is wrong to say that monetary policy has no effect at all in a small open economy under fixed exchange rates; as has been seen, an attempt to expand the money supply via open market purchases leads to reduction in the nation's foreign exchange reserves. Hence, if the central bank persists in conducting open market purchases, then it is likely that the ensuing foreign exchange reserve losses over time will undermine the ability of the authorities to keep the exchange rate fixed.

The conclusion that under the conditions specified monetary policy can have little or no effect on equilibrium income may have surprised some readers (especially those accustomed to thinking in terms of closed economies) but — as long as the small economy under a fixed exchange rate remains truly open and as long as there is relatively free mobility of goods and of financial assets across its frontiers — that conclusion is incontrovertible.

In Chapter 12 the creation of money in a closed economy was analysed. Given the assumptions at that stage (especially the assumption of a closed economy) that analysis was broadly correct. However, it was indicated in Chapter 12 that such analysis would have to be modified when we came to consider a small open economy under a fixed exchange rate. The analysis of the creation of money in Chapter 12 is misleading or wrong when applied to a small open economy under a fixed exchange rate. In small open economies under fixed exchange rates, attempts by the domestic central bank to control the money supply by open market operations must, other things being equal, break down. For such economies, open market operations will generally not lead to permanent multiple expansion (or multiple contraction) of the domestic money supply (as outlined for a closed economy in Chapter 12). At the risk of offending the reader by repetition, that is because:

(1) If the central bank buys bonds, the money supply, in the first instance, will increase, tending to cause the domestic interest rate to fall. But this will cause capital outflows, and capital outflows imply automatic contraction of the domestic money supply. (Be sure that you understand why this is so). The capital outflows will continue — the domestic money supply continues to contract — so long as the domestic rate of interest is below that abroad in countries with which the small open economy maintains fixed exchange rates. These capital outflows and the resulting monetary contraction will cause the domestic rate of interest to rise. The capital outflows induced by the initial interest rate differentials will cease only when the domestic rate of interest has returned to its initial equilibrium level, which must (in effect) be the same as the interest rate prevailing in the larger countries with which the small economy has fixed exchange rates.

(2) If the small open economy under fixed exchange rates tries to reduce its money supply independently of the rest of the world via open market sales of securities, its interest rate, in the first instance, will rise. Because its equilibrium rate of interest must be roughly in line with that abroad, a result will be capital inflows in response to the higher interest rate obtainable in the small economy, and downward pressure on that rate of interest. The capital inflows in response to interest rate differentials will cease only when the domestic rate of interest has returned to its initial level — and that rate of interest must be approximately the same as that prevailing in the larger countries with which the small open economy has fixed exchange rates.

In sum, in a small open economy under fixed exchange rates, any attempt by the central bank to control the money supply independently of the rest of the world is likely to be thwarted: in effect, its equilibrium rate of interest is that prevailing abroad (in countries with which a fixed exchange rate is maintained). If the monetary authorities *cannot control the price of money* — the rate of interest — then they *cannot control the quantity of money*. Thus the analysis of the creation of money along the lines of Chapter 12 is most misleading if applied to small open economies under fixed exchange rates. The central conclusion at this stage is that a small open economy under fixed exchange rates (if it really is open) cannot control its money supply independently of the rest of the world.

POLICIES UNDER FREELY FLOATING EXCHANGE RATES
Fiscal Policy

Assume excess capacity and fiscal policies in the form of increased government expenditure on goods and services, financed by taxation or by borrowing from the non-bank public. If income does start to increase, this will cause an increase in the transactions demand for money, placing upward pressure on the rate of interest. But any rise in the rate of interest will attract capital inflows from abroad. These capital inflows increase the supply of foreign exchange: the supply curve of foreign exchange would shift to the right. The price of foreign exchange would then fall: the domestic currency would appreciate. But, given foreign prices, this would mean that exporters (in the small economy) would be paid less in terms of domestic money for goods sent abroad. If (as in a short-run situation) domestic factor prices stay constant, the profit margin obtainable on exports, and hence the volume of exports, will fall. The appreciation of the domestic currency also means that imports, and hence importables, will be cheaper than before in terms of domestic money. If domestic factor prices stay more or less constant (as in a short-run situation), both potential exports and domestically produced goods which compete with imports on the home market will become cost-uncompetitive. Some domestic suppliers to the home market will therefore cut back their outputs or close down entirely. Consumer demand for such goods would be satisfied by increased imports. Imports would therefore increase in volume while exports would decrease in volume. The increase in government expenditure would in fact tend to be fully offset by an equivalent deterioration in the current account balance of payments. Under such circumstances there would be no net change in the level of aggregate demand. Thus, from the standpoint of rapidly driving the economy toward full employment, fiscal policy is of little importance in a small open economy under a system of freely floating exchange rates. Note how this contrasts with what happens under fixed exchange rates.

As before, the focus in the foregoing has been on the short-run alone. Thus, in the short-run, the expansion of the government sector was exactly offset by a contraction of private sector output. In consequence, the expansionary fiscal policy generated no net change in output. Longer-run effects may differ. For example, if the increase in government expenditure on goods and services is permanent, then the government sooner or later will have to increase tax rates in order to meet interest payments on the debt; in itself, this would tend to have a contractionary impact on aggregate demand. However, given that output and employment would be falling, the assumption that factor prices are absolutely rigid in a downward direction would be unlikely to hold for very long. Following the expiration of old wage contracts, etc., if factor prices do respond to downward pressure on the prices of final products, then the output of the private sector is unlikely to incur a permanent contraction in the manner suggested by short-run considerations alone.

Monetary Policy

Consider now an expansionary monetary policy, in the form of open market purchases, in a small open economy under freely floating exchange rates. As before, assume some excess capacity. The increase in the money supply will initially put downward pressure on domestic interest rates. That will lead to capital outflows to take advantage of the relatively higher interest rates abroad. These capital outflows increase the demand for foreign currency. The demand curve for foreign exchange will therefore shift to the right, leading to a rise in the price of foreign exchange — a depreciation of the domestic currency. This means that in terms of domestic money, export prices will rise. Assuming a short-run situation in which domestic factor prices are more or less given, the profit margin obtainable on exports therefore increases; hence the volume of exports increases. The depreciation of the domestic currency also means that the prices of imports, in terms of domestic money, will increase. Therefore, the prices of domestically produced goods which compete with imports on the home market also increase. Again assuming a short-run situation with rigid domestic factor prices (domestically produced) importables become more cost-competitive. The output of such goods is therefore increased and a greater share of the home market is supplied from domestic sources. The volume of imports accordingly falls. Because of increased exports and decreased imports, the balance of payments on current account will have become more favourable, and aggregate demand will have increased. Thus, from the standpoint of driving the economy closer to full capacity utilisation in the short-run, monetary policy is of more importance under floating exchange rates than under fixed exchange rates.

The short-run focus in the above analysis of monetary policy under freely floating exchange rates should be fairly obvious: monetary policy was effective in generating increased output because it brought about an increase in the ratio of output prices to factor input prices, which were assumed to remain constant. In the longer run (following the expiration of old wage contracts, etc.) factor prices are unlikely to stay constant. In fact, although there may be some lags, it is likely that they will increase in phase with, and in proportion to, the increase in output prices. If that is the case, *real* profit margins — and therefore the incentive to increase aggregate supply — will not have changed, and therefore output will not have *permanently* changed. Thus, the increased output brought about by expansionary monetary policy under freely floating exchange rates may be of short-run duration only: the long-run effect may be nil.

Very briefly, the key points in the present chapter up to now have been as follows: Assuming some slack in the economy to begin with, characterise a short-run policy as "effective" if it tends to generate changes in output and employment *in the short run*. Then, under fixed exchange rates, fiscal policy is effective and monetary policy is ineffective. The opposite holds under freely floating exchange rates: fiscal policy is ineffective and monetary policy is effective. However, these results do not necessarily hold in the medium run or in the long run.

MONEY SUPPLY AND INFLATION IN SMALL OPEN ECONOMIES

In the earlier discussion of inflation in Chapter 13 it was stated that inflation could not proceed for long unless the money supply were increasing. Thus, increase in the money supply (by affecting the level of aggregate demand) might be an initiating cause of inflation, or it might be an effect of inflation. In the case of a small open economy under fixed exchange rates, increases in the money supply must be mainly effects of inflation. From the standpoint of the small open economy with a fixed exchange rate, the ultimate causes of an internal inflationary process lie outside the country. Thus expansion in the money supply in a small open economy which remains indefinitely under fixed exchange rates could not be the cause of (sustained) inflation. In fact, the supply of money in the small open economy under fixed exchange rates must react passively to the increased demand for money to finance successively higher nominal levels of transactions, generated by the externally determined inflation. That can be seen as follows:

Recall the quantity theory of money, $MV(i, \dot{P}) = PY$. Assume that the prices of tradables are increasing by 20 per cent a year, in line with inflation abroad. If V is constant (and according to the quantity theory of

money it will be approximately constant from year to year as long as both
the rate of inflation and the real rate of interest are approximately constant) and if Y is constant or increasing (because of economic growth),
then it must be the case that M is increasing. In fact, the rate of increase
in M must roughly equal the rate of increase in PY. Thus the central bank
must passively allow the money supply to increase in line with inflation
abroad.

Suppose for simplicity that there is some constant rate of inflation
abroad, that the real rate of interest is approximately constant, that the
small open economy has a fixed exchange rate, and that its central bank
attempts to hold the money supply constant. It is easy to see that this
policy must break down. With M given, with V in the long run varying
only slightly and with P increasing in line with inflation abroad, Y would
be decreasing. Also, the *real* money supply would be decreasing. On this
count the domestic rate of interest would tend to increase in the short
run. The decreases in Y and therefore decreases in real income and
imports in each time period would lead to successively larger current
account balance of payments surpluses. These earnings of foreign
exchange would be converted into domestic money, thereby increasing
the domestic money supply. Also, the short-run rise in domestic interest
rates would induce capital inflows. These too would increase the domestic money supply, lowering the rate of interest back toward its initial
level (i.e. that level prevailing in countries with which the small economy
maintains fixed exchange rates).

It might be argued that the central bank could prevent the money
supply from increasing (through the channels just mentioned) by conducting open market sales. However, it could not attain such an objective. Open market sales would lead to upward pressure on the interest
rate, inducing capital inflows. Such inflows would cause the supply
curve of foreign exchange to shift to the right. Given the commitment to
fixed exchange rates, the central bank would then need to buy foreign
currency in exchange for domestic money. Thus, the hands of central
bankers in small open economies with fixed exchange rates are tied: in
an environment of inflation generated by forces abroad, the central bank
must passively allow the domestic money supply to increase.

For as long as a small economy remains open and maintains a fixed
exchange rate with any large country with which there is free trade (a) it
cannot independently control its money supply and (b) it cannot independently determine its rate of inflation. Opting for a freely floating exchange rate régime has some *potentially* attractive features: it is the *only*
way in which the small country could determine the rate of expansion of
its money supply and its rate of inflation, *independently* of what might be

happening in the rest of the world.

Suppose that the central bank of the small country, Home, held the money supply constant, that Home operated a freely floating exchange rate régime with the rest of the world, and that the rest of the world was inflating by, say, 10 per cent annually. Under such circumstances, Home's currency would tend to appreciate — that is increase in value against other currencies — by about 10 per cent annually. With foreign inflation at 10 per cent annually and Home's currency appreciating at the same rate, the prices of Home's exportables and importables, and the prices of imports, all denominated in Home's currency, would be constant. Thus, under the conditions specified, Home would tend to have zero inflation.

The key determinant of Home's rate of inflation under freely floating exchange rates would be the rate of increase of its money supply (which, under a freely floating exchange rate system, would be controllable by Home's central bank). By monetary restraint and freely floating exchange rates Home could opt for a very low rate of inflation or no inflation. On the other hand, by rapid expansion of the money supply under a freely floating exchange rate régime, Home could create hyperinflation, independently of inflation in the rest of the world. (Home's currency would then be depreciating against other currencies.)

Under a freely floating exchange rate régime there might be political pressures imposed on Home's central bank to cause high inflation by rapid monetary expansion. Thus, suppose that productivity and the terms of trade are given, that Home operates a freely floating exchange rate system, and that trade unions annually demand and obtain high money wage awards. If the price level remained constant, such increases would imply *real* wage increases (and declines in real profit margins). If the central bank did not increase the money supply, thereby inducing increases in the price level (and thereby moderating the rise in real wage rates), a consequence would be increased unemployment. It does not require much political insight to see that the Central Bank of Home might be pressured into averting this unemployment. How? By increasing the money supply, thereby generating inflation (and getting real wages down) which would have as its counterpart a steady depreciation of Home's currency on foreign exchange markets. It is because the consequences just mentioned might well be very real probabilities that we would not recommend that Ireland independently determine its own rate of inflation by opting for freely floating exchange rates within the European Union.

Two final remarks, which should already be apparent:

(1) A small open economy may decide to maintain a fixed exchange rate with some large country with which there is free trade. But if it does so,

it cannot independently control its rate of inflation or the rate of expansion of its money supply. Its rate of inflation will tend to be high or low depending on whether it keeps a fixed exchange rate with a country, or is in a currency union, which has high or low inflation.

(2) A small open economy may decide to control its rate of inflation, independently of what is happening in the rest of the world, by appropriate control of its money supply. But if it does so, it cannot independently control its exchange rate.

DEVALUATION AS A STABILISATION POLICY INSTRUMENT IN A SMALL OPEN ECONOMY

Consider a small open economy under (quasi-) fixed exchange rates. It is sometimes suggested that a once-and-for-all currency devaluation would improve the current account balance of payments, thereby simultaneously increasing output and employment in the small open economy. It is easy to see that such a proposition, as a statement about the long run, is likely to be erroneous; however, it does have some validity in the short run.

As before, we start with the small open economy in equilibrium below full capacity utilisation. Call the small open economy Home and call the rest of the world Abroad. Assume that a particular exchange rate prevails initially. Call Home's currency the pound and Abroad's the dollar, and suppose that the initial exchange rate is £0.5 to $1. Suppose that Home now devalues to a new fixed exchange rate so that £1 now exchanges against $1.

Because the small open economy is a price-taker in the case of tradable goods, the dollar prices of such goods will remain unchanged after the devaluation; however, their prices in terms of pounds will double. If, as is likely, factor prices are more or less given in the short run, the rise in the domestic currency price of exportables will raise the profit margins of firms in the exportables sector. Such increases in the cost-competitiveness of domestic firms in the exportables sector will generate an increase in exports.

The domestic price of importables has also doubled. If domestic factor prices are given, that causes an increase in the profit margins of domestic firms in the importables sector. The increased cost-competitiveness of such firms leads to increased domestic output in substitution for imported goods. Thus imports fall in the short run.

Hence, in the short run — for as long as domestic factor prices stay more or less constant — the balance of payments on current account, (X - M), improves and that increase in aggregate demand is likely to generate an increase in domestic employment. There is also a gain in the level of foreign exchange reserves in the small open economy.

In the long run, however, neither the factor market nor the non-tradables sector can be insulated from the devaluation:

(1) If, as indeed will be the case, the domestic currency prices of tradable goods rise in phase with the devaluation, firms in the tradables sector will be willing to pay more for the factors of production; they will, accordingly, *bid up* factor prices. Also, because the prices of food and other tradable goods will have increased (by 100 per cent in the example given), trade unions and other organisations on behalf of factor owners, are likely to *push up* factor prices in order to maintain their real incomes. These two considerations mean that in the long run, factor prices are likely to adjust and to increase by the full extent of the devaluation; in the present example they will increase by about 100 per cent.

(2) Firms in the non-tradables sector must pay the same prices for inputs as firms in the tradables sector. Because the value of the output of the non-tradables sector must equal the value of all inputs used (value added), and because the prices of inputs will tend to have increased by the full extent of the devaluation (by 100 per cent in the present example), the prices of non-tradables will increase by about 100 per cent in full long-run equilibrium, in response to the devaluation.

Hence it is concluded: If a small open economy devalues, *all* internal prices — those of tradables, of non-tradables and of the factors of production — will tend to increase by the full proportionate extent of the devaluation in full long-run equilibrium. Because there would then be no change in *relative* prices, there would be no change in *real* wages or in *real* profit margins and hence, in full long-run equilibrium, there would be no change in the structure of output. Hence, other things being equal, in full long-run equilibrium, real exports and real imports, and production of tradables and non-tradables, will be the same as they were before the devaluation.

It follows that devaluation by a small open economy may have no effect on *real* variables (such as real exports, real imports, real output and employment) in the long run. Its only long-run effects then are (a) a once-and-for-all increase in the prices of all goods and factors of production and (b) a once-and-for-all gain in the level of foreign exchange reserves. The latter gain is obtained in the short-run disequilibrium in which (X - M) is improved in response to the devaluation. But in the long run, real exports and real imports return to their initial levels; that is why the gain in foreign exchange reserves is a "once off" phenomenon.

PART FOUR

HIGHER LEVEL
MACROECONOMIC THEORY

CHAPTER 17

DEMAND-SIDE IN A CLOSED ECONOMY: IS AND LM

The macroeconomic analysis of the preceding chapters has been elementary. In particular, the approach adopted was *sequential* rather than *simultaneous*. Thus, Chapters 10 and 11, which involved the goods market alone, investigated models of income determination quite independently of any explicit consideration of money or the rate of interest. This meant that, for the most part, we were forced to regard investment demand as entirely autonomous/exogenous (i.e. determined by forces outside the model under analysis). Money and the rate of interest were later brought into the investigation, but this was done in sequential fashion, without due emphasis on the simultaneous interaction between the goods market and the money market.

A further deficiency of the approach adopted until now is that when income determination through aggregate demand and aggregate supply was investigated in Chapter 14, the exposition necessarily excluded any rigorous derivation of the aggregate demand curve in the (P, Y) plane. The four chapters which immediately follow will help rectify these deficiencies in methodology. It will be found that although the analyses of Chapters 10 to 16 lacked rigour and were in some respects logically defective, the higher-level of analysis to be initiated will not invalidate most of the central conclusions already attained; however, apart from strengthening the logical basis for the key conclusions already reached, it will yield a great many additional insights.

Until further notice, it will be assumed that the economy is *closed*, that the price level is *given*, and that there is *no government expenditure* and *no taxation*. These assumptions, which are made at this stage only to facilitate understanding of key conceptual issues, will be relaxed at a later stage. Furthermore, along the lines of Chapters 10 and 11, consideration of the supply side of the economy will be deferred until later (in Chapter 20). The economy under investigation will now be decomposed into two principal markets or sectors, *the goods market* and *the money market*.

A little thought will suggest that if the economy is really in macroeconomic equilibrium, it must simultaneously be in equilibrium in both markets. The goods market equilibrium condition is that planned savings equal planned investment. The money market equilibrium condition is that the supply of money must equal the demand for money. If one of those markets is in an apparent equilibrium, while the other market is not, then the economy cannot be in full equilibrium: disequilibrium in one market will force the other market out of equilibrium. For example, suppose that the goods market equilibrium condition, $S = I$, momentarily applies, but that the money market is not in equilibrium. Specifically, suppose that the demand for money exceeds the supply of money (so there is an excess demand for money). The excess demand for money will cause the rate of interest to increase. If the rate of interest rises, then investment demand will fall, thereby disturbing the initially assumed equilibrium in the goods market.

GOODS MARKET EQUILIBRIUM: THE IS CURVE

As was explained in Chapter 10, a necessary condition for macroeconomic equilibrium is that planned savings equal planned investment. But the earlier analysis was facile in pretending that this condition alone enabled us to determine what equilibrium Y must be. Write the equilibrium condition as

(1) $S(Y) = I(i, \exp)$

with $\Delta S/\Delta Y > 0$ and $\Delta I/\Delta i < 0$, where the inequalities indicate that planned savings are an increasing function of income, and planned investment is a decreasing function of the rate of interest. The expression on the left-hand side of (1) merely recognises that planned savings are a function of income. That on the right-hand side expresses investment demand as a function of the rate of interest, i, given the state of expectations in regard to the future (exp). Given exp, it is plausibly assumed that investment demand is inversely related to the interest rate: if the interest rate rises, investment demand will fall. Given the costs of financing an investment project, the level of investment demand also depends on the flow of expected net returns (net receipts) — perhaps over years far into the future — which the project is expected to yield. It is important to observe that such returns are those which are expected (not necessarily realised). Hence, they depend on the prevailing mood of optimism or pessimism of entrepreneurs. Unless otherwise indicated, we will take the "state of expectations" held by entrepreneurs as given. The goods market equilibrium condition can then be written simply as

(2) $S(Y) = I(i)$,

with $\Delta S/\Delta Y > 0$ and $\Delta I/\Delta i < 0$.

It is assumed that statisticians/econometricians have estimated the functional form of the investment function — the manner in which investment demand depends on the interest rate, given expectations. The trouble is that one cannot then determine I unless one knows what i is. But analysis of the goods market alone cannot tell us the value of i. In fact, (2) is one equation in two ultimate unknowns — i and Y — and it will be recalled from elementary algebra that such an equation has an infinite number of solutions: there is an infinite number of (i, Y) combinations which satisfy equation (2). Alternatively phrased, equation (2) only enables us to solve for Y as a function of i (itself as yet in the analysis another unknown).

The economy's IS curve is a pictorial representation of all relevant (i, Y) combinations which satisfy equation (2). It depicts an infinity of solutions to the goods market equilibrium condition: it shows all the (i, Y) combinations at which planned savings equal planned investment, given expectations. One expects an inverse relationship between the solution values i and Y: if i rises, I will fall, and therefore Y will fall. Thus, the economy's IS curve will slope downwards, as in Figure 1 though of course it need not be linear.

Figure 1

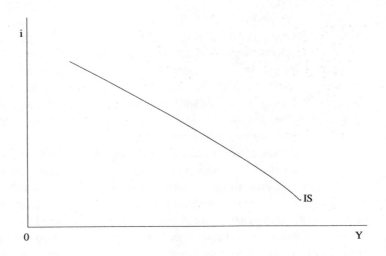

Rather than rely on algebra (which some readers might not like), one can derive the economy's IS curve from first principles graphically, as follows:

Figure 2a   Figure 2b

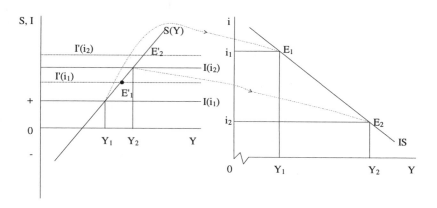

Figure 2a is a savings-investment diagram similar to Figure 3b in Chapter 10; however, it is now explicitly recognised that investment demand depends on the (as yet undetermined) rate of interest. (Note that, as drawn, we have exaggerated the steepness of the slope of the S(Y) locus, purely in the interests of visual clarity.) $I(i_1)$ represents investment demand at some particular interest rate i_1. The ensuing equilibrium Y — the solution to equation (2) corresponding to that interest rate — is then Y_1. Mapping these values of i and Y into the (i, Y) plane generates the point E_1 in Figure 2b. Hence, E_1 in Figure 2b indicates that if the interest rate is i_1, then equilibrium Y is Y_1. (Note that the scale of the horizontal axis in the second diagram is not necessarily the same as that in the first.)

Next, suppose that the interest rate were lower than i_1; $i_2 < i_1$. In response to such a *fall* in the interest rate, the initial investment demand function in Figure 2a would shift *upwards* to, say, $I(i_2)$, and the resulting equilibrium for income would be an increased value of Y, Y_2. Mapping the new i and Y values into the (i, Y) plane yields point E_2 in Figure 2b; this is another set of solution values for equation (2). It shows that if i = i_2, then the level of Y at which planned savings equal planned investment — at which the goods market is in equilibrium — is Y = Y_2.

Two points on the economy's IS curve — two sets of solutions to equation (2) — have now been traced. We could likewise consider further variations in i, and hence in I (with I moving in the opposite direction to variations in i), and trace the resulting solution values for Y in Figure 2a. If we did so, and mapped the equilibria into Figure 2b, we would be deriving a downward-sloped locus like that labelled IS in the diagram. Note that in the above derivation, $i_1 > i_2$ implies $I_1 < I_2$, which implies $Y_1 < Y_2$. The IS curve is a (partial) graphical depiction of the infinity of solutions to equation (2), and although it is not necessarily linear, it plausibly slopes downwards. It is important to understand what determines the *slope* and the *level* of the IS curve.

Slope of IS: Suppose that the state of expectations stays constant and consider a given IS curve, say that in Figure 2b. The slope of the curve is

$$(3) \ \Delta i/\Delta Y = 1/(\Delta Y/\Delta I)(\Delta I/\Delta i)$$

The absolute value of (3) will be lower — the IS curve will be flatter — the larger the national income multiplier $\Delta Y/\Delta I$ and the greater the degree of sensitivity of investment demand to changes in the rate of interest (represented in Figure 2a by the extent to which the investment demand function shifts when the interest rate changes), $\Delta I/\Delta i$.

Level of IS: The level of the IS curve in the (i, Y) plane is determined by the level of autonomous (otherwise termed exogenous) demand. Autonomous demand in any given model is that part of aggregate demand which is determined outside the model (rather than determined, or explained, by the model). For example, in the present model the state of expectations, exp, is taken as given. This means that part of investment demand is possibly independent of the rate of interest. Suppose this is the case, and that the state of expectations improves, which implies that (at any interest rate) potential investors become more optimistic in regard to the future. Looking back at Figure 2a, this means that the investment function, as originally drawn, would shift upwards: firms in general would seek to invest more at any particular interest rate. Thus, $I(i_1)$ would go to $I'(i_1)$, $I(i_2)$ would go to $I'(i_2)$, etc. As is indicated by the new equilibria E'_1 and E'_2, the ensuing equilibrium level of Y corresponding to each i would be higher than before. The reader should be able to see that the entire IS curve would have shifted to the right. In short, IS shifts to the right if autonomous demand increases; it shifts to the left if it decreases.

(If government is brought into the model, the basic conceptual meaning of the IS curve is unchanged; only its derivation is more complicated. IS then indicates the locus of (i, Y) combinations at which the goods market equilibrium condition — equation (5) of Chapter 11 — is satisfied. Then, if G is increased — if an expansionary fiscal policy is implemented — IS will shift to the right. This merely reflects the fact that at an unchanged interest rate, the level of Y at which the goods market is in equilibrium will be higher than before. Similarly, if the model is extended further to include foreign trade, IS is to be interpreted as the locus of (i, Y) combinations at which equation (18) of Chapter 11 is satisfied. In all cases, IS shifts to the right if autonomous demand rises.

Thus, if investors become more optimistic in regard to the future, if consumers become more spendthrift, if government increases its expenditure or reduces tax rates, or if net exports increase because of an emerging boom abroad, then the home economy's IS curve will shift to the right.)

MONEY MARKET EQUILIBRIUM: THE LM CURVE

The IS curve expresses goods market equilibrium Y as a function of the rate of interest. To determine that Y, we must know the rate of interest. The trouble in a proper specification of the present closed economy model is that in general, i cannot logically be taken as given (i.e. it is *not* autonomous/exogenous; rather, it is an *endogenous* variable, determined in the model). The reader might now suggest an investigation of the money market in isolation, in order to determine the equilibrium rate of interest. However, it will be found that a further problem of indeterminacy — similar to that encountered in dealing with the goods market — will arise in an investigation of the money market: in general, it will be impossible to determine equilibrium i unless Y is known. But, as already seen, we cannot not determine Y unless we know what i is.

The rate of interest is the price (opportunity cost) of holding money. Like any other price, it is determined by supply and demand. The money market is in equilibrium — the interest rate shows no tendency to change — when the supply of money, M (as set by central bank policy in the present closed economy model) is equal to the demand for money, L(i, Y), where the functional notation L(..., ...) is used to remind us that we are referring to the community's liquidity preference function. Formally, the money market equilibrium condition is:

(4) $M = L(i, Y)$

with $\Delta L/\Delta i < 0$ and $\Delta L/\Delta Y > 0$.

M can be taken as exogenously given. Assume also that the functional form of L(..., ...) on the right-hand side of (4) is known, as a result of statistical/econometric studies. The alert reader hopefully sees that (4) is one equation in two unknowns; therefore, it has an infinite number of solutions. Phrased otherwise, given the money supply, there is an infinite number of (i, Y) combinations which yield an equilibrium in the money market. Therefore one cannot determine i unless one knows what Y is. So, given M and the L(..., ...) function, the best one can do at this stage of the analysis is to express equilibrium Y as a function of i. It should be clear that the present problem of indeterminacy is very similar to that encountered above when dealing with equation (2) in the context of the goods market. The reasoning just outlined can be repeated and extended using graphical methods.

$\overline{M}$ in Figure 3a is the supply of money, as exogenously set by central bank policy. The demand for money depends on both i (reflecting speculative demand) and Y (reflecting mainly transactions demand). Thus, at any interest rate one cannot determine the community's demand for money unless one knows what Y is.

Figure 3a   Figure 3b

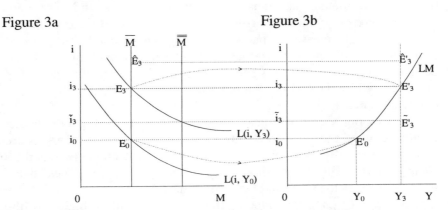

In Figure 3a, $L(i, Y_0)$ represents the demand for money if Y is at some level Y_0; the corresponding equilibrium interest rate is i_0. The point E_0 therefore represents money market equilibrium if $Y = Y_0$. The point E'_0 in Figure 3b is simply a mapping of the (i, Y) combination at E_0 into the (i, Y) plane. Thus, E'_0 is one possible representation of money market equilibrium — given the money supply, it depicts one solution to equation (4): at that point, the demand for money, L, is equal to the supply of money, $\overline{M}$.

Next, suppose that $Y = Y_3 > Y_0$. Reflecting mainly higher transactions demand requirements, the corresponding demand for money function lies above that initially drawn in Figure 3a. The equilibrium interest rate is then i_3. The equilibrium depicted at point E_3 can be mapped into the (i, Y) plane, thereby generating point E'_3, the co-ordinates of which are (i_3, Y_3). Given $\overline{M}$, the point E'_3 represents another solution to equation (4); it indicates another (i, Y) combination at which the money market is in equilibrium. Note that, given $\overline{M}$, $Y_3 > Y_0$ implies $i_3 > i_0$.

Two points at which the money market is in equilibrium — points at which the demand for money, L, equals supply of money, $\overline{M}$ — have now been derived. What we have seen is that given the money supply, a higher level of Y is associated with a higher equilibrium interest rate. One could likewise consider further levels of Y — which would mean further levels of the L(..., ...) function in Figure 3a — and derive the corresponding money market equilibria in Figure 3b. If one did so, one would trace an upward sloping locus like that labelled LM in Figure 3b.

Given M, the LM curve is simply a (part of the) graph of the infinity of solutions to equation (4); it illustrates all the (i, Y) combinations which yield an equilibrium in the money market — combinations at which the demand for money, L, equals the supply of money, M. It slopes upwards because a higher level of Y implies a higher demand for money (mainly to facilitate higher transactions demands) and, given M, the equilibrium interest rate must then rise. But what value of i *is* the equilibrium interest rate? The answer is that we cannot yet know: conducted in isolation, analysis of the money market equilibrium condition yields indeterminacy; all we can do is solve for equilibrium i as a function of Y (as expressed by the LM curve), but unless we know what Y is, we cannot determine what i must be.

The way out of the dilemma — indeterminacy of both goods market equilibrium and money market equilibrium when those two markets are treated sequentially *in isolation* — involves dealing with the two markets *simultaneously*. But before this is done, it is appropriate to investigate what determines the slope and the level of the LM curve.

The Slope of LM: The slope of the LM curve will be higher — the curve will slope upward more steeply — (a) the *more* sensitive the demand for money is to changes in the level of income and (b) the *less* sensitive the demand for money is to changes in the rate of interest.

The validity of assertion (a) is easily seen. Suppose that the demand for money were *more* sensitive to changes in Y than was assumed in moving from $L(i, Y_0)$ to $L(i, Y_3)$ in Figure 3a. In that case the L(..., ...) curve corresponding to Y_3 would lie above the level depicted in the diagram, and the corresponding intersection between $\bar{M}$ and L(..., ...) would be at a point like $\hat{E}_3$ in that diagram. In the (i, Y) plane, the counterpart to that point would be $\hat{E}'_3$ in Figure 3b. Clearly, an LM curve going through both E'_0 and $\hat{E}'_3$ would be steeper than that drawn in the diagram.

The credibility of assertion (b) in regard to the slope of LM is left to the reader to work out. Unfortunately, graphical methods are much more awkward than straightforward mathematics (not pursued in this text). However, in the context of assertion (b), the following observations should help:

First, note that in a neighbourhood of any particular point — say E_0 in Figure 3a — the demand for money is *less sensitive* to changes in the rate of interest, the *steeper* the L(..., ...) function in that neighbourhood. Consider now two hypothetical scenarios in regard to the slope of L(...,

...) around E_0 — one in which the slope is relatively steep, the other in which it is flat. Next, consider a given increase in income which (in each case) would cause the two curves to shift upwards. Suppose that the *shortest* distance between the new and the old steeply-sloped $L(\ldots, \ldots)$ curves is exactly the same as the *shortest* distance between the new and the old more flatly-sloped $L(\ldots, \ldots)$ curves. It will be found that the rise in the equilibrium interest rate in the first scenario would exceed that in the second: although the rise in income and the sensitivity of $L(\ldots, \ldots)$ to the change in income would have been the same in each case, the rise in i corresponding to the steeper $L(\ldots, .)$ functions would exceed that corresponding to the case in which the $L(., \ldots)$ functions were relatively flat, thereby implying a steeper LM curve in the first case than in the second.

The Level of LM: Given the public's demand for money function $L(\ldots, \ldots)$, the level of LM — whether it lies to the left or to the right of that drawn in Figure 3b, for example — is determined by the level of the money supply. This is easily shown: Consider the level of Y represented by Y_3 in Figure 3a. With $M = \overline{M}$, $i = i_3$. Holding $Y = Y_3$, suppose that the money supply is now increased to $\overline{\overline{M}}$. It can be seen from the same diagram that the equilibrium interest rate falls to $\tilde{i}_3$. The new money market equilibrium is represented by point $\tilde{E}'_3$ in Figure 3b. This is located to the *right* of the old LM curve, implying that the LM curve corresponding to the increased money supply lies to the right of that drawn in the diagram. It can similarly be shown that a reduction in the money supply would cause LM to shift to the *left*. In short, if the money supply is increased (reduced), a given Y will be associated with a lower (higher) equilibrium i, represented by a shift of LM in the relevant direction.

INTERACTION OF IS AND LM: SIMULTANEOUS SOLUTION

As one equation in two unknowns, the IS curve is a graph of the infinity of solutions to the goods market equilibrium condition. Alternatively expressed, it shows equilibrium Y as a function of i. But we could not solve for Y by looking at conditions in the goods market alone: to tell what Y would be, we need to know the value of i. A similar problem arose when we examined the money market in isolation. As another single equation in two unknowns, the LM curve is a graph of the infinity of solutions to the money market equilibrium condition. It showed equilibrium i as a function of Y. But we could not solve for i from consideration of the money market alone: to tell what i would be, we need to know the value of Y. The fairly obvious way out of this dilemma is to put the two equilibrium conditions — equations (2) and (4) — together. They

form two simultaneous (though not necessarily linear) equations in two
unknowns, i and Y. Given the assumed properties of the functions involved — so that IS slopes downward and LM slopes upward — a solution plausibly exists and it is unique. Hence Y and i are solved simultaneously rather than sequentially — a complication which was mainly
swept under the carpet in the very elementary expositions in Part Three.

For given M and L(..., ...) functions (which underlie money market
equilibrium and yielded the LM curve), and for given autonomous demands (which underlie goods market equilibrium and yield the IS curve),
the simultaneous interaction between the goods market and the money
market is depicted in Figure 4, where i_e and Y_e are the equilibrium
values, *simultaneously* determined.

Figure 4

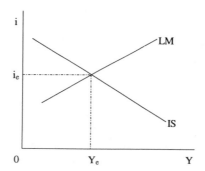

Figure 5

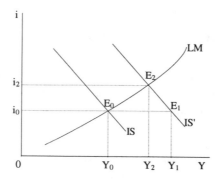

It is clear from Figure 4 that anything (any change in autonomous
demand) which causes a shift in the IS curve will have effects in the
money market (in general, it will cause the interest rate to change);

similarly, anything (typically, a change in the money supply) which causes a shift in the LM curve will have effects in the goods market (it will change the level of Y). The IS/LM approach clarifies many issues which we were not equipped to investigate using only the analytical framework of Part Three. For example, considerations involving aggregate supply aside, it clearly indicates why use of ordinary multiplier theory (as in Chapters 10 and 11) will generally *overpredict* the response of output to increases in autonomous demand.

For example, suppose that the economy is initially in equilibrium at point E_0 in Figure 5, and that next, an improvement in the state of expectations in regard to prospects for profits causes investment demand to increase (so the investment function in the savings-investment diagram shifts upward). The IS curve in Figure 5 therefore shifts to the right, to IS'. Use of ordinary multiplier theory predicts that income would increase, from Y_0 to Y_1 — because Y_1 is the level of Y at which planned savings would equal planned investment if the interest rate stayed *unchanged*. However, we are now equipped to see that this will *not* occur, because of interaction between the goods market and the money market leading to a rise in the rate of interest: so-called "crowding out" will choke off some investment demand. Some elaboration on this concept is appropriate.

As income starts to increase following the upward shift in the investment function (in the savings and investment diagram at an unchanged interest rate), the transactions demand for money increases (in the supply and demand for money diagram). Given the money supply, the interest rate must therefore rise. This in turn chokes off some part of investment demand (by an amount reflecting the sensitivity of investment demand to changes in the interest rate), which, in itself, would cause income to fall (by an amount determined by multiplier theory). Hence, the ultimate increase in investment demand will be *less* than that suggested by the upward shift of the investment function in the savings–investment diagram. It can be seen from Figure 5 that the interest rate will be bid up to a new equilibrium level i_2, and that income increases from Y_0 to Y_2, which is less than the amount predicted using ordinary multiplier theory.

ADDING GOVERNMENT TO THE MODEL

Let government (and the possibility of taxation) now be brought into the model. Although its derivation is now more complicated, the conceptual basis of the IS curve is unchanged: it still denotes the locus of (i, Y) combinations at which the goods market equilibrium condition — in the present context, equation (5) of Chapter 11 — is satisfied. Because it represents an increase in autonomous demand, an increase in government expenditure causes a shift to the right of the IS curve, the *extent* of the shift being influenced by whether or not the increase in G is financed by increased taxes. (The shift would be greater in the absence of financing through increased taxation). However, the multiplier theory of Chapter 11 will overestimate the ensuing increase in Y — because that earlier analytical framework ignored the repercussion in the money market, given the money supply. Again, Figure 5 can be used to illustrate.

Let the economy be at an initial equilibrium at point E_0 in Figure 5. At an unchanged level of i, an increase in G (financed by some means other than bank borrowing, i.e. financed by taxation and/or borrowing from the non-bank public) would cause Y to increase from Y_0 to Y_1. But the diagram indicates that E_1 is *not* an overall equilibrium, because at that point the demand for money is not equal to the supply of money — the economy is off the LM curve. The rate of interest will therefore rise. Assuming that the planned increase in G is attained, the rise in G will choke off some of private sector investment demand. Hence, the increased size of the public sector "crowds out" some private sector expenditure, and income will increase by less than use of ordinary government expenditure multipliers would predict. (Income rises to Y_2, which is less than Y_1 predicted by ordinary multiplier theory.)

The IS/LM framework clearly highlights the distinction between a *pure monetary policy* and a *pure fiscal policy* (as distinct from a combination of the two). In a closed economy model with government, a pure fiscal policy (e.g. an increase in government expenditure financed by increased taxation) causes IS to shift, with *no* shift in LM. A pure monetary policy (e.g. an increase in the money supply brought about by open market purchases by the central bank) is one which causes LM to shift, with no shift in IS. If an increase in government expenditure is financed by borrowing from the central bank ("printing money"), then *both* IS and LM will shift to the right. These observations indicate that the effects of an increase in G depend crucially on the manner in which the increased G is financed: if it is financed by borrowing from the non-bank public, then only IS will shift to the right; if it is financed by increased taxation, only IS will shift to the right, but by a smaller amount; if it is financed by printing money, *both* IS and LM shift to the right, and "crowding out" would be of less significance than would otherwise be the case.

In Figure 6 an increase in G causes IS to shift to IS'. Use of ordinary multiplier theory alone predicts that Y will increase to Y_1. If the increased G is financed by means not involving change in the money supply, crowding out will restrain the rise in Y, which will go to Y_2. However, if the rise in G is financed by an increase in the money supply (borrowing from the central bank), LM will also shift, to the right — to, say, LM', and because of a smaller extent of crowding out (or no crowding out in a very special case) the interest rate rises by less than it would have risen had M been held constant. In Figure 6 the interest rate then rises to i_3 and Y rises to Y_3 (which exceeds Y_2 but is still less than Y_1). The main point is that less crowding out will apply if the increase in G is financed by monetary means. Note, however, that this would be a case of neither a pure monetary policy nor a pure fiscal policy, but a *combination* of monetary and fiscal policies.

Figure 6

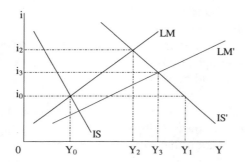

MONETARISTS VERSUS KEYNESIANS: A STERILE DEBATE

Some years ago there were major debates among economists, politicians and journalists on the issue of whether monetary policy (which generates shifts in LM) or fiscal policy (which shifts IS) was more important in changing output. An extreme version of the *monetarist* argument was that only monetary policy mattered; fiscal expansion, the monetarist argument ran, would be neutralised by complete crowding out so that, for example, an increase in G would be exactly offset be a reduction in private sector demand. (In that case, it would lead to change in the *composition* of output, but to no change in the *level* of output.) In support of their claim that only fiscal policy mattered, extreme *Keynesians* ("fiscalists") argued that monetary policy would be ineffective because they believed that investment demand was not sensitive to changes in the rate of interest. At least in the early years of the debate, both sets of protagonists tended to ignore explicit consideration of the supply side of the economy, an approach which will also be adopted in the brief exposition which follows here. Rather than involving any fundamental conceptual questions in economic theory, it turns out that the debate really revolved around the *empirical* questions of just how steeply the IS curve slopes downward and just how steeply the LM curve slopes upward. (In fact, it is suspected that the social/political philosophies of some participants in the debate coloured their alleged economic logic: monetarist arguments were usually expressed by political conservatives who did not like direct government intervention in the economy, whereas Keynesian arguments were more often heard from those holding more radical political views. As is often the case in debates involving policy issues, "the heart appears to have dominated the head" in the case of many participants in that debate.) Before proceeding, it is remarked here that it seems that most economists have held an intermediate ground between the two extreme schools, which will now be illustrated using a "straw man" Keynesian approach and a "straw woman" monetarist argument. So remember: we are going to illustrate fairly extreme versions of the arguments.

Monetarists argued that the demand for money was extremely sensitive to changes in income but insensitive to changes in the interest rate; the LM curve, therefore would be very steep — in a sense, close to vertical. They argued that investment demand was very sensitive to changes in the rate of interest; therefore, IS would be flat. The implications of these views in regard to extremes of slope can be seen using Figure 7a. It is easy to see from the diagram that expansionary fiscal policies (which shift IS to the right) would have little effect, because they would lead to almost complete crowding out, and that monetary expansion, which shifts LM to the right, would be much more effective.

Figure 7a: Monetarist Approach   Figure 7b: Keynesian Approach

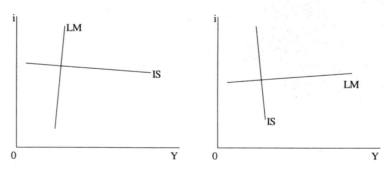

Keynesians made the contrary assumptions in regard to the demand for money and the sensitivity of investment demand to changes in i. Under such circumstances, IS would be very steep and LM would slope upwards only very moderately (if at all), as in Figure 7b. Shifts in IS could then be very effective, but shifts in LM would merely cause significant change in the interest rate combined with negligibly small change in Y.

This text will make no further reference to these extreme models of monetarists and Keynesians, partly because, as already argued, most economists have tended to hold the middle ground between them. It will therefore be assumed that IS slopes downward but that its slope does not approach either zero or minus infinity; similarly, it will be assumed that LM slopes upwards, and that the slope does not approach either extreme limiting value.

CHAPTER 18

DEMAND-SIDE IN AN OPEN ECONOMY: IS, LM AND BP

The IS/LM framework of Chapter 17 can be extended to the case of an open economy. The following assumptions will be made until further notice:

(1) The economy is small and open.

(2) It maintains a fixed exchange rate with its trading partners. If the economy is also really open in a meaningful sense, it is reasonable to assume that the home currency is fully convertible, meaning that the country's central bank agrees always to trade, and to permit trade, between home currency and foreign currency at the fixed exchange rate, thereby ensuring that the rate applicable to official transactions is the same as that available to the private sector.

(3) The price level abroad and the interest rate abroad are given. It will *not* necessarily be assumed that the domestic interest rate, and the domestic price level, must be exactly the same as those abroad. However, it should be clear that the home price level can respond to domestic economic conditions only subject to constraints imposed by assumptions (1) and (2). Until the possibility of limited variation in the price level is considered in an explicit manner, it will therefore be assumed that:

(4) The home price level stays constant.

Finally, in line with the approach in Chapter 17:

(5) The operation of the supply side of the domestic economy will be deferred for investigation in a later chapter.

In order to be in full equilibrium, an open economy must be in equilibrium in the goods market, in the money market *and* in its balance of international payments. Let BP denote the balance of payments equilibrium locus (shortly to be explained in detail). Then, for full macroeconomic equilibrium, the economy must be on its IS, LM and BP curves *simultaneously*. To illustrate the need for simultaneity, suppose for example that the goods and money markets are in an apparent equilibrium (with IS intersecting LM) but that the balance of payments is not in equilibrium. Suppose that the balance of payments is in surplus (which, as the reader will recall from Chapter 15, means that the home economy is a net recipient of foreign exchange). Such net receipts of foreign currency will be sold to the central bank in return for domestic money at the fixed exchange rate, thereby throwing the money market into clear disequilibrium. This example illustrates the need for simultaneous equilibrium in each of the main markets if the economy is to be in full macroeconomic equilibrium. It will be shown below that simultaneous equilibrium would not be a mere fluke, because such overall equilibrium is plausibly *stable* (at least in the kind of short-run model which we are about to investigate). But first, it is necessary to consider in some detail the balance of payments equilibrium locus.

THE BALANCE OF PAYMENTS EQUILIBRIUM LOCUS, BP

If price levels are constant in a short-run model of an open economy with a fixed exchange rate, then exports can plausibly be taken as exogenous: they depend largely on marketing efforts in earlier time periods and on income abroad (determined outside the model). Imports to the home country, on the other hand, depend on income at home — they are endogenous — as explained in Chapter 11. Hence, the balance of payments on current account depends on Y; in the short-run model under fixed exchange rates, it moves inversely to Y. A rise in Y will be associated with a reduction in (X - M) — a deterioration in the balance of payments on current account. Turning to the capital account of the balance of payments, net capital inflows are an increasing function of the domestic rate of interest: given interest rates abroad, an increase in the domestic rate of interest induces increased net capital inflows. It follows that the balancing item in the overall balance of payments accounts — the change in the level of foreign exchange reserves — moves in the *opposite* direction to changes in Y and in the *same* direction as changes in i. (Recall Table 1 in Chapter 15 above.) In Chapter 15 it was indicated that the value of this balancing item is what is usually meant by a balance of payments surplus or deficit; by this criterion, if foreign exchange reserves are constant, the external sector accounts are balanced (or "in equilibrium"); if foreign exchange reserves increase (decrease), the balance of payments is said to be in surplus (deficit).

Other things being equal, it follows, if we start from a position of balance of payments equilibrium, that an increase in Y will cause a deficit to emerge, and, given interest rates abroad, that an increase in i will cause the balance of payments to move into surplus. Hence, starting from a position of balance of payments equilibrium (at some (i, Y) combination), if Y increases, then there will exist some offsetting increase in i that will maintain balance of payments equilibrium. These considerations now enable us to consider the balance of payments equilibrium locus BP — the locus of (i, Y) combinations at which the balance of payments is in equilibrium — more explicitly.

Figure 1

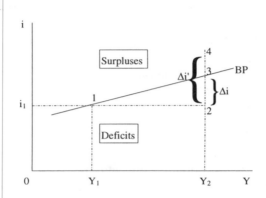

In Figure 1, suppose that point 1 is a position of balance of payments equilibrium. This implies that if the current account balance of payments is in deficit (surplus) at $Y = Y_1$, then the interest rate i_i is just sufficiently high (low) to induce enough capital inflows (outflows) to offset the foreign exchange losses (gains) which the current account deficit (surplus) would in itself entail. Thus, the change in the home country's holdings of foreign exchange reserves equals zero at the (i, Y) combination represented by point 1. If Y were to increase at an unchanged interest rate, then (X - M) would deteriorate, but capital inflows would be unchanged. The point labelled 2 in the diagram therefore denotes a position of balance of payments deficit. However, at $Y = Y_2$ there will then exist some rise in the domestic interest rate i which (given the interest rate abroad) will be just sufficient to induce enough capital inflows to restore balance of payments equilibrium. This Δi is as indicated in the diagram. Hence, point 3 is also a position of balance of payments equilibrium.

Two points — those labelled 1 and 3 — on the balance of payments equilibrium locus have now been traced. Starting at point 3, we could proceed exactly as we did starting at point 1, and thereby derive further (i, Y) combinations yielding balance of payments equilibrium. If we did so, we would then be tracing a generally upward-sloping locus (or, only in an extreme case, a zero-sloped locus) like that labelled BP in Figure 1. This merely represents the infinity of (i, Y) combinations which yield overall equilibrium in the balance of payments.

On reflection, it should be clear from the derivation of point 3 that points below BP involve deficits in the balance of payments. Points above BP imply surpluses. This can be illustrated as follows:

As already seen, point 2 was a position of deficit, and the interest rate needed to be raised by an amount Δi in the diagram in order to restore equilibrium. But suppose, starting at point 2, that the interest rate was raised by $\Delta i'$, an amount larger than that needed to restore equilibrium. The resulting level of capital inflows would mean that the country's foreign exchange reserves were increasing; hence, a point like that labelled 4 in the diagram would be an (i, Y) combination at which the balance of payments is in surplus. Similarly, the set of all points located above BP denotes balance of payments surplus.

The Slope of BP: The slope of BP turns out to be of some importance in understanding the effectiveness of policy. It will be *flatter* the greater the degree of sensitivity of international capital movements to changes in the domestic rate of interest, given the foreign rate of interest. For example, starting from point 2 in Figure 1, suppose that the increase in the interest rate necessary to induce a level of capital inflows sufficient to restore equilibrium were *smaller* than Δi depicted in the diagram. The corresponding equilibrium point would lie *below* point 3 as drawn. The BP locus would then have a flatter slope than that shown in the diagram. In the very special case in which the domestic rate of interest could not at all diverge from that abroad — so that an infinitesimally small rise in i would always induce enough capital inflows to restore equilibrium — then the slope of BP would approach zero; (in the limit) it would be perfectly flat. This would be the special case of so-called "perfect capital mobility". By way of contrast, if relatively large increases in i were necessary in order to attract significantly increased net capital inflows, then BP would be relatively steep. Note that there is no presumption that the slope of BP is constant; thus BP need not be linear.

The Level of BP: The level of BP — whether it lies to the left or to the right of that drawn in Figure 1 — reflects the choice of (level of the) exchange rate. In the short-run models to be considered, a change in the exchange rate would generate a shift of BP. However, in all subsequent references to the BP locus in this text, the exchange rate will be taken as given; hence, the level of BP will be assumed constant.

FULL DEMAND-SIDE EQUILIBRIUM

The slope of BP has just been investigated and a brief observation has been made in regard to its level. Before entering IS, LM and BP in the same diagram, a few further remarks in regard to IS and LM are appropriate in the context of an open economy with a fixed exchange rate. First, openness combined with a fixed exchange rate implies that the level of LM can be influenced by domestic monetary policy to a very limited extent only; this statement will be clarified when the interaction of IS, LM and BP come to be considered (shortly). Second, it still remains true that the slope of IS will be steeper (a) the less sensitive investment demand is to changes in the rate of interest and (b) the lower the multiplier. However, in the open economy fixed exchange rate case, the slope of IS will be steeper than in a closed economy model, because a non-zero marginal propensity to import (which partially determines the import "leakage") makes the numerical value of multipliers lower than they would otherwise be. Furthermore, the magnitude of the horizontal shift of the IS curve in response to an increase in autonomous demand will be lower in the open economy case — again because national income multipliers are lower. Drawing the IS, LM and BP loci in the same diagrams yields the three possibilities depicted in Figures 2a, 2b and 2c.

Figure 2a: Case A   Figure 2b: Case B   Figure 2c: Case C

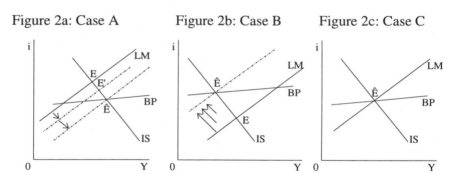

Suppose that the goods market and the money market are in *apparent* equilibrium at point E in the cases depicted in Figures 2a or 2b — Case A and Case B, respectively. (We will refer to the simultaneous equilibrium in Figure 2c as Case C.) It will now be shown that Case A is not a full demand-side equilibrium; nor is Case B, but Case C is, and it is not a mere fluke among an infinity of possibilities.

In Case A (Figure 2a), point E is located *above* the BP locus; hence, the balance of payments is in surplus — the economy is a net earner of foreign exchange. Because we are assuming an open economy which has a convertible currency, this foreign money will be sold — ultimately to the central bank — in exchange for domestic money. Therefore, the money supply will *automatically* increase — the LM curve will automatically shift to the right. Suppose that LM shifts to the right until point

E' is attained. The same argument then still applies: the balance of payments is still in surplus (though that surplus is now smaller than before). Hence, LM would automatically shift to the right until overall demand-side equilibrium — represented by point Ê in Figure 2a — is reached.

In Case B (Figure 2b) point E lies *below* the BP locus; hence the balance of payments is in deficit and the central bank is losing foreign exchange. Importers and others are selling local currency (ultimately) to the central bank in exchange for foreign money — and the Bank has no option but passively to sell them that foreign exchange because, by assumption, unrestricted currency convertibility applies. Therefore, as the domestic money supply automatically decreases, the LM curve continues to shift, automatically to the left, until simultaneous equilibrium at point Ê in Figure 2b is reached.

It follows from the foregoing that simultaneous equilibrium like that depicted for Case C, at point Ê in Figure 2c, is no mere fluke: It has just been shown that if the balance of payments of an open economy under fixed exchange rates is in surplus or deficit, and if the economy continues to maintain fixed exchange rates, then the monetary effects of the surplus or deficit tend automatically to eliminate the disequilibrium in the balance of payments. It is very important to observe that the exposition just sketched, and the key conclusion just stated, implicitly assumed that the monetary authority (the central bank) remained passive throughout: the central bank did not engage in any new, discretionary, policies. Rather, it merely responded to market forces under a régime of convertible fixed exchange rates, by honouring requests from the market to buy or to sell foreign currency in exchange for domestic money. Hence, provided the central bank allows market forces to work — in particular — provided that the Bank does not meddle with the system by trying to neutralise market-induced changes in the money supply — balance of payments disequilibrium under fixed exchange rates tends automatically to eliminate itself, because of the monetary effects of such disequilibrium.

Leaning against the Wind: Meddling with the Money Supply

The immediately preceding analysis indicates that if the central bank does not try to meddle with the system in an open economy under fixed exchange rates, balance of payments surpluses or deficits tend to eliminate themselves automatically. (Note that this is *not* saying that passive behaviour by the central bank could always avert devaluation, for example, but if speculators knew that the Bank was really committed to implementing a passive policy, thereby always *allowing* the money supply to contract automatically whenever the balance of payments was in deficit, then they would be less inclined to speculate — they would be less inclined to pursue actions which would possibly precipitate devaluation.) We know that, in fact, central banks do sometimes try to neutralise (offset or "sterilise") the monetary effects of balance of payments disequilibrium — for example, by open market operations. This may sometimes reflect myopic political pressures, or such policies may be implemented from time to time as purely transitory smoothing operations. The main point to be illustrated at this stage is that under fixed exchange rates, attempts by a central bank *permanently* to neutralise the monetary effects of a balance of payments surplus or deficit are doomed to failure, or are inconsistent with the maintenance of fixed exchange rates in the long run.

Figure 3

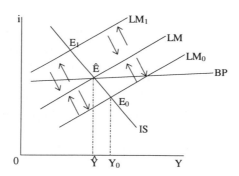

Suppose that we start with the economy at point E_0 in Figure 3, a point involving a balance of payments deficit. The corresponding level of income is Y_0. We know that if the central bank acts passively, and does not interfere, then the LM_0 curve will automatically shift to the left, until (a simultaneous) equilibrium is reached at $\hat{E}$. But note that this would result in reduced output (and reduced employment), from Y_0 to $\hat{Y}$, reflecting the fact that as the monetary contraction proceeds, the rate of interest rises, and investment demand is therefore choked off as the economy moves up (and to the left) along the IS curve. This might be politically unpopular — especially if a general election is imminent — so the central bank might be pressured into trying to prevent this from occurring. Suppose that the central bank reacts by relentlessly engaging in open market purchases (buying domestic securities). The automatic effects of the deficit would then be shifting LM_0 to the left, but the discretionary policies of the Bank would be driving it back to the right. Suppose for the sake of argument that this neutralisation policy is fully successful for a while; then the economy stays at E_0 over that time interval. But E_0 is a position of deficit, implying that the Bank is losing foreign currency reserves, and the longer the time-period that the deficit is sustained — the longer the Bank is successful in its neutralisations — the lower the level of foreign exchange holdings at the Bank. No central bank has infinite holdings of foreign exchange reserves. Hence, sooner or later, the Bank will run out of foreign currency reserves, and will be forced to devalue. But this result is inconsistent with the assumptions of the model at present under discussion.

Alternatively, suppose that the economy is initially at E_1 in Figure 3, a point involving balance of payments surplus. If the Bank stayed passive, transformation of the corresponding foreign exchange earnings into domestic money would cause that money supply to increase — LM_1 would continue to shift to the right — until simultaneous equilibrium at $\hat{E}$ was attained. Why might the Bank be pressurised into trying to prevent this? One answer is that the home country's surplus (which implies symmetric deficits abroad) might merely be in consequence of higher inflationary pressures abroad, reflecting loose monetary policies in those countries as a group. Given fixed exchange rates, the home country might *try* to insulate itself from such inflationary forces, by trying to prevent its own money supply from increasing. Suppose that the central bank is for a while successful, through open market sales of domestic securities, in preventing LM_1 from moving to the right. This apparent success cannot be sustained indefinitely, because no central bank has an infinite supply of securities (and to obtain more of such assets, it would have to increase its own liabilities, which would mean an increase in the money supply). Thus, the Bank must ultimately abandon its attempt to neutralise the monetary effects of the surplus, *or* it must revalue its currency. (In the context of the latter option, the reader may think of the motivation underlying the behaviour of the German monetary authorities over the period from the 1950s to the early 1990s.)

It should not be inferred from the foregoing — which referred to sustained discretionary policies by the central bank — that all neutralisation operations are nonsense. For example, suppose that a temporary shift in IS (perhaps due to a transitory boom or slump in export demand) causes balance of payments disequilibrium. The central bank may then sensibly try to neutralise the monetary repercussion, thereby minimising a short-run destabilising shock from outside the economy and smoothing fluctuations in output and employment. Of course, a problem in this context is that it is often difficult to know when an externally-imposed shock is of temporary duration only. If it is not temporary, neutralisation operations introduced purely as smoothing devices may become sustained, in which case they must ultimately be abandoned, and/or the target level for the exchange rate will have to be altered.

EFFECTIVENESS OF MONETARY AND FISCAL POLICIES ONCE AGAIN

Use of the analytical framework just outlined confirms and clarifies earlier observations, made in Part Three, in regard to the effectiveness of monetary and fiscal policies in a small open economy under fixed exchange rates. Note that explicit treatment of the *supply side* of the economy is still being deferred; hence, the focus remains on IS-LM-BP alone. Furthermore, it is still being assumed that goods price levels and the exchange rate are fixed.

Monetary Policy

Consider first the extreme case of a small open economy under fixed exchange rates — one which is a perfect price-taker in every market, implying that its equilibrium interest rate could not possibly diverge from the foreign interest rate. Any divergence of the domestic rate of interest from the foreign rate would be extremely transitory. This case is illustrated in Figure 4, where $i^{SOE} = i^F$ follows from the assumption of perfect capital mobility between the home country and abroad ($i = i^F$; F for foreign). Suppose, starting from full demand-side equilibrium at point E, that the central bank tries to increase the money supply, engaging in open market purchases. The LM curve quickly shifts to LM_1, the interest rate falls, and a balance of payments deficit rapidly emerges. But this cannot last for long: the deficit means that the money supply automatically shifts to the left and (consistent with the assumptions of the model) there is nothing that the central bank can do to prevent LM going back and intersecting at point E. Hence, the initial money supply increase is purely a disequilibrium phenomenon which is unlikely to last for long. The level of central bank liabilities (the monetary base) goes back to what it was initially. Hence, comparing equilibrium positions, the level of central bank assets is unchanged. But because the central bank's holdings of domestic assets have increased, while its holdings of foreign assets have fallen by an equal amount, the only *permanent* effect of the "expansionary" monetary policy is a change in the *composition* of the assets of the central bank; in effect, it has merely exchanged some of its foreign assets for more domestic assets. Note that the expansionary policy has no effect at all on equilibrium Y. It is left to the reader to see that the analysis is not substantively altered if capital is less than perfectly mobile. (In that case, BP would have a low, but non-zero, slope.)

Figure 4

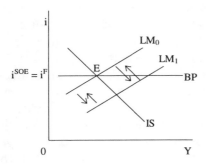

Fiscal Policy

It was seen in Chapter 17 that in the case of a closed economy, the effectiveness of an expansionary fiscal policy would be constrained by induced crowding out: given the money supply, increased government expenditure, for example, would cause the rate of interest to rise, thereby choking off some of private sector investment demand and causing income to rise by less than use of ordinary multiplier analysis would predict. It will now be demonstrated that in the present open economy fixed exchange rate model, *either* crowding out will not occur at all (in the limiting case of perfect capital mobility) *or*, if there is some crowding out, it will be of less importance than if international capital mobility were zero (as in the closed economy case). Hence (still deferring supply-side considerations for investigation later on) in the present model, fiscal expansion will cause income to increase exactly as predicted by ordinary multiplier analysis *or*, as a lower bound estimate, it would cause income to increase by more than it would if the economy were closed.

Figure 5a

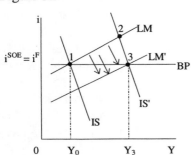

Figure 5b

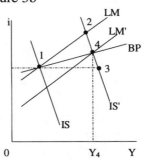

Figure 5a illustrates fiscal expansion in the case of perfect capital mobility: BP is zero-sloped. Starting at the point labelled 1, an increase in G (for example) causes IS to shift to the right a horizontal distance equal to (the government expenditure multiplier)(ΔG) — to IS'. If the economy were closed, the system would move to an equilibrium at point 2 in the diagram. But, taking account of openness and fixed exchange rates, this will not occur because point 2 implies a balance of payments surplus. The LM curve would therefore *automatically* shift to the right (to LM') until that surplus disappears, as at point 3 in the diagram. Note that the corresponding level of Y, i.e. Y_3, is the new level of Y at which planned (public, private and external sector) savings equal planned (public, private and external sector) investment, at an unchanged interest rate. Hence, (Y_3 - Y_0) equals (the government expenditure multiplier)(ΔG), as predicted using ordinary multiplier analysis.

A similar chain of reasoning — but not quite the same — applies in Figure 5b, where capital is not perfectly mobile internationally. Starting at point 1, the economy would go to an equilibrium at point 2 if it were a closed system. On the other hand, use of ordinary multiplier analysis would predict that the economy would go to point 3, because ordinary multiplier analysis assumes a constant rate of interest. Taking account of capital mobility (imperfect, as indicated by the moderate positive slope of BP) it can be seen that the economy goes to a point strictly between 1 and 3 — labelled point 4 in Figure 5b. Hence, less crowding out would occur than in the closed economy case. But because *some* crowding out applies, income increases by less than use of ordinary multiplier analysis would predict.

(It is noted in closing that the two paragraphs immediately above did not distinguish between IS in open and closed economies in which the price level is constant. As explained earlier, the slope of IS differs in the two cases, but this consideration does not qualitatively affect the conclusions of those two paragraphs.)

CHAPTER 19

DERIVATION OF THE AGGREGATE DEMAND FUNCTION, AD = AD(P)

Until now in Part Four of this text it has been assumed that the price level is constant in the economy under investigation. The operation of the supply side of the economy has not yet been considered in Part Four (though Part Three did include some fairly intuitive observations on supply-side issues). A strict interpretation of the symbol Y as used in the preceding two chapters is that it denoted real demand rather than real output; it denoted output only insofar as aggregate supply somehow responded to match that demand, or only insofar as aggregate supply was infinitely elastic at the prevailing price level (an assumption implicitly made at various stages of the text). Detailed investigation of the variables underlying aggregate supply is still deferred. In regard to demand, it has not yet been possible to derive aggregate demand as a function of the price level, AD = AD(P), given autonomous demand. To do so, it is necessary to drop the assumption that the price level is constant, and to consider it as a variable. Now that we propose to let the price level change, it is necessary to be clear on the distinction between *real* income, Y, and *nominal* income, PY. The investigation will start with a closed economy and will then proceed to an open economy under fixed exchange rates.

THE AGGREGATE DEMAND FUNCTION
IN A CLOSED ECONOMY

Consider an initial demand-side equilibrium in a closed economy at a given price level, say P_1. In order to illustrate how variation in the price level affects LM, it is assumed (purely to aid in exposition) that real income is at some particular level, say $\overline{Y}$. The first thing to note at this stage is that the transactions demand for money depends on the level of nominal income rather than on real income: if the level of real income is $\overline{Y}$, and if the price level (say) doubles, more money will be demanded under the transactions motive in order to facilitate day-to-day transactions, and the overall demand for money would therefore increase.

Given the money supply, this will impose upward pressure on the rate of interest. Resort to graphical analysis is now desirable to progress further.

Figure 1a   Figure 1b

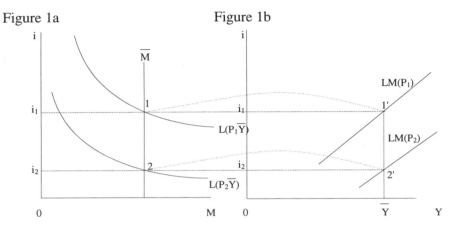

Given the price and real income levels P_1 and $\overline{Y}$, respectively, and given the money supply $\overline{M}$, suppose that the money market is in equilibrium at the point labelled 1 in Figure 1a. The locus $L(P_1\overline{Y})$ denotes the demand for money, $\overline{M}$ is at a level set by central bank policy, and i_1 is the ensuing equilibrium rate of interest. Because point 1 denotes money market equilibrium, the $(i, \overline{Y})$ values generating that point are also a point located on some LM curve: let this be represented by point 1' on the LM curve $LM(P_1)$ in Figure 1b.

(In the interests of visual clarity, only one point on the $LM(P_1)$ curve has been explicitly derived: in principle, the entire $LM(P_1)$ locus could have been derived by considering variations in Y in Figure 1a, given $P = P_1$, and tracing the equilibrium interest rate i associated with the very many $L(P_1Y)$ functions.)

Next, suppose that the price level was lower than that assumed in deriving (at least one point on) $LM(P_1)$. Suppose $P_2 < P_1$, and consider the *same* level of Y as before, $Y = \overline{Y}$. Because the level of *nominal* income is now lower than before (even though the level of *real* income is unchanged) the transactions demand for money is lower than that implied by $L(P_1\overline{Y})$. Hence, the new overall demand for money curve — which must lie *below* the $L(P_1\overline{Y})$ locus — is indicated by $L(P_2\overline{Y})$ in Figure 1a, where the corresponding equilibrium point is labelled point 2 and the implied equilibrium interest rate is $i = i_2$. We now wish to map the (i, Y) combination generating point 2 into the (i, Y) plane — Figure 1b. Straightforward derivation generates the point labelled 2' in that diagram. Note that because Y has been held constant at $Y = \overline{Y}$, point 2' must lie directly below point 1', which means that 2' must be one point on an LM curve which itself lies below, and to the right of, $LM(P_1)$. This new LM curve in Figure 1b is labelled $LM(P_2)$.

Generalising from the above, it follows that given the money supply, a fall in the price level will cause LM to shift to the right; similarly, a rise in the price level will cause it to shift to the left. Taking these findings and those pertaining to shifts in LM in Chapter 17 together, it has been shown that other things being equal, LM shifts to the right if (a) the money supply is increased, given P, or if (b) the price level falls, given M. A feature common to both (a) and (b) is that in either case, the real money supply, (M/P), would have increased. In the event of either cause of an increase in the real money supply, any given Y will be associated with a lower i for equilibrium in the money market. Hence, an *increase* in the real money supply causes LM to *shift to the right*; a *decrease* in the real money supply *shifts it to the left*. The shift to the right of the LM curve in Figure 1b has been caused by a reduction in P. To emphasise that fact, the two LM curves have been labelled as functions of the level of P — P_1 and P_2 in the illustration — and this practice will now be adopted throughout.

At this stage the reader should have adequate background understanding necessary for derivation of an aggregate demand curve for a closed economy. Because what is sought is the demand for output as a function of the price level, other things being equal, it is assumed that:

(1) All components of autonomous demand — those elements of demand that depend on neither i nor on Y in the current time period — are given.

(2) Apart from the price level itself, all factors influencing the LM curve — in particular, the money supply as determined by central bank policy — are given.

(3) Purely for ease in exposition, the possibility that the IS curve in a closed economy might be influenced by variation in P will be ignored. (At a more advanced level, one would probably resort to so-called "real balance effect" arguments which would cause IS to shift to the right if the price level fell. However, incorporation of such arguments at this stage would possibly confuse rather than illuminate. Besides, making IS dependent on P in a closed economy model would *not* alter the core conclusions attained in what immediately follows.)

With $P = P_1$, let the economy be at an initial equilibrium at point 1 in Figure 2a. The (P, Y) values implied by that equilibrium point are mapped into the (P, Y) plane in Figure 2b, where they are represented by point 1', which is one point on the economy's aggregate demand curve.

Next, suppose that the price level fell to P_2, $P_2 < P_1$. Given the (nominal) money supply, the real money supply would have increased. Hence, LM would have shifted to the right to, say, $LM(P_2)$ in Figure 2a, where the corresponding equilibrium in that diagram is indicated by point 2. Proceeding as before, this yields another point — labelled 2' in Figure 2b — on the economy's aggregate demand curve. Similarly, if the price level fell once again, to $P_3 < P_2$, one could trace points like those labelled 3 and 3' in the two diagrams, and if one continued to consider an indefinitely large number of variations in the price level, one would derive a downward-sloping locus like that labelled AD in Figure 2b.

Figure 2a   Figure 2b

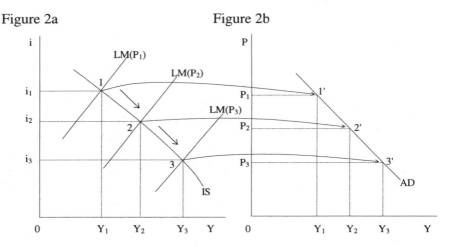

The AD curve slopes downward reflecting the monetary effects of a reduction in the price level, given the (nominal) money supply: a fall in P means that the real money supply has increased; the equilibrium rate of interest therefore falls. In response, investment demand rises by an amount determined by the sensitivity of investment demand to changes in the rate of interest, and Y increases by a further amount determined by the numerical value of the investment multiplier. (Recall the earlier discussion of the slope of the IS curve.) Thus, as the price level falls, LM shifts to the right, the rate of interest falls and the economy slides down the IS curve in (i, Y) space, which implies an inverse relationship in (P, Y) space.

Note that the foregoing exposition makes no reference whatsoever to the supply side of the economy; thus, what has been derived is the economy's aggregate demand curve, $AD = AD(P)$, with $\Delta AD/\Delta P < 0$. This relationship is merely a decreasing function; it is not necessarily linear. It should be clear that, strictly speaking, the symbol Y at this stage is to be interpreted as "equilibrium demand" rather than "equilibrium output"; however, the distinction will be largely ignored until further notice.

A SMALL OPEN ECONOMY, FIXED EXCHANGE RATES

The investigation now turns to a small open economy under fixed exchange rates. Because the small country does not significantly affect either the price level or the rate of interest prevailing abroad, these will be taken as constant throughout. In the more elementary, more intuitive, exposition of Chapter 14, it was argued that in the case of an economy of the kind now under discussion, the aggregate demand curve in (P, Y) space would be relatively flat, reflecting the fact that internal economic conditions could influence the domestic price level only to quite a limited extent (given fixed exchange rates). A more rigorous foundation for that conclusion will now be provided. In particular, it will be shown that the AD = AD(P) function for the small open economy under fixed exchange rates will be much less steeply sloped than in the case of a closed economy, and it would be perfectly flat in an extreme limiting case. (Note: We do not want to be drawn into the mathematical operation of taking inverse functions. Therefore, reference throughout will be on visual interpretations of slope, given the economics convention of locating price on the vertical axis and quantity (output) on the horizontal axis.) Before proceeding, it will be recalled from Chapter 14 that by aggregate demand in an open economy we mean the demand for the home country's output — which is not necessarily the same as the total demand by persons resident in the home country; thus, it denotes C + I + G + (X - M) as interpreted in equation (16) of Chapter 11. However, unlike the approach in Chapter 11, this magnitude will now be expressed as a function of the home country's price level, given the price level abroad.

In order to commence the derivation, denote the initial price level by $P = P_1$, and suppose that the economy is at an initial (demand-side) equilibrium at point 1 in Figure 3a. The corresponding starting point on the aggregate demand curve is denoted by 1' in Figure 3b. Next, suppose that the price level falls to $P_2 < P_1$. If the economy were closed, the system would move to points like those labelled 2 and 2' in the two diagrams. (The reason for the tilde (~) over the new LM curve will be indicated later.) Joining the two relevant points, the aggregate demand curve of the closed economy looks like AD_c in Figure 3b. But much more than this will occur in response to the price level reduction in the open economy model.

Figure 3a

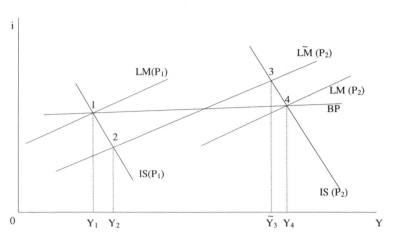

Figure 3b

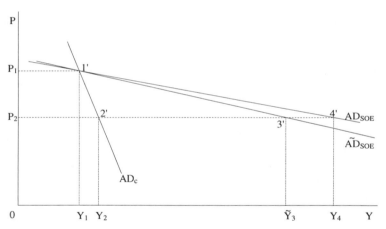

Recall that the economy is close to being a price-taker: given the foreign price level and fixed exchange rates, a reduction in the domestic price level means that home-produced goods become more attractive to foreigners, whilst foreign-produced goods become less attractive to residents of the home country. Hence, export demand would increase (by "an infinite amount" if the economy were in the extreme category of being a perfect price-taker) whilst import demand would fall as domestic consumers substitute home-produced goods for previously competing foreign-made goods. Thus, *net* exports, $(X - M)$, would increase — the extent of the increase being governed by the extent to which the home country is really a price-taker. (The reader might usefully think of a Cork or Galway versus Dublin analogy: what would occur if prices of tradable goods in Cork or Galway were significantly below those charged in Dublin?) Unlike the closed economy case, IS will therefore shift to the right, and because of this, it is now necessary to label IS to indicate its dependence on the price level through net export demand, (X - M). The extent of the shift of IS to the right is determined by the sensitivity of net exports to changes in the domestic price level, given the foreign price level. The shift would be substantial if that sensitivity were high — it "would be infinite" if the home economy were a perfect price-taker. One thing we can be sure of is that the IS curve will shift sufficiently far to the right such that it will cause the balance of payments to move into surplus in the first instance; therefore, it will intersect LM above BP in the first instance (because the balance of payments was initially in equilibrium and net exports increased following the price reduction).

Suppose that the increase in net exports is such that it generates the $IS(P_2)$ curve depicted in Figure 3a. On the basis of the reasoning outlined in the present chapter up to now, the point labelled 3 *appears* to be the new equilibrium; this has its counterpart at point 3' in the (P, Y) plane, Figure 3b. Joining points 1' and 3' in that diagram yields the curve labelled $\tilde{AD}_{SOE}$, which *appears* to be the aggregate demand curve of the open economy. However, we still have not reached the end of the story.

The point labelled 3 in Figure 3a is not a true equilibrium because the balance of payments is in surplus at that point, and we now recall from Chapter 18 that the monetary effects of the surplus will cause LM to shift further to the right. Hence, $\tilde{LM}$ and $\tilde{AD}$ are relevant in a very transitory sense only. In Figure 3a the LM curve will shift to the right until the point labelled 4 is attained. Mapping this into the (P, Y) plane yields point 4' in Figure 3b. It follows that the "true" (equilibrium) LM curve associated with $P = P_2$ is $LM(P_2)$ in Figure 3a, and the true aggregate demand curve for the output of the small open economy is like that labelled AD_{SOE} in Figure 3b.

It has been shown that the aggregate demand curve of a closed economy slopes downward — but with a relatively steep slope, reflecting the effects of the induced increase in the real money supply, given the nominal money stock. An extreme limiting case for the moment aside, it has also been demonstrated that the aggregate demand curve of a small open economy under fixed exchange rates slopes downward, but more moderately than in a closed economy, reflecting a combination of three key forces:

(1) As in the closed economy case, a reduction in P increases the real money supply, thereby shifting LM to the right.

(2) A reduction in P leads to an increase in net export demand, shifting IS to the right. The more sensitive the location of IS to changes in P, the flatter the ensuing aggregate demand curve.

(3) Combined with the shift of LM in (1), the increase in net exports in (2) causes the balance of payments to move into surplus in the first instance. But this is transitory only, because the monetary effects of the surplus cause LM to shift further to the right, reducing the rate of interest which applied when the balance of payments was in surplus, thereby inducing some increase in private sector investment demand (compared to the level of such investment when the balance of payments was in surplus) and causing the system to move some distance down the new IS curve.

The combined operation of the forces in (1) to (3) above implies a relatively flat AD curve. The reader should see that a limiting case of an infinitely elastic (perfectly flat) aggregate demand curve would apply under the following circumstances:

(1) If the BP locus was zero-sloped, i.e. if the home country was a perfect price-taker in financial markets, implying that the domestic rate of interest could not rise above that prevailing abroad (except in a most transitory sense), *and*

(2) If the country was a perfect price-taker in goods markets, implying that domestic prices could not possibly diverge from foreign prices (again, except in a most transitory sense). Then — and referring to limiting values — an epsilon (infinitesimally small) reduction in the price level would induce an infinitely large increase in export demand.

It is hoped that the determinants of the *slope* of the aggregate demand curve are now understood. In an open economy under fixed exchange rates, its *level* is determined mainly by the level of autonomous demand. The reader should check the credibility of this assertion by going back to Figure 3a, supposing that the level of government expenditure (for example) is increased starting at the point labelled 1, and working out the effects. Any reader who cannot show that the economy's aggregate demand curve would shift to the right following such an increase in autonomous demand should at this stage return to the beginning of this chapter, at least.

Some readers might with good reason ask: why spend so long studying the geometry of the aggregate demand curve of a small open economy under fixed exchange rates? The answer can be seen by bringing aggregate supply into the picture — albeit only briefly because it is the central subject-matter of the next chapter —and by first considering the extreme or limiting case of an infinitely elastic AD curve. Such a case is illustrated in Figure 4. We know that an "expansionary" fiscal policy generally shifts the AD curve to the right. But in the present limiting case this is impossible, or at best it is only a shift in the most trivial sense — it is a shift on top of itself. In this case so-called demand-management policies, such as variation in tax rates or changes in government expenditure, would have absolutely no effect on the equilibrium level of output. *Only* supply-side policies — which influence the level of the AS curve — would matter.

Figure 4

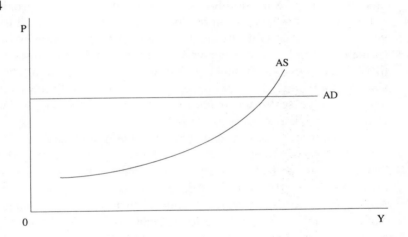

Figure 5

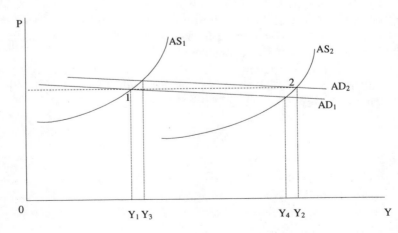

Moving away from the extreme case of a small open economy under fixed exchange rates for which the aggregate demand curve is infinitely elastic (as in Figure 4), consider the more realistic case in which the AD curve slopes strictly downward, but only very moderately, as in Figure 5. With $AD = AD_1$, and $AS = AS_1$, suppose that the economy is at an initial equilibrium at the point labelled 1, and consider the relative effectiveness of demand-management versus supply-side policies. Suppose that the government implements a massive increase in its expenditures, causing AD to shift to the right, an amount indicated by the horizontal distance (2 - 1) in the diagram. (For the moment, the reader should ignore the locus AS_2 in the diagram.) Use of ordinary multiplier analysis alone would predict an increase in equilibrium output from Y_1 to Y_2 (approximately), but even then, the increase in output might be fully accounted for by the volume increase in G itself, due to a high marginal propensity to import. (It may be recalled from Chapter 11 that multipliers in an open economy like Ireland could not be much greater than unity.) But taking the supply-side response into account makes it clear that equilibrium income is likely to increase by much less: with the aggregate supply curve unchanged, income rises only as far as Y_3 in the diagram.

The flatter an aggregate demand curve, the more a shift to the right of that curve approximates a shift on top of itself — it has already been seen that if AD were perfectly flat, the approximation would be exact — and the lower the likely effectiveness of demand management policies (unless the AS curve is infinitely elastic). It follows that supply-side policies — in particular, those which shift AS to the right — are likely to be much more potent in a small open economy under fixed exchange rates (where AD tends to be relatively flat). For example (instead of resorting to demand expansion, which implies that AD_2 as drawn in Figure 5 is now irrelevant) if some policy could be devised which would shift AS a horizontal distance (2 - 1) in Figure 5, then equilibrium income would rise from Y_1 to Y_4. This policy would be far more effective than the contrasting massive demand expansion measures just considered.

It should be apparent that it is now appropriate to investigate the factors underlying aggregate supply in greater detail than earlier (in Chapter 14). That is the principal theme of the next chapter.

CHAPTER 20

AGGREGATE SUPPLY ONCE AGAIN
(AND AGGREGATE DEMAND)

Unemployment in a modern economy can be classified as frictional, structural, demand-deficient or cost-constrained. Frictional unemployment simply reflects the fact that at any point in time some people are in the process of moving from one job to another. Government can help reduce frictional unemployment by improving information in regard to job availability. Structural unemployment reflects "mismatches" between the endowment of skills and the demand for skills, and/or immobility of labour across regions of the economy. It can be reduced by manpower training programmes and policies in regard to industrial location. The primary interest in macroeconomics is on so-called demand-deficient or cost-constrained unemployment. Therefore, in most of what follows, the first two kinds of unemployment will be ignored.

To highlight the central issues involved in deriving aggregate supply, assume homogeneous labour, a closed economy and, unless indicated to the contrary, given factor endowments. Until explicit indication is given to the contrary, it will also be assumed that the state of technology is constant, and that labour is the only ultimate factor of production which can be varied in use in the short-run. Potential output is then a function of the level of employment of labour.

DOWNWARD MONEY WAGE RIGIDITY
IN A CLOSED ECONOMY

Suppose that all markets — including the labour market — are perfectly competitive; thus, there are no institutional forces such as trade unions, minimum wage laws or unemployment relief payments ("dole") from the state, preventing real wages from being determined by free market forces. (Of course such institutional forces do exist in most economies, but in order to develop an understanding of the effects of these departures from competition, it is desirable to see what would happen if they did not exist.) It will be shown that given the foregoing assumptions, the only possible equilibrium for the system is at full employment — where everyone who is willing to work at the market-clearing wage actually finds work. (Note that the present notion of "full employment" differs from that of earlier chapters.)

We start the analysis with the supply and demand for labour as depicted in Figure 1. Microeconomics suggests — see Chapter 29 — that firms will hire labour up to a point at which the marginal revenue product of labour equals the money wage, W. Under the assumption of perfect competition in all markets, this is equivalent to saying that firms hire labour up to a point at which the marginal physical product of labour (MPP_L) equals the real wage (W/P). Hence, the MPP_L locus is the demand curve for labour in (real wage, employment) space. Full employment applies in labour market equilibrium, at $L = L_F$ and $(W/P) = (W/P)_F$ in Figure 1: under the assumptions specified, all persons willing to work at the equilibrium real wage would find work.

Figure 1

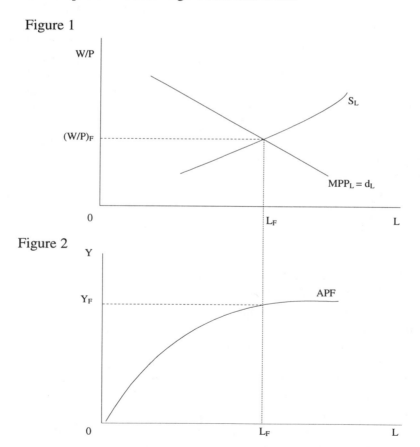

Figure 2

Assuming that labour is the only factor of production which is variable in use, Figure 2 depicts the economy's aggregate production function

(APF): it shows the maximum level of output Y as a function of varying amounts of employed labour, given the state of technology. (The reader who does not like the implicit assumption that the stock of capital in use is the same as the stock of capital in existence is asked to wait a while. But be assured that such an assumption should not bother us in the present context.) The slope of APF at any level of L is simply MPP_L. It is drawn as a strictly concave (bow-shaped) function reflecting the assumption that MPP_L is strictly decreasing. The full employment level of output, Y_F, can be read off directly, given that L_F has already been determined by the labour market equilibrium condition. Under the conditions specified, the equilibrium solution at full employment is entirely independent of the price level, for perfect competition in the labour market implies that at any price level, P, the money wage will adjust so as to generate L_F in Figure 1. For example, given some price level, suppose that the money wage was such as to imply a real wage higher than $(W/P)_F$ in Figure 1. The supply of labour would then exceed the demand for labour, and competition among the labour force seeking jobs would cause W to fall until $(W/P) = (W/P)_F$ was attained. Hence, assuming unrestrained perfect competition, equilibrium output is independent of the price level. But this would mean that the aggregate supply curve, AS, would be vertical at the single point in its domain in (P, Y) space — at Y_F in Figure 3.

Figure 3

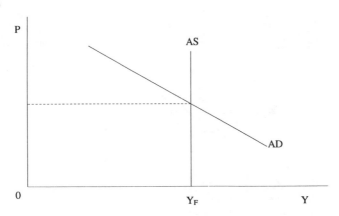

Consistent with the general practice throughout this text, assume that the relevant equilibria are stable. Then, with perfect competition in all markets — in the labour market in particular — the economy would automatically tend to full employment, and aggregate demand would have no effect other than on nominal variables (prices). For example, starting from an equilibrium in Figure 3, if government increased its expenditure the aggregate demand curve would shift to the right, causing the price level to rise. In the first instance, this would reduce the real wage below $(W/P)_F$ in Figure 1. However, the labour market would then be in disequilibrium — the demand for labour would exceed the supply of labour — and competition among employers would bid the money wage upward, in the same proportion as the rise in P, until $(W/P)_F$ was restored.

Figure 4

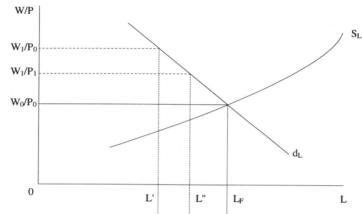

Figure 5

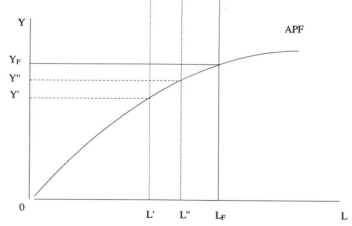

Suppose that a situation involving perfect competition, with $P = P_0$ and $W = W_0$ at the full employment equilibrium, initially applied, but that then, trade unions (or the availability of high dole payments) force up the money wage to a level W_1. From Figures 4 and 5 it can be seen that with $P = P_0$, employment would fall to L' while output would fall to Y'. Thus, point Z in Figure 6 is a point on the new aggregate supply curve. Figure 4 also indicates that given $W = W_1$, if P were to increase (to, say, P_1), the real wage would fall, employment would rise and firms would expand supply. Figure 6 shows that such a price increase would in fact occur, because of the excess of AD over AS at the old price level P_0. Hence, given $W = W_1$, the aggregate supply curve would now have a strictly positive slope. It is depicted by AS' in Figure 6; however, it overlaps the original curve AS in the diagram, for sufficiently high P. Figures 4 to 6 show that given $W = W_1$, the economy approaches a new equilibrium at Z', with output at Y", below the initial full employment level. Employment has fallen to L" at the new equilibrium.

Figure 6

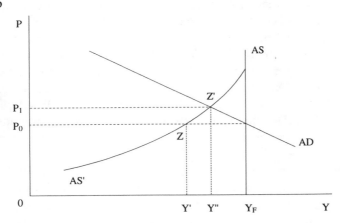

Is the unemployment implied by Z' in Figure 6 cost-constrained or is it demand-constrained? The answer is that in a sense it is either or both.

Those holding conservative political philosophies may tend to blame whatever force has caused the money wage to be rigid at $W = W_1$. If this is due to trade union bargaining, they would therefore blame trade unions, and might argue, with some justification, that the ensuing unemployment is in some sense voluntary on the part of the unions: people are unemployed because supposedly rational unions have decided to demand a money wage which generates a real wage inconsistent with full employment. Those same political conservatives might also argue (with some justification) that the government should do nothing to try to alleviate the unemployment situation, except to leave the unions to learn a lesson: if the unemployment is sustained for long, the unions might decide to settle for a lower real wage by reducing their money wage demands. The conservatives might even urge legislation reducing the bargaining powers of the trade unions. The downward money wage rigidity might alternatively be due to high dole payments from the state, which tend to set a floor on the wage rate at which people are willing to work, except covertly and illegally, even in the absence of trade unions. It could then be argued, with some justification, that the government's policy in regard to the dole is the key cause of unemployment, an argument which would lead some advocates to urge reduction in the rates of dole payments. Finally, the downward money wage rigidity may be due to minimum wage legislation, in which case the policy recommendations of conservatives would be similar to those revealed by their attitudes toward high dole payments. It is hopefully recognised that the diagnoses just outlined may be quite correct; however, the policy prescriptions (like almost all policy recommendations — recall Chapter 2) are ascientific, being matters reflecting one's sociological-political philosophy. Under the leadership of Prime Minister Margaret Thatcher, government policy in Britain throughout the 1980s was guided by diagnoses and philosophies along the lines of those just outlined. Given the behaviour of trade unions and government in Britain in the preceding decades, given the expectations which such behaviour generated and sustained, and given Mrs Thatcher's overwhelming desire to get inflation under control, the general thrust of the policies adopted by her administrations made a good deal of sense.

By way of contrast, and with some justification, individuals and interest groups holding less conservative political philosophies could ignore the notion of cost-constrained unemployment and argue that the unemployment implicit at point Z' in Figure 6 is due to too little aggregate demand. They would therefore be inclined to call on government to implement expansionary demand-management policies, thereby shifting AD to the right in the diagram. But note that with AS' having a positive slope as drawn in that diagram, the ensuing increases in output and employment would involve some increase in the price level. If the government did not care about inflation — if it did not regard erosion in the purchasing power of money as in itself "a bad thing" — such policies of expanding aggregate demand could be perfectly sensible.

It is worthwhile observing that as long as the aggregate supply curve is positively sloped, both the supply-side and the demand-side policies discussed in the immediately preceding two paragraphs are effective in increasing output only to the extent that they involve a reduction in real wages. In summary, Figure 6 implies that, given money wage rates which are rigid, output and hence employment can be increased by a policy of expanding aggregate demand — but only at a possible cost in the form of a higher price level. However, the diagram indicates that output and employment would also increase if money wage rigidity were eliminated. As an important addendum at this stage, it remains to be seen that (starting from an output level below full employment) output and employment would increase if the money wage were reduced from one level of rigidity to another.

It has already been shown that point Z in Figure 6 is a point on the economy's aggregate supply curve when the price level is P_0 and when the money wage is W_1. From Figure 4, the corresponding level of employment is L'. Still focusing on Figure 4, suppose next that with $P = P_0$, the money wage is reduced to some level W_2 strictly between W_1 and W_0. Even though the price level has not changed, the real wage has fallen. Employment will therefore increase to some level strictly between L' and L_F in Figure 4, and from Figure 5 it will be found that output will increase to some level strictly between Y' and Y_F. This means that with the lower money wage and at $P = P_0$ in Figure 6, the relevant aggregate supply curve goes through some point to the right of point Z. Extending this reasoning to arbitrary initial points on the upward-sloping part of AS' in Figure 6, and subject to one qualification, it can be seen that a reduction in W at any P shifts the aggregate supply curve to the right. The qualification pertains to the vertical part of the aggregate supply curve: a reduction in the level of downward rigidity in W cannot cause this to shift to the right, because it represents full employment in an otherwise competitive labour market. Instead of saying that a reduction in W shifts the aggregate supply curve to the right (which in not quite accurate), we will therefore say that a reduction in the level of rigidity in money wages causes the aggregate supply curve to swivel to the right: its asymptote — the vertical part — does not shift, but in other respects the aggregate supply curve does shift to the right.

Figure 7

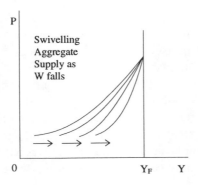

The swivelling of the aggregate supply curve in response to successive money wage reductions (until a real wage level consistent with full employment is attained) would be as depicted in Figure 7. The validity of the final statement in the preceding paragraph should now be clear.

REAL WAGE RIGIDITY IN A CLOSED ECONOMY

Next, instead of supposing that trade unions bargain for a higher money wage, assume (starting from an initial situation of perfect competition) that they demand and get a higher real wage, supposing as before that the state of technology stays constant. Furthermore, assume that the government regularly pursues policies of demand expansion in the hope that the ensuing higher price level will get the real wage down, but that the trade unions are consistently successful in their bargaining by indexing the money wage to any increase in the price level. Thus it is being assumed, following an initial money wage increase at the initial price level (hence a real wage increase), that every x% increase in the price level caused by demand expansion will invoke successful compensatory demands by the unions for an x% increase in money wage rates. It is easy to see that under such circumstances demand management can do *nothing* to restore output and employment, at least on a sustained basis.

Figure 8

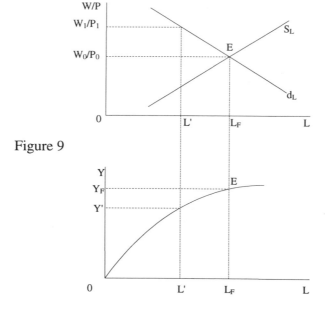

Figure 9

Figure 10

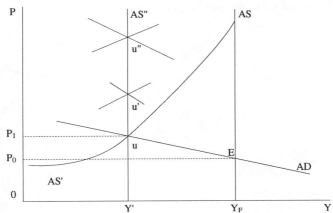

Let the initial position be at point E in Figures 8 to 10. Given P_0, trade unions force the wage up to $W_1 > W_0$. The aggregate supply curve swivels to the left to AS', output falls to Y' and the price level rises to P_1. If the government now expands demand, the price level will rise further and (given $W = W_1$) employment will rise. But if the trade unions respond by forcing wages upwards again so as to compensate for the higher P, the positively-sloped part of the aggregate supply curve will shift to the left, causing employment to fall again. Suppose, in response to successive doses of demand expansion, that the trade unions manage to index the real wage at the ratio W_1/P_1. Successive equilibria are represented by points such as u, u', u'', etc. in Figure 10: in effect, the aggregate supply curve has been shifted to a vertical locus like AS'', which is to the left of the full employment locus, AS. With such indexation, successive doses of demand expansion bring no recovery in employment, but only inflation.

PRODUCTIVITY GROWTH (TECHNICAL CHANGE), REAL WAGES AND AGGREGATE SUPPLY

Some observations on the role of technical change are now in order. Suppose, as before, that we start with perfect competition and ensuing full employment, and that next, trade unions push up the real wage to a level inconsistent with full employment, given productivity. The initial equilibrium is at point E in Figures 11 to 13. After the unions push up and index the real wage at W_1/P_1, the system goes to point J in the three diagrams. It has already been seen that assuming that the indexation is maintained, demand management policies, raising P, would be fruitless.

However, supply-side policies of an appropriate form can both restore full employment and improve living standards.

Figure 11

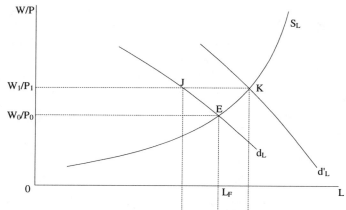

Figure 12

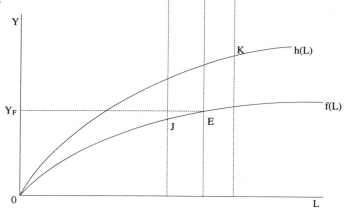

Figure 13

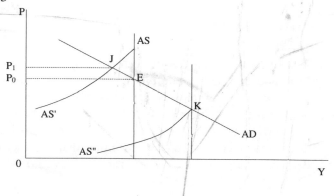

Supply-side policies can operate through technical improvement, which increases the marginal productivity of labour. Thus, the aggregate production function (the slope of which under present assumptions is labour's marginal product) swivels upwards from its origin, from f(L) to h(L) in Figure 12. A technical improvement is defined as *any* change which causes the aggregate production function to swivel upwards (i.e. in the present context, any change which causes the MPP_L curve to shift to the right). Hence, the term is used to denote anything which increases the potential output obtainable from given inputs. Therefore, it can take the form of an improvement in the "state of the technical arts" (technical change in a narrow conventional sense), improvement in work effort ("less featherbedding"), improved administration, abolition of a variety of restrictive practices, etc.

As drawn in the diagrams (Figures 11 to 13), the productivity increase exactly validates the permanently higher real wage. The new equilibrium is at point K in the three diagrams. The new aggregate supply curve is AS", implying that output and employment have increased, and the price level has fallen, despite the higher real wage.

Of course, taken together, Figures 11 to 13 illustrate only a special case of technical change. But the reader should be able to use the analytic tools now developed to see that in general, and so long as more labour-hours are offered as the real wage rises (i.e. so long as S_L is a strictly increasing function of the real wage), technical improvement:

(1) Increases equilibrium output.

(2) Increases equilibrium employment.

(3) Increases equilibrium real wages.

(4) Is a necessary precondition if an economy is simultaneously to experience increased real wages and increased employment, all sustainable over time. Thus, if policy-makers want *both* higher living standards for those at work *and* higher employment, they must promote rather than obstruct technical change. In that case, defensive tactics designed to protect existing jobs through obstruction of technical change are contrary to the national interest (as perceived by the policy-makers).

If necessary, the reader should use pencil and paper to check understanding of the foregoing propositions.

UNEMPLOYED CAPITAL AND AGGREGATE SUPPLY: LARGELY A DIGRESSION

As a representation of one aspect of macroeconomic structure in the

short run, the derivation of the aggregate supply curve up to this stage in
the present chapter has been along fairly conventional lines: it is similar
to (but in one respect more explicit than) the derivation found in other
textbooks. But some readers might reasonably feel uneasy about that
derivation: in essence, it assumed that labour is the *only* factor of production which is variable in employment in the short run. Hence, it assumed
that the amounts employed of all other factors of production — which we
will call "capital" by way of proxy, are constant. In particular, it assumed
that the capital stock *in use* is the same as the capital stock *in existence*.
In reality, if the economy is operating well below capacity at historically
low levels of output, then both capital and labour are likely to be idle. As
the economy expands starting from such a position, more capital as well
as more labour will be brought into use. Under such circumstances, the
demand curve for labour (as a function of the real wage) will not be the
MPP_L curve, as derived under the earlier assumption that the amount of
capital employed is fixed. If there is plenty of excess capacity, variation
of capital employed is likely to maintain labour productivity as more
labour is hired. Indeed, it is conceivable that even in the short run the
economy might experience returns to scale as both labour and capital are
varied in use, even if the economy's endowments of both capital and
labour are fixed.

In the short run (i.e. when the capital stock is fixed) it is reasonable to
assume that the economic cost (the opportunity cost) of employing an
extra unit of capital is zero — fixed costs do not affect short-run marginal costs. Therefore, firms will still tend to hire labour up to a point at
which the change in output due to hiring a marginal unit of labour
(combined with a marginal adjustment of capital in use) is approximately
equal to the real wage. In (Y, L) space, the observed short-run relationship between aggregate output and employment (given that capital in use
may also be varied as labour is varied) is plausibly similar to that
depicted in Figure 14. We will continue to use the words aggregate
production function, APF, to describe this curve (though some people
might object to such nomenclature on the correct grounds that for some
of its domain its slope really reflects what mathematicians call a total
differential, as labour and capital in use are both varied, rather than an
ordinary partial derivative — which is what its slope would denote if
capital in use were fixed). It will be noted that, as now drawn, the aggregate production function has a constant slope for much of the domain.
However, it becomes strictly concave at a level of output and employment where fixity of the capital stock in existence becomes a bottleneck
on expansion: it is only then that diminishing marginal productivity of
labour comes into play (and it is only then than the slope of the locus

depicted in Figure 14 is the marginal physical product of labour, MPP_L).

Because the change in output due to hiring a marginal unit of labour (whilst simultaneously bringing idle machines into use) is approximately constant for as long as there is much excess capacity in the economy, the demand curve for labour, depicted in Figure 15, will in fact be approximately zero-sloped for much of its domain in (real wage, employment) space, but will become strictly decreasing when fixity of the capital stock in existence starts to become a bottleneck on further increases in output. It is only then that the capital stock in use is the same as the capital stock in existence.

Figure 14

Figure 15

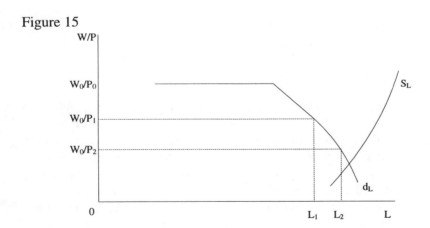

Turning now more explicitly to questions of supply, suppose that the free-market supply of labour curve is as depicted by S_L in Figure 15. Suppose, however, that the money wage is rigid downwards (due to minimum wage legislation, dole payments or trade unions) at some level

W_0 and that the initial price level is P_0. Given the information provided in Figures 14 to 16, the demand for labour by firms is then indeterminate, and the output which firms in aggregate would want to supply is therefore also indeterminate: in (P, Y) space, the aggregate supply curve is zero-sloped (perfectly flat). If the price level were to increase, the real wage would fall, and the demand for labour would become determinate. For example, given W_0, if the price level increased to P_1, the demand for labour would be L_1 in Figure 15. Similarly, a further rise in P, to P_2 given $W = W_0$, would increase the amount of labour demanded to L_2. Hence, the aggregate supply curve would be like that in Figure 16: approximately zero-sloped at first and then becoming positively sloped. Recall that this was how the aggregate supply curve was drawn in Chapter 14 above — but at that stage the analysis was developed using more primitive analytic tools.

Figure 16

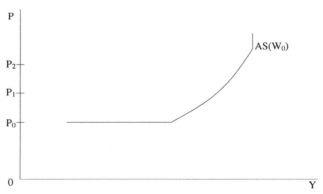

From now on (and as in Chapter 14) it will be assumed that the aggregate supply curve is like that drawn in Figure 16: approximately flat at first, then positively sloped and then vertical. Assuming money wage rigidity, its location depends on the money wage; therefore, to avoid confusion, the money wage being assumed in constructing any given AS curve will be indicated by the notation describing that curve. As reasoned earlier (in Chapter 14 and in more detail in the present chapter) a reduction in the money wage will cause the AS curve to swivel to the right, with no change in its asymptote. A technical improvement, by contrast, will cause the entire curve to shift downward and to the right; the asymptote itself would shift, reflecting the fact that potential output per worker at any level of employment of labour would have increased.

The reader may wonder why so much time has been allocated to investigation of the shape of the AS curve, given technology and the money wage rate. One reason is that most macroeconomics texts fail to investigate the matter adequately: in fact, they usually confuse the capital stock in use and the capital stock in existence. In effect, they assume that the capital stock is always employed and that labour is the only important factor of production which could be idle. A more profound reason for investigation along the lines just pursued is apparent when we come to understanding the effects of macroeconomic policy decisions. We can think of the AS curve as a short-run marginal cost curve for the entire economy. Recalling from microeconomics the relationship between marginal and average (i.e. unit) costs, we know that if marginal cost exceeds unit costs, then unit costs must be rising; if marginal cost is less than unit costs (and whether or not marginal cost is itself rising or falling), then unit cost must be falling. Recall also from microeconomics that fixed costs are included in unit costs but are *not* included in short-run marginal cost.

The policy relevance of all this is as follows: If the AS curve is *always* strictly increasing, and unless output is very low indeed, macroeconomic policies of demand deflation (e.g. contractionary fiscal policies) would tend to *reduce* unit costs in the economy as a whole, given wage rates. On the other hand, if short-run marginal costs are approximately constant — if AS is flat — policies of demand deflation will have the opposite effect: they will surely raise unit costs, given wage rates.

It follows that economists who make policy recommendations (e.g. on demand deflation) on the assumption that AS is strictly increasing, when in fact it is not, will often be offering advice which is simply wrong, given the objectives of policy-makers.

Finally in this section, it might reasonably be asked: Why has so much space been allocated to the short-run *macroeconomic* implications of unemployed capital, while this text allocates little or no time to the same issue in a *microeconomic* context?

The response is brief: The public policy implications of unemployed capital are more extreme at the economy-wide level than at the level of the firm. Although there are some exceptions, little theoretical research has been published on the microeconomic implications of unemployed capital. Sooner or later it will be forthcoming — but not in an elementary exposition such as that in the present text.

BRINGING IT ALL TOGETHER

It remains only to bring together findings from earlier investigations in this chapter and from Part Three.

For a closed economy, it has now been established that, given factor endowments:

(1) $AS = AS(P, W, T)$

where P is an index of the price level; W, an index of the wage rate is a proxy for the prices of the factors of production because (directly or indirectly) payments to the factor of production labour account for the bulk of production costs; T denotes the state of technology, broadly interpreted as indicated earlier in this chapter and measured in such a manner that a technical improvement will be indicated by a rise in T. The following has also been established:

$\Delta AS/\Delta P \geq 0$.

$\Delta AS/\Delta W < 0$.

$\Delta AS/\Delta T > 0$.

The main conclusions have been:

(1) The equilibrium level of national income is determined by aggregate supply and aggregate demand.

(2) If perfect competition applied in all markets, the only possible equilibrium for the system would be at full employment. However, in what follows it will be assumed that money wages are rigid.

(3) Given the economy's factor endowments, the variables governing aggregate supply are those on the right-hand side of equation (1). Hence, in (P, Y) space, the variables affecting the location of the aggregate supply curve (given factor endowments) are W and T. The variables affecting the aggregate demand curve are those which underlie the economy's IS and LM curves, from which $AD = AD(P)$ was derived.

(4) If aggregate supply were infinitely elastic, reliance on ordinary multiplier analysis will over-predict the response of equilibrium output to an increase in autonomous demand, to the extent to which there is "crowding out" in the money market.

(5) Even if there were no "crowding out", and if AS has a positive slope, reliance on ordinary multiplier analysis overstates the response in output to increases in autonomous demand.

(6) If technology is constant, and unless aggregate supply is infinitely elastic, policies of demand expansion operate through a mechanism which tends to involve a reduction in the real wage. However, this may not occur

if there is plenty of excess capacity or if an expansion in demand involves implementation of technical change. (In fact, demand expansion is often associated with investment demand, and new technologies tend to be embodied in new machines; in consequence, demand expansion often implies simultaneous implementation of new technology. However, when in what follows we refer to demand-side policies, we will be referring to effects on aggregate demand alone, given technology. Measures affecting technology will be described under supply-side policies.)

(7) Given technology, a reduction in money wage rates will cause the AS curve to swivel to the right, with no change in asymptote. Unless the system is already at full employment, output and employment will therefore increase (but living standards for those already in employment will fall). Hence, given technology, reduced living standards may be necessary if the economy is to experience higher employment.

(8) Technical improvement (broadly defined) is the *only* mechanism through which an economy can simultaneously experience *both* higher real wages and higher employment.

(9) Given technology, if real wages are indexed at some level inconsistent with full employment, there is nothing that demand-management policies can do to improve the situation. Supply-side policies which promote the implementation of technical change are then of crucial importance.

Complications Due to Openness

Turning to an open economy, under freely floating exchange rates there is not a great deal to add to the foregoing, except:

First, recall from Chapter 16 that, in the short-run and assuming that the economy starts from an equilibrium below full employment, fiscal expansion would tend to be ineffective while expansionary monetary policies would be effective — on the assumption that *money* wages are rigid. However, if *real* wages are rigid, no demand-side (whether monetary or fiscal) policy will be of use in boosting output and employment. An increase in the money supply would cause exchange rate depreciation and a rise in the price level; but if the wage rate (as a proxy for all internal factor prices) rose in the same proportion, then nothing would have changed in real terms.

Second, openness means that the specification of the AS function — equation (1) above — should be changed, the reason being as follows:

As in microeconomics, the amount which firms in aggregate are willing to supply depends on the relationship between output price and the price of inputs, given T (and given factor endowments). In the closed

economy case it was sensible to let W denote the price of inputs —
because all inputs would then have been domestically-produced and the
bulk of value added would have accrued as payments to labour. However,
in the case of an open economy it is important to distinguish between
those inputs which are domestically produced and those which are
imported. We will now let W — the wage rate — act as a proxy for the
price of domestically-produced inputs, and will denote the price of imported inputs by the symbol P^{MRM} (RM: "raw materials"). Hence, given
factor endowments, the aggregate supply function is represented as:

$$(2) \ AS = AS(P, W, P^{MRM}, T)$$

where it is added that $\Delta AS/\Delta P^{MRM} < 0$ — a rise in the price of imported
inputs, like a rise in money wage rates, would cause AS to swivel to the
left, in (P, Y) space. Having introduced equation (2), further comment on
the open economy will be confined to the case of fixed exchange rates.

Using the analytic framework of Part Four of this text as developed up
to now, the reader should be well equipped to analyse a wide range of
short-run policy issues in a small open economy under approximately
fixed exchange rates. Combined with lower national income multipliers,
and as has already been explained, the relative flatness of the open
economy's aggregate demand curve means that supply-side policies —
those which cause the aggregate supply curve to swivel (e.g. wages
policy) or to shift (policies affecting productivity) are more important
than in the closed economy case. However, consideration of the terms of
international trade highlights a further role for supply-side policies.

The Terms of Trade and Aggregate Supply

The terms of (international) trade reflect the amount of imports which an
economy obtains in exchange for a unit of exports. If (relative to some
base period) fewer imports can be obtained per unit of exports, then the
terms of trade are said to have moved adversely, or unfavourably; if the
opposite occurs, then the terms of trade have moved in a favourable
direction. In practice, reference to the terms of trade usually involves
resort to indices of the prices of exports, P^x, and of imports, P^m, in units
of domestic currency and relative to some base year. Units of exports and
of imports and the base year are chosen such that the *terms of trade
index*, P^x/P^m, equals one unit (usually 100) in the base year. If that index
rises over time, the terms of trade have moved favourably; if the index
falls, an adverse movement in the terms of trade has occurred. A rise in
the terms of trade is "favourable", a fall "unfavourable".

It is important to note that a small open economy (SOE) *cannot* influence its terms of trade to any significant extent, at least from one year to

the next. For purposes of exposition we will ignore the qualification and simply say that the SOE is a perfect price-taker insofar as tradable goods are concerned. Then the prices received for exports and paid for imports equal foreign ("world") prices multiplied by the exchange rate. Under such circumstances, a change in the exchange rate would have no effect on the terms of trade — and being economically small, the home country does not usually influence prices abroad. (If it did, we would not regard it as economically small.)

Even though it is a price-taker insofar as tradable goods are concerned, the terms of trade of a small country could vary because the kinds of goods the country exports generally differ from the kinds of goods it imports. In fact, the smaller the home country in a geographic sense, and hence the more limited the pattern of its natural resource endowments tends to be, the greater its exposure to terms of trade fluctuation. To take an extreme example, consider a small country which can export only beef and which must import all of its oil requirements. Then, if the world price of oil doubled, while world prices of beef stayed constant, the terms of trade of the small country would collapse. (If the index were 100 in the base year, it would have fallen to 50, implying that the home country would now obtain only 50 units of oil in exchange for 100 units of beef.) In the absence of large-scale foreign borrowing, its living standards would also tend to collapse: more of the economy's output of beef would have to be exchanged in order to obtain a given volume of oil. A key question which we now want to address is: What would happen to output and employment?

In order to analyse issues of this kind, it is desirable to economise on notation. To do so, it seems reasonable to assume that the price of exports is embodied *directly* in P, the price of the home country's output, but that all imports consist of materials for further production, implying that the price of imports, P^m, can be treated like W, the price of the domestic factors of production. Hence, the price of output will be denoted by P, as before; however, the prices of inputs to the productive system will be indicated by P^m and W. Note that under fixed exchange rates, P^m is beyond the control of the small country; W, on the other hand, may be subject to some degree of influence by domestic policy-makers. The aggregate supply function will now be represented by:

$$(3)\ AS = AS(P, W, P^m, T)$$

where an adverse movement in the terms of trade — a rise in P^m relative to P, must have the same kinds of effects as those of a rise in W, given P. In either case, production costs would have risen relative to output price, and the AS curve would therefore swivel to the left.

The alert reader is now well equipped with the tools necessary for an understanding of how a small open economy under fixed exchange rates might sensibly respond to an adverse movement in its terms of trade. Suppose that we are concerned with an energy-dependent economy which must import all of its energy requirements, say oil, and that the state of technology, the country's terms of trade and the wage rate are all initially given. Let W_0 denote that wage rate. Let processed beef products be the country's principal export. Assume that the economy is operating fairly close to full employment. In Figure 17, $AS(W_0)$ denotes the economy's initial aggregate supply curve, and Y_0 is the initial equilibrium level of output.

Figure 17

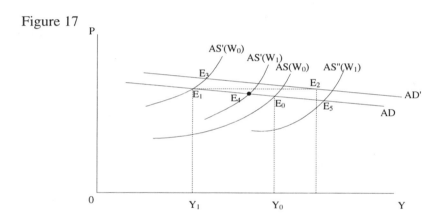

Next, suppose that the economy's terms of trade collapse. Of course, this reflects no fault of the domestic policy-makers: it is something beyond their control. Perhaps the world price of the key oil input has risen by, say, 300 per cent. Because the home country (as a close approximation) is a price-taker on world markets, its exporters cannot sensibly respond by marking up their export prices just because they must pay more for their oil inputs. (If they tried to do so, their exports would fall toward zero.) Because input prices have risen, the aggregate supply curve shifts to the left — to $AS'(W_0)$ in Figure 17. However, there is no presumption that anything has happened which will cause any significant shift in the aggregate demand curve, AD. (It is acknowledged that an ensuing change in the market demand for non-tradables might cause a small shift in the aggregate demand curve. But because the aggregate demand curve is fairly flat to begin with, this can be taken to be of minor importance. In order to focus on the substantive issues, any such shift in the aggregate demand curve will be ignored entirely.)

It can be seen from Figure 17 that equilibrium income falls, to Y_1. Unemployment therefore rises, and because there is some upward pressure on the price level (if AD is at all negatively sloped) real wages also fall. Hence, living standards of all, whether employed or unemployed, deteriorate.

Note that in a sense, the terms of trade collapse is both "inflationary" and "deflationary". Even if the money wage rate stays constant, it is "inflationary" in the sense that it causes the price level to rise, though it should be added that in itself this is a "once-and-for-all" increase (and therefore "inflationary" is not an appropriate term); it is "deflationary" in the sense that it causes a contraction in output and employment. It should be clear that the crisis would be rendered even more severe if trade unions sought and obtained a higher money wage, to compensate for the higher price level: In that event, the aggregate supply curve would shift even further to the left, and the contraction in output and employment would exceed the amounts implied by the point E_1 in Figure 17. It will now be shown that a sensible policy response would be one which concentrates on aggregate supply rather than on aggregate demand.

First, suppose that the government responds to the new equilibrium at E_1 by implementing expansionary fiscal policies — demand-side measures. Perhaps the government's economic advisers have discovered the potency of such policies for a closed economy with plenty of excess capacity; perhaps also those advisers simply do not understand much about the macroeconomics of small open economies, and the government is therefore led to believe that a massive programme of public expenditure, financed by borrowing abroad, will solve the problem; suppose that the government acts in accordance with such beliefs. This causes the aggregate demand curve to shift to the right from AD to AD' in Figure 17. (Mistaken) application of ordinary multiplier analysis at an unchanged interest rate would predict that the economy would move from E_1 to E_2 in the diagram. Note that in the case of an economy with as high a marginal propensity to import as that of Ireland, it is likely that the relevant multiplier would be quite close to unity; thus, the increase in G implied by the shift in aggregate demand would itself approximate the horizontal distance between E_2 and E_1. An important counterpart to this would be a large increase in foreign debt, the burden for repayment of principal and interest being imposed on future generations.

However, from the vantage point of the short run alone, it is unlikely that such an expansionary fiscal stance would have had great success. Figure 17 shows that even at an unchanged interest rate, when the supply-side response is taken into account, the new equilibrium is not at E_2 (as would have been predicted by naive application of multiplier analysis) but at E_3. If the aggregate demand curve is fairly flat, it is very likely that point E_3 would lie to the left of point E_0. This would imply that despite the huge fiscal injection financed by foreign borrowing, output and employment at the new equilibrium would be lower than that which applied before the adverse movement in the terms of trade. Under the circumstances just outlined, the main effects of the fiscal expansion would be adverse rather than favourable, and long-term rather than short-term. These adverse effects would be represented by the burden imposed on future generations, who would be faced with the problem of having to pay the interest on the increased external debt incurred in the process of financing the fiscal expansion. The financing of such interest payments implies additional taxation on those future generations.

The scenario just outlined is a fair representation of the behaviour of Irish governments in the 1970s in response to the terms of trade collapse (the oil crisis) of 1973/4. Through high taxation in the 1990s, the Irish workforce is still paying for such policy responses. Further comment on those policies is deferred until Chapter 23.

Suppose now, instead of opting for demand management policies — expansionary fiscal policies — that the government responds to the crisis by concentrating on supply-side measures. To remind the reader: in Figure 17, the aggregate supply curve has shifted to the left, to $AS'(W_0)$, and under the policy stance now proposed, the aggregate demand curve is unchanged; the government now seeks a way of moving the aggregate supply curve back to the right. There are two kinds of measures which it might sensibly try to implement: (a) wage cuts and (b) policies promoting technical change (productivity growth), broadly conceived.

If government advisers truly understand the implications of the terms of trade collapse, and if the government itself were strong and responsible (alas, none of these qualifications seem to have described circumstances at policy-making levels in Ireland in the 1970s) the government might emphasise the seriousness of the economic crisis and negotiate a general wage reduction with the trade union movement. If this were successful, and if the wage rate were reduced from W_0 to W_1, the aggregate supply curve would swivel to the right, causing the economy to move to the right along the initial aggregate demand curve. As drawn in Figure 17, the aggregate supply curve has swivelled to $AS'(W_1)$, and E_4 denotes the ensuing equilibrium. Note that the resulting stabilisation of output and employment would then have been attained without resort to foreign borrowing, and therefore without imposing a burden on future generations. If the wage reduction at a given level of productivity were sufficiently large, AS' could swivel sufficiently far to the right to offset exactly the terms of trade collapse and to restore the economy to its initial equilibrium point, E_0.

A second kind of supply-side policy open to the government would be the promotion of productivity growth. In practice, this would tend to reveal its effects more slowly than in the case of a wage reduction; however, for purposes of exposition we will suppose that this policy is implemented concurrently with the wage reduction, and that it is quickly effective. For example, legislation could be enforced or enacted to reduce restrictive practices, "featherbedding", etc. by employers, by self-employed professional groups and by ordinary workers (in the latter case, possibly in conjunction with negotiations with the trade union movement), and the government might decide no longer to tolerate those interest groups who seek to obstruct the immediate implementation of technical change in the narrow sense. To the extent to which such a policy is successful, the aggregate supply curve would shift (not swivel) to the right. Indeed, it is possible, over a period of a few years, that the policies emphasising productivity growth would more than offset the adverse effects of the terms of trade collapse; it is possible, therefore, that both real wages and employment would increase over time despite the initial adverse movements in living standards due to the terms of trade collapse. As drawn in Figure 17, the aggregate supply curve has shifted to $AS''(W_1)$, and E_5 is the new equilibrium. As compared to the initial equilibrium at E_0, output has increased, and employment has possibly increased — see the subsection which follows. The diagram itself cannot tell us whether real wages have increased because, although the price level has fallen, we have assumed that the policy emphasising growth in productivity has been implemented along with the policy of reducing money wage rates. All we can sensibly say for the moment is that both employment and real wages *may* have increased.

Supply-side Measures: Further Observations on Small Open Economies

The present chapter has attached special emphasis to supply-side rather than demand-side measures as appropriate instruments for increasing output, employment and living standards in small open economies. The discussion pertained mainly to the case of fixed exchange rates, partly because it is easiest to understand the issues affecting policy effectiveness in such an environment, but also because Ireland — the country which is the main focus for applications in this text — has in fact sought to maintain approximately fixed exchange rates with *some* large country ever since the 1820s. Purely from a geometric standpoint, it is easy to see that supply-side measures are likely to be of more importance than those affecting aggregate demand *because* the aggregate demand curve of the kind of economy which has been under particular investigation is fairly flat: the flatter the aggregate demand curve, the more a shift of that curve would approximate a shift on top of itself. In the limiting case of a complete price-taking small economy, where the aggregate demand curve would be perfectly flat, the approximation would be exact, implying that an "expansionary" fiscal policy would lead to no expansion at all in aggregate demand, and output would be entirely supply-determined.

Two general kinds of supply-side measures were discussed: (a) wages policies and (b) policies affecting productivity. It was shown that if the objective is to increase output and real wages over time, then policies of type (b) are to be preferred to those of type (a).

A reader accustomed to thinking along fairly conventional lines might fear that policies increasing productivity might in themselves cause un-employment. In part, this fear might be due to confusion between micro-economic and macroeconomic effects of technical change. At least in the short run, it is true that implementation of new technologies can cause frictional and structural unemployment. However, provided government policy does not undermine incentives for work, and provided the labour force is willing to be mobile and to learn new work methods, such prob-lems would tend to be only transitory in a flexible labour market environ-ment. It is also true that policies tolerating the obstruction of technical change can perpetuate employment *in the short run* at the microeconomic level. But in the long run, the more pervasive the "defensive" tactics against technical change, and the longer they are maintained, the more the economy in question is undermining its own competitiveness: Imagine interest groups in a primitive economy banning the use of the wheel and wheel-based technologies, and then (following the opening of their economic system) trying to compete in internal and international markets against products of more advanced economies, the competitive-ness of which have been assisted by the existence of the wheel and by the subsequent technologies based on the invention of the wheel.

In the long run, in a competitive world where all countries are imple-menting technical change, those countries most prone to toleration of interest groups which seek to obstruct implementation of new technolo-gies must be undermining their own competitiveness. In such a world, it is precisely those countries which have had the *fastest* rates of technical change which have had the least difficulties in increasing employment or maintaining near full employment. (Think of some Far Eastern countries since World War II.) Such countries have been increasing their *shares* of world markets, mainly at the expense of countries where technical change has been slowest. The key point to bear in mind is that the *world* is the potential market for the output of a small economy. Although it would be unwise to discount the role of marketing effort, whether or not a small country can take advantage of its world market potential depends on its unit costs. Thus, at given levels of real wages, it depends on the state of productivity in the country in question — relative to the productivity levels in the countries with which it is most closely competing.

The importance of competitiveness in the tradables sectors of an open economy is obvious. However, given that the output of a small open economy consists of non-tradables as well as tradables, it may be felt that the state of productivity in the economy's non-tradables sectors does not affect overall competitiveness. This view is simply wrong, and very fundamentally and dangerously so. In Ireland, over one half of all employment is in the services sector (as distinct from the two other traditional sector classifications, agriculture and industry). The bulk of services sector output — which consists of Public Administration and Defence, and Marketed Services — is conveniently classified as non-tradable. However (as will be explained in Chapter 23) in Ireland over one half of the gross output of Marketed Services is used as an *input* to the productive system, which includes those sectors of the economy producing tradables; it does not flow *directly* into final demand. Hence, efficiency in the non-tradables sectors (as in all other sectors) is important in determining the overall competitiveness of the economy.

The present chapter has referred to the wage rate as a variable subject to potential influence by policy-makers within a small open economy like that of Ireland. This makes sense mainly in the short run — from one year to the next. But *in the absence of policy concerning growth in productivity, it does not make sense for Ireland to pretend to have a long-term policy for employment while at the same time it purports to be part of a Common (European labour) Market.* If real wages in Ireland remain below those elsewhere in the European Union, there will be a persistent tendency for labour to flow out of Ireland to other regions of the EU, where productivity (and hence real wages) are higher; that would merely reflect the requirements for efficient operation of the labour market. Lower real wages in Ireland reflect lower productivity in Ireland. Appropriate utilisation of so-called structural (or cohesion) transfer payments from the rest of the EU is a possible mechanism through which productivity in Ireland may be raised. In spite of an apparently endless debate, in spite of much lip-service and inconsistent behaviour at policy-making levels, and in spite of a great deal of confused and erroneous thinking, a very simple fact remains: If Ireland does want higher employment *and* higher real wages, and if these are to be sustained over time, then *the only* mechanism through which its objectives can be attained is through steady increases in productivity.

PART FIVE

MONEY AND BANKING,
AND MACROECONOMIC POLICY ISSUES
IN IRELAND

CHAPTER 21

MONETARY POLICY IN IRELAND: ANALYTICAL CONSIDERATIONS

Martin Kenneally

This chapter elaborates on some analytical aspects of money and monetary policy. It is essential to observe that, in contrast with earlier chapters, *all* goods and services are assumed to be *tradable* and policy effectiveness is analysed in a model framework which emphasises the underlying equilibrium long-run forces operating in the economy. This results in a *longer-term perspective* on policy effectiveness and an increased emphasis on the nature of the supply-side response in conditioning the effectiveness of expansionary demand-side policies. Chapter 22 deals with some operational aspects of Irish monetary policy, including historical developments, money supply determination and control and, finally, the interpretation of official Irish money supply statistics.

MONEY: DEFINITION, PRICES AND QUANTITY

Definition

Although money performs a variety of functions its essential characteristic is that it serves as a medium of exchange; with minor exceptions, all trades in modern economies are for money. All other financial assets are less *liquid* than money. By this we mean either that they are not as readily *marketable* against other goods and services or assets or that if they are readily marketable, they entail some degree of *price risk*. In short, the liquidity of money makes it the standard and usually the sole general means of payment.

In a modern economy, money consists primarily of:

(1) *Currency* (Notes and Coin): Notes and coin are an accepted means of payment and are, therefore, part of the money supply.

(2) *Current Account Deposits*: Current account balances held by the public with the banking system are, through the issue of *cheques*, also widely used to settle debts and make payments. A cheque is a written instruction

[349]

by the drawer or writer of the cheque to their bank to make the payment stipulated on the cheque, to the payee named on the cheque. Current account deposits (also called checking deposits) are extremely liquid, being at just one remove from cash.

The sum of currency in the hands of the public plus current account deposits held by the public with the banking system is called "narrow money". It is customarily termed M1, both in Ireland and elsewhere.

(3) *Deposit Account Balances*: Strictly speaking, deposit account balances (also called savings account balances or term deposits) are not an accepted means of payment. Cheques cannot be written on a deposit account, nor is a savings account passbook generally accepted as a means of payment. Nonetheless, it is possible to meet a cheque drawn on a current account by transferring the appropriate amount from one's deposit account. Alternatively, one may also withdraw cash from a deposit account, without delay or loss of value, to be used as a means of payment. Thus, savings deposits are a very close substitute for cash or, equivalently, they are highly liquid.

If we add savings account balances, held by the public with the banking system, to "narrow money", M1, we obtain "broad money". "Broad money" is customarily termed M2 in most countries; in Ireland, for historic reasons, it is termed M3.

Note that cash and bank deposits are counted as part of the money supply *only if they are held by the public*. Specifically, vault cash held by a bank, deposits held by one bank at another bank or government deposits held by the banking system are *not* counted as part of the money supply. This is because they have not passed into general circulation and are not available to the general public as a means of payment.

Note also that, traditionally, only deposits held by the public *with the banking system* were counted as money. Specifically, deposit balances held by the public at non-banks (e.g. building societies) were *not* counted as part of the money supply. There is no clear analytical reason for this exclusion since such deposits may also be used as a means of payment. The distinction is of historic rather than analytical significance.

In recent years a broader definition of the money supply, M3E, which includes deposits held at non-banks, has been added by the Central Bank of Ireland to the list of official money supply statistics which it provides in its *Quarterly Bulletins*.

Prices

Money does not have *one* single price; four prices are distinguishable:

(1) *Its numeraire or accounting value*: Because money is a means of

payment it acts as the numeraire or unit of account in which all other goods and services are valued. Trivially, its "price" in this regard is 1 (i.e., Ir£1 = Ir£1) and is unchanging over time.

(2) *Its command over real goods and services*: This refers to the amount of real goods and services which Ir£1 will buy. A measure of the purchasing power of money depends on the precise content of the basket of goods in question. If we use a standard basket of consumer goods then the "price" or, more properly, the value of money, in this regard, is measured as the reciprocal or inverse of the Consumer Price Index, i.e. $1/P$ where P is the Consumer Price Index (CPI). Most attention on this front focuses on how well money stores its value over time. Price inflation erodes the value of money; price stability maintains it.

(3) *The price of liquidity over time*: Sectors of the economy (i.e. business and government) which spend more than their income are termed deficit-spending sectors. They fund their deficits by raising the required liquidity or cash or money from other sectors (i.e. households and abroad) which are induced to spend less than their income. Such funding can take the form of sales of *equity* (i.e. ownership claims on the assets and net earnings of the issuing company) or *debt* (marketable IOUs) by the deficit sector. For convenience *we will assume hereafter that all funding is raised by debt issuance.*

An important function of the financial system is to transfer efficiently the savings of the surplus or net lending sectors to the deficit or net borrowing sectors which (usually) spend them on capital goods. In a closed economy, this process is revealed in the identity of total realised savings and total realised investment.

The inducement offered to the lender of funds for foregoing consumption opportunities, transferring liquidity to the borrower and placing capital at risk, is the prospect of interest or gain in addition to the return of the capital lent. "The" *loan rate of interest* is the price of liquidity per unit of time and is expressed as the percentage return per annum on the funds lent. The return includes periodic coupons or dividends together with any prospective terminal capital gain. In practice, there are innumerable rates of interest, each corresponding to the differing lengths of time over which funds are lent (the maturity of the loan) and the different degrees of default risk posed by the borrower. However, since interest rates tend, on the average, to rise and fall together in line with some key indicator rate of interest, it is a convenient simplifying fiction to characterise the *loan market* as trading in *one* single risk-free (i.e. default-free) fixed dividend irredeemable loan instrument or *bond,* and to refer without out ambiguity to the associated rate of interest as "the" rate of interest.

If the bond pays a fixed dividend of £5 per annum and its price is £100, then the interest rate is 5 per cent, i.e. the issuer of the bond receives £100 and pays out £5 per annum to the holder thereafter. If, say, a year later, as a result of additional demand, bond prices rise to £125, then the interest rate will fall to 4 per cent (i.e. £5/£125). [The original bond holder can then sell the bond for £125 and thereby experience a £25 capital gain in addition to the £5 dividend, yielding a total *holding period* return of 30 per cent. A rise in interest rates has the opposite effect on capital gains and holding period returns].

Note, in particular, that the lender is swapping money which is a means of payment which does *not* earn interest for a less liquid asset, the borrower's bond, which is not a means of payment but which *does* earn interest.

[In reality the distinction between money and non-money financial assets is blurred: an interest-bearing deposit account balance would have to be counted as a bond under the above rubric and interest-bearing current accounts would be unclassifiable. However, the watertight distinction drawn above between money and bonds is precisely that which is implicit in the ISLM model used in this text].

(4) *The price of foreign currencies*: Foreign trade is usually invoiced or billed in a foreign currency (most frequently US dollars or Sterling). Thus, an Irish importer will sell Irish money and buy foreign currency to effect payment for the import. Similarly, an Irish exporter who receives a foreign currency payment will frequently sell the foreign currency, thus obtained, for Irish money. These considerations apply to all foreign transactions, be they current merchandise trade or capital transactions involving the purchase or sale of real or financial assets. The market in which Irish money is traded for foreign money is called the foreign exchange market. The Irish balance of (international) payments accounts record all such foreign currency receipts and payments and thereby record the principal sources of supply and demand in the foreign exchange market.

Neither Chapter 15 nor subsequent chapters on macroeconomics distinguished between the *spot* and *forward* exchange rate. What was called the exchange rate, e, was, in fact, the spot exchange rate. Now that this distinction is being made we will denote the spot exchange rate by the symbol S (identical to "e" of earlier chapters) and the forward rate by F.

The bilateral *spot* exchange rate, S, as defined earlier in this text, is the Irish pound *price* of one unit of foreign currency (Direct Quotation or American definition) when the currencies are exchanged immediately. We can conceptualise this exchange rate either as "the" exchange rate against "the rest of the world" (i.e., a weighted average exchange rate) or, alternatively, as the Irish pound/sterling spot exchange rate, assuming that Ireland and the UK are the only two economies of relevance in the particular context being analysed. *The latter interpretation is adopted, hereafter, for convenience.*

The crucial importance of the exchange rate on the demand for net exports (exports minus imports) has been dealt with earlier in Chapter 15.

The bilateral *forward* exchange rate, F, is defined as the Irish pound price, *set today*, of one unit of foreign currency, where the currency exchange is set to take place *at the end of a specified period* after the date of contract.

While there are many forward exchange rate contracts, we restrict our present attention to the 90-day forward Irish pound/sterling exchange rate. If an Irish exporting company has granted 90 days credit on a UK sterling sale, say of £5m sterling, then the company can, *today*, sell the sterling forward. This means that the company enters a contract which obliges it to sell and the buyer (usually an Irish bank) to buy the £5m sterling from it in 90 days' time at an exchange rate, the currently quoted forward rate, *which is set today*, say, F = Ir£1.10/£1stg. The advantage of this seemingly complicated arrangement is that the Irish company can, today, *fix with certainty* the Irish pound value of the sterling it will receive in 90 days' time, i.e., Ir£5.5m. To be sure, the exporter could simply wait for 90 days, receive the sterling and then sell it at the *then prevailing spot exchange rate*, but, today there is no way of knowing with certainty what that rate will be. It could turn out to be more favourable or less favourable than the currently quoted forward rate. The important point is that it is risky, whereas the forward sale *eliminates the foreign currency risk*. Forward exchange markets are used to manage foreign currency risk and also play an important role in the determination of Irish interest rates which is taken up below. When traders use the forward exchange market as illustrated above they are said to be *hedging* or *covering* their foreign currency positions or exposures.

Nominal Interest Rate Parity

Consider a one-year Irish (financial) investor who can today ($t = 0$), either invest Ir£1 at home in Irish bonds or who may, alternatively, convert to sterling, invest in UK bonds and reconvert the proceeds to Irish pounds and thereby repatriate at year end ($t = 1$). These possibilities are represented below:

Let r = the nominal 1-year Irish interest rate at $t = 0$,
r^* = the nominal 1-year UK interest rate at $t = 0$,

S_0 = the Irish pound/sterling spot exchange rate at t = 0,
S_1 = the Irish pound/sterling spot exchange rate at t = 1,
F   = the 1-year forward Irish pound/sterling exchange rate at
     t = 0.

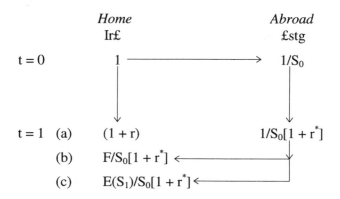

If the investor invests at home, $(1 + r)$ Irish pounds are obtained at t = 1.
If, at t = 0, the investment is converted into sterling, £1/S_0stg will be
obtained for Ir£1. This is invested, at t = 0, in a UK bond and yields
£1/S_0[1 + r^*]stg at t = 1. If, *at t = 0*, the investor sells £1/S_0[1 + r^*]stg forward, Ir£F/S_0[1 + r^*] will be obtained at t = 1. Both investments are zero-
risk opportunities since all relevant interest rates and exchange rates are
known at t = 0. It follows that they should yield identical returns. If this
were not so, say (b) > (a), then the investor could issue a Ir£1 (Irish)
bond at t = 0 and convert the proceeds to sterling and invest in a UK
bond as before. The investor will then *owe* Ir£$(1 + r)$ and *receive*
Ir£F/S_0[1 + r^*] at t = 1, giving a net profit of Ir£[(b) - (a)]. Note that this
is a *zero-cost risk-free profit*, since there is zero net cash outlay at t = 0
and, at t = 1, the certain Irish pound return on the UK investment more
than meets the certain Irish pound liability on the Irish borrowing, and it
is known as an *arbitrage*. Efficient bond markets are called *no-arbitrage*
markets precisely because they do not allow such opportunities.

In efficient markets if (b) > (a) investors would issue Irish bonds
immediately, thereby driving their price down and the Irish interest rate
up. The additional demand for sterling by such investors to purchase UK
bonds would drive the spot exchange rate, S, up; the forward sale or
supply of sterling arising from the maturing UK bond investments would
drive the forward exchange, F, down. The effect is to increase (a) and
reduce (b). Because of the speed and efficiency of bond markets (millions of pounds can be moved in seconds and at tiny cost) bond returns

(a) and (b) are brought to equality *instantaneously*.

Equating (a) and (b) and dividing through by $(1 + r^*)$ gives,

$$(1 + r)/(1 + r^*) = F/S_0$$

Subtracting 1 from each side gives the exact covered interest rate parity condition [CIRP],

$$(r - r^*)/(1 + r^*) = (F - S_0)/S_0$$

This is called *covered* since the foreign currency risk associated with the UK investment is covered or hedged by use of the forward currency market. It is convenient, for analytical purposes, to write the above equation in *approximate* form (letting $\cong$ denote "approximately equals"):

$$r \cong r^* + (F - S_0)/S_0$$

This states that the domestic interest rate equals the foreign interest rate plus the forward discount on the Irish pound. The latter is $(F - S_0)/S_0$ and the Irish pound is said to be at a discount when $F > S_0$ (sterling is then said to be at a premium) and conversely when $F < S_0$. Note that when the exchange rate is fixed and expected to remain so, then $F = S$ as traders will not pay more or accept less for forward currency than the current spot rate which is unchanging over time. In fact, the forward market would become redundant and vanish in these circumstances. However, the implied forward rate and expected future spot rate will each equal the current spot rate. Since $F = S$ under truly fixed exchange rates there can be no forward discounts or premia on the Irish pound, and it follows that $r = r^*$ under truly fixed exchange rates. *In short, the domestic interest rate will necessarily equal the foreign interest rate in a permanently fixed exchange rate small open economy.*

The investor need not use the forward exchange market but may instead sell the sterling proceeds of the UK bond investment at $t = 1$, at the then prevailing spot exchange rate, S_1. Both the domestic and foreign investment opportunity must, however, be appraised at $t = 0$ when the investment is being selected. The investor must then *take a view* or *form an expectation* of what the spot exchange rate will be at $t = 1$. This future expected exchange rate is termed $E(S_1)$ where E signifies the expectation formed at $t = 0$. Note that the return on the UK investment is no longer risk-free since it now entails some foreign currency risk, i.e. the *actual* future spot exchange rate, S_1, may turn out to be different from what was expected, i.e. $E(S_1)$. However, if investors are *risk-neutral* or indifferent to this risk then (a) = (c). Substituting and simplifying, as before, we obtain, in *approximate* form,

$$r \cong r^* + \{E(S_1) - S_0\}/S_0$$

where $\cong$ is again used to denote "approximately equals". This is called uncovered interest rate parity (UIRP) and states that the Irish interest rate will equal the UK interest rate plus the expected rate of currency depreciation of the Irish pound, $\{E(S_1) - S_0\}/S_0$. The intuition is simple: if the 1-year UK sterling interest rate is, say, 5 per cent and the Irish pound is expected to depreciate by, say, 3 per cent against sterling over the year [e.g. $E(S_1)$ = Ir£1.03/£1stg and S_0 = Ir£1/£1stg], then the Irish interest rate must equal 8 per cent to generate a competitive return. Our earlier result, that $r = r^*$ *under truly fixed exchange rates*, still holds since $E(S_1)$ = S_0 and no depreciation of the domestic currency is expected, provided that the fixed exchange rate is credible and believed by the market.

Note, finally, that if *both* covered and uncovered interest rate parity hold it follows, as inspection of both formal expressions shows, that $F = E(S_1)$, which implies that in risk neutral markets the forward exchange rate, F, is, in fact, the spot exchange rate that the market expects to occur at $t = 1$. Inspection of the forward rate relative to the current spot rate provides a useful indicator of state of market expectation on the likely future course of the spot exchange rate.

[In macroeconomics the term "investment" refers to the purchase of additional *goods*, such as plant, equipment and inventory, which are not used up in the current production period; the term "savings" refers to income which is not consumed but instead takes the form of additional *financial claims*, such as money and bond holdings, accumulated by the saver. For consistency, in the above account of interest rate parity, a bond purchaser should be referred to as a "saver" and bond holdings as accumulated "savings". The terms "investor" and "investment", while misleading, are used instead because that usage, imported from the finance literature, is now so common that it cannot be avoided].

The Quantity or Stock of Money in an Open Economy

The Irish Money supply or money stock has been defined as the liquid liabilities of the *consolidated* Irish banking system. The consolidated banking system consists of the Central Bank and all commercial banks treated, for accounting purposes, as one large bank. Some useful insights may be obtained by examining a simplified balance sheet representation of the banking system.

The balance sheet is a statement of everything the banking system owns (its assets) and everything it owes (its liabilities) at a point in time. By the principle of double entry accounting, total assets and total liabilities are always identically equal.

Consolidated Banking System: Balance Sheet

Assets	*Liabilities*
Domestic Credit ≡ D	Currency
Foreign Currency Reserves ≡ R	Deposits
D + R ≡	M

When the banking system grants a customer a loan, say for £1,000, the customer signs a loan form or IOU which is then an asset of the bank. The category of bank assets termed Domestic Credit, D, increases by £1,000. The bank, in turn and simultaneously, either pays £1,000 currency to the customer or credits the customer's deposit account with £1,000, or some combination of the two. The categories of bank liabilities termed Currency and Deposits increases by £1,000. Assets and liabilities increase identically. So also does the money supply. In fact, this is the most common way the money supply is increased — a bank grants a customer a loan and expands its credit.

Assume that an Irish importing company pays £800stg for imports and that the spot exchange rate is Ir£1.25 = £1stg. (i.e. S = 1.25). The company buys £800stg from the bank. This costs Ir£1,000. The bank debits the company's deposit account by Ir£1,000 and provides it with £800stg. This the company pays to the UK bank account of the UK exporter. Irish bank deposits decline by Ir£1,000 and the foreign currency reserves of the Irish banking system also decline by Ir£1,000. [Although the drop in foreign currency reserves is £800stg, its equivalent Irish pound value is used for balance sheet purposes since all balance sheet assets and liabilities are expressed in Irish pounds]. Bank assets and liabilities decline equally as does the money supply. The receipt by an Irish exporter of a sterling payment has an opposite effect.

It fact, the Irish money supply is the sum of Domestic Credit, D, and Foreign Currency Reserves, R, which are known as the *counterparts of the money supply*. Formally,

$$M \equiv R + D.$$

The change in the money supply between any two balance sheet dates, say over a calendar year, must be identically equal to the sum of the changes in its counterparts. Formally,

$$\Delta M \equiv \Delta R + \Delta D.$$

The change in the foreign currency reserve counterpart of the money supply, ΔR, arising from all foreign receipts into the Irish economy less all foreign currency payments out of the Irish economy is, in fact, the balance of (international) payments as defined in chapter 15, Table 1. The change in the level of domestic credit over the course of the year, ΔD, is termed Domestic Credit Expansion.

A Central Bank uses a variety of monetary instruments (dealt with in chapter 12) to control domestic credit expansion. Since money is a means of payment, expanding domestic credit is likely to exert a powerful effect on the scale of expenditure on goods, services and on the purchase of bonds. As such, the rate of credit expansion is a useful indicator of the thrust of the Central Bank's monetary policy.

THE DETERMINATION OF MONEY PRICES AND QUANTITIES IN AN SOE
Fixed Exchange Rates

The numeraire price of money is fixed and unchanging. If the exchange rate is fixed, so also is the foreign currency price of money. If the spot exchange rate is expected to remain fixed, then the forward foreign exchange market ceases to exist as it would become redundant, as noted earlier. Chapter 13 has shown that, via commodity arbitrage, the equilibrium money price of commodities (and their inflation rate) in a small open economy will necessarily tend to equal that of its major (fixed exchange rate) trading partner. This is known as the doctrine of Purchasing Power Parity (PPP) and was formally expressed as equation 9 in Chapter 13. Thus, a fixed exchange rate economy tends to import passively the inflation rate of its major trading partner. Finally, the time price of money or the domestic interest rate has been shown to be necessarily equal to that of its major trading partner via interest rate parity (IRP).

Chapter 13 has also shown that an economy's inflation rate is caused or facilitated by a broadly corresponding rate of monetary expansion. We might therefore expect that as an SOE under fixed exchange rates cannot independently control its price level or inflation rate, neither can it independently control its money stock or its (total) rate of monetary expansion. This indeed turns out to be true as demonstrated below. We also show that the capacity of the SOE to sustain a fixed exchange rate and impart *credibility* to the fixed exchange rate policy imposes constraints on the conduct of *both* domestic credit policy (monetary policy) and fiscal policy.

The Monetary Approach to the Balance of Payments
In order to see the central points at issue under the present subheading consider the following model:

(1) $M^s = R + D$

$$+ + -$$
$$(2)\ M^d = f(y, p, r)$$

$$(3)\ M^s = M^d = M$$

Equation 1 repeats the money supply identity, already explained. Equation 2 states that the demand for money depends positively on the level of income, y, and the domestic price level, p, and negatively on the domestic nominal interest rate, r (which incorporates the effects of expected inflation), as explained in chapter 13. Equation 3 is an equilibrium condition for the money market.

Differentiating equation 1 gives,

$$(1')\ \Delta M^s = \Delta R + \Delta D$$

similarly differentiating the remaining equations, substituting and rearranging gives,

$$(4)\ \Delta R = \Delta M^d - \Delta D$$

Equation 4 is termed a *reserve-flow equation* and implies that if domestic credit is expanded beyond the increase in the demand for money, then it leads to a *fully-offsetting* loss of foreign currency reserves. To illustrate, let the demand for money initially be £100m, i.e. M^d = £100m. By equation 3 the supply of money must also equal £100m (i.e., M^s = £100m) of which, say, reserves, R, equals £40m and domestic credit, D, equals £60m. Starting from this initial equilibrium, suppose that domestic credit is expanded by £10m, i.e. ΔD = £10m. Assume, for the moment, that there is no increase in the demand for money, i.e. ΔM^d = 0. It follows from the reserve-flow equation (4) that:

$$\Delta R = \Delta M^d - \Delta D = 0 - £10m$$

We can deduce that reserves will fall by £10m, i.e. the fall in reserves exactly matches the increase in credit.

Given the important assumption that the credit expansion does *not* affect the demand for money, we can now draw the following critical inferences:

(1) The domestic banking system under fixed exchange rates *cannot* control the (level of the) money supply. The final money supply, in the above example, is £100m which was also the opening money supply. This result is general, as inspection of equation (1') shows. Movements in the two counterparts of the money supply exactly offset each other. In technical terms, the money is said to be *endogenous* in a small open economy under a fixed exchange rate régime. Hence the loss of sovereignty in the conduct of monetary policy to which we earlier referred.

(2) The monetary authority (Central Bank) can conduct a reserves or balance of payments policy by setting credit expansion at the appropriate rate. For example, if the Central Bank wished to increase (foreign currency) reserves from £40m to £55m, with unchanged money demand, it should reduce domestic credit from £60m to £45m, i.e. impose a credit squeeze. Using the reserve-flow equation, again, gives:

$$\Delta R = \Delta M^d - \Delta D = 0 - (-£15m) = + £15m.$$

Monetary policy or, more exactly, credit policy is thus very important in achieving balance of payments policy targets. The reserve-flow equation provides a valuable insight into how this type of policy might be formulated by the Central Bank of Ireland. The growth in money demand might be forecast by the Central Bank and an appropriate limit might be then set for domestic credit expansion to yield the desired change in reserves.

(3) Most countries periodically run both surpluses and deficits on the balance of (international) payments. In the former case the country's banking system gains foreign currency reserves and in the latter case it loses them. As Figure 1 below illustrates, a balance of payments deficit is essentially an excess market demand for foreign currency. This excess demand is met by the Central Bank (or the commercial banking system) selling its foreign currency reserves to customers in exchange for domestic Irish pound deposits at the *existing exchange rate*, S_0.

Figure 1

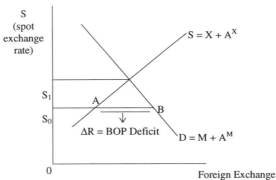

Note: X   = Exports of Goods and Services.
           M   = Imports of Goods and Services.
           A^X = Exports or Sales of Financial Assets to Non-residents.
           A^M = Imports or Purchases of Financial Assets from Non-residents.
           ΔR = Change in Foreign Currency Reserves.
           AB = Excess demand for foreign exchange
                 = $(M - X) + (A^M - A^X)$ = BOP Deficit = ΔR.

The Central Bank, of course, can only sell foreign currency reserves provided it has them or can readily borrow them in sufficient amount. If a country persistently runs a balance of payments deficit, the market rightly expects or speculates that its foreign currency reserves will soon be exhausted and that in the then absence of future official support, the excess demand will drive the exchange rate to its equilibrium level, i.e. it will depreciate; the Irish pound price of (say) sterling will rise to S_1. The fear of impending depreciation will cause investors to switch out Irish pound bonds into sterling bonds. Consideration of interest rate parity shows why this is so, and why Irish interest rates will begin to rise as the market dumps Irish bonds. If investor fears prove correct, they can switch back after the depreciation and make a currency gain in the process; if their fears prove incorrect, they can switch back without significant gain or loss. It is a one-way bet. The additional demand for foreign currency to buy sterling bonds speeds the rate of reserve depletion and the devaluation becomes a self-fulfilling prophesy. [The demand for sterling is a function, inter alia, of the expected rate of currency depreciation and when the latter expectation increases, the demand curve moves rightwards].

The foregoing account implies that for a fixed-exchange rate policy to be sustainable and reasonably free from speculative attack it must enjoy *credibility*. That credibility in turn requires that credit growth must be disciplined and not persistently lax or excessive, relative to the demand for money.

(4) A credible fixed-exchange rate policy requires discipline in the conduct not only of monetary policy but also of fiscal policy. Domestic credit is extended not only to the private sector but also to government to help fund the government budget deficit, (G - T), which is also termed the Exchequer Borrowing Requirement (EBR). It follows that in order to maintain an overall target or ceiling for domestic credit, the greater the lending to the government, the smaller must be the lending to the private sector. If the government runs increasingly large EBRs, as Ireland did from the early 1970s to the early 1980s, then bank lending to the private sector must be squeezed. The Central Bank, however, will be reluctant to restrict credit availability in the private sector severely, for fear of inducing liquidity crisis and recession. Some sectors (e.g. housebuilding and the car industry) are particularly sensitive to credit availability. However, if the private sector is not squeezed, then the domestic credit expansion target must be breached with subsequent reserve depletion and pressure on the exchange rate.

The implication is that the size of the EBR and, in particular, bank funding of the EBR or fiscal deficit, should be consistent with both overall credit policy and the credit needs of the private sector. Discipline and harmony in the conduct of fiscal and monetary policy facilitate these goals and ensure credibility.

The implications drawn from the reserve-flow equation, equation (4), hinge critically on the assumption made that domestic credit expansion does not affect the demand for money. If this assumption is not true then our policy conclusions would be considerably weaker. For example, if credit expansion increased real incomes in Ireland and *did* expand the demand for money, then reserve losses would fall short of the initial credit expansion, and the money supply would increase.

In order for credit expansion to have *no* effect on the demand for money, it follows from equation 2 that it must have *no* effect on Irish prices, Irish interest rates or Irish real income levels. We have earlier established that domestic prices and interest rates are externally determined via PPP and IRP. Hence domestic credit expansion can have no (lasting) effect on either. It remains to be established why domestic credit expansion can have no effect on domestic real income in the context of this model. Consider Figure 2 below.

Figure 2

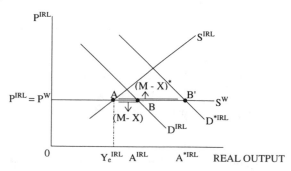

Note: Y^{IRL} = Domestic Real Output.
        A^{IRL} = Domestic Absorption, i.e., C + I + G.
        (M-X)   = Net Imports.
        P^{IRL} = Irish Price Level.
        P^W = World Price Level.

The supply of domestic real output, S^{IRL}, is plotted as an increasing function of the domestic price for conventional reasons (see Chapter 14). The downward sloping demand schedule, D^{IRL}, refers to real gross domestic expenditure (or absorption). It equals the sum of Consumption, Investment and Government spending by *Irish residents* (i.e., C + I + G). The negative slope arises because at lower price levels the real net value of nominal wealth and the real money supply are higher and thereby encourage higher domestic spending. [Note carefully that absorption refers to spending by *Irish residents*, $C + I + G$, and is not equal to the demand for *Irish goods* which is $C + I + G + X - M$]. The world supply curve, S^W, is perfectly elastic at the world price level, signifying that Ireland can import as much as it wishes at the world price, P^W. Assume for convenience that the exchange rate is unity. Then, via PPP, $P^{IRL} = P^W$. In equilibrium the supply of Irish goods, Y_e^{IRL}, will equal the demand for Irish goods, $C + I + G + X - M$. It follows that the excess demand, $D^{IRL} - S^{IRL}$, is $\{C + I + G\} - \{C + I + G + X - M\}$ which is $(M - X)$ or the current account balance of payments deficit.

(The alert reader may have observed that the methodology introduced in Figure 2 and in the paragraph immediately above differs from that of earlier chapters on open economy macroeconomics. In order to ensure an understanding of the two alternative methodologies, the reader is urged to refer back to the digression at the end of Chapter 14: we are now adopting what was there described as "the alternative model" in which all goods and services are tradable, as has been indicated at the very beginning of the present chapter.)

A credit expansion in Ireland shifts the demand schedule to D^{*IRL}. The effect is merely to expand the current account balance of payments deficit to $(M - X)^*$. The reason is straightforward. Domestic suppliers will only increase domestic output (and hence real income) if offered a higher domestic price. Because of PPP this will not occur. The extra domestic spending generated by the credit expansion is on imports which can be bought at the existing world price and, hence, more cheaply than if they were sourced from Irish suppliers. Thus, equilibrium domestic real income is independent of domestic credit policy.

The domestic credit expansion may, of course, lead to an excess demand not for goods, but for bonds (as envisaged in the ISLM model). The result is similar. The domestic interest rate is $r = Div/(Bond\ Price)$; the foreign interest rate is $r^* = Div^*/(Bond\ Price)^*$. We assume for simplicity that the exchange rate is unity and that the *fixed* annual dividends on domestic and foreign bonds are the same (i.e. $Div = Div^*$). Since interest rate parity implies that $r = r^*$ it follows that in equilibrium, Irish and UK bond prices must be equal. (Along the lines of earlier parts of the present chapter, we are assuming, for the purposes of illustration, that Ireland and the UK are the only two economies of relevance in the fixed exchange rate context being analysed.) Using the same diagram, Figure 2 above, let P^{IRL} now refer to the Irish bond price and let P^W refer to the UK bond price. The supply curve now represents the supply of Irish bonds. It is upward sloping since, for a given fixed dividend, higher bond prices imply lower interest rates or borrowing costs and a larger supply of bonds to fund the additional investment projects that become marginally profitable at lower interest rates. The demand curve now represents the demand by Irish residents for bonds (from whatever source — domestic or foreign). It is negatively sloped since, for a given fixed dividend, lower bond prices imply higher interest rates, which reduces the demand by Irish residents for non-interest-bearing money and increases their demand for bonds. The flat world supply curve signifies that, given the smallness of the Irish economy, there exists an infinitely elastic supply of UK bonds to Irish residents at existing world prices and interest rates.

A credit expansion, by creating an excess supply of money, leads to an excess demand for bonds to the same extent. As before, the demand schedule shifts to D^{*IRL}. Irish companies are, however, only willing to supply additional Irish bonds at higher prices; at existing interest rates, marginally unprofitable investment projects remain unprofitable and no additional domestic bonds are issued. If Irish residents increased their demand for Irish bonds, this would raise their price and drive down the interest return available to them. It makes more sense to purchase UK bonds. The additional Irish demand for UK bonds is so small relative to the size of the UK bond market that they can be bought at existing prices and interest rates. The excess demand, $D^{IRL} - S^{IRL}$, is the net capital outflow, i.e. the net imports of bonds. Credit expansion increases the net capital outflow to the same extent if all the additional credit is spent on bonds.

Thus, whether the credit expansion is spent on goods or bonds, the effect is the same. Foreign currency reserves are lost to the same extent in either case, through the current account balance of payments in the former case and through the capital account in the latter case.

Recall, from chapter 15, Table 1, that the balance of (international) payments equals the sum of the current account balance, (X - M) and the net capital inflow, NKI. Thus:

$$\Delta R = (X - M) + NKI = BOP = -\Delta D$$

Limitations: As with all models, the monetary approach model is a crude but insightful approximation to reality. In order to achieve clarity, we are forced to adopt simplifying assumptions. Under a fixed exchange rate, it makes more sense to adopt the polar or extreme assumption that Irish prices are effectively equal to UK prices than to adopt the opposite polar assumption that Irish prices can vary completely independently of UK prices. (The reader is again reminded that we have been referring to "the

UK" only as shorthand for whatever large countries with which the SOE, Ireland, might maintain fixed exchange rates.) It is precisely because the assumption of PPP is more likely to hold in the long run than in the short run that we claim that the model provides a longer term perspective on the effectiveness of economic policy.

The assumption of PPP may not and usually does not hold in the short run. When this is so, then credit-driven domestic expenditure may, indeed, drive traded commodity prices in Ireland above international levels *for a period* and hence increase domestic output. In such circumstances some autonomy and effectiveness attaches to monetary policy *for a period*.

Also, some credit-based expenditures may be on services such as policing, the army, haircuts etc., which are *non-traded* internationally and not subject to PPP. Credit-driven expenditure on these services may have real output effects if the price of non-traded commodities and services can be increased relative to traded commodities. However, where non-traded goods and services (for example, transport infrastructure, tele-communications and electricity) form productive inputs to the traded sector of the economy an increase in their price will, by increasing the costs of the traded sector, lead to some offsetting reduction in its output. Where non-traded goods and services are consumer oriented — such as electricity, health and education — an increase in their price may lead to an increase in wage demands and production costs, which will also moderate, if not eliminate, any output effect. The funding of increased public spending on non-traded services may, of course, be reflected, sooner or later, in higher taxation rather than higher prices, with similar effects.

It is for these reasons that we have stressed the role of the supply-side response. The supply curve, being essentially a marginal cost curve, is dominated by the costs of productive inputs, gross of taxation, such as electricity, transport, telecommunications and labour costs.

Finally, if expenditure in some sectors of the domestic economy (i.e. housing and cars) is *credit-constrained,* then additional mortgage and instalment credit may facilitate the expansion of output in these sectors at existing prices.

The model at least helps to identify the narrowed scope and *potential impermanence* of such policy effects. It also motivates the need to distinguish between the traded and non-traded expenditure sectors of an SOE, the nature of the supply-side of the economy and its dynamic response pattern to policy measures in a more elaborated model.

Fiscal Policy: The principal result above — monetary policy in an SOE under fixed exchange rates is ineffective (in affecting output or interest rates) — is perfectly consistent with the analysis provided in Chapter 16. The analysis of fiscal policy provides an interesting point of contrast. A fiscal expansion also shifts the absorption curve, D^{IRL}, outwards to D^{*IRL} and with identical effect — a corresponding increase in net imports and no change in real output or prices. This result is in stark contrast to that provided in Chapter 16 which claimed *some* effectiveness for fiscal policy in a fixed exchange rate SOE. The difference arises from the assumed supply response. In both cases fiscal policy is clearly effective in increasing domestic spending or absorption. In Chapter 16, however, it was assumed that domestic supply *passively* increased to meet the extra demand at *existing prices* (see Chapter 16, pp. 270, 271) whereas in the above analysis we have assumed that it is international and not domestic supply which is perfectly elastic. Domestic supply, being an increasing function of price, is anchored by PPP and, thus, it is imports which passively increase at the existing price level. This new focus shifts the emphasis away from the demand-side issue as to whether monetary or fiscal policy is more effective in increasing domestic expenditure (a *policy assignment problem*), to the likely domestic *supply-side* response to any increase in expenditure from *whatever* source. It also allows the theoretical analysis to sit more comfortably with the fact that while Irish fiscal policy was strongly expansionary for the early 1970s through to the early 1980s, the output response was weak.

Note also that the *funding* of the fiscal expansion can be analysed by using Figure 2 to represent the bond market. The supply curve of Irish bonds shifts out and generates a corresponding net capital inflow at existing interest rates. The fiscal expansion is funded by foreign residents buying Irish government bonds. Since the current account balance of payments deficit and the capital inflow offset each other, there is no *short-run* effect on either the balance of payments or the money supply. Thus it is a pure fiscal expansion. However, over time, as interest and capital repayments are made to foreign holders of Irish bonds and converted to sterling for repatriation to the UK, there will be downward pressure on the balance of payments and the money supply. Short-run analysis ignores these important longer-term effects on the balance of payments, the money stock (and also on stability and taxation) arising from the growth in international indebtedness.

The preceding analysis can also be viewed from another perspective by regarding Ireland as analogous to a firm in perfect competition, as in Figure 3.

In contrast to the general thrust of earlier chapters, Ireland is here conceived as a *perfect price-taker* and faces a perfectly flat or infinitely elastic demand curve, which is *exogenous* to it. The equilibrium level of output depends critically on Ireland's own supply or cost conditions. To be sure, a decrease in demand due to, say, an international recession, will reduce output. The analogy suggests that instead of seeking to increase demand, over which it has little influence, the SOE might more fruitfully attempt to ensure more flexibility in its supply response, over which it is likely to have greater influence. The potential scope for such action is taken up in Chapter 23.

Figure 3

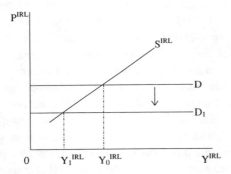

Notes: 1. $D = C + I + G + (X - M)$, i.e., the demand for Irish goods equals absorption, $C + I + G$, plus net exports $(X - M)$.
  2. The demand curve is completely flat because net exports are assumed to be perfectly price elastic. The absorption curve, D^{IRL} in Figure 2 is negatively sloped because $C + I + G$ is not perfectly price elastic.
  3. Demand shifts are exogenous to the SOE. Their effect depends on the supply response (i.e., on the position and slope of S^{IRL}), which may be subject to policy influence.

Floating Exchange Rates

The foregoing pages of the present principal section have pertained to fixed exchange rates. Since our focus is primarily on monetary policy, the following sub-section briefly sketches some implications of a monetary expansion in an SOE under floating exchange rates, additional to those outlined in chapter 16. That chapter noted that a monetary expansion causes an incipient net capital outflow, which in turn causes the currency to depreciate and thereby *increases net foreign demand* (i.e. exports less imports) for Irish output, which was assumed to respond passively to meet the extra demand.

However, if the exact analogy between the SOE and the firm in perfect competition is correct, then domestic export firms, being perfect price-takers, sell abroad at the same given foreign currency price, P^w, as before the devaluation or depreciation. The *domestic currency value* of each unit exported rises in proportion to the depreciation. So also does the domestic currency price of imports. Competition causes domestic product prices to be bid up *over time* to restore PPP: domestic producers benefit from the increased value of existing export sales volumes and divert output from home to export markets, until domestic commodity prices rise to match the increased domestic currency price of competing imports.

Following the depreciation, the marginal revenue from domestic output rises. If the marginal cost does not rise to the same extent, domestic firms experience increased *profitability* and will expand their output. In short, it is *not* increased net foreign demand but rather increased domestic supply which increases net exports. Notice the emphasis being placed on the domestic supply-side response to the devaluation and not on demand-side effects. The marginal cost of domestic output has two principal inputs, raw materials and labour. Imported raw material costs (and through competition domestic raw material costs) rise in line with the devaluation. The scale and duration of the effects of the monetary expansion, therefore, depend heavily on the domestic labour market and, in particular, on how quickly and how much domestic salaries and wages respond to the devaluation. This issue is taken up in Chapter 23.

By extension, since a fiscal expansion generates an incipient net capital inflow causing the domestic currency to appreciate, analysis of the nature of the supply-side response, provided in Chapter 23, is also necessary to gauge fully the effects of a fiscal expansion under floating exchange rates.

Finally, note that the effects of policies depend on whether they are expected by market participants. For example, if an excessive monetary expansion is expected, then currency depreciation and subsequent price inflation will also be expected to ensue. Uncovered interest rate parity implies that, given foreign interest rates, domestic interest rates rise *in anticipation* of the expected currency depreciation. If the monetary expansion is not anticipated (i.e. if it is a surprise) then interest rates do not rise until the policy is adopted and becomes known. The size and timing of such interest rate and many other important policy effects thus depend on the timing of the public's knowledge and anticipation of them.

CHAPTER 22

MONETARY POLICY IN IRELAND: OPERATIONAL CONSIDERATIONS

Martin Kenneally

HISTORICAL DEVELOPMENTS IN MONEY AND BANKING

The Banking System

At the turn of the nineteenth century rural Ireland had only a rudimentary banking system and was not fully monetised. Rent was often paid by labour services, and commodity exchange was often conducted by tally payments. When banknotes and large gold coins penetrated to rural areas they were frequently pawned for small denomination coin, pending later redemption at distant banks or agencies. Some banks had established in larger towns and portal cities. The most notable was Bank of Ireland, which received its charter in 1782 and with it a near monopoly on the issue of banknotes in Ireland. Private banks — that is, banks with six or fewer partners — could also issue banknotes but legal restrictions governing their establishment obliged them to be small and weak; Guinness and Mahon alone survives from that period.

Banks issued their own banknotes on the *unlimited liability* of their shareholders. If a bank failed, the shareholders were *personally* liable for any sums due to depositors in excess of bank assets. Banks were obliged to redeem their banknotes, when presented by note holders, with gold, at the official mint price of £3:17:9 per ounce. Issued banknotes were secured by the bank's general assets and were termed the bank's *fiduciary* issue.

During the 1820s and 1840s a succession of bank acts was passed which restricted the Bank of Ireland monopoly to a 50-mile radius of Dublin, conferred limited liability on banks (called joint-stock banks) and eased their conditions of establishment. They also required that further issues of banknotes, called a bank's *secured* issue, be secured against holdings of gold bullion. Banking grew rapidly in the wake of these

liberalisations. The remaining banks which now form the Bank of Ireland
and Allied Irish Banks groups were all established in that 20-year period,
except the Munster and Leinster bank which was established in 1887
(from the ashes of the Munster Bank, which had formed in 1864 but
crashed in 1885). The Northern Bank, The Belfast Bank and the Ulster
Bank, together with others which subsequently failed, were also
established during this period.

Outside Dublin, where Bank of Ireland dominated, Belfast quickly
developed its banking system. Manufactured exports were paid with
trade bills. A trade bill is an unconditional order in writing by (say) a
London buyer (the drawer of the bill) to their London bank (the drawee)
to make the payment stipulated on the bill to the party named on the bill
(the payee) at a specified future date, say, 3 months forward from the
date of the bill. The London buyer or drawer signed the bill and forwarded it to the bank. The London bank then signed or "accepted" the
bill and returned it to the drawer, who forwarded it to the payee in
exchange for the goods. Such bills were *assignable*, which meant that
payees could endorse the bills by signing them, and sell them or discount
them ahead of the due payment date, to their own bank. They were also
negotiable which effectively meant that if the London buyer failed to pay
on the due date their bank, as acceptor, was liable to pay the holder of the
bill. This device allowed the buyer time to sell the goods and lodge the
proceeds to their bank account while providing the seller a bank guarantee of future payment. The bills were discounted, that is, sold below their
face value to Belfast banks by the exporter for immediate payment. Payments to industrial workers took the form of banknotes issued by Belfast
banks or drafts drawn on them. These passed into more general circulation at provincial markets encouraged by the establishment of provincial
bank agencies which redeemed or exchanged their notes as required. The
liquidity of the trade bills underpinning these banks' fiduciary note issue
ensured early *confidence* in them and rapid *monetisation* of the Belfast
economy.

Cork's economy was largely commercially rather than industrially
based. In addition to brewing at Beamish & Crawford, whose output
exceeded Guinness through to the 1830s, it also provisioned naval
vessels with butter and beef. Trade in the latter, which had swollen
during the Napoleonic war, declined dramatically at its cessation. The
closure of one Munster bank in 1820 sparked off the closure of seven of
the fourteen Southern banks in a two-week period.

A bank's borrowings (i.e., its note issue and acceptance liabilities)
were redeemable for gold on demand or at short notice. Its assets consisted of securities, loans and some gold holdings. Securities, when they

could be sold suddenly and in large amount, frequently entailed capital loss, and loans could not be "called in" on demand. Because a bank's assets are less liquid than its liabilities a *loss of confidence* would lead all note holders to seek redemption in gold, thereby causing a *liquidity* crisis and leading to bank failure.

Such crises could spread to neighbouring banks. A loss of confidence in banknotes caused trade to be conducted in gold, and neighbouring banks' notes were also encashed for gold. This process is called *bank contagion* or *systemic risk*.

Dublin banks largely avoided the 1820 contagion because Bank of Ireland lent them its own banknotes, which still enjoyed public confidence, against the security of their bills. This is known as providing *a discounting facility* and it provided the liquidity required by distressed banks to meet large-scale withdrawals. Ulster-based banks largely avoided the crisis because 300 merchants and important holders of northern banknotes signed public manifestos declaring their continuing confidence in the notes.

Because bank loans yielded higher interest than government securities, the profit motive provided continuing temptation for some banks to place too high a proportion of their assets in illiquid loans and too few in liquid assets, thereby impairing their capacity to meet unexpected withdrawals and increasing their vulnerability to a liquidity crisis. Over time, banks improved their *liquidity management* skills to prevent such crises.

If a bank's loans were heavily concentrated with one customer or loan sector (say, farming), then failure of that customer or sector (due to, say, bad harvests or poor trading conditions) would lead to heavy bank losses. If those losses exceeded the bank's *equity* or *share capital*, then *insolvency* and bank failure resulted. Depositors, at most, received part-payment of deposits they had placed with the bank. In other words, their banknotes were redeemed at less than their face value. Over time, banks also improved their *prudential management*, spreading their loan portfolio over many customers and sectors to reduce the risk of default loss, and increasing their equity or *capital adequacy* to provide cover against possible trading losses.

The Savings Banks also originated in the early nineteenth century and were originally run on a part-time voluntary basis as a form of *noblesse oblige* to inculcate the savings habit amongst the industrial or working classes and indigent poor. Their assets were restricted, principally, to holdings of government securities.

Building Societies were established mainly in the later decades of the nineteenth century. Originally, they comprised groups of artisans and

newly urbanised workers who pooled their savings and drew lots for the
order in which mortgage loans would be granted to members. The
members also provided labour services in the construction of the houses.
Ultimately, when the loan (made from the continuing pool of savings and
repayments) of the last member was paid, the societies terminated. Ter-
minating societies were later replaced by permanent societies (e.g. the
Irish Permanent, formed in 1912) where depositors, borrowers and
management became distinct groups. Their titles, the Educational, the
Civil Service etc., are indicative of the occupational groups to which they
catered. Because their depositors were originally drawn from the less
well off, they were later (i.e., in the twentieth century when income tax
came fully into force) allowed to deduct tax on deposit interest at source
at less than the standard rate and to forward it to the Revenue Commissioners. Both the tax privilege and non-disclosure of members'
deposits later provided them with a competitive edge over banks in the
retail deposit market. The societies' assets were restricted to mortgage
loans, together with some government securities and cash.

Life Insurance companies covered the contractual savings market.
"Industrial" (meaning working class) insurance premiums were collected
door to door, weekly, and, on maturity or death provided a lump sum,
usually for a decent burial. Later this form of insurance was replaced by
"Ordinary" life assurance to cater for the improving material circumstances of the emerging middle classes. Premiums were larger: deducted
monthly by bank standing order over a long period, they entailed reduced
collection costs and larger terminal values for maturing policies. The
policies provided life insurance cover (against mortality risk) which was
later officially encouraged by the tax deductibility of premiums. Life
policies, however, were increasingly dominated by the savings component of the policy, since the bulk of the premiums have been used by life
companies to buy stocks, bonds and other investments on behalf of
policy holders. More recently, insurance companies have begun to operate unit funds which compete more sharply with bank deposits for personal savings, as they are more liquid than traditional life policies.

In 1927, five years after the emergence of the Irish Free State, a
Currency Commission was formed which progressively replaced sterling
and private Irish banknote issues with the newly issued Saorstát Punt.
The Industrial Trust Company, later to become the Industrial Credit
Company (ICC), and the Agricultural Credit Company (ACC) were also
set up by statute in the late 1920s, as temporary expedients to provide
long-term developmental credit. The Currency Commission evolved to
become the Central Bank in 1943.

Twentieth-century Irish banking was marked by the stability of *existing* Irish banks and their consolidation into smaller numbers through merger and acquisition. The UK-based National Westminster Bank acquired the Ulster Bank in 1917. The UK-based Midlands Bank took over the Belfast Bank in 1917. It sold its branches in the Republic of Ireland to the Royal Bank in 1923, and subsequently merged the Belfast Bank with the Northern Bank, which it acquired in 1965. In 1958, the Bank of Ireland acquired the Hibernian Bank. In 1966, the Bank of Ireland group was formed by merger of Bank of Ireland, the Hibernian Bank and the newly acquired National Bank. The Provincial Bank, the Royal Bank and the Munster and Leinster Bank merged to form Allied Irish Banks (AIB), partly as a defensive measure against the size of the Bank of Ireland group. The mergers of Irish-controlled clearing banks occurred partly also as a defensive measure against the growing incursion of foreign investment banks in Ireland. Foreign banks had followed their large manufacturing clients, who had established industrial bases in Ireland, on foot of the growth of direct foreign investment. The Northern Bank was sold by the Midlands Bank to National Australia Bank in 1988 and renamed the National Irish Bank.

Investment banks focus on the provision of foreign exchange services, merger and acquisition advice, corporate treasury, underwriting and other specialist services for medium- to large-scale corporate clients. They have few branches, are not active in the retail deposit market and raise their funds from foreign parents and on domestic commercial paper and (mainly) inter-bank markets. Allied Irish Investment Bank (AIIB), part of the AIB group, and Investment Bank of Ireland (IBI), part of the Bank of Ireland group, were formed to counter competition from foreign banks. They also formed separate banking entities to compete on the leasing and instalment credit markets.

Ireland became a member of the European Economic Community, EEC, (now European Union) in 1973. In the sphere of banking the vision of a "Europe without Frontiers", which underpinned the EEC's founding treaty (Treaty of Rome, 1957), gradually crystallised into a series of banking co-ordination directives which passed into the domestic legislation and regulations of Member States, including Ireland. Directives (in 1977, 1983 and 1989) established the right of a bank in one Member State to set up in another Member State (*mutual recognition*), harmonised the accounts conventions and reporting formats of banks, and established minimum solvency (i.e., capital adequacy) and liquidity ratios. Prudential regulation of bank branch operations was henceforth to be exercised on a consolidated basis by the competent authority (i.e., the Central Bank) of the country in which the parent had its head office. This principle is known *as "home country control"* and eliminated the need for a bank to maintain separate endowment capital in respect of branches of the bank operating in other Member States. Moreover, any banking services offered by a parent bank in its home country might also be offered by a branch of that bank in any other Member State, provided that services fell within an agreed list of banking activities. This provision is popularly referred to as *"the single banking license"*.

The *minimum* capital adequacy ratios established by the EC largely parallel those formulated by the Bank of International Settlements (BIS) in Basle in 1988 and which have wider application to OECD banks. Long term "own funds" (equity and disclosed reserves), called Tier 1 Capital, must constitute at least 4 per cent of weighted risk assets and the sum of Tier 1 plus Tier 2 capital (for example, long-term bank debt and preference shares) must constitute at least 8 per cent of weighted risk assets. Higher weights are attached to those bank assets (and contingent or off-balance sheet liabilities) which are subject to greater price risk in calculating total weighted risk assets.

New derivative financial securities such as swaps, options and futures as well as the more traditional underwriting obligations are "contingent" or "off balance sheet" liabilities. Traditionally banks were obliged to make capital adequacy provisions only against their on-balance sheet assets. For example, if a bank sold a *call option* on a currency to a client, then it received up front a fee or *premium* from the client and, in return, agreed to sell the client foreign currency for an agreed price, called the *exercise price*, at some date in the future, called the *exercise date*, if the client so wished. If, at the exercise date, the spot price of foreign currency was lower than the exercise price, then the client would simply tear up their option contract and buy the required foreign currency more cheaply on the spot market; if, however, the spot price of foreign currency was higher than the exercise price, then the client would exercise their option. This obliged the bank to buy the currency at the high spot price and sell it, to the client, at the lower exercise price. The bank would then incur a loss. At the date the option was sold, the bank received a premium which appeared as income in its Profit and Loss account. The liability being "contingent" on future spot exchange rates would not appear on the face of its balance sheet, and thereby escaped the costly capital adequacy provisions required of banks in respect of their on-balance sheet assets. Banks could and did expand business in derivative securities areas without having to acquire additional bank capital to do so. The lack of regulatory prudential provision for derivative securities led to fears that bank capital was becoming increasingly inadequate. The *weighted risk assets* in the Basle risk asset ratio included provisions for such derivatives, with weights proportional to their riskiness.

Increased international regulation also resulted from the growing liberalisation of international banking, which necessitated uniform rules of minimum safety and even competition.

In order to protect depositors from the potential hazards of increased banking competition, an EC-wide system of *deposit protection* was introduced which insured depositors' funds against bank failure. A mandatory small levy or insurance premium, currently 0.2 per cent in Ireland, is applied to all bank and other credit institutions deposits and the proceeds maintained in a Deposit Protection account at the Central Bank. Depositors are reimbursed to a maximum limit, currently £10,000 on a deposit of £15,000 or more in Ireland, in the event of bank failure.

The current regulatory position in Irish banking is that the Central Bank of Ireland formulates prudential policy for Irish licensed banks subject to their adherence to *minimum* EU-wide capital adequacy ratios and depositor protection provisions. It also provides some surveillance of the branches of foreign banks, registered in another Member State but operating in Ireland; the responsibility for the prudential supervision of these branches, however, rests mainly with the Central Bank of their home and not their host country. The right of Irish residents to engage freely in cross-border banking has been recognised, since 1 January 1993, (at which date the EC 2nd Banking Co-ordination Directive came into operation in Ireland) and the range of bank services available to them on this basis has been extended. *The Central Bank of Ireland retains responsibility for the operation of Irish monetary policy.*

The 1989 Central Bank Act gave legal expression to the above measures. It also provides for the supervision by the Central Bank of Ireland of the Irish Futures and Options Exchange (IFOX), and money-brokers and financial institutions operating in the International Financial Services Centre (IFSC). Associated legal acts in 1989 for Building Societies and Trustee Savings Banks also drew these deposit-taking institutions under Central Bank supervision.

The intended effect of these regulatory provisions is to provide a single competitive European banking market and to "level the playing field" as between banks and competing deposit-takers, all of whom are termed *credit institutions* in EU nomenclature. The traditional boundaries between these institutions had declined as had *specialisation* in particular financial products by particular financial intermediaries. Banks now provided insurance products and stockbroking services (in the wake of the "Big Bang" reform of the UK stock market in 1986) through affiliates and were now more actively engaged in mortgage lending, securities and foreign exchange trading and fund management. Building societies and state banks broadened the traditional base of their activities, and insurance companies increased their share of the retail savings market through contractual savings schemes and increased their focus on more liquid life-assurance-related savings products as distinct from traditional insurance. The EU also permits access by non-member states to EU banking markets on a *reciprocating* basis. This regulation is currently interpreted liberally in the interest of encouraging bank competition.

Regulations under earlier Acts also gave the Central Bank responsibility for licensing and supervising Undertakings for Collective Investment in Transferable Securities (UCITS). These are mainly Unit Trusts and financial investment companies.

The four banks — AIB, Bank of Ireland, National Irish Bank and Ulster Bank — which operate the cheque-clearing or money transmission services in Ireland are known as the *Associated Banks*. They have multiple retail branches and service the retail deposit and loan markets. Bank of Ireland and AIB dominate with approximately equal market shares, totalling around 80 per cent.

Other than the four banks mentioned immediately above, the remaining banks are known as the *Non-Associated banks*. AIIB, IBI, Ulster Investment Bank and National Irish Investment Bank are members of this group, the former two having a dominant share of investment banking in Ireland. The group consists of around thirty banks, licensed within the state, many being subsidiaries of large foreign banks. A further ten foreign banks provide banking services in Ireland on a branch basis and a further thirty provide services to Irish residents on a cross border basis. Competition is stronger than on the retail market.

In the current (1994) banking environment in Ireland there is vigorous competition between banks, building societies and insurance companies for wholesale and retail deposits and small savings. *Cross-border banking*, formally liberalised in 1993, provides an additional source of competition. (This liberalisation motivated the reduction of deposit income retention tax (DIRT) from 29 per cent to 10 per cent on special savings accounts and special investment accounts (SSAs and SIAs) in order to discourage the flight of small savings, bank deposits and investments to other Member States.)

There is also competition for medium to large corporate and farm loans. The heavy concentration of money transmission services (cheque clearing and credit cards) and retail lending (personal and small business loans) in the hands of the dominant (cheque) clearing banks, AIB and Bank of Ireland, has led to a perception that these services are uncompetitive and overpriced and to calls for the formation of a third banking force in the retail market to be formed from an amalgamation or sale of ACC, ICC and the Trustee Savings Banks.

The current position, in 1994, as regards small loans is that there is an informal understanding between the Central Bank and the Associated Banks that the highest personal overdraft and term loan rates charged should not exceed the average one month inter-bank rate, at the time the loan is made, by more than 5.5 percentage points. Banks are required to inform the Central Bank and obtain its approval for any changes in money transmission *charges*. They must also post their approved charges publicly.

The Currency System

By proclamation in 1701, the Irish exchange rate was fixed at one shilling and one penny Irish to one shilling British. Both countries shared the same lawful gold coinage. Thus, one gold guinea was worth 22 shillings and 9 pence Irish and 21 shillings British. This 13:12 exchange rate prevailed to the turn of the nineteenth century and was said to be *at par* when the surplus per cent of Irish currency exchanged for British was $8^1/_3$ per cent, i.e., [(13 - 12)/13 x 100] per cent.

At the onset of the Napoleonic war, the convertibility of banknotes into gold was suspended. Bank of Ireland increased its banknote issue considerably, with the result that in 1797 they depreciated against London to 16 per cent. Belfast banknotes appreciated to 5 per cent *against* London or 11 per cent *on* Dublin. The 1804 currency commission, led by Henry Thornton, concluded that the Dublin depreciation was caused by excessive note issue by Bank of Ireland. Its preferred solution was the restoration of the gold standard or convertibility. Excessive note issue, it reasoned, would pressure Irish prices upwards, lead to a trade and balance of payments deficit and, as Irish banknotes were converted to gold by British exporters, the reduction in Bank of Ireland gold holdings would inhibit further note issues by it. However, given the legal restrictions on convertibility, it recommended instead that Bank of Ireland should hold an *exchange equalisation account* at the Bank of England where Bank of Ireland notes would be exchangeable for Bank of England notes at rates gradually reduced to par. In short, given the legal restriction on the operation of a gold standard, it recommended instead the operation of a sterling standard. Bank of Ireland was thus required to hold external assets (e.g., British Treasury bills) in the account which could be exchanged for its own notes, if presented. These recommendations were implemented.

In 1817 the Irish and British exchequers were amalgamated and, by law, Irish and British government stocks were made *interchangeable at the par rate of exchange*. This was, perhaps, the first example of a dual currency bond. If Irish banknote issues were excessive and drove Irish bond prices above British levels, then investors could buy the cheaper British stock, convert it at par to Irish stock which could be sold in Dublin for profit and thereby depress Irish bond prices to UK levels. This ensured interest rate parity and obviated the need for a forward exchange market. The capital outflow of Bank of Ireland notes to pay for the stock reduced the assets in its exchange equalisation account as British stock sellers encashed Irish banknotes for sterling. It therefore exerted downward pressure on its note issue (on domestic credit). Gold convertibility was gradually resumed beginning in 1820; the Irish pound price of gold being initially set above the official mint price of gold. However, the Irish pound price of gold was gradually reduced to the official mint price, as parity was restored.

The assets of the exchange equalisation account were built up seasonally during the Irish export season and drawn down during the rest of the year when the Irish trade balance reversed. The convertibility of Irish banknotes to UK banknotes at par obviated the necessity for private gold movements, and the Bank of Ireland seldom withdrew gold from its London account. The predictability of the drawdown permitted Bank of Ireland to switch some of its exchange equalisation account assets out of Exchequer bills to longer dated and higher yielding government stocks.

The amalgamation of the two exchequers in 1817 progressively eliminated the supply of Irish government bonds. This was followed by a secular build-up of Net External Assets; domestic loan demand was either weak or unsatisfied by Irish banks.

In 1826 the currencies of both countries were assimilated; the Irish unit of account changed, with one Irish pound now equalling one British pound. Additional Irish pound banknote issues thereafter were secured against gold bullion at the official mint price.

In 1914, as a wartime contingency, an Act allowed British banknotes to be held as backing or cover for the issue of Irish banknotes in place of gold, as maritime shipping of gold was hazardous. Bank of England and Irish banknotes were given full legal tender status in Ireland. This status was withdrawn from Irish banknotes in 1919.

When the Irish Free State was formed in 1922 it sought to establish an independent currency. It set up a Banking Commission in 1926 which recommended the issue of a new Saorstát Punt with a one-to-one no margins parity link to sterling. To this end the newly founded Currency Commission established a *Legal Tender Note Fund*. This fund issued Irish pounds as its liabilities on a one-for-one basis against the receipt of sterling assets or of Irish banks' secured note issue, which were redeemed by the Commission on a one-for-one basis for sterling. The asset base of the fund thereby ensured full and perfect convertibility to sterling. The Commission also issued new Consolidated Bank Notes on a one-for-one basis against the receipt of the banks' fiduciary or unsecured note issues. The new legal tender notes were first issued on 10 September 1928 by the Commission, which appointed the Bank of England as its London agent. To launch an independent currency successfully and to ensure public acceptability and confidence in it was a difficult task, then as now. It is a tribute to the Commission's work that these features of the currency became taken for granted in the decades that followed.

The Commission was acutely aware of the loss of monetary sovereignty imposed by the fixed exchange rate, especially as Britain's return to the gold standard in 1925, at prewar parity, had caused recession and unrest. When Britain came off the gold standard in 1931 and allowed the pound sterling to float, it depreciated by 30 per cent within 3 months and with it the dollar value of external (sterling) assets held in the Legal Tender Note Fund. Nonetheless, the Commission regarded the issuing of punts against the receipt of sterling *only* as sound practice. To issue against the receipt of other foreign currencies, it argued, would involve it unduly in currency speculation and might endanger the sterling link if those currencies depreciated against sterling.

Following the Second Banking Commission, which was established in 1934 and reported in 1938, the Central Bank of Ireland was formed in 1943. It was granted limited powers to *expand* but not to contract Irish bank credit. It could *rediscount* bills for banks in an "emergency". The legal tender notes (Irish pounds) used by the Commission in rediscounting were to be drawn from a *General Fund* with an adequate sterling reserve in order to avoid diluting the one-to-one sterling cover against the issue of Irish pounds. Such a dilution would otherwise have occurred since the discounted bills were domestic Irish pound bills. It could also take mandatory non-interest bearing deposits from banks who underlent in Ireland (banks whose domestic assets fell below their domestic liabilities by a given proportion).

Irish commercial banks had accumulated large holdings of net external assets which could be exchanged one-for-one for Irish pounds at the Central Bank. Hence, the rediscount rate could not effectively exceed the London discount rate; if it did Irish banks would simply sell some UK treasury bills at lower cost and convert the proceeds to Irish pounds.

When the Central Bank was founded, the commercial banks' equity holding in the Currency Commission was repaid and the total Central Bank share capital of £24,000 was vested in the Minister for Finance.

The Central Bank also had responsibility for advising and commenting on public spending when it had monetary implications. The exercise of that responsibility earned it the derisory title of the "Banshee of Foster

Place" but failed to stem the growth in public spending and the emergence of balance of payments deficits in the late 1940s and early 1950s. In fact, the public capital and current budget deficits were first distinguished by government in 1951, in order to emphasise the high capital content of public spending and to justify the recourse to public borrowing to fund it. Notwithstanding this, the Central Bank, at that time, argued that expansionary fiscal policy could not be justified by Keynesian economics in a small open economy where instead of depression caused by underinvestment and oversaving, the opposite was the case.

In 1958, the Central Bank assumed the function of Central Clearing Agency for the settlement of inter-bank balances; a function previously performed by Bank of Ireland. In 1960 the interest rate on these clearing balances was set at 1/8 per cent below the average tender rate for UK Treasury Bills. The rediscount rate was set 1/16 per cent above the highest Treasury Bill rate at the preceding tender.

In 1956, US dollar securities were added to the list of securities that might be held in the Legal Tender Note Fund. In 1961, a "Balance in the General Fund" was added to the list of assets which could be held in the Legal Tender Note Fund. Since the General Fund contained domestic punt securities this, indirectly, allowed the issue of Irish pounds against the backing of domestic securities. It is from this date (barring a minor once-off exception in 1959) that the dilution in the full external asset backing of the Irish pound effectively occurred. [In 1989 the General Fund and Legal Tender Note Fund were finally merged].

In 1965, the Central Bank issued the first of a series of a letters of advice to the associated banks (and also to the non-associated banks) which set guidelines for the expansion of domestic credit. The letters also indicated a minimum Central Bank ratio which the associated banks should observe. The Central Bank ratio (CBR) was defined as:

$$CBR = \frac{\text{Net External Assets} + \text{Bankers' Deposits at Central Bank}}{\text{Domestic Current and Deposit Account Liabilities}}$$

The numerator was intended to provide a measure of bank liquidity, and, by fixing a value for the ratio, it was intended that a fall in bank liquidity would trigger a fall in domestic lending (proxied by the denominator). Because the numerator could not be predicted with accuracy and because domestic lending could not be precisely related to the denominator, the *quantitative guideline* additionally set out the overall desirable level of credit. These letters of advice ("moral suasion"), however, did not have force of statute and were frequently breached.

In the 1968 Basle agreement, the UK government offered official holders of sterling (Central Banks) guarantees as to the exchange value of their sterling assets. Sterling had devalued in 1967 and this UK measure was intended to inhibit further sales of sterling and pressure on its exchange rate. As commercial banks were ineligible for the guarantee, they transferred their sterling assets to the Central Bank in exchange for interest-bearing deposits at the Bank. By 1970, the transfer was complete and the commercial banks thereafter held only working balances in London. The Central Bank thereby became custodian of the Foreign Currency reserves of the Irish banking system.

In 1969, the Money Market Committee, established by the Central Bank, reported to the effect that Irish banks held relatively small amounts of Irish gilts (i.e., government bonds) compared with their holdings of UK gilts. This, the committee reasoned, was due to the illiquidity of Irish gilts, which could not be sold in appreciable amounts by domestic banks without depressing their price. This feature made them unattractive to hold compared with UK gilts, which did not suffer this disadvantage. To overcome this obstacle the committee recommended, inter alia, that the Central Bank should act as market-maker in short-dated gilts (0–5 years), buying and selling from its own account as the market required, and that the Department of Finance should act as market-maker in the longer-dated gilts. Dealing limits were increased, dealing spreads (i.e., the spread between the buying or bid price and the selling or offer price) were cut and the liquidity of the Irish gilt market improved. (In November 1990, the National Treasury Management Agency (NTMA or "Auntie Mae") assumed responsibility for all *primary* gilt issues.)

In 1970, the Central Bank established a foreign exchange market to meet the requirements of banks.

The 1971 Central Bank Act conferred important additional powers on the Central Bank:

(1) It became the licensing authority for commercial banks, a function heretofore performed, without much supervision, by the Department of Finance.

(2) The Government Exchequer Account was transferred to the Central Bank, completed in 1972, from the Bank of Ireland, where it had resided since 1782. The Central Bank was now banker to the government.

(3) It acquired statutory powers to impose liquid asset ratios on banks.

In 1972, the Central Bank prevailed on the licensed banks to introduce a new system of *term lending* to replace, except for seasonal purposes, the overdraft system which allowed borrowers, at their discretion, to call at will on the unutilised facilities. The intention and effect was to increase the scope for effective control of domestic credit.

During 1972/3 the Central Bank began to implement two liquid asset ratios. The *Secondary Ratio* required banks to hold government paper (e.g., gilts) up to some minimum proportion of their deposit liabilities. To the extent that this obliged banks to hold government paper in excess of their wishes, it constituted a tax on banks and conferred a privileged access to domestic funding by government. The secondary ratio was progressively emasculated by the Central Bank by reducing its size and increasing the forms of assets which might be counted as government paper. It was terminated completely in January 1994 in compliance with Article 104A of the Maastricht Treaty which prohibits privileged access by public bodies to financial institutions.

The Primary Liquidity Ratio is the ratio of a bank's vault cash and its deposits at the Central Bank to *relevant resources*. Relevant resources are the sum of a bank's current and deposit account liabilities plus its net external liabilities (adjusted for exemptions) less its inter-bank deposits.

The imposition of the primary liquidity ratio was intended to promote competition by relating a bank's lending capacity to its ability to attract deposits which, other things constant, would generate surplus liquidity and increase a bank's lending, its size and profitability. (See the next section of this chapter for a fuller account.) It inhibited banks lacking the required liquidity from creating new deposits by way of additional lending.

More importantly, the total bank *system liquidity* comprises *un-borrowed liquidity* and *borrowed liquidity*. A principal source of un-borrowed system liquidity is the balance of payments. When Ireland runs a balance of payments deficit, the excess demand for, say, sterling, is met by the Central Bank of Ireland selling the foreign currency to the licensed banks at the fixed exchange rate. The licensed banks' deposits at the Central Bank are debited to pay for the sterling. The licensed banks in turn are paid by debiting their customers' deposits. Finally, the sterling is paid to the UK bank accounts of UK exporters. The result is a reduction in bankers' deposits at the Central Bank — that is, a reduction in total or system primary liquidity. With a given binding primary liquidity ratio in place, this obliges banks to reduce their customers' deposits, which is achieved by reducing domestic credit.

The Central Bank can vary the primary liquidity ratio to control the level of domestic credit. For example, if there is a balance of payments surplus, then the Central Bank may consider it desirable to increase the primary liquidity ratio as a means of absorbing the surplus primary liquidity generated, and, thereby, inhibiting an increase in domestic credit. Another possibility is that licensed banks might attempt to attract inflows of foreign funds by engaging in foreign borrowing and exchanging such funds for deposits at the Central Bank, thereby increasing their primary assets and lending capacity. After 1973, the Central Bank, on occasion, obliged licensed banks to place 50 per cent of any such funds on deposit at the Central Bank at uncommercial rates of interest and did not count them as primary assets. This is known as *sterilising* the balance of payments surplus so that it does not lead to an increase in domestic credit. Other sources of unborrowed liquidity are considered in the remaining sections of this chapter. The Central Bank may lend the licensed banks primary liquidity by rediscounting bills for them. However, it regards the rediscounting mechanism as a privilege, not a right. As such, it discourages the use of borrowed liquidity by banks by providing it on terms which are unprofitable to them. In short, it sets the rediscount rate (that is, the interest rate at which it lends primary liquidity to banks) sufficiently high, relative to the loan interest rate which banks charge their customers, to make it unprofitable.

On 13 March 1979, Ireland joined the Exchange Rate Mechanism (ERM) of the European Monetary System (EMS) along with the remaining EC members, other than the UK. The ERM is the centrepiece of the EMS. Each participating country in the ERM was given a *central exchange rate* against the European Currency Unit (ECU). The ECU is a synthetic currency unit composed of a basket of the EMS member countries' currencies, where the share of each currency in the basket is broadly proportional to that country's size. A country's central ECU exchange rate, therefore, is a weighted average exchange rate against the EMS currencies.(Although the UK was not an ERM participant, the pound sterling was included in the calculation of the ECU). The exchange rate of a participating currency in the ERM was allowed to fluctuate by 2.25 per cent on either side of its central rate. (The Italian Lira was permitted a 6 per cent fluctuation limit). Sterling appreciated against other EMS currencies later in the same month and on 29 March 1979 the 51-year-old one-to-one link of the Irish pound with the pound sterling was broken.

An important motivation in joining the ERM was the desire to have a broadly fixed exchange rate link to countries which enjoyed low inflation rates. It was hoped that this would, over time, through PPP and IRP, cause Ireland to import a low inflation rate and low interest rates. UK inflation and Irish inflation had been relatively high throughout the 1970s.

For Ireland, the early years of the EMS were marked by rapid fiscal expansion, adverse balance of payments deficits and excessive credit growth. Irish inflation was slow to wind down to Continental European levels against which we lost competitiveness. The Irish pound realigned or devalued against its ECU central rate on repeated occasions through the early 1980s.

By the mid-1980s Ireland had reversed the fiscal stance from expansion to retrenchment and the exchange rate stabilised against its ECU central rate. Inflation abated and interest rates fell below UK levels. In 1986, however, the Irish pound appreciated against the pound sterling, impairing Irish competitiveness on the UK market. The Irish pound realigned, devaluing by 8 per cent against sterling to restore competitiveness on the UK market.

The break with sterling in 1979 also increased the scope, but within narrow limits, for independent domestic monetary policy. Partly encouraged by the imposition of outward foreign exchange controls against sterling, and partly to avoid foreign currency risk, Irish bank customers increasingly sought to match their Irish pound assets and liabilities by borrowing domestically. As domestic credit expanded, so also did required system primary liquidity which could not be met in full from unborrowed sources. The Central Bank became a consistent net provider of *borrowed primary liquidity* in the 1980s and early 1990s. By altering the interest rates at which it made this liquidity available to licensed banks it made its view known on the desirability of emerging trends in domestic credit and exerted some short-term influence on Irish interest rates.

Banks having surplus primary liquidity at the Central Bank, frequently the Associated banks, lent this to banks experiencing a shortage of primary liquidity, frequently the non-associated banks, on the *Inter-bank Market*. The Inter-bank market is, thus, a wholesale market for primary liquidity and Inter-bank interest rates are a measure of the marginal cost of funds to banks. An Inter-bank interest rate is a money market interest rate, which means that the deposits are lent for short periods (usually a maximum of three months but frequently for shorter periods) and bid and offer rates are quoted competitively to all participating banks.

In the early years of EMS membership, the Central Bank imposed binding *quantitative guidelines* on domestic credit expansion by Irish Banks. By the mid-1980s, it had abandoned these in favour of a more market-led approach. Tight monetary conditions were reflected thereafter by an increase in the spread of Irish market interest rates over foreign interest rates. Moreover, the practice of commercial banks in setting uniform deposit and loan rates of interest as a cartel, subject to Central Bank approval, was abandoned in 1985. Thereafter, loan interest rates were more closely tied to money market interest rates, particularly inter-bank rates. In 1991, the Central Bank set a *maximum* spread of 5.5

percentage points over the average one-month inter-bank interest rate to the loan rate that banks may charge their ordinary customers at the time the loan is made. Banks are free to compete within that limit. Prime lending rates to corporates are exempted from this arrangement, competition between the non-associated banks for corporate loans being sufficiently strong to ensure competitive corporate loan rates.

In 1989, the Delors Committee on European Monetary Union, (EMU), proposed a three-stage progression towards full monetary union between Member States. Stage 1 entailed completing the Single European Market and received formal expression and consent from the Member States in the adoption of the Maastrict Treaty. Existing exchange control regulations between Member States were rescinded with derogations or delays granted to some Member States, including Ireland. Stage 2 envisaged the transfer of national monetary policy decision-making to a European System of Central Banks (ESCB). In Stage 3, exchange rates between Member States were to be irrevocably fixed with a full transfer of monetary policy decision-making to the ESCB, and the setting of agreed rules and procedures for budgetary and macroeconomic policy.

The UK joined the ERM on 8 October 1990 and initially experienced a benign régime of declining interest rates, triggered by falling German interest rates. The costs of German reunification, however, exerted upward pressure on German interest rates in 1992 which, in turn, placed upward pressure on UK rates. Moreover, uncertainty as to the future of EMU developed with the initial failure of Denmark, in June 1992, to adopt the Maastrict Treaty. (it ultimately did so on 18 May 1993). There were fears that other countries might follow suit. On 16 September 1992, in the face of increased pressure against sterling, the UK decided against raising interest rates to maintain its ERM commitment; it devalued. Initially, Ireland maintained its exchange rate commitment *vis-à-vis* the German mark, allowed interest rates to increase, and the Irish pound appreciated sharply against sterling. The loss of Irish competitiveness in the UK, particularly for labour-intensive price-sensitive goods, together with the rise in mortgage servicing costs which had been deferred to January 1993, dampened public enthusiasm for continuance of the exchange rate policy. The elimination of remaining Irish exchange controls on 1 January 1993, together with rapid reserve depletion, weakened the Central Bank's capacity to withstand increased speculation against the Irish pound. It devalued by 10 per cent on 30 January 1993. Confidence in the ERM reached crisis point in August 1993. The permitted band of fluctuation for ERM currencies was widened to 15 per cent (from 2.25 per cent). The French franc, Danish krone and Belgian franc depreciated sharply within days, and all currencies floated within the wider band thereafter. Since the declared intention of the Delors plan was a progressive narrowing and ultimate elimination of currency fluctuation, it follows that progress towards EMU was thrown into disarray and, to date, remains in Limbo. Since August 1993, all ERM currencies have floated more widely than previously, but well within the new wider band of permitted fluctuation.

Responsibility for the setting of Irish exchange rate policy, as confirmed in the 1989 Central Bank Act, lies with the Minister for Finance who consults with the Central Bank in formulating exchange rate policy and delegates to the Central Bank responsibility for implementing that policy. In its *Annual Report* for 1993, the Central Bank states, "The ultimate objective of Irish monetary policy is to achieve price stability" and that this requires a "firm" exchange rate policy. It also noted that, in August, the Minister for Finance "reaffirmed that the central objective of Irish exchange-rate policy was price stability". In practical terms this means that the Central Bank will not use the increased scope for independent monetary policy, conferred by floating exchange rates, to take the lead in easing domestic credit conditions unduly. It fears that such action would result in higher inflation, worsening balance of payments, currency depreciation and higher interest rates. Neither does it wish to encourage a return of fiscal laxity by easing the availability and terms under which the government might borrow from domestic banks. It therefore tends to follow rather than lead international interest rate reductions and to maintain the Irish pound in the centre or upper half of the ERM band.

A final point to note is that Central Banking is extremely profitable. The cost of printing banknotes is but a fraction of their face value. These are bought by licensed banks with interest-bearing government stock. The income from this and other sources (£209m in 1992) substantially exceeds expenditure on pay and non-pay (£19m in 1992) so that, having allowed for depreciation and transfers to reserves, the Central Bank has substantial Surplus Income (£168m in 1992). Traditionally the surplus income of the Central Bank in a particular year is transferred to the Exchequer a year later. In recent years advance payments have been provided by the Central Bank to help finance the exceptional costs of the Public Service Early Retirement/Redundancy Scheme.

A Note on Historical Sources

In preparing the foregoing principal section, the following sources have been drawn on, chronologically, for historical details: George O'Brien, *The Economic History of Ireland from the Union to the Famine*, Longmans, Green, London, 1921; G.L. Barrow, *The Emergence of the Irish*

Banking System, 1820-1840, Gill and Macmillan, Dublin, 1975; Maurice Moynihan, *Currency and Central Banking in Ireland, 1822-1960*, Gill and Macmillan, Dublin, 1975; Davy, Kelleher and McCarthy, *The Control of Banking in the Republic of Ireland*, Mount Salus, Dublin, 1984.

MONEY SUPPLY DETERMINATION

A Commercial Bank's Balance Sheet

The balance sheet is a record, at a point in time, of the assets and liabilities of the bank. Assets are everything which the bank owns and Liabilities are everything it owes. By the principle of double entry accounting, total assets and total liabilities are identically equal. This does not mean that the banks' shareholders owe as much as they own. The bank is treated in law as having a separate "legal" personality to its shareholders. Shareholders are that group of claimants to whom any excess of assets over liabilities accrues. This excess or surplus is referred to as the reserves or capital or net worth of the bank. Letting ACC denote a shorthand for "account", the balance sheet of an individual commercial bank might be like that which follows:

Commercial Bank's Balance Sheet

	Assets	£IR		*Liabilities*	£IR
$a.1_i$	Cash	10	1.1_i	Capital & Reserves	50
$a.2_i$	Deposits at CB	85	1.2_i	Current ACC Deposits	150
$a.3_i$	Gilts	255	1.3_i	Savings ACC Deposits	800
$a.4_i$	Loans	650			
$\sum_{j=1}^{4} a_{ji}$	Total Assets	1,000	$\equiv \sum_{j=1}^{3} l_{ji}$	Total Liabilities	1,000

Liabilities

"Capital & Reserves" are the funds subscribed by the shareholders and the accumulated undistributed profits of the bank. They provide a certain level of cover against the risk of trading losses by the bank. Banks are obliged to pay their depositors interest and capital when due. If these payments cannot be met from loan interest and capital repayments received by the bank, the shortfall is met by drawing down "Capital & Reserves". Shareholders' funds are, thus, the risk capital of the bank's owners and are held for prudential reasons.

The bulk of funds raised by banks are customer deposits. In the example above, shareholders fund 5 per cent of the assets for the bank, depositors fund 95 per cent.

Assets

Banks hold a spread of assets. More grandiosely, they hold a diversified portfolio of assets. Assets vary along a spectrum or scale of liquidity. Liquidity is a measure of an asset's nearness to cash. If an asset is readily marketable for cash and at little price risk, then it is liquid. The market in which the asset is first issued is called the *primary* market. Many financial assets are traded in a second-hand or *secondary* market: this improves their liquidity.

Generally, *bank loans* earn the highest rate of interest for the bank. They are the least liquid of the bank's assets, having average maturities of three years or more, and do not enjoy a secondary market. This means that banks must wait, on average, that length of time for full repayment unless the borrower elects to make an early repayment. The bank itself cannot "call-in" the loan ahead of time, nor can it sell the loan for cash to a third party. Because of their illiquidity, bank loans are charged out at higher rates of interest.

The purchase by the bank of a freshly issued gilt or government bond is a loan by it to the government. The gilt is the government's IOU. The nominal maturities of gilt loans made by the bank are generally longer than the maturities of bank loans made to the private sector. However, gilts are traded on a secondary market. They can be bought and sold for cash at little notice and with little *capital or price risk*. They are more liquid than bank loans. They are also less prone to *default or credit risk*. Furthermore, they entail smaller transactions, credit assessment and administration costs than bank loans. For both of these reasons, the interest rate earned on gilts is less than bank loans to the private sector.

The bank also holds money on deposit at the Central Bank. This money earns a lower return than either loans or gilts. It is highly liquid.

Finally, the bank holds vault cash in order to meet the requirements of its customers. Cash is pure liquidity but the bank earns no interest on its cash holdings.

It is clear from the foregoing that a bank which wishes to maximise earnings will tend to place a large proportion of its funds in illiquid high-yielding loans and to hold the bare minimum in low-yielding liquid assets. Provided that the loan rate charged covers the bank fully for the additional costs involved in making illiquid loans, its profits will also increase. In short, there is generally a trade-off between liquidity and profitability.

The Commercial Banks' Aggregate Balance Sheet

Assume that there are ten commercial banks called bank A, bank B, bank C etc., and that the balance sheet of each is identical to that described above.

This simplifying assumption of identical balance sheets implies that the aggregate balance sheet for the commercial banks is simply a 10-fold "blow up" of the individual bank's balance sheet.

Commercial Banks' Aggregate Balance Sheet

	Assets	£IR		*Liabilities*	£IR
A.1	Vault Cash	100	L.1	Capital & Reserves	500
A.2	Deposits at CB	850	L.2	Current ACC Deposits	1,500
A.3	Loans	6,500	L.3	Savings ACC Deposits	8,000
A.4	Loans	2,550			
$\sum_{j=1}^{4}a_j$	Total Assets	10,000	$\equiv \sum_{j=1}^{3}l_j$	Total Liabilities	10,000

The Central Bank's Balance Sheet

A simplified version of the Central Bank's balance sheet is given below. Consistent with the above table pertaining to the commercial banks, suppose that the Central Bank's liabilities consist of Ir£600 of currency (notes and coin) issued by it and Ir£850 of bankers deposits placed with it, Ir£85 from each of the 10 commercial banks. It is paid for its currency issue with gilts. It credits bankers' deposits on receipt of gilts, which are its assets.

Central Bank's Balance Sheet

	Assets	£IR		*Liabilities*	£IR
A.5	Gilts	1,450	L.4	Currency Issued	600
			L.5	Bankers' Deposits	850
				of which:	
				Bank A = 85	
				Bank B = 85	
				Bank C = 85	
				...	
				Bank J = 85	
A.5	Total	1,450	$\equiv$	(L.4 + L.5) Total	1,450

The Consolidated Banking System's Balance Sheet

The consolidated banking system consists of the Central Bank and the 10 commercial banks represented, for accounting purposes, as if they were simply one combined bank. Inter-bank assets and liabilities are "washed-out" in the consolidation.

From the construction of the balance sheets it follows identically that:

$$A.1 + A.2 + A.3 + A.4 + A.5 \equiv L.1 + L.2 + L.3 + L.4 + L.5$$
$$A.2 \equiv L.5$$

$$A.3 + (A.4 + A.5) \equiv (L.4 - A.1) + L.1 + L.2 + L.3$$

Banking system assets and liabilities are identically equal. Commercial Bank deposits at the Central Bank, A.2, are necessarily equal to bankers' deposits held at the Central Bank, L.5, and are netted out and to give the Consolidated Banking System's Balance Sheet.

The Consolidated Banking System's Balance Sheet

	Assets	£IR		Liabilities	£IR
			(L.4–A.1)	Cash held by Public	500
			L.2	Current ACC Deposits	1,500
A.3	Loans	6,500	L.3	Savings ACC Deposits	8,000
(A.4 + A.5)	Gilts	4,000	L.1	Capital & Reserves	500
	Total Assets	10,500	≡	Total Liabilities	10,500

Of the Ir£600 currency issued by the Central Bank, Ir£100 is held by the commercial banks as vault cash; that Ir£100 "washes out" in the consolidation. The remaining Ir£500 is held by the public as pocket cash; the banking system has issued Ir£500 currency which is held by the public.

The first three liabilities of the consolidated banking system are "broad" money, M3, and the remaining items are referred to collectively as the *counterparts of the money supply* and consist of bank loans and gilts less bank capital and reserves.

An Algebraic Model of Money Supply Determination and Control

The money supply, M, consists of cash, C, and bank deposits, D, held by the public. Formally,

$$(1)\ M \equiv C + D$$

Assume that the public holds a fixed fraction, h, (say, h = 5 per cent) of its deposits as cash. Formally,

(2) $C = h \times M$

Liquid assets, L, are the sum of banks' vault cash plus bankers' deposits held at the Central Bank. The liquidity ratio, LR, is the *minimum* ratio of liquid assets, L, to customer deposits, D, which the Central Bank obliges the commercial banks to hold. Assume that total commercial bank deposits are at their maximum size (i.e., banks are fully lent) which is the value of liquid assets (L = Ir£950) divided by the required liquidity ratio (say, LR = 1/10). That is, total bank customer deposits are Ir£9,500. Formally,

(3) $D = L/LR$

The (liquid) liabilities of the Central Bank, (L.4 + L.5), are called the Monetary Base, B, and consist of Cash held by the public, C, and Liquid Assets, L, held by commercial banks (i.e. Vault Cash and Bankers' Deposits at the Central Bank),

(4) $B = C + L = G_{cb}$

The money base is also, in our simplified representation, gilt holdings by the Central Bank, G_{cb}. It follows that,

(4') $L = B - C$

Substituting equations (2), (3) and (4') into (1) and rearranging gives,

(5) $M = [1/\{1 - (1 - h)(1 - LR)\}] \times B$

Equation (5) states that the money supply is a "multiplier" times the Monetary Base, where the latter is the gilt holdings of the Central Bank.

Monetary Control in a Closed Economy

It is instructive to restate equation (5) as,

(5'). $M = m \times G_{cb}$

where the money multiplier, $m = [1/\{1 - (1 - h)(1 - LR)\}]$ and the monetary base $B = G_{cb}$. This highlights the fact that the money supply depends on the Gilt holdings of the Central Bank. In fact, it is a multiple of them; since h and LR are fractions it follows that the multiplier must exceed 1.

It follows that the money supply can be controlled if *monetary policy instruments* can be used to control the money multiplier or the monetary base.

The Instruments of Monetary Policy

The fraction of its money which the public holds as cash, h, is assumed fixed by practice and tradition in the short run. We abstract from very short-run seasonal increases in h at Christmas and from a long-run tendency of h to decline, because of improvements in banking technology, such as credit card usage.

(1) The Required Liquidity Ratio, LR: The liquidity ratio is an important instrument of monetary policy. If the liquidity ratio is reduced by the Central Bank the money multiplier increases and with it, given the monetary base, so does the money supply. The money supply is reduced by increasing the liquidity ratio. Formally, $\Delta M/\Delta LR < 0$.

(2) Open Market Operations: The monetary base changes when the Central Bank changes the level of its gilt holdings. When it does so, voluntarily, on the open market and at its own initiative, this is termed an *open market operation*. The Central Bank increases the monetary base and — given the money multiplier — the money supply when it makes an open market purchase of gilts. It reduces the monetary base and the money supply when it makes an open market sale of gilts. Formally, $\Delta M/\Delta G_{cb} > 0$.

(3) Rediscounting: The Central Bank acts as Lender of Last Resort to those commercial banks which, given their deposit base, lack the required Liquid Assets to meet the mandatory liquidity ratio. It buys gilts from them, *at their initiative*, at a reduced or discounted price, *temporarily*. It credits their deposit accounts at the Central Bank on receipt of the gilts, which provides the commercial banks with the required liquidity shortfall. The Central Bank later sells the acquired gilts back to the commercial banks at an increased price. In short, the Central Bank makes a secured loan, called a *repo*, which is an abbreviation for a sale and repurchase agreement.

The increase in the Central Bank's gilt holdings from rediscounting expands the monetary base and the money supply in like fashion to an open-market purchase of gilts by it. Formally, $\Delta M/\Delta G_{cb} > 0$.

The implied interest rate on a repo is the rediscount rate. For example, if a commercial bank sells a gilt to the Central Bank for £100 and agrees to buy it back one month later for £101, then the secured £100 loan from the Central Bank costs it £1 for the month or 12 per cent per annum.

The liquidity ratio is altered infrequently. When it is reduced it frees up or creates surplus *unborrowed liquidity*. Open market operations are used regularly by the Central Bank to manage the level of unborrowed liquidity. Rediscounting is used by banks to alter their borrowed liquidity. A Central Bank will usually discourage the use of rediscounting as a permanent source of bank liquidity since it would impair Central

Bank control of the monetary base and the money supply. It does so by raising the rediscount rate relative to the loan rate of interest, thereby making marginal lending unprofitable to banks. Bank lending declines and with it bank deposits and the money supply.

The Process of Monetary Expansion and Contraction

Assume that the Central Bank makes an *open market purchase* of Ir£100 of gilts from Seán Bloggs who banks at Bank A. Seán receives a cheque drawn on the Central Bank to the value of Ir£100 in exchange for the gilts he has transferred to it. He countersigns and presents the cheque at Bank A. He withdraws £5.00 (1/20th) as cash and lodges the remaining £95.00 (19/20ths) to his current account. [the cash/money ratio, h, is assumed throughout to be 5 per cent]. Bank A takes possession of the cheque which now becomes its property. It presents the cheque for clearing at the Central Bank. The Central Bank accepts the cheque and credits Bank A's account at the Central Bank with Ir£100. It then tears up the cleared cheque.

The Consolidated Balance Sheet for the Banking System will now look as follows:

The Consolidated Banking System's Balance Sheet

Assets	£IR	Liabilities	£IR
		Cash	505
		Current ACC Deposits	1,595
Loans	6,500	Savings ACC Deposits	8,000
Gilts	4,100	Capital & Reserves	500
Total Assets	10,600 ≡	Total Liabilities	10,600

The public, in the person of Seán Bloggs, holds an extra £5 in cash and an extra £95 on current account. In short, the money supply has risen by £100. The asset side of the banking system's balance sheet shows that the gilt holdings (at the Central Bank) have risen by £100. Assets and liabilities, necessarily, have risen equally.

The Central Bank's open market purchase involves it swapping a money asset, the cheque drawn on itself, for a non-money asset, the gilt. The effect illustrated thus far is, however, merely the *instantaneous* effect on the money supply. To see this, consider the current state of Bank A's balance sheet which now looks like this:

Bank A's Balance Sheet

Assets	£IR		Liabilities	£IR
Cash	5		Capital & Reserves	50
Deposits at CB	185		Current ACC Deposits	245
Gilts	255		Savings ACC Deposits	800
Loans	650			
Total Assets	1,095	≡	Total Liabilities	1,095

Bank A's liquid assets are now Ir£190. Its total deposits are now Ir£1,045. The required liquidity ratio of 10 per cent implies that Ir£104.50 is the required level of liquid assets; the remaining Ir£85.50 is Bank A's surplus or excess liquidity. Bank A will, generally, not wish to hold surplus liquidity since loan assets are higher yielding. Provided suitable loan opportunities exist, the bank will lend the surplus liquidity to a customer.

The Central Bank's balance sheet currently looks like this:

Central Bank's Balance Sheet

Assets	£IR		Liabilities	£IR
Gilts	1,550		Currency Issued	600
			Bankers' Deposits	950
			of which:	
			Bank A = 185	
			Bank B = 85	
			Bank C = 85	
			…	
			Bank J = 85	
Total	1,550	≡	Total	1,550

Its gilt holdings have risen by Ir£100 and so has the value of bankers deposits held with it.

Assume that Bank A now makes a loan of Ir£85.50 to Dave Horton. Dave needs the loan to pay a medical bill owed to Dr Wills. Consider, first, the effect of the loan on Bank A's balance sheet. The *incremental* balance sheet below shows the *changes* in the balance sheet resulting from the loan.

Bank A's *Incremental* Balance Sheet

Assets	£IR	Liabilities	£IR
Cash	—	Capital & Reserves	—
Deposits at CB	—	Current ACC Deposits	
		(Dave Horton)	+85.50
Gilts	—	Savings ACC Deposits	—
Loans	+85.50		
Total Assets	+85.50	≡ Total Liabilities	+85.50

Dave Horton signs a loan form for the bank once he has negotiated the loan. This is his IOU which is now held as an asset of the bank. Hence, Loans are "written up" by Ir£85.50. The bank credits Dave's current account with Ir£85.50; it stands ready and liable to pay out Ir£85.50 at his instructions, which he will give, most likely, by way of cheque. This is the most common way in which money is created — a loan is advanced to a customer.

Dave now writes a cheque for Ir£85.50 payable to Dr Wills who banks at bank B. Dr Wills signs and presents the cheque at his bank, withdraws Ir£4.275 in cash (i.e. 5 per cent) and lodges Ir£81.225 to his current account (i.e. 95 per cent). Bank B presents the cheque for clearance at the Central Bank. The Central Bank debits Bank A's deposits by £85.50 and credits Bank B's deposit account by £85.50. It forwards the cleared cheque to Bank A with notification of its reduced deposit balance at the Central Bank. Bank A debits Dave's current account by £85.50 and returns the cleared cheque to him. Bank A's incremental balance sheet now has two additional entries:

Bank A's *Incremental* Balance Sheet

Assets	£IR	Liabilities	£IR
Cash	—	Capital & Reserves	—
Deposits at CB	-85.50	Current ACC Deposits	
Gilts	—	(Dave Horton)	+85.50
Loans	+85.50		-85.50
(Dave Horton)		Savings ACC Deposits	—
Total Assets	—	≡ Total Liabilities	—

Essentially, Bank A's surplus liquidity is eliminated and converted to a higher yielding asset — a bank loan. The final position on Bank A's balance sheet is:

Bank A's Balance Sheet

Assets	£IR	Liabilities	£IR
Cash	5	Capital & Reserves	50
Deposits at CB	99.50	Current ACC Deposits	245
Gilts	255	Savings ACC Deposits	800
Loans	735.50		
Total Assets	1,095	≡ Total Liabilities	1,095

Bank A's liquid assets, Ir£104.50 are now exactly 10 per cent of its total customer deposits, Ir£1,045, as is required. Had Bank A lent Dave an amount in excess of its surplus liquidity, then it would experience a liquidity shortfall once Dave wrote a cheque for that amount to a customer of Bank B. In short, *a bank may only safely lend amounts equal to its surplus or excess liquidity.*

Turning to bank B its balance sheet now looks as follows:

Bank B's Balance Sheet

Assets	£IR	Liabilities	£IR
Cash	5.725	Capital & Reserves	50
Deposits at CB	170.50	Current ACC Deposits	231.225
Gilts	255	Savings ACC Deposits	800
Loans	650.00		
Total Assets	1,081.225	≡ Total Liabilities	1,081.225

Note that Bank B has total customer deposits of Ir£1,031.225 and hence required liquid assets of Ir£103.1225. Its actual liquid assets are Ir£176.225 and hence it has surplus or excess liquidity of Ir£73.1125. As with Bank A, it will prefer to loan its surplus liquidity rather than keep it in lower yielding liquid assets. The surplus liquidity, initiated by the open market purchase of gilts, has created a chain reaction with surplus liquidity passing from one bank to another, albeit in diminishing amounts. The process of loan creation, drawdown and clearance proceeds for Bank B in identical fashion to Bank A. A loan of £73.11 is made by Bank B to a customer. Its deposits and loan book are written up by that amount. A cheque for £73.11 is paid by the Bank B borrower to a customer at Bank C. When the cheque is cleared, Bank B's current account deposits are debited by £73.11, as is its deposit at the Central Bank. Its closing balance sheet will then be:

Bank B's Balance Sheet

Assets	£IR	Liabilities	£IR
Cash	5.725	Capital & Reserves	50
Deposits at CB	97.388	Current ACC Deposits	231.225
Gilts	255	Savings ACC Deposits	800
Loans	723.112		
Total Assets	1,081.225	≡ Total Liabilities	1,081.225

Note that Bank B is now fully lent. Its liquid assets of £103.113 are just sufficient to support its deposits.

At Bank C the payee of the £73.11 cheque will have taken £3.655 (5 per cent) as cash and lodged the remaining £69.445 (95 per cent) to his current account. When the cheque has cleared at the Central Bank the deposit account of Bank B is debited by £73.10 and the deposit account of Bank C is credited with £73.10.

Bank C's Balance Sheet

Assets	£IR	Liabilities	£IR
Cash	6.345	Capital & Reserves	50
Deposits at CB	158.11	Current ACC Deposits	219.455
Gilts	250	Savings ACC Deposits	800
Loans	655		
Total Assets	1,069.455	≡ Total Liabilities	1,069.455

Bank C now has surplus liquidity of £62.51. It advances a loan of this amount to a customer and the process passes on to bank D.

The process of money creation may be summarised as follows:

Change in M3 =		(Algebraically)	£m
Change in Money Base +		$\Delta B +$	£100 +
Net New Lending at			
Bank A	+	$[(1-h)(1-LR)] \times \Delta B$ +	£85.5 +
Bank B	+	$[(1-h)(1-LR)]^2 \times \Delta B$ +	£73.1 +
Bank C	+	$[(1-h)(1-LR)]^3 \times \Delta B$ +	£62.5 +
Bank D	+	$[(1-h)(1-LR)]^4 \times \Delta B$ +	£53.4 +
Bank E	+	$[(1-h)(1-LR)]^5 \times \Delta B$ +	£45.7 +
....		....	......
....		....	......
....		....	......
....		....	......
TOTAL		$[1/\{1-(1-h)(1-LR)\}] \times \Delta B$	£689.65

Note: The totals given in the final row are strictly limiting values of the deposit expansion process. This implies that we either require a larger number of banks than 10 for the approximation to be accurate, or that the expansion process recycles from Bank J back to Bank A. In the later case the effects described in the table are first-round rather than final effects.

The algebraic expression for the change in the money supply given in the final row above can also be obtained by differentiating equation (5) with respect to B,

$$(6)\ \Delta M/\Delta B = [1/\{1 - \{(1 - h)(1 - LR)\}\}] = 6.89$$

The rationale underlying the expansion process is straightforward. For every £1 of base money, B, that the Central Bank creates by an open market purchase of gilts, the gilt seller will withdraw £h as cash from their bank and deposit £(1 - h) to their current account. The bank's liquid assets rise by £(1 - h). Since deposits have risen by £(1-h); *required* liquid assets rise by £(1 - h) x LR. It follows that *surplus* liquid assets are £(1 - h)(1 - LR). This equals the net new lending which the bank will undertake and is the algebraic entry given for Bank A with $\Delta B = 1$. The borrower issues a cheque to that amount to a payee who banks at Bank B. The payee withdraws £h x [(1 - h)(1 - LR)] as cash and deposits £(1 - h) x [(1 - h)(1 - LR)]. Liquid assets also rise by the latter amount at Bank B. *Required* liquid assets rise by £LR(1- h) x [(1 - h)(1 - LR)] and hence *surplus* liquid assets rise by £[(1 - h)(1 - LR)] x [(1 - h)(1 - LR)] i.e. by $[(1 - h)(1 - LR)]^2$. Net new loans to that amount are made by Bank B and so on ad infinitum.

Limitations
We have assumed that all banks are fully lent and hold no surplus liquidity.

When a bank lacks suitable loan applicants of its own it will lend its surplus liquidity on the inter-bank market to other banks. But if suitable loan applicants are generally not available, because of depressed market conditions, then banks may elect to hold surplus liquidity. The actual liquidity ratio will then exceed the required *minimum* liquidity and the money multiplier and money supply will be smaller than represented by equation (5).

The Central Bank also acts as banker to the government. If a government can "lean on" the Central Bank, it may run large budget deficits and "encourage" the Central Bank to fund it by buying freshly issued gilts. If the Central Bank lacks the independence to refuse, it loses control over the level of its gilt holdings, the monetary base and the money supply. It is precisely because the short-run (output and political) effects of monetary expansions are frequently beneficial while their long-run (inflation) effects are frequently deleterious that governments are "kept away from the (money) printing presses" and Central Banks are granted varying degrees of independence, as a check against imprudent fiscal action.

The focus on monetary control ignores the possible effects of prudential regulation. The Central Bank fixes a *minimum capital adequacy ratio* of Capital & Reserves to Total Assets for commercial banks. The deposit expansion process outlined above assumes that banks have sufficient Capital and Reserves to meet the ratio as its loan book and total assets expand.

In a small open economy, the Central Bank holds both domestic and foreign currency (say, UK) gilts. An open market purchase of domestic gilts by the Central Bank creates surplus liquidity and causes credit to expand as illustrated above. However, if the exchange rate is fixed, then the excess supply of credit creates a corresponding balance of payments deficit, as illustrated in Chapter 21, and results in the Central Bank selling its foreign currency holdings (i.e., its UK gilts) to meet the excess demand for currency at the existing exchange rate. The monetary base contacts to its initial level. The Central Bank cannot control the monetary base in a fixed exchange rate SOE. What it can control is its domestic and foreign reserve counterparts.

Note, finally, that in practice commercial banks hold *correspondent* accounts with each other and operate the clearing or payment system themselves by debiting and crediting their correspondent accounts appropriately. Movements in the *aggregate net balance* of such accounts only are cleared at the Central Bank.

A BRIEF INTRODUCTION TO OFFICIAL IRISH MONEY SUPPLY STATISTICS

The Central Bank of Ireland is the primary source of Irish money supply statistics. Each quarter it publishes a detailed account of economic and monetary developments in Ireland, together with a comprehensive statistical appendix, in the *Central Bank Quarterly Bulletin* (*CBQB*). We will consider below a few key tables in the *CBQB*, which give full applied expression to the analytical measures and concepts dealt with in earlier sections of the current and the preceding chapter.

The Money Supply and Counterparts

Table 1: Irish Banking System: Consolidated Balance Sheet

		31 Dec. 1992	31 Dec. 1991		1992
	Liabilities	Ir£m	Ir£m		Ir£m
L.1	Currency	1,410.2	1,381.4	+	28.8
L.2	Borrowing from Other Credit Institutions	712.3	713.4	-	1.1
L.3	Non-Government Current Accounts	1,817.5	1,813.3	+	4.2
L.4	Non-Government Deposit Accounts	10,005.9	8,893.4	+	1,112.5
L.5	Accrued Interest on Non-Government Deposits	257.4	223.2	+	34.2
L.6	Capital Employed	2,685.0	2,432.1	+	252.9
L.7	Government Deposits at the Central Bank	639.3	1,248.3	-	609.0
L.8	Net External Liabilities of Licensed Banks	2,226.9	3,858.2	-	1,631.3
L.9	Acceptances	74.3	74.6	-	0.3
L.10	Other Liabilities	1,964.7	951.9	+	1,012.8
	Total	21,793.5	21,589.8	+	203.7
	Assets				
A.1	Lending to Other Credit Institutions	303.4	331.9	-	28.5
A.2	Non-Government Credit	14,410.7	13,553.2	+	857.5
A.3	Interest Accrued on Non-Government Credit	149.5	133.0	+	16.5
A.4	Government Credit	3,541.6	3,075.5	+	466.1
A.5	Official External Reserves	2,112.8	3,256.0	-	1,143.2
A.6	Fixed Assets	645.4	611.0	+	34.4
A.7	Other Assets	630.1	629.2	+	0.9

Source: CBQB Summer 1993, Table C1.

The *actual* consolidated balance sheets for the Irish Banking System at 31 Dec. 1991 and 31 Dec. 1992, together with the *incremental* balance sheet for the calendar year 1992, are given in Table 1. The consolidated banking system refers to the Central Bank and the within-the-state offices of all licensed banks (see *CBQB* for a full listing). "Other Credit Institutions" refers to other non-licensed bank deposit-takers, namely, the TSB, ACC, ICC, POSB and Building Societies.

The balance sheet identity in Table 1 is:

$$L1 + L2 + L3 + L4 + L5 + L6 + L7 + L8 + L9 \equiv A1 + A2 + A3 + A4 + A5$$

It can be simplified by rearranging it as:

$$[L1 + L2 + L3 + L4 + L5] \equiv [\{A1 + A2 + A3 - L9\} + \{A4 - L7\} \\ + \{A6 + A7 - L6 - L10\} + \{A5 - L8\}]$$

Table 2 clarifies the money supply identity, $M \equiv D + R$. The sum of the first three *domestic* counterpart assets in the Table is, D, the net domestic assets of the banking system: the net foreign assets, R, equals the sum of the net *foreign* asset positions of both the Central Bank and the licensed banks.

Table 2: Irish Banking System: Consolidated Balance Sheet

	31 Dec. 1992	31 Dec. 1991		1992
Liabilities	**Ir£m**	**Ir£m**		**Ir£m**
Broad Money, M3				
L1 + L2 + L3 + L4 +L5	14,203.3	13,024.7	+	1,178.6
Total	14,203.3	13,024.7	+	1,178.6
Assets				
Domestic Counterparts				
Private Sector Credit				
A1 + A2 + A3 - L9	14,789.3	13,943.5	+	845.8
Net Government Lending				
A4 - A7	2,902.3	1,827.2	+	1,075.1
Net Non-Monetary Assets				
A6 + A7 - L6 - L10	- 3,374.2.5	- 2,143.8	-	1,230.4
Foreign Counterpart				
Net Foreign Assets				
A5 -L8	- 114.1.6	- 602.2	+	488.1

During the calendar year 1992 broad money, M3, increased by £1,179m. Domestic Credit Expansion (DCE) was £1,921m and consisted of an increase in Private Sector Credit of £846m and an increase in net Government Lending of £1,075m. Net non-monetary assets of the banking system fell by £1,230m. The domestic counterparts of the money supply, D, thus increased by £691m. The net foreign assets of the banking system, R, rose by £488m and consisted of a reduction in the net external liabilities of the licensed banks of £1,631m and a reduction in the Official External Reserves of the Central Bank of £1,143m.

The Counterparts of the Money Supply

Private Sector Credit: Inspection of the preceding tables will confirm that Private Sector Credit is dominated by Non-Government Credit. Non-government credit is usually measured over a non-calendar year in order to avoid possible distortions of underlying credit trends due to timing of "Christmas" sales. The figures for outstanding credit at February 1992 and February 1993 and for credit growth over that one-year period are given in Table 3.

Table 3: All Licensed Banks: Sectoral Distribution of Advances

£m	Resident Non-Government Credit				
	Feb. 1993	(%)	Feb. 1992		Feb. 1993/ Feb. 1992
1. Agriculture, Forestry & Fishing	1,304.5	(9)	1,403.9	-	99.4
2. Energy	162.6	(1)	107.3	+	55.3
3. Manufacturing	1,594.8	(12)	1,687.3	-	92.5
4. Building & Construction	406.9	(3)	412.3	-	5.4
5. Distribution, Garages, Hotels & Catering	1,780.2	(12)	1,746.7	+	33.5
6. Transport	413.1	(3)	328.5	+	84.3
7. Postal Services & Communications	29.7	(—)	41.4	-	11.7
8. Financial	2,596.2	(18)	1,864.0	-	732.2
9. Business & Other Services	1,769.0	(12)	1,687.2	+	81.8
10. Personal	4,345.4	(30)	4,226.9	+	118.5
TOTAL	14,402.4	(100)	13,505.4	+	898.8

Source : Table C8, *CBQB* 1992(Q4) and *CBQB* 1993(Q2).

The *stock* of outstanding non-government credit at February 1993 was £14.4bn. About 30 per cent of this was accounted for by private sector borrowing (around half of which was mortgage borrowing). Financial companies, business, distribution, manufacturing and agriculture were the other large credit sectors. Their percentage shares in non-government credit at February 1993 are given in Table 3. A more detailed account is provided in the *CBQB* which shows that farming, food co-ops, retail distribution, hotels & catering, leasing companies and mortgage lending were the largest credit subsectors. Non-government credit *increased* by almost £900m over the period. Note that non-government credit refers to the net change in credit outstanding, which is new or gross loan advances less repayments of existing loans. It follows that gross advances, in any period, exceed credit by the amount of loan repayments over the same period. Lending to "other credit institutions" plus accrued interest are added to non-government credit and "Acceptances" are netted from it to yield Private Sector Credit. Private Sector Credit grew by £846m in the calendar year 1992.

Net Government Lending: Bank lending to the government grew by £466m in the calendar year 1992 and took the form of increased holdings of gilts and Exchequer bills by the licensed banks. The government also drew down its Deposit account at the Central Bank by £609m over the same period. Net Government Lending was, thus, £1,075m.

Net Non-Monetary Assets: This category in Table 2 is the sum of Fixed Assets and Other Assets less Capital Employed and Other Liabilities. Illustrative examples of how these items can change the money supply are as follows:

(1) If a bank buys premises and credits the seller's deposit account, then bank deposits and the money supply rise on foot of an increase in a non-monetary asset — the newly acquired bank building.

(2) If a bank depositor buys newly issued bank shares and pays by cheque, then their current account is debited and Capital Employed is increased correspondingly — the increase in Capital Employed reduces bank deposits and the money supply. An increase in Net Non-Monetary Assets increases bank deposits and the money supply correspondingly. These assets are called non-monetary because they can not be quickly liquidated. Net Non-Monetary Assets fell by £1,230.4m in 1992.

Overall, the net domestic assets of the licensed banks increased by £690.5m in 1992.

Net Foreign Assets: This category in Table 2 is the sum of the net foreign assets of the licensed banks and the Central Bank. The within-the-state offices of licensed banks' liabilities *vis-à-vis* non-residents exceed their assets *vis-à-vis* non-residents. In short, they have positive net external liabilities or, equivalently, they have negative net external assets. These result from the normal banking activity, *vis-à-vis* non-residents, of domestic bank offices and arise mainly from the fact that non-resident bank deposits at those offices exceed lending to non-residents by those offices. An aggregate balance sheet which provides a detailed listing of the gross assets and liabilities *vis-à-vis* non residents of the within-the-state offices of licensed banks for 1992 is provided in the *CBQB* 1993 (Q2), Table C4. The net external liabilities of the licensed banks fell by £1,631.3 in 1992; it follows identically that their net external assets increased by £1,631.3m.

The net foreign assets of the Central Bank are termed the "Official External Reserves". These consist principally of external balances and securities held by the Central Bank together with some Gold, ECU (European Currency Units) and its reserve position at the IMF (International Monetary Fund). Official External Reserves declined by £1,143.2m in 1992. A detailed account of the constituents and movements in Official External Reserves in 1992 is provided in *CBQB* 1993 (Q2), Table C2. Overall, the Net Foreign Assets of the Banking System increased by £488.1m in 1992.

In summary, in 1992 Net Domestic Assets of the banking system increased by £690.5m, its Net Foreign Assets increased by £488.1m and the broad money stock, M3, increased by £1,178.6m.

Table 4: Money Aggregates M1, M3 and M3E

£m	M1	M3	M3E
31 Dec. 1992	3,227.7	14,203.3	20,834.2
31 Dec. 1991	3,194.6	13,024.6	18,576.8
Changes, 1992	33.1	1,178.7	2,257.4

Source: CBQB 1993(Q2), Table A3.

As can be seen from Table 4, Narrow Money, M1, consisting of cash and current account balances held by the public at licensed banks, increased by £33m in 1992. Broad Money, M3, which additionally includes deposit account balances held by the public at licensed banks plus borrowing by licensed banks from other credit institutions, increased by £1,178.7. The expanded broad money series, M3E, also includes current and deposit account balances held by the public at other credit institutions net of those institutions' cash holdings and lending to licensed banks. It increased by £2,257.4m. The variation in money growth remains large even when expressed in percentage terms and highlights the care required when seeking to determine the degree of monetary ease or restraint.

The Monetary Base and Bank Liquidity

A simplified version of the balance sheet of the Central Bank is set out in Table 5.

Table 5: Central Bank's Balance Sheet

	£m	31 Dec. 1992	31 Dec. 1991	End Dec. 1992/ End Dec. 1991	
	Liabilities				
L1	Currency	1,604.4	1,568.2	+	36.2
L2	Bankers' Deposits	447.7	670.7	-	223.0
L3	Government Deposits	638.9	1,247.8	-	608.9
L4	EMCF Debtor Position	716.1	0.0	+	716.1
L5	Other Liabilities	1,200.1	1,053.2	+	146.7
	TOTAL	4,607.3	4,540.0	+	67.3
	Assets				
A1	Official External Reserves	2,112.8	3,256.0	-	1,143.2
A2	Liquidity Support Assets	2,074.5	817.1	+	1,257.4
A3	Other Assets	420.0	467.0	-	47.0

Source: CBQB 1993(Q2), Table C2 condensed.
Note: Liquidity Support Assets are Repos, Secured Advances and Short Term Facility (STF) drawings.

It follows identically from Table 5 that:

$$L1 + L2 + L3 + L4 + L5 \equiv A1 + A2 + A3$$

Rearranging gives:

$$L1 + L2 \equiv A1 + A2 + A3 - L3 - L4 - L5$$

In table format this gives Table 6.

Table 6: The Monetary Base 1992

£m		31 Dec. 1992	31 Dec. 1991	End Dec. 1992/ End Dec. 1991	
	Liabilities				
L1	Currency	1,604.4	1,568.2	+	36.2
L2	Bankers' Deposits	447.7	670.7	-	223.0
	MONETARY BASE	2,052.1	2,238.9	-	186.8
	Assets				
A1	Official External Reserves	2,112.8	3,256.0	-	1,143.2
A2	Liquidity Support Assets	2,074.5	817.1	+	1,257.4
A3	Other Assets	420.0	467.0	-	47.0
Less Liabilities					
L3	Government Deposits	638.9	1,247.8	-	608.9
L4	EMCF Debtor Position	716.1	0.0	+	716.1
L5	Other Liabilities	1,200.1	1,053.2	+	146.9

Source: Table 5.

In 1992, the Monetary Base declined by £186.8m. Factors reducing the monetary base were the decline in Official External Reserves of £1,143.2m, the growth in the Central Bank's indebtedness to the EMCF of £716.1m and the decline in its Other Net Assets of £193.7m. Factors increasing the monetary base were the rundown in Government deposits at the Central Bank of £608.9m and the injections of liquidity by the Central Bank, through the use of support measures of £1,257.4m.

Note that the currency figures contained in the Monetary Base in Table 6 refer to the total currency issued by the Central Bank and is held *either* as vault cash by banks *or* as pocket cash by the public.

Since primary bank liquidity consists of bank vault cash plus bankers' deposits at the Central Bank it follows that the licensed banks' primary liquidity is obtained by deducting currency held by the public from the monetary base. This is done in Table 7 and shows that primary bank liquidity fell by £215.6m in 1992.

Table 7: Primary Bank Liquidity 1992

£m		31 Dec. 1992	31 Dec. 1991	End Dec. 1992/ End Dec. 1991
1.	Monetary Base	2,052.1	2,238.9	- 186.8
2.	Currency Held by Public	1,410.2	1,381.4	+ 28.8
3.	Primary Bank Liquidity (1 - 2)	641.9	857.5	- 215.6

Source: Table 1 and Table 6.

Market Liquidity, the EBR and the Balance of Payments

A licensed bank gains liquidity when it increases its cash holdings or gains a deposit at the Central Bank. Movements in the latter dominate overall movements in bank liquidity and have three principal sources.

First, the government, on foot of its deficit spending, is a *net* issuer of cheques through its Exchequer/Paymaster General account, held at the Central Bank. These are lodged, by payees, with domestic banks who credit the payees' deposit accounts. Each countersigned cheque becomes an asset of the receiving bank. When the cheques are cleared at the Central Bank, the Exchequer/Paymaster General account is debited and the receiving bank's deposit account at the Central Bank is credited. Licensed banks gain deposits at the Central Bank.

Second, when net external receipts, arising from a balance of payments surplus, are placed by a licensed bank at the Central Bank, its deposit account is credited. This is often effected by a foreign exchange swap between the licensed bank and the Central Bank. The licensed bank swaps foreign currency for an Irish pound deposit at the Central Bank with provision for the swap to be reversed in the future, at agreed rates.

Third, the Central Bank may add to bank liquidity by buying securities from licensed banks i.e., through open market operations and re-discounting. On receipt of the security, the licensed bank's deposit account at the Central Bank is credited. The Central Bank possesses a number of specific liquidity support measures to effect this end. We will not consider these in detail but simply note that repos are the dominant instrument which the Central Bank uses.

The preceding subsection on the monetary base and bank liquidity provided a partial and incomplete account of the *net* effects which the government, the Central Bank and the balance of payments have on bank liquidity. We now complete the picture by considering, in turn, the funding of the EBR, and the balance of payments, and drawing these together in an account of the underlying forces affecting *system* liquidity. In particular, the underlying *gross* foreign exchange *market* pressure on bank liquidity in 1992 and the *gross* non-market effects of government borrowing and Central Bank support in alleviating it are distinguished.

Funding the EBR

In 1992, total current Government expenditure was £9,806m and total current revenue was £9,360, giving a current budget deficit of £446m. The government's capital deficit was £267m; hence the total deficit, or EBR, was £713m. This was financed as set out in Table 8.

Table 8: Financing of the Exchequer Borrowing Requirement (EBR)

£m			End December 1991/ End December 1992
1.	**Raised on Domestic Market**	-	947
a)	Net Sales of Securities to		
—	Non-bank public		282
—	Banks		435
—	Non-residents	-	1,809
b)	Small Savings		145
2.	**Other Financing**		**1,660**
a)	Direct external borrowing		1,008
b)	Reduction in balances at the Central Bank		652
3.	**Exchequer Borrowing Requirement (1 + 2)**		**713**

Source: CBQB, Summer 1993, Table 7.

As can be seen, the government raised £1,087m in *cash* through the sale of government securities to the licensed banks (£435m) and by running down its deposits at the Central Bank (£652m).

A Technical Digression: The consolidated balance sheet for the banking system has earlier shown that bank lending to government increased by £466m, whereas the above EBR table gives a figure of £435m. The apparent discrepancy arises because of the difference in the *cash* proceeds from a security at its date of sale and its *valuation* at the balance sheet date. For example, suppose the government sells a one-year bill with a face or redemption value of £100 for £90 on 2 January 1992. The cash received is £90, whereas its valuation at 31 December 1992 is £100. Thus, the government raised £435m in cash from issuing securities to banks in 1992 but the market value of government securities held by banks over the course of the calendar year 1992 increased by £466m.

The reduction in government balances at the Central Bank, given as £652m in the above EBR table, is a balancing item. It differs from the figure of £609m given in the consolidated balance sheet of the banking system, partly for the reason given above but also because *timing differences* between sanctioning government expenditure (used in calculating the EBR) and its associated *cash drawdown* (reflected in government deposits at the Central Bank) and partly because of other, relatively small, non-exchequer government accounts held at the Central Bank.

The total EBR was £713m in 1992. The exchequer made *net domestic* (i.e., Irish pound) *payments* of £1,606m. These were net of the receipt of Small Savings of £145m. It follows that the domestic or Irish pound component of the EBR was £1,751m and the net foreign currency component of the EBR was -£1,038m, i.e., foreign currency receipts of the exchequer exceeded foreign currency payments by the exchequer by £1,038m. Net domestic payments is the difference between domestic expenditure and domestic (tax) revenue. Net foreign currency receipts is, principally, the difference between international (EU) transfers to the government and foreign debt interest payments by it. It is worth noting that international transfers are made directly to the Government account at the Central Bank and do not pass through the foreign exchange markets. The Central Bank credits the exchequer Irish pound deposit account by the amount of the transfer (the Central Bank's liability) and holds the foreign currency as part of its Official External Reserves (the Central Bank's counterpart asset). Debt interest payments to non-residents are also made directly and do not pass through the foreign exchange markets. The corresponding credits and debits are as above, with reversed signs.

The government made net domestic (Irish pound) payments of £1,606m in 1992 and also bought back net £1,092m of its Irish pound gilts. The latter was occasioned by the impending devaluation of the Irish pound which led to capital flight from Irish pound assets. Non-residents dumped Irish pound gilts and converted the proceeds to foreign currency. The government thus made total Irish pound market payments for these purposes of £2,698m. It funded £652m of this by running down its deposits at the Central Bank: it funded £1,038m from its net foreign currency receipts and the remaining £1,008m by direct foreign borrowing. It is also worth noting in passing that the foreign currency receipts from direct foreign borrowing by the government do not pass through the foreign exchange market but are lodged directly to the Central Bank.

In summary, Irish pound net payments from the exchequer account provided the Irish banking system with a liquidity injection of £2,698m. It funded £2,046m from net foreign currency receipts and foreign currency borrowing; the balance of £652m from a rundown of its deposits at the Central Bank.

The Balance of Payments

The £1.7bn current account surplus shown in Table 9 was more than offset by the £4.6bn *market* capital outflow, of which £1.6bn was accounted for by a net reduction in the external liabilities of banks. The remaining market items were triggered by a flight out of Irish pound securities on foot of the expected Irish pound devaluation, which materialised on 30 January 1993. *Non-market* foreign currency capital inflows increased by £1.7bn on foot of external borrowing by government and by the Central Bank from the European Monetary Co-operation Fund (EMCF). Overall the official foreign currency reserve holdings of the Central Bank fell by £1.1bn to £2.1bn.

Table 9: Balance of Payments *Estimates*

£m	End Dec. 1991/ End Dec. 1992
Current Account	
1. **Current Account Surplus**	**1,739**
of which:	
— Non-Government Market Surplus	701
— Government Non-Market Surplus	1,038
Capital Account	
2. **Market Flows**	**- 4,617**
of which:	
— Uptake of Irish Pound Securities by non-residents	- 1,809
— Net flows through banks	- 1,558
— Net flows through other institutions	170
— Net external borrowing of state-sponsored bodies	131
— Private-Capital/residual bodies	- 1,551
3. **Non-market flows**	**1,667**
of which:	
— Government direct foreign borrowing	1,035
— Other official capital	- 74
— EMCF debtor position	716
4. **Valuation adjustment to reserves**	**58**
5. **Change in official external reserves (1 + 2 + 3 + 4)**	**- 1,143**
6. **Level of reserves (end-period)**	**2,113**

Source: CBQB 1992 (Q2), and own estimate of current account breakdown as between market and non-market components.

Note that of the £1,739m current account surplus, approximately £1,038m relates to the excess of government foreign currency receipts (from international transfers, for example) over foreign currency payments (foreign debt interest payments, for example). Since these do not pass through the foreign currency market we refer to them as *non-market*. The remaining £701m component of the current account surplus does pass through the foreign exchange market and we term it "Non-Government Market Surplus" above. Total market *outflows* through the balance of payments were £3,916m being the sum of the current and capital account market outflows.

System Liquidity

Table 10: Sources of Change in Licensed Bank Liquidity

£m		End Dec. 1991/ End Dec. 1992	
1.	**Government**		
—	Net Domestic (Irish Pound) Payments	+	1,606
—	Net Purchases of (Irish Pound) Gilts	+	1,092
2.	**External**		
—	Market Foreign Exchange Transactions	-	3,925
3.	**Central Bank**		
—	Liquidity Support Measures	+	1,258
—	Other	-	218
4.	**Change in Monetary Base (1 + 2 + 3)**	**-**	**187**
5.	*Less* **Increase in Currency held by Public**	**-**	**36**
6.	**Change in Licensed Bank Deposits at the Central Bank (4 + 5)**	**-**	**223**

Source: CBQB 1993 (Q2), Table 5 (rearranged).

Note 1: Central Bank Liquidity Support of £1,258m comprises repos (+£1,180m), secured advances (+£96m) and Short Term Facility (STF) drawings (-£18m).

Note 2: The reduction of £223m in licensed bank liquidity comprises a reduction of £222m in their mandatory deposits at the Central Bank, and a reduction of £1m in their "Other Deposits" at the Central Bank.

Note 3: Vault cash at banks increased by £7.4m so that their total primary liquid assets fell by £215.6m

Table 10 is a rearranged version of our earlier tables for the monetary base and bank liquidity (See Tables 6 and 7). Being an accounting identity, it does not directly admit behavioural conclusions, but it does provide some revealing insights into the sources of change in Irish bank liquidity in 1992. Foreign exchange market outflows reduced licensed bank liquidity by nearly £4bn. These were principally mediated by foreign currency swaps between the licensed banks and the Central Bank (at rates within the permitted ERM band) and reflect the strain on bank liquidity imposed by the currency crisis at the end of 1992. We have earlier noted that non-residents unloaded £1.8bn of Irish pound gilts and no doubt converted the Irish pound proceeds to foreign currency. These were "abnormal" capital outflows. The degree of strain on the foreign exchange market is masked in the balance of payments table by the recourse of Government to direct foreign borrowing and other non-market net foreign currency receipts. The Government provided a substantial net injection of domestic liquidity, almost £2.7bn, by writing (net) Irish pound cheques on its Central Bank account to fund its net domestic payments and buy-back of Irish pound gilts. This was insufficient to staunch the liquidity outflow through the balance of payments. The Central Bank provided additional gross liquidity support of £1.25bn to Irish banks, principally through the use of sale and repurchase agreements (repos). The Central Bank provided sufficient liquidity to staunch the liquidity outflow and limit it to £223m. This was sufficient to maintain bank liquidity at the reduced mandatory level which the Central Bank required of the licensed banks.

The underlying foreign exchange market drain on bank liquidity at end-1992 pressured domestic interest rates upwards. Interest rate parity implies that, given foreign interest rates, a newly expected devaluation will produce such an effect. When the remaining exchange controls *vis-à-vis* EU countries were dismantled on 1 January 1993 the pressure increased, and the Irish pound devalued by 10 per cent relative to sterling on 30 January 1993. This eliminated expectations of further currency depreciation, and bank liquidity and official external reserves improved dramatically in 1993. This was driven by external foreign exchange market flows. The government scarcely provided any liquidity in 1993 and the Central Bank absorbed over £2bn in market liquidity in 1993. (See *CBQB* 1994 (Q2), Table 2 and text for a fuller account).

This completes our brief introduction to the key money supply statistics and liquidity flow tables, which are provided by the Central Bank. The text and remaining tables in the Central Bank's *Quarterly Bulletins* can be read with comparative ease and profit and are highly recommended.

CHAPTER 23

ASPECTS OF DEMAND-SIDE AND SUPPLY-SIDE POLICIES IN IRELAND

Depending on the exchange rate régime, monetary and fiscal measures are the principal potential instruments of public policy in influencing aggregate demand in the short run. Ever since the creation of the State, Ireland has always maintained either fixed exchange rates or a managed floating exchange rate régime with its main trading partners. For these reasons, monetary policy measures have not been the principal instruments used in Ireland for the regulation of aggregate demand; rather, monetary measures have been targeted toward influencing the level of foreign exchange reserves and the exchange rate. Hence, fiscal policy — discretionary variation in public sector revenues and expenditures — has been the dominant mechanism through which the authorities have sought to regulate aggregate demand in the short run.

PUBLIC FINANCE IN IRELAND

The Public Sector

The public sector in Ireland consists of central government, local authorities and agencies or enterprises commonly called state-sponsored bodies.

State-sponsored bodies engage in three kinds of activity: they provide public utilities (as in the case of the ESB and Aer Lingus), they engage in manufacturing and trade, and they engage in other activities which it is felt are best conducted by the public sector; the brief of Forbairt (a division of what was formerly called the Industrial Development Authority — IDA) is an example. Some of them are financed entirely by central government; others are largely or entirely self-financing.

Local authorities (such as county councils) engage locally in activities such as construction of housing, construction and repair of subsidiary roads, provision of water and sewage facilities, rubbish disposal, and to some extent in provision of education and health services. Grants and loans from central government are among their sources of finance.

Central government provides social security, defence, and law and order. It also transfers large sums in grants to local authorities and state-sponsored bodies. Its expenditure is financed mainly by taxation and

[413]

borrowing, and through transfer payments from the European Union. Virtually all of the receipts of *central government* are paid into a fund called the *Exchequer* — the state money box. Also, almost all of the money required by central government to make payments is withdrawn from the Exchequer.

The Budget

The annual Budget is a statement of the government's expenditure programmes. Broken down into current and capital components, it also indicates how it is intended to finance those expenditures.

The *Current Budget* is concerned with central government current revenues and expenditures. Current revenues consist mainly of receipts from taxation. Current expenditures are outlays by central government on activities other than the creation of fixed capital assets. They consist largely of wage and salary payments to the civil service, the army and the police, and payments such as interest on money borrowed by central government and unemployment assistance. In Ireland the budget is said to be *balanced* if *current* revenue is equal to *current* expenditure; but note that this convention diverges from that of some other countries.

The *Capital Budget* is concerned with the entire public sector's expenditures on fixed assets and with the financing of such expenditures. What is called the Public Capital Programme accounts for almost the entire Capital Budget on the expenditure side. Much of expenditure under the Capital Budget is financed by Exchequer borrowing, and by transfer payments from the European Union. However, the Public Capital Programme also includes items financed from internal resources of state-sponsored bodies and through borrowing on the market by those bodies, as well as some capital expenditures financed by local authorities.

The details of public finance in Ireland can be exhaustive and of course they vary from year to year; for such details the reader is therefore referred to the budget documentation published each year and to public finance statistics in *National Income and Expenditure*, also published annually. (However, the reader who does wish to consult such references should note that the classification of categories in *National Income and Expenditure* is not in all cases directly comparable with that in the budget documentation.) Only a relatively small amount of detail will be provided here.

Tables 1 and 2 focus on the Current Budget out-turn for 1993 — the latest year for which data are available at time of writing.

Table 1 outlines the principal classes of central government current expenditure. Service of Public Debt refers mainly to interest on monies borrowed by central government. Other entries pertain to remuneration of public servants, or to expenditures on goods and services or in the form of transfer payments, by the respective government departments. Public services remuneration comprises the pay of civil servants, national and secondary school teachers, the defence forces, police, and the Exchequer contribution to the pay of health-board employees and vocational teachers.

Table 1: Central Government Current Expenditure, 1993, £m.

		% of total gross exp.
Service of Public Debt	2,390	(18.3)
Social Services		
Social Welfare, Health	5,666	(43.4)
Education	1,733	(13.2)
Economic Services		
Agriculture, Forestry, Fisheries	625	(4.8)
Industry, Labour, Tourism	350	(2.7)
Security, Infrastructure, Other	2,282	(17.6)
Gross Expenditure	13,046	(100.0)
Less Supply Service Receipts	2,527	
Net Current Expenditure	10,519	

Source: Budget 1994, Pn 457, Stationery Office, Dublin, 1994, p. 148.

Table 2: Central Government Current Receipts, 1993

	£m	% of total
Tax Revenue		
Income Taxes	3,791	36.0
Value-Added Tax	2,332	22.2
Customs and Excise Duties	1,916	18.2
Corporation Tax	952	9.1
Motor Vehicle Duties	238	2.3
Stamp Duties	227	2.2
Other Taxes	248	2.3
Total Tax Revenue	9,704	92.3
Non-Tax Revenue	436	4.1
Budget Deficit (financed by borrowing)	379	3.6
TOTAL RECEIPTS	10,519	100.0

Source: Budget 1994, p. 148.

Table 2 shows how the net expenditure in Table 1 was financed. More than one-third of central government current revenue is raised by *Income Taxes*. As in many other countries, the structure of the income tax code is such that higher rates of tax have been applicable to higher levels of taxable income. Note that social security revenues (from PRSI contributions) and expenditures are *not* included in the budget and are therefore *not* included in Tables 1 or 2. These are considered as "extra-budgetary" items. (However, in line with an earlier observation, they *are* included under government revenue and expenditure in *National Income and Expenditure*.)

Over 20 per cent of the government's current revenue comes from *Value-Added Tax*, which is levied at different rates on different categories of goods and services. The meaning of value-added taxes is simple. In the course of production and distribution, goods pass through several stages before reaching the consumer. At each stage value is added — it comprises the payments to factors of production in the form of wages, rent, interest and profit. This is the "value added" which is taxable under a value-added tax. Taxpayers arrive at their liability by first taking the full amount charged by them for taxable goods sold or taxable services rendered and applying the rate of value-added tax appropriate thereto. From the resultant sum they deduct the value-added tax already paid on goods and services they have bought. The difference is the tax payable to the Revenue Commissioners.

The third major category of tax receipts listed in Table 2 is that under *Customs and Excise*. Excise duties account for almost all of this revenue. Before Ireland joined the EC there was a wider variety of duties than at present imposed on imported goods. Although all had the effect of raising revenue, some had been introduced to protect industry from foreign competition; others were in place primarily to raise revenue. However, now that we are part of the EU, we have little control over the structure of our customs duties. That is because all Member States of the EU must maintain free trade between each other, while applying a Common External Tariff against countries outside the EU. Excise duties are raised on a small variety of goods: they are directed toward the "old reliables" — tobacco, alcoholic drinks and hydrocarbon oils, the principal reason being that such commodities tend to be price inelastic in demand.

The fourth principal category listed in Table 2, *Corporation Tax*, is levied on the profits of companies. *Non-Tax Revenue* in Table 2 consists mainly of the Surplus Income of the Central Bank and the Surplus Income of the National Lottery. These categories are akin to the distributed profits of a private company, with the Exchequer as sole shareholder. In the case of the Central Bank, interest from the Bank's holdings of foreign government securities (which are part of Ireland's foreign exchange reserves) has been the principal source of this income.

The Public Capital Programme

Table 3 provides a summary of the provisional out-turn of the Public Capital Programme in 1993. The first category listed, *sectoral economic investment*, was broken down as follows: Industry (£340m); Agriculture and Food (£137m); Tourism (£52m); Forestry and Fisheries (£51m). These figures include not only investment conducted directly by the public sector, but also loans to those sectors from the Industrial Credit Company and the Agricultural Credit Corporation — two state-sponsored banks — and outright grants through public sector bodies such as the IDA. The allocation within the category *productive infrastructure* was as follows: Roads and Sanitary Services (£433m); Energy (£355m); Telecommunications, RTE and Postal Service (£192m); Transport (£123m). Finally, the breakdown of public investment in *social infrastructure* was Housing (£190m); Government Construction (£85m); Education (£81m); Hospitals (£44m).

Table 3: Public Capital Programme, Provisional Out-turn 1993, £m

Sectoral Economic Investment	579
Productive Infrastructure	1,103
Social Infrastructure	402
TOTAL	2,084

Source: Budget 1994, p. 160.

A quick glance at the breakdown of the aggregates listed in Table 3 suggests that the construction industry is immediately and extensively affected by the level and the composition of the public capital programme. This inference is correct: in fact, in recent years close to two-thirds of the public capital programme has consisted of output from the construction industry. It follows that output and employment in the construction industry are particularly sensitive to changes in the level and composition of the public capital programme.

Public Sector Borrowing

When the Exchequer's current revenue falls short of its current expenditure, the resulting Current Budget deficit must be met by borrowing. It will be seen from Table 2 that in 1993 the Current Budget deficit came to £379 million. Although transfer payments from the EU for capital

purposes have become increasingly important in recent years, a significant proportion of Capital Budget expenditures must also be met by
borrowing. Not all of this is by the Exchequer. In 1993 the total Exchequer Borrowing Requirement (EBR) came to £690 million. Because
£379 million of this pertained to the Current Budget deficit, the remaining £311 million represents the contribution of borrowing by the
Exchequer in financing the Capital Budget. A further sum, £172 million,
was borrowed for capital purposes, from sources other than the
Exchequer, by state-sponsored bodies and by local authorities. Thus, in
1993, the Public Sector Borrowing Requirement (PSBR) came to £690m
+ £172m = £862m.

Table 4 provides some summary details of the extent of deficit financing in Ireland in 1976 and 1993. The EBR and the PSBR are two often-
cited indicators of the stance in fiscal policy — i.e. the extent to which
the levels of public sector revenue and expenditure are being used to
boost or curtail aggregate demand. Other measures of the contribution of
fiscal policy to aggregate demand have been proposed in the literature.
However, investigation of more sophisticated measures of fiscal stance is
left to a subsequent course in Economics. Nevertheless, Table 4 suggests
that relative to GNP, fiscal policy was more expansionary in 1976 than in
1993.

Table 4: Budget Details, 1976 and 1993, £m

		1976	1993
i	Current Budget Deficit	259	379
	(As % of GNP)	(4.4)	(1.4)
ii	Exchequer Borrowing for Capital Purposes	342	311
	(As % of GNP)	(6.6)	(1.1)
iii	**Exchequer Borrowing Requirement (i + ii)**	601	690
	(As % of GNP)	(11.0)	(2.5)
iv	Borrowing by State-sponsored Bodies and Local		
	Authorities	71	172
	(As % of GNP)	(1.9)	(0.6)
v	**Public Sector Borrowing Requirement (iii + iv)**	672	862
	(As % of GNP)	(12.9)	(3.1)

Source: *Budget 1994*, p. 125.

The years chosen for Table 5 are representative in showing trends in
deficit financing in Ireland since the mid-1970s.

Table 5: Deficit Financing as % of GNP

Year	Current Budget Deficit	EBR	PSBR
1976	4.4	11.0	12.9
1982	7.9	15.6	19.8
1988	1.6	3.1	3.8
1994	0.9	2.7	3.4

Source: Budget 1994, p. 125.
Note: The entries for 1994 are those projected early in that year in the
    1994 Budget documents.

In Ireland what is officially called the *National Debt* represents the total debt of the Exchequer outstanding on monies which it has borrowed from all sources over the years, both in Ireland and abroad. Thus, as officially defined in this country, the National Debt does *not* include that part of the debt of state-sponsored bodies or of local authorities which is owed by them to sources other than the Exchequer. (The debt of state-sponsored bodies and local authorities reflecting loans to them from the Exchequer is indirectly reflected in the official National Debt, because the Exchequer generally has had to borrow in order to lend to them.) It should be clear, when account is taken of the debt of state-sponsored bodies and local authorities other than that due to the Exchequer, that the total public sector debt is in excess of what is officially termed the National Debt.

In effect, the National Debt represents the sum of all past Current Budget deficits plus the sum of all past Exchequer borrowings to finance capital expenditure, less all repayments of such indebtedness by the Exchequer. Substantial sums in interest payments must be made each year in servicing this debt.

The National Debt has risen rapidly in recent decades, reflecting both extensive borrowing by the Exchequer to finance capital programmes and Current Budget deficits since the 1970s. As a percentage of GNP, the Debt increased from about 60 per cent in the early 1970s to over 100 per cent in the 1980s. By international standards among developed economies, these debt ratios are very high. Corresponding to the rapid rise in the Debt, both in absolute terms and as a percentage of GNP, there has been a substantial increase in the cost of servicing the Debt — in paying interest to holders of the Debt and in making provision for repayment. The cost of servicing the National Debt is a charge on the Current Budget.

The bulk of these charges consist of interest payments. From Table 6 it can be seen that these charges came to over 90 per cent and to about 65 per cent of receipts from Income Tax in 1985 and 1994, respectively.

Table 6: Service of Ireland's National Debt, 1977–94

Year	Service Charge (£m)	As a % of Income Tax
1977	334	64
1980	661	65
1985	1,967	93.5
1990	2,300	76
1994	2,229	59

Source: *Budget 1994*, p. 126. Entries for 1994 are provisional.

The Exchequer borrows from a large variety of sources in Ireland, including the Central Bank, commercial banks, other financial institutions and the public. One consequence of the high levels of the EBR in recent decades is that the government has not been able to raise all the money at home and it has therefore had to borrow abroad. In consequence, the proportion of Ireland's National Debt held by foreigners has increased since the 1970s and has averaged around 40 per cent in the period 1980–93.

The servicing of the Debt not only involves the stream of service charges on the Current Budget but may also involve friction in the economy associated with raising taxes and redistribution of income in the community. Increased taxation, needed to finance Debt service charges, may lead to some loss of real output because of its *disincentive effects* on economic activity, even though the redistribution of income from taxpayers to recipients of interest is a domestic transfer payment insofar as that part of the Debt which is held in Ireland is concerned. Thus, in a closed economy, a high Debt/GNP ratio would presumably impose a "burden" on economic activity because the high taxation which it would entail, in order to generate transfer payments (in the form of interest) to Debt-holders, would presumably have an adverse effect on work incentives. However, in referring to the "burden" of the National Debt in an open economy, it is crucial to distinguish between externally held Debt and that which is held by domestic residents. The key point is that externally held Debt entails direct loss of real resources, because payment of interest abroad is made in foreign exchange, and in the long run that foreign exchange is obtained by exporting more or importing less. Thus, the liability of having to pay interest abroad involves loss of potential consumption in Ireland, even at given levels of output.

In view of the fact that a high National Debt may have implications of the forms just discussed, the reader may be wondering why Ireland's National Debt was accumulated in the first place. The principal reasons are twofold:

(1) A high proportion of the Public Capital Programme has been financed by borrowing (and, in recent years, by capital transfers from the EU) rather than from current revenue. One rationale for this deficit financing has been that much of the expenditure under the Public Capital Programme is on the creation of assets which provide flows of goods and services over time. In principle such increased production should, directly or indirectly, create the means by which the Exchequer can repay the debt incurred in creating the assets in question.

(2) Until the early 1970s, Irish governments sought to balance the Current Budget. If a deficit appeared in the out-turn, this was unplanned, reflecting underestimation of expenditure or overestimation of revenue. In 1972, for the first time, the government budgeted for a Current Budget deficit. The objective was to stimulate the level of aggregate demand. The departure in 1972 from the tradition of balancing the Current Budget was maintained over many subsequent years: government sought to boost aggregate demand by planning Current Budget deficits. Hence the National Debt increased much more rapidly in the 1970s than would otherwise have been the case. However, the resulting increase in Debt service charges brought difficulties in public finance, had adverse effects on work incentives, and therefore had adverse effects on aggregate supply and output for several years after the apparently "expansionary" demand-side policies were implemented. As will be shown in the section which immediately follows, the governments' new-found obsession with stimulating aggregate demand in the 1970s, and their failures to recognise what was happening to the supply-side of the economy, led to policies which were fundamentally misconceived.

MISMANAGEMENT THROUGH AGGREGATE DEMAND
Ideas and Institutions

Outside Ireland, demand management policies — sometimes perhaps misleadingly called *Keynesian* policies because they embodied *some* of the ideas of the great economist J.M. Keynes who had died in 1946 — designed to steer the economy along a stable full employment growth path, were at the peak of academic and political popularity in the 1950s and 1960s. In those decades, the prevailing textbook models typically assumed a closed economy (or added openness as a fairly minor afterthought) and largely ignored the incentives of firms to produce, and

hence aggregate supply. Popular textbook expositions of macroeconomics often seemed to assume that firms did not care about profits
(or that aggregate supply was infinitely elastic), a topic which in any case
was considered as belonging to what some regarded as the quite distinct
discipline of microeconomic theory. Lectures adapting the approach of
such textbooks began to be offered in the Republic's universities in the
middle and late 1960s. And with a lag — as time enabled such thinking
to filter through to the top of the Civil Service — Irish governments in
the early 1970s began to implement demand management policies,
largely based on the aforementioned thinking,. Given what has just been
stated, it is not surprising that the policies were quite inappropriate.

As was emphasised by the formal models of just a few economists (in
particular, Milton Friedman and William Baumol in the US) in the 1950s
and very early 1960s, apparently sensible demand management policies
may make economic prospects worse rather than better. The main problems which concerned such economists (who tended to analyse an
economy as a dynamical stochastic system, as distinct from the conventional approach — comparative static equilibrium analysis of deterministic systems) pertained to the lags of *recognition, decision, implementation and effect* surrounding discretionary demand management policy.
(For example, partly because of delays in the availability of economic
statistics, policy-makers tend to recognise a macroeconomic problem
only some time after it has arisen. By the time that any ensuing discretionary policy takes effect, the problem may have automatically disappeared. In that case, discretionary policy could *amplify* economic instability.) These problems were accentuated in the open economy of
Ireland in the early 1970s because, questions of dynamics aside, a fundamentally wrong basic model was being used to formulate and guide
policy — a model more appropriate to a relatively closed economy with a
great deal of excess capacity.

By the time that single-minded focus on demand management was at
its peak in Irish policy circles — in the middle and late 1970s — a
number of younger and mainly academic economists had begun to argue
that Ireland was in fact an open rather than a closed economy, that
supply-side incentives did matter, that the economy should be modelled
as such, and that policy-makers should incorporate such a model in their
approach to policy formation. For a while the arguments of these economists were neglected, but ultimately their ideas did filter through to
policy circles, gradually in the late 1970s and more completely in the
1980s. These observations should remind us of the famous passage from
J.M. Keynes about the ultimate power of ideas, quoted at the end of
Chapter 1 of this book. They also emphasise the dangers of inflexible

"tunnel-visioned" views of the world, and of the economic system in particular.

Although perhaps oversimplifications in some respects, and in full awareness that dead men cannot reply while old men may be too serene to do so, the main points to be inferred from the foregoing are as follows:

(1) Formal training in macroeconomics in Ireland lagged behind that in other developed countries. This may have reflected the more relaxed environment which prevailed in our universities, as elsewhere in Ireland, up to the mid-1960s.

(2) When, in the late 1960s, formally-structured macroeconomics did become a subject of university lectures in Ireland, the assumptions made were typically more appropriate for the underemployed, more closed economies of the 1930s. Thus, the overwhelming focus was on aggregate demand as a policy variable.

(3) The ideas in (2) filtered through to the minds of policy-makers in Ireland in the early 1970s. But they applied such (for Ireland, mis-specified) ideas in regard to aggregate demand with the over-enthusiasm of novices and discounted the role of openness and supply-side incentives.

(4) Some academic economists in Ireland did begin to emphasise the importance of openness and the supply side by the mid-1970s, but they were young people and their expositions were at first disregarded. However, with the usual (but by then shortening) time lags as the quality of the Civil Service and other advisory bodies improved, policy in the 1980s gradually evolved to the macroeconomic implications of openness and began to consider supply-side issues more explicitly.

Policy Responses to Supply-side Shocks

Consider now the context of the demand-side policies of the 1970s, some consequences of which still impinge on the economy in the early 1990s. In Ireland, 1972 was the first year in which an Irish government delibe-rately planned a Current Budget deficit in order to shift the aggregate demand curve to the right. By the standards of subsequent years, the deficit was insignificant. But the *timing* of the switch to more explicit interventionist demand management policies turned out to be very un-fortunate. In fact, two kinds of boost caused the aggregate demand curve to shift rightwards in 1972/3: fiscal policy through planned deficit finan-cing of part of the Current Budget *and* an unexpected upswing in the world economy (a matter which is entirely beyond the control of a small open economy). Thus, the fiscal injections inadvertently added to pressure on capacity. (In this context, recall the warnings in regard to pitfalls in counter-cyclical policy due to the various kinds of lags mentioned earlier.)

But much worse was to follow: In 1973–4, also due to factors entirely beyond Ireland's control, we experienced sharp supply-side shocks in the form of very adverse movements in the terms of trade (a collapse in our export/import price ratio) because of unprecedented increases in the price of imported energy, upon which we were — and are — heavily dependent. (In 1973–4, the Organisation of Petroleum Exporting Countries, OPEC, acted as a cartel in setting quotas on oil production and in generating an unprecedented increase in world oil prices.)

Given the new-found obsession with aggregate demand at policy levels, the macroeconomic implications of the terms of trade shocks were not understood. One suspects that they still are not widely understood in Ireland. Because it is probable that Ireland will experience further swings in its terms of trade in the decades ahead, and because some of the policy problems of the 1980s and 1990s in part reflect unfavourable inheritances from the policies of the 1970s, some examination of the mismanagement of the mid-1970s is worthwhile.

The core of the problem can be illustrated both arithmetically and graphically. Consider first an arithmetic illustration in which we will resort to extremes in order to highlight the central issues. Consider a hypothetical small open economy (SOE) which produces 100 units of a single commodity (and nothing else), say beef, the entire output of which is exported in exchange for, say, 100 units of oil, which is the only product which it consumes. Let the initial terms of trade index (export/import price ratio index) be 1. Next, suppose that import prices suddenly double, due, say, to the actions of an OPEC-type organisation abroad. The terms of trade index has fallen to 1/2, and the SOE now gets (and can consume) only 50 units of oil for the 100 units of beef which it produces. In the absence of (a) a doubling of the rate of domestic production or (b) annual foreign borrowing by the SOE (or annual decumulation of assets held abroad by the SOE) equal in amount to the initial level of domestic production or (c) specific combinations of (a) and (b), living standards in the SOE must fall.

This was the kind of policy problem faced by Ireland following the 1973–4 oil crisis. In its concentration on aggregate demand, the government failed to focus seriously on supply-side measures in order to induce increased output. Although some politicians called for wage restraint and "belt-tightening" (often phrased confusingly and wrongly, as though such restraints would cure an *externally determined* inflation, rather than directly reducing unemployment through a shift to the right of the aggregate supply curve), it was decided to maintain living standards by borrowing abroad. Fiscal deficits, designed to neutralise the supply-side shocks, were themselves financed abroad. For several years, competition for votes by the political parties postponed supply-side action in order to redress what had been a supply-side shock; hence the deterioration in the public finances implicit in Table 5 above. The Irish public was not sufficiently aware of the inevitable consequences, and the inevitability of the enforced fiscal contractions of the 1980s and into the 1990s was largely ignored. Some competent economists did warn of the consequences — increased taxation and reduced consumption in the future in order to pay for the debts myopically being incurred. But too few wanted to understand and too few were encouraged to listen. In fact, some politicians dismissed the warnings and the criticisms. Therein lies much of the genesis of the fiscal crises in Ireland in the 1980s and carried forward into the 1990s. It seems to have been a combination of the ultimate power of ideas (recall the passage in Keynes to which reference has already been made), as well as blatant necessity, which led Ireland's political leaders ultimately to relax their emphasis on aggregate demand and to assign more recognition to supply-side measures.

Much of the foregoing can be illustrated using the AS/AD framework introduced in Chapter 14. Recall the AS function, $AS = AS(P, P^{MRM}, W, T)$ and recall the meaning of the independent variables and the signs of the derivatives. Point E in Figure 1 represents macroeconomic equilibrium in 1973 just before the oil crisis. The terms of trade shock — the rise of P^{MRM} in the AS function — shifted AS to the left, to AS'; thus it was inflationary in pushing prices up but deflationary in pushing output and employment down, to, say, the levels represented by point F in 1974. The responses of the prevailing and subsequent governments were to increase aggregate demand, using deficit financing. Thus, new equilibria, like that at point G in Figure 1, were attained for years in the middle and later seventies. It should be clear from the diagram that it was unlikely that demand-side policies could quickly get the economy back to the level of output which prevailed at E or to the right of E. In the meantime debts were being persistently incurred to sustain the level of aggregate demand. It was inevitable that the longer this situation was allowed to continue, the more would the need to pay interest (and principal) have further adverse effects on aggregate supply: the corresponding ultimate increases in the tax burden tended in themselves to cause further shifts to the left of the aggregate supply curve, through their effects on the incentives to work (at least in fully legal forms) and through their effects on (after-tax) real wage bargaining, and therefore on costs.

It should be fairly clear from Figure 1 that what was needed after

1973–4 was a portfolio of policies to shift the AS' curve continuously to the right. This could have included wage restraint in the short run, possibly through legal enforcement but preferably through education in regard to the central macroeconomic implications of a major change in the terms of trade. Such an approach could have been supplemented in the medium term by policies designed to maximise the pace of technical change — to increase T in the AS function in the general sense discussed in Chapter 14. In the out-turn, the Irish people were forced to incur years of retribution for the myopic macroeconomic policies which were implemented on their behalf in the 1970s and into the early 1980s.

Figure 1

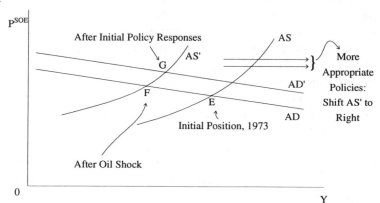

Figure 2

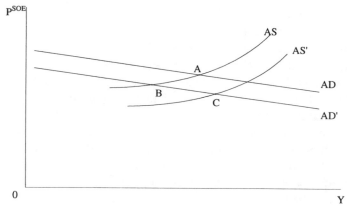

The Irish economy was adversely affected by a further discrete shock in the price of imported energy — an immediate terms-of-trade deterioration — in 1979–80. As the reader should recognise by now, in itself this operated in such a manner as to shift the aggregate supply curve to the left, thereby tending to contract output and to increase unemployment. In turn, the rising level of unemployment payments (the rising level of "dole" payments) was one factor in increasing the EBR and the PSBR. (Thus, changes in the EBR and the PSBR can be very misleading measures of the stance in fiscal policy: to an extent, they are *effects* of the level of economic activity.) As was indicated in Table 6 above, the cost of servicing Ireland's National Debt absorbed almost all of the government's revenue from Income Tax by 1985. Close to one half of the payments in interest where to foreigners. Hence, the Irish authorities were *forced* to face a crisis in the public finances in the 1980s and into the early 1990s. At first they sought to do so — without much success — by increasing taxation; in the later 1980s the emphasis shifted to cutbacks in public expenditures.

As is suggested by the entries for the EBR and the PSBR in Table 5, the later 1980s and early 1990s can be characterised as a period of enforced fiscal contraction. If aggregate demand were all that mattered, one would therefore expect that output would have been falling over those years. In fact, although unemployment remained very high, the Irish economy experienced unusually fast rates of growth in the final few years of the 1980s. Although this experience has surprised some observers, it should not be at all surprising when aggregate supply is brought into the picture. Apart from investigation of the demand side, and along the lines suggested in Chapter 14, a comprehensive analysis of Ireland's growth experience in the late 1980s would examine the key supply-side variables — real wages as perceived by employers, the terms of international trade, and technical change broadly defined. Here it is merely noted that following the adverse terms-of-trade movement in 1979–80, Ireland's terms of trade became progressively more favourable in the 1980s and in the years 1986 to 1989 in particular. (With the terms-of-trade index equal to 100 in 1980, the index had risen to 110 by 1989.) Thus, as illustrated in Figure 2, the effect of demand contraction through fiscal policy — a shift of the aggregate demand curve from AD to AD' — is to move the economy from point A to point B; however, a significant improvement like that experienced in the terms of trade — illustrated by a shift of the aggregate supply curve from AS to AS' — could cause the economy to move from point B to point C in the diagram. As drawn in Figure 2, point C lies to the right of point B: the net effect is an expansion of output. (However, as an explanation of Ireland's experience in the late 1980s, the above exposition is incomplete, not least because it ignores other supply-side variables — the real wage as perceived by employers and employees, and the pace of technical change, broadly defined.)

There is plenty of evidence to suggest that at policy-making levels and elsewhere, *the macroeconomic implications of terms-of-trade changes are not adequately recognised* in Ireland's extremely exposed economy. But for an economy like Ireland, where the sum of exports and imports comes to almost 140 per cent of net domestic product at factor cost, the issues are important. It is easy for policy-makers to allow living standards to improve when the aggregate supply curve shifts to the right because of favourable terms-of-trade movements. Indeed, the potential gains in output and employment may be nullified in such circumstances if there is also a weakening in resistance to nominal wage demands. (In that case, reduction in one kind of cost relative to output price would be offset by the other type of cost.) But because of contracts, or due to other forms of ratchet, to political ineptitude, etc., it may prove difficult to depress living standards (through real wage reductions) when the terms of trade move adversely. If that is the case, supply-side measures aimed at improving productivity will be all the more important. Indeed, for any given terms of trade ratio, it is *only* through steady increases in productivity that we can expect to experience steady and simultaneous increases in employment *and* in living standards.

ON NATIONAL WAGE AGREEMENTS, AGGREGATE SUPPLY AND EXCHANGE RATES

It has not always been the case in Ireland that wage rates have been outcomes of bargaining under free competition, or of collective bargaining between individual employers and employees alone — though the latter arrangements did tend to apply through most of the decades immediately preceding the mid-1960s. A National Wage Agreement was made in 1964, and from time to time this was followed by further centralised Agreements until the end of the 1970s. Centralised bargaining through National Wage Agreements was abandoned for most of the 1980s. A key feature of such agreements — tripartite between government, employers' organisations and bodies representing the trade unions — was the establishment of agreed norms for wage increases of different categories of workers, applicable over a specified period (typically two or three years) from the date of an Agreement.

Ireland returned to centralised wage agreements in 1987. These (three to date) have been embodied in documents entitled the *Programme for National Recovery* 1987–1990, the *Programme for Economic and Social Progress* 1991–1993 (*PESP*) and the *Programme for Competitiveness and Work*, January 1994 to June 1997 (*PCW*). That these documents embodied social as well as economic objectives will be ignored in what follows.

The present section, which summarises and updates a paper delivered by the author (Small Firms Association Annual Conference at Kinsale) in November 1993, focuses on only some of the macroeconomic implications of the kinds of National Wage Agreements which we have had in Ireland in recent years. Key points are that centralised wage agreements can be crucial in affecting aggregate supply, and hence the level of employment; that (in the national interest) sensible agreements must be flexible rather than predetermined and *must be linked to exchange-rate developments*; and that recent agreements — in particular the PCW in force at the time of writing (summer 1994) — have involved an element of *gambling* with the level of national output and employment.

The points just mentioned suggest that at this stage the reader should be reminded of some facts in regard to the external environment of the Irish economy:

(1) As a rough approximation, one third (a gradually shrinking share) of Ireland's external trade is with the UK; a third is with the rest of the EU; the remaining third is with the rest of the world.

(2) In regard to exchange-rate arrangements, throughout the 1980s Ireland operated on a quasi-fixed exchange rate régime *vis-à-vis* most of the EU countries. This was reflected in Ireland's participation in the Exchange Rate Mechanism (ERM) of the European Monetary System (EMS). The *numeraire* currency unit of the ERM is the European Currency Unit (ECU), which is a weighted average of the national EU currency units (including the pound sterling); thus, as the ERM operated in the 1980s, participating countries sought to maintain fixed central rates between their national currency unit and the ECU, and hence approximately fixed exchange rates with each other. Most countries outside the EU floated against the ECU. Note that although sterling was one of the currencies which had (and still has) a weight in the composition of the ECU, the UK authorities did not participate in the ERM. Instead, the UK authorities operated on a broadly managed floating exchange rate régime between sterling and the ECU. Indirectly, this meant that the Irish pound passively participated in a managed float against the pound sterling (with most of the management being conducted by the UK authorities).

(3) The ERM was fundamentally altered in the late summer of 1993, when the participating countries in effect agreed to operate on a managed float of their currencies against each other. Under this revised ERM, the

participating countries agreed to maintain their currencies within a band of plus or minus 15 per cent of a fixed central rate between a country's national currency unit and the ECU (instead of within a very narrow band of plus or minus 2.25 per cent around a central rate as had previously been the norm). As in the 1980s, sterling stayed outside the new ERM arrangements. Thus, under the present arrangements, it would be possible that the Irish pound could appreciate substantially against sterling, while simultaneously experiencing a significant depreciation against the most important currency in the ERM, the German Mark. If this were to happen, among the consequences would be downward pressure on the Irish pound prices of goods traded with the UK, and upward pressure on the Irish pound prices of goods traded with Germany. If wage rates stayed constant, Ireland would therefore tend to lose in competitiveness against the UK, but we would tend to gain in competitiveness against Germany. This observation underlines the *importance of wage flexibility*, not only upward but also in a downward direction.

In most of the contexts which follow in the present section, references to "the" wage will pertain to the cost of hiring labour as seen by the employer; hence, "the" wage equals employee remuneration including taxes on employment creation through employer's contribution to social insurance, less any employment subsidy (as under the Market Development Fund mentioned later) received by the employer. In the light of the recent and present economic environments, as a strategic contingency against possible external developments, and given what appear to be the objectives of Irish economic policy, we will be arguing that National Agreements which set wage norms for a few years in advance *may* be sensible, provided that such agreements satisfy certain criteria: in particular, only if the agreements provide for *rules* for wage revision during the duration of an Agreement or a satisfactory *institutional framework for revision* of any wage norms which may be provisionally agreed. Thus, the rigid framework of the PESP and the subsequent PCW is inappropriate given Ireland's external environment: they lacked the kind of built-in flexibility discussed below. Such flexibility should be a necessary rather than a sufficient characteristic of National Agreements; otherwise the author would feel inclined to recommend their abandonment.

A few more preliminary remarks are desirable before advancing this argument.

Preliminary Remarks

Define the trade-weighted exchange rate, e, as the price of a "unit" of foreign currency; it is the number of Irish pounds which must be paid for a unit (a mix) of foreign currencies, where the weights applicable in the definition of that "unit" reflect the structure of Ireland's trade. Then, subject to qualifications which are unimportant for present purposes, and as an approximation,

$$(**) \ P \cong eP^F$$

where $\cong$ denotes "approximately equal to", P is an index of the Irish price level (measured at factor cost), e is the trade-weighted exchange rate and P^F is an appropriate index of the price level abroad. Brushing aside fairly minor issues of controversy, the main points to note, because of openness and smallness of the Irish economy, are that:

(1) For any given P^F and e, Ireland's price level is largely determined by forces beyond our control.

(2). A devaluation/depreciation of the Irish pound means a rise in e, and hence a rise in the Irish price level.

(3). An appreciation or "strengthening" of the Irish pound (implying a depreciation or "weakening" of foreign currency) — a reduction of e — does the opposite: it imposes downward pressure on the Irish price level, for any given level of foreign prices.

Competitiveness does not depend on output prices alone or on input prices alone. Rather, it depends on the *relationship* between output prices, input prices and productivity. In Ireland, excluding the agricultural sector, employee remuneration (the "wage" bill) comes to over 70 per cent of *domestic* production costs. The (indirect-tax-exclusive) price of output can be decomposed into the following components: (a) wage costs to employers; (b) other domestic cost items — interest, rent etc.; (c) non-domestic costs reflecting the prices of imported inputs; (d) *as a residual*, profits, which would be negative — i.e. losses would apply — if a + b + c exceed price, p.

Because employee remuneration forms the bulk of domestic production costs, we will take "the" wage rate as a proxy for domestic production costs, and we will take the terms of international trade (which are beyond our control) as constant. Given P^F and e it follows, at given levels of productivity, that a rise in the wage rate *must* cause profits to fall — it *must* cause a loss in competitiveness and hence it *must* cause a reduction in employment. Furthermore, dropping the assumption that P^F and e are fixed, it is easy to see that there is only *one* way in which *real* wages can steadily increase over time while employment *also* increases — and that is when the rate of increase in real wages is no greater than the rate of productivity growth.

Consider now three possible scenarios for wage negotiation.

Scenario I: Free Competition

Scenario I would involve enforcement of a framework like that of perfect competition in the labour market, and would leave wage determination to the free forces of supply and demand alone; thus, the price of labour services would be determined like, say, the price of carrots. This would involve removing "imperfections" from both sides of the labour market: both labour unions and employers' unions would have to go — and so too would the dole. This scenario would ensure a situation close to full employment (at least relative to the present situation): if the supply of labour exceeded labour demand, competition would bid the wage rate down (thereby reducing the amount of labour offering its services, while also operating on employers' incentives and increasing the amount of labour services demanded by them) until the demand for labour matched the supply of labour (i.e. those seeking work). Under this institutional framework, neither the price of output nor the choice of exchange rate would be of much relevance to the outcome — employment for all of those willing and able to work at the ensuing competitively-determined wage structure. Those who were not willing to work under the institutional framework specified would either emigrate to avail of the higher wage (or dole) rates elsewhere, or they would be deemed to be in *voluntary* unemployment.

Although the extreme scenario just sketched is unacceptable in a social democracy like ours, it merits attention because it highlights some of the implications of our present institutional framework. For example, the level of dole would impose a floor on wage determination even in an otherwise competitive labour market. Because it reduces the *demand* for labour (by creating a floor on the wages of the lowest paid) it causes unemployment. But the dole also increases the *supply* of labour: some of those at present in receipt of dole would not be in the Irish labour force if the dole were abolished. Thus, by reducing labour demand and by increasing its supply, government action increases unemployment through the system of dole payments. Note that if one were to go further and considered the *financing* of the dole system (including the taxation of employers on the employment they do provide) one would find a *further* mechanism through which the dole causes unemployment. Scenario I also highlights some implications of wage rigidities due to collective bargaining.

Scenario II: Decentralised Bargaining

In the social democracy in which we have chosen to live, there are of course "imperfections" on both sides of the labour market, on top of the system of dole payments. Subject to those constraints, wage determination could be left to fairly decentralised bargaining, as in Ireland in the earlier years of the 1980s. From the standpoint of minimising unemployment, this might be the best attainable, but it would be sensible to strive for a superior alternative — see Scenario III below. The main problem under Scenario II is that (unlike those which would apply under Scenario I) competitiveness, and hence the employment/unemployment outcomes, *would* depend on exchange rates and hence on the price level. Scenario II (decentralised bargaining) would probably lead to *wage contracts* for periods of one to three years into the future. Even if such contracts provided for no change in present wage rates — and suppose for purposes of argument that this would be the case — they would constitute a gamble which (in terms of employment growth/unemployment reduction) *might or might not pay off*. For example, suppose that the currency of the UK — the country with which we conduct one third of our trade — were to depreciate substantially during the next three years. With low inflation in other EU countries, this would impose *downward pressure on the Irish price level*; in particular, the prices of those goods dependent on UK markets, or on competition from the UK, would tend to fall. With wage rates rigid by contract, reduction in prices would mean loss in competitiveness and contraction in output and employment. Of course the opposite could happen (i.e. sterling could appreciate). The main point is that opting for rigid wage contracts not linked to exchange rate developments would be tantamount to having our hands tied and taking a gamble that exchange rate developments might or might not be conducive to output and employment creation in Ireland.

Scenario III: A Particular Form of Centralised Solution

A centralised wage agreement — a National Agreement — would be attractive *only* to the extent to which it is likely to yield a set of solutions superior to the effective "market" solution (decentralised bargaining like that discussed under Scenario II). Given Ireland's present exchange rate arrangements, to be superior it would have to be *flexible* — wage rates would have to be flexible downward if exchange rate developments imposed downward pressure on prices. This implies that the Agreement would have to be linked to exchange rate developments. For example, suppose for sake of argument that Ireland continues to maintain a fixed central rate between the Irish pound and the ECU, subject to a margin of plus or minus 15 per cent around the ECU central rate. Because both sterling and the German Mark are components of the ECU, even keeping our currency exactly at the ECU central rate could be consistent with a substantial general depreciation of sterling combined with a significant general appreciation of the Mark. Under such circumstances, the Irish pound prices of Irish produced goods dependent on the UK, as well as of Irish goods which compete with imports from the UK in the Irish market, would tend to fall; on the other hand, those traded with Germany would tend to rise in price. Note that for Ireland, the UK is a far more important market than Germany. If wages were rigid because of (centralised or decentralised) contracts, the net effect would be an increase in structural and cost-constrained unemployment in Ireland. Under the present exchange rate arrangements, it therefore seems that any sensible National Agreement must provide for rules linking wage adjustments to any significant changes in relevant exchange rates; in this way it could provide an improvement on the decentralised solution (Scenario II). Alternatively, if explicit rules cannot be devised in advance to ensure wage flexibility, an acceptable National Agreement must provide for frequent monitoring and revision of any initial contingent agreement in the face of changes in exchange rate relativities. These characteristics were absent from the three Agreements in Ireland since 1987. In the absence of flexibility along the lines suggested, and given the volatility of key exchange rates, the case in favour of National Wage Agreements is very dubious.

On the Wage/Price Crisis, late 1992

The desirability of having rules for wage revision under a centralised wage agreement such as the PESP (or the PCW which followed it in 1994) was underlined by developments in the autumn and winter of 1992. The key problem which emerged for many Irish producers was that some prices became too low relative to wage contracts under the PESP: *the wage/price ratio of such firms had fallen.* Depreciation of sterling late in 1992 meant that at unchanged prices denominated in sterling, Irish exports to the UK fetched a lower price denominated in Irish pounds; similarly, competing imports from the UK became cheaper in terms of Irish pounds. A solution to this loss in competitiveness had to involve *either* a rise in prices (obtainable through devaluation) *or* a reduction in the effective wage paid by the employer *or* a sufficient rise in productivity: only then could real profit margins, and competitiveness, have been restored. Operations on the productivity front were not feasible in the short run; thus, the resolution had to involve *either* wage reductions (with wages as defined from the viewpoint of those who hire labour) *or* devaluation (or both). Hence, at least at the early stages of the crisis, devaluation of the Irish pound within the ERM was not inevitable: wage revision was an alternative option.

It is worthwhile to consider in some detail what happened, because it highlights the shortcomings of the PESP in regard to flexible rules. Following an initial depreciation of sterling in the second half of September 1992, the Irish government did respond, outside the PESP, on the issue of wage rates (as perceived by the employer) through a programme called the Market Development Fund. This provided for up to £50 million in wage subsidies, payable between October 1992 and March 1993, to firms adversely affected by exchange rate changes. Up to 800 firms availed of such wage subsidies, which were temporary only. The so-called currency crisis — it was a wage/price crisis — oscillated on a generally accelerating trend through November and December 1992. There were calls for a devaluation of the Irish pound within the ERM, expressed in such a manner as to suggest that devaluation was the only option; *this of course distracted attention away from the option of wage revision.* Spokespersons for the trade union movement firmly opposed the devaluation option. Although their motives are unknown to this author, the logic of their stance seemed to suggest that they might be willing to renegotiate some of the agreed agenda on the wages front. However, no automatic rules for wage readjustment had been specified under the PESP, and between 5 November 1992 (when the Dáil was dissolved) and 12 January 1993 (when a new government was formed) there was *in effect* no government (in the absence of rules already agreed) with whom or through whom the unions could negotiate wage flexibility. A small team from the International Monetary Fund came to Ireland (not on a mere courtesy visit) around the end of November 1992. It was of the firm conviction that wage flexibility rather than devaluation was the appropriate policy stance, if that were possible. However, for several weeks the nominal government of Ireland was more concerned with inter-party dialogue than with attempting to deal jointly with the trade unions and employers.

The logic of the stance of the trade unions highlighted the need for wage revision when the new government was formed early in January 1993. However, by that time the calls for devaluation were reaching a crescendo, and even if its advisors did understand the importance of wage flexibility, the new government seems to have been distracted away from action on the wages front. It is therefore not surprising that the expectations of speculators became self-fulfilling prophesies at the end of that month, when the Irish pound was devalued within the ERM. However, it would seem that the new government failed to learn much from the wage/price crisis: within a year it had negotiated a further National Wage Agreement under the PCW, which set norms for wage increases up to June 1997, *independent of whatever might happen to relative exchange rates.* As has been warned above, this is a *gamble* with output and employment which might be successful in the out-turn, but in failing to provide for wage flexibility linked to possible exchange rate developments, it may reflect a lingering lack of appreciation, at policy-formation levels, of the paramount importance of supply-side issues in a small open economy.

NON-TRADED SERVICES ARE IMPORTANT FOR COMPETITIVENESS

The present chapter has dealt in some detail with the variables P, P^{MRM} and W in the aggregate supply function, and on the ratios between some of these variables. The remaining variable T in the aggregate supply function first introduced in Chapter 14 denotes technology, very loosely defined: it represents all of those things which determine the *potential* output of the economy. Thus, a technical improvement, represented by a shift to the right in the asymptote of the AS curve, could take the form of an increase in the capital stock of the economy (and recall that new capital equipment usually embodies designs which are superior to those of old equipment, implying that fixed investment is a mechanism through which technical innovation is transmitted to the economy); an improvement in "the state of the industrial arts" even if the capital stock is constant in amount; or simply greater efficiency in the use of existing inputs.

The importance of productivity growth was emphasised in Chapter 14, and subsequently. It was also observed that abolition of restrictive practices — by employers as well as employees — was one means of generating productivity growth. Defensive strategies by workers in individual industries attempting to prevent the implementation of technical change in the narrow sense, and restrictive practices by owners/employees/professions, are likely to impede growth in output and employment in the long run. Indeed, it is precisely those economies which have maximised the pace of technical change, and where competition (possibly backed by legal enforcement) has swept aside restrictive practices, that have increased their shares of world markets and grown the fastest.

Some aspects of the importance of productivity growth in agriculture and manufacturing industry, the two principal (internationally) traded sectors of our open economy, have long been recognised in the implementation of Irish economic policy. (Partly for reasons of space, such policies are not surveyed in this text. However, the reader may consult the more descriptive literature on the National Economics of Ireland, including the many relevant official publications.) But what about the services sectors, the output of which is mainly non-traded internationally, but which now accounts for the bulk of employment in Ireland?

In Ireland, sectoral employment shares are approximately as follows: Agriculture (including Forestry and Fishing), 16 per cent; Industry, 24 per cent; Services, 60 per cent. The Services category can be decomposed into Marketed Services and Non-marketed Services (such as Public Administration and Defence, etc.). Marketed Services account for about 40 per cent of all employment in the state. Thus, the marketed services sector is the most important source of employment in Ireland, and its share in the total has been rising over time. Figure 3 provides a summary of the general international experience on the relationship between sectoral employment shares and per capita income. Note that based on the general international experience, shrinkage of the industrial sector's share in employment — often regarded as a symptom of economic decay — is quite normal rather than exceptional as an economy matures.

Figure 3: The General International Experience

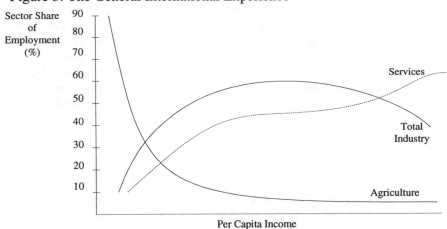

Per Capita Income

Input–output studies consider intersectoral flows between the producing sectors of an economy, as well as flows from the producing sectors into final demand. Such studies indicate that in Ireland since around 1975, in accordance with the experience of other economies, and contrary to notions widely held, the bulk of the output of marketed services has been as *inputs* to the productive system, rather than as flows into consumption demand: they are what are called *producer services*. Hence, even though most of the marketed services subsectors are sheltered in the sense that they do not directly compete in international trade, inefficiencies in the provision of such services can undermine the competitiveness of the more exposed trading sectors of the economy.

Some years ago this author made the following observations:

> Ireland has articulated policies for agriculture, manufacturing industry and the
> public sector, but it has had no clear and sustained policy for the marketed
> services sector. That has been an anomaly, especially in view of the increased
> relative importance of marketed services and of producer services in particu-
> lar. Perhaps it reflected the mistaken view that services sector outputs are
> mainly non-tradable internationally and hence — and this is the error — that
> the competitiveness of the economy is little dependent on the efficiency of the
> marketed services sector. Because marketed services do influence the com-
> petitiveness of the internationally traded goods sectors — indeed, increas-
> ingly so — it would seem desirable that Ireland articulate a clear and sus-
> tained policy for private sector services.... *The central feature of general
> policy towards private sector services should be emphasis on competition
> and the dismantling of restrictive practices and price maintenance.*
>
> That would not only benefit the Irish consumer directly; it would also
> increase the competitiveness of traded goods and hence, in the long run, it
> would promote job creation. It would be folly for policy to put a brake on the
> pace of technical change in private sector services with a view to saving jobs
> in the short run.... In a world of rapid technical change it is precisely those
> countries which innovate the fastest which are likely to increase their shares
> of world markets by most: in a sense, standing still would be moving back-
> wards." ("Public Policy for Private Sector Services", *Journal of Irish Busi-
> ness and Administrative Research*, October 1984. Emphasis in original.)

At policy levels in Ireland, there is now a much greater awareness of the
importance of efficiency in the services sectors — even in the case of
those subsectors which are themselves mainly non-tradable — in determining the overall competitiveness of the economy. For example, a statement under "Competition Policy" in the *Programme for Economic and
Social Progress, 1991–1993* (p. 86) noted that new legislation would be
enforced "so that the traded sectors will not have to bear the costs imposed by anti-competitive practices in the more sheltered local businesses." The emergence of an active competition policy in Ireland is surveyed by Patrick McNutt in Chapter 28 below.

PART SIX

MICROECONOMIC ANALYSIS

CHAPTER 24

THE THEORY OF DEMAND

It was seen in Part Two that in a perfectly competitive market the equilibrium price is determined by the intersection of the supply and demand curves. It was assumed that demand curves slope downwards. This chapter provides an explanation of the demand curve in terms of the structure of consumers' tastes and their budgets, leaving further analysis of supply until later chapters. Here we focus on two central questions in demand theory:

(1) How must consumers with given tastes, a fixed money income and facing given market prices, allocate their expenditure between goods in order to maximise satisfaction?

(2) Why do demand curves usually slope downwards? Can we be sure that they will *always* slope downwards?

MARGINAL UTILITY THEORY

The theory of demand, like the science of economics itself, is of relatively recent origin. Until the publication in 1871 of W. S. Jevons' *Theory of Political Economy*, most economists adhered to some form of cost-of-production theory of value. They believed that the exchange value (i.e. the price) of a good was determined by its production costs, particularly its subjective cost in terms of the necessary labour time embodied in its production. Cost of production is a major determinant of supply. On the role of demand and utility the early economists had relatively little to say. By utility we mean the satisfaction which consumers derive from possession of a good. The early economists did agree that there is some connection between the demand for a good and its utility: they felt that without utility a good would not be demanded at all. But they saw little direct relationship between utility and price. What they believed, in sum, was that, possessing utility, the price of a good is determined by its cost of production.

The Paradox of Value

Because he did not understand the role of utility in price determination,

Adam Smith was led to his famous "paradox of value" when in 1776 he wrote that goods

> which have the greatest value in use have frequently little or no value in exchange; and ... those which have the greatest value in exchange have frequently little or no value in use. Nothing is more useful than water, but ... scarcely anything can be had in exchange for it. A diamond, on the contrary, has scarcely any value in use; but a very great quantity of other goods may frequently be had in exchange for it. (*The Wealth of Nations*, Bobbs-Merrill abridged ed., Indianapolis 1961, pp. 29, 30).

No cost of production theory could rigorously explain why the price of diamonds is high and that of water low, even zero. However, by his distinction between total utility and marginal utility, Jevons resolved the paradox of value.

Total Utility and Marginal Utility

The total utility of n units of good x to a consumer is the total satisfaction from possession on n units of that good. The marginal utility of x, when n units of x have been purchased, is the *change in total* utility due to the possession of n instead of (n - 1) units of x.

The Law of Diminishing Marginal Utility

The marginal utility theorists went beyond total utility by invoking the law of diminishing marginal utility. According to this hypothesis, the more one has of any good x per period of time, the smaller is the increase in total utility due to the possession of a further unit of x, the amount possessed of all other goods remaining constant. Alternatively, the law states that total utility increases at a diminishing rate as one obtains more of a good. The relationship between total utility and marginal utility can be seen in Figures 1a and 1b. Note that q represents quantity *per period of time*.

Figure 1a

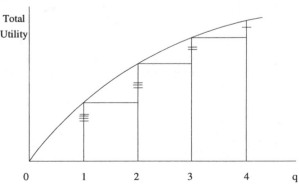

Figure 1b

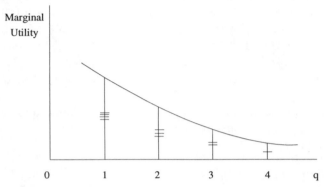

The Paradox of Value Resolved

Marginal utility analysis quickly resolves the paradox of value. Because they are very scarce relative to demand, diamonds have high marginal utility. Consumers are therefore willing to pay a high price for them. Water, because it is abundant, has a low marginal utility and hence a low or even zero price. *Given supply*, the determinant of price is thus seen to be marginal utility rather than total utility.

The Consumer's Allocation Problem

Using marginal utility theory we now consider the consumer's allocation problem. In order to maximise satisfaction or utility, a consumer, with given tastes, a fixed money income, and facing given market prices, must allocate expenditure between various goods in such a manner that the last unit of expenditure on each good brings to the consumer the same increase in total utility (yields the same marginal utility). This is equivalent to saying that consumers must spend their money in such a manner that for all goods purchased, marginal utilities are proportional to prices.

Suppose, for simplicity, that a consumer buys only two goods, x and y. To maximise satisfaction he must allocate his expenditure in such as manner that

(1) $MU_x/p_x = MU_y/p_y$

If the consumer allocated his expenditure in any other manner he would not be maximising utility. If, when he had spent all his money on the two goods, $MU_x/p_x > MU_y/p_y$, he could have increased his utility by buying more x and less y. Define a unit of x as that amount of x which costs £1, and define a unit of y as that amount of y which costs £1. Thus $p_x = p_y$. But $MU_x > MU_y$: the last £1 spent on x yields a greater increase in utility than the last £1 spent on y. The rational consumer must therefore transfer expenditures from y to x. As he buys less y and more x, MU_x will fall and MU_y will rise (because of the law of diminishing marginal utility). Eventually a point will be reached at which $MU_x = MU_y$. The consumer can then no longer gain by transferring expenditures from y to x. Hence, allocation in accordance with condition (1) is necessary for utility maximisation.

If the consumer spends his money on N goods, then, in order to maximise satisfaction, he must allocate his expenditure among those goods in such a manner that

$$(2) \qquad MU_x/p_x = MU_y/p_y = \ldots = MU_N/p_N$$

— marginal utilities, for all goods bought, must be proportional to their prices. The pattern of behaviour implicit in conditions (1) and (2) is called the *equimarginal principle* of consumer's behaviour.

The Consumer's Demand Curve

We now turn to the second question in demand theory posed at the beginning of the chapter. It is often stated that demand curves slope downwards because of the law of diminishing marginal utility. Given tastes and money income, and given the prices of all goods except that in which we are directly interested, if the law of diminishing marginal utility as applied to goods were the *only* factor determining the slope of a demand curve, then all demand curves must slope downwards. Consider the reasoning behind such a conclusion.

The equimarginal principle showed how a rational consumer with given tastes, a fixed money income and facing given market prices for all goods, would allocate expenditure between N goods. The consumer would act in accordance with the principle in condition (2). Now examine the adjustment in the consumer's purchase plan for some good n as its price (p_n) varies. The set of ratios in condition (2) must equal some number. Let this number be k (k for constant). Then,

$$MU_n/p_n = k, \text{ or}$$

$$(3) \; p_n = MU_n/k$$

which implies a unique relationship between the price the consumer is willing to pay for good n and its marginal utility to her. Thus, it *seems* that the price the consumer is willing to pay for good n can be derived directly from the MU curve of good n: from equation (3), it seems that the consumer demand curve for good n would be simply a transformation of the MU_n curve. *If* it can be derived from the law of diminishing marginal utility, the individual's demand curve must slope downwards. If, given money income and the prices of all other goods, diminishing marginal utility as applied to goods were the only factor determining the shape of individual demand curves, then every individual's demand curve for any good would slope downwards. Because a market demand curve for any good is the horizontal sum of the individual demand curves for that good, the market demand curve, derived from marginal utility theory, would slope downwards. Marginal utility analysis thus suggests that *all* demand curves *must* always slope downwards.

Some Problems

The above analysis is defective on a number of counts. First, it was assumed that utility, and hence marginal utility, is *cardinally* measurable — just as height and distance are cardinally measurable (i.e. it was assumed that one could quantitatively compare the difference in total utility obtainable from, say, six units and seven units of a good, just as one could quantitatively compare the average height of six-year-old and seven-year-old children). Many have objected to marginal utility analysis on the grounds that utility is not cardinally measurable. Secondly, marginal utility analysis led to the conclusion that demand curves must always slope downwards. In a more refined analysis that conclusion is *not necessarily true*. Indifference curve analysis helps to provide more rigorous solutions to the two questions posed at the beginning of this chapter.

INDIFFERENCE CURVE ANALYSIS

In indifference curve analysis it is not assumed that utility is *cardinally* measurable. However, it is assumed that the consumer makes his purchases in accordance with a *scale of preferences*, by which he is able to *rank* all conceivable bundles of goods in order of importance to him. This implies that he is able to indicate the bundles of goods between which he is indifferent. But instead of making statements of the form "the consumer obtains 100 units of utility from purchase plan A and 100 units of utility from purchase plan B, but only 50 units of utility from purchase plan C" (the *cardinal* utility approach), in indifference curve analysis we need only make statements of the form "the consumer is indifferent between A and B and prefers either to C, but it is not necessary and it may not be possible to know by how much he prefers B to C" (the *ordinal* utility approach). In what follows it is assumed for simplicity that there are only two goods, x and y, entering the consumer's purchase plan.

Indifference Curves

The concept *indifference curve* owes its origin to the Irish economist Francis Ysidro Edgeworth (1845–1926). An indifference curve shows the combinations of two goods between which an individual is indifferent (i.e. they yield the consumer the *same level* of satisfaction). The curve IC_1 in Figure 2 shows combinations of goods x and y between which the consumer is indifferent. It is assumed that more goods are preferred to less (the assumption of non-satiety). It is obvious, in Figure 2, that bundle C will be preferred to bundle B (or A): if the consumer had bundle C, he would have more of both goods than if he had bundle B. There are several combinations of goods which would yield the consumer the same level of satisfaction as commodity bundle C. These all lie on the indifference curve of bundle C, IC_2.

Figure 2

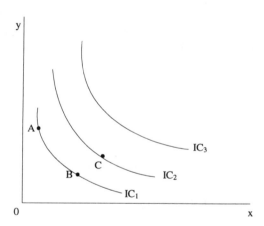

The consumer is indifferent between all combinations of x and y which lie on IC_2. But every point on IC_2 is preferred to any point on IC_1. However, we cannot, or need not, say *by how much* (by how many units of utility) the consumer prefers a bundle on IC_2 to a bundle on IC_1; we merely say that the utility of bundles on IC_2 (along which the level of utility is constant) *exceeds* that of bundles on IC_1 (along which utility is also constant, though at a lower level). The locus IC_3 in Figure 2 represents yet another level of consumer satisfaction. All commodity bundles on this locus are equally attractive to the consumer. But every point on IC_3 is preferred to any point on a lower indifference curve. The higher the indifference curve, the greater the level of utility or satisfaction.

On the assumption that all conceivable bundles of goods can be ranked according to preference or indifference (this is called the axiom of completeness) the rational consumer has infinitely many indifference curves. These indicate all commodity bundles between which the consumer is indifferent, the commodity bundles which are preferred to any given bundle, and the bundles which give less satisfaction than any given commodity bundle. The whole series of indifference curves is the consumer's *indifference map*. An indifference map is a graphical depiction of a consumer's *preference ordering* among goods.

Figure 3

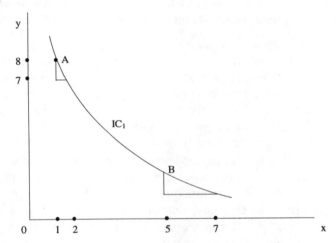

Figure 4

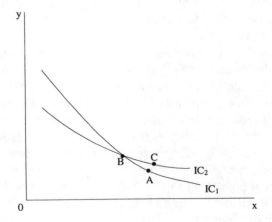

The higher the indifference curve, the higher the level of utility, but utility is constant along a given indifferent curve. Thus, in indifference

curve analysis we need attach only ordinal rather than cardinal significance to the utility of one bundle of goods as compared to another. We
can say that the utility on one bundle is greater than (less than or equal
to) that of another; this is merely *ranking* bundles in order of preference
and indifference; it does not require any assumption of cardinally
measurable utility.

Properties of Indifference Curves

Three properties of indifference curves are as follows:

(1) Indifference curves slope downwards. (Any other shape would be
inconsistent with the assumption that more goods are preferred to less.)

(2) Indifference curves are strictly convex, reflecting the diminishing
marginal rate of substitution of good x for good y, $DMRS_{xy}$. ($DMRS_{xy}$,
explained below, which implies strict convexity of indifference curves, is
an assumption concerning consumer tastes, rather than something which
is necessarily true.) The MRS_{xy} is the rate at which the consumer is
willing to substitute x for y consistent with feeling no better or worse off
(i.e. while staying on the same indifference curve). The MRS_{xy} is the
slope of an indifference curve (we ignore the negative sign of slope). For
example, consider the indifference curve in Figure 3, and suppose that
initially the consumer has commodity bundle A. It can be seen that the
consumer is willing to give up 1 unit of y for an extra 1/2 unit of x: the
consumer is made no better or worse off by making such a substitution,
for he has remained on the same indifference curve. But note that in a
neighbourhood of point A, the absolute value of the slope of the indifference curve (approximated by $\Delta y/\Delta x$) equals 2, approximately. This
indicates that the consumer is just about willing to forego 2 units of y if
he were given 1 more unit of x.

Note also that as the consumer obtains more x, the absolute value of
the slope of the indifference curve diminishes. This reflects the assumption that the marginal rate of substitution is *diminishing*. If, for example,
the consumer has a lot of y but little x (as at point A in Figure 3), it is
likely that for a unit reduction in his holdings of y he will accept a small
increase in holdings of x. However, as his holdings of y are reduced and
those of x are increased, it is likely that the consumer will require progressively larger increments in his holdings of x to offset reduction in his
holdings of y. If, as at point B in Figure 3, he has 5 units of x but only 2
units of y, he will be willing to sacrifice an additional unit of y only if he
obtains an additional 2 units of x. Hence, the consumer is willing to
forego progressively fewer units of y in substitution for progressively
more units of x.

We assume that the consumer's MRS_{xy}, as represented by the absolute value of the slope of an indifference curve, will always diminish as one moves down an indifference curve. If that is the case indifference curves must be strictly convex.

(3) Indifference curves cannot intersect. Suppose for only a moment that they can intersect, as in Figure 4. This is contradictory. Bundle C is preferred to bundle A, because C contains more of both x and y than does A. The consumer is indifferent between A and B: they both lie on the same indifference curve (IC_1). The consumer is also indifferent between C and B, because they too lie on the same indifference curve (IC_2). The consumer is, therefore, indifferent between A, B, and C. But C is preferred to A. Thus an assumption that indifference curves can intersect is contradictory.

THE CONSUMER'S ALLOCATION PROBLEM ONCE AGAIN

Indifference curve analysis can aid us in answering the first question posed at the beginning of this chapter: how will a consumer with given tastes, with a fixed money income, and facing given market prices, allocate his expenditure among goods if he is to maximise satisfaction? For simplicity it will be assumed that the consumer spends all his income on two goods, x and y.

If the consumer spent all his money income on good y, he could buy an amount of that good equal to his money income divided by the price of good y. Let that amount be 0A in Figure 5. Thus 0A = (money income)/p_y. If the consumer spent all his money income on good x, he could buy an amount of that good equal to his money income divided by the price of good x. Let that amount be 0A' in Figure 5. Thus 0A' = (money income)/p_x. The consumer could buy, with his fixed money income, any of the combinations of x and y on the locus AA', which is called the consumer's *budget constraint* — it is the constraint imposed on the consumer's purchases by his fixed money income, given market prices. Ignoring the negative sign, the slope of the budget constraint is the price ratio. Thus, slope of AA' = 0A/0A' = (money income/p_y)/(money income/p_x) = p_x/p_y.

Given market prices, the level of the budget constraint is determined by the level of money income. If the consumer obtains an increase in money income while prices are unchanged, the budget constraint will shift upwards, perhaps to BB' in Figure 5. If his money income is reduced, while prices stay constant, his budget constraint will shift downwards, perhaps to CC' in Figure 5.

Figure 5

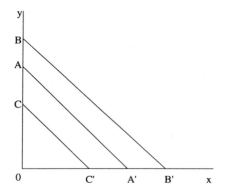

Figure 6

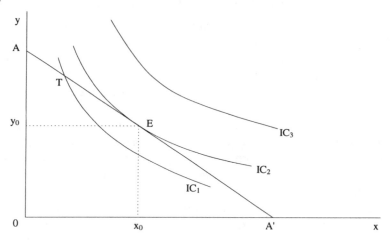

We now superimpose the consumer's budget constraint on his indifference map, as in Figure 6. The indifference map depicts the consumer's preferences, which are assumed given. The consumer has fixed money income and faces given prices for x and y. The corresponding budget constraint is AA'. The consumer's problem is to get to the highest indifference curve attainable, consistent with that budget constraint.

In Figure 6, the consumer could not get to IC_3, which lies above his budget constraint. He could attain IC_1 by buying bundle T but he would not be maximising satisfaction. It is clear that given his budget constraint, the highest indifference curve which the consumer can attain is IC_2. The consumer can attain IC_2 by buying the bundle E, represented by the tangency of an indifference curve to the budget constraint.

The tangency of an indifference curve to the budget constraint gives the highest level of satisfaction attainable by a consumer with given tastes, with a fixed money income, and facing given market prices. The slope of an indifference curve is the MRS_{xy}. The slope of the budget constraint (again ignoring the negative sign) is p_x/p_y. Thus, at point E, $MRS_{xy} = p_x/p_y$. Hence, if a consumer with given tastes, a fixed money income, and facing given market prices is to maximise satisfaction obtainable from the fixed money income, he must allocate expenditure in such a manner that, for *any* two goods x and y bought,

(4) $MRS_{xy} = p_x/p_y$

Condition (4) is the indifference-curve-theory version of the equi-marginal principle, stated earlier as condition (2).

CHANGES IN CONSUMER EQUILIBRIUM

The consumer is in equilibrium at point E in Figure 6. Buying bundle E (x_0 of x and y_0 of y), he has no incentive to change his purchase plan, for he is obtaining maximum satisfaction consistent with his tastes, his money income and market prices. The conditions underlying equilibrium may change. In what follows it is assumed that the consumer's tastes or preferences remain constant — that his indifference map remains unchanged.

Suppose that all prices change by some proportion but that money income changes in the same proportion, and in the same direction, as the changes in prices. This will cause no change in the rational consumer's behaviour. Suppose, for example, that prices and money income double. The budget constraint was initially $p_x x + p_y y =$ money income, where p_x, p_y and money income are initially given. After the changes in prices and money income, the budget constraint becomes $2p_x x + 2p_y y = 2$(money income), which is identical to the initial budget constraint. The consumer's behaviour will not change because neither of the factors underlying that behaviour — his tastes or the budget constraint — will have changed.

Assuming tastes to be constant, there are three general ways in which the conditions underlying consumer equilibrium may change:

(1) Either (a) absolute prices might remain constant but the money income of the consumer might change, or (b) relative prices (the price of one good relative to others) and money income might stay constant, but absolute prices might change. Although (a) and (b) would cause no change in the slope of the budget constraint (which reflects relative

prices), they would cause that constraint to shift upwards or downwards. Because real income would have changed, the consumer would be made better or worse off. The adjustment in the consumer's purchase plan due to a change of type (1) — a change in real income without change in relative prices — is called the *income effect*.

(2) Money income might be constant but relative prices might change in such a manner that the consumer is made no better or worse off — he remains on the same indifference curve. A change of this kind could occur if, for example, a tax were imposed on y and if a subsidy, sufficient in amount to offset exactly the welfare-reducing effects of the tax — were granted on x. Although, in this case, the consumer remains on a particular indifference curve, he will substitute the good which has become relatively cheaper for that which has become relatively dearer. The adjustment in the consumer's purchase plan due to a change in relative prices which causes no change in attainable utility is called the *substitution effect*.

(3) Money income might stay constant but relative prices might change in such a manner that the consumer is made better or worse off. For example, the price of one good might change while prices of all other goods stay constant. The adjustment in the consumer's purchase plan due to such a change is called the *price effect*.

The Income Effect

We start the analysis with the consumer in equilibrium at point E in Figure 7. Suppose that the consumer's money income is increased, while both absolute and relative prices stay constant. The consumer's budget constraint shifts upwards to BB'. The rational consumer will try to get to the highest indifference curve consistent with this new budget constraint: he will buy bundle E'.

If the consumer obtains a further increment in income, the budget constraint will again shift upwards, to CC' in Figure 7. The bundle which the rational consumer will buy is then E"

There is an infinity of possible tangency points between successively higher budget constraints and successively higher indifference curves. If we could plot all of these points we would obtain the smooth curve labelled ICC in Figure 7. This is called an *income consumption curve*. It shows how much of x and y the rational consumer would buy at different levels of money income, given his tastes and market prices.

Note that both x and y in Figure 7 are "normal" goods: higher income increases purchases of both. The income effect for both is positive.

Alternatively, it can be said that the income elasticity of demand for both is positive.

Figure 7

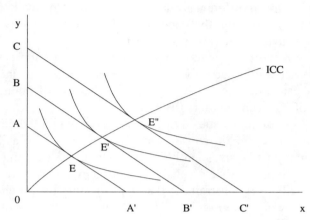

Figure 8

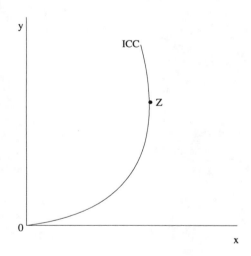

Recall from Chapter 5 that the income elasticity of demand for some goods is negative — all else remaining constant, an increase in money income leads to reduction in purchases of certain goods. A good is technically described as *inferior* if increased money income reduces purchases of that good. In Figure 8, good x is inferior beyond point Z — purchases of x are reduced after income rises beyond the level implied by point Z. The term inferior good pertains to the direction of the income effect: a good is inferior if the income effect is negative.

The Substitution Effect

The substitution effect pertains to the adjustment in the consumer's purchase plan when a change in relative prices just enables the consumer to
remain on the same indifference curve as initially. However, the consumer would then substitute the good which becomes relatively cheaper
for that which is made relatively more expensive.

We start with the consumer in equilibrium at E in Figure 9. Next,
suppose that a tax is imposed on y. Because money income is unchanged,
the consumer can now buy less y than before. Instead of being able to
buy 0A units of y he can buy only 0B units.

However, suppose that a subsidy is simultaneously granted on good x.
If the consumer is to remain on the same indifference curve as initially,
the subsidy on x must be sufficiently large to enable the consumer to buy
0B' units of x. Suppose that a subsidy of this amount is granted. The
consumer's new budget constraint is BB'. By adjusting his purchase plan
from E to E', he can remain on IC_1. The substitution effect is the movement along the indifference curve from E to E'

Figure 9

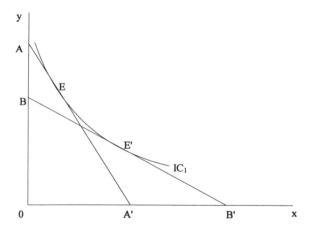

The Price Effect

The price effect is concerned with the adjustment in the consumer's
purchase plan due to a change in relative prices which leaves the consumer better or worse off. Suppose, given his money income, tastes and
the price of good y, that the price of x changes. Relative prices will then
have changed. The price effect analysis focuses on the relationship
between quantity demanded of x and variations in its price. It is, therefore, concerned with the individual's demand curve for good x.

Figure 10

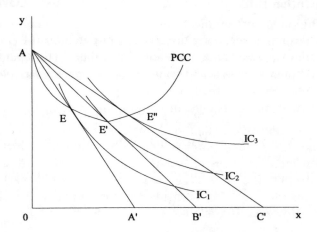

We start with the consumer in equilibrium buying bundle E in Figure 10. If p_x is now reduced, the consumer will be able to purchase, with his given money income, more of x — an amount 0B' (if he spent all of his budget on good x). Because p_y has not changed, the consumer could still buy 0A of y (if he spent all of his money on good y). The locus AB' is the consumer's new budget constraint. The rational consumer will move to the highest indifference curve consistent with that budget constraint — he will buy bundle E' in Figure 10.

If p_x fell further, the consumer's budget constraint would fan further out along the x axis — to a point like C'. AC' would then be the budget constraint, and the consumer would buy bundle E".

There is an infinity of budget constraints corresponding to different possible prices of good x. With each of these budget constraints the rational consumer will buy that commodity bundle indicated by the tangency of the budget constraint to an indifference curve. The curve PCC — called a *price consumption curve* — is the locus of tangency points between successive budget constraints and successively higher indifference curves as p_x is reduced. It shows the amount of x (and y) bought as p_x varies.

The observant reader will notice that, in the present case, a reduction in p_x increases purchases of x. Therefore, the demand curve for x must slope downwards.

Our immediate concern is the relationship between p_x and quantity of x demanded. To see how changes in real income, *due to price changes*, affect the slope of the demand curve, it will now be shown that the price effect is a combination of income and substitution effects.

THE PRICE EFFECT IS A COMBINATION OF INCOME AND SUBSTITUTION EFFECTS

There are two forces affecting the consumers purchases of x when p_x is reduced, all else remaining constant. In reality both operate simultaneously. However, in order to facilitate an understanding, consider the two forces separately:

(1) If p_x is reduced, while all other prices (p_y in the present example) and money income remain constant, the consumer experiences an increase in *real* income: his general purchasing power would have increased. Increased real income, taken in isolation, causes an upward shift of the budget constraint. The price effect thus involves an income effect. If x is "normal", this income effect (considered in isolation) will increase purchases of x. However, if x is inferior, the income effect of a price reduction will tend to reduce purchases of x.

(2) If p_x is reduced, all other prices and the consumer's money income remaining constant, then relative prices have changed. Good x is now relatively cheaper and good y is relatively dearer than before. The consumer will therefore substitute x for y. Thus the price effect involves a substitution effect. Because indifference curves are assumed to be strictly convex, the substitution effect, considered in isolation, always increases purchases of the good the price of which has fallen.

Shown graphically in Figure 11, the price effect (the movement from A to B) is a combination of an income effect (a movement up an income consumption curve to a higher budget constraint and to a higher indifference curve) and a substitution effect (a movement along a given indifference curve).

Figure 11

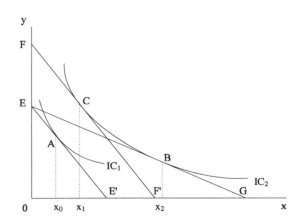

When p_x is reduced, all else remaining constant, the consumer experiences an increase in real income. The income effect, treated in isolation, is represented by an upward shift of the budget constraint. The consumer moves along the ICC to point C in Figure 11. Note that the income effect on good x is here positive — in itself, it increases purchases of x, by an amount $(x_1 - x_0)$.

Having examined the income effect in isolation, we now turn to the substitution effect. The income effect has brought the consumer to point C on IC_2 in Figure 11. The substitution effect is a movement along IC_2. If we now recall that relative prices have changed, the consumer's budget constraint, FF', will pivot to the right — to EG. Note that EG is tangent to the same indifference curve (IC_2) as FF'. The substitution effect, in isolation, causes the consumer to move along IC_2, from C to B. The substitution effect of the price change increases purchases of x by an amount $(x_2 - x_1)$.

The movement from A to B in Figure 11 (the price effect) is a combination of movement from A to C (the income effect) and from C to B (the substitution effect). The income effect increased purchases of x by an amount $(x_1 - x_0)$. The substitution effect increased purchases by $(x_2 - x_1)$. The total increase in purchases of x due to the price reduction is $(x_2 - x_0)$. Hence, for the range of price variation considered, the demand curve for x must slope downwards.

Inferior Goods

Figure 12

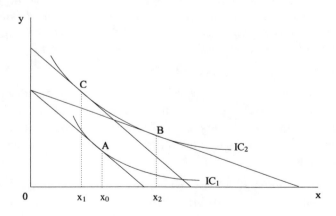

If x is an inferior good, we cannot be sure that a reduction in its price will increase quantity demanded. The negative income effect of the price change, by itself, would reduce purchases. Then, whether or not the price effect increases purchases hinges on the relative sizes of the negative income effect and the substitution effect. If the substitution effect is strong enough to offset the negative income effect, the demand curve will slope downwards in the normal way, implying that a reduction in price increases quantity demanded.

Figure 12 depicts the price effect for an inferior good. The income effect (the movement from A to C), by itself, would reduce purchases, from x_0 to x_1. The substitution effect (the movement from C to B) by itself would increase purchases, from x_1 to x_2. However, the full price effect increases purchases of x because the substitution effect ($x_2 - x_1$) is strong enough more than to offset the negative income effect ($x_1 - x_0$). Hence, although good x is inferior, the individual's demand curve slopes downwards, at least for the range of price variation considered.

Giffen Goods

Some goods might be so inferior that the negative income effect of a price reduction (which, by itself, reduces purchases) would more than offset the substitution effect of the price reduction (which, by itself, increases purchases). A price reduction would then *reduce* purchases of such a good. Such goods are called *Giffen goods*. A Giffen good is one for which a negative income effect of a price reduction is so strong that it dominates the substitution effect, causing the demand curve to slope *upwards* rather than downwards, for some range of price variation.

A Giffen good is an inferior good (meaning that its income effect is negative), but not all inferior goods are Giffen. The term Giffen good pertains only to the price effect. An inferior good is Giffen if and only if it is so inferior that the negative income effect of a price change is so strong that it more than offsets the substitution effect, leading to a perverse price effect — a demand curve which slopes upwards.

The Demand Curve Once More

The foregoing has examined the relationship between quantity demanded by an individual of any good x, and its price. It was assumed that the consumer had given tastes and a fixed money income, and that the prices of all goods, other than that under analysis, remained constant.

We conclude:

(1) Individual demand curves generally slope downwards (a) because both the income and substitution effects of a price reduction may increase purchases, or, (b) if the income effect is negative, the substitution effect will usually be strong enough to offset the negative income effect.

(2) If for an individual a good is Giffen over a certain range of price

variation, that individual's demand curve for the good will slope upwards over the range of price variation in question.

A *market demand curve* for a good is the sideways sum of the individual demand curves. The market demand curve will generally slope downwards for reasons (a) and (b) in (1) above. A market demand curve may, for some ranges of price variation, slope upwards for reason (2) above. However, cases of upward sloping market demand curves must be extremely rare.

We now see why the statement that "demand curves must slope downwards because of the law of diminishing marginal utility" is not precise. The central reason for the inadequacy of the marginal utility approach to demand curves is that it cannot adequately handle the income effect of price changes. We have at last provided a solution to question (2), posed at the beginning of the chapter.

CHAPTER 25

THE FIRM: PRODUCTION AND COSTS

Chapter 4 outlined the elementary theory of price determination by supply and demand in perfectly competitive markets. Chapter 24 left supply in the background and examined demand in greater detail than earlier. The present chapter leaves demand in the background and investigates production, costs and supply. The chapters which immediately follow will then consider the determination of price and output in different market structures.

PROFIT MAXIMISATION

Economic theory usually assumes that firms seek maximum profits. Economists do not believe that profit maximisation is the sole objective of all firms. Why then do they make that assumption? First, all theory must simplify in order to attain general conclusions. Second, experience suggests strongly that the assumption of profit maximisation yields predictions which are broadly consistent with reality. Third, if the assumption of profit maximisation is rejected, it is not clear what should take its place, consistent with being able to make predictions which are both general and empirically plausible. For these reasons we assume that firms maximise profit.

Cost and Profit

Profit is the difference between revenue and cost. We define the cost of a factor of production to a firm as that payment necessary in order to keep the factor in employment with the firm. This definition draws on the notion of opportunity cost. Thus, as an approximation, firm A must pay for the services of a factor just as much as that factor could earn in its most lucrative alternative employment, with, say, firm B. Suppose firm B were just willing to pay the factor £x per period; if all markets are competitive and in equilibrium, that must be because, in some sense to be defined later, the factor would "produce" £x of output for firm B. Therefore, if the factor is currently employed by firm A, firm A must pay the factor £x in order to maintain its services; if A offered less than £x, the factor would transfer to firm B. Sometimes the economist's notions of factor costs are implicit rather than explicit; sometimes they diverge from, sometimes they correspond to, the accountant's measures of costs.

Consider the *cost of hiring labour*. This is an explicit cost; labour services are hired at some wage rate (which includes employer's contribution to social insurance) and it might reasonably be assumed that this is the amount labour would earn in its best alternative employment. The economist's measure of labour costs is similar to the accountant's. However, in the case of *capital costs,* economists diverge from the conventions of accountants: instead of looking at the historical cost to a firm of, say, a machine, economists regard the implicit (economic) cost of the machine's services per period as what someone else would be willing to pay for its use. Thus the (economic) cost of a machine-hour in any use is the rental rate for that machine in its most lucrative alternative use: by continuing to use the machine itself, the firm is implicitly foregoing the rental rate someone else would be willing to pay for its use. The economic *cost of using land* is similar to capital cost. It is an implicit or an explicit rental cost, depending on whether the firm owns the land.

Turning to the *costs of entrepreneurial services* (the services of the owner of the firm, which include risk-taking), note that much of what accountants call "profit" is regarded by economists as a cost of production. Profit is a payment to the owner of a firm, and that part of the payment necessary to keep the owner in a particular business, called "normal profit", is a cost to that business. To an economist, economic or "supernormal" profit is entrepreneurial income in excess of "normal profit".

Thus, we define economic profit — profit in the sense of the economist rather than the accountant — from the sale of goods as the difference between revenues from sale and the opportunity costs of the factors (including entrepreneurial services) used in their production. It follows that although an accountant might say that a firm is experiencing a profit, an economist would say that (economic) profit is negative — that the firm is incurring a loss — if profit in the accountant's sense were less than "normal profit".

THE PRODUCTION FUNCTION

Throughout this chapter we will be investigating the production and costs of *a single firm*. In the interests of simplicity, it will be assumed that the firm produces only one kind of product. Suppose that the firm can increase or decrease the amount used of all inputs. How must it use inputs if it is to minimise the cost of producing any given level of output? The answer has two aspects — a technical aspect and a financial aspect. The central concept on the technical side, which will be considered first, is the production function.

A production function shows the *maximum* levels of output obtainable from alternative combinations of inputs. It also shows the extent to which one input can be substituted for another in the production of a given output. It indicates how inputs may be transformed into outputs, consistent with technical efficiency.

Suppose, for purposes of illustration, that only two inputs — labour and capital — are used to produce a certain good. The production function, representing the relationship between technically efficient input use and output, might be:

(1) $q = f(x, y) = 2xy$

where q represents quantity produced, and x and y are the amounts used of labour and capital, respectively. Knowing the production function (1), we could plot the relationship between the amounts of inputs used and the resulting output on a three-dimensional diagram. However, it is easier to regard q as a parameter. We might, for example, think of setting quantity produced at ten units, in which case (1) would become

(2) $10 = 2xy$

We could now solve for the non-negative combinations of x and y satisfying (2). In doing so we would be finding the combinations of labour and capital use which could produce ten units of output in a technically efficient manner. Looking at (2) we see that (as approximations):

If $x = 1$; $y = 5$	If $x = 5$; $y = 1$
$x = 2$; $y = 2.5$	$x = 6$; $y = 0.8$
$x = 3$; $y = 1.7$	and so on.

There is an infinite number of combinations of x and y which satisfy (2). If it were possible for us to plot them all, we would get a smooth curve like I_{10} in Figure 1.

Isoquants

The curve I_{10} in Figure 1 is called an equal product curve, or more briefly, an *isoquant*. Total product along this curve is constant at ten units. Formally, if two inputs, x and y, are used in the production of a given good, an isoquant is the locus of combinations of x and y which produce the same level of output in a technically efficient manner.

In order to trace the input combinations which produce twenty units, set $q = 20$, in which case (1) becomes

(3) $20 = 2xy$

Now find the non-negative combinations of x and y which are solutions to (3). Thus, as approximations:

If x = 2; y = 5	If x = 10; y = 1
x = 4; y = 2.5	x = 12; y = 0.8
x = 6; y = 1.7	and so on.

Plotting these values in Figure 1 gives an isoquant like that labelled I_{20}. We could likewise set q = 30 in (1) and plot the input combinations which yield thirty units of output. There is an infinity of levels at which we could set q. For any of these we could plot the corresponding iso-quant. If we did so for many levels of q, we would obtain an *isoquant map*, like that in Figure 2. An isoquant map is merely a (partial) *graph of the production function*.

Figure 1

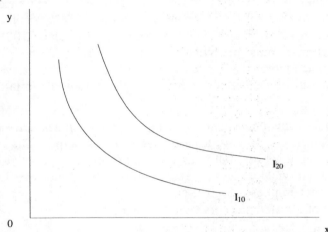

Figure 2

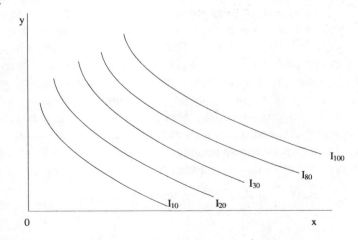

Properties of Isoquants

The isoquants in Figure 2 are downward sloping, strictly convex, and non-intersecting. The reasons are as follows:

(1) The isoquants slope downwards reflecting an assumption that if less of one input is used, more of the other must be used in order to keep output constant. The slope of an isoquant is the marginal rate of technical substitution of one input for another (of x for y), $MRTS_{xy}$. It is the rate at which x can be substituted for y (using the inputs in a technically efficient manner, and keeping output constant).

(2) The isoquants are strictly convex, reflecting an assumption of diminishing $MRTS_{xy}$. It is assumed that as production is made more x-intensive, it becomes progressively more difficult to substitute x for y (more difficult in the sense that each unit increment in x can be offset by only progressively smaller reductions in y) if output is kept constant. For example, both labour and capital are required to produce 100 pairs of shoes. Starting at some particular capital/labour ratio, if the production process is made more labour-intensive, it will become progressively more difficult to substitute labour for machinery and tools if output is kept constant.

(3) Isoquants cannot intersect. An isoquant shows *technically efficient* input combinations yielding a particular level of output. Thus, corresponding to any level of input x, an isoquant shows the *minimum* level of input y that will yield a specific level of output. To assume that isoquants could intersect implies a logical contradiction. (Recall the reasoning in the context of indifference curves, in Chapter 24.)

Marginal Physical Products and MRTS

We define the marginal physical product (MPP) on the nth unit used of input x as the change in total physical product caused by using n instead of (n - 1) units of x, the state of technology and the amount used of all other inputs remaining constant. The slope of an isoquant at any point is approximated by $\Delta y/\Delta x$, where Δx is small. If use of input x changes by a small amount, then the resulting change in output is approximated by $MPP_x\Delta x$. If use of input y changes by a small amount, the change in output will be approximated by $MPP_y\Delta y$. It follows, if x is varied by a small amount, Δx, and if y is also varied by a small amount, Δy, then the change in output is approximately $\Delta q = MPP_x\Delta x + MPP_y\Delta y$. Because output is constant along an isoquant, $\Delta q = 0$. Hence, along an isoquant,

$$MPP_x\Delta x + MPP_y\Delta y = 0, \text{ or, rearranging terms,}$$

$$(4) \ \Delta y/\Delta x \ (= MRTS_{xy,}) = - MPP_x/MPP_y$$

Thus, the slope of an isoquant ($MRTS_{xy}$) is the negative of the ratio of the marginal physical products of the two inputs.

Isocost Curves

We now turn to financial aspects of production. If the firm could buy as much as it might wish of all inputs — of just x and y in the present case — it could buy various combinations of those inputs for any particular cost outlay. Suppose, for example, that it decides to spend £1,000 on inputs. With £1,000 it could buy, say, 0A of x if it bought only input x (see Figure 3). If it spent the whole £1,000 on y it could buy 0B of y. Alternatively, it could buy, for £1,000, any of the combinations of x and y given by locus AB — as long as the cost outlay and the prices of inputs remain constant. The locus AB in Figure 3 is called an *isocost curve*: it shows the amounts of two inputs which the firm could obtain for a given cost outlay (£1,000). We know that slope AB = - 0B/0A. 0B is the amount of y which could be obtained if the whole £1,000 were spent on y: $0B = 1,000/p_y$. Similarly, $0A = 1,000/p_x$. Hence:

$$\text{Slope } AB = - (1,000/p_y)/(1,000/p_x) = - p_x/p_y$$

The higher the isocost curve, the larger the cost outlay. Assuming that per unit costs of x and y are constant, CD in Figure 4 is the isocost curve for an outlay of £1,500. Conversely, the lower the isocost curve, the smaller the cost outlay. GH is the isocost curve for £500. There is an infinity of isocost curves, each pertaining to a different cost outlay. The slope of each is - p_x/p_y.

Figure 3

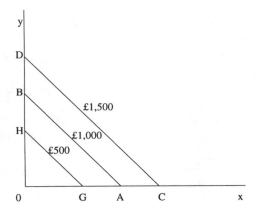

Figure 4

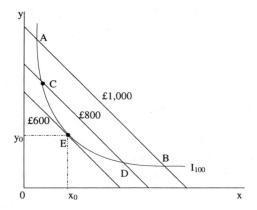

Cost Minimisation

Assuming that the firm can vary in either direction all inputs — in the present case just x and y — all we need do to find the input levels which achieve a given output at minimum cost is bring together the technical data, as represented by the production function (isoquant map), and the financial data, as represented by the map of isocost curves.

Suppose that the firm seeks to produce 100 units at minimum cost. I_{100} in Figure 4 is the relevant isoquant. We see that using input combinations A or B the firm could produce 100 units — for both points lie on I_{100} . But it would be doing so at a cost outlay of £1,000, as indicated by the isocost curve through points A and B. Factor combinations C or D, which lie on the isocost curve of £800, could also produce 100 units. But £800 is not the lowest possible cost for production of 100 units: there are many lower isocost curves (only one of which is shown in the diagram) which either intersect or touch I_{100}. Therefore, there are many factor combinations costing less than £800 which can produce the 100 units. The lowest isocost curve which at least touches I_{100} is that which is tangent to I_{100}. Using input combination E, the firm can spend £600 on inputs to produce the 100 units. But it could not produce 100 units by spending less than £600, because the isocost curves for outlays of less than £600 lie entirely below I_{100}. The tangency solution at point E therefore yields the input combination which minimises the production cost of 100 units. When two curves are tangent, their slopes are equal. At E, the slope of I_{100}, - MPP_x/MPP_y, equals the slope of the isocost curve, - p_x/p_y; thus, at E,

$$(5) \; MPP_x/MPP_y = p_x/p_y$$

Note that (5) does not hold at any other point on I_{100}. At any point other than E (e.g. at A or D), $MPP_x/MPP_y \neq p_x/p_y$. To minimise the cost of producing any given level of output when it can vary both inputs, the firm must employ those inputs in such a manner that condition (5) holds. Cross-multiplying, it can be seen that, at E,

$$(6)\ MPP_x/p_x = MPP_y/p_y$$

It has been shown that point E (x_0 of x, y_0 of y) denotes the cost-minimising input combination for production of 100 units. Generalisation indicates that the tangency of an isocost curve to whatever isoquant is relevant is the cost-minimising input combination for any level of output. Thus, if a firm is to produce any level of output at minimum cost, it must use inputs such that condition (6) holds — the marginal physical products of the (variable) inputs must be proportional to the prices of those inputs.

We have been discussing production using only two inputs, x and y, both of them variable in either direction. Nevertheless, condition (6) can be generalised further: if a firm uses any number (N) of inputs, and if each of those inputs can be increased or decreased, then, in order to minimise the cost of producing any given output, it must use those inputs in such a manner that

$$(7)\ MPP_1/p_1 = MPP_2/p_2 = ... = MPP_N/p_N$$

The principle embodied in (6) and (7) is called the *equimarginal principle* of factor employment.

THE EXPANSION PATH

All Inputs Variable

If the firm wishes to produce 54 units at minimum cost, if input prices are given and if all inputs are variable in either direction, then it will use input combination E_1 in Figure 5. If it wishes to produce 87 or 101 units it will use input combinations E_2 and E_3, respectively. The points along 0E are tangencies between successively higher isoquants and higher isocost curves: they denote the cost-minimising input combinations for successively higher output levels. There is an infinity of isoquants, each denoting different output levels. There is also an infinity of isocost curves, each implying different minimum cost outlays. The locus 0E in Figure 5 is called an expansion path. It is the locus of cost-minimising input combinations, as the firm expands output from zero to progressively higher levels. Each point on the expansion path shows two things:

(1) A certain level of output as given by the isoquant through the point.

(2) The minimum cost associated with the output in question, given by the isocost curve tangent to the isoquant at the point.

Point E_4, for example, represents the level of output indicated by the isoquant through that point. At E_4, $x = 5$, $y = 7$. Suppose $q = 126$ at E_4. That point also implies a certain minimum cost outlay, as given by the isocost curve tangent to I_{126} at E_4. Suppose $p_x = £1$ and $p_y = £2$. It is easy to calculate the value of the isocost curve tangent to I_{126} at E_4; total cost = $p_x x + p_y y$. Thus, the minimum cost of producing 126 units is $(£1)(5) + (£2)(7) = £19$. Similarly, we could read off from the expansion path the minimum cost of producing any other level of output, given that both (i.e. all) factors are variable to the firm.

Figure 5

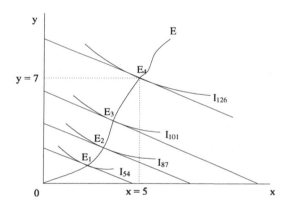

Figure 6

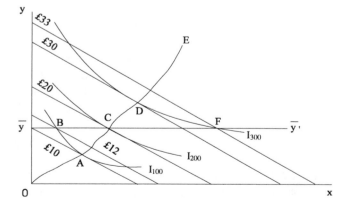

Some Inputs Fixed, Some Variable

Not all factors are necessarily variable in a given period. Suppose that the firm has a fixed amount of y (say capital equipment) denoted by $\bar{y}$ in Figure 6, but that it can expand or reduce its employment of x (say labour). 0E would be its expansion path if both (all) factors were variable. However, with y fixed at $\bar{y}$, the firm can expand output only by moving along $\bar{y}\bar{y}'$. We could call $\bar{y}\bar{y}'$ the expansion path given $y = \bar{y}$; however, to avoid confusion with the case where all factors are variable we call $\bar{y}\bar{y}'$ a *factor limitation locus*.

It can be seen from point A in Figure 6 that if both factors were variable, the minimum cost of producing 100 units would be £10; but with $y = \bar{y}$ the minimum cost of that quantity, as given by point B, is £12. It can be inferred from the diagram that with both factors variable, the minimum cost of producing any output less than 200 units would be lower than the minimum cost at which the same output could be produced if $y = \bar{y}$. The diagram also shows that there is one (but only one) output level, i.e. $q = 200$ at point C, at which the minimum cost of production when $y = \bar{y}$ is the same as when both x and y are variable. However, for outputs exceeding 200 units, the minimum cost is lower when both factors are variable than when y is fixed at $\bar{y}$. For example, when both factors are variable, the minimum cost of 300 units is £30, as at point D; but point F shows that the minimum cost of 300 units when $y = \bar{y}$ is £33.

It should be clear that with both factors variable we can read off the minimum cost of any output by moving along 0E; with $y = \bar{y}$ we read the minimum cost of any attainable output by moving along $\bar{y}\bar{y}'$.

The principal inferences from Figure 6 are quite general: if a firm employing several factors can vary its employment of some factors but cannot vary that of others, the minimum cost at which it could produce any particular output will generally be higher than would be the case if all factors were variable; however, there may be some specific level of output at which minimum cost is the same in either case (as at point C in Figure 6).

THE SHORT RUN AND THE LONG RUN

In the preceding exposition, which for simplicity assumed only two factors of production (thereby enabling us to use graphical methods), we saw how to find the minimum cost of producing different levels of output (1) when both factors were variable and (2) when one factor was fixed and one was variable. Whether or not all factors are variable depends on the period under analysis. It is unlikely that the firm will be able to vary the services of machines, warehouses, etc. (capital equipment) available to it in a given day. But within two years it probably could. Within short periods the amount of physical capital available to the firm is likely to be fixed; over long periods it is variable.

The *short run* is defined as a period in which the firm can vary only some inputs, the amount available to it of other inputs being fixed. Those inputs which it can vary are called variable inputs. Those which are fixed are called fixed inputs.

The *long run* is defined as a period of time in which the firm can vary the amount used of all inputs.

It follows that there are two types of costs in the short run — fixed costs and variable costs. Variable costs are those incurred because of hire or purchase of factors of production which can be varied in amount. In the short run, some labour costs, the cost of raw materials and that of fuel, transport and power are normally variable. Fixed costs are those which do not vary with output. They are incurred, in the short run, even if output falls to zero. Suppose that a firm faces a trade recession. Although sales fall, its fixed costs do not change. It still has to meet over-heads like rent, insurance, depreciation and maintenance costs. For a plant of a given size, these costs must be incurred regardless of the level of output. Because the scale of a firm's operations can be varied (it can go out of business or grow very large) in the long run, long-run costs are all variable. Fixed costs do not normally exist in the long run.

It should now be clear that the locus 0E in Figures 5 and 6 above — what we called the firm's expansion path — pertained to the long run; it traced the minimum cost of producing various levels of output when both (all) factors were variable. The factor-limitation locus, $\overline{yy'}$ in Figure 6, pertained to a short-run situation; it traced the minimum cost of producing higher outputs when one factor was fixed and one was variable.

If a firm used many inputs to produce some good, there would exist an expansion path analogous to 0E in Figures 5 and 6 if all factors were variable (a long-run situation); if many inputs were fixed and some were variable, there would exist a factor-limitation locus analogous to yy' in Figure 6.

Returns to Scale

The phrase "returns to scale" refers to the response in output to a *simultaneous proportionate change* in the amount used of *all* inputs. In the traditional economics literature, returns to scale are usually long-run phenomena, because not all inputs can be varied in the short run. Returns to scale are *increasing* if a simultaneous proportionate change in the amounts used of all inputs yields a greater proportionate change in output. If a 100 per cent increase in all inputs yields a 200 per cent increase in output, returns to scale are increasing. If a simultaneous proportionate change in all inputs yields a smaller proportionate change in output, returns to scale are *decreasing*. If a simultaneous proportionate change in all inputs yields an equiproportionate change in output, returns to scale are *constant*.

Inspection of the isoquant map indicates returns to scale. If isoquants are plotted so that they represent equal increments in output, and if they remain equidistant, returns to scale are constant (see Figure 7a). What do we mean by equidistant? Draw any ray from the origin through the isoquant map. If, moving along any such ray, the isoquants are equidistant, constant returns to scale prevail. The isoquant map in Figure 7a has constant returns to scale. If the distance between the isoquants progressively increases, as in Figure 7b, decreasing returns to scale prevail. If the distance between isoquants decreases, as in Figure 7c, returns to scale are increasing.

Figure 7a

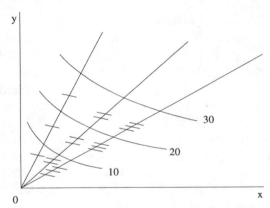

Figure 7b

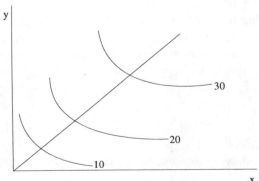

Figure 7c

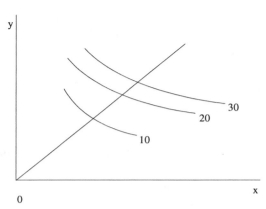

DERIVATION OF LONG-RUN COST CURVES

There is no reason why the firm's production function must always have increasing, constant or decreasing returns to scale over all levels of output. It is more likely that as the firm expands from a low level of output, it will experience increasing returns to scale, that it will then enter a phase of constant returns, and that for high outputs (perhaps not observed) returns to scale would decrease. In the analysis which follows, it is assumed that the firm's production function at first has increasing returns to scale, that a phase of constant returns is then entered, and that for very high levels of output returns to scale would be decreasing.

(It is noted in passing that the fact that returns to scale may change from increasing to constant to decreasing, as output is expanded, may seem to cause problems for the concept of returns to scale, as introduced above. Suppose, for example, that isoquants representing equal increments in output are progressively closer as output is expanded from, say, zero to 1,000 units — that increasing returns to scale prevail — and that the isoquants become equidistant over the output range 1,000–1,100 units. Our definition of returns to scale might then seem to imply that there were increasing returns to scale over the output ranges 1,000–1,100 units — which is something we do *not* wish to imply. However, if we interpret 1,000 units as the new origin, our definition causes no problems. Likewise, if isoquants representing equal increments in output become progressively further apart as output is expanded beyond 1,100 units, we regard 1,100 as the new origin, and state, consistent with the definition, that returns to scale are decreasing beyond q = 1,100.)

Some of the causes of increasing returns to scale are:

(1) There may be unavoidable excess capacity at low outputs because

certain factors of production are indivisible. For example, if a railway company wished to double services on given railway routes, it is unlikely that it would need to double the size or number of railway tunnels. Nor would it need to double its rolling stock on the routes. Managerial input is also indivisible. If output is low, it is unlikely, in order to double output, that the number of managers would need to be doubled.

(2) Both men and machines can be made more specialised as the scale of operations increases. Instead of performing several tasks, each man or machine can become more efficient on a smaller number of tasks.

A phase of constant returns to scale may be reached if all net technical advantages of further expansion are exhausted.

If output is very high, returns to scale might decrease because managerial efficiency, and communications within the firm, may break down if the firm grows beyond a certain size; that is one reason why we might not observe firms growing beyond certain sizes.

Figure 8

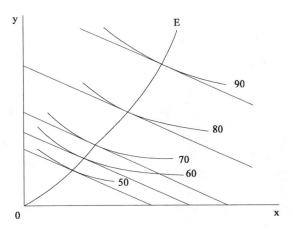

Assume that returns to scale are increasing, constant, and decreasing, depending on the scale of operations. Then, plotting isoquants for equal increments in output, the firm's isoquant map would be like that in Figure 8. Assume also that input prices are given. The isocost map then consists of a series of parallel lines, as in Figure 8. We can now construct the firm's expansion path, 0E. Each point on 0E shows two things: (a) a certain level of output and (b) the minimum cost of producing that output when all factors are variable. If we read off (a) and (b) from the expansion path, and plot them on different axes, we obtain a long-run total cost (LRTC) curve like that in Figure 9a. The firm's LRTC curve shows the minimum cost of producing each output level when all factors are variable.

Given input prices, the shape of the LRTC curve is determined by the production function. In Figure 9a the LRTC curve at first increases at a diminishing rate due to increasing returns to scale. When the phase of constant returns to scale is entered (from q = d to q = e) total costs increase at a constant rate. If the firm continues to expand output, it will experience decreasing returns to scale (which prevail for q in excess of q = e) and total costs will increase at an escalating rate.

Figure 9a

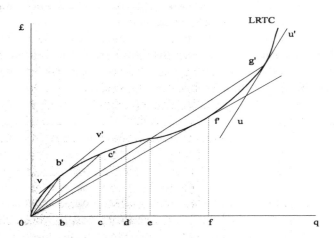

Figure 9b

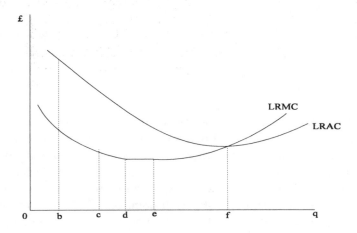

Once the LRTC curve is known, it is easy to derive the long-run average cost (LRAC) curve, because LRAC = (LRTC)/q. This is drawn in Figure

9b. The LRAC of any level of output is the slope of the ray from the origin to the LRTC curve at the output in question. For example, the LRAC of b units is bb'/0b. But bb'/0b is the slope of 0b'. Similarly, the LRAC of c units is the slope of 0c', while that of f units is the slope of 0f'. Note that the slopes of the rays from the origin to the LRTC curve are diminishing as output is expanded from 0 to f units; therefore LRAC is falling over such output ranges. Beyond f', the slopes of successive rays from the origin to the LRTC curve are increasing, so LRAC is rising over output levels beyond f units. An inference is that the LRAC curve attains its minimum when f units are produced.

Having derived long-run average costs from the LRTC curve, we now derive the long-run marginal cost (LRMC) curve. The marginal cost (MC) of the nth unit is the change in total cost due to producing n instead of (n - 1) units. The LRMC of any unit is $\Delta(LRTC)/\Delta q$, where $\Delta q = 1$; it is approximated by the slope of the total cost curve. The LRMC curve can, therefore, be derived directly from the LRTC curve. For output levels below $q = d$ in Figure 9a, the slope of the LRTC curve is falling. Therefore the LRMC curve is also falling, as in Figure 9b. Between $q = d$ and $q = e$ in Figure 9a, the slope of the LRTC curve is constant, but positive, so LRMC is constant over the same output ranges. Beyond $q = e$ the slope of the LRTC curve is rising, so LRMC is rising over those output ranges.

What is the relationship between the LRAC and the LRMC curves? In Figure 9a we see, for output levels below f units, that the slope of the LRTC curve is less than the slope of the ray from the origin to the LRTC curve at the same output (e.g. slope vv' < slope 0b'). Therefore, between 0 and f, LRMC < LRAC. At f, the slope of the LRTC curve is equal to the slope of the ray from the origin to the LRTC curve. Therefore, at f, LRMC = LRAC. But for any output level beyond f units, the slope of the LRTC curve exceeds the slope of the ray from the origin to the LRTC curve (e.g. slope uu' > slope 0g'). That is why, in Figure 9b, LRMC > LRAC for q > f.

There is an alternative explanation of the relationship between the LRAC and the LRMC curves. LRMC was defined as $\Delta LRTC$ when $\Delta q = 1$. If $\Delta LRTC$ because of producing an additional unit is less than the LRAC previously established, then LRAC is being pulled down. Hence, so long as LRMC < LRAC, LRAC must be declining. That is true whether or not LRMC itself is falling, constant or rising. If $\Delta LRTC$ because of producing an additional unit is greater than the LRAC previously established, then LRAC is being pulled up. So long as LRMC > LRAC, LRAC must be rising. That is true regardless of whether LRMC is falling, constant or rising. Hence, (a) if LRMC < LRAC, LRAC is falling and (b) if LRMC > LRAC, LRAC is rising.

It follows that the LRMC curve cuts the LRAC curve at its minimum point. Note that the statement "if LRMC is falling, then LRAC is falling, and if LRMC is rising, then LRAC is rising" is incorrect.

Given the prices of inputs, the shapes of the LRMC and LRAC curves were determined by the production function. The reason why both were U-shaped was because we assumed that the production function has increasing and decreasing returns to scale.

At this stage the informed reader might ask: why do many empirical studies suggest that the LRAC is L-shaped (rather than U-shaped, as assumed). The following considerations are relevant:

(1) Some firms may curtail expansion if rising unit costs are threatened. If that is the case, a rising LRAC curve will not be observed in empirical studies.

(2) A profit-maximising firm might have a very lengthy plateau of constant long-run average costs. It might find that its profit-maximising output is along that plateau. For such a firm, even though the LRAC curve would ultimately increase *if* output were expanded indefinitely, we would not observe such rising long-run average costs.

(3) The state of technology — and hence the firm's production function — changes over time. Empirical studies of cost and output over time — over, say, a decade — record the effects of changing technology. However, we assumed that the firm had a given production function: we assumed that the state of technology was constant. The analysis of the last several pages applies to circumstances in which (a) all factors are variable and (b) the firm's production function is given.

Having considered long-run cost structures we now turn to the short run.

THE SHORT-RUN COST STRUCTURE OF THE FIRM

The short run was defined as a period in which some factors of production are fixed, and some are variable. Assume that the firm has a plant of a given size — a fixed number of machines, a fixed amount of warehouse space, etc. Associated with a plant of fixed size, the firm must incur certain overhead costs which do not vary with output. Whether the firm produces much or little, short-run overhead costs are fixed. Such costs were earlier defined as fixed costs. Variable costs are those which vary with output. Costs incurred on unskilled labour, raw materials and on purchase of fuel and power are usually variable.

The short-run cost structure of the firm is derived from its factor limitation locus (recall Figure 6) and financial data. However, in the interests of space, the derivation will not be outlined here. We merely consider the type of cost structure to be expected in the short run. Having done so, some relationships between short-run and long-run costs will be examined.

Short-run total cost (C) at any level of output, in a plant of a given size, is the sum of total fixed cost (TFC) and total variable cost (TVC):

In the short run, $C = TFC + TVC$

Therefore, $C/q = TFC/q + TVC/q$

i.e. in the short run, $AC = AFC + AVC$

— average (total) cost consists of average fixed cost plus average variable cost. In order to construct the firm's AC curve it is necessary to consider AFC and AVC. Because TFC is a constant, the AFC curve (= TFC/q) must be a rectangular hyperbola, as in Figure 10. Discussion of the shape of the AVC curve is less straightforward. It is reasonable to assume that it is U-shaped, as in Figure 10. This assumption will now be justified.

Figure 10

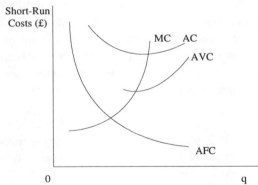

Rising average productivity of variable factors is the main reason why AVC is likely to fall. It is probable that the average product of labour will rise as output is expanded from a low level. Suppose that a clothing firm has available a cutting room, a machine and finishing room with ten sewing machines, and a general office in which packing, correspondence, and general secretarial work are conducted. If only one man is at work in the factory, he must act as cutter, machinist, finisher, packer, typist and telephone operator. He might produce five garments per week. However, if a second worker is employed, production will almost certainly rise above ten garments per week — the marginal product of the second unit of labour is likely to exceed that of the first, thereby pulling up the average product of labour. For *economies of the division of labour* can occur:

(1) Each worker can become more expert on a smaller range of tasks.

(2) There is saving in time lost in passing from one kind of work to another.

Such considerations make it probable that the average product of labour will continue to rise until the firm has at least one cutter, several machinists and finishers, and someone to attend to packing and office work. However, if the price of labour is given, rising average productivity of labour implies declining labour cost per unit. Other things being equal, AVC will fall because of rising labour productivity entailed by economies of the division of labour.

The AVC curve will eventually rise because of *the law of diminishing returns* (not to be confused with decreasing returns to scale) which states that, given the state of technology, as equal increments of one or more variable factors are combined with one or more fixed factors, total output will tend to increase, but, after a certain point at least, at a diminishing rate. If successively more workers are hired in a plant of a fixed size, declining marginal productivity of labour will eventually set in. The law of diminishing returns is axiomatic. It is obvious that, if successively more machinists are set to work on ten machines, a point will ultimately be reached at which the marginal product of machinists will start to decline. Because the marginal product of labour will ultimately decline, so also will the average product decline. (This will occur as soon as the marginal product of labour falls below the average product of labour.) Given the price of labour, labour cost per unit will therefore rise. Other things being equal, AVC will rise because of declining average productivity of the variable factors entailed by the law of diminishing returns. Thus, the AVC curve is U-shaped because:

(1) AVC will decline with economies of the division of labour.

(2) AVC will rise because of the law of diminishing returns.

It is now simple to construct the short run AC curve. Because AC = AFC + AVC, we need only add the AFC and AVC curves vertically, as in Figure 10. Note that the difference between AC and AVC is AFC. The AC and AVC curves converge as output increases, reflecting the fact that the difference between these curves — AFC — is steadily decreasing. Note also that the minimum point of the AC curve lies to the right of minimum AVC. This is because AFC continues to fall after AVC has started to rise.

The SRAC curve, like the LRAC curve, is U-shaped, but for different reasons. The LRAC curve is U-shaped because of economies and diseconomies *of scale*. Rephrasing what has already been stated, the SRAC curve is U-shaped because:

(1) The SRAC curve declines because (a) AFC falls as fixed overheads are spread over higher levels of output, and (b) AVC falls due to rising average productivity of the variable factors.

(2) The SRAC curve rises because of the law of diminishing returns.

There is a further cost of relevance in the short run — short-run marginal cost, SRMC. SRMC bears no relation to AFC. On the basis of reasoning similar to that in our discussion of LRAC and LRMC, we conclude that if AVC is declining, SRMC < AVC, and if AVC is rising, SRMC > AVC. Similarly, if AC is declining, SRMC < AC, and if AC is rising SRMC > AC. It follows that the short-run MC curve cuts the AVC and AC curves at their minima.

RELATIONSHIPS BETWEEN THE LRAC AND SRAC CURVES

When, in what follows, reference is made to a short-run average cost curve, we will be referring to the relationship between AC and output in a plant of a given size. Because plant size is fixed in the short run, the firm in the short run is confined to a given SRAC curve. In the long run, the firm can vary its plant size, thereby moving from one SRAC curve to another.

Suppose, in Figure 11, that the profit-maximising firm seeks to produce output A. In the long run it will build a plant (plant 1) which enables A units to be produced at minimum possible cost, $£AC_1$. $SRAC_1$ pertains to plant 1. If the firm is operating with plant 1, and if the firm wants to produce B units, it can do so in the short run only at an average cost of $£AC_2$, because of the law of diminishing returns. In the long run it can add to its capital stock and construct plant 2 — that plant which permits production of B units at minimum possible average cost, $£AC_1$. $SRAC_2$ is then the appropriate short-run average cost curve. If, with plant 2, the firm wishes to produce D units, it can do so, in the short run, only at an average cost of $£AC_3$. But in the long run it can adjust the scale of its plant to that (plant 3) which produces D units at minimum possible average cost $£AC_1$. $SRAC_3$ is the average cost curve for plant 3. The pattern of reasoning should be clear: if a firm wishes to produce any output at minimum average cost, it will, in the long run, construct that scale of

plant which enables it to do so. If, in Figure 11, it wishes to produce E
units, plant 4 is appropriate.

Figure 11

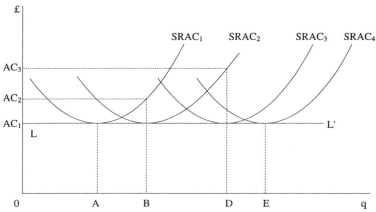

The firm's LRAC curve shows the minimum possible cost of producing
any output when all factors are variable. But in moving from one plant
size to another — from one SRAC curve to another — that is precisely
what we have been tracing in Figure 11. If plant size were continuously
variable, then (on the basis of an assumption to be made explicit immediately below) the curve LL' in Figure 11 would be the firm's LRAC
curve.

In the foregoing derivation of the long-run average cost curve, it was
implicitly assumed that the firm experienced no net economies or diseconomies of scale: it was assumed that, if all factors of production were
variable, LRAC would be constant as the firm expanded plant size. If
economies of scale prevail, then the higher the output, the lower the unit
cost that can be attained by expanding plant size. In Figure 12, for
example, the minimum possible unit cost of producing A units is $£AC_1$.
The cheapest way of producing B units is by constructing plant 2, in
which unit cost is $£AC_2$. If the profit-maximising firm wishes to produce
quantity D, it will build plant 3, which produces that output at a unit cost
$£AC_3$. Within the range 0D, larger plants can bring about expansions in
output at lower unit cost, because of economies of scale.

If diseconomies of scale prevail, larger outputs can be produced only
at rising unit costs. In Figure 12, plant 4 can produce E units at the
minimum possible unit cost, namely, $£AC_4$. The reason why the minima
of the SRAC curves are increasing as output is expanded beyond q = D is
because of diseconomies of scale (i.e. decreasing returns to scale).

Figure 12

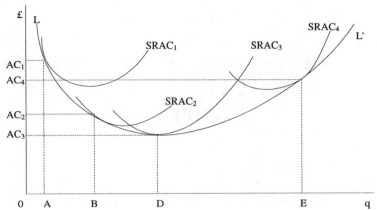

If plant size were continuously variable, the LRAC curve LL' in Figure 12 would trace the minimum possible cost of producing any level of output. It first slopes downwards due to economies of scale. Eventually it slopes upwards due to diseconomies of scale.

What, then, is the relationship between the firm's LRAC and SRAC curves? The answer is that the LRAC curve is the *envelope* of the SRAC curves for plants of different sizes. The reader can think of the LRAC curve as the nest of adjustment possibilities, through time, of the firm's SRAC curves as the firm moves from plants of small to progressively larger sizes, at a given state of technical knowledge.

CHAPTER 26

EQUILIBRIUM OF THE FIRM AND INDUSTRY UNDER PERFECT COMPETITION

In this chapter and in that which follows, we consider price and output determination in markets which are (a) perfectly competitive; (b) monopolistic; (c) imperfectly competitive; and (d) oligopolistic. Chapter 25 analysed cost structures. Before equilibrium of the firm and of the industry in different market structures are considered, it is necessary to examine the pattern of demand which the individual firm faces. Cost (supply) considerations and demand considerations will then be brought together.

In this chapter we confine ourselves to equilibrium in perfectly competitive markets. First, we clarify the meaning of equilibrium in the context at hand. A firm is in equilibrium in a given time period (short run or long run) if it has no incentive to change its decisions (e.g. its output) within that time period. The state of technology is assumed constant. A perfectly competitive *firm* is in *short-run equilibrium* if, given prices and plant size, it is producing that output which maximises profits; it is in *long-run equilibrium* if, given prices, it is operating in that plant size, and producing that output, which maximise profits. The *industry* is in (full, or long-run) equilibrium if there is no tendency towards change in the output of the industry. Two conditions are necessary for industry equilibrium under perfect competition:

(1) Each firm in the industry must be in long-run equilibrium.

(2) There must be no tendency towards change in the number of firms in the industry. If, for example, each firm were in long-run equilibrium — condition (1) — earning economic profits, then more firms would be attracted into the industry. Entry would change the industry's output. Thus, each firm must be earning only normal profits in long-run equilibrium if the industry is in full equilibrium under perfect competition.

DEMAND IN PERFECTLY COMPETITIVE MARKETS

It was seen in Chapter 4 that there are very large numbers of traders in perfectly competitive markets. Equilibrium price and quantity are determined by market supply and demand. Each firm is a price-taker; it cannot, by its own actions, influence price. In Figure 1a, P_0 and Q_0 are the equilibrium price and quantity of a particular good. The individual firm is one of a very large number of suppliers: its output is an infinitesimally small part of total supply. The firm does not affect market price by variation in its own output. The locus dd' in Figure 1b is therefore the demand curve which the *individual firm* faces in a perfectly competitive goods market. The locus dd' is also called the firm's average revenue (AR) curve. A firm's AR curve *is* its demand curve. For example, if the firm sells 100 units at £6 each, total revenue (TR) is £600; AR is TR/q = £600/100 = £6; hence price and AR are the same.

Figure 1b: The Firm   Figure 1a: The Industry

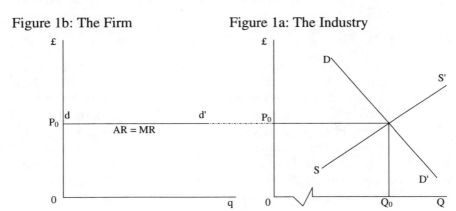

We define marginal revenue (MR) on the nth unit sold as the change in TR due to selling n instead of (n - 1) units. If price (AR) is constant, as in the case of a perfectly competitive firm, then MR = AR. For example, suppose, as before, that a firm can sell 100 units at price £6. Then TR = £600. If the firm operates in a perfectly competitive market it can sell 101 units at price £6 (AR = £6), and TR = £606. Then, MR = ΔTR = £(606 - 600) = £6 = AR; for the perfectly competitive firm, AR = MR, as in Figure 1b.

SHORT-RUN EQUILIBRIUM OF THE PERFECTLY COMPETITIVE FIRM

There are very many firms in a perfectly competitive industry. Nevertheless, we often refer to "the" firm in what follows. Thus, it will be assumed that this firm, in relevant ways, is representative of all firms in the industry. It will also be assumed that each firm is a price-taker in the factor market; thus, it is assumed that the firm regards the (explicit and implicit) prices of inputs as data beyond its control. Hence the firm, by expanding output, will not bid up factor prices against itself; however, expansion of the industry may bid up factor prices.

There are two constraints on industry output in the short run: (1) Each firm has plant of fixed size. (2) The number of firms in the industry is fixed.

In Figure 2a, SS' is the short-run supply curve of the perfectly competitive industry. Given the market demand curve DD', equilibrium price and quantity are P_0 and Q_0, respectively. The individual firm accepts that price as a datum. That is why the demand curve which the firm faces is $AR_0 = MR_0$ in Figure 2b. The firm's short-run cost structure is shown in the same diagram.

Figure 2b: The Firm   Figure 2a: The Industry

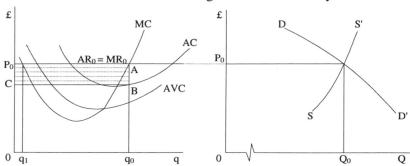

How much will the firm produce? If it produces any amount, it must produce a quantity for which MC = MR. That is a *necessary condition* for profit maximisation. Now MC = MR at both q_0 and q_1. Which of these quantities is the profit-maximising output? The answer is given by the *second-order condition* for profit maximisation, which states that the MC curve must cut the MR curve from below, as at q_0. Quantity q_0 is the firm's profit-maximising output. Given price P_0, the firm is in equilibrium when producing q_0: it has then no incentive to change its output, as it is maximising profits.

Why is the firm in equilibrium at q_0, the output level at which the MC curve cuts the MR curve from below? Consider what would happen if output were at any other level. It is clear that the firm would not produce q_1 (or any output less than q_1); if it did so, its sales price would not cover even variable cost per unit (AVC). Nor would it produce any other quantity below q_0. If output were less than q_0 (but greater than q_1), MR > MC. Hence the firm, by expanding output, would add more to TR than to TC.

The firm would therefore expand output to q_0. But it would not go beyond q_0. If the firm expanded beyond q_0, it would be adding more to its total costs than to its total revenues, because MC > MR for $q > q_0$. Thus, q_0 — the output at which the MC curve cuts the MR curve from below — is the profit-maximising output.

THE SHORT-RUN SUPPLY CURVE OF THE PERFECTLY COMPETITIVE FIRM

We have seen why the perfectly competitive firm, in the short run, would supply quantity q_0 at price P_0. If we could tell how much it would supply at every other price, we would know the firm's short-run supply curve. We therefore examine, in Figure 3b, how much the firm would produce at various hypothetical prices. Suppose, in Figure 3a, that the price of the firm's product were P_1. The corresponding AR = MR curve is the horizontal line $AR_1 = MR_1$. It is obvious that in this case the firm will produce nothing, because price is insufficient to cover unit variable costs of any possible quantity. The firm will not produce if P < AVC. Thus, short-run supply from the firm will be zero when $P < P_2$.

Figure 3b: The Firm   Figure 3a: The Industry

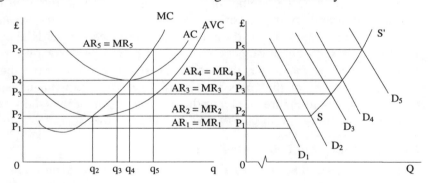

Let price now rise above P_2, to P_3. Note that P_3 < AC, so the firm will incur losses if it produces at price P_3. Note also that, at P_3, the firm can cover unit variable costs. We know that *if* the firm does produce any quantity, it will supply q_3 units, because this is the output at which the MC curve cuts the MR curve from below.

Will the firm have incentive to produce q_3 units? If output were zero, the firm would incur losses: fixed costs are incurred in the short run regardless of the level of output. If price were P_3, the firm, by producing q_3, could cover variable costs per unit. But because, at q_3, AR > AVC, the firm by producing q_3 would contribute *something* towards meeting fixed costs. By producing q_3 the firm would incur smaller losses than if output were zero. It can therefore be concluded that the firm will produce q_3 at price P_3. This kind of situation often prevails in the short run. Consider a firm during trade recession, when price has fallen, and the firm cannot cover its full costs at any level of output. The firm then faces a choice of remaining in production or temporarily closing down. If it closes down, its entire fixed costs must be met either by borrowing or by drawing on funds accumulated in the past. But if price, though less than AC, exceeds AVC, then the firm can, by staying in production, cover all variable costs and *part* of its fixed costs. In such cases it would incur smaller short-run losses by producing than by not producing. Hence, in the short run, the firm will produce to where MC = MR as long as price exceeds AVC. Thus, referring to Figure 3b, if price were P_3 or P_4 or P_5, the firm would produce q_3 or q_4 or q_5, respectively.

We have examined how much the firm would produce at various prices in the short run: as long as price exceeds AVC, it will produce to where MC meets MR from below. As price rises, the firm expands along its MC curve until MC = MR. It follows that the firm's short-run supply curve is that part of its MC curve which lies above its AVC curve.

In the short run, the number of firms in the industry is fixed. In the interests of simplicity in exposition, assume that if the industry expands its output in the short run, it does not bid factor prices upwards against itself. Under such circumstances, the *short-run supply curve* of a perfectly competitive *industry* is the horizontal (sideways) sum of the short-run supply curves of the firms in the industry. The short-run industry supply curve SS' in Figure 3a is thus the horizontal sum of the (short-run) marginal cost curves of all the firms in the industry, for MC $\geq$ AVC.

Normal Profits and Economic Profits

It has been noticed above that the perfectly competitive firm could, in short-run equilibrium, be earning economic profits (as at price P_5 in Figure 3b), incurring losses (as at P_3) or just breaking even (as at P_4). Economic profit is the difference between costs and revenues. But recall from Chapter 25 what we mean by costs. A firm's costs are those payments which it must incur in order to maintain factor supplies. There are four kinds of factors of production — land, labour, capital and enterprise. The firm's total costs include payments to each. Rent must be paid for land, wages must be paid to labour, and an implicit or explicit rental must be paid for capital. Otherwise the factors will not be supplied to the firm. The *supply price* to the firm of any factor of production is the minimum price which that factor must be paid if it is to be supplied to the firm.

Normal profit is the supply price of enterprise. Normal profits in any industry are the minimum profits an entrepreneur must receive in order to have incentive to stay in the industry in the long run. They are payments to the factor enterprise. Because they are the supply price of a factor, they are costs of production. Normal profits are therefore included in the firm's AC curve. Economic or "supernormal" profits are payments to enterprise in excess of normal profits. The firm in Figure 2b is in *short-run equilibrium* earning economic profits represented by the shaded area P_0ABC. However, it will soon be seen that in the long run these will be competed away. In long-run competitive equilibrium, each firm earns zero economic profits. That does not mean that the firm earns zero profits in the long run: in (long-run) *industry equilibrium*, the perfectly competitive firm earns normal profits; otherwise the firm would leave the industry or more firms would be attracted into the industry (implying that the perfectly competitive industry was not in equilibrium to begin with).

LONG-RUN EQUILIBRIUM OF THE FIRM, AND INDUSTRY EQUILIBRIUM

In the long run, the firm can adjust plant size to produce any output at minimum possible cost. The conditions for *long-run equilibrium of the firm* are:

(1) The firm must be able to cover all costs of production. This condition is satisfied if its AR is at least as great as its long-run average cost (AC_L). Thus, in the long run, $AR \geq AC_L$. In the long run, if the firm cannot cover its full production costs, it will go out of business.

(2) Assuming condition (1) satisfied, the firm in the long run will produce that level of output at which its long-run marginal cost (MC_L) curve cuts its MR curve from below. The perfectly competitive firm's *long-run supply curve* is that part of its MC_L curve which lies above its AC_L curve.

The long-run analysis of perfectly competitive markets is complicated: an understanding of what is to follow therefore demands concentration. In general, the long-run supply curve of the perfectly competitive *industry* is *not* the sideways sum of the long-run supply curves of the individual firms. (This assertion will be clarified in the next few pages.) Two types of adjustment in plant availability can occur in perfectly competitive markets in the long run. Suppose, because of an increase in demand, that each firm earns supernormal profits in the short run. In the long run each firm can adjust its plant size. But because of supernormal profits, and because there is freedom of entry, new firms will be attracted into the industry in the long run. The resulting increase in supply will force price down. Entry will continue until supernormal profits are no longer available — until price (AR) has been bid down to a level equal to that of the minimum point of the firm's AC_L.

In the long run, therefore, the *industry* will be in equilibrium when each firm is producing an output at which (1) its MC_L curve cuts its MR curve from below, and (2) $AC_L = AR$. Condition (1) implies that each firm is in long-run equilibrium. Condition (2) implies that there will be no tendency towards entry to, or exit from, the industry. If $AC_L = AR$, each firm in the industry is earning only normal profits, supernormal profits then being zero.

External Economies and Diseconomies

External economies occur if an increase in the size of an industry reduces unit costs of the firms in the industry. These economies are external to the individual firm — they occur because of growth of the industry as a whole, rather than because of growth of any particular firm. A firm experiences external economies if its cost curves *shift down* because of expansion in the output of the industry. For example, it is possible that the price of steel to each firm in an industry using steel as an input will be reduced if expansion of that industry enables the steel industry to avail of economies of scale. That would not be due to the expansion of any particular firm in the steel-using industry; it would be due to growth of the steel-using industry as a whole. That is why such economies are considered external to the individual firm — they are not caused by its own growth. The lower price of steel would cause the AC curves of firms in the steel-using industry to shift down, implying that each can now produce any given output at lower unit costs.

External diseconomies occur if an increase in the size of an industry increases per unit costs of the firms in the industry. For example, each firm in an industry experiences external diseconomies if expansion in the size of the industry bids up the price of skilled labour. Because of forces external to itself, the individual firm must then pay more for skilled labour. The firm could then produce a given output only at higher unit costs. External diseconomies cause *upward shifts* in the cost curves of the firms in the industry.

If (net) external diseconomies prevail in an industry, that industry's long-run supply curve slopes upwards; it is called an *increasing-cost industry*. If external economies prevail, the industry's long-run supply curve slopes downwards; it is a *decreasing-cost industry*. If neither external economies nor external diseconomies prevail, then the industry is a *constant-cost industry*; its long-run supply curve is horizontal. It is usual to assume that the long-run supply curve of a perfectly competitive industry slopes upwards: although no single firm bids up factor prices against itself, it is likely that the prices of some factors of production will be bid up (against existing firms and against new firms) as the aggregate output of an industry expands following the entry of more firms to the industry.

Industry Equilibrium in an Increasing-Cost Industry

We now consider a perfectly competitive industry's adjustment towards full equilibrium. We begin with the industry in full equilibrium, we will suppose that there is an increase in demand, and we will then examine the adjustment towards a new industry equilibrium.

With price P_0 in Figure 4a, the industry is in equilibrium because:

(1) The typical firm is in long-run equilibrium. It has adjusted plant size to produce q_0 at minimum possible cost. It is operating that plant up to the point at which the short-run marginal cost curve, MC_s, cuts the MR curve, MR_0, from below.

(2) The typical firm, in a plant of optimum size, is earning only normal profits ($AC_s = AR_0$); therefore the number of firms in the industry shows no tendency to change.

Figure 4b: The Firm   Figure 4a: The Industry

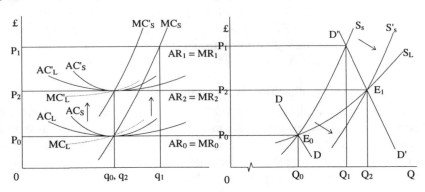

Next, suppose that the industry demand curve shifts to D'D'. In the short run, price rises to P_1. The typical firm's AR and MR curve is now given by $AR_1 = MR_1$. The firm expands along its MC_s curve and produces q_1. Note that because $AR_1 > AC_s$ at q_1, the firm earns economic, or supernormal, profits. In the long run, therefore, more firms enter the industry. As more firms enter, the short-run industry supply curve S_s, shifts to the right. This causes price to fall and eliminates some of the supernormal profits.

However, there is another force reducing supernormal profits. If, as is assumed here, external diseconomies prevail, then expansion in the size of the industry causes the cost curves of each firm to shift upwards, as in Figure 4b. Entry to the industry will cease only when the typical firm is no longer earning supernormal profits. Such a situation prevails when price has fallen to P_2 in Figure 4a. The industry is then in equilibrium because its output shows no tendency to change. Entry has caused price to fall from P_1 to P_2. But it has also caused the AC curves of the representative firm to shift up, because of external diseconomies.

Locus S_L is the long-run supply curve of the perfectly competitive industry. It traces the horizontal sum of the minimum of each firm's long-run average cost curve. The reason why, in the present case, it slopes upwards, is that external diseconomies cause each firm's LRAC curve — and hence its minimum point — to shift up as the industry expands. Point E_0 might be the horizontal sum of the minimum of each firm's LRAC curve when there are N (a very large number) firms in the industry; point E_1 might be the horizontal sum of such minima when the industry has expanded to 2N firms. The reason why E_1 lies above E_0 is that each firm's LRAC curve shifted upward as the industry expanded.

(It is noted in passing that in Figure 4b, AC'_L is drawn in such a manner that its minimum is at the same q as that of AC_L. Alert readers ask whether this is inevitable; the answer is no. External diseconomies cause upward shifts in the firm's AC curves, but that may be directly upwards or upwards to the right or left, depending on the precise form of the external diseconomies. A similar observation applies in the situation with external economies, discussed below.)

Industry Equilibrium in a Decreasing-Cost Industry

We now consider adjustment towards industry equilibrium in a decreasing-cost industry — when expansion in the size of the industry yields external economies to all firms in the industry. As before, we start with the industry in equilibrium at price P_0, and consider its adjustment after an increase in demand.

The curve S_s in Figure 5a is the industry's short-run supply curve — it shows the amounts supplied at various prices, given the supply potential of the industry in the short run. It is the horizontal sum of the short-run supply curves of all the firms in the industry (fixed in the short-run). DD is the market demand curve. Equilibrium price and quantity are P_0 and Q_0, respectively. The representative firm's AR = MR curve is $AR_0 = MR_0$ in Figure 5b.

At price P_0 in Figure 5b, the typical firm is in long-run equilibrium — it has adjusted to optimum plant size and has no incentive to change its output from q_0. Because the firm is earning no economic profits ($AC_L = AC_s = AR_0$), the industry is also in equilibrium.

Suppose that demand increases to D'D' in Figure 5a. In the short run, price rises to P_1, a datum to the representative firm. The firm's new AR = MR curve is $AR_1 = MR_1$ in Figure 5b. In the short run, the firm expands along its MC curve until $MC_s = MR_1$. The representative firm is then producing q_1. Note that the firm is now earning supernormal profits per unit, given by the distance between AC_s and AR_1, at q_1. Therefore, in the long run, firms enter the industry, causing S_s to shift to the right, which forces price down. If, as is assumed here, expansion in the size of the industry causes external economies, the cost curves of the typical firm shift downwards.

Figure 5b   Figure 5a

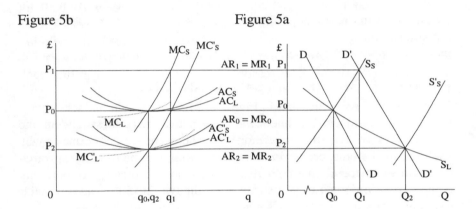

Entry continues until the representative firm no longer earns supernormal profits. Throughout this adjustment process, the industry's short-run supply curve continues shifting to the right, causing price to fall, while simultaneously, the AC curves of the representative firm continue to shift downwards, because of external economies.

Eventually a situation is reached at which the typical firm can no longer earn supernormal profits. The industry has then reached a new equilibrium. Such a situation is attained in Figures 5a and 5b when price has fallen to P_2, and industry output has increased to Q_2. The firm's AR and MR curves are now $AR_2 = MR_2$. Its cost curves — AC'_s, AC'_L, MC'_s and MC'_L — have shifted downwards because of external economies. When, at price P_2, the firm is producing q_2, the industry has reached a new equilibrium. The firm then has no incentive to change output or plant size. And because the representative firm is only breaking even (at price P_2 and quantity q_2), there is no tendency for the number of firms in the industry to change.

The locus S_L in Figure 5a is the industry's long-run supply curve. It is the horizontal sum of the minima of the LRAC curves of the firms in the industry. It slopes downwards because external economies cause each firm's LRAC curve — and hence its minimum point — to shift downward as the industry expands. The long-run supply curve of a perfectly competitive industry slopes downwards if external economies prevail.

(It is noted that the presence of external economies in a given industry could be due to unexhausted increasing returns to scale in some firm supplying inputs to the given industry. As will be made clear in the chapter which follows, this implies that the industry supplying the input in question could not be perfectly competitive.)

We have examined adjustment towards industry equilibrium in increasing and in decreasing cost industries. It is left to the reader to trace the adjustment in constant-cost industries and to show that the long-run industry supply curve is then a horizontal line (i.e. it is infinitely elastic).

PERFECT COMPETITION, EFFICIENCY AND INCOME DISTRIBUTION

It was mentioned earlier that few if any actual markets satisfy all the requirements of perfect competition. But there are several reasons why analysis of perfect competition is worthwhile. Actual markets often approximate the conditions of perfect competition. Knowledge of perfectly competitive markets gives insights into the workings of such similar markets; that was shown in Chapters 6 to 8 where some applications of supply and demand analysis were considered. Furthermore, perfect competition is a *desideratum* which yields criteria by which we may judge actual market structures.

Resource Allocation

If we assume (a) that marginal cost to the firm (MPC — marginal private cost, or, more simply, MC) corresponds to marginal social cost (MSC) and (b) that market price is a measure of marginal social value (MSV), then a necessary condition for an optimal allocation of resources from the point of view of society is that each firm produce up to the point at which MC = price. Some elaboration of this statement will now be provided.

Define the MSC of the nth unit of a good as the change in total cost, no matter by whom in society it is incurred, due to producing n instead of (n - 1) units of that good. For example, if production of an additional unit of a good involves emission of smoke which pollutes the atmosphere, then the MSC of that unit equals the change in total cost incurred by the firm in producing that additional unit (MPC) *plus* the monetary value of the damage done to all persons in the community by the air pollution.

We can think of the MSV of the nth unit of a good as the change in welfare of society due to consumption of the nth unit of that good. It is reasonable to assume that the price which individuals are just willing to pay for a good is a measure of the relative subjective value of that good to them. Therefore, if an individual's consumption does not interfere with the welfare of others, it seems reasonable to regard price as in some sense a measure of marginal social value.

A necessary condition for an optimal allocation of resources is that each firm produce up to a point at which MSC = MSV. That can be seen by considering the implications for the welfare of society if, for some good, MSC is not equal to MSV. If, when a firm is producing a given level of output, MSC < MSV, then the cost incurred by society in the production of an additional unit would be less than the increase in welfare of society due to consumption of that additional unit. The social interest therefore requires that the firm expand production, for as long as MSC < MSV. However, if, when a firm is producing a given level of output, MSC > MSV, then the additional cost incurred by society due to production of the last unit would exceed the increase in welfare of society due to consumption of the last unit. The social interest requires that the firm contract output for as long as MSC > MSV. Thus, a necessary condition for an optimal allocation of resources from society's point of view is that each firm produce an output for which MSC = MSV.

Is this requirement for optimality attained in perfectly competitive markets? Both in the short run and in the long run, the perfectly competitive firm produces an output for which MC equals price. Given assumptions (a) and (b) above, it follows that the perfectly competitive firm produces an output for which MSC = MSV. It can therefore be stated that if assumptions (a) and (b) are valid, a necessary condition for an optimal allocation of resources would be attained in perfectly competitive markets. Given those assumptions, perfectly competitive markets satisfy one of the requirements for overall economic efficiency.

Income Distribution

It has been seen that the perfectly competitive firm could be in short-run equilibrium earning supernormal profits. But such supernormal profits could not prevail for long. We saw that if the representative perfectly competitive firm earns supernormal profits in the short run, these will be competed away in the long run, by entry to the industry. When the industry is in full (long-run) equilibrium, each firm is earning only normal profits. Thus, the pattern of income distribution emerging from perfectly competitive markets might tend to be more egalitarian than that emerging from market forms in which the individual firm can continue to make supernormal profits in the long run. However, note that as *economists*, we cannot say that there is anything "good" or "bad" about the pattern of income distribution emerging from any particular form of market structure.

CHAPTER 27

DEPARTURES FROM PERFECT COMPETITION

We now turn to goods markets which substantively deviate from the conditions of perfect competition. Chapter 28, by Patrick McNutt, will review legal attitudes in Ireland concerning market structure. It will be seen that although openness implies that much of the tradable goods sector approximates perfect competition in relevant ways (recall Chapters 6 to 8), there may be very significant departures from perfect competition in certain sectors, especially in non-tradable goods and services. In such cases, the state may be a monopoly producer, or legislation seeks to foster competition.

PURE MONOPOLY

A pure monopolist is the sole seller of a good which has no close substitutes. Pure monopoly and perfect competition are extremes on a *spectrum* of market structures. Actual goods markets lie between them, some approximating pure monopoly, others closer to perfect competition.

Demand under Pure Monopoly

Because there is only one firm in the industry under pure monopoly, there is then no distinction between firm and industry. The monopolist's demand curve *is* the industry demand curve. As such, it slopes downwards. The locus DD' in Figure 1 is the monopolist's demand curve; its AR curve. It will be assumed that any advertising outlay by the monopolist remains constant. In order to sell more, the monopolist must reduce price; the monopolist is a price-maker rather than a price-taker. That is why, under monopoly, MR < AR, as in Figure 1. Note how this contrasts with the perfectly competitive firm, which is a price-taker.

Suppose, for example, that the monopolist can sell 10 units at £6 each (TR = £60, AR = £6). If the monopolist wishes to sell 11 units, then that firm must reduce price, say to £5.95, because the firm *is* the industry — and the industry faces a downward sloping demand curve. TR is then £(11)(5.95) = £65.45, and AR = £5.95. The corresponding MR (= ΔTR) is £5.45. Because the firm must reduce price in order to sell an eleventh unit, MR (£5.45) < AR (£5.95).

Figure 1

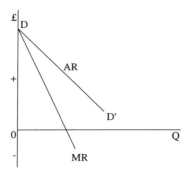

The monopolist's MR can become negative. Suppose that the firm could sell 20 units at £3 each (TR = £60, AR = £3). In order to sell 21 units, it must reduce price, say, to £2.80. The monopolist's TR is then £(2.80)(21) = £58.80, and AR = £2.80. But MR = ΔTR = £(58.80 - 60) = - £1.2; MR has become negative (implying that demand is inelastic at low prices).

The Sources of Monopoly

The central reason why monopoly exists is that other firms find it un-profitable or impossible to enter the industry. Thus, the persistence of monopoly over time is due to *barriers on entry* to an industry. Such barriers may enable the monopolist to earn supernormal profits in the long run. Conspiracies, intimidation and brute force aside, there are two principal kinds of barriers — *technical barriers* and *legal barriers.*

The prevalence of increasing returns to scale in a single firm is a major *technical barrier* on entry, and hence an important source of monopoly power. If economies of scale in a single firm prevail over all relevant ranges of industry output, then total supply can be produced most cheaply by a single firm. Such a firm is called a *natural monopoly*. Public utilities are frequently natural monopolies: a large town or city is usually best served by a single gas company, a single supplier of elec-tricity, and a single sewage-disposal authority. Competition in such mar-kets may imply wasteful duplication of resources: a natural monopoly can normally supply any level of output at lower unit cost than a large number of competing firms.

Another technical basis of monopoly is unique knowledge of a low-cost production technique. The problem of a monopolist fearing entry is then to keep this technique to itself alone. That may be difficult unless the technology is protected by a patent. Sole ownership of essential resources (e.g. mineral deposits), prohibitive transport costs or absolute cost advantages due to entrepreneurial efficiency may be other technical sources of monopoly.

Entry to an industry is often limited by *legal controls*. Patent rights are important in this context. A patent gives an inventor of a new process the exclusive right to use that process for a number of years. Patent rights thus encourage innovation. But they also restrict entry of potential competitors to an industry. High tariff protection of a small domestic market, or the provision of a licence giving a single firm exclusive rights to supply the domestic market, may be further legal sources of monopoly. Finally, the state may form a monopoly in some good if it reserves to itself the provision of that good to the domestic market. (Note, however, that state monopolies are often industries which, because of increasing returns to scale, would tend to be monopolies in the absence of state ownership; this consideration, along with the fact that they might be in a position to earn supernormal profits indefinitely, may be one of the reasons for the nationalisation of such industries.) In what follows in this chapter, the discussion will be confined to the private sector of the economy.

Price and Output under Monopoly

Assuming that the firm can cover its variable costs, the monopolist, in the short run, will produce that level of output at which its short-run MC curve cuts its MR curve from below. In the long run, it can adjust the size of its plant so as to produce any level of output at minimum cost. Assuming that the firm can cover its total costs, the monopolist, in the long run, will produce that output at which its long-run MC curve cuts its MR curve from below.

The pattern of demand which the monopolist faces is shown by the curve AR in Figure 2a. The AR and MR curves both slope downwards for reasons already indicated. The firm's long-run cost structure is also shown in the same diagram.

The profit-maximising monopolist in Figure 2a will produce Q_0 — the quantity given by the intersection of its MC_L and MR curves. It will charge the highest price consistent with that quantity, p_0. If quantity were less than Q_0, then MR > MC: the firm could add more to its total revenue than to its total cost by expanding output. It would therefore expand up to Q_0, at least. If it expanded beyond Q_0, then MC > MR: the firm would be adding more to cost than to revenue. Thus, price p_0 and quantity Q_0 are the profit-maximising price and quantity under monopoly. Charging p_0 and producing Q_0, the firm is in long-run equilibrium because it has no incentive to change the size of its plant or its output. The industry is in full equilibrium because the firm is in long-run equilibrium, and because the firm is the industry.

The firm in Figure 2a is earning supernormal profits, represented by the rectangle p_0ABC. If it remains a monopolist, it can earn such supernormal profits indefinitely; they will not be competed away by entry to the industry. However, there is no reason why a monopolist *must* earn supernormal profits in the long run, even if it tries to do so. The monopolist could not earn supernormal profits if its demand and long-run cost conditions were as depicted in Figure 2b. At best, such a firm could only break even.

Figure 2a

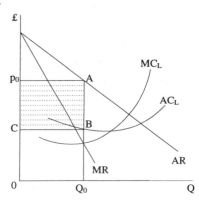

Figure 2b

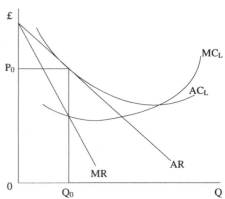

Non-existence of Supply Curves under Monopoly

It was stated in Chapter 4 that it is *only* in perfectly competitive markets that price is determined by the intersection of supply and demand *curves*.

That is mainly because a well-defined supply curve does not normally exist in market structures other than perfect competition. Recall the definition of a supply curve in Chapter 4 — a supply curve shows the various alternative quantities of a good which producers will supply at various alternative prices, other things being equal. Consider now the monopolist whose MC curve is depicted in Figure 3. It can be seen that whether its demand curve is AR_0 or AR_1, in either case the firm will supply the same output, Q_0. That is because the firm's MC curve intersects the corresponding MR curves, MR_0 and MR_1, at the same point, E. The two patterns of demand imply two different prices, p_0 and p_1; nevertheless, quantity supplied in either case is the same, Q_0. There is, in fact, an *infinity* of possible demand patterns (only two of which are depicted in the diagram) for which MR can cut MC at point E. Each of those demand patterns implies a different equilibrium price. Hence, it is concluded that a monopolist may supply Q_0 at any one of an infinity of possible prices; it will do so as long as the MR curve intersects the MC curve at point E. There is thus no *definite* relationship between price and quantity supplied under monopoly; hence a supply curve does not exist under monopoly. It would be wrong, therefore, to state that the equilibrium price under monopoly is determined by the supply and demand curves. For the supply curve does not then exist.

Figure 3

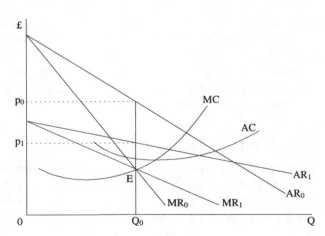

SOME ISSUES IN ASSESSING MONOPOLY
Resource Allocation
From the standpoint of society, the profit-maximising monopolist misallocates resources if (a) private costs coincide with social costs and (b)

market price can correctly be regarded as a measure of marginal social value. The monopolist produces an output for which MC = MR. But because MR is less than price (i.e. AR), the monopolist, when in equilibrium, produces an output for which MC < P. Hence, at the equilibrium level of output of a monopolist, and if provisos (a) and (b) are satisfied, marginal social cost (as defined toward the end of Chapter 26), is less than marginal social value. Recall from Chapter 26 that a necessary condition for an optimal allocation of resources throughout the economy is that each firm produce an output for which MSC = MSV. Thus, in the absence of government regulation, monopoly equilibrium yields a smaller output than the public interest requires.

It was also observed in Chapter 26 that as long as provisos (a) and (b) above are satisfied, MSC = MSV under perfect competition. This may appear to imply that, for the maximisation of social welfare, monopolistic markets must be dismembered and made perfectly competitive. However, as will shortly be shown, the latter conclusion does not follow; *if* the source of monopoly is increasing returns to scale, then it may be impossible, on any sustained basis, to transform (e.g. by legislation) a monopolistic industry into a perfectly competitive industry. Key points in this context are that (a) for technical reasons, it may be impossible to have perfect competition in an industry; (b) for technical reasons, monopoly may be inevitable, but if unregulated, the monopolistic industry will involve misallocation of resources as already explained, and (c) given that monopoly may sometimes have to be accepted as a fact of life, the only way in which government may ensure a sensible allocation of resources may have to involve regulation of monopoly. As will be shown, this might sometimes involve subsidisation of private-sector monopolies, or nationalising them and perhaps operating them at commercial losses. The reasoning under (a), (b) and (c) above will be clarified shortly.

"Excess Capacity", Price and Output

We know that the individual firm in full industry equilibrium under perfect competition produces as much as possible, and charges the lowest possible price, consistent with the firm breaking even. Because such a firm would tend to be operating at the minimum point of its AC_L, this implies, in a sense, that the individual firm under perfect competition would tend to be utilising its capacity fully. It is extremely unlikely that it would be in the interests of a profit-maximising monopolist to produce at the minimum point of its AC_L curve; it would do so only if the MR curve happened to intersect the MC curve at that minimum point. It is sometimes said that if a situation like that depicted in Figure 2b arises, then the monopolist must be operating with excess capacity, because it is producing an output below that corresponding to the minimum point of its AC_L curve. However, we cannot see anything of substance in such reasoning, because:

(1) Given the size of the market as represented by the monopolist's demand (i.e. AR) curve, it is not clear how the industry depicted in Figure 2b could possibly be made perfectly competitive;

(2) If the monopolist depicted in Figure 2b did produce at minimum AC_L, it would not only be incurring losses, but also, too much would be produced from the standpoint of efficient resource allocation: because MC would then exceed AR, i.e. price, MSC > MCV (assuming that private cost coincides with social cost, and that market price is the same as marginal social value).

Except when a situation like that depicted in Figure 2b arises, the unregulated profit-maximising monopolist charges a price in excess of average cost. On the basis of this consideration, it is often said that the price charged will be higher, and quantity produced will be lower, under monopoly than would be the case if there were a large number of competing firms in the industry. Such conclusions are not necessarily correct: they overlook the importance of increasing returns to scale as a source of monopoly. If a monopolist experiences increasing returns to scale over *all* relevant ranges of output, then the monopolist could produce any level of output at lower unit cost than a large number of competing firms. Under such circumstances it is *possible* that price will be lower under monopoly than in a more competitive environment. Furthermore, under the conditions specified, an attempt to dismember the monopolist, and to introduce something like perfect competition to the industry, would surely break down: increasing returns to scale accruing to any single firm over all ranges of industry output are inconsistent with perfect competition. Thus, *technology* may decree that perfect competition is unattainable. These propositions are illustrated in Figure 4.

The existence of increasing returns to scale over all ranges of industry output is the source of monopoly power for the firm depicted in Figure 4. The monopolist, if unregulated, would produce Q_m and would charge price p_m. Suppose that the monopolist were dismembered and that several competing firms were introduced in its place. It is reasonable to assume that the technology available to those competing firms would be the same as that of the monopolist. Suppose, shortly after the monopolist was broken up, that each of the competing firms was producing a small proportion of the previous industry output, say q_c. The average cost of the competing firms would then be very high; in the case depicted in Figure 4 it would exceed the price consumers are willing to pay for the good. Some of the competing firms would therefore leave the industry. A greater share of market demand would then accrue to those remaining. Suppose that there were only two competitors remaining, each producing q'_c. Note that average cost in each of the competing firms would exceed the AC_L which would prevail under monopoly equilibrium. Furthermore, because of increasing returns to scale, if one of the competing firms expanded its output, it could in the long run attain a lower level of average costs than its rival. The increased industry output would also mean that price would have fallen. Hence, the firm expanding output would drive its sole remaining rival out of business, and would itself become a monopolist.

Figure 4

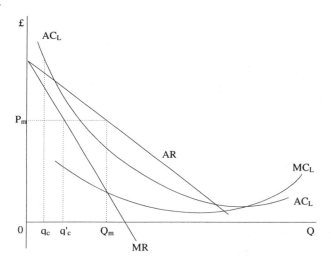

It has been shown:

(1) If increasing returns to scale are the source of monopoly, price may be lower, and industry output higher, under unregulated monopoly than in a (transitory) situation involving competition.

(2) An attempt to break up a monopoly and to introduce something like perfect competition in its place would, if increasing returns to scale were the source of the monopoly, tend to break down. Competition among firms, each with increasing returns to scale over relevant ranges of industry output, would tend to restore the initial monopolistic market structure.

Indeed, increasing returns to scale over all ranges of industry output are inconsistent with perfect competition, in the long run.

It is emphasised that the above remarks pertain to situations in which increasing returns to scale are the source of monopoly; they will frequently be invalid if other considerations, such as legal controls (e.g. patents or tariff protection) are the sources of monopoly. For example, if tariff protection in the domestic market is the source of monopoly, it will usually be possible to attain a lower equilibrium price by removing the tariff.

Income Distribution

It has been seen that except when situations like that in Figure 2b arise, an unregulated monopolist earns supernormal profits in the long run. That could not occur under perfect competition. When the industry is in full equilibrium under perfect competition, the typical firm is earning only normal profits. Thus unregulated monopolistic markets may tend to exacerbate income inequality.

REGULATION OF MONOPOLY: SOME EXTENSIONS

The preceding analysis suggests two objectives of public policy in regulation of monopoly:

(1) To induce the monopolist to produce more than it would if exempt from regulation. Without regulation, the monopolist would produce to where MC = MR (with MC intersecting MR from below). At that level of output, MC < P. Therefore (if two assumptions stated towards the end of Chapter 26 are satisfied), MSC < MSV. The objective of regulation may be to improve resource allocation by removing the divergence of MSC from MSV.

(2) A second objective of regulation may be to reduce supernormal profits.

Marginal Cost Pricing and Profits

Government may try to improve resource allocation by requiring the monopolist to produce that output at which its marginal cost curve intersects its AR curve from below; then MC = P. However, there is no guarantee that this would eliminate supernormal profits. Furthermore, if increasing returns to scale are the source of the monopoly, government may need to subsidise the firm if it is required to produce to where MC = P. Figures 5a and 5b clarify these points.

Figure 5a

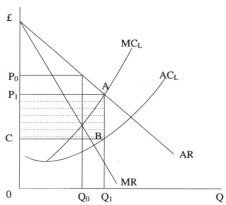

Figure 5b

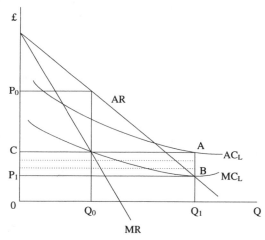

In Figure 5a, the monopolist, unregulated, would produce Q_0 and charge p_0. If the firm were required to produce Q_1 it could obtain only the lower equilibrium price, p_1. Marginal cost would then equal price, but some supernormal profits would remain. These are shown by the rectangle p_1ABC. (Of course the government could require the monopolist to supply the even larger output at which AC = AR, thereby eliminating the supernormal profits; but because marginal cost would then exceed price, this would involve misallocation of resources: the monopolist would then be producing too much.) Government could eliminate the supernormal profits attained at Q_1 by imposing a lump-sum tax per period, equal in value to the rectangle p_1ABC. Such a lump-sum tax would in effect be a charge per period for a licence or franchise permitting the firm to produce the good under consideration. Because, by definition of lump sum, the tax would not vary with output, it would in effect be a fixed cost. Precisely because it would not vary with output, it would not affect MC_L. The MC_L curve would remain as in Figure 5a, while the AC_L curve would shift upwards; if the lump-sum tax were p_1ABC per period, then the supernormal profits would be eliminated entirely, while the point at which MC_L intersects AR would remain unchanged. Under the circumstances indicated, the monopolist would be producing output Q_1, at which MC = P, earning only normal profits.

That it may be necessary to subsidise a monopolistic firm which is required to produce to where MC = P is evident from Figure 5b. In this case the monopolist, unregulated, would produce Q_0 at price p_0. Government could eliminate the supernormal profits then being earned, by requiring the monopolist to produce an output at which AC = AR, but it can be seen from the diagram that the monopolist would still be producing too little, because under such circumstances, $MC_L < P$. Suppose that the government required the monopolist to produce Q_1; then $MC_L = p_1$. However, because $MC_L = p_1 < AC_L$, the monopolist would be incurring losses, as represented by the shaded rectangle $CABp_1$. In order to give the monopolist sufficient incentive to stay in production, supplying the regulated quantity, Q_1 per period, it would be necessary for government to offer the firm a subsidy of $CABp_1$ per period.

State Ownership

Rather than regulate monopolies in the private sector, the state may nationalise them. The objectives of state monopolies in different countries have varied. Some of them are constrained to produce an output at which average cost, or even marginal cost, equals price; others seek to maximise profits, like firms in the private sector. In the latter case the primary objective may be the raising of government revenue.

IMPERFECT COMPETITION

The words "imperfect competition" are used in two senses by different authors. Sometimes they refer to any market structure other than perfect competition. However, we define imperfect competition as a market structure in which there is a *large number* of firms selling goods which are *close*, though not perfect *substitutes*, in the minds of buyers. Thus, unlike the case under perfect competition, the product traded in an imperfectly competitive market is not homogeneous. Although the firms might sell goods which are physically very similar, *product differentiation*, in the form of trademarks, brand names, colour and packaging, etc., renders different sellers' products non-homogeneous in the minds of buyers. Competitive advertising is a key characteristic of imperfect competition: each firm attempts to convince buyers that its product is better than that of rivals. To some extent, most actual goods markets are imperfectly competitive.

Imperfectly competitive markets, being intermediate between perfect competition and monopoly, have some of the characteristics of each of those extremes in the spectrum of market structures. The imperfectly competitive firm may earn large supernormal profits in the short run. But in the long run, more firms would be attracted into the industry until supernormal profits are competed away. The analysis, in that context, resembles that of perfect competition in the long run. However, each firm in an imperfectly competitive industry has some monopoly power. (It is for this reason that imperfect competition is sometimes called monopolistic competition.) Because, in the minds of at least some buyers, the products of no two firms in the industry are identical, each firm, in a sense, has a monopoly of its own product (e.g. of its brand name). If one firm raises price just a little, it will not lose *all* of its sales.

Brand names and competitive advertising are not the only reasons why consumers discriminate between the product of one supplier and that of another. Some importance may be attached to transportation costs. A further reason why buyers might become attached to a particular supplier is because of goodwill. This might arise because of the reputation of a given seller, because of personal acquaintance with the seller, or merely because of habit or custom.

Because each firm under imperfect competition has some monopoly power, the demand curve for the product of any particular firm slopes downwards, reflecting the fact that in the absence of increased advertising, the firm must reduce price of a given product if it wishes to expand sales. It follows that at any level of output of the individual firm under imperfect competition, MR < AR, as in Figure 1.

The imperfectly competitive firm can manipulate three variables in order to influence its sales: (a) It can change the *price* of its product. (b) It can change the *form* of its product. The firm changes the form of its product if it changes the size, colour, design, or packaging of its "product". (c) It can change *advertising* outlay.

In the analysis which follows, it is assumed that each firm keeps the form of its product, and the level of its advertising outlay, constant. The discussion throughout will be in terms of a representative firm. This implies an assumption that all firms in the industry have similar cost structures, and that the pattern of demand which each firm faces is similar for all firms in the industry. These assumptions are made for analytical simplicity only. It will also be assumed that the industry is a constant-cost industry — that there are no external economies or dis-economies.

Equilibrium of the Firm and Industry under Imperfect Competition

In the short run, the representative firm under imperfect competition may be in equilibrium earning supernormal profits. The pattern of demand which it faces is given by AR_0 and MR_0 in Figure 6a. The short-run cost structure of the firm is depicted by the MC_s and AC_s curves in the same diagram.

Figure 6a

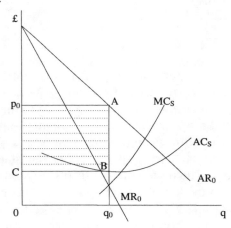

Figure 6b

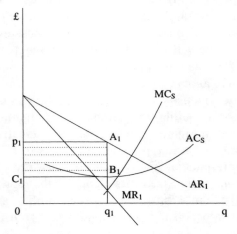

Figure 6c

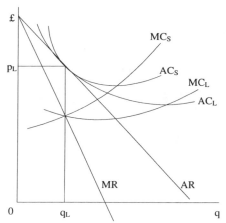

The profit-maximising firm in Figure 6a will produce that level of output at which the MC_s curve cuts the MR_0 curve from below. Thus, the firm is in short-run equilibrium producing q_0 and charging p_0. Note that the firm is earning large supernormal profits indicated by rectangle p_0ABC.

Because the representative firm in Figure 6a is earning supernormal profits, new firms enter the industry. Entry reduces the share of the market held by any one firm. The representative firm's demand (AR) and MR curves therefore shift to the left, as in Figure 6b. This is because the firm can now sell less than initially at any given price, given that there are now more firms in the industry. Producing q_1, and charging p_1, the firm still earns supernormal profits at its new short-run equilibrium, shown by rectangle $p_1A_1B_1C_1$ in Figure 6b. Although profits of the representative firm have been reduced, the industry has not yet attained equilibrium. Because the firm still makes supernormal profits, even more firms enter the industry. The AR and MR curves of the typical firm therefore continue to shift to the left. As they do so, the firm moves from one short-run equilibrium to another.

The adjustment towards industry equilibrium will be complete only when the firm is in long-run equilibrium earning zero economic profits. Such a situation is depicted in Figure 6c, where the representative firm is in equilibrium producing q_L, charging p_L. The industry is in full equilibrium because: (a) the representative firm has no incentive to change its price-quantity combination, or the size of its plant; (b) the representative firm is in long-run equilibrium earning only normal profits, and hence there is no tendency towards change in the number of firms in the industry.

Resource Allocation

Like monopoly, and for one of the same reasons, imperfectly competitive markets tend to misallocate resources. Both in the short run and in the long run, the representative firm produces an output for which MC = MR. But MR < price in imperfectly competitive markets. Therefore, MC < price. If (a) MC and MSC coincide and (b) price is a satisfactory measure of MSV, then imperfectly competitive firms produce outputs for which MSC < MSV. *On this count*, imperfectly competitive markets lead to a smaller level of production than the social interest requires.

Income Distribution: Erosion of Supernormal Profits

It has been seen that the imperfectly competitive firm could, in the short run, earn supernormal profits. In the long run these would be competed away, by entry to the industry. Imperfect competition is in this respect similar to perfect competition, unlike monopoly.

Competitive Advertising

Although it is a central characteristic of imperfectly competitive markets, advertising outlay in the foregoing analysis was treated as though it were non-existent. The case against competitive advertising has at least two aspects, one that of the moralist, the other more closely related to economic analysis.

The moral argument against competitive advertising is that it involves a breach of the privacy of the consumer's mind. It is psychological seduction which creates in the consumer wants which did not previously exist. Consumers are told what they "must" have and are convinced of new needs by forces largely independent of their minds. For example, the manufacturers of well-known brands of toiletries have long been attempting to convince us that in order to have "personality", or to be "desirable", we must use a particular firm's toiletries. If many people were not influenced by such sales tactics, the associated selling expenses would have been fruitless. Such tactics create new wants which, it can be argued, imply reduction in consumer welfare.

Perhaps want-creation through competitive advertising has gone beyond the bounds of the public interest. In developed countries we have reached a stage at which, in a given firm, "goods" are being made to satisfy what the firm might describe as "urgent human needs", while simultaneously, the marketing unit of the same firm, by means of its sales tactics, is "manufacturing" the needs. By the engineering of synthetic demand for products through advertising, scarce resources may be drawn away from vital social uses (housing for the poor, the aged or the infirm, hospitals, schools, pollution control, etc.), so as to produce products of little or no social urgency.

A less emotive argument against competitive advertising is that because firms must, in the long run, cover full costs (production costs in a narrow sense, plus selling costs) if they are to stay in an industry, competitive advertising forces prices up against consumers. Firms in imperfectly competitive markets advertise their products as being superior to those of their rivals. Suppose that no advertising exists to begin with. Firm A now advertises, attempting to convince the public that its product is superior to that of firms B, C, D.... If B, C, D.... do not follow suit, then firm A will reduce their market shares. In order to protect themselves against declining sales, B, C, D... must advertise also, thereby threatening A's share of the total market. In response, A might advertise further, in which case B, C, D..., to protect their own interests, do likewise.

However, sales of the industry (e.g., toothpaste, automobiles, or headache cures) may not have significantly increased. If that is the case, unit costs must have risen as a result of competitive advertising. The argument that advertising in imperfectly competitive markets forces up prices which consumers must pay has some validity. For this reason, some people are averse to brand names which are heavily advertised; they may cost more than the (perhaps) physically identical variant which is not backed by massive advertising outlays.

There are, however, some arguments in favour of product-differentiation and advertising. If, for example, there were only a single variant of each good, the range of consumer choice would be greatly limited. With product differentiation in imperfectly competitive markets, the consumer is faced with more variants of a good between which to make a choice. Some advertising, furthermore, is more informative than competitive; it makes consumers aware of products of which they would otherwise be unaware.

OLIGOPOLY

Neither the supply-and-demand framework of perfect competition, the simple monopoly model, nor the model of imperfect competition, is appropriate for analysing markets in which there are only a few sellers. An *oligopolistic industry* is one in which there are only a few sellers. There is no simple, generally applicable, model of oligopoly. Rather, several models have been proposed to explain certain aspects of observed oligopoly behaviour. Such models are here deferred to a more advanced course in microeconomics. What follows consists of some general observations in regard to oligopoly:

(1) Because they are few, firms in an oligopolistic industry are likely to be conscious of their *interdependence*. Suppose, for example, that oligopolist A is considering a price increase. Whether it deems it in its interest to increase price depends on what *conjectures* or guesses it makes in regard to the *reactions of its rivals*. On the one hand, the firm may feel that if it raises price, this will act as a signal for a general price increase throughout the industry, in which case A would be a "price-leader". On the other hand, the firm may feel that its rivals will not follow suit if it raises price, in which case it could lose most or all of its sales (depending on whether the product in the oligopolistic industry is differentiated or not). Similarly, in regard to the effects of a price reduction by firm A, A would consider whether its rivals are likely to follow suit: if its rivals do follow suit it may be initiating a price war, making all firms (including A itself) worse off; but if its rivals do not follow the price reduction, or do so only with a substantive lag, then A might gain by cutting prices.

(2) Sporadic episodes of cut-throat competition aside, firms in an oligopolistic industry may *collude*; they may make explicit or tacit agreements limiting forms which competition within the industry may take (i.e. establishing "rules of the game"), or restricting entry to the industry. Collusion may take many forms. It may be a tacit agreement among firms not to adopt price competition. They may enter market-sharing agreements. If, for example, there are only three firms in the industry, it may be agreed that firm A will be assigned the southern part of the country as "zone of influence" and will not compete elsewhere, while the north and midlands may be similarly allocated to firms B and C, respectively. There is also the possibility that the firms in an oligopolistic industry might agree to act *like* a monopolist. In that case, maximum-output quotas would be agreed by each firm. Total industry output could then be restricted to that which a monopolist would produce, and price could thereby be raised to that which a profit-maximising monopolist would charge. The latter kind of collusion would maximise the profits of the oligopolists *as a group*. The collusion in recent years by the members of the Organisation of Petroleum Exporting Countries (OPEC) is an example along those lines which immediately comes to mind.

MARKET STRUCTURE AND THE IRISH ECONOMY

Ireland is a small open economy in a free-trading environment within the European Union. Because Irish producers of tradable goods are close to being price-takers (in the sense that they can generally exert little control over the prices of their outputs), many markets in Ireland are, for most purposes, adequately analysed using the supply-and-demand framework of perfect competition. That remains true even though there may be only one or two domestic producers in some industries producing tradable goods; to the extent to which these firms face external competition by way of imports or potential imports, their ability to raise price by restricting output is limited. Thus, free trade enforces a degree of competition on the tradable goods sectors of the Irish economy. However, in the non-tradable goods sectors (which include many service industries as well as other activities) there is greater scope for oligopolistic or monopolistic policies.

Irish markets have not always been as competitive as in the 1990s. The Irish economy was surrounded by a wall of tariff and quota protection from the early 1930s to the early 1960s. This meant that scope for oligopolistic and monopolistic trading practices was greater than it is today. For example, referring to the textile, clothing and footwear industries in his 1952 Budget speech, the Minister for Finance remarked that "the Government some time ago reinforced the protection of these industries by increases in tariffs and reductions in quotas. The home market is now virtually reserved to the Irish manufacturer". However, legislation of 1953 for the first time ever in the Republic enabled the government to veto or regulate oligopolistic and monopolistic trading practices. The evolution of competition policy in Ireland is investigated and assessed by Patrick McNutt in the chapter which immediately follows.

CHAPTER 28

ECONOMIC LAW AND COMPETITION POLICY IN IRELAND

Patrick McNutt

The business environment in any economy operates within a legal framework. This chapter charts the history of competition legislation in the Republic of Ireland in the period 1972–91 and proceeds to identify the challenges raised by the relevant legislation to a successful overview of the conduct of business in the country. The dates have been deliberately selected; in 1972 the Restrictive Practices Act was introduced while 1991 witnessed the enactment of the 1991 Irish Competition Act which heralded a new era in Irish competition policy. The premise underpinning competition legislation in general is the attempt to curtail monopoly power under the subterfuge of protecting the consumer. The principle is inscribed in the preamble to the 1991 Irish Competition Act:

> An Act to prohibit, by analogy with Articles 85 and 86 of the Treaty establishing the European Economic Community, and in the interests of the common good, the prevention, restriction or distortion of competition and the abuse of dominant positions in trade in the State, to establish a Competition Authority.

The new rules on competition are contained in s4 of the 1991 Act which prohibits anti-competitive agreements and arrangements and s5 which prohibits the abuse of a dominant position. The Act also established a new independent body, the Competition Authority, to replace the Fair Trade Commission. The genesis of the Irish Competition Act 1991 can be explained with respect to a requirement under EC legislation towards a single European market rather than from any acknowledgement by the Irish government of any inherent weakness in the 1972 Act, the 1978 Act or the 1987 Act. Albeit, weaknesses in Irish competition policy prior to the enactment of the 1991 Act had been identified with respect to ensuring competition in the state and prohibiting anti-competitive behaviour.

The history of Irish competition policy can be traced back to the 1953

Restrictive Trade Practices Act which established the Fair Trade Commission. However, earlier legislation may have unwittingly introduced clauses which could be construed as competition clauses, although the intent of the legislation was more political than economic. For example, the Control of Manufactures Act, 1933, required that a new firm could begin operations in the state only if half of its share capital and two-thirds of its voting rights were in Irish hands. While economic historians may differ, the author is of the opinion that the Act proffered joint venture opportunities for UK firms and entry into a tariff protected Irish market. The success of Arklow Pottery Ltd., for example, can be traced back to the operations of the 1933 Act.

Under the 1953 Act, the Fair Trade Commission had the power to hold public enquires and establish Fair Trading Rules with respect to the supply and distribution of goods and services, excluding professional services. The Commission considered unfair practices on a case by case basis, following a *rule of reason* approach in pronouncing on practices and recommending prohibitions. Given the level of industrial development in Ireland at the time there was little if any reference made to monopolies. The 1953 Act, amended in 1959 to widen the scope of the Commission to enquire "into aspects of the supply and distribution of ... goods", is the same in substance as the 1972 Restrictive Practices Act.

The 1972 Act, however, introduced some important changes: (a) it extended the scope of the legislation to all services including professional services; (b) it established the statutory body of Examiner of Restrictive Practices; and (c) it changed the name Fair Trade Commission to the Restrictive Practices Commission. The Office of Examiner, in recommending which Fair Trading Rules must be applied, strengthened the role of the Commission as an investigative body of enquiry. As the number of Rules increased, the Commission's role was increasingly seen as applying the Rules rather than recommending them. The ambivalent role of the Commission was streamlined by the 1987 Restrictive Practices (Amendment) Act which established the office of Director of Consumer Affairs.

During the pre-1972 industrial development of Ireland, a government policy was adopted on price controls, which witnessed the enactment of the 1958 Prices Act amended in 1965 and in 1972. The National Prices Commission was established in 1971 by Ministerial Order to act in an advisory role to government in the supervision of prices. There was liaison between the Restrictive Practices Commission and the National Prices Commission on prices of commodities and charges for services, a liaison encouraged by government to strengthen the impact on anti-competitive business practices. The National Prices Commission was disestablished in 1986 although the Minister for Industry and Commerce (henceforth the "Minister") retains the power under the 1972 Act to impose price controls where restrictive practices result in high prices.

The question of mergers and takeovers became an issue in the later 1970s with the enactment of the 1978 Mergers, Takeovers and Monopolies (Control) Act, whereby the Examiner had a function of investigation in the case of mergers if referred by the Minister. The Examiner could recommend that the Restrictive Practices Commission hold an enquiry in the case of investigative evidence on monopolies. The 1987 Restrictive Practices (Amendment) Act implemented the following:

(1) It abolished the office of Examiner, replacing it with the office of Director of Consumer Affairs and Fair Trade (previously the Director of Consumer Affairs established under the 1978 Consumer Protection Act).

(2) The Restrictive Practices Commission became known as the Fair Trade Commission. Thus, the name of the relevant Commission reverted to what it had been between 1953 and 1972.

(3) The Fair Trade Commission's role was expanded to include enquires into banking and public utilities such as electricity supply and transport.

PRICE CONTROL AND THE PRICES ACT, 1958

The 1958 Prices Act, which repealed the Prices Commission (Extensions of Functions) Act, 1938, empowered the Minister to control prices of certain products and services where the Minister was of the opinion that such prices were excessive because of the existence of restrictive trade practices. The Prices Advisory Committee, which was established under the Act, would simply advise the Minister. The reasoning behind this rather innocuous Act was really to attempt to have some uniform administration of prices rather than to introduce price control legislation per se. The government was not particularly perturbed by firms making a profit in charging high prices during this period of early post-war industrial development.

In their approach to a prices policy it has been widely acknowledged that the Irish government was of the opinion that competition would discipline domestic firms. Reference was made in the *Second Programme for Economic Expansion (1964)* to the discipline of imports. It referred to "competitive imports as imports which compete with domestic output" (p. 145). Hence, in the view of the government, there was little need for price control. This approach, however, compared rather uncomfortably with the absence of price competition in many product-markets which remained characterised by the presence of private and public monopolies.

The *Second Programme* continued by referring to the appropriate industrial policy for "industries in which the number of firms is *large* by Irish standards as well as for "industries in which there is a *single* firm or a very small number of firms" (p. 145, our italics). It would appear that neither size of firms nor the number of firms in the market influenced government policy in regard to prices. In the early 1960s, the government, however, did encourage rationalisation through amalgamation

It was not until the Prices (Amendment) Act, 1965, that firms were obliged to notify the Minister of any proposed price changes — this was largely a reflection of the government's concern in regard to the contribution of high prices to higher wage demands. The Prices (Amendment) Act, 1972, extended "prices" to include professional and insurance charges, hire-purchase interest charges and road and rail charges. The National Prices Commission, which was established in 1971 replacing the Prices Advisory Committee, buttressed the scope of the 1972 Act in requiring applications one month in advance (later extended to two months) of any proposed price increase. In addition, every business had to display the retail price charged for the commodity or service under the Retail Price (Food) Display Order, 1972. The Commission conducted analyses of Irish industries which augmented the powers of enquiry which the Minister had under the 1972 Act. By the late 1970s, until it was disestablished in 1986, the National Prices Commission "watchdogged" on price increase applications from Irish businesses, particularly from the larger firms.

There was very little litigation in the area of competition policy. The Minister did impose Maximum Prices Orders on a range of products including flour, butter, milk, petroleum products and cigarettes, most of which have now been rescinded. Minimum Prices Orders were also introduced but to a lesser extent — the Groceries Order 1987, for example, which prohibited below-cost selling, is a more recent example of a Minimum Price Order. In 1988, the Fair Trade Commission was given responsibility for enforcing the Prices Acts. Consequently, the question of compliance with the price display Orders remained under investigation by the Fair Trade Commission, whose small staff had a remarkable inspection record, monitoring pubs, restaurants, petrol stations and grocery stores across Ireland. Nonetheless, in 1988, the Commission inspectors found in relation to petrol that 110 out of 113 petrol stations did not comply with the display Order, that 36 out of 66 restaurants failed to comply with a display Order and that 58 out of 102 pubs visited outside Dublin failed to comply with a display Order. With a small investigative staff and with advance notice of the impending visit by the Commission, failure to comply with Orders would tend to be the norm. Therefore, doubts would have to be expressed about the compliance of Irish businesses with respect to restrictive practices Orders.

MONOPOLISATION AND THE RESTRICTIVE PRACTICES ACT, 1972

The main legislation relating to competition and restrictive practice in Ireland up to 1991 was the Restrictive Practices Act, 1972, which repealed earlier legislation under the Restrictive Trade Practices Acts, 1953 and 1959. The 1972 Act covered professional services as well as the sale and distribution of goods. Businesses noticeably absent from the range of activities under the 1972 Act include banking business, the supply of electricity, the provision of public transport, services provided by local authorities and any service provided under a contract of employment. These are ranges of business activity conducive to restrictive business practices and abuse of monopoly power. After the criticism of this narrow scope by the Restrictive Practices Commission in their 1981 Annual Report, a major review of legislation occurred with the eventual implementation of the Restrictive Practices (Amendment Act), 1987. The 1972 Act did not outlaw any particular restrictive practice, but rather subjected enterprises to public examination by the Examiner of Restrictive Practices and the Restrictive Practices Commission. The Minister, on the advice from both agencies could issue an Order outlawing the particular restrictive practice. The Commission, as with the Fair Trade Commission, had the power to establish Fair Trading Rules, on the recommendation of the Examiner.

Although the 1972 Act contained no specific provisions, it did provide, under s8, for the issue of Orders prohibiting certain business practices. For example, The Restrictive Practices (Groceries) Order 1987 is the more familiar and polemical of the many Orders under the Act. As the current Order stands, it prohibits the selling or the advertising for sale of grocery goods (including alcoholic beverages) at below-cost prices. It also prohibits "hello" money, the practice whereby suppliers allegedly offer larger stores an inducement in order to have their products placed at vantage points of sale in the store. It further prohibits the withholding of the supply of grocery goods. The issue of Ministerial Orders against various business practices leads to a situation where the business practices are prohibited by the Order *ex-post*, unlike (say) legal procedure under US anti-trust wherein a per se ruling prohibits specific kinds of business practices outright.

Orders under the 1972 Act were a second-best alternative to a per se prohibition. In other words, Irish competition policy in the 1970s appeared to be *Order-lagged* rather than *Order-led*; that is, the direction of restrictive practices Orders embraced political as well as economic criteria, whereas an Order-led policy would have been less tolerant of attempts by any manufacturer to control the prices at which products were resold and of attempts to establish exclusive market-sharing agreements. The practice of below-cost selling is a familiar business practice in the grocery trade. In the US, selling below cost or predatory pricing is illegal under US anti-trust. It is contrary to s2 of the Sherman Act, 1890. In Irish restrictive practices law, the deliberation of Justice Keane in a 1979 decision over the concept of "net invoice price" implicit in the 1987 Groceries Order, is characteristic of an Order-lagged policy. Under an Order-lagged policy, for example, *any* price reduction may subsequently be caught by the Order but not every price reduction is a below-cost price or a predatory price.

In the context of specific areas of economic activity, business practices which were prohibited under the Orders provision included:

(1) Resale price maintenance, whereby the supplier recommends a resale price. This was explicitly prohibited by the Radios Order 1955, the Building Materials Order 1955, the Electrical Appliances and Equipment Order 1971 and the Groceries Order 1981.

(2) Horizontal price fixing, whereby firms arrange an agreed price. This was prohibited by the Intoxicating Liquor and Non-alcoholic Beverages Order 1965 and the Groceries Order 1981.

(3) (Second degree) price discrimination in terms of supply, whereby the terms are more favourable to large supermarkets than (say) small groceries. This was prohibited by the Groceries Order 1973, since rescinded.

(4) Market sharing, whereby firms concert to divide up the market, usually along geographic lines. This was prohibited by the Building Materials Order 1955.

(5) Exclusive dealing or tying arrangements, whereby suppliers, notably wholesalers, tie the retail outlets to supplier products. This was initially prohibited by the Motor Spirit and Motor Vehicle Lubricating Oil Order 1972, and since incorporated into a 1981 Order.

Businesses which are outside the scope of the activities described by the Orders were free to embark on an array of anti-competitive behaviour. It was only when the restrictive practice came to the attention of the Minister — an Order-lagged policy — that it was proscribed by Ministerial Order. The legislative treatment of monopolies in the state under the 1972 Act was rather lacklustre until the 1978 Mergers, Takeover and Monopolies (Control) Act, 1978. Effectively, monopolies were allowed to develop in the state, constrained only by the penalties which the Restrictive Practices Commission was empowered to impose under the 1972 Act. The political will to strengthen the proscription of monopolies was circumscribed by the belief that Irish monopoly firms which were more export-orientated and were competing in a European, principally the UK, market should be unincumbered by monopoly legislation at home. The 1978 Act, however, increased the penalties and extended the powers to include the breaking up of monopolies and making their continued existence contingent on particular provisions.

If we reflect on the Irish government's approach to monopolies pre-1978, we could infer a belief held within government circles that export-orientated monopolies in the domestic market should be outside the remit of restrictive practices legislation. This would imply that the absence of domestic competition, arising naturally from the monopoly positions of the large firms, is a requisite for success in the more competitive export markets. If this was the perceived wisdom of the Irish government in the period during the formative years of Irish competition policy pre-1972, then Alice through the proverbial looking glass can only deduce that the seeds of industrial decay were inadvertently sown long before any extra-territorial economic event like world recession or the oil crisis delivered a blow to Irish industrial development.

BIG FIRMS AND THE MERGERS, TAKEOVERS AND MONOPOLIES (CONTROL) ACT, 1978

With the growth in size of firms in Ireland, firm size soon became an issue and the 1978 Mergers, Takeover and Monopolies (Control) Act was the first serious attempt by government to deal specifically with the perceived problem. The Act, as amended by the 1991 Competition Act, provides that no proposal for a merger of a certain size can be approved until the Minister (a) has been notified, and (b) has approved the merger. The Minister under s7 of the Act can refer the merger to the Examiner of Restrictive Practices and after receiving the Examiner's report may refer it to the Restrictive Practices Commission which is obliged to comment on whether the proposed merger would be likely to behave anti-competitively with respect to a set of criteria, outlined in the schedule of the Act. These include: (a) preventing or restricting competition; (b) restraint of trade or in providing a service; (c) endangering the continuity of supplies; (d) affecting employment; (e) not in harmony with rationalis-ation plans in the industry; and (f) likely benefits in R&D, increased production and access to markets. The Restrictive Practices Commission also has to take cognisance of the varied interests of all stake-holders in the enterprise, including shareholders, employees and consumers.

The Mergers Act, 1978, extended the general powers contained in the Restrictive Practices Act, 1972, which penalised monopolies which abused their position; in the 1978 Act, such monopolies can be broken up or allowed to continue under strict conditions as laid down by Ministerial Order. However, the Order arrived after a lengthy process which began with the initial investigation by the Examiner, the writing up of the Examiner's report to the Restrictive Practices Commission, who in turn were obliged under the Act in their statutory report to the Minister to state whether they agreed with the Examiner's report. The report had to identify a restriction on competition and then argue (a) that it was unfair and, (b) that it operated against the common good. The latter criteria, in our opinion, translate the unfair practices outlined in (a) to (f) *supra* into restrictive practices which are unfair methods of competition, rather than restraints of trade which are fundamentally anti-competitive. The responsibiity for enforcement is divided between the Minister and the Competition Authority (*vide* below); full enforcement powers for the Authority would be more in keeping with a restraints of trade interpretation of the legislation and would also initiate a more speedy proscription of the anti-competitive activity.

The Definition of Monopoly pre-1991

Where the Minister is of the opinion that a monopoly exists, the Commission can be requested to hold an enquiry. The reader should supplement this section with the later section "On Mergers". The emphasis in the 1978 Act was on a national definition of a monopoly. The 1978 Act s1(1) defines a monopoly as

> [A]n enterprise or two or more enterprises under common control, which supply or provide, or to which is supplied or provided, *not less than one-half* of the goods or services of a particular kind supplied or provided *in the state* in a particular year, according to the most recent information available on an annual basis, but does *not include* any enterprise at least 90 per cent of whose output is *exported* from the State or any enterprise at least 90 per cent of whose output comprises components of products which are exported from the State [our italics].

While at least a 50 per cent market share is acknowledged as a threshold from which to define a national monopoly, it is too high to capture the enterprises, either with a unilateral market share of less than 50 per cent or a collective market share in excess of 50 per cent, who more than likely are engaging in unfair practices. The absence of a lower limit on market share continues to make it rather difficult to define objectively a single-firm dominant position in merger legislation. In other words, a quantifiable lower limit would supplement any legal inference of single-firm dominance. This problem is further compounded by the varying financial limits which at the moment exclude monopolies with sales of less than IR£6m and enterprises involved in a merger with gross assets of more than IR£5m and annual sales of at least IR£10m. Public state-sponsored bodies, the quintessential natural monopoly, did not come under the remit of the 1978 Act; commercial state-sponsored bodies are now "undertakings" as defined under s3(1) of the 1991 Competition Act.

PRÉCIS ON COMPETITION POLICY PRE-1991

The 1978 Restrictive Practices (Amendment) Act transferred the powers of the Examiner to the newly established office of Director of Consumer Affairs and Fair Trade. The Director of Consumer Affairs and Fair Trade could ask the Commission to hold an enquiry after an investigation had been carried out. The investigative powers of the Director were quite extensive as conferred by s14 and s15 of the 1972 Act. The Director's task was to enforce twelve restrictive practices Orders which included the Groceries Order 1987, the Drinks Order 1965, the Building Materials Order 1955, and the Petrol Order 1981. Apart from these four main Orders, others existed dealing with radios, carpets, motor cars, cookers and ranges, hand-knitting yarns, watches and clocks, electrical appliances and electrical equipment. But for every other sector in Irish business not covered by an Order, it remained legal under Irish competition policy to fix prices, to collude, to market-share and in general to engage in anti-competitive practices. The anomaly existed that there was no general ban on price-fixing, but some of the Orders did contain prohibitions on price-fixing in particular sectors. The Director could investigate or indeed request the Fair Trade Commission to hold a public enquiry — the outcome of which could have been a new restrictive practices Order. Many complaints were received by the Office of Fair Trade and Consumer Affairs. The 1988 Annual Report of the Director commented on two such complaints:

> [I]n relation to newspapers, we continued to try to resolve complaints from new outlets who could not get supplies of newspapers (p. 26)

> During 1988 I continued my investigations of the actions of an association of pharmacists in seeking to have supplies of various nonprescription or over-the-counter products confined to pharmacies.

The issue in Ireland pre-1991 was that the activities of both the newspapers and the pharmacies, although blatantly anti-competitive, were not in breach of Irish competition policy — in other words, there were no restrictive practices Orders dealing with those particular sectors. These are the tip of an iceberg in cases of alleged abuse, cases to be exposed under the 1991 Competition Act. The Restrictive Practices (Amendment) Act, 1987, opened new sectors to scrutiny under restrictive practices law, including the public state-sponsored bodies dealing with telecommunications, post, broadcasting and transport. Each of these sectors remained in an enviable market position to capture the supra-normal profits from an alleged abuse of their monopoly power.

Précis on the 1987 Groceries Order

One of the more contentious issues in Irish competition policy is whether the Groceries Order 1987 is still in force. It apparently is. In *HB* v. *Mars 1992,* Justice Keane implicitly supported a continuation of the Order. The government, after considerable lobbying no doubt, has allowed the Groceries Order some reprieve; however, the Press Statement of 24 September 1991 may have initially sounded the death-knell for the Order, commenting that a "decision on when this Order will be repealed will follow full consideration of the Fair Trade Commission Review of the Order". The outcome of the review, alas, has been surpassed by events.

The reader may ask: why the anguish amongst the grocery trade, which has been the subject of so much regulation in its history? It is believed that if the Groceries Order is repealed, a price war across selected food items in the grocery trade will occur. The issue on below-cost selling is far from resolved and, as alluded to earlier, the absence of a workable definition of *unfair price* will continue to hamper legislation on price disputes. The precedent in EC case law deems price to include discounts, rebates, credit terms and profit margins.

REGULATION OF BUSINESS AND THE IRISH COMPETITION ACT, 1991

The 1991 Competition Act came into effect on 1 October 1991 and represents a departure from the previous Irish competition legislation as enunciated by restrictive practices law. As pointed out above, legislation was based on a control of abuse system under which restrictive practices were prohibited by Ministerial Order. The system was recognised as cumbersome at best and was applicable to particular sectors of the economy only. The principles underpinning the Act reflect those of EU competition policy and of US anti-trust laws, namely the Sherman Act, 1890, and the 1914 Clayton Act. The principles are explicitly designed to control the abuses of monopoly power and in so doing protect competition. It is generally agreed that the main goal of anti-trust policy is to improve consumer welfare. The philosophy is contained in the 1991

Act s4(2)(c) in phrases like "allowing consumers a fair share of the resulting benefit". Universally, horizontal price-fixing, whereby firms attempt to control market prices, has been outlawed. The issue of price-fixing is dealt with in s4(1)(a) of the Act which prohibits all agreements, decisions and concerted practices which "directly or indirectly fix purchase or selling prices or any other trading conditions".

The Act also established the Competition Authority to replace the Fair Trade Commission. The role of the Authority is clearly defined in s3 of the Act to include (a) dealing with notifications for licences and certificates and (b) investigating the existence and abuse of a dominant position. However, the powers of the Authority extend beyond those enjoyed by the Examiner or the Director of Consumer Affairs and Fair Trade. On the production of a warrant issued by a District Justice, the Authority can enter a premises unannounced and seize all documents (— referred to as dawn raids). The Authority may grant either (a) a licence if an agreement or concerted practice promotes special social or economic objectives, or (b) a certificate if an agreement or concerted practice does not come under the prohibition in s4(1). The Act provides for the licence to be granted for a specified period and for the certificate to be revoked if in either case the Authority believes that the circumstances have changed in the product-market.

Price-Fixing Agreements

The 1991 Act, however, is different from any previous legislation in three important respects: (a) it has introduced a general prohibition of anti-competitive behaviour; (b) it introduced price-fixing agreements into competition legislation and (c) it offers legal redress to anyone adversely affected by anti-competitive behaviour. The prohibitions are modelled on Articles 85 and 86 of the Treaty of Rome, while the general prohibition in (a) is a radical departure for Irish competition law. The much heralded right of action under s6(1) and sections 4 and 5 open up the possibility of a court action by "an aggrieved person". While the 1991 Act does not define an aggrieved person, the Authority, in its *Annual Report* is clearly of the opinion that:

> [I]t would appear to cover persons injured by reason of the operation of an anti-competitive agreement to which they were not a party or through the abuse of a dominant position. It would also appear possible for class actions to be taken by groups or associations on behalf of their members or on behalf of some or all consumers (*Annual Report*, 1992).

However, while the Court can award damages, it cannot impose fines for anti-competitive arrangements or abuses prohibited under s4 and s5 of the Act. The plaintiff has to prove injury; this may dissuade aggrieved persons from seeking legal redress under the provisions of the Act for an alleged anti-competitive practice or abuse of a dominant position. It has been well documented in accounting for the absence of private actions under US anti-trust law that consumers have little incentive to take action because the anti-competitive tactic may have disappeared by the time of the investigation, and for other traders, there is the possibility of free riding on the anti-competitive tactic — price collusion, for example.

What is the particular significance of the provision on price-fixing agreements? Illegal price-fixing is dealt with by s(4)1(a) and s5(2)(a) which introduced the words "price", "fix" and "unfair" without elaborating on each term. The ambiguity spans across s4 to s5 with "directly or indirectly fix purchase or selling prices or any other trading condition....", to s5(20(a) with "directly or indirectly imposing unfair purchase or selling prices or other unfair trading conditions".

Section 5 of the Act does not refer directly to price-fixing, referring instead to "unfair" prices or trading conditions. Subsection 2(a) states that an abuse of a dominant position may consist in "directly or indirectly imposing *unfair* purchase or selling prices or other unfair trading conditions" (our italics). The definition of an unfair price will be a problem for the Authority; consequently, it is more than likely that any action taken under s4 or s5 of the 1991 Act will be unable to outlaw below-cost selling per se, which is one reason for retaining the Groceries Order 1987.

On Mergers

The 1991 Act amended the provisions of the Mergers, Takeovers and Monopolies (Control) Act, 1978 and the Restrictive Practices (Amendment) Act, 1987. With respect to mergers and takeovers, s8(2) of the 1978 Act as amended by s17(4) of the 1991 Act, requires the Authority, after investigation, to state whether the proposed merger or takeover would be likely to restrict competition in any commodity or service. The 1991 Act replaces the concept of a monopoly with that of "abuse of a dominant position". Section 5(1) states that:

[A]ny abuse by one or more undertakings of a dominant position in trade for any goods or services in the State or in a substantial part of the State is prohibited.

While defining neither "dominant position" nor "abuse", the Act does give instances of such an abuse. Without any definition of a dominant position, s(5) indicates some abuses of such a position which will be prohibited in law. The categories of restraint of trade — price-fixing, limiting production, market-sharing, discriminatory behaviour and tying contracts — have been reduced from five in s(4) to four in s(5).

While Articles 85 and 86 of the Treaty of Rome apply only in the case of anti-competitive behaviour as it affects trade between EU Member States, the 1991 Competition Act will apply to all anti-competitive activities in the Irish market, even when there is no external trade effect. For example, it is possible that some mergers may come within the scope of s4 or s5 of the 1991 Act. In *Woodchester/UDT Bank Limited*, the Authority had to consider an agreement for the purchase of a 100 per cent shareholding in a licensed bank by another licensed bank. The Authority in its 1992 decision stated:

> In the Authority's view such arrangements do not enjoy any *automatic exemption* [our italics] from the provisions of Section 4(1).... A merger will frequently result in a reduction in the number of competitors in a market. The Authority does not believe that this necessarily restricts competition (p78).

The Competition Authority's decision in *Woodchester/UDT* applied s4(1) to mergers where the Authority believed that there was a threat to competition. Quite simply, the Authority argued that where a proposed merger allowed the merged firm to raise prices, then s4(1) could apply. In its decision, the Authority argued that increased concentration in a market was *not sufficient* to establish a violation of s4(1). The Authority found that s4(1) did not apply in this particular case, and awarded a certificate approving the merger.

However, the decision in *Woodchester/UDT* has set a precedent: the Authority may invalidate a merger. In particular, it may invalidate a merger already notified and cleared with the pre-merger clearance system operated under the 1978 Mergers, Takeovers and Monopolies (Control) Act, much to the chagrin of the legal profession. Quite simply, a legal grey area has now emerged whereby a merger approved under the 1978 Act may not be cleared under the 1991 Act. In the case of *Woodchester/ UDT* the merger had been approved under the 1978 Mergers Act. Mergers in general are becoming a recognised business rationalisation strategy. In other words, mergers per se enable competitor firms to share the market and to improve their post-merger dominant position. In such a situation, there is a need to monitor the activities of the merged firm, particularly its pricing policy and cost rationalisation policies which tend to translate into layoffs or plant closures.

The decision to apply s4(1) to mergers in Ireland affords the Authority the luxury of "policing" modern business rationalisation plans which *may* include mergers and acquisitions, with the covert intent of lessening competition. In essence, the 1991 Competition Act has been unwittingly strengthened by the Authority's opinion in *Woodchester/UDT;* Irish competition policy is now *Order-led* which is appropriate in the emerging world of international competitiveness. Legal angst might be somewhat abated if the notification procedure under the Competition Act were more speedy in line with clearance under the 1978 Act.

SUMMARY

Modern firms of whatever nationality are wont to conceal pricing arrangements in a maze of non-price tactics which inadvertently overlap with either (second degree) price discrimination or with tying agreements. For example, volume discounts and coupons are examples of second-degree discrimination as is multi-part pricing (the six-pack phenomenon), where the price per six-pack can is lower than the regular price per can purchased. On the question of tying agreements, how, for example, does the practice of "long-term agreements" in the Irish grocery trade reconcile with the restriction on below-cost selling? Second degree price discrimination is more difficult to identify than (third degree) price discrimination; the latter is more common; examples include different prices for train tickets on different days of the week, peak and off-peak electricity and telephone charges. Third degree price discrimination is unlikely to be proscribed by competition legislation. A legal difficulty will continue to arise in showing that a charge of predatory pricing represents an abuse of a dominant position contrary to s(5) of the 1991 Act. The burden of proof requires the identification of the relevant market and demonstration that the intention of price cutting was to disadvantage rival firms in that market.

In the absence of any general proscription on anti-competitive behaviour ranging from market-sharing arrangements to tying arrangements to cross-subsidisation, the monopoly firms could have continued unincumbered by restrictive practices law. The task of the Director of Consumer Affairs and Fair Trade is to dissuade businesses from engaging in anti-competitive practices. It is clear from the Annual Reports of the Director that this state of affairs remains both frustrating and unsatisfactory. The prohibitions in most of the Orders included resale price maintenance, collective price fixing, restriction of entry and below-cost selling. By 1992, it could be reported, in the Annual Report of the Competition Authority that: "No monopoly was ever referred for investigation by the Commission and, accordingly, no order was made in respect of any monopoly" (p. 3).

It is also quite clear that apart from the grocery trade, the pubs and petrol stations, very few areas of business activity in Ireland came under the scrutiny of the Office of Consumer Affairs and Fair Trade. Alas, this was to change in 1991. The history of Irish competition policy has emerged from a restrictive practices law which proscribed certain *specified business activities in particular sectors* of the economy to a *general prohibition* under the 1991 Act. The emphasis pre-1972 was on promoting industrial policy objectives with a token gesture towards promoting competition per se. The continued existence of monopolies in the state can now be checked either internally under the aegis of the 1991 Act, or externally by the winds of international competitiveness. Our competition legislation has historically embraced political concerns, and the 1991 Act is no exception, having been framed within the context of a pan-European competition policy. The challenge for government now is to ensure that Irish competition policy continues to promote competition rather than protect the competitors.

CHAPTER 29

THE FACTOR MARKET AND DISTRIBUTION THEORY

The determination of price and output for goods traded in different kinds of product markets has been investigated in the preceding chapters. It is now appropriate to consider how factor prices, and the amounts of each factor hired by profit-maximising firms, are determined. These are the topics of distribution theory, so called because the processes which determine the pricing of the factors of production are those which determine the pattern of income distribution in the economy.

Each of the productive factors falls into one of four categories: land, labour, capital and enterprise. The payments (or returns) to these are rent, wages, interest and profit, respectively. Each of the factors has a supply price. The supply price of a factor of production is the minimum return which the factor must obtain if it is to be kept in supply. The market price of a factor may differ from its supply price (the factor may earn a surplus above its supply price).

MARGINAL PRODUCTIVITY

Marginal productivity provides the key to factor pricing. It has been seen that a necessary condition for profit maximisation is that each good be produced such that MC = MR. Alternatively, from the standpoint of the factor market, it can be said that in order to maximise profits, a firm must seek to hire each input up to a point at which its marginal revenue product equals its marginal cost (marginal factor cost). It is assumed throughout this chapter that whatever factor is under consideration at any given stage is the only variable factor. This keeps the analysis as simple as possible.

The *marginal physical product* on the nth unit of factor x used (MPP_x) is the change in total physical output due to using n instead of n - 1 units of factor x, the amounts used of all other factors, as well as the state of technology, remaining constant. MPP_x may increase at first as successively higher levels of x are combined with one or more fixed factors; in that case a more "appropriate" mix of fixed and variable factors is being approached. After a certain point MPP_x will decline, as progressively more of x is used, because of the law of diminishing returns. Thus, the relationship between MPP_x and employment of x will typically be as in Figure 1a.

The *marginal revenue product* on the nth unit of x (MRP_x) is the change in the firm's receipts from employing n instead of n - 1 units of x, the amounts used of other factors, and the state of technology, remaining constant.

If perfect competition prevails in the product market, the price of output is fixed, and $MRP_x = (MPP_x)$(price of output). We can thus derive the firm's MRP_x curve from its MPP_x curve. The shape of the MRP curve in Figure 1b is a mirror image of the MPP_x curve.

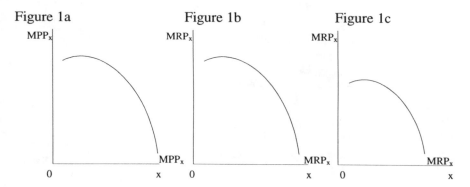

Figure 1a   Figure 1b   Figure 1c

If the firm sells in an imperfectly competitive or monopolistic product market, then $MRP_x \neq (MPP_x)$(price of output). Output price is no longer constant — the firm must lower price in order to expand sales. The MRP_x curve of a firm which is not a perfect competitor in the product market is illustrated in Figure 1c; it slopes down more rapidly than that depicted in Figure 1b (which pertains to the MRP_x curve of a firm which is perfectly competitive in the product market.)

PRICING IN PERFECTLY COMPETITIVE FACTOR MARKETS

In a perfectly competitive factor market, there are very large numbers of buyers and sellers of a factor. No individual can affect a factor's price — each must accept it as a datum. In Part Two it was shown that in perfectly competitive markets, equilibrium price is determined by the intersection of supply and demand curves; factor markets are not exceptions. In the exposition in this section, it is assumed that the commodity is labour services of a particular kind, in which case the price in question is the wage rate for that kind of labour. However, it should be borne in mind throughout that the analysis is general; the commodity, the services of

which we will be analysing, could be land or capital. Although the fundamentals of the present analysis are applicable to the pricing of services of
land and capital (as well as to those of labour), it will be recognised later
in the present chapter that land and capital have distinctive features
which merit more detailed analysis.

Wage Determination in Perfectly Competitive Labour Markets

The curves S_L and D_L in Figure 2a are the supply and demand curves for
a homogeneous type of labour (perhaps unskilled agricultural labour).
The equilibrium price is w_0, and the amount of labour hired is N_0 (N for
number of labour hours).

Figure 2b: The Firm   Figure 2a: The Market

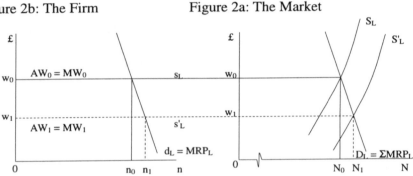

If, as is assumed, the *factor market* is perfectly competitive, each firm
must accept w_0 as a datum, determined by overall market conditions. The
individual firm is such a small part of the buyer's market for labour that
it can hire any amount of labour at the established price, w_0. The un-
broken line s_L in Figure 2b is therefore the supply curve of labour to the
firm.

Define the marginal wage (MW) as the change in the firm's total
wage bill due to employing n instead of n - 1 units of labour. If the firm
can hire any amount of labour at a fixed price, w_0, then the marginal
wage equals the average wage. Thus s_L in Figure 2b is the firm's average
wage curve as well as its marginal wage curve.

Figure 2a showed how the equilibrium wage and the overall employment level are determined in perfectly competitive labour markets. The
individual firm pays a wage w_0. But how much labour will it employ?

(Note: In order to ensure a meaningful analysis, it will be assumed
throughout that the average revenue product of labour is at least as great
as the average wage, at some level of employment.)

The profit-maximising firm will employ labour up to the point at which the MRP_L equals the MW. Thus, the firm in Figure 2b will employ n_0 units of labour. If $n < n_a$, then $MRP_L > MW$; the firm, by expanding employment, would add more to its total revenue than to its total costs. If $n > n_0$, then $MRP_L < MW$; the firm would be adding more to its total costs than to its total revenue by increasing employment. Hence, n_0 is the firm's optimal employment level.

The downward-sloping part of the MRP_L curve shows how much labour the firm would hire at any price of labour; it is therefore the firm's demand curve for labour. (Generalising, we can say that MRP_x is the firm's demand curve for any factor x.) The market demand for labour is the sum of the demands of all buyers of labour services. The curve D_L in Figure 2a is therefore the horizontal sum of the demand curves for labour of the individual firms.

(Note: The latter statement ignores the point that if all firms demand more labour, and therefore produce more, the price of output will fall, and the market demand curve for labour will not be quite the same as the sum of the MRP_L curves, as drawn. However, taking account of this point — as in more advanced courses in so-called general equilibrium theory — would complicate rather than illuminate, and it will therefore be ignored.)

Suppose now that the market supply of labour were to increase. The curve S_L in Figure 2a would shift to the right, perhaps to S'_L. If the pattern of demand for labour remained unchanged, employment would rise to N_1 and the equilibrium wage would fall to w_1. The individual firm, moving down its MRP_L curve, would expand its employment to n_1.

Non-competing Groups

The above analysis established that the price of labour services in perfectly competitive labour markets is determined by the intersection of the supply and demand curves for labour services. Perhaps the analysis was of the market for unskilled agricultural labour. The forces of competition yielded a wage, w_0. All units of labour in the category under discussion received the same wage, w_0.

Competition does tend to equalise the wages of any given category of workers. Yet, high wage differentials prevail between different kinds of labour. That is largely because the labour market is divided into non-competing groups. Competition (and hence a tendency toward wage equalisation) may indeed prevail among agricultural labourers. But there is little direct competition between that type of labour and, for example, civil engineers. The two groups are non-competing. If they could compete effectively, labourers would become civil engineers. This would bring down the wages of civil engineers and raise the wages of agricultural labourers. If competition between the two groups prevailed, the wages of the two groups would tend to be equated. The labour market is divided into non-competing groups because of trade union restrictions on entry to a trade, inequality of opportunity, differences in ability, custom, immobility, or merely because many people are ignorant of the opportunities open to them.

FACTOR PRICING UNDER MONOPSONY

Perfectly competitive and monopsonistic factor markets are extreme opposites. A monopsonist is the sole buyer of a commodity, in the present context, a factor of production. As such, the monopsonist can influence the price of the factor. Suppose that the factor of production is a particular type of labour. Assume, furthermore, that there is competition on the seller's side of the labour market. (Note that the analysis may still be generalised to cases in which the factor is land or capital.) Consider now how the wage and amount of labour employed are determined under monopsony.

In the discussion of perfectly competitive factor markets, it was seen that the supply curve of labour to the firm is represented by a horizontal line. Thus, in perfectly competitive labour markets, $MW = AW$. Such an equality does not hold under monopsony. Because the monopsonist is the only buyer of the type of labour under discussion, it bids up the price of labour as it hires more. Hence, $MW > AW$. For example, if the monopsonist could hire ten units of labour at a weekly wage of £1,000, the total wage bill (TWB) = £10,000 and AW = £1,000. Assume that in order to hire eleven units of labour, the monopsonist must offer a weekly wage of £1,200. For eleven units of labour, TWB = £13,200 and AW = £1,200. But $MW = \Delta(TWB) = £3,200$. Because £3,200 > £1,200, $MW > AW$.

Figure 3

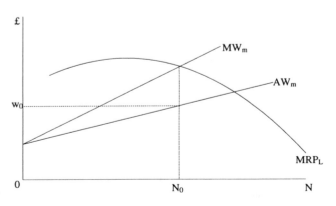

Let AW and MW in Figure 3 be the AW and MW curves of the monopsonist. They slope upwards and are unequal for the reasons indicated above. The curve MRP_L is the MRP curve for the type of labour under discussion. The firm will employ labour up to the point at which $MRP_L = MW$. The corresponding employment level is N_0. (If $N < N_0$, $MRP_L > MW$, and employment would be increased; if $N > N_0$, $MRP_L < MW$, and employment would be reduced.) At the equilibrium level of employment, N_0, the firm pays a wage w_0. Note that the wage each worker obtains, w_0, is less than the marginal wage. Thus, under monopsony labour receives a wage less than its MRP. Such a situation is sometimes termed "monopsonistic exploitation".

COLLECTIVE BARGAINING

Until now, collective bargaining has been ignored. This can take many forms. In what follows it will be assumed that a trade union demands and obtains a higher wage, without any stipulation in regard to numbers employed. Assume that the union is willing to supply as much labour as is required at the agreed wage, and examine the effect on employment in factor markets which had previously been perfectly competitive in the first case, and monopsonistic in the second.

Initially, Perfect Competition in the Factor Market

Figures 4a and 4b depict the pattern of wages and employment in a perfectly competitive factor market. Prior to demands for a higher wage, the equilibrium wage is w_0 and employment is N_0. Suppose now that a trade union demands and obtains a wage, w_1, and agrees to supply as much labour as is required at that price. The curve S_L in Figure 4a is now irrelevant. The horizontal line S'_L is the new supply curve of labour to both the industry and the firm. Figure 4a shows that equilibrium employment falls to N_1; some unemployment results.

Figure 4b   Figure 4a

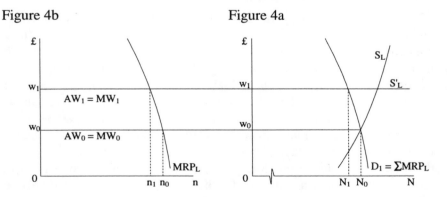

Initially, Monopsony in the Factor Market

The levels of employment and wage rates prior to collective bargaining with the monopsonist are shown in Figure 5 as N_0 and w_0, respectively. Suppose now that a trade union demands and obtains a wage w_1, and agrees to supply as much labour as is required at that price. Because the union has agreed to supply any amount of labour at wage rate w_1, the firm's AW and MW curves are now the same: it no longer bids up the price of labour as it increases employment. Thus, the supply curve of labour to the firm is now $S_L = AW_1 = MW_1$. The profit-maximising firm employs labour up to the point at which $MRP_L = MW$. The monopsonist's MW curve in Figure 5 is now MW_1. Thus, the monopsonist will employ labour up to point E. Hence, it is concluded that a rise in the wage rate, due to a very specific form of trade union activity, has led to an increase in employment, from N_0 to N_1.

Figure 5

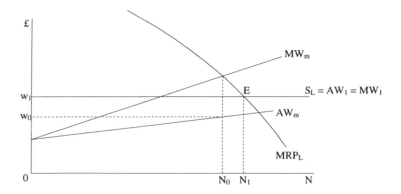

Conclusion on the Labour Market

We have seen how wage rates are determined in perfectly competitive and monopsonistic factor markets. Microeconomic effects of one form of collective bargaining have also been considered. Most factor markets are intermediate between the perfectly competitive and monopsonistic extremes. To the extent that actual labour markets are highly competitive, they approximate key characteristics of the perfectly competitive (labour market) model discussed above. It seems very likely that apart from the effects of trade union activity and government intervention, most labour markets approximate that competitive model. Labour markets in which there are only a few firms hiring a particular type of labour tend to be closer to the monopsonistic model than the perfectly competitive one.

Finally, trade unions must recognise the constraints imposed on their actions by different kinds of factor markets.

Generalisation and Extension

The manner in which the price of labour services in different kinds of factor markets is determined, in accordance with the marginal productivity theory of distribution (i.e. factor pricing), should now be clear: the profit-maximising firm seeks to employ any particular category of labour up to a point at which MRP_L equals the marginal cost of that labour to the firm (MW). The marginal productivity theory can be generalised to explain the price and amount employed of any simple factor — not only labour — which is variable in supply to the firm. Thus, the firm will employ land, or a particular kind of capital equipment, up to a point at which the MRP of the factor's services (per period of time) equals the marginal cost to the firm of those factor services (per period of time). Some factors of production have their own peculiarities. This is true of the factor land, the return to which is rent.

RENT: CONVENTIONAL AND ECONOMIC

When we use the word "rent" in the everyday sense, we mean a payment made for the use of some commodity. For example, when we refer to the rent of land or the rent of a dwelling, we normally mean the payments made for the use of those assets. In this section we refer to payments of this form — rent in the everyday sense of the word — as conventional rent, as distinct from *economic rent*. Conventional rent and economic rent may be different types of payment. Economic rent is defined as the surplus earnings over and above the supply price (or transfer earnings) of any factor of production. The supply price of a factor in any employment X is the minimum payment which that factor must receive if it is to be kept in supply to use X. If a factor of production in any employment X does not receive its supply price it will, in the long run, transfer to some other employment.

Assume, for example, that an individual is motivated solely by monetary returns. Suppose, furthermore, that his most lucrative employment is as a mechanic earning £400 a week, and that his second most lucrative employment is as a labourer earning £300 a week. As long as he is offered at least £300 per week, he will supply his services as a mechanic. His supply price as a mechanic is £300. However, if he expects to earn only £280 weekly as a mechanic, he will transfer to being a labourer. A weekly wage of £300 is the minimum that will prevent him from transferring to being a labourer. If he earns £400 per week as a mechanic,

£100 of this is a surplus above his supply price. As a mechanic, he is then earning a species of economic rent, to the extent of £100.

The Rent of Land

A much-debated question in the history of economics is whether the earnings of land are an economic rent. In what follows, those earnings will be considered from the standpoints of (a) the economy as a whole, (b) a particular industry and (c) an individual. But first, the meaning of the factor of production land should be clarified.

By the factor land we mean land in its virgin state, as originally supplied by nature. Thus, if someone rents land upon which there are farm buildings, or which has been improved by clearing or by the application of fertilisers, then part of the payment made is for the services of capital rather than for that of land per se. In discussing the rent of land in what follows, such payments for capital services will be conceptually isolated, and excluded from consideration.

Rent and the Supply of Land to the Economy

Consider an island of uniform grassland. Let this island be inhabited solely by tenant farmers, who have no contact with the outside world except when paying rents to proprietors who reside abroad. Assume that land is wanted only to grow food, and that conditions close to perfect competition prevail among landlords and tenants. Note that these assumptions are being made purely for simplicity in exposition.

The locus SS' in Figure 6 represents the fixed supply of land in the island community. Regardless of the level of rent, the supply of land to the community cannot be increased. If the island population is low, the demand for food, and hence the demand for land, will be low. Let D_1 be the demand curve for land when population is very low. Because the supply and demand curves fail to intersect in the positive quadrant, the rent of land must be zero. The community is so small that it does not want to farm the whole island. And because there is perfect competition among landlords, no farmer need pay any rent. If one landlord tries to extract rent from a tenant, then that tenant can move to some other piece of land.

Suppose now that population increases, while technology in agriculture stays constant. This will raise both the demand for food and its price. The demand curve for land will therefore shift to the right — perhaps to D_2. Note that the supply and demand curves now intersect in the positive quadrant. A positive price — rent £R_2 — is now charged per acre. Competition among tenants will bid price up to that level. The aggregate level of rent payments is shown by the shaded rectangle

$0SAR_2$. If population growth continues, the demand for food and its price will continue to increase. Perhaps the demand curve for land will shift out to D_3 in Figure 6. This pattern of demand yields a rent per acre of £R_3. Total rent payments are then given by the rectangle $0SBR_3$.

Figure 6

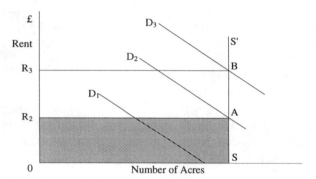

Do high rents cause high prices or do high prices cause high rents? The general view among the public is that high rents cause high prices. However, the reason why rents in the island community increased was because the demand for food, and the hence the price of food, increased. Thus, high prices cause high land rents rather than vice versa.

Economic rent was defined as the surplus earnings above the supply price of a factor of production. The aggregate amount of land is fixed in supply. From the standpoint of the economy as a whole, the supply price of land is zero. It can be seen in Figure 6 that the supply of land is fixed regardless of the level of rents. The transfer earnings of land are zero; if it is not utilised, its earnings will be zero. Thus, whatever land does earn is a surplus above its supply price. Hence, from the standpoint of the economy as a whole, conventional rents on the factor of production land are also economic rents.

Because the economic rent on any factor constitutes a surplus above the supply price of that factor, it follows that a lump-sum tax (a tax the receipts from which do not vary with output) could be imposed on economic rent without causing any change in the amount supplied of the factor in question. Thus, a lump-sum tax could be imposed on the earnings of land without causing any change in the overall supply of land.

(Note: The reader may argue that land is not quite fixed in supply, as the experience of the industrious Dutch, in filling in the sea, indicates. However, reclaimed land has more of the character of capital than of "land", as defined above.)

Rent and the Supply of Land to an Industry

Relax the assumption that land is uniform in quality and has only one use. The demand for any particular acre then depends on its fertility in different potential uses and on its location. From the standpoint of any particular industry, not all of the earnings of land are economic rents. Suppose that industry A is willing to pay £1,000 a year for the use of a certain acre of land, and that the land could earn £800 annually in its second most lucrative use, in industry B. Competition will drive the land into industry A, because industry A can pay the highest conventional rent (£1,000). The land will be supplied to industry A as long as it pays at least £800 annually. The supply price of the land to industry A is £800. If any less were paid by industry A, the land would be supplied to industry B, which will pay £800. The transfer earnings of the land in industry A are £800. Thus, the economic rent of the land in industry A is £200. Assuming that the earnings of the land in industry B would not be taxed, £200 is the maximum lump-sum tax which could be imposed on the land in industry A without causing the land to transfer to industry B.

Rent and the Supply of Land to an Individual Firm

From the standpoint of the individual producer, the economic rent of land is usually zero. Suppose that perfect competition prevails, and that the market rental of some acre of land is £800. This means that several producers, after they have paid all the other factors of production used in conjunction with the land, could just afford to pay a (conventional) rent of £800. If the land is let to one of those producers, say X, X must pay the market rent, £800. If X refuses to pay £800, X will not get the land. The supply price of the land to producer X is £800. Thus, although the conventional rent is £800, the economic rent — the surplus earnings of the land over and above its transfer earnings — is zero from the standpoint of an individual producer X.

On Lump-Sum Taxation of Land Values

It has been seen that because the supply price of land to the economy is zero, lump-sum taxes could be imposed on all land valuations without affecting the overall supply of that factor. Note that in this respect land differs substantively from the other factors of production: taxation of labour income affects the supply of effort; if all of the earnings of capital were taxed, firms would not invest; if all of the earnings of enterprise (including normal profits) were taxed, potential entrepreneurs would not undertake the risks of loss associated with production.

These considerations suggest that lump-sum taxation of land may be among the most efficient means of taxation, in the sense that it may not adversely affect the overall supply, or the allocation, of resources. That inference is correct — provided that the scheme of lump-sum land taxes is carefully designed. Note that under a system of lump-sum land taxes, it would generally be essential to assess land for taxation (in accordance with its most lucrative potential use) regardless of the uses to which the land might be assigned; otherwise the allocation of land between industries would tend to be adversely affected.

Suppose that government valuers have assessed the value of every acre of land in the country, and that each of the assessments is accurate. Thus, the valuers would have assigned to each acre the potential earnings of the land in its most lucrative possible use. On the basis of such assessments, suppose that the government demands in annual taxation a sum equal to (up to 100 per cent of) the earnings of the land in its most lucrative possible use. Land would then flow into those uses in which it produced most (if it had not been initially allocated to those uses). The supply of effort would not be affected; firms and employees would still seek to maximise the returns on labour, capital and enterprise used in conjunction with the land. Such a scheme of taxation has strong attractions: unlike most other forms of taxation, it would not adversely affect the supply of effort; thus, it would not cause a misallocation of resources. Indeed, if resources were misallocated to begin with, it would force landowners to improve the allocation of their land. However, introduction of such a system of taxation (possibly in substitution for other forms of taxation) would be tantamount to expropriation of land values by the state. The market price of land would collapse, because anyone buying land from existing owners would know that they themselves would have to pay the annual lump-sum tax on the land. Thus, although the resource-allocation effects of lump-sum land taxes are attractive, they may be deemed unsuitable on grounds of equity.

Questions of equity aside, the scheme of lump-sum land taxation, outlined above, is of course extreme; we have been merely trying to highlight the fundamental points. Not all people would like to see land always allocated in such a manner that the value of the output of measurable goods and services is maximised; most of us appreciate scenic parkland to which we have free access. However, the state could exempt allocations of land to certain uses from payment of the tax if (on non-commercial grounds) that were deemed in the public interest.

Other Forms of Economic Rent

Land is not the only factor of production which earns economic rent. *Rent of ability* is a form of economic rent accruing to persons who have some ability which is inelastic in supply. For example, if a professional footballer can earn £90,000 annually playing soccer, while his most lucrative alternative is in an occupation earning £20,000 a year, his rent of ability as a footballer is £70,000 annually. *Quasi-rent* is a return over and above the supply prices of factors of production which are inelastic in supply in the short run, but elastic in supply in the long run. If supernormal profits are earned by a perfectly competitive firm in the short run, those earnings are a species of quasi-rent. They are a surplus above the supply price of the factor enterprise (normal profit) and will be competed away by entry of firms to the industry in the long run.

The supernormal profits of a monopolist are economic rents — they may be earned in the long run as well as in the short run. As noted in Chapter 27, the imposition of a lump-sum tax on supernormal profits does not change the monopolist's output. In general, *we can tell whether any earning is an economic rent by using the test of a lump-sum tax: if the imposition of a lump-sum tax on an earning causes no change in supply, then that tax has been imposed on an economic rent.*

CAPITAL AND INTEREST

To the economist, monetary claims such as banknotes, securities or equities are not capital. To the economist, capital consists of productive assets such as railways, aircraft and equipment, ships, roads, machines and factories. Capital is the only factor deliberately made by man for productive use. Investment means addition to the capital stock. The economist, therefore, does not regard purchase of securities as investment, for these are not, in themselves, productive assets. (However, note that there is some departure from this nomenclature in the context of the balance of international payments, as well as in the area of financial economics.)

The Demand for Capital Services

Just as the demand for labour or land is a demand for the services of those factors, the demand for capital is a demand for capital services. The profit-maximising firm seeks to employ the services of any type of capital asset up to a point at which the marginal revenue product of those services equals their marginal cost. It will be assumed that the marginal cost of capital services to the firm is constant (so that the marginal and average costs of capital services are the same). The cost to the firm of the services of a capital good is the rental price of capital. If the firm does not own the capital assets it uses, it must pay an explicit rental; if it owns a capital good which it uses internally, it is implicitly foregoing the rental which it could obtain if it made the services of the capital good available to somebody else. In either case, the rental price is the economic cost of capital services to the firm. The capital rental is a composite of two, and possibly three, elements: a pure (risk-free) interest charge, depreciation, and possibly a risk premium. For the moment we ignore risk. Suppose that a firm employs a new capital good which costs £1,000, and that the interest rate obtainable on loans to government is 5 per cent. By employing the capital good for, say, one year, the firm is foregoing £50 in interest which it could have earned had it loaned the £1,000 at a risk-free interest rate of 5 per cent. Hence, interest (although in this case it is implicit rather than explicit) is one component of the cost of the services of a capital good. In addition, the capital good will be worth less than £1,000 in real terms — say it will be worth only £900 — at the end of the year, because of depreciation. That £100 in depreciation is also part of the cost of the services of the capital good.

If the firm does not own some of the capital which it employs, it is renting it. It is easy to see, considerations of risk aside, that the rental which the firm has to pay tends to be a composite of an interest charge and a charge for depreciation of the asset over the term of the rental. Although we have regarded the economic cost of using a capital good as the rental value of the capital asset, business people do not usually think of the matter in the same terms. Business people focus on the *stock of capital assets*, and on changes in the stock of such assets, rather than on the *services of capital assets*. Note, however, the following: (a) It has already been seen that a firm seeks to employ the services of a capital good (or any other productive factor) in any time period up to a point at which the MRP of those services equals their marginal costs. However, focusing on the stock of capital assets, we can say that a firm seeks to expand its capital stock (b) up to a point at which the *rate of return over cost* on a marginal unit of capital equals the rate of interest, or (c) up to a point at which the *present value* of a marginal unit of capital equals its cost. It can be shown that, under certain conditions, the three approaches are equivalent, in the sense that they lead to precisely the same decisions. In what follows we focus on approaches (b) and (c).

Present Value

Suppose that the general price level stays constant, that you have £1 million available, and that if you invested that sum in a new machine you would expect a sum of returns, over the next ten years, of £1.5 million. Whether or not you should rationally invest depends on the rate of interest. That is true whether one is contemplating using one's own funds or borrowing in order to finance the proposed project. The fact is that "time is money"; the present value of £100 in three years time is less than £100 now. (All variables are in real terms.)

The present value of £100 in three years' time is that sum X which when compounded over three years will yield £100. Suppose that the rate of interest, i, is constant. Then:

$X(1 + i)$ is the nominal value of £X invested now at the end of one year.

$X(1 + i)(1 + i) = X(1 + i)^2$ is the nominal value of £X invested now at the end of two years.

$X(1 + i)^3$ is the nominal value of £X invested now at the end of three years.

Suppose that $X(1 + i)^3 = 100$. Then $X = 100/(1 + i)^3 < 100$. X is the present value of £100 in three years' time.

The Two Approaches

On the question of methodology, there are two main approaches which firms adopt in arriving at a decision to invest:

(1) The first approach involves computing the rate of return over cost which the asset under consideration is expected to earn, and comparing that to the rate of interest which must be paid to finance the purchase (or, in the case of internally generated funds, the interest foregone by not lending).

(2) The second approach involves computing the present value of the asset and comparing that with the cost of the asset.

Suppose that we are contemplating investment in a capital asset which is expected to last N years. Then, the rate of return over cost, r, is the unknown in the following equation:

$$(1) \ C_0 = \frac{R_1}{(1 + r)} + \frac{R_2}{(1 + r)^2} + \ldots + \frac{R_N}{(1 + r)^N}$$

where C_0 denotes the cost of the asset (its present purchase price), while $R_1, \ldots, R_N$ represent the expected flow of (after-tax) revenues in excess of expected operating (i.e. non-capital) costs associated with the asset. R_N includes any scrap value of the asset. Assume that the rate of interest, i, is expected to remain constant. Then, whether investment in an additional machine (or piece of equipment) will be made depends on whether r exceeds I. (The mathematically proficient reader will note that (1) is a polynomial of degree N and therefore has N solutions. However, it can be shown that in the present context the N solutions are likely to be repeated solutions, i.e., they are likely to be the same.)

Suppose that for a marginal "machine", $r > i$: the rate of return over cost exceeds the rate of interest. Then the firm will invest in a marginal machine. Indeed, it will continue to invest in further machines up to the point at which $r = i$. Diminishing returns to capital equipment imply that there will be some finite volume of investment for which $r = i$. Clearly, the lower the rate of interest, i, the lower the rate of return required to justify further investment. We have thus established an inverse relationship between the rate of interest and the volume of planned private investment.

Consider now the second approach which a firm might adopt in appraising a potential investment project.

The present value of a potential new capital asset equals the additional (after-tax) revenues it is expected to generate in the future, minus an estimate of the additional operating costs it will incur (excluding depreciation), all discounted by the rate of interest prevailing in each time period. If the rate of interest, i, is expected to remain constant, we have, for present value (PV):

$$(2)\ PV = \frac{R_1}{(1+i)} + \frac{R_2}{(1+i)^2} + \ldots + \frac{R_N}{(1+i)^N}$$

Under this second approach, the firm will rationally plan to invest in an additional asset if the present value of that asset exceeds the cost of the asset, C_0. Indeed, it will seek to invest in additional machines up to the point at which the present value of a marginal machine exactly equals the cost of the machine. In the event that the firm cannot raise all the finance which it desires, it will seek to invest in those projects with highest PV, so long as $PV > C_0$.

Normally, if the interest rate is constant over time, we can expect that the two alternative approaches to the investment decision just outlined will yield identical results (in terms of projects selected or rejected). It has been demonstrated elsewhere in the literature that when the two decision rules do yield different results, the present-value criterion is superior to the rate-of-return criterion.

As we should expect, the present-value approach establishes an inverse relationship between the volume of investment and the rate of interest. From (2), it can be seen that if i increases, PV will decrease. This implies that some investment projects which would be chosen at a low i (because $PV > C_0$) will no longer be justified commercially (because, with a high i, $PV < C_0$).

PROFIT: THE RETURN TO ENTERPRISE

"Normal" profit is the supply price of enterprise. It is the minimum return which an entrepreneur must expect to receive in order to have incentive to risk capital by investment in any industry. Normal profit, being a cost of a factor of production, enterprise, is a cost of production.

Suppose, by way of illustration, that I am thinking of opening a small shop up the road. £300,000 of my capital would be tied up by doing so. Suppose that I own the land, provide my own capital, and employ myself, for fifty hours per week, behind the counter. I will not find it worth my while to open the store unless I earn an acceptable return on my land, capital and labour, *plus* some return for bearing the risks of enterprise.

Assume that I could earn £5,000 a year by renting the land at its market value, that if I purchased £300,000 worth of gilt-edged securities I could obtain annual interest returns of £25,000, and that I could earn £30,000 a year in wages working for someone else. The sum of these payments amounts to £60,000.

If the annual income I expect to receive as a shopkeeper is only £60,000 then, assuming that I am motivated solely by financial considerations, I will not become a shopkeeper. For I can earn £60,000 annually without shouldering the non-insurable risks and uncertainties inherent in enterprise. Perhaps, if I open a shop, sales will be below my expectations, and I will incur losses.

In deciding whether to open a shop, I will, therefore, demand some premium for risk-bearing. Perhaps I will open the shop only if I can expect an annual income of at least £70,000. If that is the case, £10,000 is the minimum return which will entice me to shoulder the non-insurable risks and uncertainties which I would face as a businessman. This £10,000 is my supply price as an entrepreneur. It is my level of "normal profit". My services as a self-employed shopkeeper will not be forthcoming unless I expect to receive that sum for incurring non-insurable risk. Normal profit is, therefore, a cost of production.

Suppose, however, that I am the only shopkeeper in my locality. Owing to lack of competition, I might now expect to earn £96,000 annually. Let us continue to assume that of this sum, £5,000, £25,000 and £30,000 are the market returns to my land, capital and labour respectively. If that is the case, then the remaining £36,000 is profit. My supply price as an entrepreneur is £10,000, so some £10,000 of the £36,000 is normal profit and is a cost of production. The residual £26,000 is a surplus above normal profit; it is supernormal profit. As such, *it is an economic rent, which could he taxed in lump-sum manner without affecting my incentives.*

CHAPTER 30

OVERVIEW OF THE MARKET MECHANISM

THE MARKET MECHANISM

In Part Two, Chapter 3, we opened the discussion of microeconomics by stating the *allocation problem* of every economy. This problem has three aspects:

(1) Decisions must be made in regard to *what* goods will be produced.

(2) Decisions must be made in regard to *how* goods will be produced.

(3) Society must establish some procedure to decide *for whom* goods will be produced.

It was indicated that society's allocation problem could, in principle, be solved by centralised planning without use of market prices. A central planning bureau could lay down commands pertaining to the quantities of all goods to be produced, as well as directions on choice of technique in their production. It could then distribute the goods among households in accordance with the government's ethical priorities.

A private enterprise economy relies on a decentralised system of markets and prices to solve its allocation problem. In such an economy, prices serve as *signals* which allocate flows of goods among competing consumers and flows of resources into different uses. Because the pricing of the factors of production determines the pattern of income distribution, it also determines for whom goods are produced. It is useful to refer to Figure 1 to see how the price mechanism solves society's allocation problem. The upper half of Figure 1 refers to the goods market; the lower half refers to the factor market.

In the factor market, firms demand land, labour and capital, in order to carry on production. The prices of these factors — land rents, wages and capital rentals — are determined by supply and demand in the factor market. Factors of production will not flow to firms which cannot pay those market prices. Thus, factor prices act as a means of allocating resources among competing firms. Because firms are assumed to seek

maximum profits, each firm, in the long run, will employ each factor
which it hires up to a point at which the factor's marginal revenue product equals marginal factor cost. Because firms minimise the cost of
producing any level of output of any good, each firm will select a choice
of technique, in the production of any good, such that for all variable
factors used, marginal physical products are proportional to factor prices.
Thus, the profit motive acting through a mechanism of factor markets
determines how goods are produced. Since factor prices, and hence the
pattern of income distribution, are determined in the factor market, the
question for whom goods are be produced is also resolved in the factor
market.

Figure 1

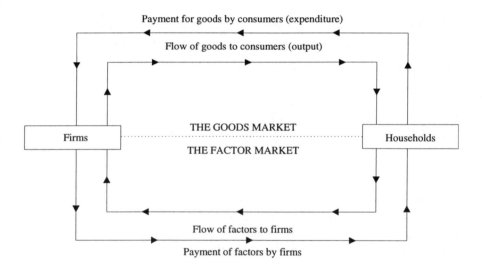

Turn now to the upper half of Figure 1. The owners of factors of production have earned their incomes in the factor market. As consumers, they
now spend their money by demanding goods from firms. Being motivated by utility maximisation, each consumer allocates their expenditure
among goods in such a manner that, for every two goods x and y
purchased, $MRS_{xy} = p_x/p_y$. Given the pattern of demand, profit-
maximising firms produce up to a point at which $MC = MR$. Given the
pattern of demand, the market thus determines what goods and how much
of each good are produced.

It should be noted that the lower and upper halves of Figure 1 are not
independent. This should not be surprising, for we know from Chapter 9

that, appropriately defined, aggregate income, output and expenditure are identically the same. Hence, the reader should now understand how the price mechanism solves society's allocation problem. Although every individual is assumed to pursue their own interests, the totality of individual actions determines: (a) what goods are be produced; (b) how goods are produced; (c) for whom goods are produced.

Note that we have not been justifying the price mechanism from a political standpoint. We do not believe that the pattern of income distribution emerging in the factor market is necessarily an equitable one. All we have been showing is that the market mechanism, in the absence of any controlling organisation such as a planning bureau, provides one way of solving society's allocation problem.

Efficiency in Resource Allocation, and Market Failure

As economists, we cannot say whether the pattern of income distribution generated by the market mechanism is "good" or "bad"; that is a question for the moralist. The question of income distribution aside, most economists believe that highly competitive market systems tend to allocate society's resources in an efficient manner; but they do not believe that this is always the case. In the latter event the state may intervene to improve resource allocation. As a first approximation, we can say that the market mechanism works efficiently to the extent that:

(1) Marginal private costs coincide with marginal social costs.

(2) Market price coincides with marginal social value.

(3) Each good is produced up to a point at which marginal social cost equals marginal social value.

It was seen in Chapter 26 that if conditions (1) and (2) are satisfied, then condition (3) would be satisfied in perfectly competitive markets; that is the central reason why perfect competition is regarded as an ideal of efficiency. Of course, conditions (1), (2) or (3) may not be satisfied in practice, in which case the market system is said to have failed, meaning that from the standpoint of society, the market system would be supplying the wrong amounts of at least some goods:

(1') If a firm pollutes the environment, and if it is not charged for the cost imposed on society by that pollution, then marginal private cost is less than marginal social cost.

(2') Market price is regarded as a measure of the marginal social value of a good because it indicates how much consumers are willing to pay for the marginal unit of that good supplied. But if an individual's consumption of a good affects the welfare of others, then there is no presumption that price paid measures marginal social value.

(3') If conditions (1) and (2) were satisfied, condition (3) would be satisfied exactly, only if markets were perfectly competitive; in other forms of market structure marginal social cost would be less than marginal social value.

The circumstances mentioned in (1'), (2') and (3') are three sources of market failure. A fourth source of failure is in the case of *public goods*. A public good is a good such that any one individual's consumption of its services does not detract from the amount available for consumption by others. Examples include the security provided by national defence and national storm-warning systems. In general, the market mechanism cannot enforce payment, from an individual, for the amount of public goods consumed by that individual. That is because there is no way to prevent someone from enjoying the services of the good if they refuse to pay for it. But government can enforce payment by all, through the tax system. The market mechanism would not supply such goods, the social benefit of which may be considerable, or if it did supply some of them, it would tend to supply too few of them.

The market *fails* in the case of public goods, and when conditions (1) to (3) break down. Hence, resource allocation may be improved by certain forms of state intervention. The state may also intervene in order to affect the pattern of income distribution.

Partial Equilibrium Analysis and General Equilibrium Analysis

The method adopted in the microeconomics sections of this text has been that of *partial equilibrium analysis*. That is, analysis of individual markets in isolation, on the assumption that conditions in all other markets remain unchanged. When we examined the determination of price and output in a particular market, we did so on the assumption that demand and supply in all other markets remained unchanged. Hence, it was assumed that the prices of all goods, other than that in which we were directly interested, and the money incomes of consumers, remained constant.

There are, however, complex interactions between markets. In a sense, all prices are interdependent. So too are the levels of production of all commodities. For example, suppose that there is an increase in demand for shipping. This will spark off a chain of reactions in other industries. As more ships are built, the demand for steel, timber, and other inputs to shipbuilding will increase. More steel production will increase demand for coking coal. Because inputs must be transported to shipyards, the increased demand for shipping implies an increased demand for transport. It is probable, indeed, that the increased demand for shipping will lead, indirectly, to increased demand for the services of water transportation. The higher output of transportation industries will increase the demand for oil — and so on.

The study of interdependence among markets is the realm of *general equilibrium analysis*, which is deferred for a later course.

PART SEVEN

INTERNATIONAL ECONOMICS

CHAPTER 31

THE GAINS FROM INTERNATIONAL TRADE

Two of the central questions in the theory of international trade are:

(1) Do countries gain by international trade?

(2) If countries do gain by trade, what determines which goods a country produces and exports, and which goods it imports?

The answers to these questions are analytically the same as those to:

(1') Do individuals gain by trade?

(2') If individuals do gain by trade, what determines the production and consumption mix of each individual?

Thus, although the specific focus in what follows will be on countries, the analysis is equally applicable to individuals who both produce and consume.

For simplicity, it will be assumed that there are only two goods, X and Y. However, the core of the analysis can be generalised to the case of any number of goods. The analysis is in terms of only two countries, A and B; however these are regarded as merely a microcosm of a world of many countries. Finally, the analysis will be static in the sense that it will be assumed, again for simplicity in exposition, that the sole purpose of production in any period is consumption in the same period.

PRODUCTION, CONSUMPTION AND ECONOMIC WELFARE IN A CLOSED ECONOMY

Consider an economy which does not trade with the rest of the world. The production possibility frontier (the transformation frontier) of this economy is the locus TT' in Figure 1. (Recall the similar diagram in Chapter 1). It shows the maximum amount of one good which the economy is capable of producing, given the amount produced of the other good.

Figure 1

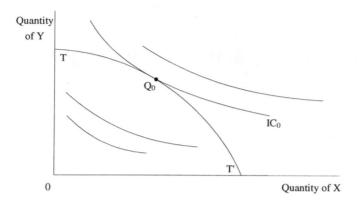

Figure 2

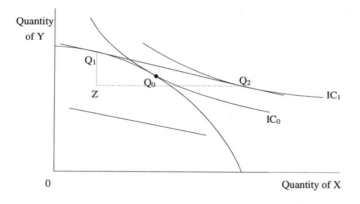

The production possibility curve has been drawn as a strictly concave (i.e. bow-shaped) locus, reflecting an assumption of diminishing returns in productive transformation. This assumption can be "justified" as follows: Suppose good Y is food and good X is non-food. It is likely, if the nation tries to become more specialised in non-food, that the production of more non-food will require sacrifice of progressively more food products. That is because some factors of production are relatively specific to food production; others are more suited to non-food production. As progressively more non-food is produced, factors of production most suited to food, but not particularly suited to non-food, must be drawn out of food production and allocated to non-food production. In that case the *opportunity cost* of non-food (in terms of food foregone) will be increasing as more non-food is produced; there will be diminishing returns in productive transformation (through reallocation of factors of production) of good Y into good X. Under such circumstances the production possibility or transformation curve will be strictly concave, as drawn.

The slope of the transformation curve is the marginal rate of transformation of Y into X, MRT_{yx}. It is the opportunity cost of X in terms of Y. On the assumption that the economy is operating on the transformation curve TT' rather than below it, the slope of TT' indicates how much of Y must be foregone per unit increase in the amount of X produced: it measures the marginal cost of X in terms of Y. Thus (ignoring the negative sign of slope)

$$MRT_{yx} = MC_x/MC_y$$

The production opportunities open to society are represented by the area bounded by TT' in Figure 1. How much will the closed economy seek to consume? (Note that, in this closed economy model, a decision on the amounts to produce *is* a decision on the amounts to consume.) The answer depends on society's preferences between Y and X. These are represented by a map of social indifference curves in Figure 1.

The indifference curves in Figure 1 are analogous to those of an individual, except that they now pertain to society. As before, they are drawn strictly convex; also, the higher the indifference curve, the more preferred the position. It is assumed that the closed economy's objective is to allocate resources in such a manner that, given its production opportunities, it gets to the highest social indifference curve attainable. The economy will therefore produce the combination of Y and X indicated by the point Q_0 in the diagram; social welfare is then being maximised. Thus, for maximisation of social welfare, that combination of goods will be produced such that

$$MRS_{xy} = MRT_{yx}$$

where MRS_{xy} is society's marginal rate of substitution of X for Y and MRT_{yx} is its marginal rate of transformation of Y into X.

PRODUCTION, CONSUMPTION AND ECONOMIC WELFARE IN AN OPEN ECONOMY

The assumption that the economy is closed will now be relaxed. What will be produced and what will be consumed therefore depends on trading opportunities. It will be assumed that the economy can export and import at fixed prices; it is a price-taker. Relative prices, p_x/p_y, are given by the slope of the parallel straight lines in Figure 2.

Will the open economy produce Q_0, as it did in the absence of trading opportunities? The answer in general is no: in order to maximise welfare (to get to the highest indifference curve attainable), the economy should produce Q_1, i.e. it should produce that output given by the tangency of a price ratio locus and the transformation frontier. At the optimum point for production:

$$MRT_{yx} (= MC_x/MC_y) = p_x/p_y$$

At the given international price ratio, p_x/p_y, the economy, by producing Q_1, can consume Q_2; it can get to Q_2 by exporting Q_1Z of Y in exchange for Q_2Z of X. At Q_2, $MRS_{xy} = p_x/p_y$, as in ordinary consumption theory. Note that trade increases the nation's welfare. Without trade the nation could at best attain only the indifference level IC_0; after trade it can get to the higher indifference curve IC_1.

In the absence of international trade, the economy could not separate its production decision from its consumption decision. But with trade the two decisions are separated. The optimum production decision is found first, by equating MRT_{yx} (= MC_x/MC_y) to p_x/p_y. The optimum consumption point, Q_2, is then found by trading, moving along the price ratio line until $MRS_{xy} = p_x/p_y$. Taken together, the optimum production and consumption decisions are represented by

$$MRT_{yx} (= MC_x/MC_y) = p_x/p_y = MRS_{xy}$$

We have not discussed what determines the international price ratio, p_x/p_y. This is determined by supply and demand internationally. Making the usual assumption that the home economy is small relative to the rest of the world, the home economy must accept the price ratio — its terms of trade — as given; as in the case of a perfectly competitive firm, it is a price-taker.

TWO OPEN ECONOMIES

How a country may gain by trade has just been demonstrated. It will now be shown that the country which has just been considered did not increase its welfare at the expense of the other countries with which it traded. For purposes of illustration, the exposition which follows will focus on only two countries, A and B, but the reader should bear in mind that these are only a microcosm of a world of many countries.

The transformation loci in Figures 3a and 3b are such that differing *factor endowments* of the two countries render country A more suited to the production of Y and country B more suited to the production of X. For example, country A might have plenty of labour relative to capital and production of good Y might be labour-intensive, while the opposite assumptions might apply to country B and to the production of good X. In the absence of international trade the two countries would produce Q_a

and Q_b, respectively. Note that MRT_{yx} in country A is then not equal to MRT_{yx} in country B., i.e. the *comparative* or the *opportunity costs* in A differ from those in B. The introduction of trade establishes some price ratio, p_x/p_y, as is represented by the slope of the price ratio locus EE in the two diagrams; because it is assumed that there is unrestricted free trade between the two countries, and because transport costs have been ignored, this price ratio is the same for both countries. To maximise its welfare under trade, country A produces Q'_a but consumes Q''_a. It exports Q'_aF of Y to country B in exchange for Q''_aF of X. Country B produces Q'_b but consumes Q''_b. It exports Q'_bG of X to country A in exchange for Q''_bG of Y. Because both countries move to higher indifference curves after trade, both countries are better off after free trade than they were previously, when national self sufficiency applied.

Figure 3a: Country A

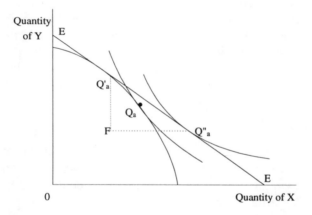

Figure 3b: Country B

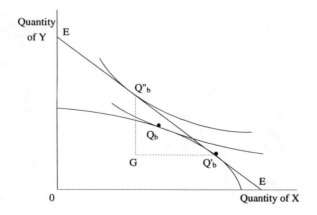

The foregoing illustrates a general proposition in regard to the circumstances under which two countries, A and B, can gain from unrestricted trade with each other: they can both gain as long as MRT_{yx} in country A before trade differs from MRT_{yx} in country B before trade. Because $MRT_{yx} = MC_x/MC_y$, we can say that countries A and B can gain from trade as long as the (marginal) opportunity cost ratios, or comparative (marginal) cost ratios, *in the absence of trade* differ between the two countries. Note that nowhere in the above exposition did we need to examine absolute costs in A or absolute costs in B; it was only the comparative or opportunity-cost ratios, rather than absolute costs, which mattered. For these reasons the theory just outlined is called the theory of comparative costs, or the theory of comparative advantage. With the opening of trade, both A and B move toward greater specialisation in the good in which they have a comparative advantage. Thus, before trade in the example in Figures 3a and 3b, (MC_x/MC_y) in country A exceeds (MC_x/MC_y) in country B; country A has a comparative advantage in the production of Y and country B has a comparative advantage in the production of X. Hence, under free trade, country A moves toward specialisation in Y while country B moves toward specialisation in X.

It is left to the reader to reason that if MRT_{yx} were the same in both countries *before trade* then the two countries would *not* gain by specialisation and trade between each other.

THE TERMS OF TRADE

Gains from international trade accrued to both countries in the above illustration of the theory of comparative costs. However, one country may gain by more than the other (though both gain). The division of the gains depends on the terms upon which trade takes place. In Chapter 14 and subsequently, the *terms of trade* were defined as the price of exports relative to the price of imports. However, they can also be defined as the amount of imported goods which may be obtained in exchange for one unit of exports. If (as in Figures 3a and 3b) country B is exporting good X and importing good Y, and if p_x increases while p_y stays constant, then B's terms of trade are said to have improved (but they would have moved unfavourably for country A).

The terms of trade, then, reflect relative prices, p_x/p_y. This price ratio emerging from international trade must lie *strictly between* MRT_{yx} in country A before trade and MRT_{yx} in country B before trade; otherwise one of the countries would not have incentive to engage in international trade. The reader should be able to see that within this interval, the closer p_x/p_y under free trade is to MRT_{yx} in country B before trade, and the further p_x/p_y under free trade is from MRT_{yx} in country A before trade, the greater the gain from trade accruing to country A and the smaller the gain accruing to country B.

GENERALISATION

The theory of comparative costs can be generalised to a world of any number of goods and any number of countries. Thus, the theory suggests that free trade is in the interests of all countries, in the sense that total world production can be increased, and that each country can be made better off by improved international allocation of resources, under free trade than under national economic independence. Hence, the theory provides a rationale for free-trading areas such as the EU. It also provides a rationale for the General Agreement on Tariffs and Trade (GATT). Under this agreement, member countries of GATT meet from time to time to negotiate reductions in tariffs. GATT has accelerated the movement toward freer world trade in the second half of the twentieth century, away from the international protectionism of the 1930s.

FREE TRADE AND PROTECTION

The theory of comparative costs suggests that unrestricted trade is in the interests of the world as a whole because it enables total world production to be higher than it would otherwise be. Hence, free trade would make it possible for every household in the world to consume more of all goods than would be the case if every nation pursued self-sufficiency. However, there are a few cases in which it might be in the interests of an *individual country* (or an organised group of countries) to interfere with the mechanism of free trade:

(1) Suppose that a country faces a price-inelastic demand curve for its exports. In this case, the country has some monopoly power in world markets. Like a monopolistic firm, it may be in the interests of such a country (or group of countries which form a cartel) to limit its exports, thereby raising their price. Such a country could not be a small open economy in the sense discussed in earlier chapters on macroeconomics, because it would not be a price-taker. By exerting its monopoly power it could improve its terms of trade. However, it is easy to see that *world* production would be higher if production of goods price inelastic on world markets were not restricted. Thus it would be *possible* for other countries as a group to compensate a country exporting a good which is price inelastic in demand for *not* restricting its exports, and yet for all countries still to be better off.

(2) The most common argument in favour of restrictions on international

trade is the so-called *infant industry argument* for protection. The argument is that an underdeveloped economy, if exposed to free trade, could not develop certain industries, the technology of which is subject to increasing returns to scale, unless those industries were given an opportunity to grow under protection; it is argued furthermore that if those industries are given an opportunity to grow in the domestic market under protection, then they may ultimately be able to survive in a free-trade environment. For example, when the Irish Free State introduced tariff protection in the late 1920s, the country was producing few manufactured goods except alcoholic beverages, partly because potential domestic industry could not withstand the competition of established industry in Britain. Resort was made to tariff and quota protection in order to give domestic Irish industry a chance to grow. Some of the industries in Ireland which were given tariff protection in the 1930s have proven themselves viable in the freer trade environment of the EU in the 1990s. However, a problem with the infant industry argument for (temporary) protection is that many infants do not grow up; for example, some of the industries in Ireland which were developed from the 1930s to the late 1950s, under the shield of tariff and quota protection, collapsed following the introduction of freer trade between Ireland and its main trading partners from the 1960s onward.

(3) Questions of efficiency in resource allocation aside, there may be social and political reasons for interfering with the free flow of goods in international trade. Considerations of defence are of particular relevance here. For example, a country may seek to protect domestic agriculture (thereby maintaining incomes in agriculture higher than they would otherwise be, and curtailing the outflow of labour from agriculture into the industry or services sectors) just in case food supplies are cut off in times of war.

(4) Tariffs and quotas may be placed on imports in order to protect the exchange rate at times of balance of payments difficulties — recall the discussion towards the end of Chapter 15. However, if tariff or quota protection is required to maintain the exchange rate over sustained periods of time, it may be in the interests of the country in question to remove such protection and allow the domestic currency to float. Alternatively, the authorities might attempt to address what very often is the underlying core of the problem, by resorting to measures which make the economy more cost competitive — through improving flexibility in the labour market and/or through implementing measures to increase productivity.

CHAPTER 32

EVOLUTION OF THE INTERNATIONAL MONETARY SYSTEM

International monetary arrangements have changed on several occasions in the twentieth century. Before World War I the principal countries of the world maintained a system of fixed exchange rates with each other by means of the gold standard. That system was abandoned in the 1930s, when exchange rates were largely determined by the market forces of supply and demand. From the post-World War II years to 1971, most countries of the world maintained relatively fixed exchange rates with each other under the so-called Bretton Woods System. However, that system broke down in 1973. Since then some countries have been operating under régimes of broadly floating exchange rates; others have sought to maintain approximately fixed exchange rates with the currencies of certain major economies.

THE GOLD STANDARD

The gold standard was a fixed exchange rate system. The way in which it operated was quite simple. Each country declared itself willing to exchange its currency for a certain weight in gold. Because each country valued its currency in terms of the *numeraire* (i.e. common denominator) gold, one country's money exchanged at a fixed rate against the money of another country. For example, in 1914 the pound sterling was convertible into 0.257 standard ounces of gold. The US dollar, on the other hand, was convertible into 0.093 standard ounces of gold. This meant that the pound was convertible into 4.86 times more gold than the dollar; thus the exchange rate between the dollar and sterling was 4.86 dollars for one pound.

The gold standard was self-regulating in the sense that balance of payments surpluses or deficits tended to be eliminated automatically by means of international movements in gold stocks and through induced changes in domestic money supplies and price levels. Suppose that country A had a balance of payments surplus and that country B had a deficit. Because gold was the standard means of international settlement, gold would flow into the surplus country A. The deficit country B, on the other hand, would be making payments of gold to foreigners, so gold would flow out of country B. Under the gold standard, the domestic money supply of each country was linked directly to gold; the bulk of the reserves of the banking system consisted of gold. Hence, the money supply would expand in the country (A) with the balance of payments surplus, and contract in the country (B) with the deficit. From the quantity theory of money we know that prices (and/or real income) in A would rise, while prices (and/or real income) in B would fall. Because exchange rates were fixed, these changes would cause A's imports to increase and its exports to fall, while B's imports would fall and its exports would increase. Thus, both countries would automatically move towards balance of payments equilibrium.

The gold standard would have worked smoothly as long as wages and prices were perfectly flexible downward. Suppose a country had a balance of payments deficit. It would then tend to lose gold; however, if prices were sufficiently flexible in a downward direction, such losses of gold would soon be arrested via the mechanism described above. However, if output prices and wage rates adjusted slowly, a deficit country might lose all of its gold holdings, in which case it would be knocked off the gold standard (because it would no longer have the gold necessary in order to redeem its currency). Furthermore, if prices were flexible downward while wage rates were rigid, increased unemployment would ensue. Problems like these arose in the early 1930s, when certain key countries abandoned the gold standard.

The 1930s were years of experimentation. Many countries allowed their currencies to float; others sought to maintain fixed exchange rates with certain key currencies. The world was experiencing the Great Depression in those years. In the hope of protecting employment by increasing exports and reducing imports, many countries introduced or increased tariffs and quotas on imports, subsidised exports, and devalued their currencies for short-run gain. These actions led to retaliation by other countries. Collapse in the volume of world trade was one result of the increased restrictions and uncertainty in regard to exchange rates in the 1930s.

THE BRETTON WOODS SYSTEM

With a view to averting the international economic chaos experienced in the 1930s, several of the leading nations of the world came together to negotiate at a town called Bretton Woods, New Hampshire, USA, in 1944. The central objective was to design for the post-war world a system of exchange rates which would encourage the free flow of international trade. The agreements reached at Bretton Woods formed the basis of the international monetary system which prevailed until 1971. Under this system countries agreed to maintain fixed exchange rates with each other; however, devaluation (revaluation) would be considered acceptable if at an existing exchange rate a country's balance of payments was in fundamental disequilibrium, that is, if it showed a persistent tendency to be in deficit (surplus).

Central features of the Bretton Woods system were twofold: (a) US dollars held by central banks were made directly convertible into gold at a fixed price (of $35 an ounce) by the US government; (b) national currency authorities declared a fixed exchange rate between their own currency and the US dollar. The rates at which national currencies were pegged to the dollar could be changed in the event of fundamental disequilibrium in the balance of payments. In order to maintain their currencies at fixed exchange rates against the dollar, the central banks of each country had to be willing and able to buy their currency with foreign exchange (along the lines outlined in Chapter 15). Thus, accumulation of foreign exchange reserves was a key factor in enabling each country to maintain its declared fixed exchange rate with the US dollar.

The International Monetary Fund (IMF) was established under the Bretton Wood's agreements. Among its tasks were (a) to ensure that countries maintained fixed exchange rates except at times of fundamental disequilibrium in their balance of payments, and (b) to make short-term loans of foreign exchange — out of funds subscribed by member nations — to enable the central banks of countries in temporary (rather than fundamental) balance of payments difficulties to defend their fixed exchange rates. The IMF still exists today, although the Bretton Woods system has collapsed.

The provision of adequate levels of foreign exchange reserves to iron out short-term fluctuations in international receipts and payments was a central problem of the Bretton Woods system. If exchange rates were free rather than pegged, fluctuations in both current and capital account payments would cause exchange rates to fluctuate. Therefore, inventories of foreign exchange were required if exchange rates were to be pegged. However, the rapid growth in international transactions in the post-war years meant that the absolute values of short-run balance of payments surpluses and deficits tended to increase over time. This implied an increase in the demand for foreign exchange reserves. But how were these reserves to be provided?

The keystone of the Bretton Woods system was gold: countries were supposed to maintain fixed exchange rates with the US dollar, which, in turn, was expressed in terms of, and was convertible into, gold. Thus gold was the ultimate means of international settlement, and hence, one reserve asset, under the Bretton Woods system. The use of gold as a reserve asset caused two serious problems. First, the world's supply of monetary gold did not expand fast enough to provide adequate reserves to finance rapidly expanding levels of world trade. That was largely because, despite generalised inflation, the dollar price of gold (i.e. the rate at which the dollar was convertible into gold by the US government) was held fixed at $35 an ounce. Secondly, given that the supply of monetary gold did not increase sufficiently fast to ensure adequate levels of international reserves, the only way (in the absence of changes in the Bretton Woods system) in which those reserves could be increased in the face of growing international transactions was by countries the currencies of which were generally acceptable as means of international settlement — mainly the US and the UK — running balance of payments deficits; in this way the foreign exchange holdings of the rest of the world were increased. But as the US pumped more reserves into the world economy by running balance of payments deficits, it was inevitably destroying the attractiveness of the dollar as a reserve currency.

Thus, the Bretton Woods system, immediately based on the dollar but actually based on gold, contained the germs of its own destruction. In the earlier years of the system the nations of the world were happy to make and to accept international payments in US dollars because (given that the dollar was convertible into gold at $35 an ounce) the dollar was in effect "as good as gold". But US deficits, increasing foreign exchange reserves and hence increasing the means of international settlement, inevitably undermined confidence in the dollar: the longer the US deficits continued, the less able was the US to ensure convertibility of the dollar into gold. For this reason, the US lost more and more of its gold stocks as the 1960s progressed; doubting the ability of the US authorities to maintain convertibility of the dollar into gold, more net earners of dollars began to demand payment for their dollar holdings in the form of gold.

The desire to provide an additional reserve asset not linked to the currency of any particular country led to the introduction in 1969 of so-called Special Drawing Rights (SDRs) at the IMF. Each member country of the IMF was assigned a quota of SDRs which was denominated in terms of a fixed gold value (hence SDRs were referred to as "paper gold") which it could use to buy an equivalent amount of foreign exchange from other member countries. SDRs could and have been used to finance balance of payments deficits. They have, furthermore, outlived the Bretton Woods system which they were initially designed to assist.

The Collapse of the Bretton Woods System

Gold, US dollars and the pound sterling were the principal reserve assets of the nations of the world under the Bretton Woods system. However, the balance of payments deficits of the UK and the USA, which in the short run facilitated the operation of the system by increasing foreign exchange reserves in the world economy, inevitably undermined it. They increased the means for speculation against the pound and the dollar. At first it was the pound that tended to be under pressure. In the 1950s and 1960s holders of sterling had reasons for believing that the UK might not be able to maintain convertibility at a fixed exchange rate between the pound and the currencies of countries such as the US, Switzerland and West Germany. This led to speculative rushes to sell sterling before its anticipated devaluation. However, such speculation only exacerbated the forces making it necessary for the UK to devalue against the dollar. When sterling was forced into devaluation (as in 1949 and in 1967) many countries with strong trading links with the UK also devalued against the dollar.

The other principal reserve currency, the US dollar, was tending to become weaker in the 1960s. In those years the US experienced growing balance of payments deficits, partly related to Vietnam War expenditure. People therefore rushed to buy gold because they believed that an inevitable devaluation of the dollar would take the form of a rise in its gold price.

In the late 1960s pressure to buy gold could not be resisted, and the major economies of the world were forced to stop pegging the free market price of gold at $35 an ounce. From 1968 onwards, there were two prices of gold. One was the official price at which monetary authorities settled debts between each other by transferring gold holdings. The other was the free market price, determined by the forces of supply and demand independently of intervention by central banks. The free market price quickly rose far above the official US price of $35 an ounce.

Once the free market price of gold was allowed to be determined independently of the official price, speculation in favour of gold against the dollar shifted in favour of those currencies which were clearly undervalued relative to the dollar. The task of central banks to maintain fixed exchange rates in the face of such speculation became more difficult.

The core of the Bretton Woods system came to an end in the autumn of 1971 when the US announced suspension of the convertibility of the dollar into gold. However, speculation against the dollar (in favour of "strong" currencies such as the German mark) had earlier become so severe that some countries had already allowed their currencies to float, and thereby to appreciate against the dollar. The suspension of convertibility of the dollar into gold accentuated such speculative rushes, in response to which several other countries decided to join Germany and the Netherlands in allowing their exchange rates to float.

The so-called Smithsonian agreements of December 1971 sought to restore the world to fixed exchange rates. Under these agreements the US devalued the dollar by raising its official gold price by 7.9 per cent while at the same time the currencies of some countries which had persistent balance of payments surpluses were revalued against the dollar. A régime of fixed exchange rates with a nominal gold base was thereby renewed, but because the free market price of gold remained substantially above the official price, central banks were generally unwilling to use gold to settle debts among themselves. Thus, immediately after the Smithsonian agreements the world was on a *de facto* dollar standard. Central banks held some of their reserves in the form of dollars, which were no longer convertible into gold.

THE PRESENT INTERNATIONAL MONETARY SYSTEM

The devaluation of the dollar in December 1971 did not end speculation against that currency. In the first few months of 1973 there were massive speculative flows from the US to Europe and Japan. In February 1973 the US indicated intent to devalue again. This exacerbated speculative flows out of the dollar. There had also been pressure on the pound sterling, resulting in a decision around the middle of 1972 to float the pound. The currency chaos of 1972 and early 1973 led to abandonment of the world-wide system of fixed exchange rates. Since then, the world's economies have operated under exchange rate régimes which have combined aspects of fixed exchange rate systems and managed floating: there has been a great deal of central bank intervention in foreign exchange markets. The principal objectives of such intervention have been to limit the amplitude of exchange rate fluctuation and, in the case of groups of countries opting for approximately fixed exchange rates with each other (such as those of "the Snake" in the 1970s and of the ERM in the 1980s and early 1990s — see below), to maintain approximately fixed exchange rates within the groups. Thus, central banks still hold reserves in the form of foreign currencies and SDRs, in order to be able to influence exchange rate levels. What follows in the present chapter pertains mainly to exchange rate developments within Europe.

The Snake, and the Goal of Monetary Union in the EEC

The Bretton Woods system did not seek to maintain precisely fixed exchange rates; rather, each central bank was expected to maintain the exchange rate of its national currency within a band of plus or minus 1 per cent of a fixed rate against the US dollar. However, the Smithsonian agreements widened the band within which each nation's exchange rate could fluctuate, to plus or minus 2.25 per cent of a fixed central rate against the dollar. (Thus, the Smithsonian agreements sought to restore the economies of the world to a régime of approximately fixed exchange rates.)

By 1970, the member countries of the EEC recognised that further integration of the Community, once the industrial customs union had been achieved and once the Common Agricultural Policy had been initiated, involved progress towards monetary integration of member countries. An ultimate goal of many EEC politicians was full economic and monetary union by 1980. A report to that effect (the Werner Report of October 1970) was endorsed in February 1971 by the EEC Council of Ministers. As perceived by Werner, economic and monetary union would imply a supranational central bank, a single EEC currency or *irrevocably* fixed exchange rates between the currencies of EEC member countries, a central fiscal authority and the virtual elimination of national central banks.

In 1972, as a first stage in the gradual evolution toward monetary union, the EEC nations sought to narrow the margins of fluctuation in the exchange rates between member countries: their currencies were to vary against each other only within a band of plus or minus 1.125 per cent, but the whole Community band could move within the wider band of plus or minus 2.25 per cent against the dollar as provided for in the Smithsonian agreements. Those EEC exchange rate arrangements initiated in 1972 constituted the *Snake*. (This nomenclature reflected the narrow band of fluctuation to which the participants agreed, that band itself being inside the wider band or "tunnel" of plus or minus 2.25 per cent.) In anticipation of their entry to the EEC, the UK, Ireland and Denmark joined the Snake in May 1972; however, speculation against sterling forced the UK to withdraw some weeks later. (Because it then opted to maintain its fixed exchange rate with sterling, Ireland also withdrew from the Snake in the summer of 1972.)

In 1973, when the system of approximately fixed exchange rates against the US dollar was finally abandoned, five of the member countries of the EEC decided to continue the attempt to stabilise their currencies against each other, but to float against the dollar: thus, after 1973, the Snake was a *joint float* of some EEC currencies against outside currencies, especially the dollar. The monetary authorities of a number of EEC countries continued to intervene in exchange markets to keep the exchange margins of Snake currencies relative to each other within narrow limits. However, the UK stayed outside the amended Snake system and allowed sterling to float against all major currencies. Because Ireland remained tied to sterling, we floated in unison with the UK currency against the currencies of the rest of the world.

As an attempt to maintain approximately fixed exchange rates between the currencies of EEC member countries, the Snake was not an unqualified success. As already indicated, UK and Irish membership of the Snake (actually prior to their entry to the EEC) was very brief. France withdrew from the Snake in January 1974 and returned in 1975 but withdrew again in 1976. And Italy was an even more occasional member of the Snake system than was France.

A number of considerations made it difficult, or impossible, for the countries of the EEC to maintain (approximately) fixed exchange rates with each other in the 1970s, and thereby to progress toward monetary union. In this context, the observations in the three paragraphs which immediately follow in the present subsection were expressed by the author in 1979 (in *Economic Analysis for an Open Economy: Ireland*, pp. 393, 4). Although the EEC is now called the EU, these observations are still of relevance in the 1990s:

(1) As was seen in Chapter 16, monetary expansion by the central bank of a small open economy under fixed exchange rates tends to result in losses in that country's foreign exchange reserves. (It was also observed that such reserve losses, by their effects on the domestic money supply, tend to offset the initial monetary expansion, but they also weaken the ability of the country in question to maintain its fixed exchange rate arrangements). The effects are similar under (nearly) fixed exchange rates if the central bank of a single country attempts to increase the domestic money supply more rapidly than in the case of other countries with which it has approximately fixed exchange rates. Hence, for a Snake-type exchange rate system to be viable, there must be co-ordination of monetary policies between member countries. In practice there was insufficient co-ordination in the Snake system: some countries sought to expand their money supplies more rapidly than some of their partners in the Snake. The ensuing reserve losses induced speculation against the currencies of the countries pursuing the more expansionary monetary policies; such speculation exacerbated the losses of foreign exchange reserves, thereby leading to decisions to devalue the currencies in question *vis-à-vis* other Snake currencies.

(2) *In the short run*, and at given levels of labour productivity, cost-push wage pressure in one country may exceed that in another country with which there is a fixed exchange rate. However (because of free trade and fixed exchange rates), the rate of inflation of tradable goods would tend to be the same in both countries. Profits, output and employment would therefore tend to fall in the country with the higher cost-push wage

pressure. The increased unemployment would in itself tend to abate the cost-push pressure on the real wage. However, such an adjustment mechanism (through increased unemployment) may be politically unpopular; the country in which money wage rates are increasing most rapidly might seek to get real wages down by wilfully forcing prices up — by *devaluation* of the domestic currency. *This, of course, would tend to be only a short-run, and generally myopic, palliative: it would tend to reflect failure to address fundamental supply-side problems, namely wage rigidity in the labour market and inadequate growth in productivity.*

(3) *In the long run*, under (approximately) fixed exchange rates within a multinational Community in which both goods and factors of production are mobile, prices of tradable goods would tend to increase at roughly the same rate in all member countries, and factor prices (especially money wage rates) would also tend to increase at the same rate across member countries. However, suppose that labour productivity is increasing more slowly in one of the countries than in others. With money wages and prices in the low-productivity growth country increasing at about the same rates as in the high-productivity growth countries, real profit margins in the low-productivity growth country will be falling over time, leading to reductions in output and employment in that country and inducing outflows of the excess supply of labour to the high-productivity growth countries. Such emigration might be politically unpopular in the low-productivity growth country. To avert declining real profit margins and declining employment, the low-productivity growth country might be tempted to try to maintain its competitiveness by means of a sequence of devaluations. However, the perceived political necessity for such devaluations, which are inconsistent with monetary union, could be averted if countries in the Community were willing to assist in raising productivity growth in member countries which would otherwise lag behind. They could do so by aiding the (otherwise) lagging countries to increase and modernise their capital stocks by means of resource transfers to those countries. To some extent such resource transfers were being implemented in the EEC even before the 1980s, through the European Regional Fund, which was designed to assist lagging regions (countries) of the Community. (Ireland negotiated resource transfers over and above the very limited amounts provided to it by the European Regional Fund, in arranging for its membership of the European Monetary System in March 1979.)

The EMS, 1979

The Snake arrangements brought little progress toward monetary union in the EEC. That was largely because individual countries were not willing to pursue monetary and supply-side policies consistent with the maintenance of (approximately) fixed exchange rates between EEC member countries: rather than handle their macroeconomic problems by way of such internal policies, some of them found it politically more palatable to devalue their currency or to let it depreciate in the context of a floating rate against their EEC partners. However, the EEC's second scheme to lock the currencies of member countries, after about nine months of negotiation, finally came into existence in March 1979. This new system, which replaced the Snake arrangements, is called the European Monetary System (EMS). In some respects, the EMS is merely a reform of the old Snake; in others, it appears to be much more. Some details follow:

Under the Exchange Rate Mechanism (ERM) of the EMS as originally established in 1979, France rejoined the five surviving members of the old Snake (Germany, Belgium, the Netherlands, Luxembourg and Denmark) in a system of nearly-fixed exchange rates (fluctuation limited to plus or minus 2.25 per cent around central rates). Ireland finally broke the so-called "sterling link" — the fixed exchange we had had kept with the pound sterling — and joined the EMS on the same terms in regard to exchange rate margins as France. A looser arrangement was made for Italy, permitting fluctuation of up to plus or minus 6 per cent around the central rate set for the lira. But the UK did not join the ERM of the EMS. Thus, no limits on fluctuation were set for the ninth EEC member. (In 1979, the EEC consisted of only nine countries.)

However, the ERM as originally devised was not just a set of eight currency units with nearly fixed exchange rates between them. Each of the eight original participants in the ERM also had a fixed central rate against a new currency unit, the European Currency Unit (ECU). In fact, the ECU was the agreed numeraire for the system, with reference to which the band for permissible fluctuation of each currency within the ERM was set.

From its beginning, the ECU consisted of a weighted average of the national currency units of each of the members of the Community, including the pound sterling. The weight assigned to individual national currencies in the composition of the ECU reflected a country's economic importance within the EC. For example, the German mark was assigned a weight of about one third, but the weight attached to the Irish pound was just a little above 1 per cent. Thus, although the UK was a participant in the EMS in the 1980s in the sense that its currency was included in the composition of the ECU, in those years the UK did not participate in the ERM of the EMS.

The composition of the ECU was extended from nine to twelve currencies following the accession to the Community of Spain, Greece and Portugal in the 1980s. It was not until 1990 that the UK decided to participate in the ERM: like Spain (in 1989), the UK then agreed to maintain its currency within a band of plus or minus 6 per cent of a fixed central rate against the ECU.

As was the case with the Snake which preceded it, the ERM was not successful in maintaining approximately fixed exchange rates among the participating countries: there were several realignments of the central rates between national currency units and the ECU in the period up to 1986. It will be recalled that although sterling is a component of the ECU, the UK did not participate in the ERM in the 1980s. Thus, it was possible for sterling to fluctuate — and to depreciate — significantly against the ERM currencies. Given wage inflexibility, depreciation of sterling meant a loss in competitiveness of Ireland *vis-à-vis* her main trading partner, the UK. Ireland devalued her central rate against the ECU on two occasions in the 1980s — in 1983 and in 1986; on each occasion the devaluation followed depreciation of sterling relative to the ERM currencies.

The later 1980s were years of relative stability in the ERM: there were few realignments of central rates in the system. The end of the decade saw increased emphasis on movement toward full monetary union (EMU) within the EC. The Delors Report (so named because the committee from which it originated was chaired by the EC Commission President Jacques Delors) was published in April 1989. It recommended that full monetary union of EC countries should be attained in three discrete stages — that is, gradually, as had been proposed in the Werner Report of 1970. Under the Maastricht Treaty at the beginning of 1992, the Member States of the Community agreed to implement most of the key recommendations of the Delors Report: they agreed to a timetable of measures so as to make transition to EMU irreversible by 1999. However, the unfolding of events late in 1992 and into 1993 has meant that the timetable for EMU, as agreed at Maastricht, now appears to have been shelved.

Following the Werner Report of 1970, the EU (as the former EEC is now called) has spent almost one quarter of a century aspiring to create a monetary union among Member States. A key point to note (under the Snake and the ERM) is that this was to be attained *gradually* rather than all at once. A fundamental problem with a gradual approach to monetary union — EMU by stages — is that until monetary union is attained, independent national currency units still exist. Governments may therefore act myopically and may take the easy option of devaluation if wage/price rigidity threatens unemployment or emigration of labour from the national territory (an event which in Ireland is often described as a "national disgrace" despite that fact that Ireland claims to be part of a common EU labour market): in this context recall the analysis in the second half of Chapter 23 above. In fact, it seems that *the very existence of national currency units within the EU distracts the attention of politicians, of their advisers, of popular commentators and hence of the general public, away from the crucial role of wage/price flexibility, of convergence in rates of productivity growth and of labour migration, as preconditions for a workable monetary union.*

A few months after the EMS was established, this author wrote as follows:

> There are strong arguments to the effect that if the EEC does want a stable monetary union, it will have to be by way of monetary union all at once rather than via the gradualist approach pursued to date. Monetary union all at once has been described by [the Australian economist Max] Corden as follows: 'On one day a Community central bank is established, it takes over the foreign-exchange reserves of the member countries, and it acquires the sole right to manufacture legal tender and hence base money. If this is seen as a decisive, irrevocable transformation, then expectations will be immediately adjusted' and the costs of adapting to a common rate of inflation would be minimised. Monetary union all at once, and hence convergence to a common rate of inflation, has been politically unacceptable because some countries [within the EEC] have been unwilling to accept the short-run adjustment costs which would be involved. Hence it would seem that we shall experience periodic revaluations and devaluations in the EMS. But the prospects of such parity changes will encourage speculation. The danger then is that the EMS will end up in a series of exchange rate crises and collapse. ("Monetary Union and the EMS", *Journal of Irish Business and Administrative Research*, April 1980, p. 10.)

These fears expressed late in 1979 came close to full realisation in 1992/3. Having joined the exchange rate mechanism of the EMS in 1990, the UK left the ERM in September 1992. Sterling quickly depreciated against the ERM currencies, including the Irish pound. As has been reviewed in Chapter 23 above, a result was a wage/price crisis in Ireland, calls from sources within Ireland for devaluation in order to maintain competitiveness, and a further devaluation of the Irish pound within the ERM in January 1993. It should be mentioned at this stage that the Irish pound was not the only ERM currency under pressure in the autumn of 1992 and in the winter which followed. Further tensions, focusing mainly on the French franc, led in July 1993 to a general widening of the ERM bands to plus or minus 15 per cent around central rates against the ECU.

Thus, although the ERM survives, at the time of writing the system within most of the EU constitutes a broadly managed float around fixed central rates between national currency units and the ECU — one in which the margin for permissible fluctuation is now broader than it was before mid-1993. Hence, the aspiration of a gradual approach to EMU — originally to be attained (in the 1970 Werner Report) by 1980, later to be attained (in the Delors Report and under the Maastricht Treaty) by 1999 — now seems to have faded into the twenty-first century.

The present chapter has avoided many of the details pertaining to the EU's aspirations in regard to economic and monetary union: some of these are discussed by Rory O'Donnell in the chapter which follows.

CHAPTER 33

EUROPEAN INTEGRATION

Rory O'Donnell

1. INTRODUCTION

This chapter provides an overview of an aspect of international economics which is of particular importance to Ireland–European economic and monetary integration. The formation and development of the European Union are briefly described in Section 2. Section 3 outlines the economic analysis of market integration. It identifies several models of economic integration and explains how the possible effects of integration are derived from the economic theories of international trade and integration. Section 4 explains Ireland's adjustment to membership of the European Union, by examining which of the possible effects, outlined in Section 3, have actually materialised in Irish manufacturing (the adjustment of Irish agriculture to EU policy is considered in Chapter 8). This shows that, although Ireland's adjustment differs from that experienced by the original members, it is consistent with a modern understanding of how trade and integration work where there are initial differences in levels of development, technology and scale of production. Section 5 considers the programme to complete the internal market of the European Union. It explains the origin and elements of the programme and the way in which it is conceptualised in economic analysis. The section finishes with an explanation of why the market integration of mixed economies is, unavoidably, a highly political process. Section 6 provides a brief explanation of the "cohesion" issue in the European Union and the policies which aim to reduce regional and social disparities. However, given our focus on economic analysis, greater attention is given to the way in which the regional effects of economic and monetary integration are analysed by economists. This is done in Section 7. This section highlights the emergence of a new perspective on the regional effects of integration, in which the emphasis has moved from the regional effects of *monetary* integration to the regional effects of free trade, and capital and labour mobility. The final section considers European co-ordination of monetary policy and plans for transition to Economic and Monetary Union (EMU). The achievements and limits of the European Monetary System (EMS) are documented and the plan for transition to a single currency — embodied in the Treaty on European Union — is explained. The chapter finishes with consideration of the prospects for EMU after the financial and exchange rate crisis of 1992–93.

2. THE FORMATION AND DEVELOPMENT OF THE EUROPEAN UNION

The Treaty of Rome, signed by Belgium, France, Germany, Italy, Luxembourg and the Netherlands in 1957, expressed the determination to "lay the foundations of an ever closer union among the peoples of Europe". In the face of problems on both the political and military fronts, the means chosen to achieve this aim were economic — the establishment of a European Economic Community (EEC). The central element of this was to be the creation of a common market — an integrated market without obstacles to the movement of goods, persons, services and capital. Another important feature of the Treaty was agreement to adopt a common policy in the spheres of agriculture and transport, and to devise a system to ensure that competition in the common market was not distorted. In addition, it was agreed that Member States would approximate their laws and co-ordinate their economic policy to the extent necessary to ensure the proper functioning of the common market and to attain other objectives of the Treaty.

By the time Ireland joined in 1973, the Community's economic policy contained additional areas. Nevertheless, the initial agenda — the common market, the Common Agricultural Policy, competition policy (and to a lesser extent, transport and energy policy) — continued to form the core of Community economic policy. Indeed, some of the additional economic policies were developed because they were considered necessary to achieve the central economic objective of a common market. This can certainly be said of fiscal or taxation policy, some elements of which entered the Community agenda early on. While some saw monetary union as necessary for a genuine common market, it was equally true that it would greatly deepen the degree of integration and require political as well as economic institutions and developments.

European Union industrial and regional policy were viewed as necessary if the achievement of the common market was not to create excessive economic and social disruption and not to be threatened by national, regional or industrial resistance. The Union's technology and environmental policies developed somewhat later, in response to problems which were not perceived at the outset.

These new policies — reflecting greater focus on original objectives — received formal status in the revision of the Treaty of Rome, introduced by the Single European Act (SEA) of 1986. As well as codifying policies which already existed, the SEA provided the constitutional basis for the completion of the European internal market. It set December 1992 as the target date for establishing the internal market and provided for a move from unanimity to qualified majority voting on many issues related to the internal market. In addition, the SEA contained new Treaty articles stating that Community action should strengthen economic and social cohesion and, in particular, aim at reducing disparities between regions and the backwardness of the least favoured regions. The Treaty basis of European economic integration was further advanced by the 1992 Treaty on European Union (TEU), otherwise known as the Maastricht Treaty. Much the most important economic element was the plan for transition to a single currency. The TEU also advanced the EU's competence in infrastructural policy, industrial policy, R&D policy and environment policy.

Note should be made of the terminology used in this chapter. The term European Union (EU) is generally used to refer to the formal structures of European integration, even though the EU did not legally come into existence until the Treaty on European Union (1992). A brief chronology should make this usage clear. The European Coal and Steel Community (ECSC) was established by the 1957 Treaty of Rome (ECSC). The European Atomic Energy Community (Euratom) was established by the 1957 Treaty of Rome (Euratom). The European Economic Community (EEC) was established by the 1957 Treaty of Rome (EEC). From the early 1970s, these three Communities came collectively to be known as the European Community (EC). The European Union, created by the 1992 Treaty on European Union (TEU), contains as one of its three "pillars" (the other two being common foreign and security policy, and co-operation in the field of justice and home affairs) what came to be known as the European Community. In addition, and somewhat confusingly, one of the TEU amendments involved renaming the European Economic Community the European Community. Consequently, the name European Community now refers to only one of the three European Communities, whereas up until 1992 it was the commonly accepted term to describe all three. Throughout this chapter the formal structures, laws and policies of European integration are described as the European Union, even where reference is made to policies which existed before 1992. The only exception is where this practice would make statements of historical chronology blatantly inaccurate. Up to the end of 1994 the Member States of the EU were: Belgium, Denmark, France, Germany, Greece, Ireland, Italy, Luxembourg, the Netherlands, Portugal, Spain and the United Kingdom. Accession agreements were signed with Austria, Finland, Norway and Sweden, and these were due to join the EU in 1995.

3. THE ECONOMIC ANALYSIS OF MARKET INTEGRATION

In thinking about Ireland as an open economy, it is important to take note of the way in which European integration has been analysed and understood by economists. The conceptual framework used in understanding European economic integration has changed significantly since the early 1960s and continues to develop (see NESC, *Ireland in the European Community: Performance, Prospects and Strategy*, 1989, Chapters 2 and 3).

Three Models of Economic Integration

Although integration is a complex process, which can vary in a large number of ways, three different levels of integration can be defined for the purposes of analysis:

The Customs Union Model involves only the elimination of tariffs and quotas and adoption of a common external tariff.

The Common Market Model involves not only free trade but free movement of capital and labour. It also involves some common market-regulating policies, such as competition policy, which in turn implies that some revenue be raised for a central budget.

The Economic and Monetary Union Model (EMU) involves free trade, free movement of capital and labour, plus monetary integration (either a common currency or fixed exchange rates, with close co-ordination of the states' macroeconomic policies). In addition, in an EMU many of the policies originally undertaken by the Member States are now of concern at the union level. This implies the existence of a much more substantial union budget.

Identifying and Measuring the Effects of Integration

In order to evaluate the impact of the EC it is necessary to identify the possible effects which economic integration might have. The possible effects can be identified by drawing on economic theories of international trade and integration. In recent years there have been important developments in these theories — as a result of recognition of the significance of a number of factors which were excluded in traditional, textbook, international trade theory. Taking account of recent developments, we can identify five possible effects of the removal of tariff and non-tariff barriers (Table 1).

Table 1: Possible Effect of the Removal of Tariff and Non-Tariff Barriers

1.	Inter-industry adjustment and trade
2.	Trade creation and trade diversion
3.	Cold-shower effect of improved technical efficiency
4.	Intra-industry adjustment and trade
5.	Increased firm size and restructuring

Orthodox Trade Theory: Inter-Industry Adjustment and Trade

As explained in Chapter 31, orthodox or traditional international trade theory explains the pattern of trade between two countries by reference to their relative endowments of resources such as labour, capital and land. Without international trade, each country must produce the full range of goods it wishes to use in consumption or investment. When trade is allowed, then the theory predicts that the country which has relatively abundant labour will find it advantageous to concentrate on labour-intensive goods and to purchase capital-intensive goods abroad — where they are produced more cheaply. Likewise, the capital-rich country will find that it cannot produce labour-intensive goods as cheaply as the labour-rich country, and will purchase them abroad rather than produce them. Thus, each country specialises in the products to which it is most suited — and acquires the other products through trade. This trade between countries is known as *inter-industry* trade, because each country imports and exports very different products of *different* industries. The international pattern of production which is involved is called *inter-industry specialisation*.

The Theory of Customs Unions: Trade Creation and Trade Diversion

This theoretical approach produces predictions concerning three phenomena: the patterns of trade, the welfare gains from trade and the effects of trade on distribution between labour and capital (see Chapter 31). When applied to the formation of a free trade area, a customs union or a common market a distinction is made between trade *creation* and trade *diversion*. These forms of economic integration are not a move to complete free trade, since the countries forming the union exclude other countries by maintaining, or increasing, tariffs against them. Consequently, as well as "trade created" as the member countries specialise, there may, against this, be "trade diverted", as trade with non-member countries is reduced, or stopped altogether (see item 2 in Table 1). Whether the formation of the customs union increases or decreases total world welfare depends on the relative size of "trade created" and "trade diverted".

Research suggests that, in the EC, trade creation far exceeded trade diversion — a finding which reflects the fact that the EC was established in a period of general trade liberalisation. A striking feature of the many estimates of the welfare effects of European economic integration, derived using traditional trade theory, is the smallness of the welfare, or efficiency, gains. Most studies have produced estimates of welfare gains ranging from 0.15 per cent of GNP to, at most, 1 per cent of GNP, realised after the transition period had been completed. In the face of these results, researchers have asked why policy-makers and the European public attach such significance to European integration, when the verdict of conventional economists is that the economic benefits are derisory. Has the public been deluded, or have traditional economists been missing something important? It was eventually realised that the real arguments for market integration must be looked for outside the basic framework of customs union theory. This was done by introducing factors which are excluded from the neo-classical theory of trade.

The Cold-shower Effect of Increased Technical Efficiency

A possibility not included in the orthodox trade theory is that, prior to the opening of trade, firms employ inefficient practices and processes. By inefficient we mean that more output could be achieved with the same inputs. The assumption of technical efficiency (prior to integration) is part of the reason why the gains from integration are so narrowly defined in the conventional theory. Those who have studied the process of European integration are in no doubt that, prior to trade liberalisation, many firms in various European countries were not maximising the output they achieved from the inputs they used. Consequently, European industrial market integration could have a "cold-shower" effect on the behaviour of industrial firms. They could respond to increased international competition by increasing their efficiency. This would lead to a reduction in costs of production which would constitute a gain to society. Indeed, the welfare consequences of an improvement of technical efficiency after the reduction of protection seem likely to be many times larger than the rather trivial gains from improving price-efficiency.

It is very difficult to measure this technical inefficiency and hence to quantify the beneficial effect of market integration. Nevertheless, some consideration must be given to the possibility that one of the effects of the various stages of European integration, including the current one, is the impact of increased cross-border competition on the efficiency of firms (see item 3 in Table 1).

Intra-industry Adjustment and Specialisation

One of the major innovations in recent approaches to the analysis of international trade and economic integration is the inclusion of *economies of scale*. Economies of scale exist where the cost of producing a good is *lower*, the larger the scale of production. Remarkably, the conventional approach to trade, and most of orthodox economics, is premised on the assumption that cost of production is either constant or *increasing* as output increases (but see Chapter 27). However, there is much evidence to show that manufacturing and some kinds of agriculture experience economies of scale and that these economies of scale play a significant role in international trade. Including economies of scale in the analysis has significantly altered economists' views on the likely effects of trade and integration. The reason for this is explained in all modern textbooks on trade theory or European economic integration. Here we concentrate on the practical implications. Theoretical argument shows that the presence of economies of scale encourages *product differentiation* and *intra-industry trade* (IIT). Product differentiation arises where firms compete more on the basis of specialised design and quality than on the basis of price. Intra-industry trade arises where there is two-way international exchange of very similar goods. The trade occurs *within* a given industry and involves specialisation *within* industries rather than *between* them.

These developments in the theory of international trade were necessary because it had become impossible to explain the pattern of trade between advanced industrial countries by reference to their endowments of land, labour and capital. For example, both Sweden and Germany sell each other luxury cars, high-technology equipment and food products. Indeed, most of the trade in the EU and in Western Europe consists of very similar products going in both directions. Of course, when looked at in great detail, these products have fine distinctions, in terms of technical specifications and consumer appeal.

In the late 1950s, it was widely predicted that, with the formation of the EEC, the German steel industry would effectively wipe out the steel industries in Belgium, Italy and France, because, even by then, Germany had a leadership position in that industry. This did not happen. What happened was that Germany, Belgium, Italy and France, all retained steel industries, but they specialised, within the steel industry, in narrower segments. Individual firms and, connected to that, individual countries, found themselves specialising into narrow segments and products, foregoing other segments and products within the industry. Those products were then traded between the countries, reflecting intra-industry specialisation. A similar story would be told of many other industries.

Intra-industry specialisation and trade is now a major feature of research on the effects of European integration. A number of reasons can be identified for this. Many European economies (and especially the original EC-6) are at very similar levels of development and have similar endowments of labour, land and capital. Consequently, there is little basis for inter-industry specialisation and they are, indeed, found to conduct two-way-trade in most products. This intra-industry trade suggests that their patterns of competitive advantage and specialisation are based on product differentiation. In addition, the internal market programme (see Section 5 below) is targeted at high-technology manufactures and services — since it is in these sectors that the greatest non-tariff barriers are found. Competition in high-technology manufactures, and increasingly in services, is very largely based on technology, design and product differentiation. Intra-industry trade and specialisation is most likely in precisely these sectors.

Increased Firm Size and Restructuring

Once economies of scale are introduced into the analysis, then other new phenomena must be allowed in also. Where economies of scale exist, it is unrealistic to view each industry consisting of very many small producers, as is assumed in traditional theory. Instead, industries with economies of scale tend to be highly concentrated — that is, dominated by a few firms (see Chapter 27). It follows that, in analysing the effects of integration, attention must be given to the size structure of firms and industries, and to the market power of corporations. This subject is known in economics as market structure or *industrial structure* (see Chapter 28).

One very important proposition concerning industrial structure has emerged in modern research on economic integration. It has been argued that the reduction of barriers to trade will bring about an increase in the concentration of industry. The idea is that access to foreign markets increases the incentives for large-scale producers in each country to drive out marginal producers by increasing capacity and thereby lowering cost. Furthermore, firms which are threatened by the low cost of the dominant producers will presumably search for counter-strategies, such as product differentiation, product innovation, process innovation, and mergers or takeovers. But most of these strategies also imply a slow but steady reorganisation of industry towards large-scale production, with weeding out of fringe producers. Consequently, there are solid reasons to expect market integration to lead to a rise in domestic producer concentration.

Empirical research confirms the accuracy of this prediction for the Six after the formation of the EEC, and subsequent work shows that the growth of trade between 1963 and 1978 further increased the size of production units in Germany, Italy, and the United Kingdom. It is clearly of some interest to ask whether the increase in trade prompted a similar process of concentration in Ireland.

4. IRELAND'S ADJUSTMENT TO MEMBERSHIP OF THE EUROPEAN UNION

In order to identify the effects of European integration in Ireland, we must now ask which of the possible effects, listed and explained above, have actually materialised in the Irish case. Since the internal market removed many tariff and non-tariff barriers to trade in *manufactured* goods, but until very recently left in place most barriers to trade in services, the main focus is on the effects of EC membership on manufacturing in Ireland. The results of detailed study of trade, output and employment in manufacturing industry are summarised in Table 2 and explained in the remainder of this section (see NESC, *Ireland in the European Community*, Chapters 4–7).

Table 2: Developments Since Freeing of Trade

1.	Trade creation and diversification
2.	Cold-shower effect
3.	Some intra-industry adjustment
4.	Large inter-industry adjustment
5.	Reduction in firm size

Overall Economic Performance

As in other European countries and regions, the period since 1973 has been a turbulent one. Ireland's entry to the EEC in 1973 coincided with a major slow-down in economic growth in all OECD countries. However, Ireland's recovery from the recession of 1974–5 was very strong and, consequently, the Irish economy was relatively buoyant during most of the 1970s. By contrast, Ireland had, perhaps, the worst economic performance in Europe during most of the 1980s, as a result of international recession, reinforced by a dramatic domestic adjustment to reduce public finance and balance of payments deficits. Since 1987, overall economic performance has been much stronger, with growth above the European average in most years, movement of the balance of payments on current account into a strong surplus and gradual reduction of the debt/GNP ratio. However, a resumption of economic growth and stabilisation of the public finances was not sufficient to prevent continuing problems of large-scale emigration (when foreign labour markets are buoyant) and per-sistent unemployment of almost 20 per cent of the labour force.

Trade Creation and Diversion

Despite the difficulties of measuring trade creation and trade diversion, we can say with some confidence that trade diversion, and hence the distinction between trade creation and trade division, was of little significance in Ireland's adjustment to EC membership. This is because prior to membership Ireland did not import extensively from non-EC-12 countries and Ireland's major trading partner, the UK, joined the EC at the same time.

Although adherence to EC external trade policy was an extension of the approach adopted by Ireland from 1958, membership of the Community did imply significant changes in Ireland's external trade régime. Consequently, membership had important effects on Irish trade, some of which should be reported.

Levels and Patterns of Trade

Because of the small scale of the home market, the importance of agriculture and a lack of other natural resources, Ireland has, for a very long time, been a trading country. Nevertheless, there has been a remarkable increase in the openness of the economy since accession to the EC: exports increased from 38 per cent of Gross Domestic Product (GDP) in 1973, to 63 per cent in 1993; imports increased from 45 per cent of GDP in 1973, to 52 per cent in 1993. The share of Irish exports going to the UK fell from 62 per cent in 1970 to 31 per cent in 1992, while the share going to EU countries other than the UK rose from 13 per cent to 43 per cent over the same period. The origin of Ireland's imports shows less change. The UK never provided as large a share of Irish imports as it took of Irish exports, but neither has that share declined as rapidly.

The commodity composition of Irish exports has shown equally dramatic changes. Although food, drink and tobacco accounted for over 45 per cent of the value of exports in 1972, these were soon overtaken by the value of manufactured exports, and now stand at around 24 per cent. The exports of the chemicals and engineering industries grew from 15 per cent of total exports in 1972, to over 46 per cent of total exports (67 per cent of manufactured exports) in 1992. This reflects the profound changes in the structure of the economy which have occurred since

Ireland's switch to an outward looking economic strategy, and especially since membership of the EC (see below).

The Cold-Shower Effect

Despite the difficulties of measurement, experts are in no doubt that the substantial gains made by both France and Italy after the formation of the EEC are explained by a drastic increase in technical efficiency, induced by the competitive threats and opportunities of the common market. Given that the Irish economic structure in 1973 was one which had developed behind high protective tariffs, it is likely that similar inefficiencies existed. Official studies of Irish manufacturing during the 1960s provided evidence of such inefficiencies, and economic performance during the gradual reduction of protection suggests that efficiency was improved in a typical cold-shower effect.

Some Intra-Industry Adjustment

There is clear evidence of an intra-industry adjustment in Ireland following the reduction of tariffs. The index of Intra-Industry Trade (IIT) rose sharply in the late 1960s and throughout the 1970s (see NESC, *Ireland in the European Community,* Chapter 6). This suggests that firms in Ireland reacted to free trade by specialising in particular segments of their industry. It was noted above that in the case of the EC-6, this was found to be the main adjustment to market integration.

A Large Inter-Industry Adjustment

A significant feature of Ireland's adjustment to European market integration has been a substantial inter-industry adjustment. This was initially highlighted by the fact that the index of intra-industry trade, having risen in the 1960s and 1970s, fell in the 1980s. On closer inspection, it emerged that a strong inter-industry adjustment had, in fact, occurred throughout the period of tariff reduction. The nature of this adjustment is best illustrated by identifying three groups of industries, each of which had a different pattern of response to free trade:

(1) foreign-owned, grant-aided, export-oriented;

(2) industries in which the domestic market is naturally protected;

(3) internationally-traded, relatively large scale.

The first group consists of industries such as chemicals, pharmaceuticals and electrical machinery. These experienced continued expansion, and rapid export growth, throughout the period of EU membership. Because of their reliance on the domestic market, the industries in the second group, (which include paper and printing, drink and tobacco, some food industries and small-scale metal and woodworking firms) fared well in the 1970s, when domestic demand was buoyant, but suffered severe contraction in the 1980s, when the Irish economy languished in prolonged recession. The third group comprises textiles, clothing, footwear, leather, parts of chemicals, motor vehicles and parts, electrical engineering, ship-building, bread, biscuits, flour and confectionery and other food industries. Many of Ireland's relatively large manufacturing firms were in these industries. After the removal of tariff protection, import penetration was rapid and, in this highly competitive international environment, these industries suffered secular decline in which the larger Irish producers were eliminated. The drastic removal of these industries — and their replacement by foreign-owned firms in high-technology segments of chemicals, pharmaceuticals and electrical machinery — constituted a much more significant inter-industry adjustment than was found in the case of the EC-6 or, indeed, in Britain or Denmark. The Irish experience lends some credence to the expectation that the effect of economic integration on Spain, Greece and Portugal may involve a disruptive, costly, inter-industry adjustment, rather than the relatively smooth, intra-industry specialisation, which characterised the earlier phases of European market integration.

Reduction in Firm Size

The fifth possible effect of market integration listed in Table 1, industrial concentration, was not observed in Ireland. There was, in fact, a fragmentation of indigenous manufacturing industry. The opening of trade induced a sharp reduction in average manufacturing firm size in the 1970s and 1980s, thereby reversing a slow process of industry concentration which had operated since the 1930s. The nature of this change can be illustrated by reference to a single sector, metals and engineering. After the freeing of trade, new start-ups and employment growth in indigenous firms in this sector were heavily concentrated in sub-sectors like metal articles and engineering, which are mostly small-scale activities serving local markets in products which are somewhat protected from international competition. At the same time, large Irish establishments, in activities where there are economies of scale, and which are open to international competition, closed or contracted. Together these trends ensured that the tendency of integration to encourage concentration did not occur in Ireland. Instead of integration stimulating dominant indigenous firms to exploit economies of scale, and thus eliminate the tail of smaller high-cost producers, the larger Irish manufacturers would seem to *have been part of the tail* eliminated by producers in other countries (see NESC, *Ireland in the European Community*, Chapter 6).

Interpretation

It is possible to interpret the radical adjustment in the structure of the Irish economy in terms of the response of firms to European market integration. The removal of inefficient practices (the cold-shower effect) and an element of specialisation on particular products *within* their own industry (intra-industry specialisation) offered some breathing space to indigenous manufacturers, but did not, as in other countries, complete the process of adjustment. Because Irish firms' basic scale was too small relative to their competitors, and because they suffered a range of other competitive disadvantages, that breathing space was only temporary. Competitive pressure for further adjustment built up, forcing further contractions of output and employment. In industries where economies of scale exist, contractions of employment (except where they removed basic inefficiencies or introduced new technologies), and contractions of output, tend to *raise* costs rather than *lower* them. Consequently, such "adjustments", rather than re-establishing competitiveness on a new basis, were the start of the process of long-run decline, inherent in international specialisation *between* industries. The experience of Irish manufacturing industry since 1973, can be seen to be consistent with a modern and realistic understanding of how trade and integration work where there are initial differences in the levels of development, technology and scale of production (NESC, *Ireland in the European Community*, Chapter 7).

The Role of Domestic Policy

Research on Ireland's economic experience of European integration also draws attention to the role of domestic factors, and this is important in the overall perspective on EU membership which has emerged in recent years. In particular, mention has been made of Irish industrial development and macroeconomic policies. First, it has been argued that the earlier policy of industrial protectionism left a legacy of under-sized firms, involved mainly in the assembly of products for sale on the small home market. Second, it has been shown that, after the removal of protection, Irish industrial policy failed to overcome some of the barriers facing indigenous industry. A third factor which may have some role when explaining the run-down of much indigenous industry, and its replacement by foreign firms in a narrow range of sectors, is the uneven growth of domestic demand. During the 1970s, Ireland pursued an expansionary fiscal policy which was frequently pro-cyclical. The resulting severe imbalances in both the public finances and the balance of payments dictated that deflationary macroeconomic policies be pursued throughout the 1980s. In this period of prolonged depression, a major contraction of indigenous manufacturing industry and a doubling of Irish unemployment occurred. A final factor which must be considered is the change in exchange rate régime which resulted from the decision to join the European Monetary System in 1979 (see Section 8 below).

5. THE INTERNAL MARKET PROGRAMME

The Crisis of the Community and the Costs of "Non-Europe"

In response to the economic difficulties which were experienced in Western Europe in the 1970s and early 1980s, the European Parliament and the European Commission undertook detailed analysis of the economic position of the EC. That study confirmed that the economic performance of the EC was significantly worse than that of its major trading rivals, Japan and the US. The analysis suggested that the main obstacle to the economic growth of European countries was "non-Europe". By "non-Europe" was meant the low level of co-operation between Community members and the weakness of common policies. States had resorted to measures which, though they did not contravene the Community's rules, amounted to protection via non-tariff barriers (NTBs). Important examples were the use made of state-aid to industry, state procurement and national technical and professional standards. In addition, Member States had been less co-operative, with the result that Europe was for ten years virtually paralysed by hair-splitting and protracted disputes and interminable budgetary debates, all of ridiculously small importance compared with the major challenges which faced it.

In devising a strategy for recovery, the Commission laid stress on two sets of measures: the creation of a unified internal market and new Community-level co-operation in a number of important fields — specifically high-technology sectors such as information technology, energy, biotechnology, aircraft and space research. These two elements became the central thrust of the initiatives which culminated in the Commission's 1985 White Paper, *Completing the Internal Market* and the 1986 Single European Act (SEA).

The *1992* Project: Completing the Internal Market

In 1985 the incoming Commission, led by Jacques Delors, presented a White Paper to the European Council entitled *Completing the Internal Market*. It explained that completing the internal market had three aspects:

(1) Welding together the twelve individual markets of the Member States into one single market of 320 million people;

(2) Ensuring that this single market is also an expanding market;

(3) Ensuring that the market is flexible so that resources, both of people and materials, and of capital and investment, flow into areas of greatest economic advantage.

The White Paper set out in great detail the measures necessary to achieve the first of these objectives and to adopt a timetable for the legal enactment of these measures. The White Paper grouped under three headings the 300 measures necessary to complete the internal market:

(1) The removal of *physical* barriers to trade and competition, including the removal of border posts;

(2) The removal of *technical* barriers to trade and competition — the most obvious of these barriers being different national standards adopted for health or safety reasons or for environmental or consumer protection.

(3) The removal of *fiscal* barriers to trade and competition — in particular, the harmonisation of indirect taxes across the EC.

An important innovation in the White Paper was the adoption by the Commission of a "new approach" to the removal of technical barriers. Up to that point the attempt to remove technical barriers had taken the form of complete *harmonisation* of all countries' technical standards. This proved to be an extremely lengthy and difficult process. The "new approach" moved away from the concept of harmonisation to that of *mutual recognition*. The principle of mutual recognition means that Member States must give access to their market to any product which satisfies the requirements of any Member State.

Another important innovation in the White Paper was action on public procurement. In principle, public bodies were already forbidden to discriminate between suppliers from EC countries and were required to advertise major contracts, but public procurement in all countries favoured national companies wherever possible. In addition, important areas such as telecommunications, water, energy and transport, were exempt from the requirements for open tendering. The White Paper proposed that existing regulations for open competition would have to be enforced and that these exemptions would be eliminated.

While the White Paper was concerned mainly with completion of the internal market, it did link this to three other policy approaches. It stressed that the suspension of internal borders must be accompanied by actions which strengthen the research and technological base of the Union's industry. It argued that the integration of national markets must be accompanied by a strengthening of the co-ordination of economic policies and the European Monetary System (EMS). Finally, the Commission noted the risk that, by facilitating the movement of resources to areas of greatest economic advantage, the completion of the internal market could widen the existing discrepancies between the regions of Europe. In the Commission's view this enhanced the importance of the Community's Structural Funds (see Sections 6 and 7 below).

Most of the measures in the White Paper were adopted by the December 1992 deadline, and attention has since moved to the Member States, which have to transpose the EU directives into national law and ensure implementation. The Commission has identified delays in five areas: suppression of border checks, indirect taxation, the creation of an EU patent and trademark, abolition of double taxation on firms, and company law. Over the years a number of measures have been added to the internal market programme as originally outlined by the Commission. For example, a greater realisation of the link between external trade policy and internal market fragmentation has led to changes in EU import quotas. Proposals for a single market for energy were also added and recently, the role of infrastructure and, in particular, trans-European networks, in making the single market a reality has been emphasised by the Commission.

Conceptualising the Internal Market

In 1988 the Commission undertook a major study on the completion of the internal market, *The Economics of 1992* — often referred to as the Cecchini Report (available as M. Emerson et al., *The Economics of 1992*, OUP, Oxford, 1988). This included an inventory of the major non-tariff barriers, estimation of the losses in welfare resulting from the fragmentation of European markets — the so called "costs of non-Europe" — and analysis of the likely effects of completion of the internal market. While numerical estimates of the growth and employment effects were important in the Commission's highly successful selling of *1992,* what remains particularly relevant is the economic analysis used by the Commission. This incorporated recent developments in both trade theory and industrial economics and should be understood by any student of Ireland in its European context. This analytical framework is outlined schematically in Figure 1 and is explained below (for a more detailed account see NESC, *Ireland in the European Community*, Chapter 8). The completion of the internal market works through two main channels — "size" and "competition" — each of which contains both direct and indirect effects.

Figure 1: Size and Competition
Two Channels of Direct and Indirect Effects of Internal Market
Completion

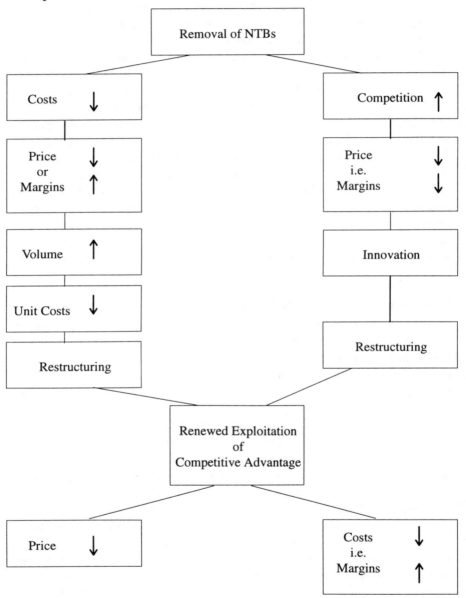

Direct Effects of Market Completion

The "size" channel — on the left-hand side of Figure 1 — begins with the cost reductions which result from the removal of non-tariff barriers (NTBs). For example, firms are able to find cheaper inputs, transport and insurance; packaging and labelling costs fall, and the cost of traded goods is reduced by the removal of bureaucratic obstacles, etc. As shown in Figure 1, these cost reductions facilitate price reduction and, consequently, increased demand and output. Turning to the right-hand channel of Figure 1, *increased competition* results from the improved market access of firms in all countries. Firms which could previously operate high price-cost margins or price discrimination find this ability curtailed by increased competition. The relative strength of these two direct effects differs from industry to industry. It is, however, possible to identify some of the factors which determine the strength of the two direct effects.

The extent of immediate *cost reduction* clearly depends on the heights of NTBs in different industries. Some NTBs affect all industries which produce tradable products — the most obvious example being customs costs. Others affect only some industries — for example, national packaging, labelling or technical standards and national government procurement practices. In general, NTBs are relatively less in low-technology products than in high-technology markets. *Price reductions* resulting directly from increased competition are a function of the degree of concentration of an industry. Despite the presence of NTBs, many industries contain a large number of firms, and competition ensures that price does not depart excessively from costs. Commonly cited examples include textiles, clothing, and footwear. By contrast, other industries were highly concentrated, or market entry was restricted, and firms in individual national markets had scope for monopoly pricing, price discrimination and inefficiencies. Examples are pharmaceuticals, man-made fibres, office machinery, domestic electrical appliances and motor vehicles.

Indirect Effects of Market Completion

These two direct effects may be the start of two chains of causation which create substantial *indirect* effects. These have been labelled "size" and "competition" in the Cecchini Report are depicted schematically in Figure 1.

It was noted above that the first *direct* effect of removal of NTBs is to reduce costs and, consequently, price. As the quantity demanded and supplied increases, the firm may find costs of production falling again because of *economies of scale*. This facilitates further price reductions and output growth. The process of increasing output and exploiting economies of scale involves larger, low-cost, producers eliminating smaller high-cost firms and can, consequently, initiate a major restructuring of industry. This is the first possible indirect effect of market completion.

A major restructuring of business, with further growth in firm size, depends on the extent of economies of scale and the degree to which firms in the EU were operating below the minimum efficient scale prior to the *1992* programme. The extent of economies of scale varies between production, distribution, financing, R&D and innovation. It follows that the overall importance of economies of scale and, consequently, the extent of restructuring, depends on which activity is important in a given industry at a given time. The size of economies of scale determines what kinds of firms reap the greatest medium to long-term benefit from completion of the European market, and also what kinds of firms will emerge in Europe. If economies of scale are very substantial, then larger firms have had an initial advantage and very large firms will ultimately emerge. If economies of scale are not so significant, then small to medium-size enterprises (SMEs) will benefit and competition will take some form other than scale-based cost reduction.

The second direct effect of *1992,* the effect of increased *competition* on price-cost margins, is expected to stimulate a second indirect effect, in the form of a spur to *innovation* (see Figure 1). Firms faced with more aggressive competition seek not only to *match* the competition, but also to *evade* it by repositioning themselves. They can do this by differentiating their product from that of their rivals. Product differentiation usually requires innovation. A view emerging from some recent work on industrial economics is that increased competition has a positive impact on technical progress and the diffusion of innovation. This is at variance with a traditional idea that monopoly, despite its attendant costs, was more conducive to R&D and innovation. The new view denies that large firm *size* is conducive to innovation and argues instead that rapid market *growth* strongly stimulates innovation in industry. This view led to the expectation that completion of the European internal market, by increasing competition, would have a major dynamic impact on those sectors in which NTBs were high, technological development is significant, and the outlook for market growth is good.

In using this framework for analysis of the European internal market, three propositions should be borne in mind. First, the indirect effects of market completion are likely to be more substantial than the direct effects. Second, and most significantly, the relative size and nature of the direct and indirect effects differs between sectors of the economy. Third, account must be taken of the *perception* of firms and, more generally, of the very significant *psychological* effect of the internal market programme.

Firm Size, the Internal Market and Europe's Competitiveness

This effect of increased competition on innovation was given considerable emphasis in *The Economics of 1992*. If increased competition causes more innovation, then it would seem to be exactly what is required to address the key problem of the European economy — the failure of Europe's high technology industries to match the performance of the Japanese and the Americans. Of course, independent of market completion in Europe, a tremendous wave of technical change is occurring and this is clearly affecting not only those high-technology sectors which generate innovation and produce high-technology products, but also many industries producing traditional products.

While exploitation of economies of scale and increased competition are not necessarily inconsistent — as long as the market can sustain enough firms — there are, in fact, considerable differences in thinking between those who stress *economies of scale* and those who emphasise *competition* and *innovation*. This was reflected in the *Economics of 1992*, which was assembled from the research of many different economists. In the report there was a clear tension between the view that further concentration of industry would be likely (because significant economies of scale remained to be exploited) and the view that the larger market will increase the *variety* of products available, and hence that small and medium-sized enterprises would benefit most (because they suffered most from non-tariff barriers and they have a particular ability to innovate). This is one of the most important questions concerning the European economy and the impact on it of the European Union. If a significant part of the increased competition created by completion of the market takes the form of cost reduction based on scale expansion, then the fear naturally arises that small firms will find it very difficult to compete. Furthermore, if completion implies increased firm size, then *barriers to entry* of various sorts may increase — even though market completion also means increased competition *between those dominant firms* in a given industry. If, on the other hand, those who stress competition and innovation are correct, then the increased competition will take a number of other forms, such as technological activity aimed at product and process development, product differentiation, market segmentation, and redefinition of firms' specialisation. The argument between these two views turns on a number of theoretical and empirical points concerning the effects of the internal market on the size of firms, the relationship between competition and innovation, the historical significance of economies of scale, the effects of technical and organisational change on scale economies and the role of small firms in economic development (see NESC 1989, *Ireland in the European Community*, Chapter 8).

The Internal Market Programme in Perspective

The legislative programme to complete the internal market was a very significant step in European economic integration. Whether it will fulfil the hopes of its authors, by reviving the competitiveness and dynamism of Europe, remains to be seen and certainly cannot be taken for granted. In this, and a number of other respects, it is important to keep the internal market programme in perspective.

First, research suggests that while the terms "completion of *the* internal market" and "*single* European market" are unavoidable, they may create the misleading impression that since January 1993 there has been a single or unified European market of 360 million people for almost all manufactured goods and services. But the fragmentation of the European market is only partly a result of the trade barriers which have been removed in the internal market programme. Much of the fragmentation arises from the diversity of cultures, traditions and consumption patterns in Europe and, consequently, remains. Conversely, there was already a unified European market for some commodities, such as aircraft and oil. The extent to which the internal market programme is creating a unified market in each product is a question for expert industry-specific analysis. Second, it is important to appreciate that economic analysis cannot predict the precise effects of the internal market on each industry and country in Europe. The traditional factor-proportions theory of trade explains comparative advantage at a high level of aggregation, not at the level relevant for deciding industrial production or policy. With the *new* approach to understanding trade, this problem is even more acute. Intra-industry trade is a more complex phenomenon which does not lend itself as readily as the inter-industry trade model to predictions of shifts in comparative advantage. Third, the completion of the European internal market must be seen in the context of other changes in the general economic environment, such as technical change, organisational change, macroeconomic conditions, and the emergence of important new producers from Asia. One of the most significant features of current technological change, and the associated organisational restructuring, is that it seems to be *inherently international* or, perhaps more accurately, supra-national. National markets, particularly small national markets, seem to be a hindrance to the full deployment of the new technologies. Recognition of these facts allows us to see the internal market programme as Europe's response to a set of changes which are occurring in any event and which will inevitably increase the international aspect of economic life.

Integration of Mixed Economies: The "Economic Order"

Early in the analysis of European integration, a distinction was made between *negative* and *positive* integration. *Negative* integration refers to the *removal* of obstacles to the movements of goods, labour or capital. *Positive* integration refers to the *establishment* of common policies and institutions in order to achieve economic integration or to pursue other objectives of the union. It used to be said that creation of a common market required primarily negative integration. However, this assumes that the only significant government intervention in the economy is the setting of tariffs and quotas and the imposition of restrictions on the international movement of capital and labour. In modern mixed economies government intervenes in a myriad of ways, ranging from market regulation, social policy, labour market policy, industrial policy, technology policy, to direct provision of goods and services and active macroeconomic management. Many of these public policy interventions significantly affect the competitive conditions in each country. It follows that a common market — which implies free and undistorted movement of goods, labour and capital — could not be achieved merely by *removal* of tariffs, quotas and purely legal obstacles to the movement of labour and capital.

Creating a common market for goods requires not only the removal of tariffs, but also elimination of border interventions — such as customs controls. But this requires harmonisation of indirect tax and removal of national technical standards. These changes are extremely complex and politically demanding. If the numerous domestic policy interventions are similar in their effects to border interventions, then a common market also requires some harmonisation of national government influences on competitive conditions in Member States. This is very ambitious, since it undermines national industrial policy, regional policy, public procurement practices and the financing of state-owned enterprises. Achievement of a single labour market requires change in national social and labour market policies. Integration of financial markets will tend to undermine national stabilisation and redistribution policies, and may be dependent on co-ordination of macroeconomic policies, concerning the money supply, exchange rates and budget deficits. In short, creation of a genuine *common market,* seems virtually to involve creation of full *economic and monetary union.*

An important implication of the fact that European integration involves a *process* of integration of *mixed* economies is that the question of integration becomes linked to questions about the "economic order". An economic order can be defined as a coherent set of laws, institutions and customs concerning the management of economic life, and includes some balance between markets and the state. Although the societies of Western Europe have adopted a broadly similar economic order — the mixed economy — it is not clear whether national approaches to the detailed relationships and institutions of the economic order are sufficiently compatible for European economic integration to be possible.

This has a number of implications. First, it largely accounts for the fact that integration tends to begin with *negative* integration such as trade liberalisation. *Positive* integration measures would require detailed agreement on many of the allocative and possibly redistributive and stabilising functions of government in the economy. But even with negative integration — the lowest common denominator of what all Member States can agree — the fundamental issue of the desirable economic order still arises. Even negative integration will tend to change the economic order, pushing more interventionist countries in a liberal, free market, direction. Faced with this tendency for *integration* to imply *deregulation*, many argue that national regulation should be replaced by *re-regulation* at the European level. Consequently, it is not surprising that deepening European integration gives rise to fierce debate on the desirable economic order for Europe.

The requirements for the market integration of mixed economies also explains the close connection between economic and political integration. Market integration tends to undermine complex packages — concerning market regulation, income redistribution and macroeconomic management — which are at the heart of national politics. Integration as *de*regulation alters these domestic political compromises, while integration as *re*-regulation involves the irrevocable transfer of national jurisdiction to European institutions. Either way, the process of market, or economic, integration is clearly intensely political.

6. THE COHESION ISSUE AND EU STRUCTURAL POLICIES

Introduction

In recent years, the term "cohesion" has come to denote the European Union's objective of reducing spatial and social disparities in living standards, employment and unemployment. This term should be distinguished from the word "convergence", which tends to be used to refer to convergence of economic magnitudes such as inflation rates and interest rates. Much Irish analysis and discussion of the European Union concentrates on the cohesion issue and, particularly, on EU expenditures under the Structural Funds. For three reasons, this section is confined to a brief account of the origin and structure of EU cohesion policies. First, these policies, and their application to Ireland, are well documented elsewhere (see A. Matthews, *Managing EU Structural Funds in Ireland,* Cork University Press, 1994). Second, the impact of EU cohesion policies is probably less than the impact of market and monetary integration. Third, the focus of this textbook on economic theory and principles, suggests that greater emphasis should be placed on analysis of the *regional effects* of economic and monetary integration (see Section 7 below).

The Cohesion Policies of the European Union

Although the Treaty of Rome made no provision for a regional policy, it did contain implicit references to regional problems and regional objectives. The Treaty established the European Social Fund (ESF) to address employment problems and this gradually acquired a regional function as well. Much the most significant regional instrument created by the Treaty of Rome was the European Investment Bank. Plans for movement to economic and monetary union in the early 1970s — combined with the enlargement to include the UK, Ireland and Denmark, in 1973 — prompted the development in 1975 of a European regional policy. Since then, EU regional policies have developed along three main lines: first, the co-ordination of the national regional policies of Member States to ensure their conformities with the Treaties; second, an attempt to make other EU policies and financing instruments more sensitive to regional disparities; third, establishment of specific regional policy instruments at European level. The most significant reform of EU regional policy was that which followed the Single European Act (1986). The Act strengthened the objective of reducing disparities between regions and called for the cohesion objective to be taken into account in the implementation of other policies. It also led to a doubling of the Structural Funds and their concentration on a set of five specified objectives, which focused the funds on areas most in need of support. The Treaty on European Union — commonly known as the Treaty of Maastricht — further developed the EU's approach to cohesion. It stipulated that the Commission must submit a report every three years, indicating how EU policies have contributed towards economic and social cohesion. The Treaty also established the new Cohesion Fund, providing financial support to projects in the fields of environment and trans-European networks, particularly transport infrastructure. Following the Treaty of Maastricht, the negotiation of a new financial package for the years 1994–99 has led to a slight increase in the EU budget, a two-thirds increase in the Structural Funds available to the least prosperous regions which, with the new Cohesion Fund, implies a doubling of structural support to the four poorest countries (Greece, Ireland, Portugal and Spain) as a whole.

As a result of these developments, the European Union now has four sets of structural policies aimed at economic and social cohesion. First, the social policy aims at improving the employment opportunities and working conditions of EU citizens. Payments from the ESF are used to fund training and retraining of workers whose skills are inadequate because of industrial change, regional problems or social disadvantage. Second, the agricultural guidance policy is intended to address the structural problems in the agricultural sector and is funded by the Guidance Section of the EU's agricultural fund, EAGGF — also established in 1957 (see Chapter 8). Third, EU regional policy provides grants for infrastructural and industrial projects in less prosperous regions, and is funded by the European Regional Development Fund (ERDF), established in 1975. Although most ERDF money has, in all countries, been spent on infrastructure, especially transport infrastructure, there has, in recent years, been a move into new areas. These include initiatives to foster regional development through improving telecommunications, technology, research and development, energy supply, environment and local economic initiatives. Fourth, the EU Cohesion Fund, providing financial support to environmental projects and trans-European networks — is available to Member States which have an average income per head less than 90 per cent of the EU average.

One very important feature that the three Structural Funds and the Cohesion Fund have in common is their small size relative to the total EU budget, relative to total EU GDP and, most significantly, relative to the scale of inequalities and structural problems in the European economy. The EU budget has only recently passed 1 per cent of GDP of the 12 member countries. The EU budget has been, and remains, dominated by agricultural outlays — spent mainly on buying up unwanted food and subsidising exports to the world food market (see Chapter 8). This accounts for the small share of the Structural Funds in the overall EU budget. The doubling of the Structural Funds, between 1987 and 1993, brought them to about 25 per cent of the EU budget and 0.3 per cent of EU GDP.

EU Cohesion Policies in Economic Context

The cohesion provisions emerging from the Treaty of Rome, the Single European Act and the Treaty of Maastricht must be seen in the context of the overall set of forces which shape the regional pattern of economic activity and income in Europe. Given their size and nature, the regional pattern of economic activity and income in Europe is determined to a very small extent by EU cohesion policies. Other EU policies, such as the internal market, the CAP, external trade policy, technology policy and monetary policy are likely to have much more significant regional effects. National policies also have a significant impact on how a country or region performs within the international competitive environment. Finally, and most significantly, aside from policy altogether, the regional pattern is very largely shaped by international economic forces such as industrial growth and decay, foreign direct investment, technical and organisational change and labour migration. The regional effects of some of these forces, and the way in which they are influenced by economic integration, are considered in Section 7.

7. REGIONAL EFFECTS OF ECONOMIC AND MONETARY INTEGRATION

Changing Perspectives on the Regional Effects of Integration

The recent deepening of economic and monetary integration in the European Community has re-opened discussion of the regional distribution of the costs and benefits of integration. Policy-makers at national and EU level are confronted with a bewildering range of opinions on the likely regional effects of the removal of non-tariff barriers, a single financial area, free mobility of labour and currency union. The purpose of this section is to explain the emergence as a new perspective on the regional effects of integration. Our concern, throughout, is to identify the analytical arguments which support the various perspectives. For the purpose of analysis we make use of the well-known definition of three different levels of integration — a customs union, a common market and an economic and monetary union (EMU) — outlined earlier in this chapter.

The central argument of the section is that there has, in recent years, been a distinct shift in perspective on the regional effects of integration. Developments in microeconomics, macroeconomics and regional theory have served to undermine the perspective which dominated discussion through most of the post-war period. The view which dominated was that it is the *monetary* stage of integration which presents weaker regions with the greatest problems. As a result, most discussion by economists of the regional implications of economic integration focused on the *monetary* stage and, within that, concentrated on the loss of exchange rate autonomy. While it is commonly noted that this traditional view was based on a particular body of macroeconomic theory which many now reject, it is important to see that it was also based on a particular perspective on *free trade* (the customs union stage) and *capital and labour mobility* (the common market stage). In particular, it was based on analytical approaches to free trade and factor mobility which suggested that these stages of integration would be relatively benign.

Consequently, in assessing the adequacy of the traditional view, and in devising a new perspective on the regional effects of integration, it is necessary not only to update the macroeconomics analysis of the monetary issue, but also to take note of new approaches to trade and the mobility of labour and capital. It is when all three are considered that a genuine shift is perspective on the regional effects of integration can be discerned. At the cost of some simplification, this central argument can be neatly portrayed in Table 3.

Table 3: Views on the Regional Effects of Integration

Integration Stage	Traditional View	New View
Free Trade (Customs Union).	All regions gain. Adjustment costs only.	Uneven costs and benefits.
Capital and Labour Mobility (Common Market).	All regions gain. Regional differences eroded.	Costs as well as benefits.
Economic and Monetary Union.	Possible deflationary effects.	Limited effects on output and employment.

The Traditional View

The view of the regional implications of EMU which has dominated discussion of European monetary union, from the late 1960s until very recently, is that it is the *monetary* stage of integration which presents weaker regions with the greatest problems. This view results from the following arguments. First, it was considered that the allocation of economic activity between Member States would differ substantially depending on whether the states had formed a customs union, common market, or an EMU. The second important element of this viewpoint is that this difference was considered to have significant implications for the regional pattern of economic activity in a monetary union. Third, combining Keynesian macroeconomics with the orthodox theory of international trade and factor mobility led many economists to focus their analysis of the regional effects of integration on the monetary stage. This is described in the table as the traditional view. In particular, it was argued that in weaker states and regions, which previously used exchange rate devaluation to support output and employment, adherence to a single monetary standard would be deflationary for significance periods. It is also because of these arguments that many economists consider that monetary union should include a federal budgetary mechanism which would cushion regions from the worst effects of shocks, in the way that exchange rate variation did before monetary union.

An Alternative Perspective on EMU

In the light of recent developments in microeconomics, macroeconomics and regional theory, it is possible to identify an alternative perspective on the pattern and timing of the overall costs and benefits of integration for weaker regions. This involves, first and foremost, a different view of the regional implications of *free trade* (the customs union stage) and *capital and labour mobility* (the common market stage). It suggests that even *free trade* can generate large and unevenly distributed costs and benefits in both the short and long run. Furthermore, it indicates that international movements of labour and capital may widen rather than narrow the differences between regional economies. It is within this context that the third element of the traditional view — the specifically monetary argument concerning the macroeconomic effects of a single currency — should be evaluated. In addition, it is possible to extend the analysis of the monetary element beyond issues of *macroeconomics* management to consideration of the implication of monetary union for financial flows and the availability of finance in different regions of a single monetary zone. This line of argument suggests that, as a first approximation, we can consider the *economic* forces, unleashed by free trade and mobility of labour and capital, as separate from the monetary factors.

Regional Tendencies in an Economic Union: Trade and Factor Mobility

This section presents, in summary fashion, arguments concerning tendencies for regional convergence and divergence which can be found in regional economics and the economics of international trade. These arguments are spelled out in more detail in the NESC report *Ireland in the European Community* (1989, Chapters 2 and 11). On the basis of these arguments, it is possible to question two important elements of the traditional view outlined above — first, that, unlike monetary integration, the effects of free trade and factor mobility are fairly benign and, second, that the international pattern of economic activity will be very different depending on whether countries form a customs unions, a common market or an EMU.

Regional Convergence by Market Forces

Mainstream economic theory, based on the notion of the economy as a self-adjusting mechanism, formulates the regional dimension in a way which stresses the tendency to regional balance. According to this theory, the normal functioning of supply and demand will tend to achieve full utilisation of all resources within each region and, more significantly in the current context, tend to eliminate disparities between different regions. This theory of regional convergence is widely considered to be invalid since it is based on some highly unrealistic assumptions. The implication of this is that any easy extrapolation of "invisible hand" ideas to the real world of regional economics in the context of European integration is unwarranted in the light of economic history and theory.

Forces Making for Regional Concentration of Economic Activity

A much more promising approach to understanding the existence and persistence of regional inequalities is that which invokes the "principle of cumulative causation". If there are "economies of scale in production" (the cost of production of goods falls as output increases) or if there are "economies of agglomeration" (the cost of production is lower because of the proximity of other firms), then a region which gets an initial advantage will find that advantage reinforced as its level of production increases. Each time output is increased, costs fall and other regions find it more difficult to catch up. If the strong region attracts capital and labour from weaker regions, this will further enhance its productive potential and, because of the economies of scale and of agglomeration, strengthen its competitive advantage. Hence, the label "cumulative causation": output growth, by lowering costs, developing skills and know-how, inducing innovation and specialisation creates a self-sustaining growth process in certain regions; but other regions may find themselves in a cycle of decline. In this view, economic disparities, far from being self-adjusting or self-correcting, as in the orthodox vision, tend to be *self-reinforcing*. Thus, contrary to an assumption of comparative static equilibrium analysis, an inter-regional equilibrium may be *dynamically unstable*. (Recall the qualifications in Chapters 4 and 7 in regard to the limitations of the method of comparative statics.)

The existence and importance of economies of agglomeration is related to one of the most fundamental processes of economic development — the division of labour. In recent work on the regional distribution of economic activity, access to information networks is given even more emphasis than economies of scale in production. Other factors which reinforce the tendency to concentration are advantageous labour market characteristics (enhanced by migration from poorer regions) and economies of scale in the provision of infrastructure. Yet another recently studied advantage of concentration is *innovation leadership*. Empirical work has revealed evidence of remarkable concentration both of industrial research activity by private and public sector organisations, and of actual manufacturing innovations in core regions.

In recent years, these ideas — which have long been central in regional economics — have become more widely known and accepted in economics generally. In an influential book, *Geography and Trade* (MIT Press, 1991), Paul Krugman argues that the tendency for industry to co-centrate in the large "central" economies depend on three factors: *economies of scale, transport costs and the size of the manufacturing sector*.

> If transportation costs are high, return to scale weak, and the share of spending on manufactured goods low, the incentive to produce close to the market leads to an equal division of manufacturing between the regions. With lower transport costs, stronger scale economies, or a higher manufacturing share, circular causation sets in: the more manufacturing is located in one region, the larger that region's share of demand, and this provides an incentive to locate still more manufacturing there.

This formidable list of arguments would seem to justify the conclusion that there are considerable forces making for concentration of advanced economic activity. If this is what emerges from *regional economics*, it is of interest to ask how consistent it is with what is found in the *economics of international trade* and economic integration.

The New Economics of International Trade

One reason why the conventional theory of economic integration viewed monetary integration as more likely to exacerbate regional problems was that the relative costs and benefits of a customs union, a common market and an economic and monetary union were assessed by applying the traditional theory of international trade. That traditional theory was based on very restrictive assumptions and these had a major role in generating the benign view of trade in the conventional literature. In recent years, significant developments have occurred in the theory of international trade and integration. The new approach takes account of important real world phenomena — such as economies of scale, external economies, the market power of firms and learning by doing — which were long used to explain uneven regional development. In doing so, these new approaches inevitably alter views on the gains from trade and integration.

In general, the new approaches to trade indicate that the overall gains from trade and integration are potentially larger than in the conventional analysis. In addition, the new theories provide some reasons to believe that the *costs of adjusting* to free trade will be *more evenly* distributed between regions, and some reasons why the *long-run benefits* of trade will be *less evenly* distributed — depending, to a large extent on the initial economic structures of the countries and regions entering into integration. Krugman summarises this difference by saying that trade based on economies of scale, the market power of firms and product differentiation, "probably involves less conflict of interest within countries and more conflict between countries than conventional trade". This statement is explained in Chapter 2 of the report, *Ireland in the European Community* (NESC, 1989). (Krugman's paper, "Economic Integration in Europe: Conceptual Issues" is reprinted in A. Jacquemin and A. Sapir (eds) *The European Internal Market: Trade and Competition*, Oxford University Press, 1989).

Thus, the general view of uneven regional development outlined above is one which finds a clear echo in the new theories of international trade. Furthermore, this view is also found in the vast majority of recent studies which consider the regional distribution of the benefits and costs of European market integration.

Two Qualifications

The existence of a strong tendency to regional concentration of advanced economic activity should not be understood as implying that industry will definitely concentrate and regional fortunes will definitely diverge. The process of regional development and change is not as deterministic as some accounts of "cumulative causation" suggests. This is so for two distinct reasons. First, it would be very surprising if there were not also counter tendencies. There are, indeed, some forces making for *diffusion* of activity, especially manufacturing branch-plants. Second, the process of regional change, just like the process of economic development, is not a steady journey along a path of either concentration or dispersal. It is an inherently uneven process which progresses in bursts of progress and sharp reversals. This unpredictability and contingency is reflected in the more interesting recent research in regional economics, the economics of trade and integration and development economics.

In regional economics, it is recognised that although there are tendencies to concentration (and, to a lesser extent, tendencies to dispersal) there is, in fact, a *shifting hierarchy* of leading and lagging regions. Although analysis of these shifts is at a very rudimentary level, this line of enquiry suggests that a region's fortunes are not fully determined by external or immutable forces making for concentration. It is recognised that factors indigenous to a region or country can influence the role which it assumes in the international division of labour. In the new approach to international trade, this non-deterministic outlook is reflected in the fact that simple economies of scale in production and market size are not the only factors influencing the pattern of trade and

production and the relative gains from trade. It is recognised that important sources of economies of scale and the market power of firms, lie in
the *dynamic* process by which firms and industries improve their technologies. This emphasis on innovation suggests the significance of firms'
strategies, but also of the institutional factors which support or inhibit
innovation. In addition, the emphasis on strategic sectors, which emerges
in the new analysis of trade, strongly suggests an important determining
role for policy within a state or region (see R. O'Donnell, *Ireland and
Europe: Challenges for a New Century*, ESRI, Dublin, 1993).

Regional Aspects of the Monetary Union

Having reviewed the traditional and new views on trade and factor
mobility, we must now briefly consider the monetary question itself. The
main question concerns the effects of permanently foregoing the option
of exchange rate devaluation or revaluation. In the run up to European
negotiations on the new Treaty, the Commission published a major study,
One Market, One Money, evaluating the potential benefits and costs of
forming an economic and monetary union (special issue of *European
Economy*, No. 44, October 1990). While many of the issues examined in
that report are considered in Section 8 below, here we concentrate upon
the regional effects of EMU.

Monetary Union and the Loss of Exchange Rate Autonomy

The traditional pessimistic view of the regional implications of monetary
union has two components. First, if weaker regions have a worse underlying trade-off between inflation and unemployment, then imposing the
same inflation rate on all regions, which is one effect of monetary union,
will imply higher unemployment in weaker regions. Second, when
economic fluctuations occur which affect some regions more than others,
commonly referred to as "asymmetric shocks", the impossibility of exchange rate devaluation means that output, employment and unemployment in the unlucky region will bear the full brunt of the shock. For a
reason that will emerge presently, these two propositions should be kept
distinct from one another.

The monetarist and new classical revolutions have severely
challenged the analytical foundations of this traditional view. Put most
simply, monetarist theory says that devaluation offers no protection to
output and employment, but simply changes prices in the country devaluing. This alone suggests that the loss of the exchange rate instrument
is no loss. While many economists are now persuaded that devaluation
has limited ability to defend employment, in the case of monetarists and
new classicists, this idea is linked to a much more general proposition

about the determination of output and employment, and the relationship between money supply and the level of real activity in the economy. That general proposition is that the real economy in each country (or in a monetary union) has a natural tendency to *full* employment and, consequently, it would be logically impossible for a change in the exchange rate, or any other macroeconomic policy, to increase output and employment further. In short, this theory says that there is no trade-off between inflation and unemployment, in either strong or weak regions, and hence disposes of the first component of the pessimistic view of monetary union. Carried to its logical conclusion this theory also dismisses the second component of that view: it suggests that wages and prices will adjust to restore rapidly full employment after an asymmetric shock — a performance which could not be improved upon by exchange rate devaluation.

What are we to make of this wholesale dismissal of all traditional anxieties about the effect of monetary union on unemployment? Three points provide a perspective on the issue.

First, experience does indeed suggest that devaluation is a less powerful instrument than was once assumed (see Chapter 16). Rather than make a very general statement, it may be sufficient to say that, in the circumstances prevailing in Ireland (a small economy with a very high propensity to import), exchange rate devaluation offers policy-makers a very limited instrument for increasing output and employment and makes it more difficult to achieve low inflation.

But, second, the evidence does not support the view, which is suggested by some, that the exchange rate is *completely powerless* to influence competitiveness, output and employment. The authors of *One Market, One Money* say that "nominal exchange rates may have an impact on real exchange rates for, say, two to five years, but this does not persist in the long-run" (Commission, 1990, p.140). Indeed, the strong theoretical position against the significance of the exchange rate is undermined by the historical evidence of successful devaluations, and more emphatically, disastrous over-valuations. This does not make the case for devaluation, but it disposes of an absolute rejection of the idea. When assessing the merits of devaluation, other considerations arise which suggest that it could only be successfully used *infrequently* — but that, in certain crisis situations, it could provide a breathing space, either to ride out a temporary crisis or to undertake adjustment to a permanent shift in economic conditions.

Third, regardless of the effectiveness or ineffectiveness of devaluation at the current stage of integration, it is important to know whether in EMU there are likely to be problems which affect different regions

differently, and which therefore generate regional macroeconomic imbalances. Not surprisingly, much of the recent debate on EMU has
focused on the likelihood of asymmetric shocks and, if they occur, the
best method of dealing with them. In *One Market, One Money*, it is
argued that asymmetric shocks are unlikely and that wage and price
flexibility can protect regional economies. Others argue that — given
differences in economic structures, behaviour and policies — asymmetric
shocks are probable and that the problems they cause will be no more
likely to solve themselves rapidly and painlessly, by means of price and
wage adjustment, than they are now (see P. De Grauwe, *The Economics
of Monetary Integration*, Oxford University Press, 1992). Consequently,
it has frequently been argued that a European monetary union would
work more effectively if it were also a fiscal union. The raising of union
revenue, and its expenditure on a range of Union policies, would provide
an automatic adjustment mechanism which would tend to cushion
regions from the worst effects of asymmetric shocks.

General Principles for a Currency Area: Size and Social Unity

Perhaps the most general analysis of the relative merits of currency independence and monetary union is that of Goodhart in *Money, Information and Uncertainty* (Macmillan, London, 1989). He attempts to reduce
various analytical approaches to a few general principles:

> There appear to be two common factors here determining whether the
> balance-of-payments adjustments of some geographical area would be more
> easily solved as a region within a common-currency area or as an independent
> country with a separate and potentially-variable exchange rate. They are size,
> and social unity with surrounding, contiguous regions (p. 420).

The smaller the size of the region, the easier it will adjust within a common currency and the harder it will find it to run an effective independent
monetary and exchange rate policy. In Goodhart's judgment, the more
important factor is social unity. The reason is that if this exists, then
fiscal mechanisms will be in place which will ease, and possibly solve,
regional disparities. He considers that an attempt to impose an exchange-
rate union without the support of a strong, centralised, or at least inter-
regionally co-ordinated, fiscal policy could have serious regional effects.

In discussing this subject, Goodhart puts his finger on a problem
which is very relevant to the current position of the European Union.
This is what he refers to as a chicken and egg problem:

> I have argued both that a single-currency area requires a strong, centralised
> fiscal authority, ready and able to ease regional adjustment problems, and also
> that it will be difficult to establish any effective centralised fiscal authority

covering areas with independent, separate currencies (Goodhart, *Money*, p. 424).

This inter-dependence between monetary and fiscal union leads him to say emphatically that "Fiscal and monetary harmonisation will march together, or not at all". While Goodhart does not offer any way out of this chicken and egg problem, it is clear that the factor which links fiscal and monetary union, and which is indispensable to them, is political union. This is clear when we consider European economic and monetary union in more detail.

8. ECONOMIC AND MONETARY UNION

EMU in the Treaty of Rome and the Single European Act

The Treaty of Rome made very little reference to monetary integration. References to monetary integration were confined to those considered, at that time, to be necessary to achieve the Community's main concrete objective — a common market. Article 104 set out the macroeconomic policy objectives of the EC; it is noteworthy that these objectives were described in *national* terms and it was stipulated that each *Member State* shall pursue its economic policy in such a way as to ensure equilibrium of its overall balance of payments, confidence in its currency, a high level of employment and a stable level of prices. While the Treaty left the core of economic policy with the Member States, it did specify that Member States will "co-ordinate their economic policies" and regard their conjunctural policies and exchange rate policies as "a matter of common concern" (Articles 105(1), 103 and 107(1)). This limited approach can be explained by the economic conditions of the period: the Bretton Woods system of fixed exchange rates was functioning smoothly and the European economies were in an extended period of economic growth (see Chapter 32). It also reflected the prevailing perception that limited economic policy integration, and almost no macroeconomic policy integration, were necessary to achieve a common market (see Section 5 above).

These minor macroeconomic and monetary provisions of the Treaty were extended somewhat by the Single Act of 1986. It noted that "convergence of economic and monetary policies ... is necessary for the further development of the Community" (Article 102a), but it stipulated merely that Member States "should co-operate in accordance with the objectives of Article 104" and build on the experience of EMS. It was explicitly stated that further institutional developments in the monetary area would require another revision of the Treaty.

The European Monetary System (EMS)

After revaluations of the mark and devaluation of the French franc in the 1960s, the 1969 Hague summit of Community leaders decided that the Community should seek to move towards EMU. The Community then quickly entered the first stage towards EMU — restriction on the exchange rate movements — but this project was doomed to failure and was effectively shelved at the Paris summit of 1974. A much more modest attempt to limit exchange rate volatility, the Snake, had only very limited success between 1972 and 1979. Nevertheless, there was a general dissatisfaction with the floating exchange rate system which had replaced the fixed rates of the Bretton Woods era. Exchange rate movements disrupted production and trade and seemed to reflect speculative whims more than underlying economic conditions. This was the context in which the EMS was devised in 1978 and introduced in early 1979.

The purpose of the EMS is to minimise fluctuations between currencies, thereby creating a "zone of monetary stability". A central feature of the system is the European Currency Unit (ECU). This is a composite currency made up of specified amounts of all Member-State currencies. At any point in time, each currency participating in the EMS has a given value — called a "central rate" — in relation to the ECU. These values, once fixed collectively, have to persist until a decision is made by the participating states to alter them. The central rates, expressed in terms of the ECU, are then used to establish a grid of exchange rates between each pair of currencies in the system. The obligation on a country participating in the system was, until August 1993, to prevent its currency diverting more than 2.25 per cent above or below these central rates. This +/- 2.25 band was known as the EMS narrow band. The general means for achieving this is the conduct of national fiscal and monetary policy in such a way as to ensure that the currency's market value does not rise or fall out of this narrow band. However, should this occur, the countries concerned are obliged to intervene in the foreign exchange markets or to undertake other measures, such as changes in interest rates or fiscal policy. In order to facilitate these interventions, the EMS has some shared foreign exchange reserves and has facilities to provide credit to countries having to undertake balance-of-payments financing.

Although all Member-States' currencies are represented in the ECU, only eight countries — West Germany, France, Belgium, Luxembourg, the Netherlands, Denmark, Ireland and Italy — initially participated in the exchange rate mechanism of the EMS. Spain joined the system in June 1989, the UK joined in October 1990 and Portugal joined in April 1992, all three opting for the wider, 6 per cent, band. The system experienced severe turbulence in 1992 and 1993. In September 1992, sterling was "suspended", the Italian lira was withdrawn from the exchange rate mechanism and several other currencies realigned. In August 1993, the fluctuation margin for the whole system was widened to +/-15 per cent.

The EMS has been the subject of a vast literature, examining its creation, its working and its ability to achieve its goals. This voluminous literature is now cast in a new light by the crisis which hit the system in September 1992 and led to its dramatic alteration in August 1993. The crisis, and its implications for EMS and EMU, has now become the subject of analysis. It is not possible here, in an overview of the economics of European integration, to provide a thorough account of the EMS and the way it has been understood by economists. However, students should be aware of some of the key features of the system and the issues which it has thrown up.

One of the most important features of the EMS is that it has functioned in different ways at different times during the period from 1979 to the present. Consequently, there are few general propositions which are true of EMS per se. The following chronology has been suggested for the EMS.

- From 1979 to 1983, inflation differentials were broadly accommodated by frequent realignments.

- From 1983 to 1987, the system experienced more stability and less frequent realignments. Anxieties about asymmetry (see below) led to reform of the system in 1987.

- From 1987 to 1992, there was significant convergence of inflation rates, interest rates and budget defects and *no* realignments.

- In 1992 and 1993, the system came under severe strain as a result of remaining differences in inflation, high interest rates associated with German unification and political doubts about the ratification of the Maastricht Treaty.

- Despite increased intra-EMS exchange rate stability, over the years, from 1979 to 1993 there was a significant cumulative appreciation of the mark (and the Dutch guilder), and a trend depreciation of the lira, the French franc and the Irish pound.

Economic analysis of the EMS, has focused on six questions (see D. Gros and N. Thygesen, *European Monetary Integration*, Longman, London, 1992, and P. Honohan, *An Examination of Irish Currency Policy*, ESRI, Dublin, 1993). Did it succeed in creating a zone of monetary stability? How important were capital controls in creating the stability of the system? Did the EMS help reduce the cost of disinflation (i.e. getting inflation down)? Does the EMS operate as a mechanism jointly to absorb shocks coming from outside? To what extent, and in what ways, is EMS an asymmetric system? Does the EMS contain a deflationary bias? Here, the focus is on those findings which are fairly widely agreed and which are relevant to any future attempt at European-level management of the macroeconomic and monetary environment.

- Although the EMS probably assisted disinflation in some countries, and the maintenance of low inflation in many, there is little evidence that it reduced the *cost* of disinflation, in terms of increased unemployment.

- The EMS displayed significant asymmetry, in that Germany retained the ability to set monetary policy independently, and other countries pegged their currencies to the deutschmark.

- This asymmetry was not constant. After 1987, monetary leadership was more widely shared. But leadership shifted back to Germany after reunification, because of Germany's need to conduct the tightest monetary policy in the EC.

- Asymmetry has both advantages and disadvantages. It is the asymmetry of an exchange rate system which produces its disciplinary, anti-inflationary, role. But it can also increase volatility in peripheral economies.

- There is some evidence that EMS lends a deflationary bias to the European economy, because each county believes that the benefits of fiscal expansion would accrue to its neighbours.

Pressure for a German-led fiscal expansion was averted in the late 1980s by some reform of the EMS and a dramatic improvement in the economic climate resulting from a decline in oil prices, a relaxation of monetary policy following the 1987 stock exchange crash and the internal market effect. But tension reappeared as growth faltered in 1990. This was greatly exacerbated by the shift in the German policy-mix following reunification. An insistence on one-to-one conversion of ostmarks for deutschmarks, and a refusal to meet the high costs of reunification by increasing taxes, led to inflationary pressure and a growing budget deficit. This moved the Germans to restrict monetary growth which, in turn, imposed high interest rates on other ERM countries. This occurred in a situation in which several EMS countries had experienced a progressive overvaluation of their currencies — largely in a conscious effort to put downward pressure on inflation. In addition, the convergence criteria for transition to EMU (explained below) tied several governments to restrictive fiscal policies. This set of circumstances created the crisis which led to the departure of sterling and the lira from the system and the widening of the fluctuation margin to +/-15 per cent.

EMU in the Treaty on European Union

The 1992 Treaty on European Union (TEU) — often referred to as the Maastricht Treaty — contains a blueprint for European economic and monetary union. Three reasons can be identified for the willingness to proceed to EMU. First, after a period of naïve and dogmatic belief in general floating of exchange rates in the 1970s, there developed widespread disillusionment with this idea in Europe and, by and large, this remains. Second, the liberalisation of capital markets as part of the internal market project, in the context of fixed exchange rates, is widely believed to alter the conditions for the conduct of domestic monetary policy, in such a way that it requires either the abandonment of fixed exchange rates or greater co-ordination of monetary policy. Third, the more the internal market programme has proceeded, the more have influential people come to believe that many of its possible benefits will be lost if separate currencies continue to exist.

The Treaty articles which deal with EMU may be classified into five categories: objectives; principles; instruments; rules; and transitional provisions. The *objectives* of the EC, as modified in the new Treaty, are:

- Balanced economic development;
- Sustainable and non-inflationary growth respecting the environment;
- A high degree of convergence of economic performance;
- A high level of employment and of social protection;
- The raising of the standard of living;
- Economic and social cohesion and solidarity.

In designing the Treaty basis of EMU, several economic and monetary *principles* were agreed and these are now incorporated in the Treaty:

- The parallel development of economic and monetary integration;
- Price stability as the main objective of monetary policy;
- Central bank independence;
- Sound public finances and monetary conditions;

- A sustainable balance of payments;

- An open market economy with free competition.

In order to pursue the objectives outlined above in accordance with these principles, the EU requires certain policies and instruments. Although the full range of Union policies are relevant to pursuit of the stated objectives, the incorporation of EMU into the Treaty has resulted in the definition of new or enhanced *policy instruments* in two particular areas:

Monetary Policy:

- Establishment of a single currency, the ECU;

- Establishment of a European Central Bank to manage this currency, and definition of its rules.

Macroeconomic Policy:

- Surveillance of national macroeconomic policy and performance, formulation of broad guidelines for the economic policy of the Member States and the Community and control of "excessive" budget deficits.

The Treaty defines certain *rules* governing both membership of monetary union and behaviour within it. In order to participate in the adoption of the single currency, a country must meet the following "convergence criteria":

- Inflation close to the three best-performing Member States;

- Public finances without excessive deficits or debt;

- A currency within the normal EMS fluctuation margins for at least two years, without devaluation;

- Interest rates which suggest that the convergence is durable.

Within EMU and, indeed before the final stage is reached, Member States must conduct their economic policies as a matter of common concern and, specifically:

- In accordance with the broad guidelines set by the European Council and the Council of Finance Ministers;

- Without monetary financing of budgetary deficits;

- Without being bailed-out by the Community;

- Avoiding "excessive deficits".

The Treaty, and an attached protocol, define an excessive deficit as either a government deficit significantly above 3 per cent of GDP, and not declining substantially and continuously towards that level, or public debt greater than 60 per cent of GDP and not approaching that value at a satisfactory pace.

The final element of the Treaty concerns the transition to EMU. There are two dimensions to the transition to a single currency. The first is definition of the *method* of transition; the second concerns the *speed* of transition and *the procedures* for moving forward. In defining the *method* of transition, the TEU follows closely the three stages suggested in the 1988 Delors Report. Stage I, which began in 1990, involved adherence to the EMS and gradual removal of controls on the movement of capital between member countries. Stage II, as defined in the Treaty, involves closer co-ordination of macroeconomic policies and some development of the institutions which will eventually manage monetary policy and the new currency, the ECU. In the third, and final, stage, exchange rates will be locked irrevocably, EU rules on macroeconomic and budgetary policy will become binding and the new European Central Bank (ECB) will prepare the transition to a single currency.

In defining the *speed* of transition, the Treaty set January 1994 as the start of Stage II. That stage saw the establishment of a European Monetary Institute (EMI), rather than a European System of Central Banks (ESCB) as proposed by the Delors Report. A most important element of the Treaty is the provisions governing movements to the third and final stage. It stipulates that the European Council must decide, before the end of 1996, whether a majority of Member States fulfils the necessary conditions for the adoption of a single currency and, if so, set a date for the beginning of Stage III. But the Treaty makes clear that "if by the end of 1997 the date for the beginning of the third stage has not been set, the third stage will start on 1 January 1999" (Article 109 J.4). At that point, any number of states can proceed to EMU. The Treaty ensures that non-participating states cannot prevent the Union moving to the third stage and lays down that their position will be reviewed every two years.

The British Conservative Government has consistently opposed the idea of a single currency. In recognition of this, the EU has designed a special procedure for the UK and attached this to the Treaty in a "Protocol". The procedure stipulates that the UK "shall notify the Council whether it intends to move to the third stage of economic and monetary union before the Council makes its assessment", towards the end of 1996. If the UK notifies the Council that it does not intend to move to the third stage, then it will be excluded from the majority and weighted majority voting procedures on matters concerning EMU. The Treaty also contains a Protocol on Denmark — in recognition of the fact that the Danish constitution may require a plebiscite prior to Danish participation in the third stage of EMU. Following the June 1992 referendum in Denmark, in which ratification of the TEU was narrowly defeated, the Danish government was, in December 1992, granted a clearer "opt-out" from EMU.

EMU after the Crisis of 1992–93

There can be no doubt that the exchange rate crises of 1992–3 significantly changed the European macroeconomic and monetary environment. The most significant change is in the UK and Italy, which have not only had a large devaluation and a reduction in interest rates, but have moved from a pegged to a floating exchange rate régime. In other countries, a devaluation *vis-à-vis* the deutschmark and a move to a fluctuation margin of +/- 15 per cent were, of course, important changes, but their significance may lie more in the relief they afford from speculative attacks, and the associated high interest rates, than in increased exchange rate volatility. There is little evidence that governments wish to use the wider margins of fluctuation actively to pursue a devaluation strategy. Consequently, one possible change in the macroeconomic environment — a switch from an anti-inflation policy involving real appreciation, to a growth-oriented policy of competitive devaluations — seems not to have transpired.

However, it seems unlikely that the EU states will, in future, be able, or indeed be willing, to defend exchange rate parities by means of an asymmetric system such as the EMS. The problems of monetary control which arise in an asymmetric system are, as De Grauwe argues in *The Economics of Monetary Integration* (1992), likely to lead to conflicts about the kind of monetary policy to be followed for the whole system:

> Pressure on the centre country will certainly be exerted. These conflicts of interest have to be dealt with in one way or another. [This] suggests that an asymmetric system may not survive in the long run. Too much conflict will exist about the appropriate monetary policies for the system as a whole. Peripheral countries especially if they are similar in size to the centre country (as is the case in the present EMS), may not be willing to subject their national interest to the survival of the system. In the end, more explicit co-operative arrangements may be necessary (p. 121).

The events of 1992 and 1993 suggest that a central issue in the economics of European integration is whether more explicit co-operative arrangements will be designed.

One thing that has changed since the late 1980s and, indeed, since the design of the Maastricht Treaty, is the level of European governments' concern about unemployment and economic growth. While control of inflation was the primary policy goal in the 1980s, this was largely achieved by the early 1990s. Indeed, there was a considerable degree of inflation convergence in the EU in 1993 and 1994. While unemployment remained high by historical standards in most EU countries in the 1980s, the recession of the early 1990s produced a new surge in unemployment in Europe. In consequence, there was something of a change in policy priorities, which was marked at the EU level in December 1993, by the presentation of the Commission's White Paper *Growth, Competitiveness and Employment* to the Brussels European Council. However, neither the White Paper, nor the reactions of governments to it, produced any consensus on how the problem should be tackled. Proposals for a coordinated expansion were, once again, rejected because of existing deficits and doctrinal rejection of Keynesian ideas on the role of effective demand. It seems more likely that the EU will follow individual European governments in reacting to problems of slow growth and unemployment with supply-side measures, rather than with more general macroeconomic policy. Indeed, the EU initiative on growth, unemployment and competitiveness has brought forward arguments for deregulation of European labour markets, increased training and the enhancement of European infrastructure. If common policies are not implemented, or do not work, the danger is that Member States will resort to supply-side measures which undermine the internal market.

Turning to the prospects for transition to a single currency, one finds even greater uncertainty. Since the political and exchange rate crisis which developed in the EU in 1992, the plan for EMU embodied in the Treaty on European Union has come under critical scrutiny. The possibility of a gradual transition to EMU by means of a progressive convergence of macroeconomic performance, and tightening of the ERM, has been questioned. Related to this, it has been argued that the minimal institutional developments envisaged in Stage II could not produce a sufficient pooling of instruments and responsibilities to advance beyond the achievements of Stage I. Some economists have argued that the convergence criteria and the Treaty rules governing national fiscal policy are arbitrary, unnecessary, and likely to lend a deflationary bias to the European economy throughout the 1990s. Indeed, in 1993 and 1994 only Luxembourg simultaneously met the convergence criteria on public debt and deficits. The experience of 1992–3 has also re-awakened fears that the Treaty has designed a somewhat unbalanced system, in the sense that there may be more coherent institutions and policy on the *monetary* than on the *economic* side. Will the Union's economic policies be sufficient to pursue goals other than price stability — especially employment, growth, competitiveness and cohesion? Concern has also been expressed about the fiscal requirements for a successful EMU: can the European Union hope to create an economic and monetary union without the system of fiscal federalism which is found in almost all successful monetary unions? Finally, several of these questions are closely related to issues of political union. Many would doubt that the, largely inter-governmental, decision-making procedures which apply to the EMU provisions of the TEU, have the authority, legitimacy or effectiveness to progress to and, more importantly, *govern* an economic and monetary union (see R. O'Donnell (ed.) *Economic and Monetary Union*, Institute of European Affairs, Dublin, 1991).

Faced with these doubts, many economists doubt that the EU, or even a majority of its Member States, will proceed to EMU in accordance with the Maastricht plan. While some see recent problems as evidence that a European economic, monetary and political union was never meant to be, it seems likely that this reflects a prior opposition to the idea. Indeed, many still believe that the *eventual* monetary integration of Western Europe is virtually inevitable. But no one seems clear on how and when this might be achieved. If the crises of 1992–3 simply implied a slower transition to EMU, there may be no great difficulty. However, questions have been raised which cast doubt on the *strategy* and *method* of transition chosen in the Treaty on European Union. Consequently, the prospects for EMU may depend on the design of an alternative strategy and the achievement of political agreement on it. This confirms the extent to which EMU is a political project, dependent on political will as much as economic convergence.

GLOSSARY

absorption: the sum of private sector consumption and investment expenditure plus government expenditure on goods and services in an economy.

aggregate demand curve: (a) a curve relating the demand for output produced by the economy under analysis, to the price level in that economy, or, (b) a curve relating demand by residents of the economy under analysis, to the price level in that economy. Interpretation (a) is adopted throughout this text, except in pp. 252–4 and in Chapter 21, where interpretation (b) is adopted.

aggregate supply curve: a curve relating the supply of goods and services produced in an economy, to the price level, given money wage rates, the prices of any imported inputs, and the state of technology.

appreciation: reduction in the domestic currency price of foreign currency.

arbitrage: an opportunity for profit or gain from buying a good or asset in a low-price market and simultaneously selling it in a higher-price market.

autonomous variable: a variable the value of which is determined outside the model under investigation; it is alternatively described as exogenous.

bank rate: the term, used generically in this text, to describe the rate of interest at which the central bank is willing to lend to the commercial banks.

barriers on entry: phenomena which deter or prevent entry to a market, such as patent rights or increasing returns to scale accruing to existing participants in the market.

capital: the stock of physical productive assets, such as machines, buildings and raw materials. This meaning is extended in the area of finance to include the stock of financial claims.

capital gain: the increase in the value of an asset between the time of purchase and the time of sale.

cartel: a group of producers who have colluded to restrict output and raise prices, collectively.

central bank: the bank which is responsible for the implementation of monetary policy, and which serves as banker to the commercial banks.

change in demand: a shift of a demand curve.

change in quantity demanded: a movement along a demand curve.

change in quantity supplied: a movement along a supply curve.

change in supply: a shift of a supply curve.

closed economy: an economy with no significant economic relationships with the rest of the world.

commercial banks: the banks with which the public normally deals.

commercial bank reserves: money held by the commercial banks to meet the contingency of withdrawals by depositors.

comparative advantage: a country has a comparative advantage in the production of a good if the relative or opportunity costs of producing the good are lower in that country than in other countries.

comparative static equilibrium analysis: the study of equilibrium solutions at a point in time, and, following a disturbance to equilibrium, the comparison of one static equilibrium solution with another static equilibrium solution.

complementary goods: two goods are complements if the demand for one (at a given price) moves in the opposite direction to changes in the price of the other good.

consumer price index: an index of the price of a basket of goods and services bought by a representative consumer.

consumption function: the relationship between consumption demand and disposable income.

correlation: the extent to which changes in one variable are consistently associated with changes in another variable.

cost-push inflation: inflation associated with persistent increases in the prices of factors of production.

cross elasticity of demand: a measure of the degree of responsiveness in the demand for a good to changes in the price of some other good.

crowding out: reduction in private sector investment demand due to an increase in government expenditure.

demand curve: the relationship between the quantity demanded of a good and its price.

demand deposits: deposits which can be drawn upon without advance notice.

demand-pull inflation: inflation associated with persistent excess in the level of aggregate demand over and above the supply potential of the economy.

depreciation: (a) increase in the domestic currency price of foreign currency, or, (b) the amount by which productive assets decrease in value as they are used, and become older.

devaluation: a discrete increase in the domestic currency price of foreign currency.

domestic income or **domestic product:** a money measure of the total production of final goods and services in an economy in a given period, usually one year.

economic rent: the earnings of a factor of production over and above the level of earnings necessary to induce the supply of that factor.

elasticity: *see* cross elasticity, income elasticity, price elasticity.

endogenous variable: a variable the value of which is determined within a given model; it is explained by the model.

equilibrium: a set of phenomena are in equilibrium when they show no inherent tendency to change: they are in a position of rest.

excess demand: a situation in which, at a given price, quantity demanded exceeds quantity supplied.

excess supply: a situation in which, at a given price, quantity supplied exceeds quantity demanded.

exchange rate: the domestic currency price of foreign currency.

exogenous variable: a variable the value of which is determined outside a given model.

factor of production: an input to the production process. Directly or indirectly, all of such inputs can be decomposed into the categories of land, labour, capital or enterprise.

fiscal policy: public policy in regard to government revenue and expenditure.

fixed costs: those costs which do not vary with the level of output — sometimes called overhead costs.

fixed factors: those factors of production the availability of which cannot be varied in the short run.

foreign exchange reserves: foreign currency or securities held by a central bank in order to protect the exchange rate.

free rider problem: the problem which arises when an individual gains something, through the action of others, without paying for it, and therefore fails to contribute to its cost.

freely floating exchange rates: a system in which exchange rates are determined by the free market forces of supply and demand, without any intervention by a central bank.

full employment: a situation in which the levels of real wage rates are such that the demand for labour equals the supply of labour.

full employment output: (a) the maximum level of output which the economy is capable of producing under normal peacetime conditions, or, (b) the level of output corresponding to full employment as defined above.

general equilibrium analysis: a simultaneous solution for equilibrium in all markets of the economy; thus, this methodology attempts to capture the complex interactions between individual markets and between individual sectors of the economy.

imperfect competition: a market structure in which there is a large number of firms selling products which are close but not perfect substitutes for each other; thus, the individual firms face downward-sloping demand curves for their products.

import function: the relationship between imports to an economy and its national income.

income effect: the variation in demand for goods due to a change in real income, given relative prices.

income elasticity of demand: a measure of the responsiveness in the demand for a good to a change in the level of real income.

income velocity of money: the ratio of nominal income to the money supply, PY/M.

infant industry argument: the argument that in the early stages of their development, some industries need protection from foreign competition in order to acquire skills and avail of economies of scale, and that thereby they will ultimately be able to survive in the face of international competition.

inferior good: a good the demand for which falls as real income increases.

infinitely elastic demand: the demand for a good is infinitely elastic if any amount can be sold at a particular price, but none of it will be demanded if price is increased to the smallest extent conceivable.

infinitely elastic supply: with price on the vertical axis and quantity on the horizontal axis, a supply curve would be infinitely elastic if it were perfectly flat (i.e. has a slope of zero).

inflationary gap: in a closed economy, an excess of aggregate demand over and above the supply potential of the economy.

inflation rate: the proportionate or percentage (equals proportionate multiplied by 100) rate of increase in the price level.

investment: that part of output in a given period which is not consumed (by the private sector or by government) in the same period; the change in the capital stock. Note that in the literature on finance this definition is extended to include the change in the stock of financial claims.

law of diminishing marginal utility: the hypothesis that as an individual consumes progressively more of the same good in a given time period, the increment in total utility or satisfaction progressively decreases.

law of diminishing returns: the hypothesis which states that as the amount of one input is increased, total output increases at a diminishing rate (the amount used of all other inputs and the state of technology remaining constant).

liquidity: the ease with which an asset can be converted into purchasing power.

lump-sum taxes: taxes the receipts from which are fixed; in particular, the receipts do not vary with output.

M1, M3: measures of the money supply used in Ireland. Narrow money M1 consists of cash and current account balances held by the public at licensed banks. Broad money supply M3 additionally includes deposit account balances held by the public at licensed banks plus borrowing by licensed banks from other credit institutions.

macroeconomics: the study of aggregate or overall economic activity.

marginal cost: the change in total cost incurred in producing an additional unit of output.

marginal physical product: the change in total physical product due to employing an additional unit of a variable factor, the amount employed of all other factors remaining constant.

marginal propensity to consume: the amount by which consumption demand increases when disposable income increases by one unit (£m).

marginal propensity to import: the amount by which imports increase when national income increases by one unit (£m).

marginal propensity to save: the amount by which planned savings increase when disposable income increases by one unit (£m).

marginal rate of substitution: the extent to which a consumer is willing to substitute one good for another, while remaining no better or worse off.

marginal rate of technical substitution: the extent to which one input can be substituted for another, consistent with economic efficiency and maintaining the level of output constant.

marginal rate of transformation: the extent to which one good can indirectly be transformed into another, through reallocation of the factors of production and consistent with economic efficiency.

marginal revenue: the change in total revenue due to the sale of an additional unit.

marginal revenue product: the change in total revenue from sales arising from the marginal physical product.

marginal tax rate: the amount by which net tax receipts automatically increase when national income increases by one unit (£m).

marginal utility: the change in total utility or subjective satisfaction due to consuming an extra unit of a good in a given time period.

market failure: a situation in which a market economy fails to attain full economic efficiency.

medium of exchange: anything which is generally accepted as a means of payment.

microeconomics: the study of the individual elements (firms, households and markets) which, taken together, comprise the aggregate variables of macroeconomics.

monetary policy: public policy (usually implemented by a central bank) which affects the supply of money or which directly affects the composition of the assets of the banking system.

money: anything which generally serves as a medium of exchange.

monopoly: a market structure in which there is only a single supplier.

monopsony: a market structure in which there is only a single buyer.

national income or **national product:** a money measure of the total production of final goods and services, by factors of production resident in an economy, in a given period, usually one year.

national income multiplier: in a model of the goods market, the coefficient relating the change in equilibrium national income to a change in the value of some exogenous component of aggregate demand.

normal good: a good the demand for which increases as income increases.

normative analysis: analysis in regard to what ought to be.

oligopoly: a market structure in which there are only a few sellers.

open economy: an economy which is relatively dependent on international trade.

open market operations: purchase or sale of securities in the open market by a central bank.

opportunity cost: the opportunity cost of any decision is the next-best alternative foregone as a result of implementing that decision.

partial equilibrium analysis: analysis of equilibrium in individual markets in isolation, on the assumption that conditions in other markets remain unchanged.

patent: a legal privilege giving an inventor an exclusive right to use, produce or sell the invention.

perfect capital mobility: mainly in the finance and balance of payments literature, a situation in which movement of capital responds instantly and substantively, to differences in rates of return on investment between countries, thereby equating those returns.

perfect competition: a situation in which each individual firm is a perfect price-taker; therefore it can sell any quantity at the prevailing market price, but if it were to raise price, then it would lose all of its sales.

portfolio: mainly in the finance and balance of payments literature, an investor's set of net assets.

positive analysis: analysis of what was, what is or what conceivably could be; it purports to describe rather than prescribe.

present (discounted) value: how much a sum of money or some other asset, to be received in the future, is worth now.

price ceiling: a maximum on the price which may legally be charged.

price discrimination: a practice whereby a seller charges different prices for the same good or service.

price elasticity of demand: a measure of the degree of responsiveness in quantity demanded of a good to changes in its price.

price elasticity of supply: a measure of the degree of responsiveness in quantity supplied of a good to changes in its price.

price floor: a minimum price below which market price may not fall.

price index: a measure of the price of a basket of goods and services over time, relative to the prices which prevailed in a base year.

production function: the relationship showing the maximum level of output obtainable from various alternative combinations of inputs.

production possibility curve: a relationship showing the maximum amount of any one good which the economy is capable of producing, given the amount produced of all other goods; sometimes called a transformation curve or frontier.

public good: a good such that any one individual's consumption of its services does not detract from the amount of its services available for consumption by others.

quantity theory of money: the theory that the income velocity of money, which reflects the speed with which people on average get rid of money, is a function of the costs of holding wealth in perfectly liquid form.

real income: the purchasing power of nominal income, relative to some base period (year).

real rate of interest: equals the nominal rate of interest minus the rate of inflation.

returns to scale: refers to the response in output to a simultaneous proportionate change in the amount used of all inputs; if returns to scale are increasing (decreasing), then a given proportionate change in all inputs will lead to a larger (smaller) proportionate change in output.

revaluation: a discrete reduction in the domestic currency price of foreign currency.

stable equilibrium: an equilibrium for a set of phenomena is stable if, when the phenomena are not in equilibrium but are in a neighbourhood of equilibrium, they gravitate towards equilibrium.

substitute goods: two goods are substitutes if an increase in the price of one of them causes an increase in the demand for the other.

substitution effect: the change in a consumer's purchase plan when a change in relative prices just about enables the consumer to remain on the same indifference curve as initially.

supply curve: the relationship between the quantity supplied of a good and its price.

terms of trade: in an open economy, the amount of imported goods which may be obtained in exchange for a unit of exports.

terms-of-trade index: an index of the price of exports divided by the price of imports.

transfer payment: a payment made for reasons other than the provision of productive services by the recipient.

transformation curve: *see* production possibility curve.

unstable equilibrium: any equilibrium solution other than a stable equilibrium.

utility: the level of satisfaction which an individual obtains from consumption.

variable costs: those costs associated with the employment of variable factors.

variable factor: a factor of production which can be acquired or released in a given time period.

wage rigidity: a situation in which wage rates do not fall in response to an excess supply of labour.

windfall gain: *see* capital gain.